Manhwa Novella Collection Volume 2

9 Faces of Love

WANN

NETCOMICS

Manhwa Novella Collection Volume 2

9 Faces of Love

Story and Art by WANN

English translation rights in USA, Canada,
UK, NZ, Australia arranged by
Ecomix Media Company
395-21 Seogyo-dong, Mapo-gu,
Seoul, Korea 121-840
info@ecomixmedia.com

- Produced by **Ecomix Media Company**
- Translator **Jennifer Park**
- Editors **Jeffrey Tompkins, Ernest Woo**
- Managing Editor **Soyoung Jung**
- Cover Design **purj**
- Graphic Design **Soohyun Park, Eunsook Lee**
- Pre-Press Manager **Youngsook Hwang**
- President & Publisher **Heewoon Chung**

P.O.Box 16484, Jersey City, NJ 07306
info@netcomics.com
www.NETCOMICS.com

ISBN: 1-60009-161-X

First printing: August 2006
10 9 8 7 6 5 4 3 2 1
Printed in Korea

From the author

The short pieces in this collection are traces of my work from 1998 to 2005. Looking at them now, I am ashamed, but proud, as well. (The emotions are getting mixed up. Ahem....!)

Though I work in serials now, the short form also has a charm all its own, and I was completely absorbed as I drew these.

They are pleasant memories of mine.

As I drew them at the time with such devotion, one short after another, the weight of a complete book feels quite hefty.

And I am that much more attached to them. I hope they give you, the readers, the same kind of good feeling. And, though the details may be forgotten, may that feeling remain with you long after....

August 2006

WANN

CONTENTS

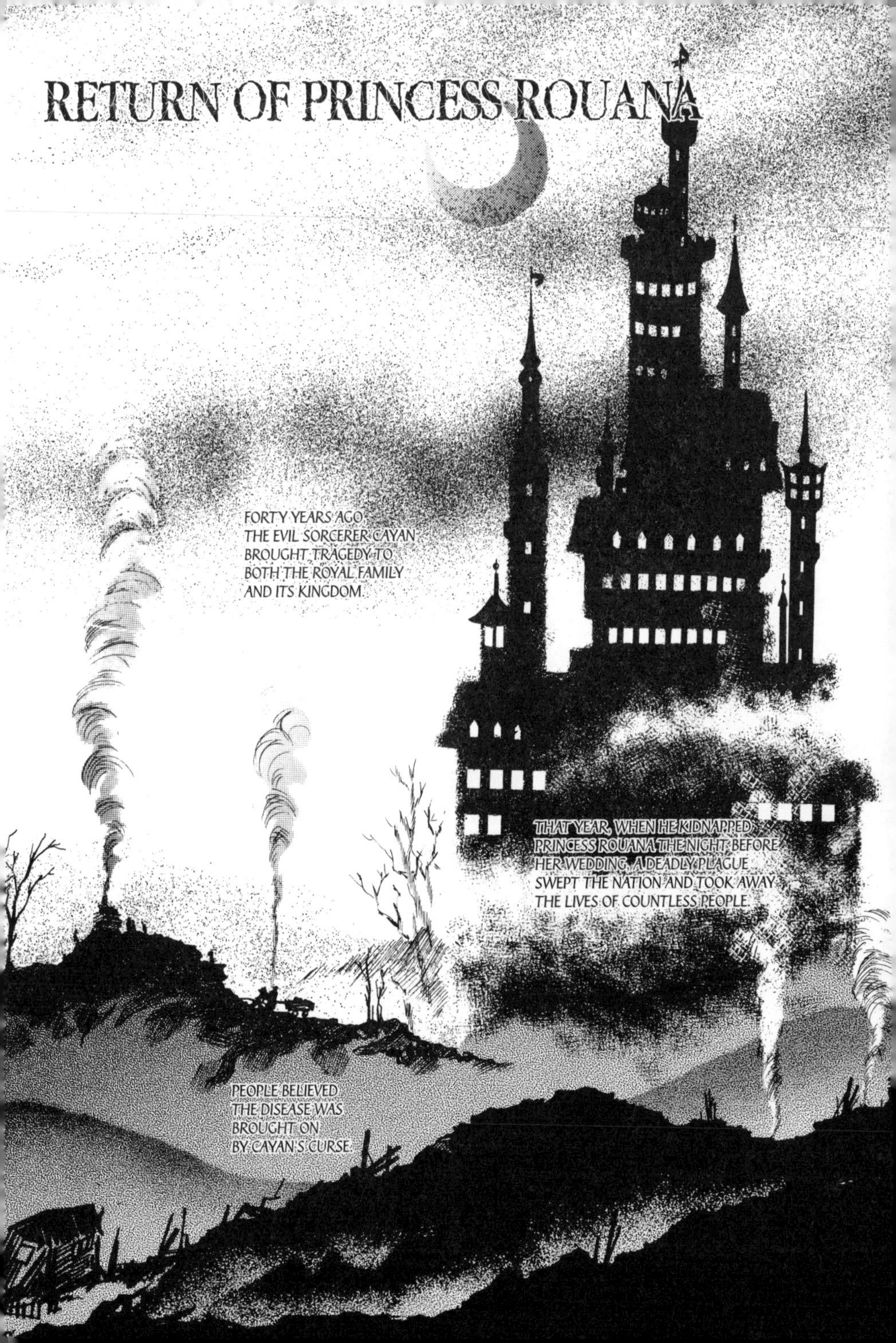
RETURN OF PRINCESS ROUANA
FORTY YEARS AGO THE EVIL SORCERER CAYAN BROUGHT TRAGEDY TO BOTH THE ROYAL FAMILY AND ITS KINGDOM.
THAT YEAR, WHEN HE KIDNAPPED PRINCESS ROUANA THE NIGHT BEFORE HER WEDDING, A DEADLY PLAGUE SWEPT THE NATION AND TOOK AWAY THE LIVES OF COUNTLESS PEOPLE.
PEOPLE BELIEVED THE DISEASE WAS BROUGHT ON BY CAYAN'S CURSE.

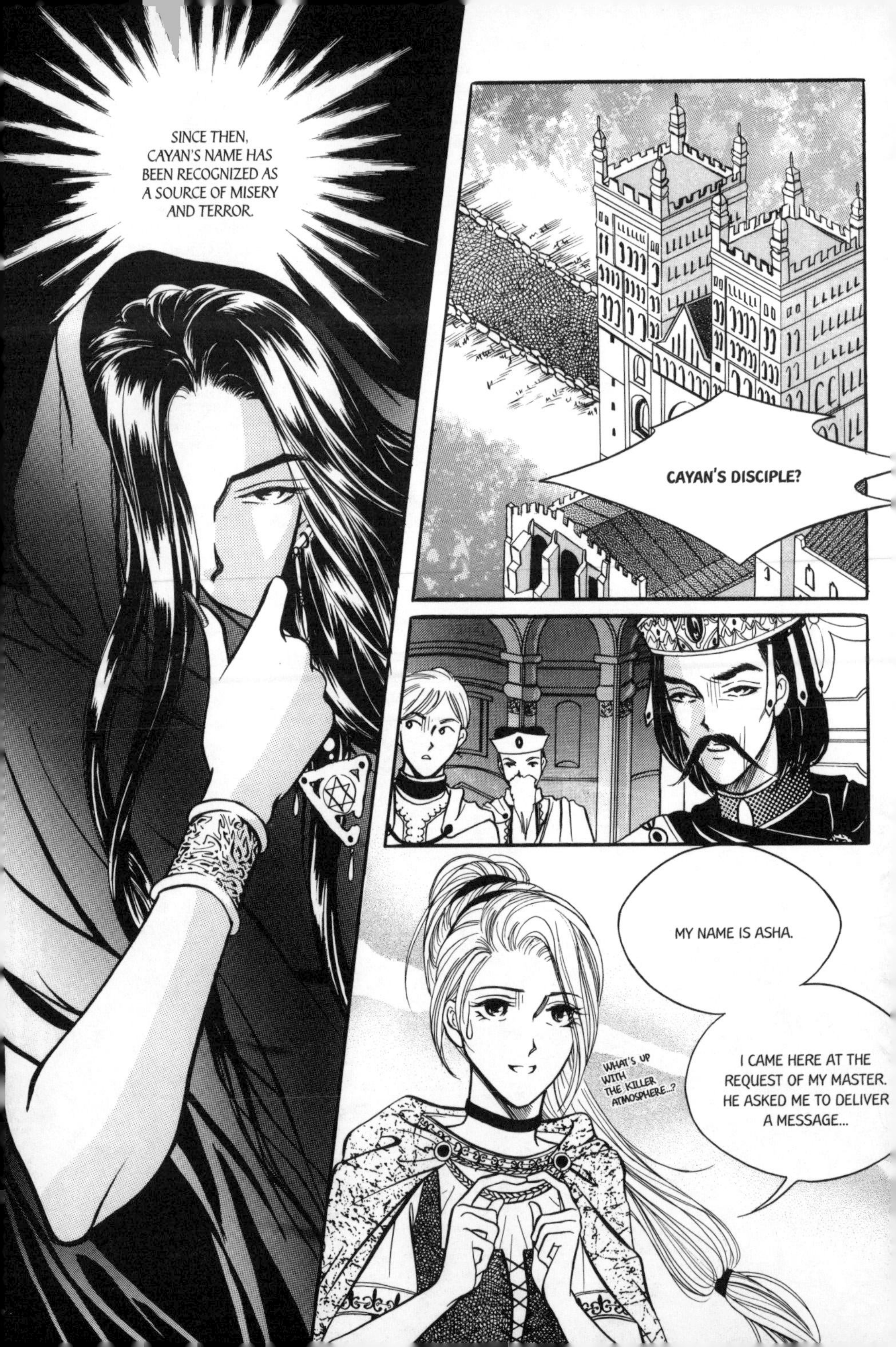
SINCE THEN, CAYAN'S NAME HAS BEEN RECOGNIZED AS A SOURCE OF MISERY AND TERROR.
CAYAN'S DISCIPLE?
MY NAME IS ASHA.
WHAT'S UP WITH THE KILLER ATMOSPHERE...?
I CAME HERE AT THE REQUEST OF MY MASTER. HE ASKED ME TO DELIVER A MESSAGE...

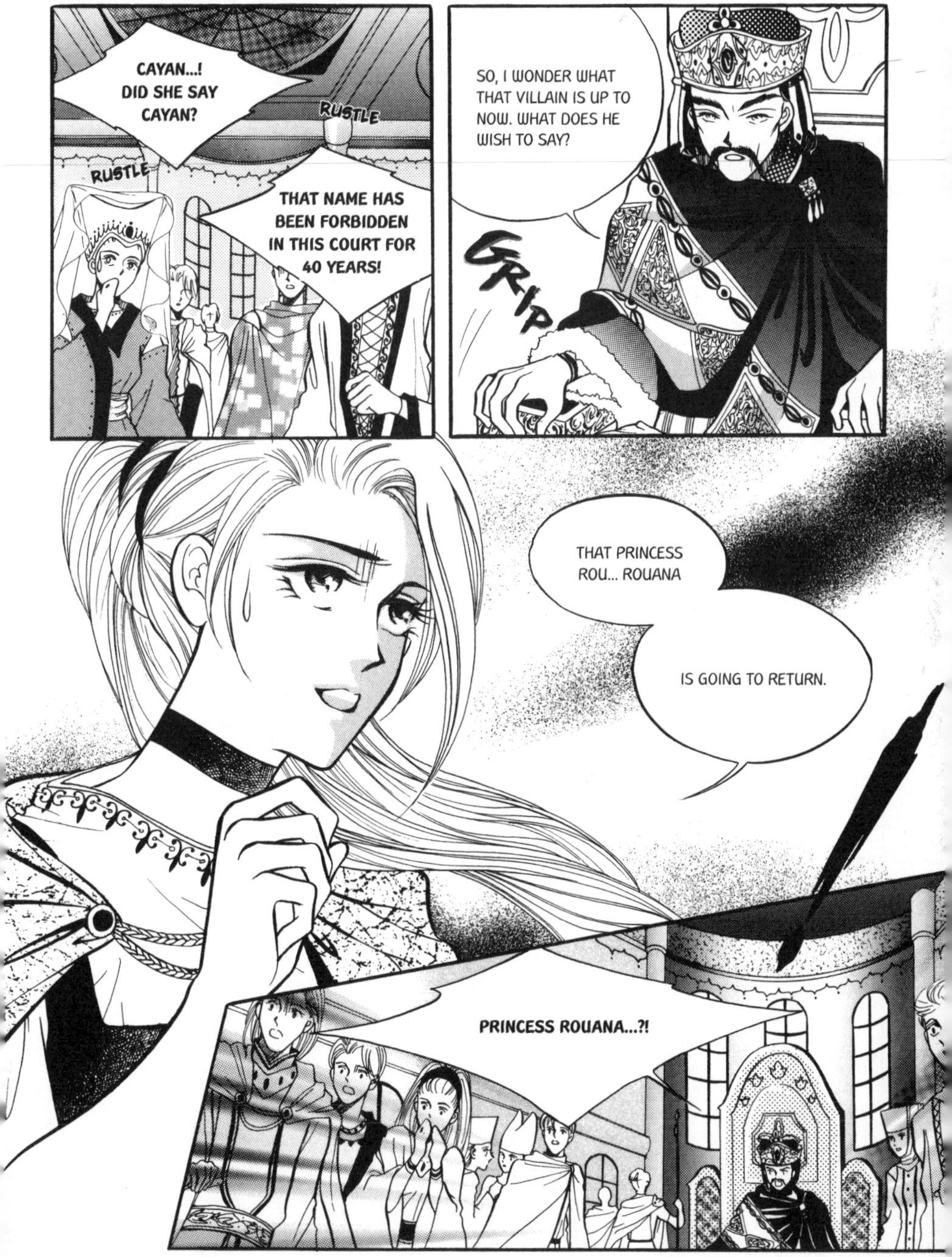
CAYAN...! DID SHE SAY CAYAN?
RUSTLE
RUSTLE
THAT NAME HAS BEEN FORBIDDEN IN THIS COURT FOR 40 YEARS!
SO, I WONDER WHAT THAT VILLAIN IS UP TO NOW. WHAT DOES HE WISH TO SAY?
GRIP
THAT PRINCESS ROU... ROUANA
IS GOING TO RETURN.
PRINCESS ROUANA...?!

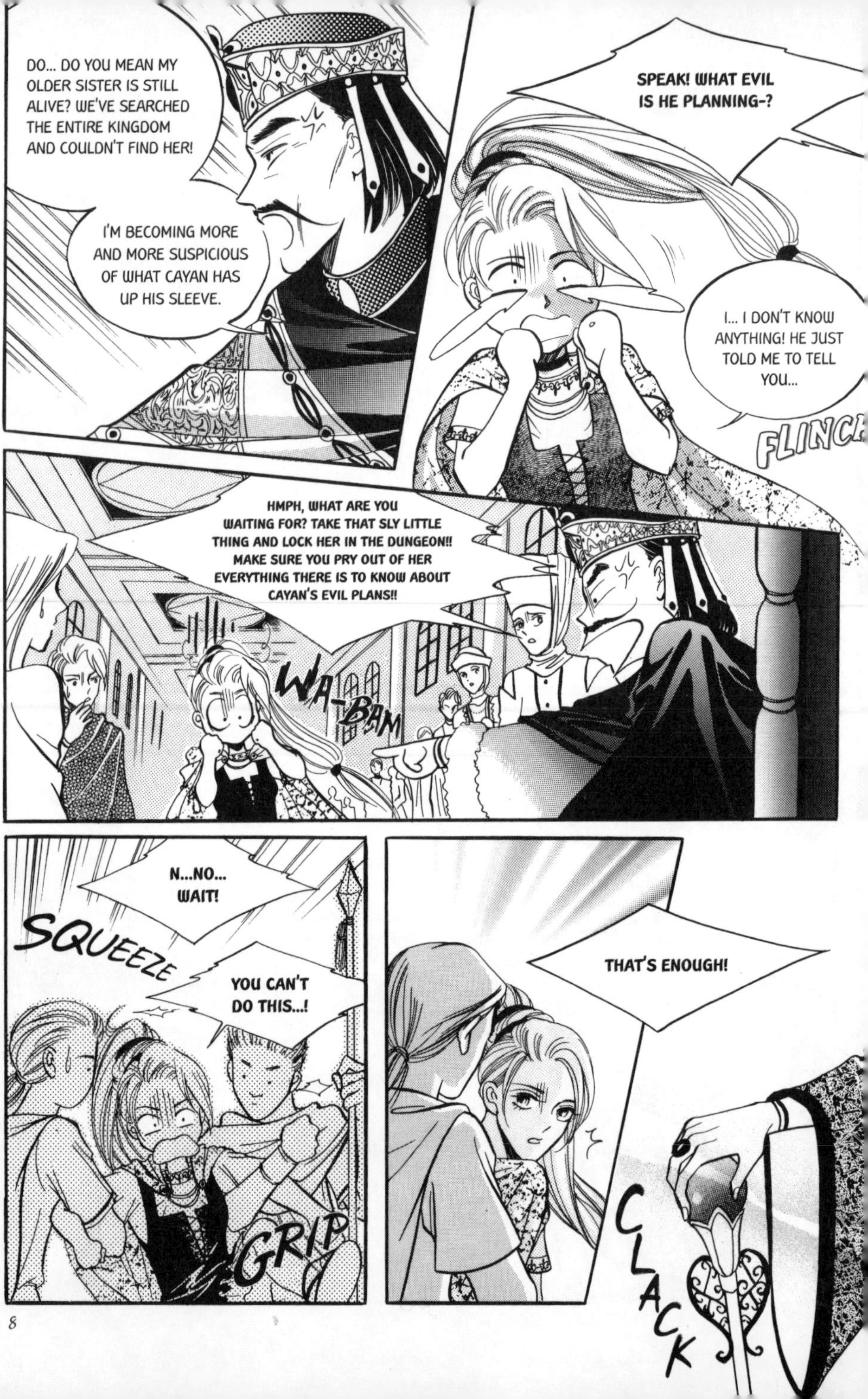
DO... DO YOU MEAN MY OLDER SISTER IS STILL ALIVE? WE'VE SEARCHED THE ENTIRE KINGDOM AND COULDN'T FIND HER!
I'M BECOMING MORE AND MORE SUSPICIOUS OF WHAT CAYAN HAS UP HIS SLEEVE.
SPEAK! WHAT EVIL IS HE PLANNING-?
I... I DON'T KNOW ANYTHING! HE JUST TOLD ME TO TELL YOU...
FLINCH
HMPH, WHAT ARE YOU WAITING FOR? TAKE THAT SLY LITTLE THING AND LOCK HER IN THE DUNGEON!! MAKE SURE YOU PRY OUT OF HER EVERYTHING THERE IS TO KNOW ABOUT CAYAN'S EVIL PLANS!!
WA-BAM
N...NO... WAIT!
SQUEEZE
YOU CAN'T DO THIS...!
GRIP
THAT'S ENOUGH!
CLACK

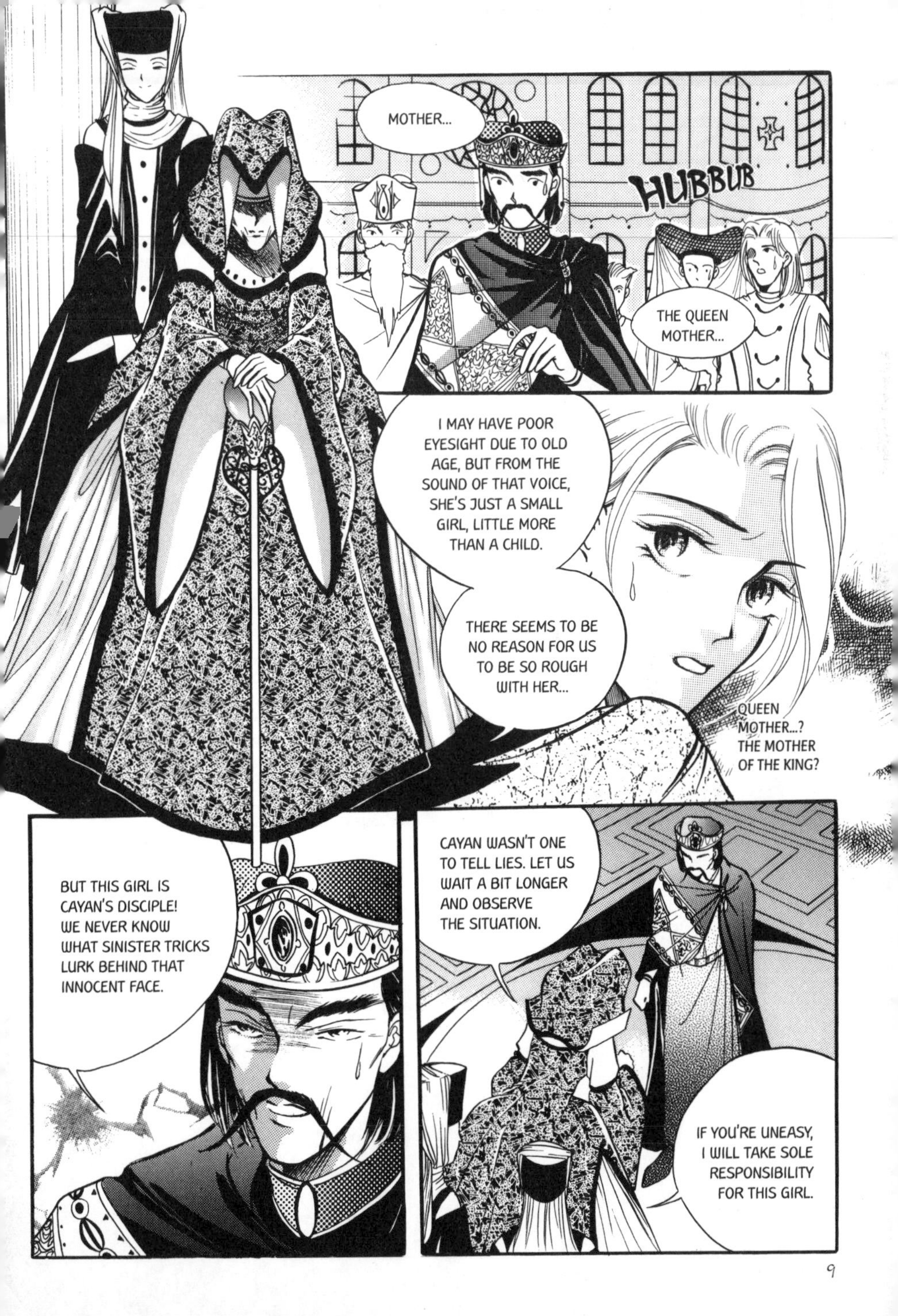
MOTHER...
HUBBUB
THE QUEEN MOTHER...
I MAY HAVE POOR EYESIGHT DUE TO OLD AGE, BUT FROM THE SOUND OF THAT VOICE, SHE'S JUST A SMALL GIRL, LITTLE MORE THAN A CHILD.
THERE SEEMS TO BE NO REASON FOR US TO BE SO ROUGH WITH HER...
QUEEN MOTHER...? THE MOTHER OF THE KING?
BUT THIS GIRL IS CAYAN'S DISCIPLE! WE NEVER KNOW WHAT SINISTER TRICKS LURK BEHIND THAT INNOCENT FACE.
CAYAN WASN'T ONE TO TELL LIES. LET US WAIT A BIT LONGER AND OBSERVE THE SITUATION.
IF YOU'RE UNEASY, I WILL TAKE SOLE RESPONSIBILITY FOR THIS GIRL.

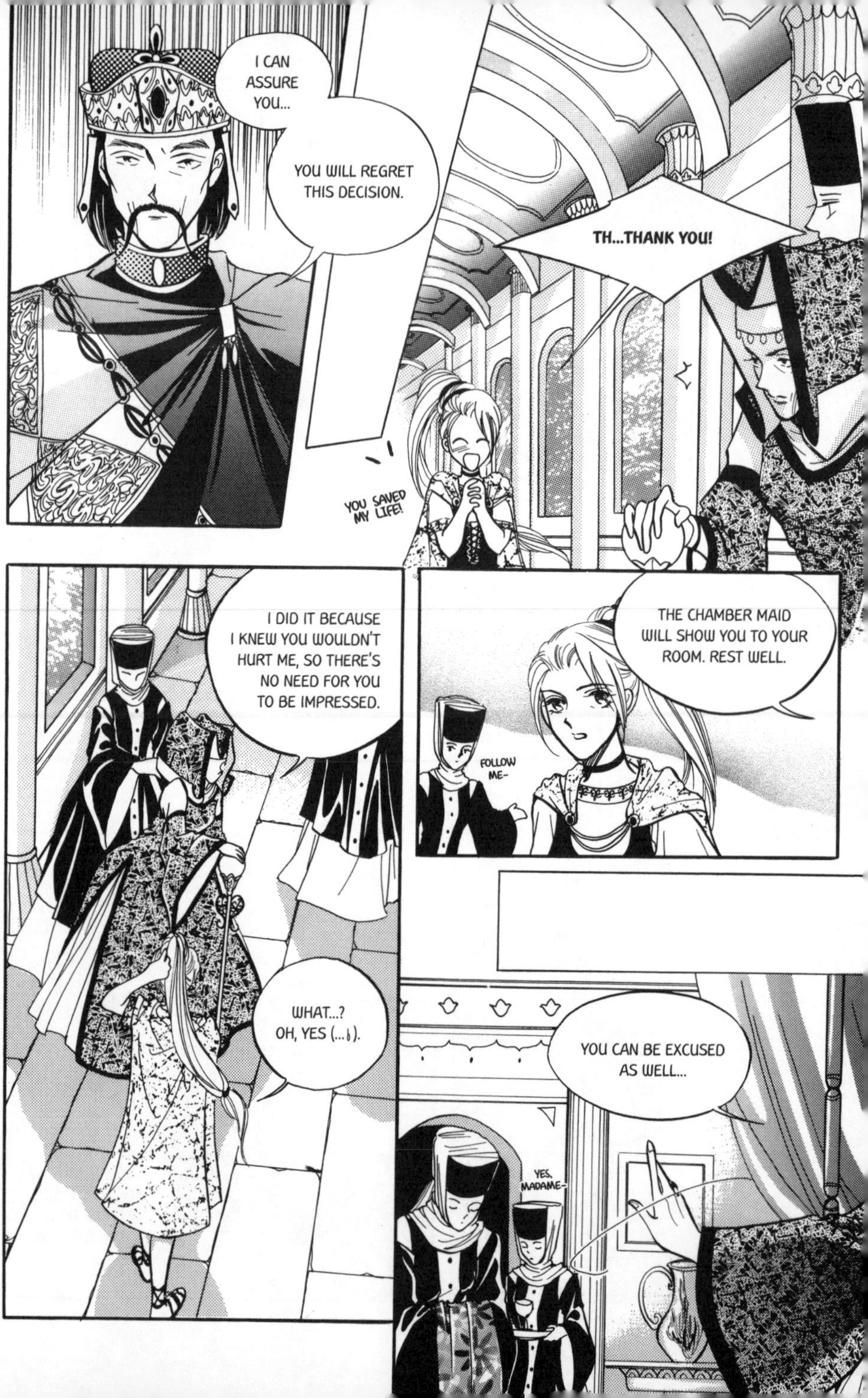
I CAN ASSURE YOU...
YOU WILL REGRET THIS DECISION.
TH...THANK YOU!
YOU SAVED MY LIFE!
I DID IT BECAUSE I KNEW YOU WOULDN'T HURT ME, SO THERE'S NO NEED FOR YOU TO BE IMPRESSED.
WHAT...? OH, YES (...).
THE CHAMBER MAID WILL SHOW YOU TO YOUR ROOM. REST WELL.
FOLLOW ME-
YOU CAN BE EXCUSED AS WELL...
YES, MADAME-

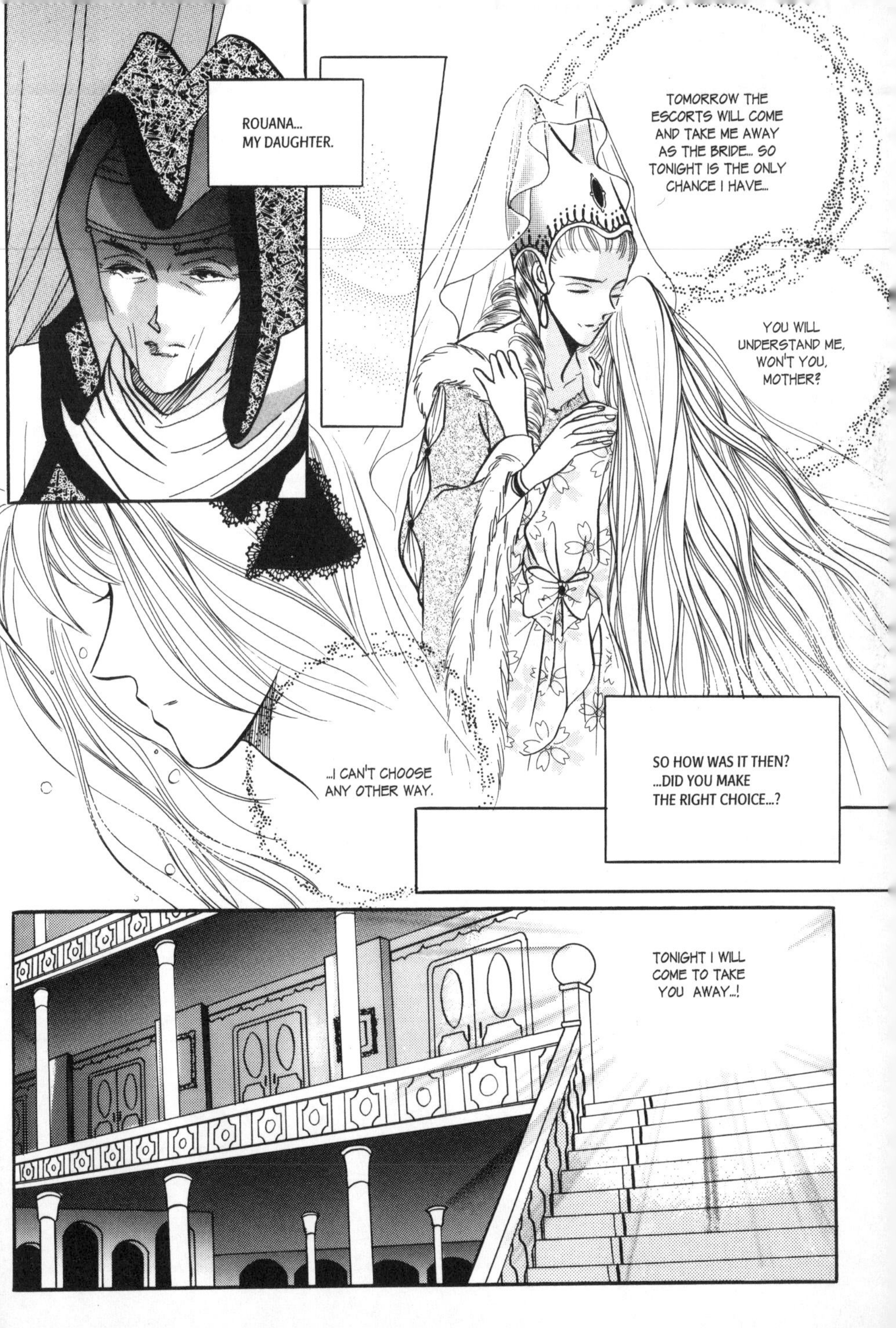
ROUANA... MY DAUGHTER.
TOMORROW THE ESCORTS WILL COME AND TAKE ME AWAY AS THE BRIDE... SO TONIGHT IS THE ONLY CHANCE I HAVE...
YOU WILL UNDERSTAND ME, WON'T YOU, MOTHER?
...I CAN'T CHOOSE ANY OTHER WAY.
SO HOW WAS IT THEN? ...DID YOU MAKE THE RIGHT CHOICE...?
TONIGHT I WILL COME TO TAKE YOU AWAY...!

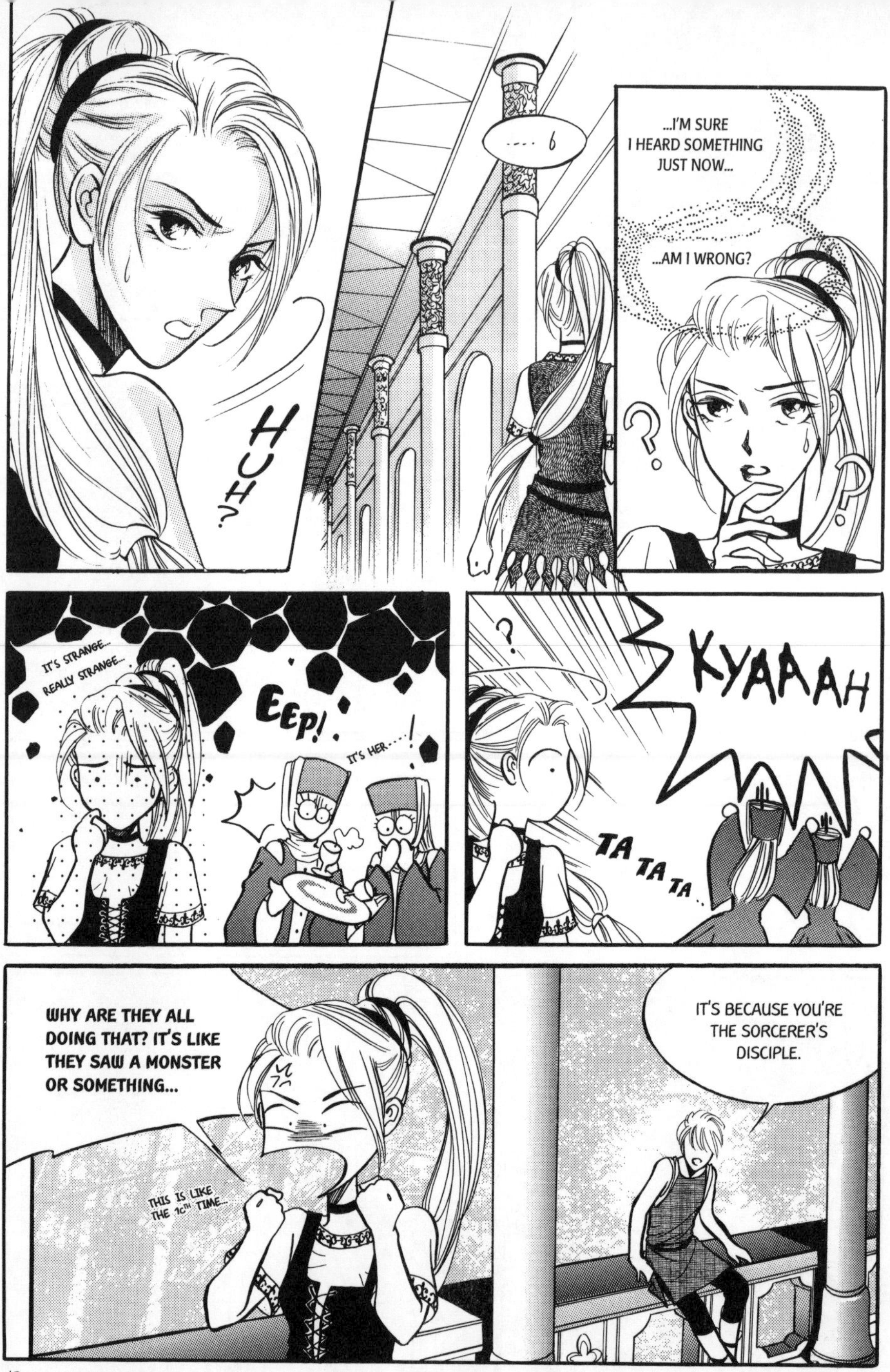
HUH?
...I'M SURE I HEARD SOMETHING JUST NOW...
...AM I WRONG?
IT'S STRANGE... REALLY STRANGE...
EEP!
IT'S HER....!
KYAAAH
TA TA TA...
WHY ARE THEY ALL DOING THAT? IT'S LIKE THEY SAW A MONSTER OR SOMETHING...
THIS IS LIKE THE 10TH TIME...
IT'S BECAUSE YOU'RE THE SORCERER'S DISCIPLE.

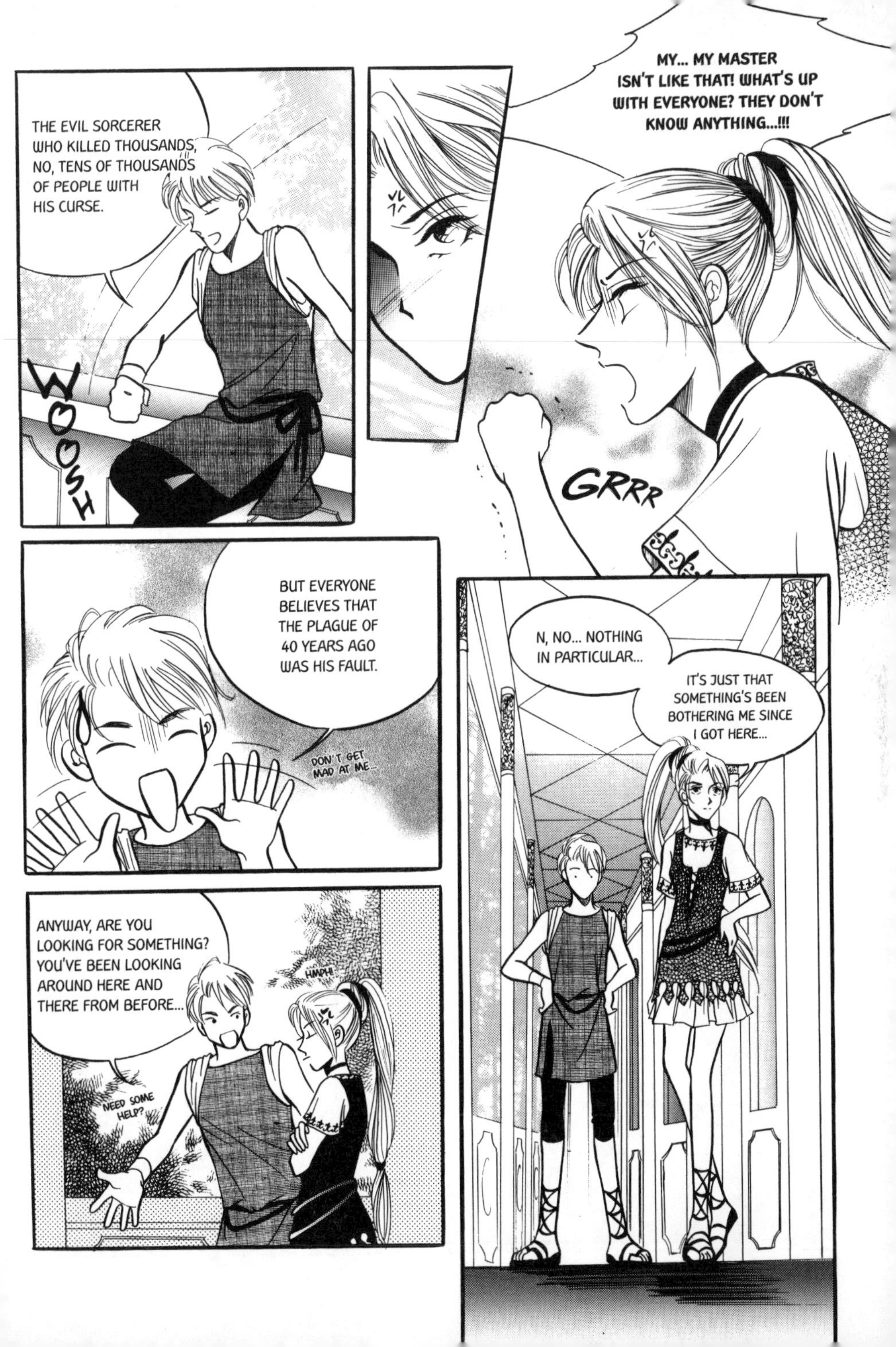
THE EVIL SORCERER WHO KILLED THOUSANDS, NO, TENS OF THOUSANDS OF PEOPLE WITH HIS CURSE.
WOOSH
MY... MY MASTER ISN'T LIKE THAT! WHAT'S UP WITH EVERYONE? THEY DON'T KNOW ANYTHING...!!!
GRRR
BUT EVERYONE BELIEVES THAT THE PLAGUE OF 40 YEARS AGO WAS HIS FAULT.
DON'T GET MAD AT ME...
ANYWAY, ARE YOU LOOKING FOR SOMETHING? YOU'VE BEEN LOOKING AROUND HERE AND THERE FROM BEFORE...
HMPH!
NEED SOME HELP?
N, NO... NOTHING IN PARTICULAR...
IT'S JUST THAT SOMETHING'S BEEN BOTHERING ME SINCE I GOT HERE...

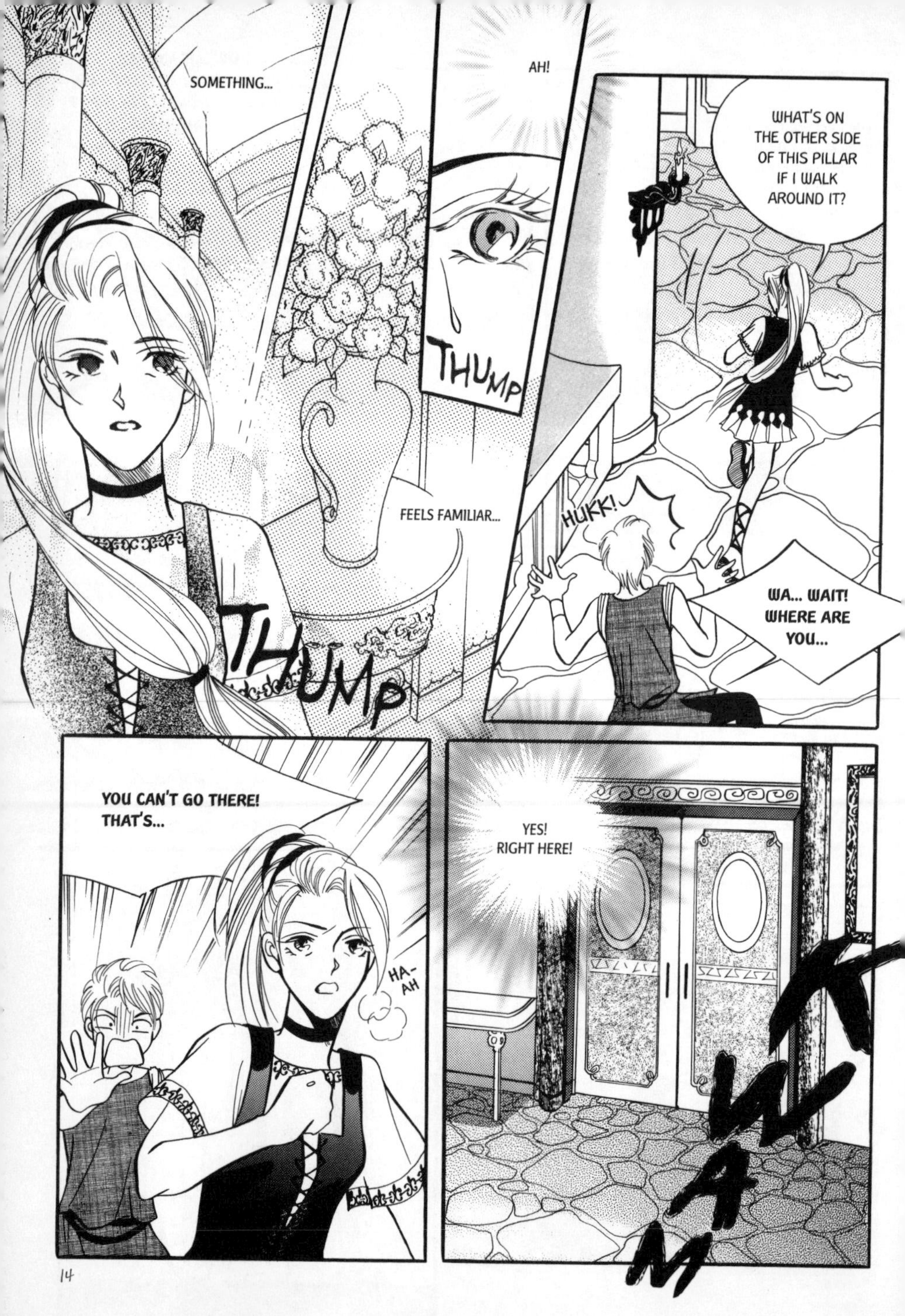
SOMETHING...
FEELS FAMILIAR...
THUMP
AH!
THUMP
WHAT'S ON THE OTHER SIDE OF THIS PILLAR IF I WALK AROUND IT?
HUKK!
WA... WAIT! WHERE ARE YOU...
YOU CAN'T GO THERE! THAT'S...
HA-AH
YES! RIGHT HERE!
KWAM

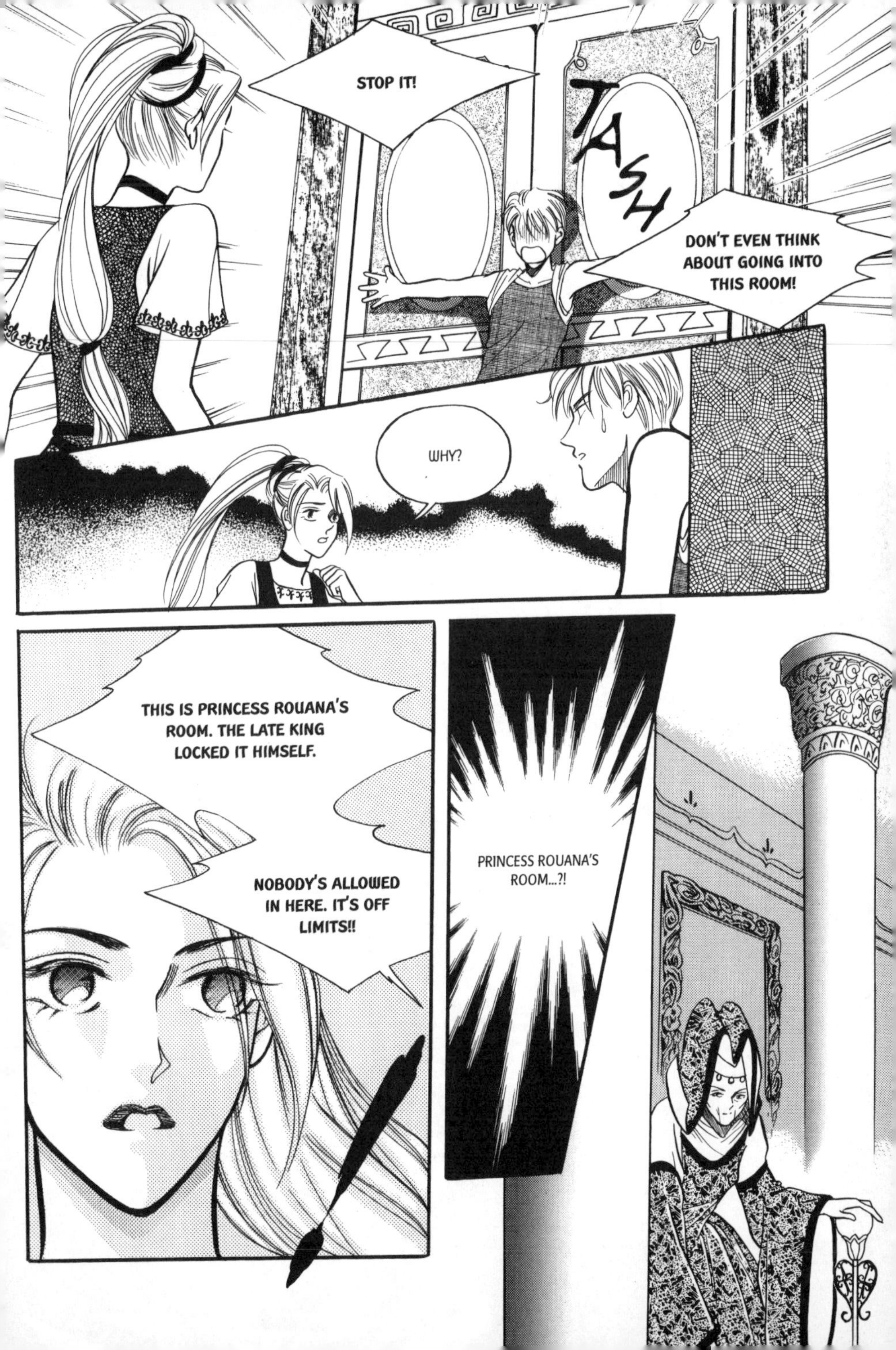
STOP IT!
TASH
DON'T EVEN THINK ABOUT GOING INTO THIS ROOM!
WHY?
THIS IS PRINCESS ROUANA'S ROOM. THE LATE KING LOCKED IT HIMSELF.
NOBODY'S ALLOWED IN HERE. IT'S OFF LIMITS!!
PRINCESS ROUANA'S ROOM...?!

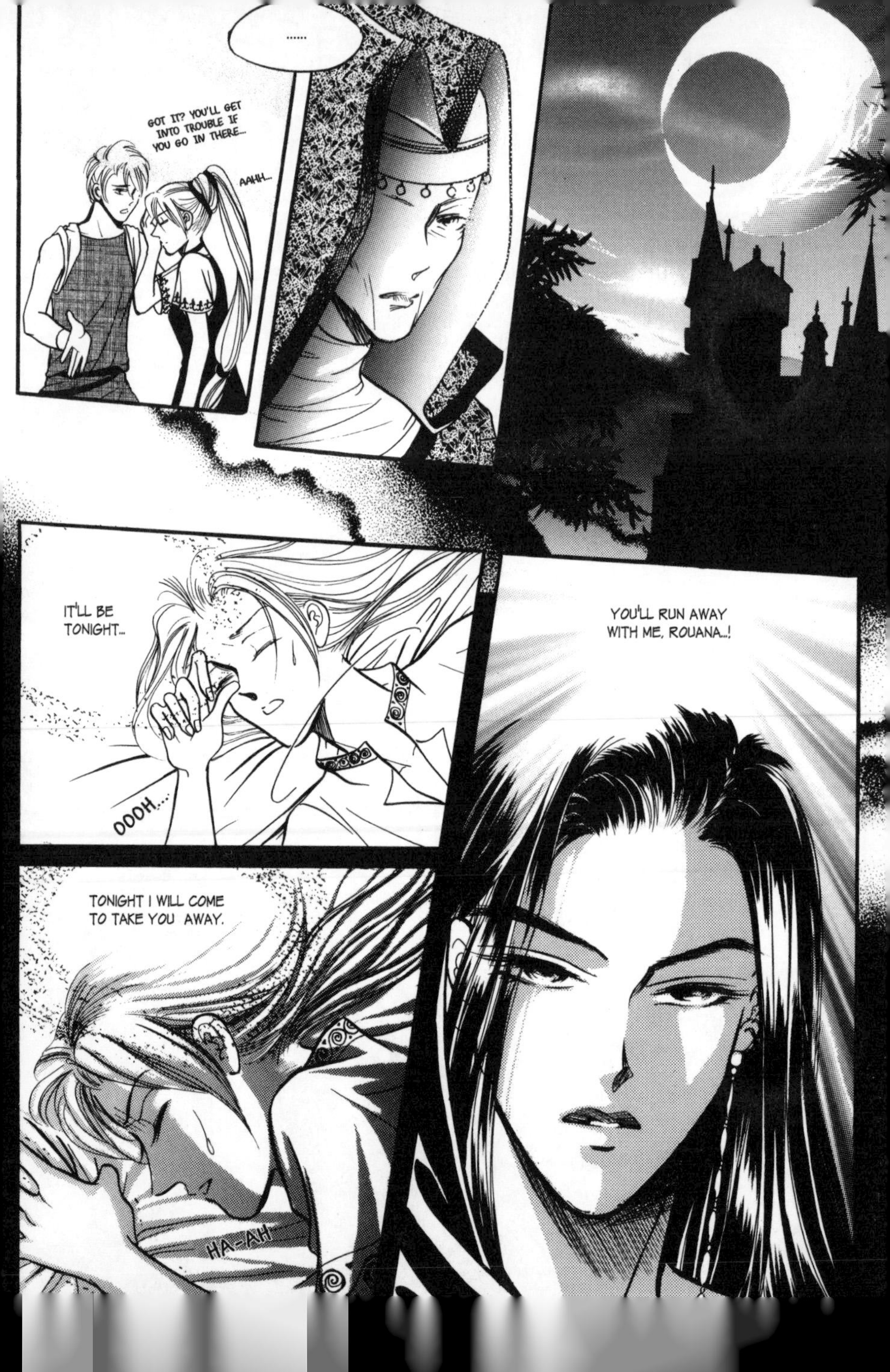

......
GOT IT? YOU'LL GET INTO TROUBLE IF YOU GO IN THERE...
AAHH...
IT'LL BE TONIGHT...
OOOH...
YOU'LL RUN AWAY WITH ME, ROUANA...!
TONIGHT I WILL COME TO TAKE YOU AWAY.
HA-AH

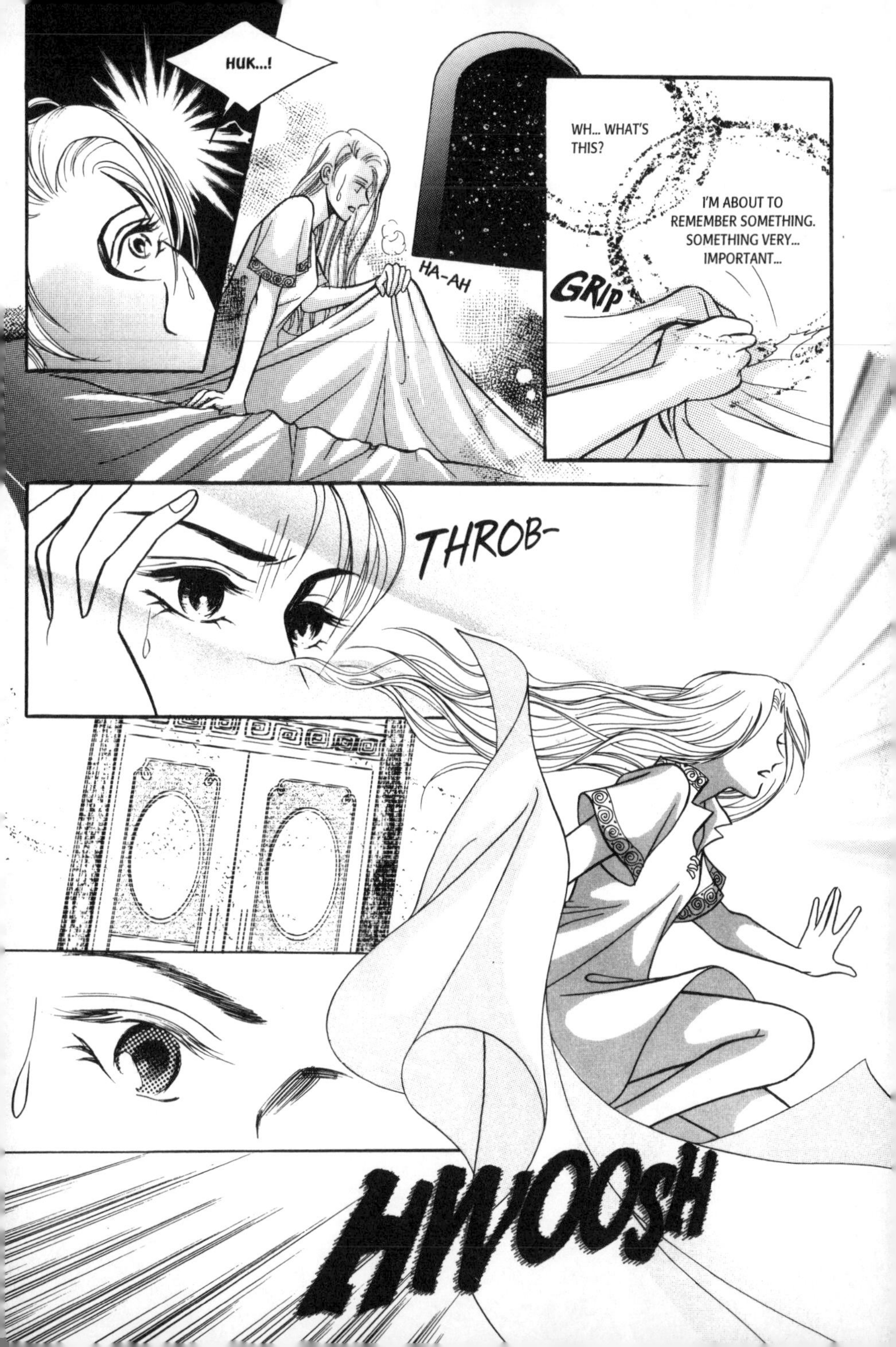

HUK...!
HA-AH
WH... WHAT'S THIS?
I'M ABOUT TO REMEMBER SOMETHING. SOMETHING VERY... IMPORTANT...
GRIP
THROB-
HWOOSH

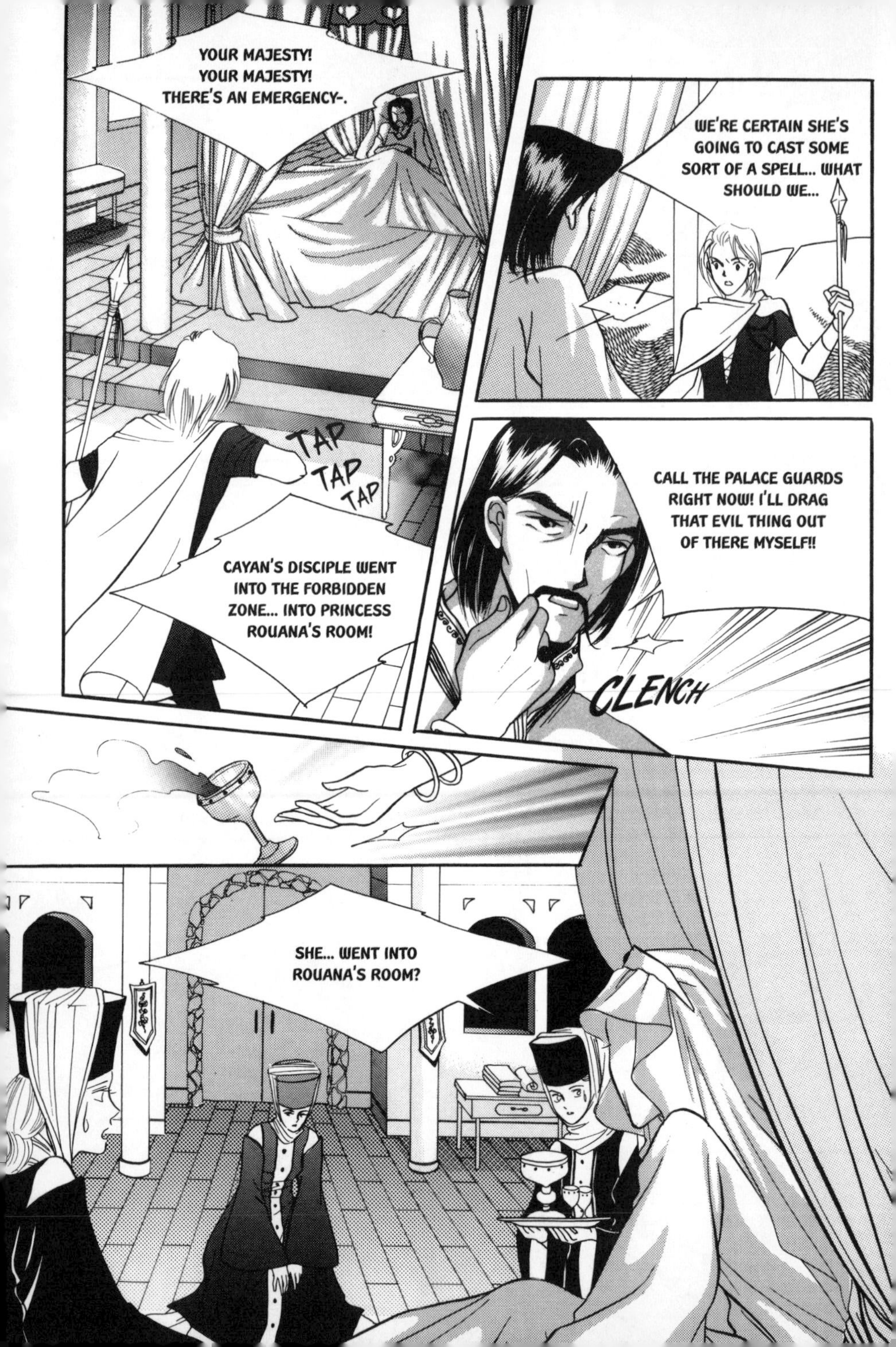
YOUR MAJESTY! YOUR MAJESTY! THERE'S AN EMERGENCY-.
TAP TAP TAP
CAYAN'S DISCIPLE WENT INTO THE FORBIDDEN ZONE... INTO PRINCESS ROUANA'S ROOM!
WE'RE CERTAIN SHE'S GOING TO CAST SOME SORT OF A SPELL... WHAT SHOULD WE...
CALL THE PALACE GUARDS RIGHT NOW! I'LL DRAG THAT EVIL THING OUT OF THERE MYSELF!!
CLENCH
SHE... WENT INTO ROUANA'S ROOM?

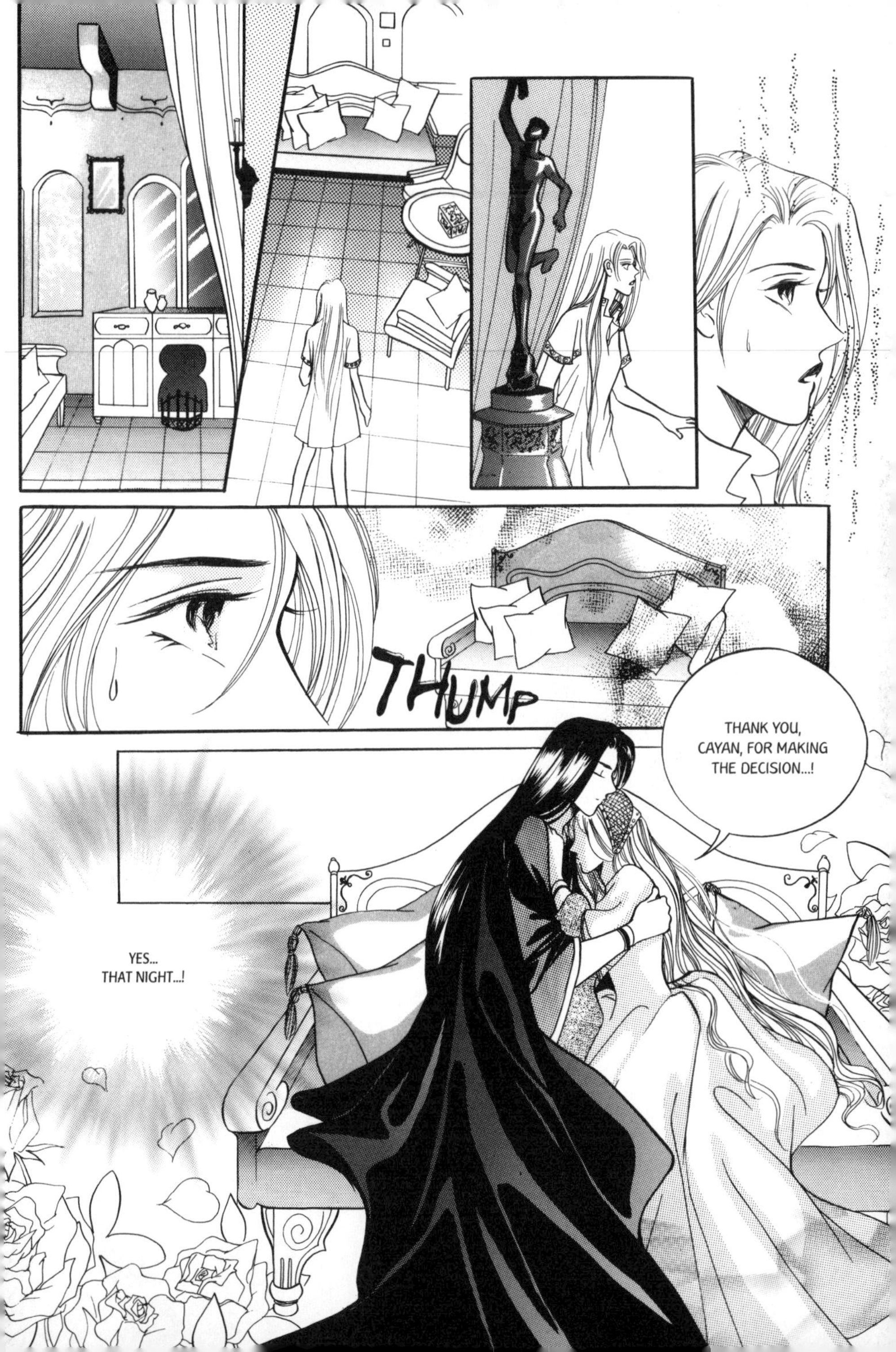
THUMP
THANK YOU, CAYAN, FOR MAKING THE DECISION...!
YES... THAT NIGHT...!

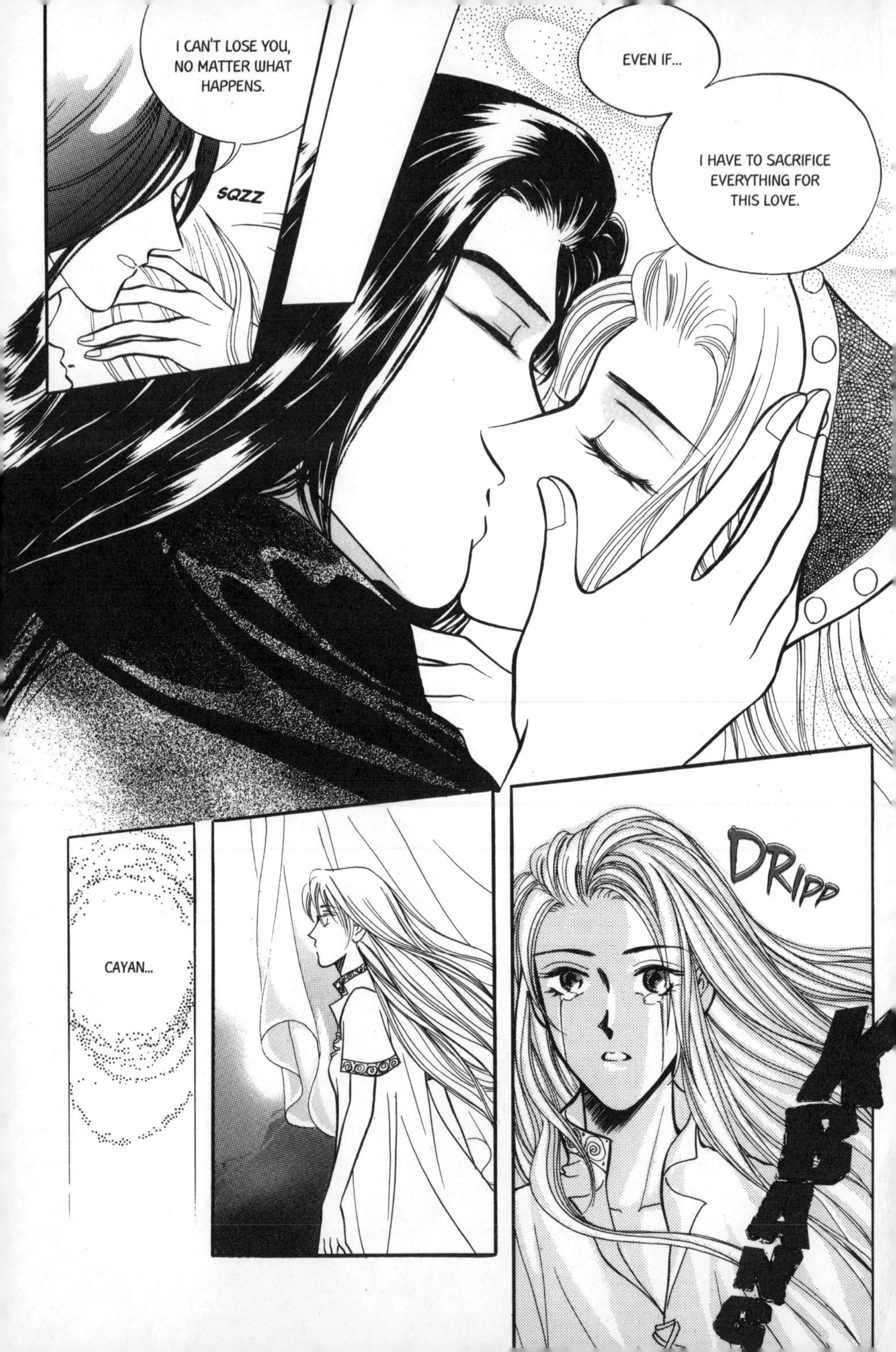
I CAN'T LOSE YOU, NO MATTER WHAT HAPPENS.
SQZZ
EVEN IF...
I HAVE TO SACRIFICE EVERYTHING FOR THIS LOVE.
CAYAN...
DRIPP

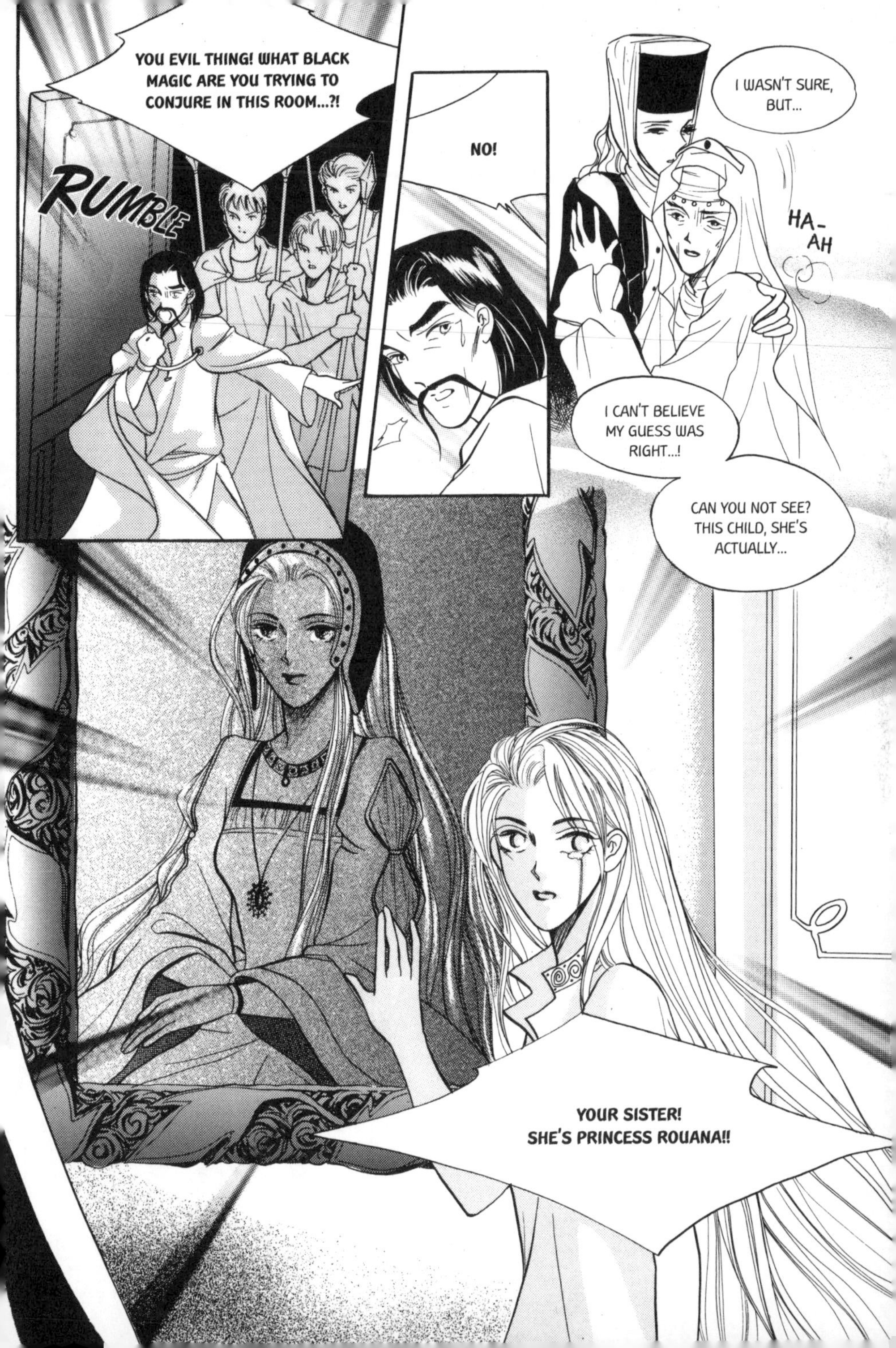
YOU EVIL THING! WHAT BLACK MAGIC ARE YOU TRYING TO CONJURE IN THIS ROOM...?!
RUMBLE
NO!
I WASN'T SURE, BUT...
HA-AH
I CAN'T BELIEVE MY GUESS WAS RIGHT...!
CAN YOU NOT SEE? THIS CHILD, SHE'S ACTUALLY...
YOUR SISTER! SHE'S PRINCESS ROUANA!!

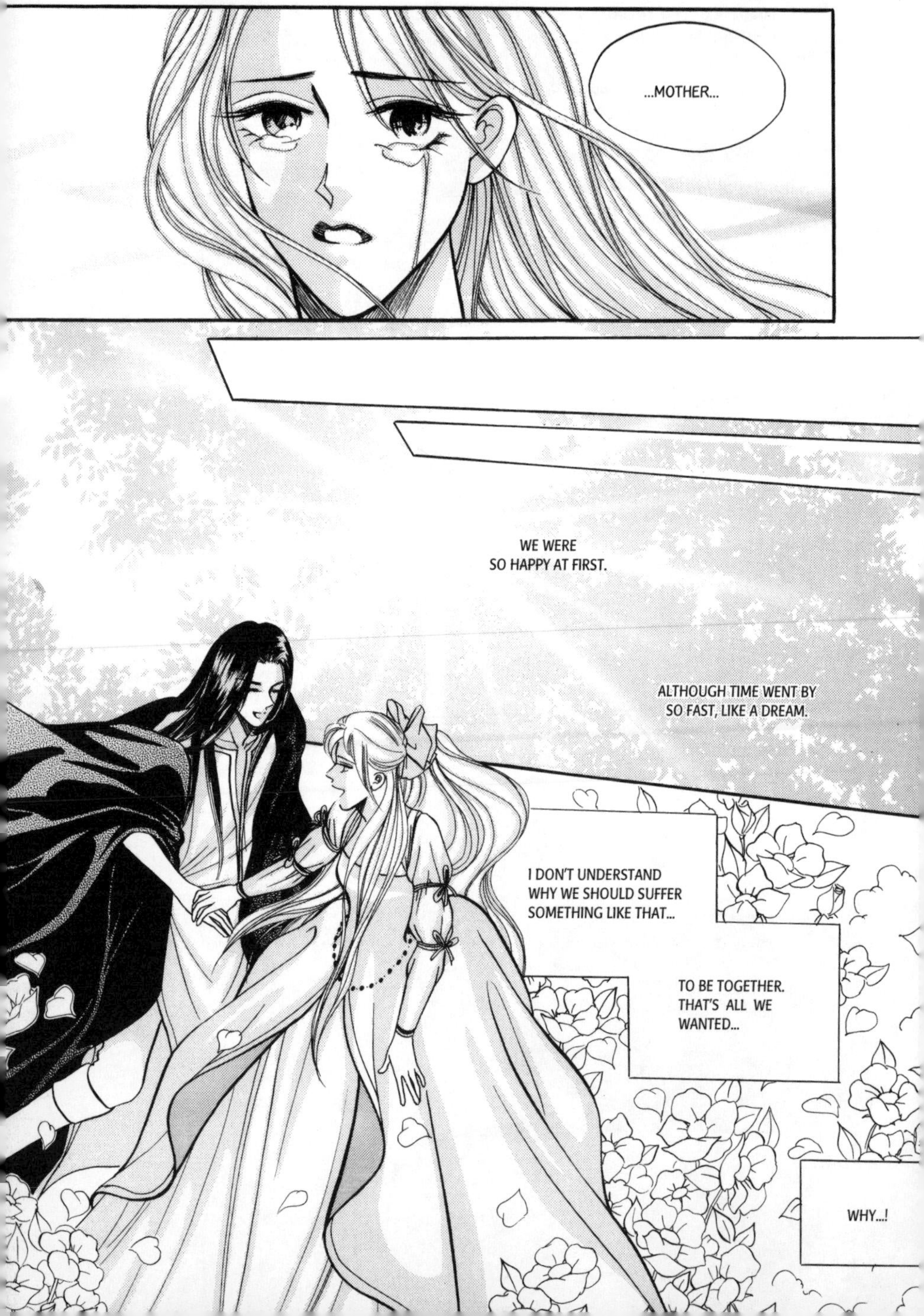
...MOTHER...
WE WERE SO HAPPY AT FIRST.
ALTHOUGH TIME WENT BY SO FAST, LIKE A DREAM.
I DON'T UNDERSTAND WHY WE SHOULD SUFFER SOMETHING LIKE THAT...
TO BE TOGETHER. THAT'S ALL WE WANTED...
WHY...!

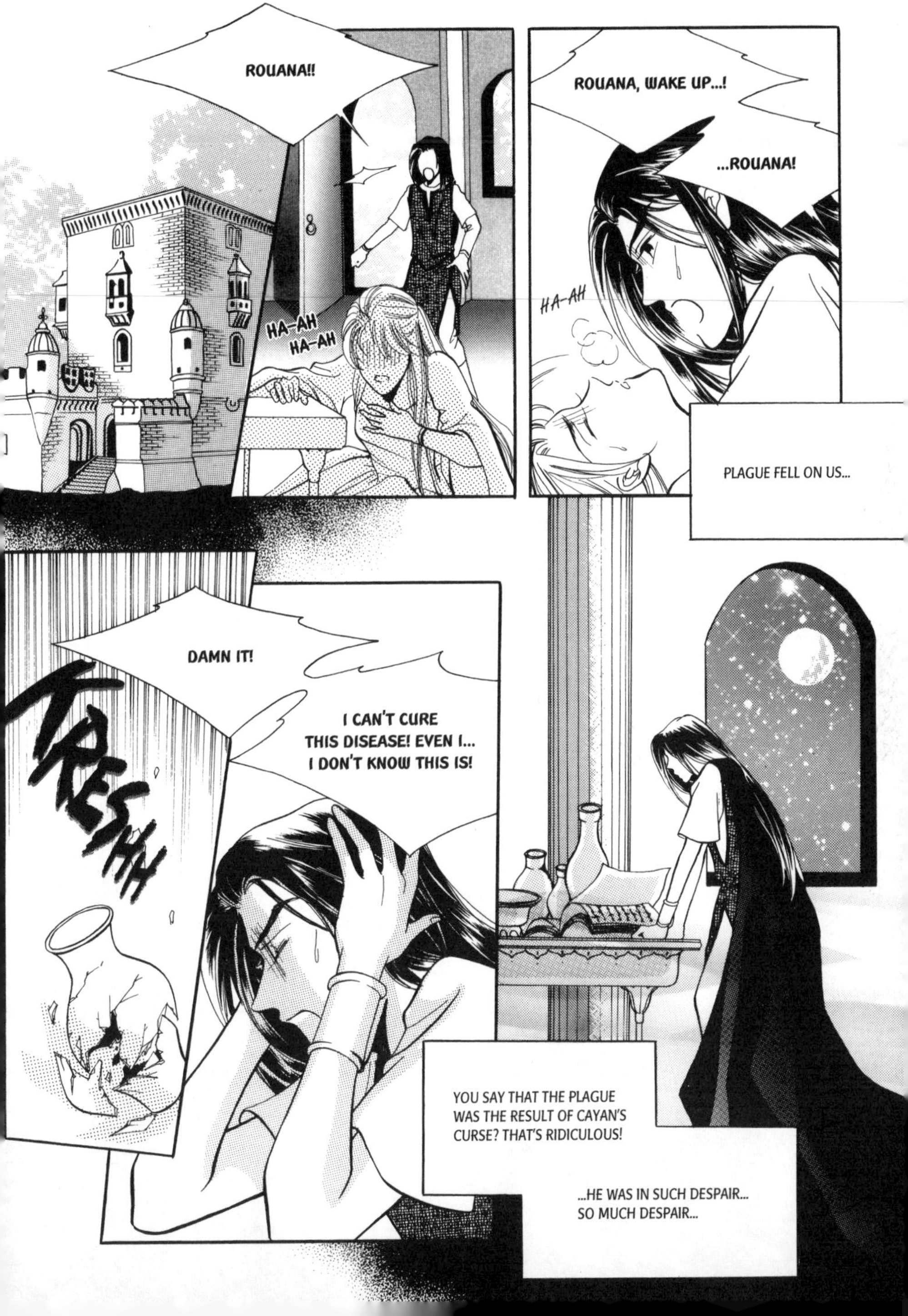
ROUANA!!
HA-AH HA-AH
ROUANA, WAKE UP...!
...ROUANA!
HA-AH
PLAGUE FELL ON US...
DAMN IT!
FRESHH
I CAN'T CURE THIS DISEASE! EVEN I... I DON'T KNOW THIS IS!
YOU SAY THAT THE PLAGUE WAS THE RESULT OF CAYAN'S CURSE? THAT'S RIDICULOUS!
...HE WAS IN SUCH DESPAIR... SO MUCH DESPAIR...

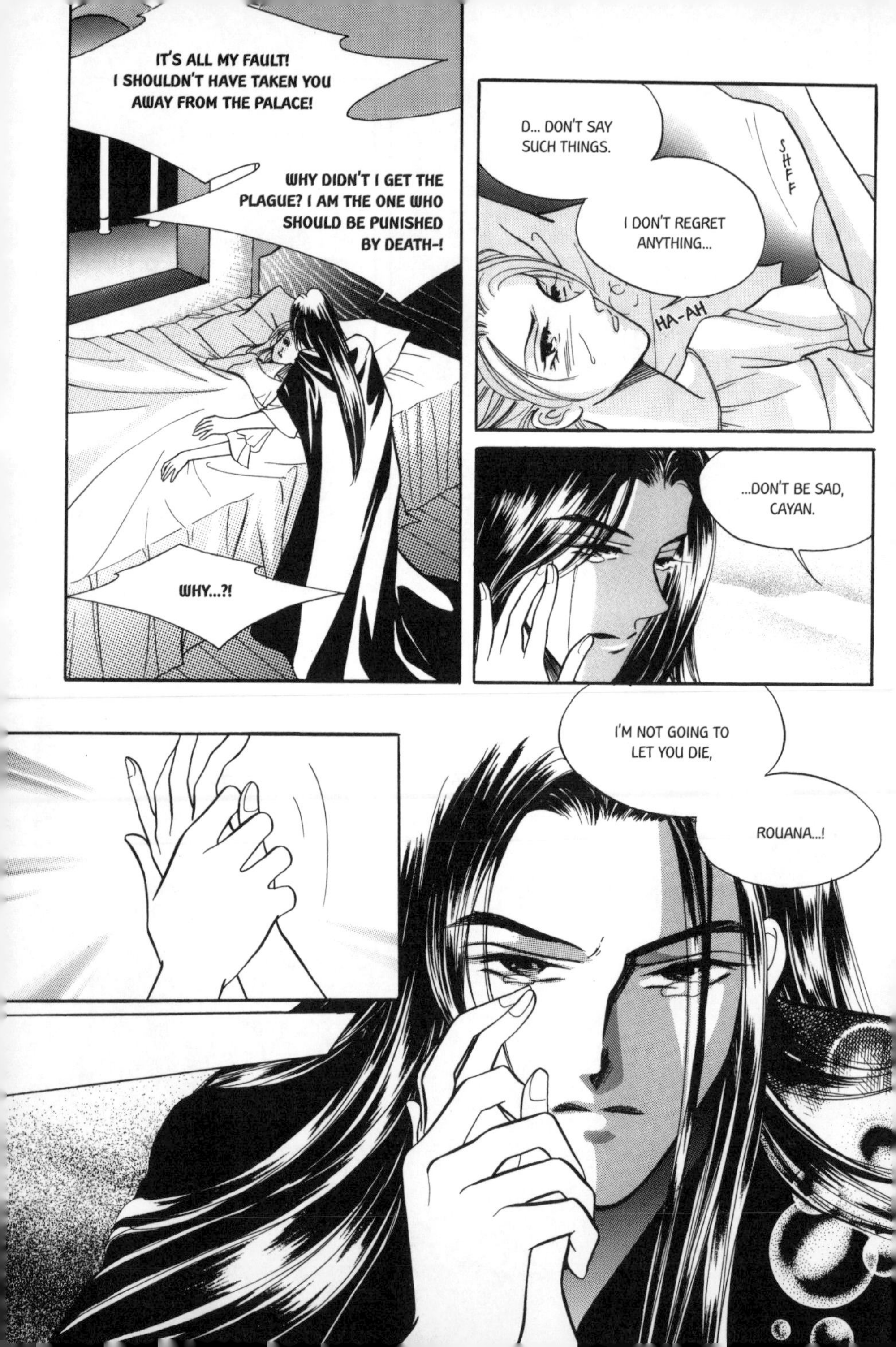
IT'S ALL MY FAULT! I SHOULDN'T HAVE TAKEN YOU AWAY FROM THE PALACE!
WHY DIDN'T I GET THE PLAGUE? I AM THE ONE WHO SHOULD BE PUNISHED BY DEATH-!
WHY...?!
D... DON'T SAY SUCH THINGS.
SHFF
I DON'T REGRET ANYTHING...
HA-AH
...DON'T BE SAD, CAYAN.
I'M NOT GOING TO LET YOU DIE,
ROUANA...!

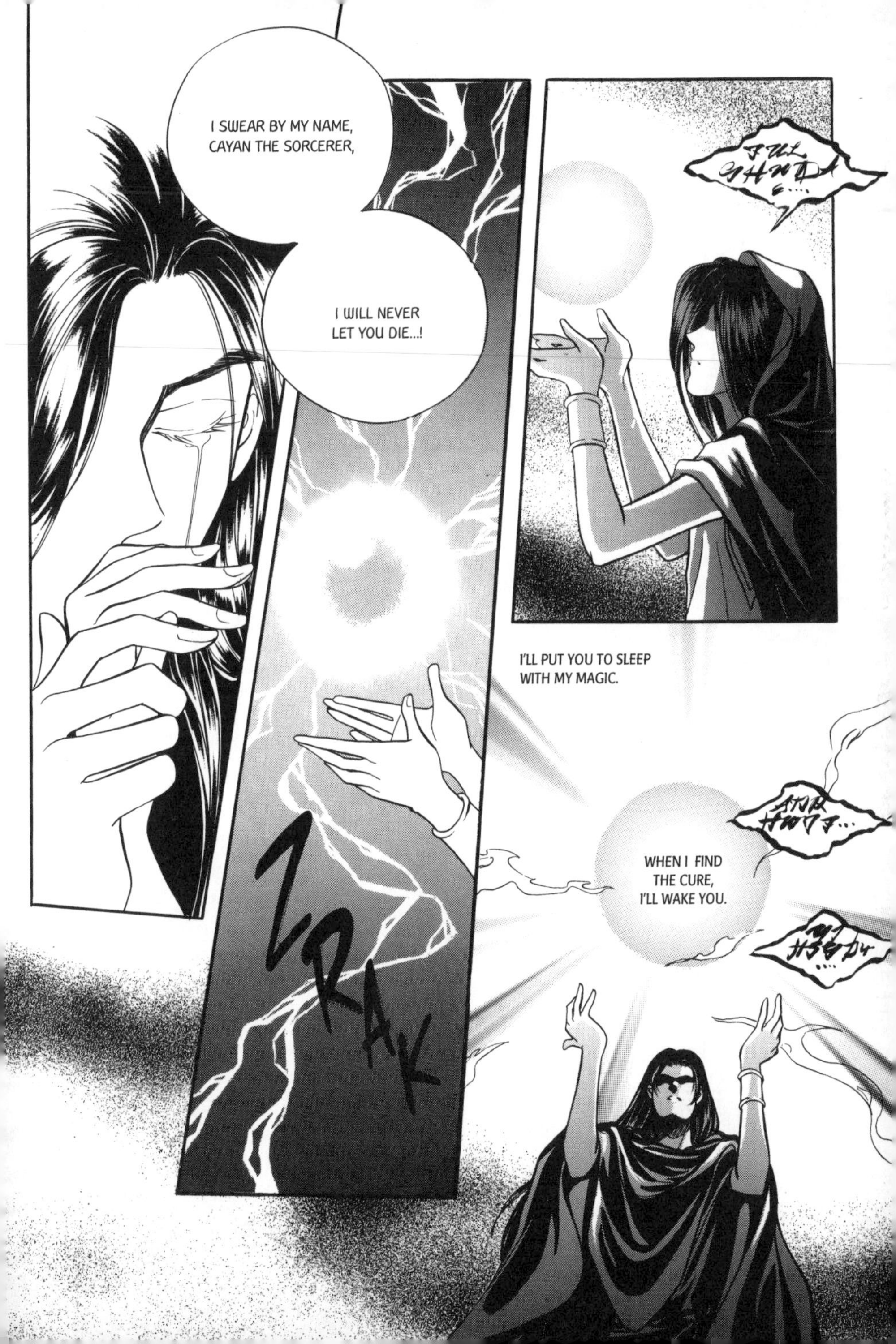
I SWEAR BY MY NAME, CAYAN THE SORCERER,
I WILL NEVER LET YOU DIE...!
ZRAK
I'LL PUT YOU TO SLEEP WITH MY MAGIC.
WHEN I FIND THE CURE, I'LL WAKE YOU.

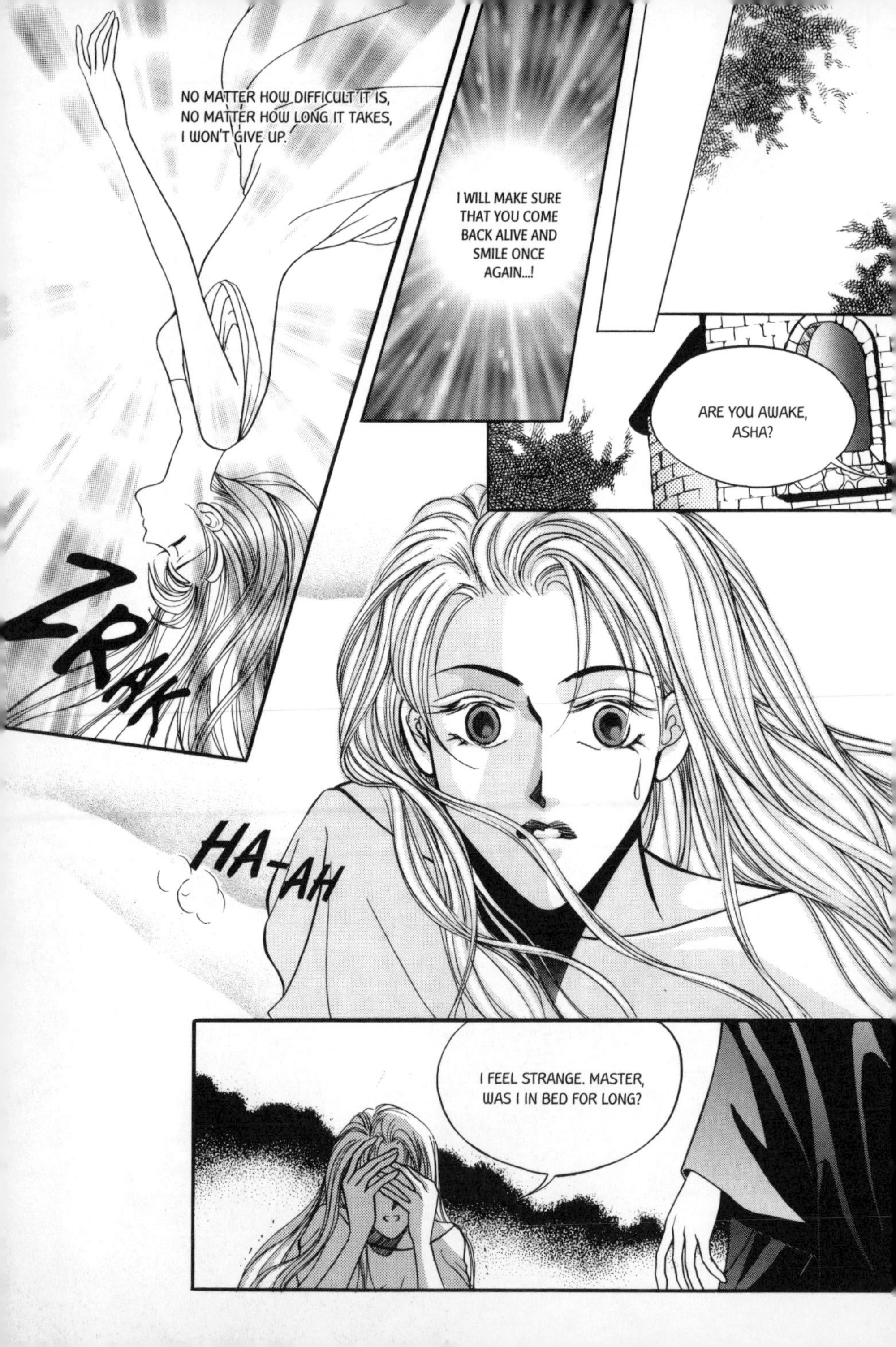
NO MATTER HOW DIFFICULT IT IS, NO MATTER HOW LONG IT TAKES, I WON'T GIVE UP.
I WILL MAKE SURE THAT YOU COME BACK ALIVE AND SMILE ONCE AGAIN...!
ZRAK
ARE YOU AWAKE, ASHA?
HA-AH
I FEEL STRANGE. MASTER, WAS I IN BED FOR LONG?

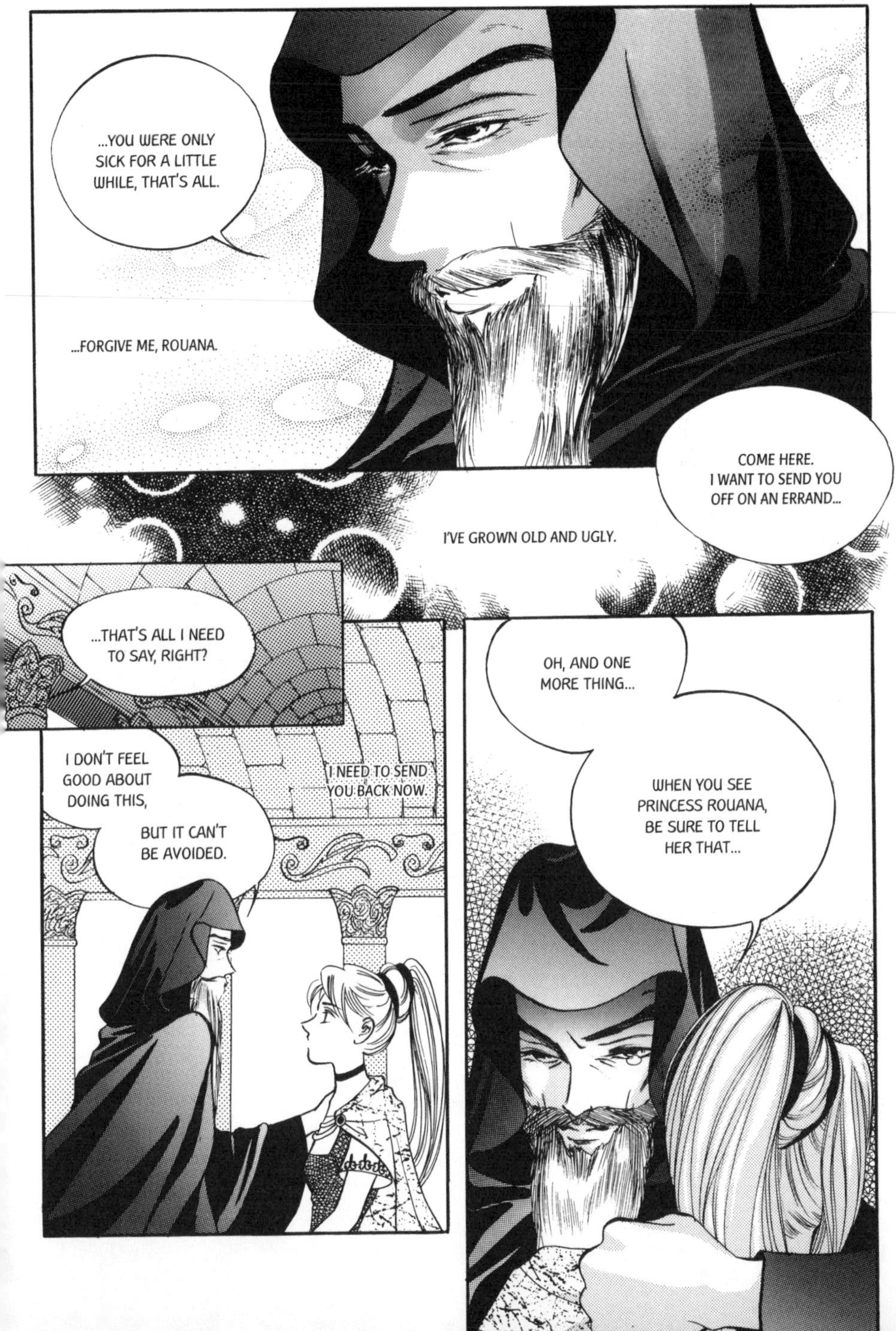
...YOU WERE ONLY SICK FOR A LITTLE WHILE, THAT'S ALL.
...FORGIVE ME, ROUANA.
I'VE GROWN OLD AND UGLY.
COME HERE. I WANT TO SEND YOU OFF ON AN ERRAND...
...THAT'S ALL I NEED TO SAY, RIGHT?
I DON'T FEEL GOOD ABOUT DOING THIS,
BUT IT CAN'T BE AVOIDED.
I NEED TO SEND YOU BACK NOW.
OH, AND ONE MORE THING...
WHEN YOU SEE PRINCESS ROUANA, BE SURE TO TELL HER THAT...

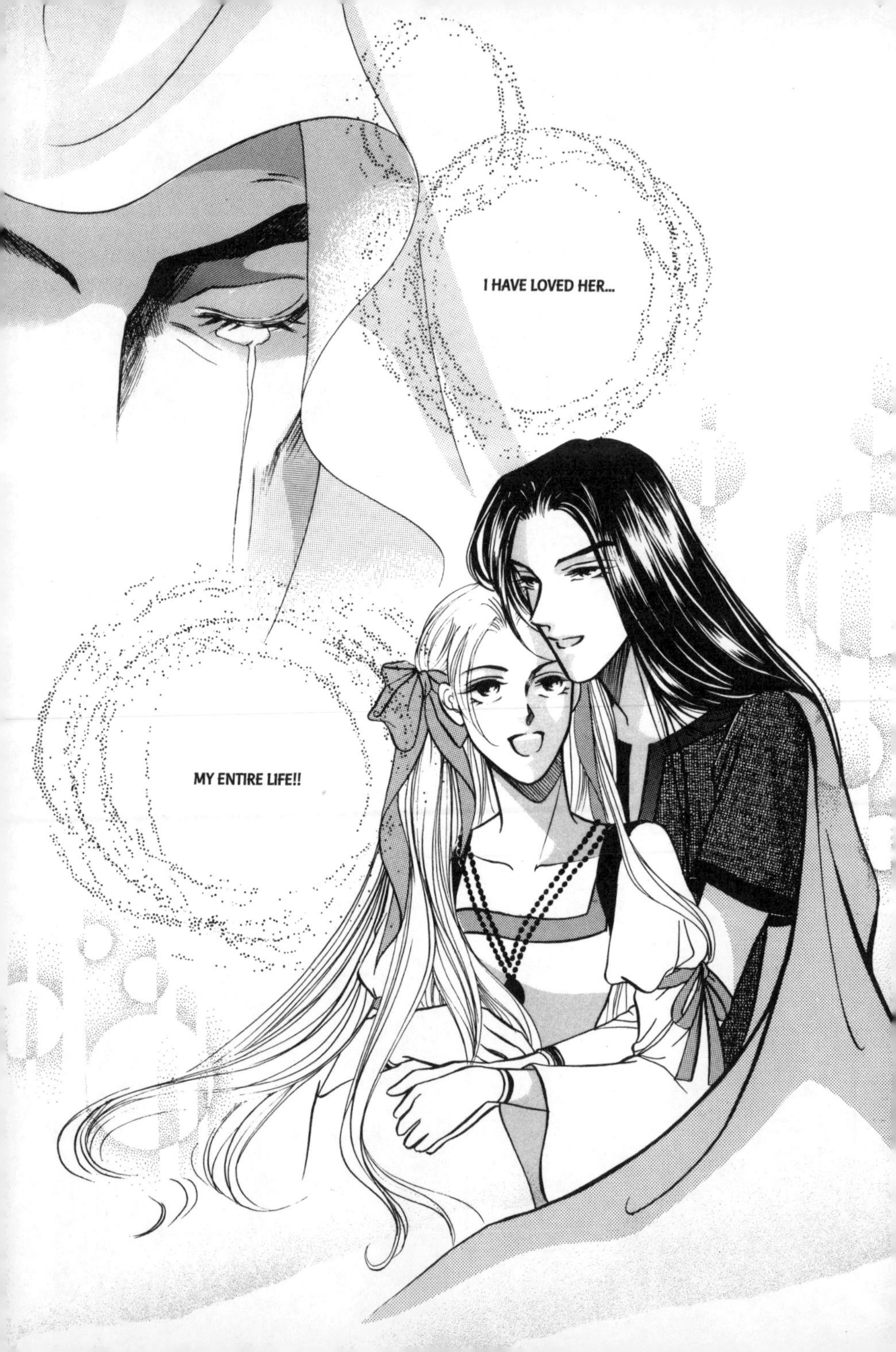
I HAVE LOVED HER...
MY ENTIRE LIFE!!

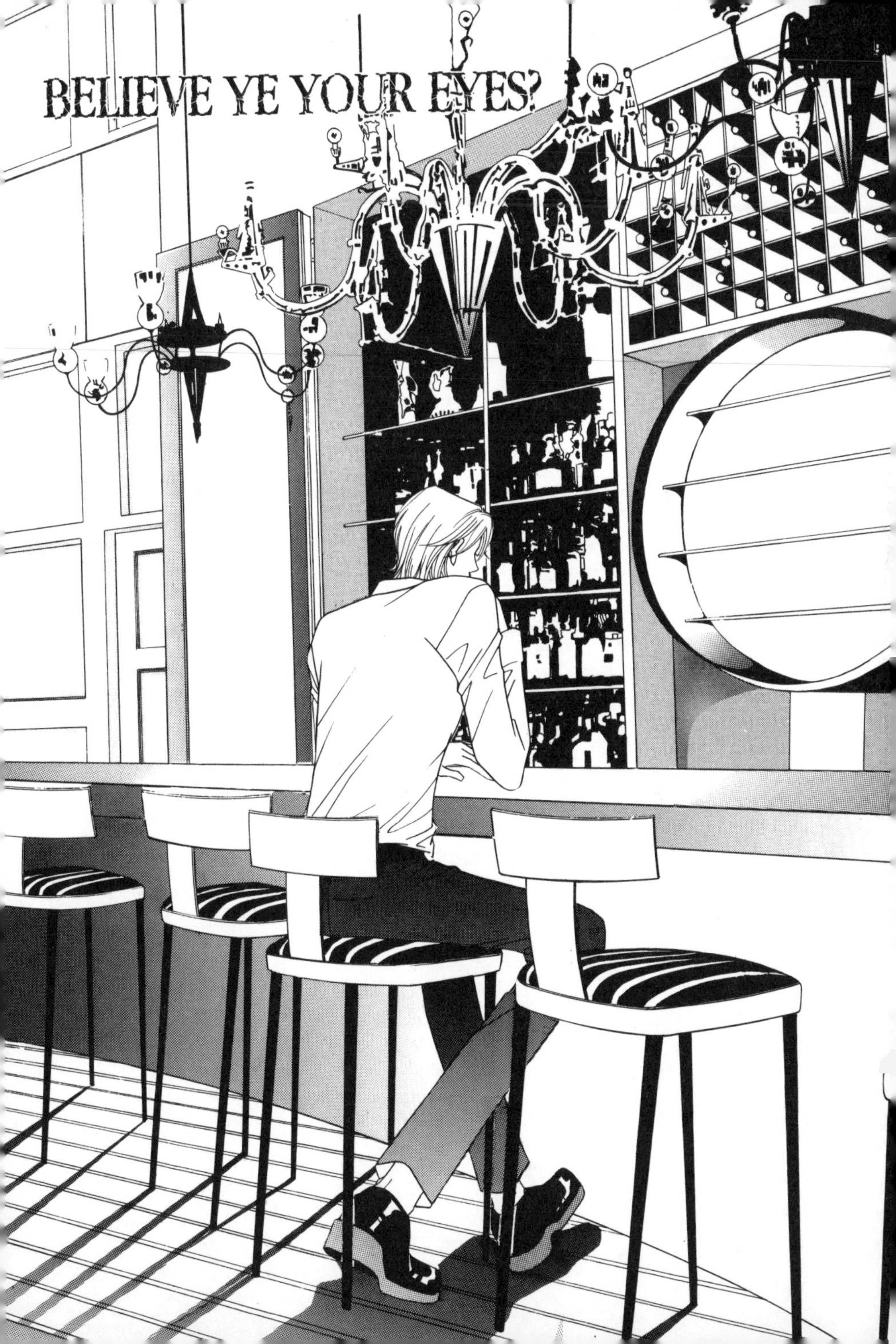
BELIEVE YE YOUR EYES?

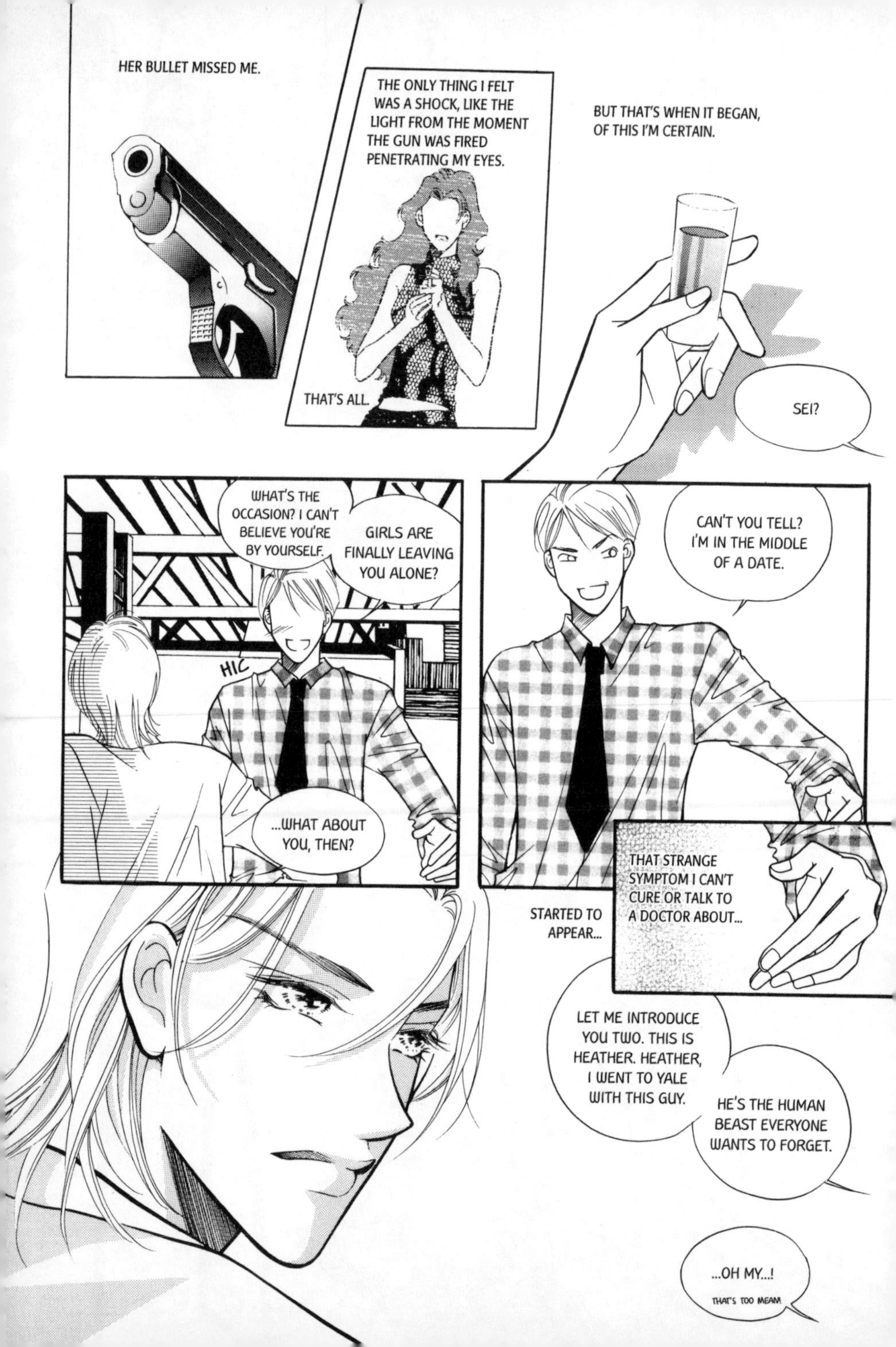
HER BULLET MISSED ME.
THE ONLY THING I FELT WAS A SHOCK, LIKE THE LIGHT FROM THE MOMENT THE GUN WAS FIRED PENETRATING MY EYES.
THAT'S ALL.
BUT THAT'S WHEN IT BEGAN, OF THIS I'M CERTAIN.
SEI?
WHAT'S THE OCCASION? I CAN'T BELIEVE YOU'RE BY YOURSELF.
GIRLS ARE FINALLY LEAVING YOU ALONE?
HIC
...WHAT ABOUT YOU, THEN?
CAN'T YOU TELL? I'M IN THE MIDDLE OF A DATE.
THAT STRANGE SYMPTOM I CAN'T CURE OR TALK TO A DOCTOR ABOUT...
STARTED TO APPEAR...
LET ME INTRODUCE YOU TWO. THIS IS HEATHER. HEATHER, I WENT TO YALE WITH THIS GUY.
HE'S THE HUMAN BEAST EVERYONE WANTS TO FORGET.
...OH MY...!
THAT'S TOO MEAN!

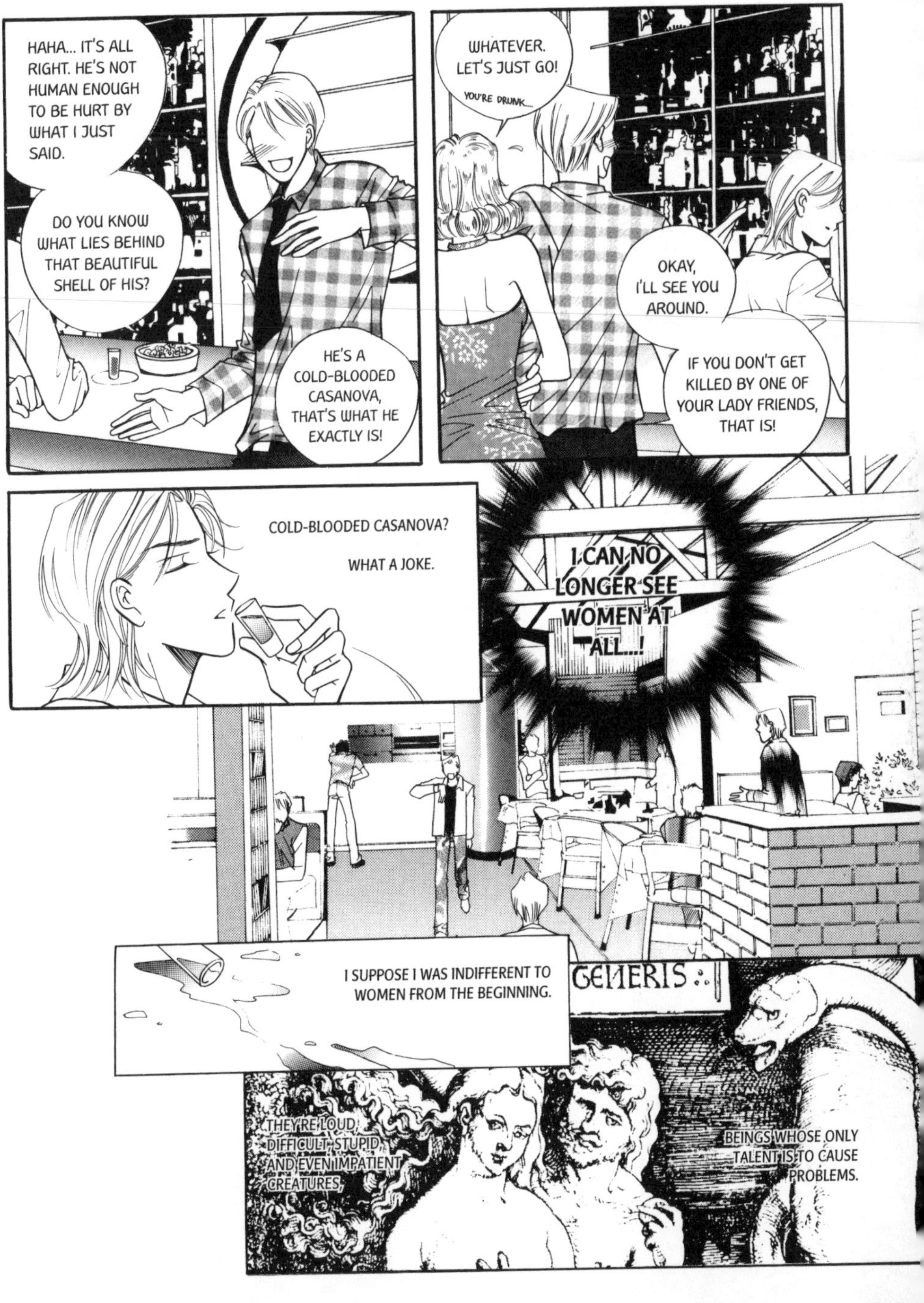
HAHA... IT'S ALL RIGHT. HE'S NOT HUMAN ENOUGH TO BE HURT BY WHAT I JUST SAID.
DO YOU KNOW WHAT LIES BEHIND THAT BEAUTIFUL SHELL OF HIS?
HE'S A COLD-BLOODED CASANOVA, THAT'S WHAT HE EXACTLY IS!
WHATEVER. LET'S JUST GO!
YOU'RE DRUNK....
OKAY, I'LL SEE YOU AROUND.
IF YOU DON'T GET KILLED BY ONE OF YOUR LADY FRIENDS, THAT IS!
COLD-BLOODED CASANOVA?
WHAT A JOKE.
I CAN NO LONGER SEE WOMEN AT ALL...!
I SUPPOSE I WAS INDIFFERENT TO WOMEN FROM THE BEGINNING.
GENERIS
THEY'RE LOUD, DIFFICULT, STUPID AND EVEN IMPATIENT CREATURES,
BEINGS WHOSE ONLY TALENT IS TO CAUSE PROBLEMS.

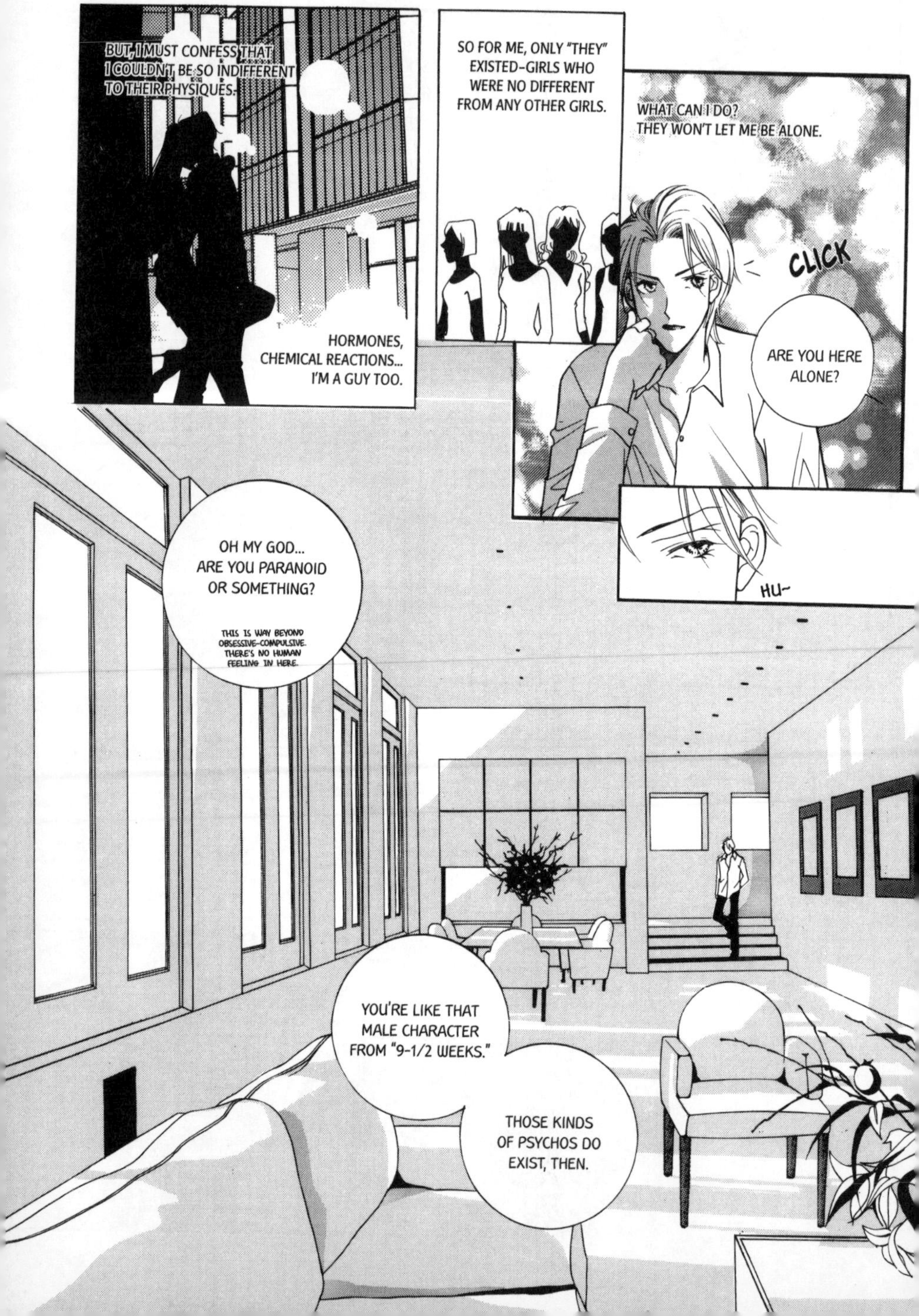
BUT, I MUST CONFESS THAT I COULDN'T BE SO INDIFFERENT TO THEIR PHYSIQUES.
HORMONES, CHEMICAL REACTIONS... I'M A GUY TOO.
SO FOR ME, ONLY "THEY" EXISTED-GIRLS WHO WERE NO DIFFERENT FROM ANY OTHER GIRLS.
WHAT CAN I DO? THEY WON'T LET ME BE ALONE.
CLICK
ARE YOU HERE ALONE?
HU~
OH MY GOD... ARE YOU PARANOID OR SOMETHING?
THIS IS WAY BEYOND OBSESSIVE-COMPULSIVE. THERE'S NO HUMAN FEELING IN HERE.
YOU'RE LIKE THAT MALE CHARACTER FROM "9-1/2 WEEKS."
THOSE KINDS OF PSYCHOS DO EXIST, THEN.

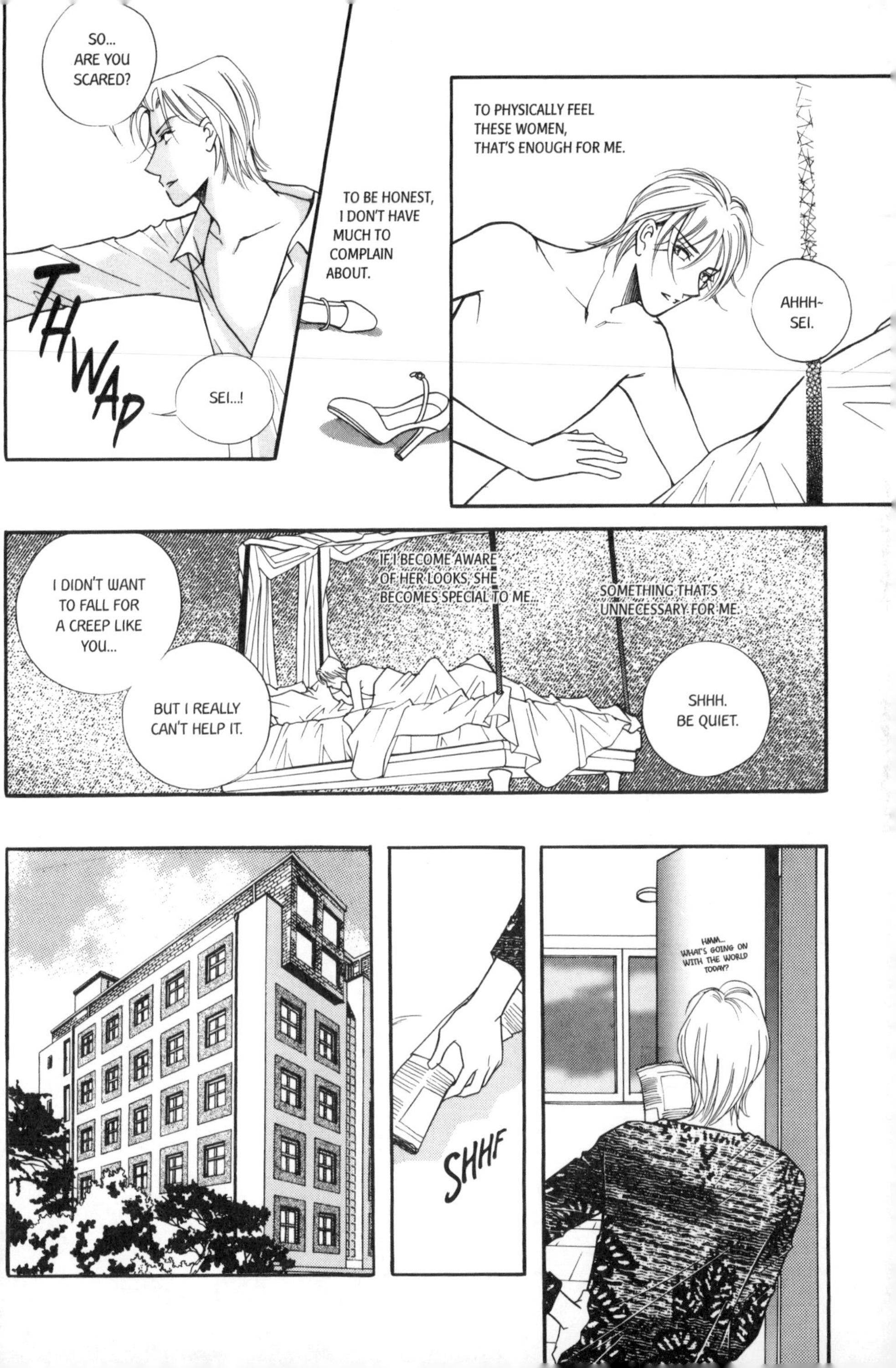

SO... ARE YOU SCARED?
TO BE HONEST, I DON'T HAVE MUCH TO COMPLAIN ABOUT.
THWAP
SEI...!
TO PHYSICALLY FEEL THESE WOMEN, THAT'S ENOUGH FOR ME.
AHHH~ SEI.
I DIDN'T WANT TO FALL FOR A CREEP LIKE YOU...
BUT I REALLY CAN'T HELP IT.
IF I BECOME AWARE OF HER LOOKS, SHE BECOMES SPECIAL TO ME...
SOMETHING THAT'S UNNECESSARY FOR ME.
SHHH. BE QUIET.
SHHF
HMM... WHAT'S GOING ON WITH THE WORLD TODAY?

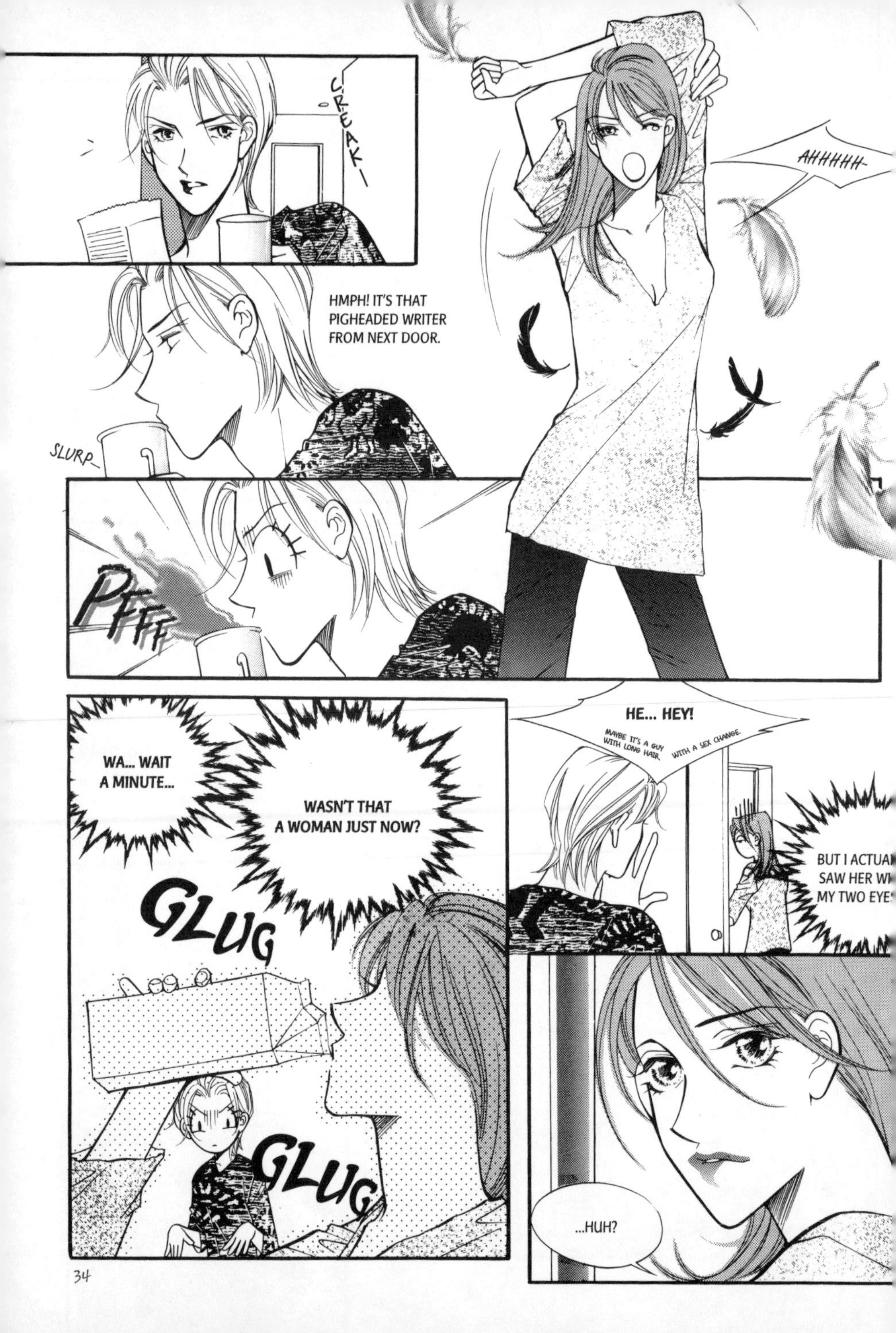
CREAK!
HMPH! IT'S THAT PIGHEADED WRITER FROM NEXT DOOR.
SLURP
AHHHHH-
PFFFF
WA... WAIT A MINUTE...
WASN'T THAT A WOMAN JUST NOW?
GLUG
GLUG
HE... HEY!
MAYBE IT'S A GUY WITH LONG HAIR.
WITH A SEX CHANGE.
BUT I ACTUA
SAW HER W
MY TWO EYE
...HUH?

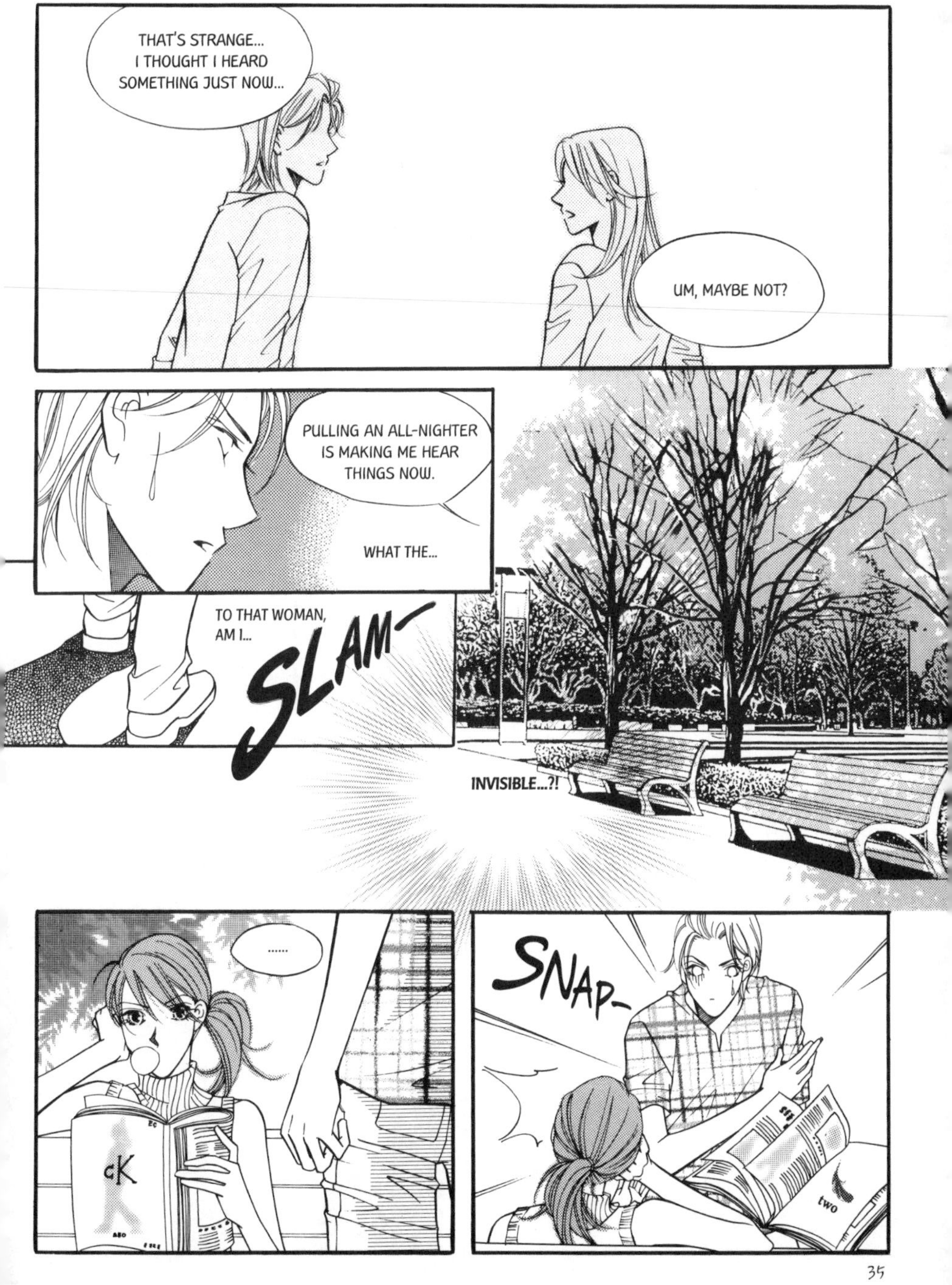

THAT'S STRANGE... I THOUGHT I HEARD SOMETHING JUST NOW...
UM, MAYBE NOT?
PULLING AN ALL-NIGHTER IS MAKING ME HEAR THINGS NOW.
WHAT THE...
TO THAT WOMAN, AM I...
SLAM-
INVISIBLE...?!
......
SNAP-

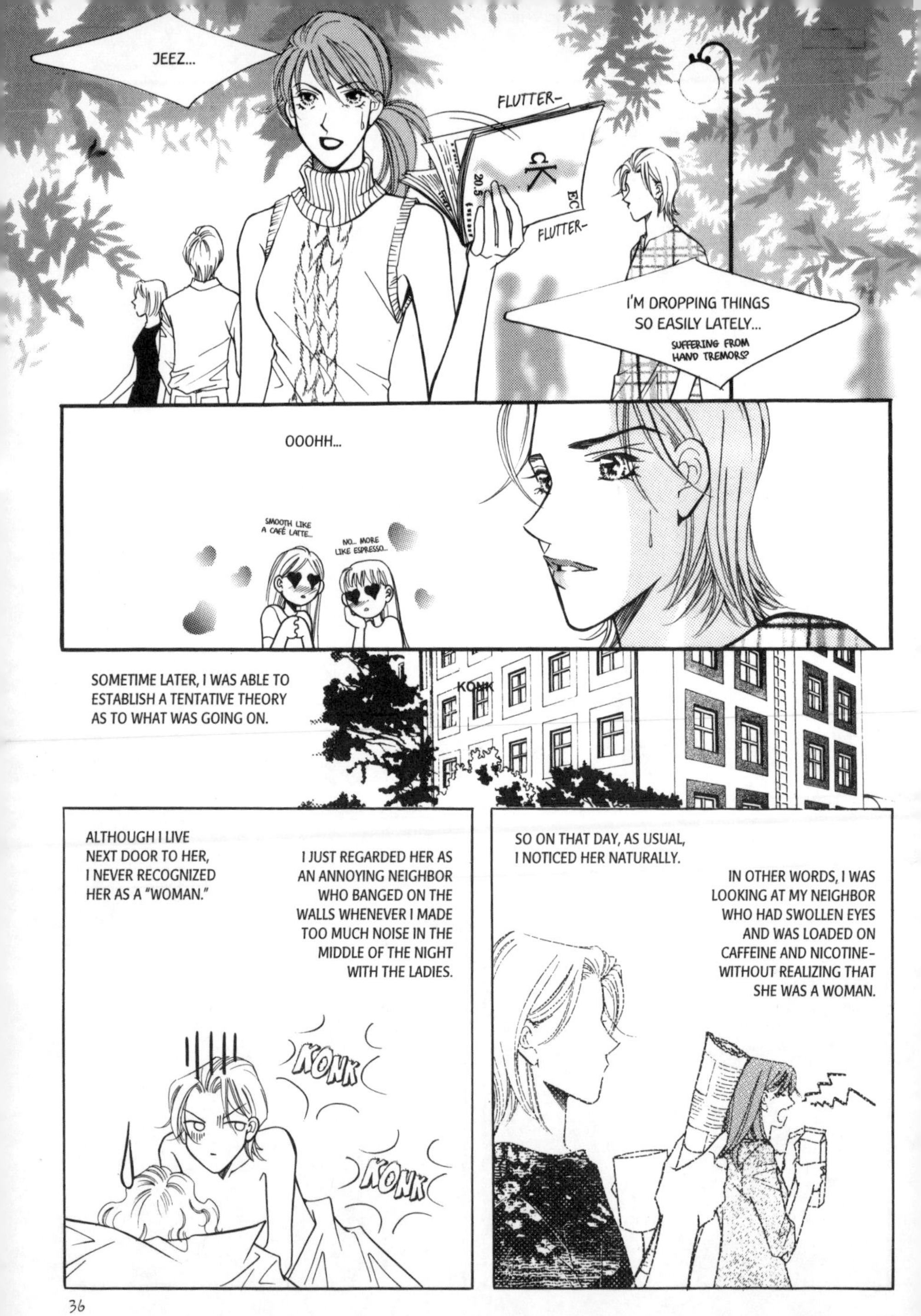
JEEZ...
FLUTTER-
FLUTTER-
I'M DROPPING THINGS SO EASILY LATELY...
SUFFERING FROM HAND TREMORS?
OOOHH...
SMOOTH LIKE A CAFÉ LATTE...
NO... MORE LIKE ESPRESSO...
SOMETIME LATER, I WAS ABLE TO ESTABLISH A TENTATIVE THEORY AS TO WHAT WAS GOING ON.
KONK
ALTHOUGH I LIVE NEXT DOOR TO HER, I NEVER RECOGNIZED HER AS A "WOMAN."
I JUST REGARDED HER AS AN ANNOYING NEIGHBOR WHO BANGED ON THE WALLS WHENEVER I MADE TOO MUCH NOISE IN THE MIDDLE OF THE NIGHT WITH THE LADIES.
KONK
KONK
SO ON THAT DAY, AS USUAL, I NOTICED HER NATURALLY.
IN OTHER WORDS, I WAS LOOKING AT MY NEIGHBOR WHO HAD SWOLLEN EYES AND WAS LOADED ON CAFFEINE AND NICOTINE-WITHOUT REALIZING THAT SHE WAS A WOMAN.

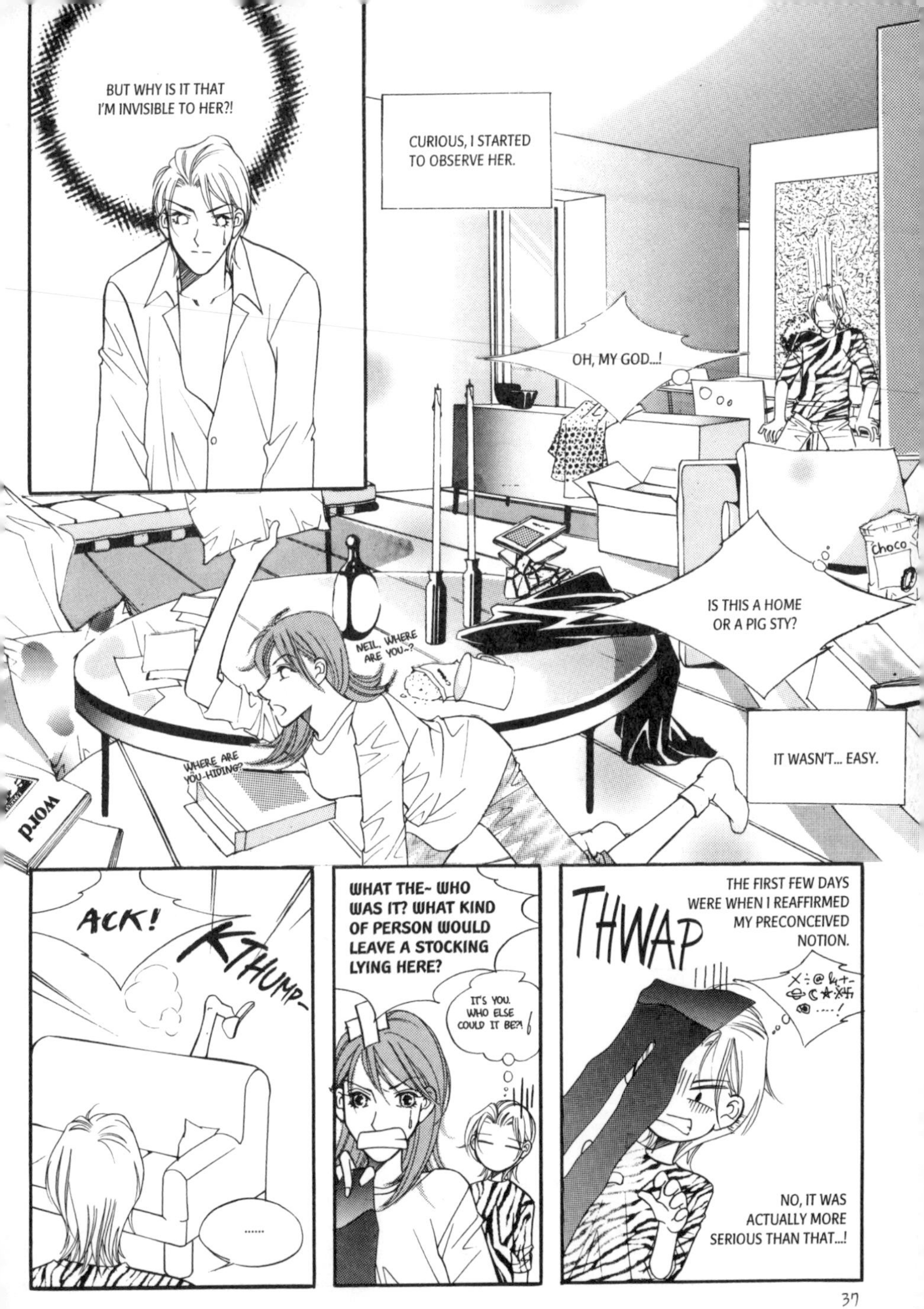
BUT WHY IS IT THAT I'M INVISIBLE TO HER?!
CURIOUS, I STARTED TO OBSERVE HER.
OH, MY GOD...!
choco
IS THIS A HOME OR A PIG STY?
NEIL, WHERE ARE YOU~?
WHERE ARE YOU-HIDING?
word
IT WASN'T... EASY.
ACK!
KTHUMP-
......
WHAT THE~ WHO WAS IT? WHAT KIND OF PERSON WOULD LEAVE A STOCKING LYING HERE?
IT'S YOU. WHO ELSE COULD IT BE?!
THWAP
THE FIRST FEW DAYS WERE WHEN I REAFFIRMED MY PRECONCEIVED NOTION.
NO, IT WAS ACTUALLY MORE SERIOUS THAN THAT...!

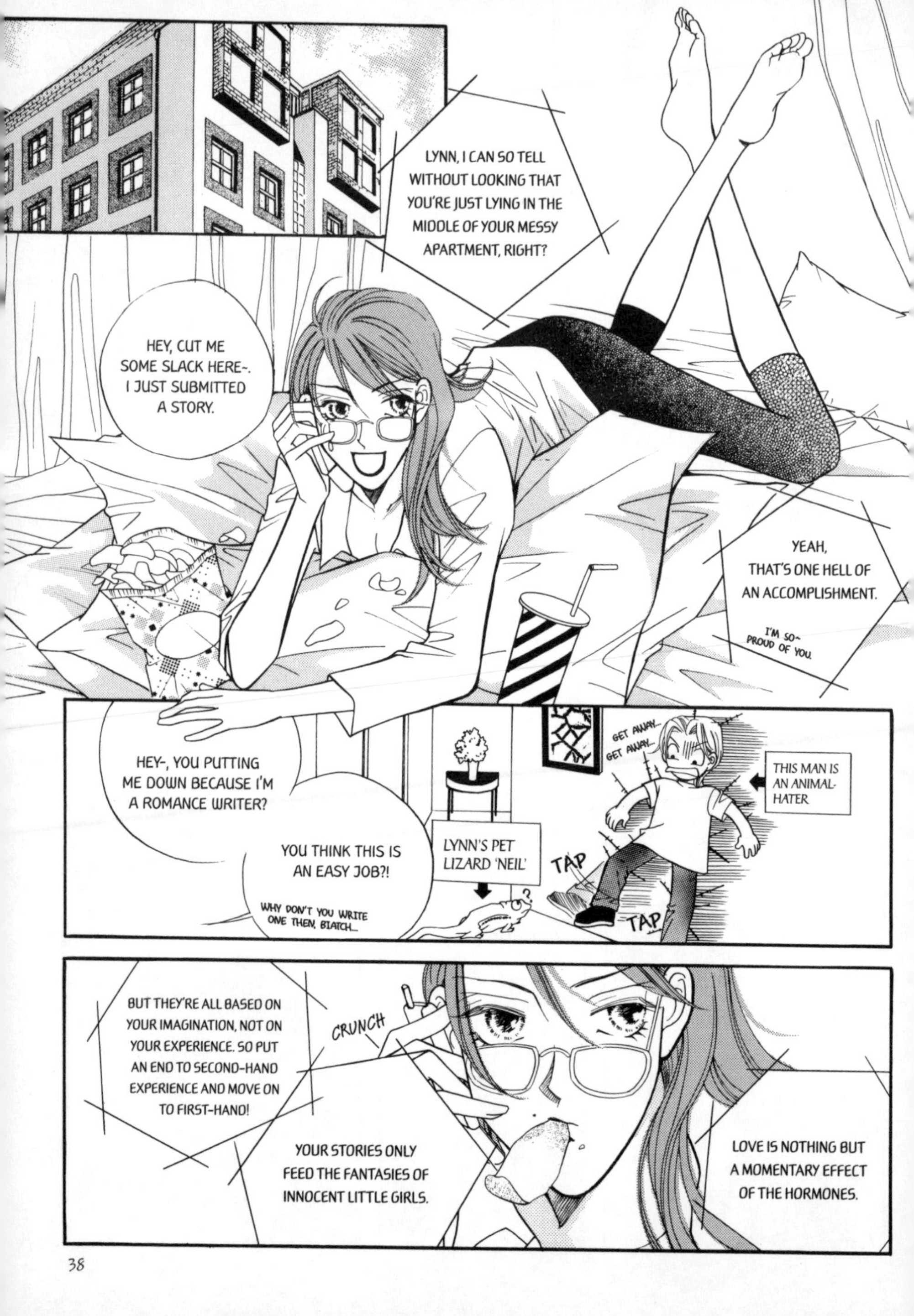
LYNN, I CAN SO TELL WITHOUT LOOKING THAT YOU'RE JUST LYING IN THE MIDDLE OF YOUR MESSY APARTMENT, RIGHT?
HEY, CUT ME SOME SLACK HERE~. I JUST SUBMITTED A STORY.
YEAH, THAT'S ONE HELL OF AN ACCOMPLISHMENT.
I'M SO~ PROUD OF YOU.
HEY~, YOU PUTTING ME DOWN BECAUSE I'M A ROMANCE WRITER?
YOU THINK THIS IS AN EASY JOB?!
WHY DON'T YOU WRITE ONE THEN, BIATCH...
LYNN'S PET LIZARD 'NEIL'
GET AWAY... GET AWAY...
THIS MAN IS AN ANIMAL-HATER
TAP
TAP
BUT THEY'RE ALL BASED ON YOUR IMAGINATION, NOT ON YOUR EXPERIENCE. SO PUT AN END TO SECOND-HAND EXPERIENCE AND MOVE ON TO FIRST-HAND!
CRUNCH
YOUR STORIES ONLY FEED THE FANTASIES OF INNOCENT LITTLE GIRLS.
LOVE IS NOTHING BUT A MOMENTARY EFFECT OF THE HORMONES.

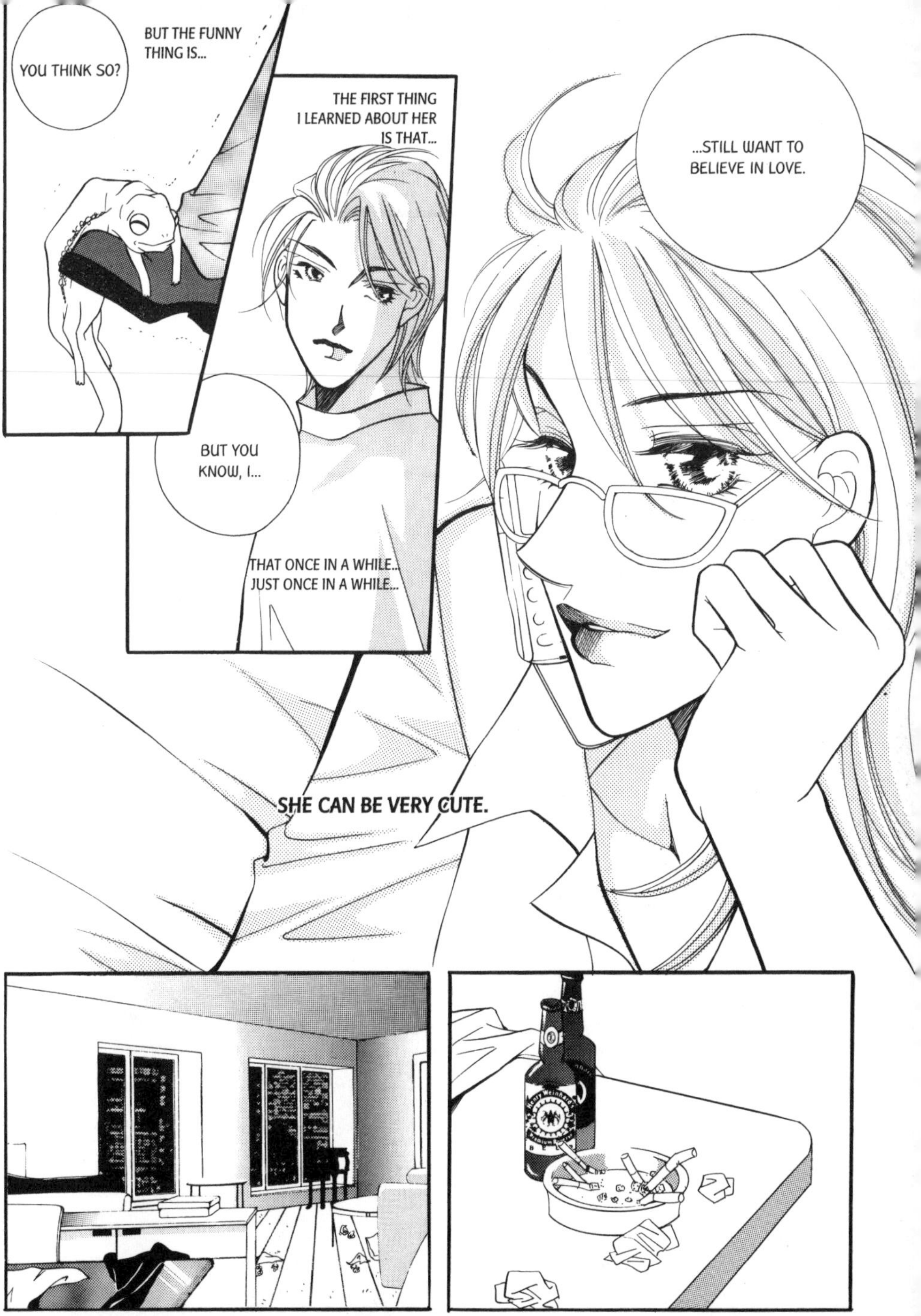
BUT THE FUNNY THING IS...
YOU THINK SO?
THE FIRST THING I LEARNED ABOUT HER IS THAT...
...STILL WANT TO BELIEVE IN LOVE.
BUT YOU KNOW, I...
THAT ONCE IN A WHILE... JUST ONCE IN A WHILE...
SHE CAN BE VERY CUTE.

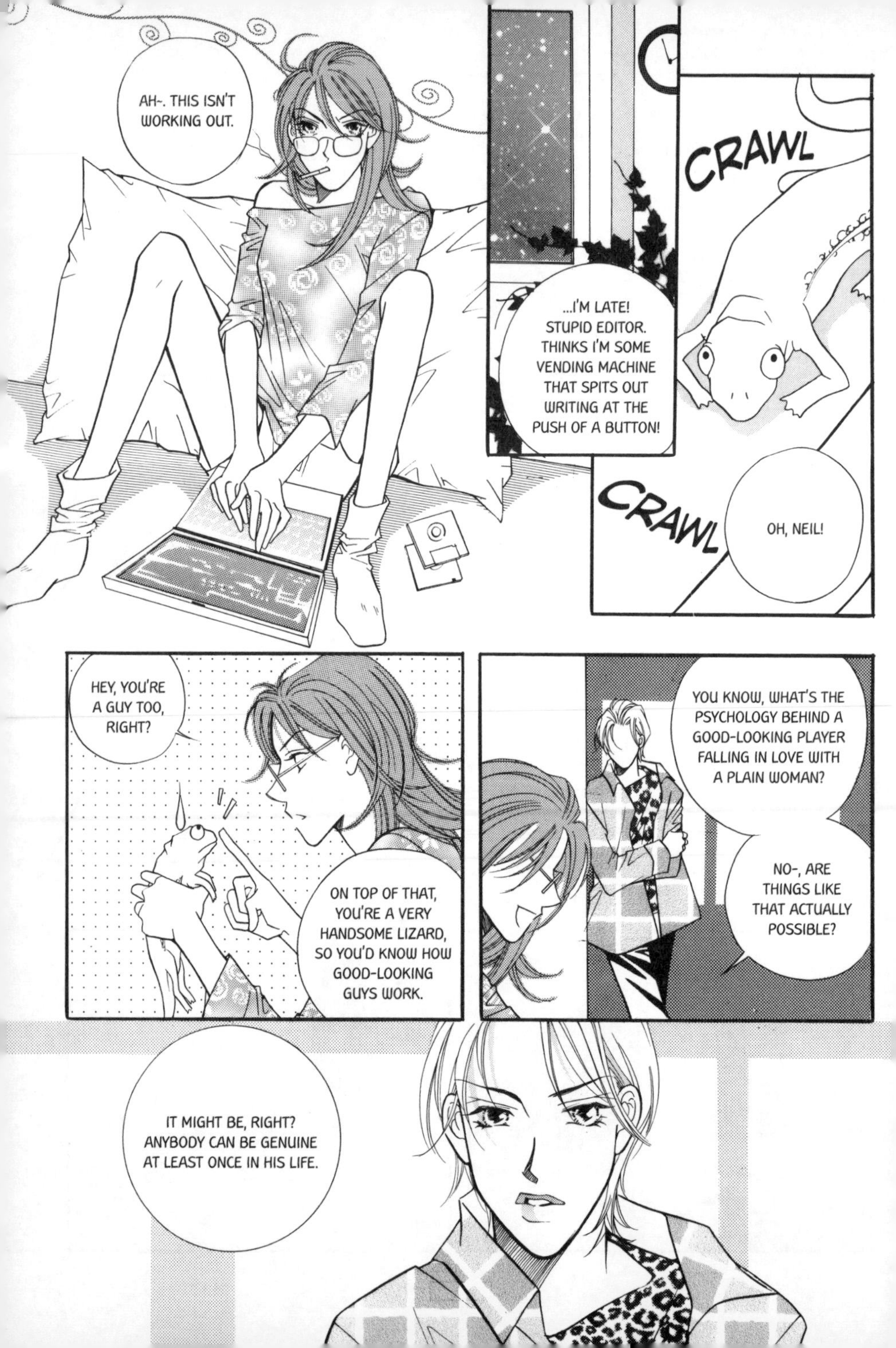
AH-. THIS ISN'T WORKING OUT.
...I'M LATE! STUPID EDITOR. THINKS I'M SOME VENDING MACHINE THAT SPITS OUT WRITING AT THE PUSH OF A BUTTON!
CRAWL
CRAWL
OH, NEIL!
HEY, YOU'RE A GUY TOO, RIGHT?
ON TOP OF THAT, YOU'RE A VERY HANDSOME LIZARD, SO YOU'D KNOW HOW GOOD-LOOKING GUYS WORK.
YOU KNOW, WHAT'S THE PSYCHOLOGY BEHIND A GOOD-LOOKING PLAYER FALLING IN LOVE WITH A PLAIN WOMAN?
NO-, ARE THINGS LIKE THAT ACTUALLY POSSIBLE?
IT MIGHT BE, RIGHT? ANYBODY CAN BE GENUINE AT LEAST ONCE IN HIS LIFE.

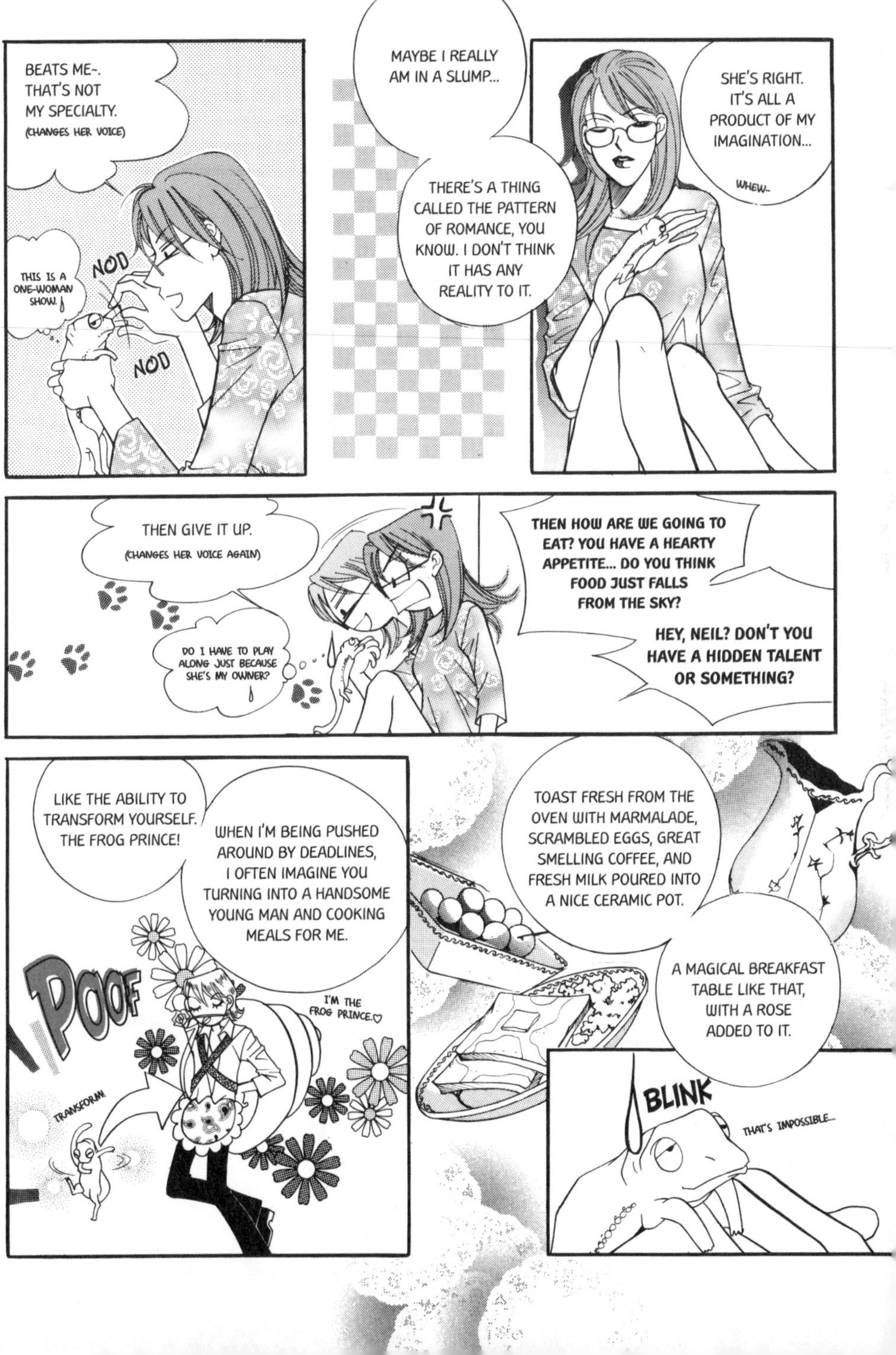
BEATS ME~. THAT'S NOT MY SPECIALTY.
(CHANGES HER VOICE)
THIS IS A ONE-WOMAN SHOW.
NOD
NOD
MAYBE I REALLY AM IN A SLUMP...
THERE'S A THING CALLED THE PATTERN OF ROMANCE, YOU KNOW. I DON'T THINK IT HAS ANY REALITY TO IT.
SHE'S RIGHT. IT'S ALL A PRODUCT OF MY IMAGINATION...
WHEW~
THEN GIVE IT UP.
(CHANGES HER VOICE AGAIN)
DO I HAVE TO PLAY ALONG JUST BECAUSE SHE'S MY OWNER?
THEN HOW ARE WE GOING TO EAT? YOU HAVE A HEARTY APPETITE... DO YOU THINK FOOD JUST FALLS FROM THE SKY?
HEY, NEIL? DON'T YOU HAVE A HIDDEN TALENT OR SOMETHING?
LIKE THE ABILITY TO TRANSFORM YOURSELF. THE FROG PRINCE!
WHEN I'M BEING PUSHED AROUND BY DEADLINES, I OFTEN IMAGINE YOU TURNING INTO A HANDSOME YOUNG MAN AND COOKING MEALS FOR ME.
POOF
I'M THE FROG PRINCE.♡
TRANSFORM!
TOAST FRESH FROM THE OVEN WITH MARMALADE, SCRAMBLED EGGS, GREAT SMELLING COFFEE, AND FRESH MILK POURED INTO A NICE CERAMIC POT.
A MAGICAL BREAKFAST TABLE LIKE THAT, WITH A ROSE ADDED TO IT.
BLINK
THAT'S IMPOSSIBLE...

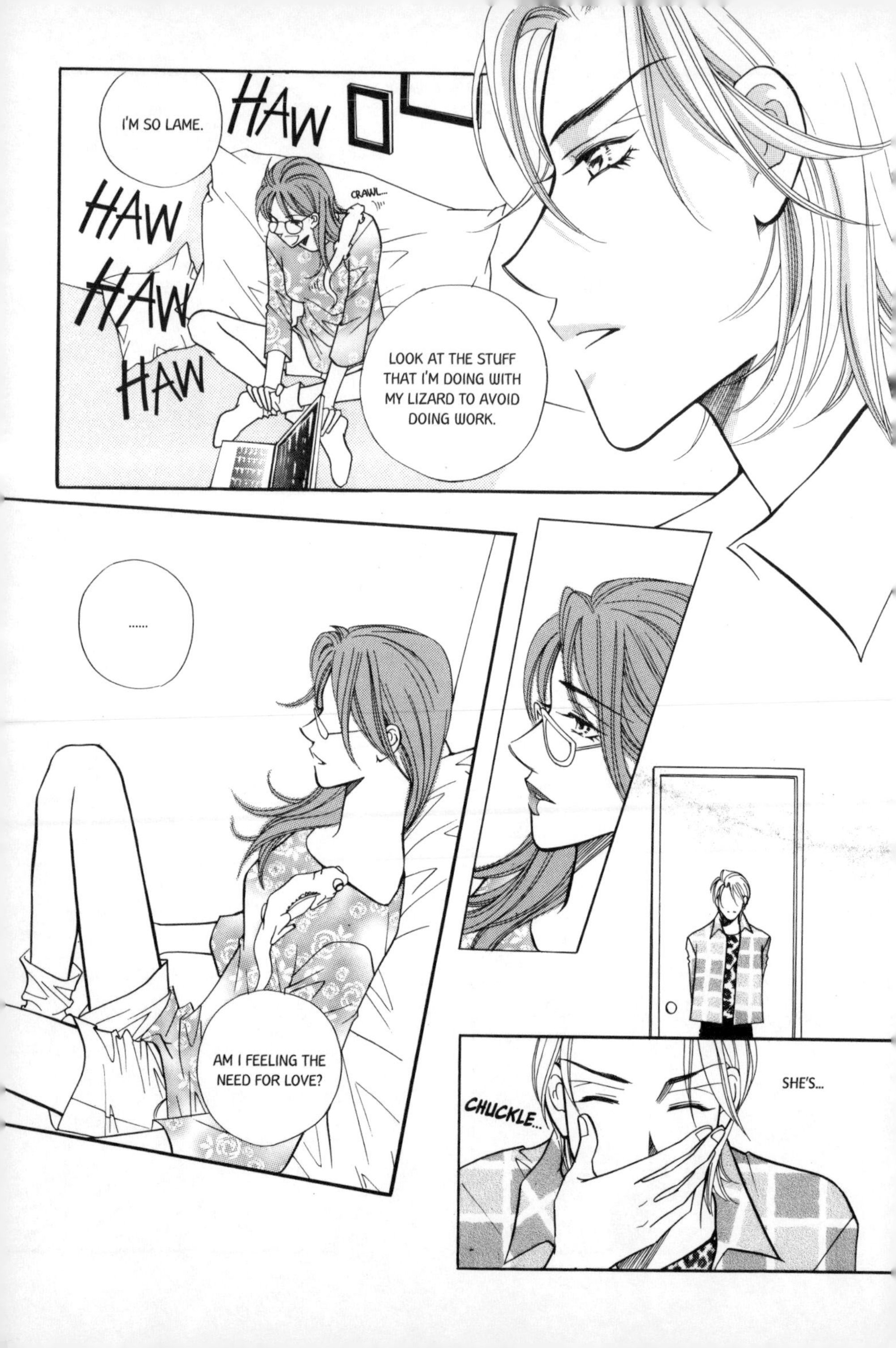
I'M SO LAME.
HAW
HAW
HAW
HAW
CRAWL...
LOOK AT THE STUFF THAT I'M DOING WITH MY LIZARD TO AVOID DOING WORK.
......
AM I FEELING THE NEED FOR LOVE?
CHUCKLE...
SHE'S...

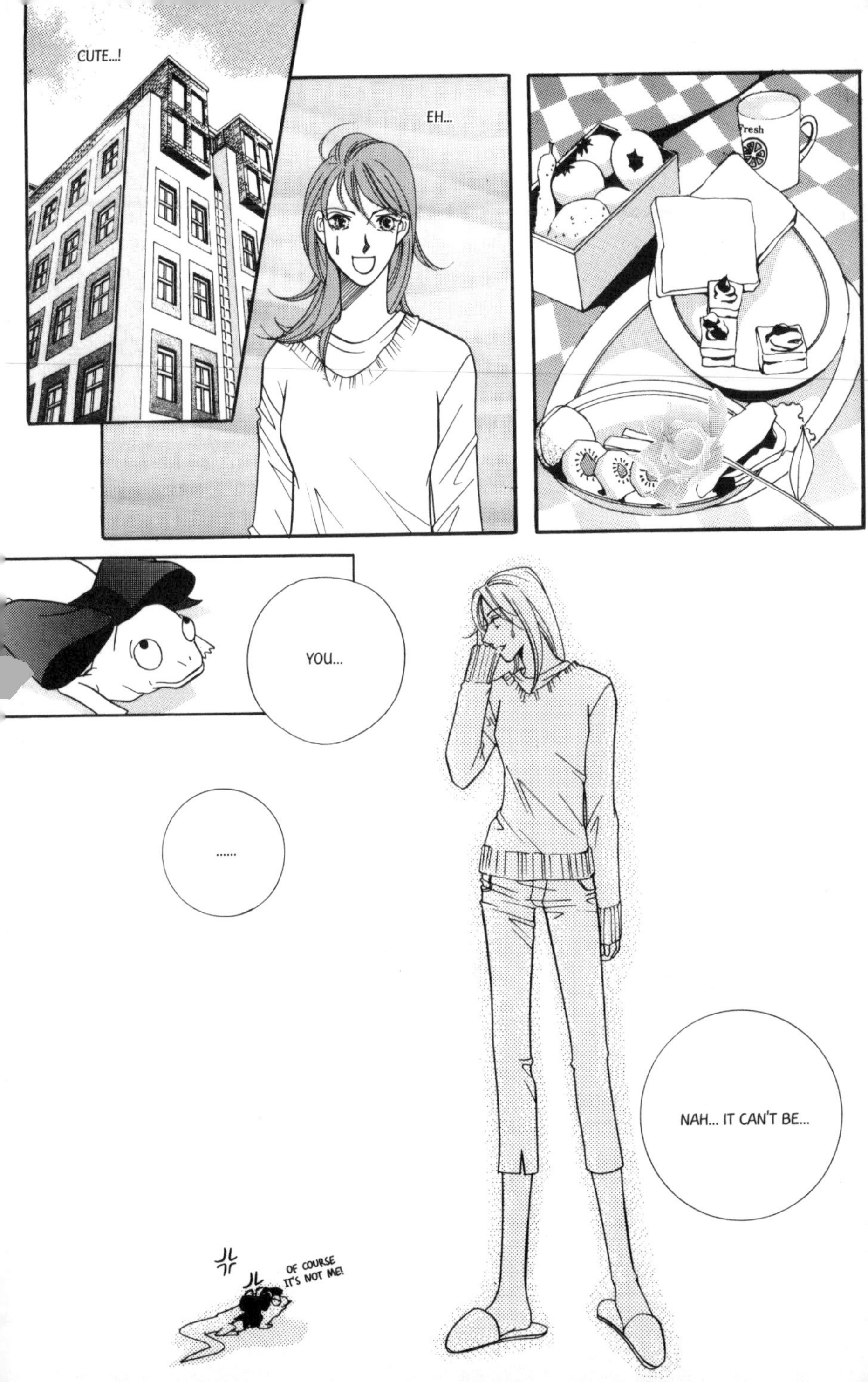
CUTE...!
EH...
Fresh
YOU...
......
NAH... IT CAN'T BE...
OF COURSE IT'S NOT ME!

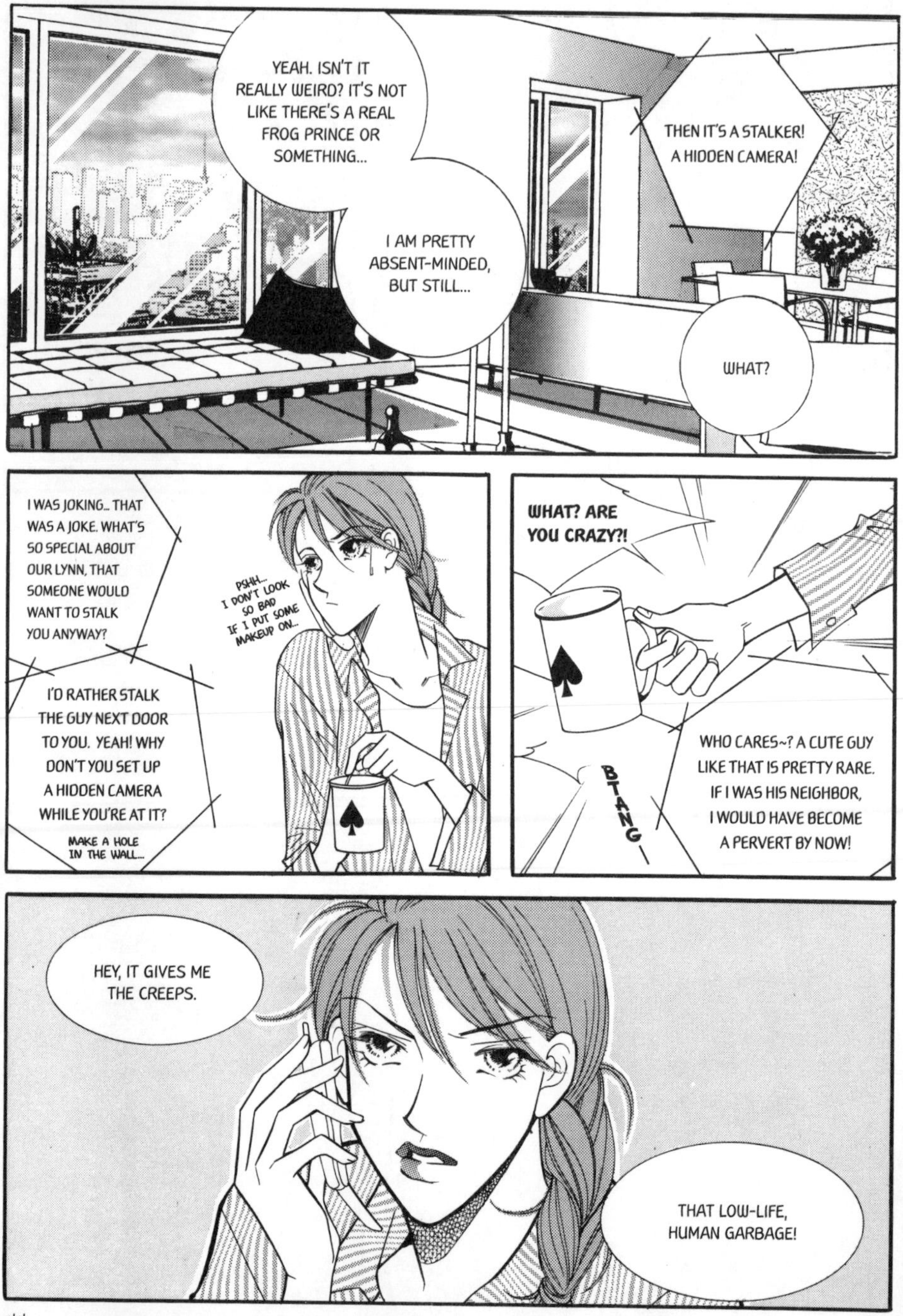
YEAH. ISN'T IT REALLY WEIRD? IT'S NOT LIKE THERE'S A REAL FROG PRINCE OR SOMETHING...
I AM PRETTY ABSENT-MINDED, BUT STILL...
THEN IT'S A STALKER! A HIDDEN CAMERA!
WHAT?
I WAS JOKING... THAT WAS A JOKE. WHAT'S SO SPECIAL ABOUT OUR LYNN, THAT SOMEONE WOULD WANT TO STALK YOU ANYWAY?
PSHH... I DON'T LOOK SO BAD IF I PUT SOME MAKEUP ON...
I'D RATHER STALK THE GUY NEXT DOOR TO YOU. YEAH! WHY DON'T YOU SET UP A HIDDEN CAMERA WHILE YOU'RE AT IT?
MAKE A HOLE IN THE WALL...
WHAT? ARE YOU CRAZY?!
BTANG
WHO CARES~? A CUTE GUY LIKE THAT IS PRETTY RARE. IF I WAS HIS NEIGHBOR, I WOULD HAVE BECOME A PERVERT BY NOW!
HEY, IT GIVES ME THE CREEPS.
THAT LOW-LIFE, HUMAN GARBAGE!

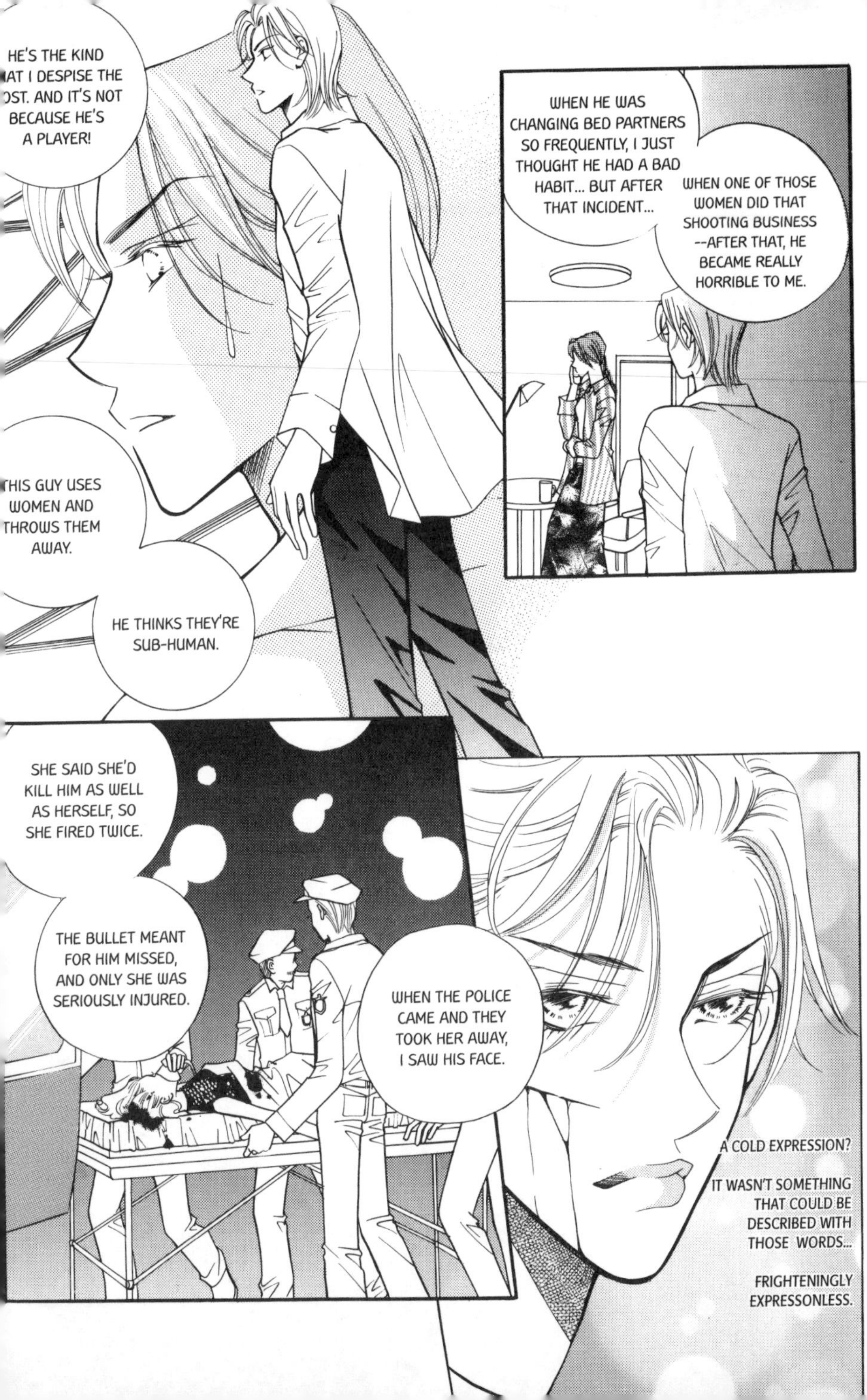

HE'S THE KIND AT I DESPISE THE OST. AND IT'S NOT BECAUSE HE'S A PLAYER!
THIS GUY USES WOMEN AND THROWS THEM AWAY.
HE THINKS THEY'RE SUB-HUMAN.
WHEN HE WAS CHANGING BED PARTNERS SO FREQUENTLY, I JUST THOUGHT HE HAD A BAD HABIT... BUT AFTER THAT INCIDENT...
WHEN ONE OF THOSE WOMEN DID THAT SHOOTING BUSINESS --AFTER THAT, HE BECAME REALLY HORRIBLE TO ME.
SHE SAID SHE'D KILL HIM AS WELL AS HERSELF, SO SHE FIRED TWICE.
THE BULLET MEANT FOR HIM MISSED, AND ONLY SHE WAS SERIOUSLY INJURED.
WHEN THE POLICE CAME AND THEY TOOK HER AWAY, I SAW HIS FACE.
A COLD EXPRESSION?
IT WASN'T SOMETHING THAT COULD BE DESCRIBED WITH THOSE WORDS...
FRIGHTENINGLY EXPRESSONLESS.

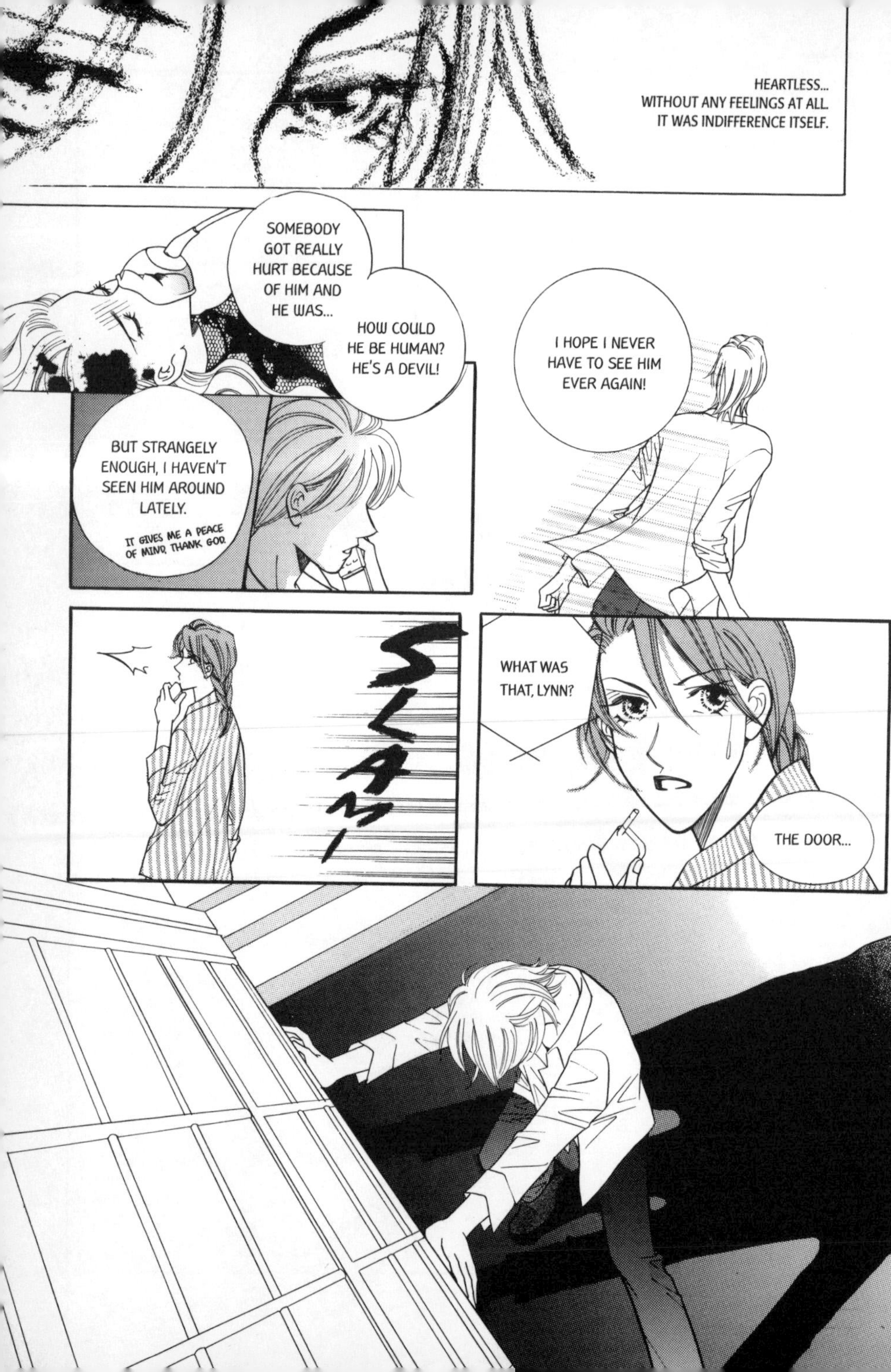
HEARTLESS...
WITHOUT ANY FEELINGS AT ALL.
IT WAS INDIFFERENCE ITSELF.
SOMEBODY GOT REALLY HURT BECAUSE OF HIM AND HE WAS...
HOW COULD HE BE HUMAN? HE'S A DEVIL!
BUT STRANGELY ENOUGH, I HAVEN'T SEEN HIM AROUND LATELY.
IT GIVES ME A PEACE OF MIND, THANK GOD.
I HOPE I NEVER HAVE TO SEE HIM EVER AGAIN!
SLAM!
WHAT WAS THAT, LYNN?
THE DOOR...

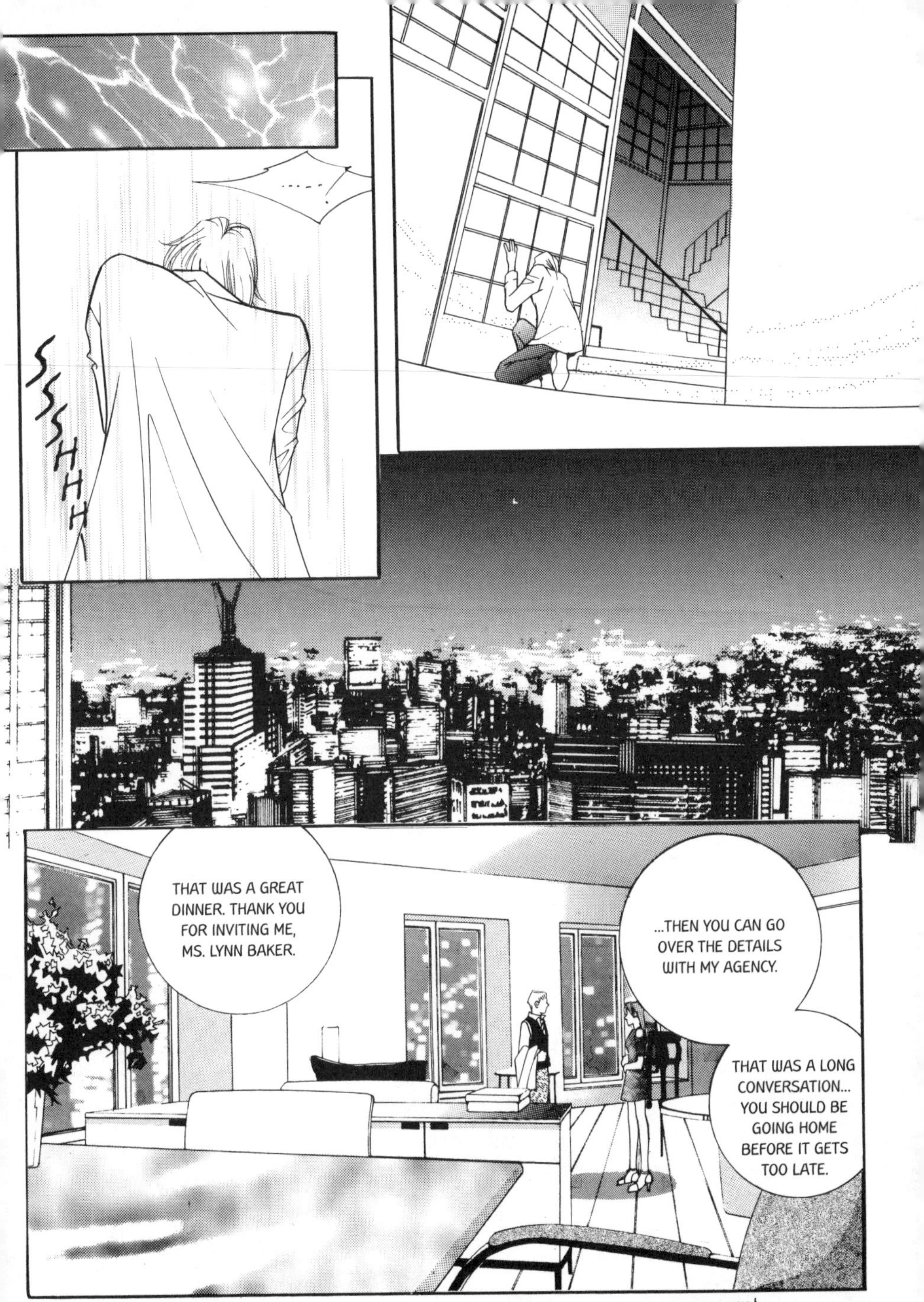
SSSHHH
THAT WAS A GREAT DINNER. THANK YOU FOR INVITING ME, MS. LYNN BAKER.
...THEN YOU CAN GO OVER THE DETAILS WITH MY AGENCY.
THAT WAS A LONG CONVERSATION... YOU SHOULD BE GOING HOME BEFORE IT GETS TOO LATE.

LYNN CLEANED UP HER PLACE BECAUSE OF THE GUEST.

NO, NO. THAT'S NOT THE WAY IT'S SUPPOSED TO GO.

...EXCUSE ME?

STOP PLAYING INNOCENT HERE. YOU'VE KNOWN I WANTED YOU FROM THE BEGINNING.

YOU INVITED ME OVER BECAUSE YOU HAD SOMETHING IN MIND, NO?

DON'T PRETEND YOU'RE NAÏVE.

.......!

KAACK~! LET ME GO!

SHFF—

...HUH?

WHO... WHO ARE YOU?!

I'M GOING TO KILL YOU, YOU SON OF A BITCH~!!

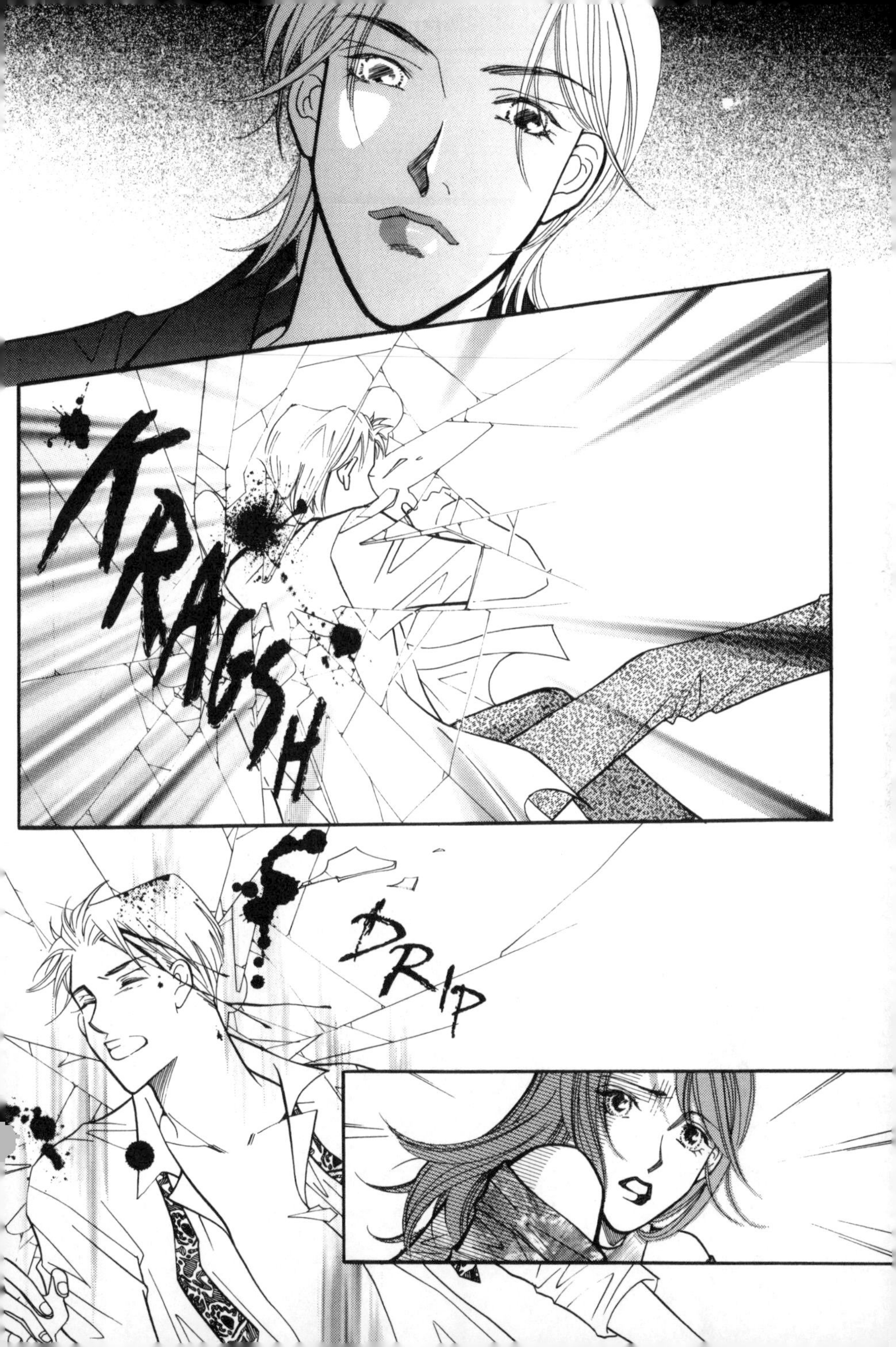
KRASSH
DRIP

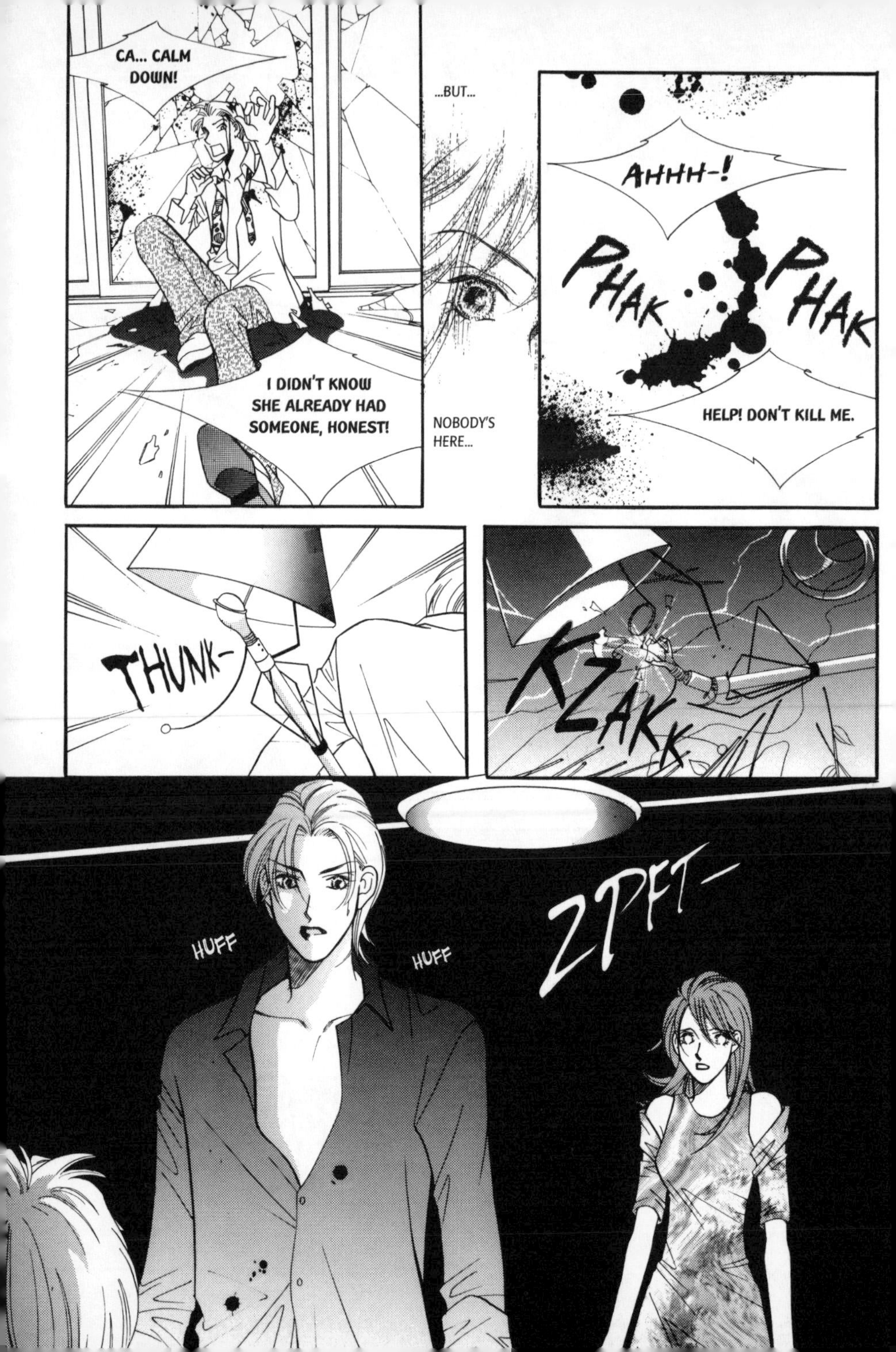
CA... CALM DOWN!
I DIDN'T KNOW SHE ALREADY HAD SOMEONE, HONEST!
...BUT...
NOBODY'S HERE...
AHHH-!
PHAK
PHAK
HELP! DON'T KILL ME.
THUNK-
KZAKK
HUFF
HUFF
ZZPFT-

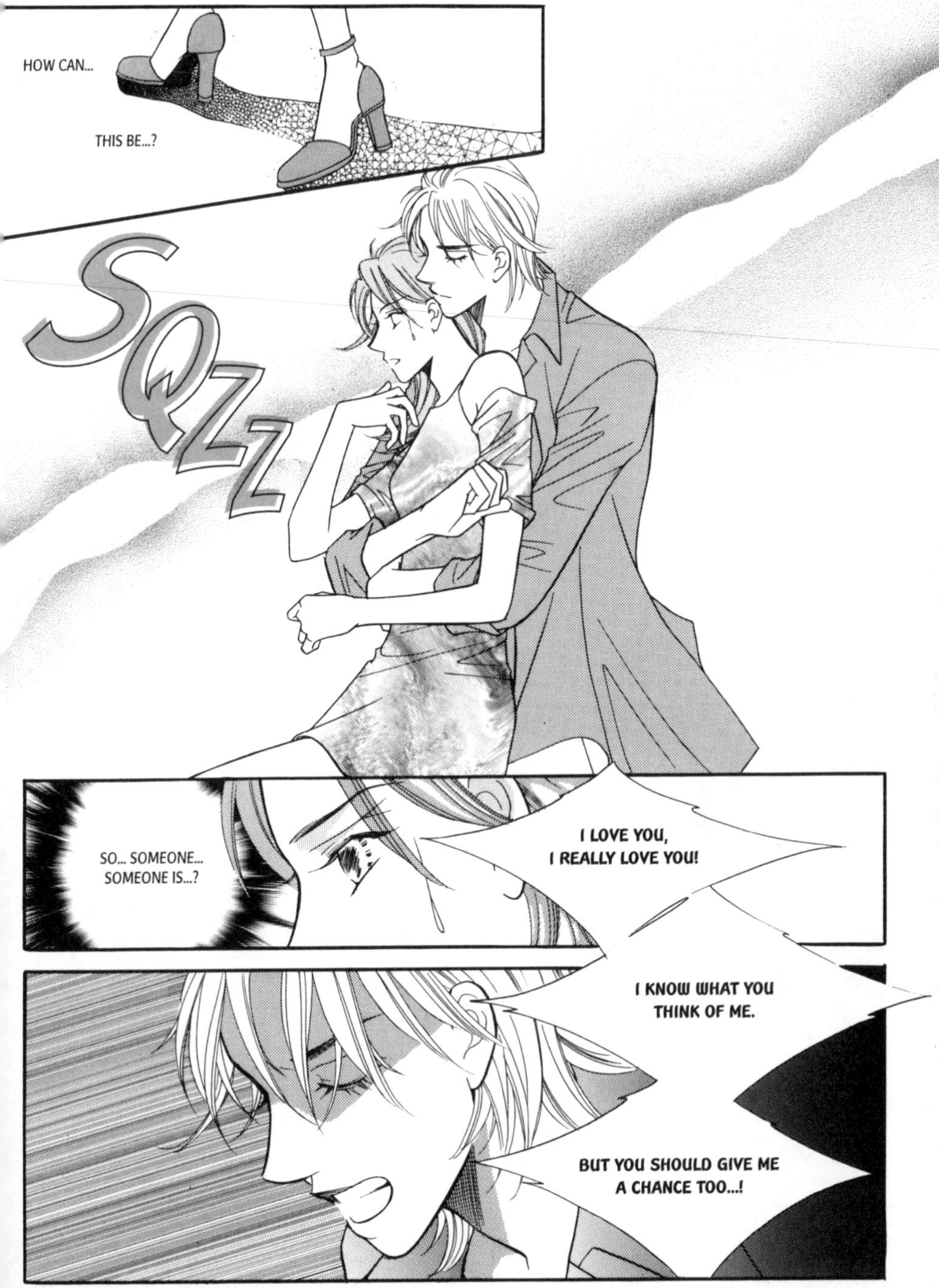
HOW CAN...
THIS BE...?
SQZZ
SO... SOMEONE...
SOMEONE IS...?
I LOVE YOU,
I REALLY LOVE YOU!
I KNOW WHAT YOU
THINK OF ME.
BUT YOU SHOULD GIVE ME
A CHANCE TOO...!

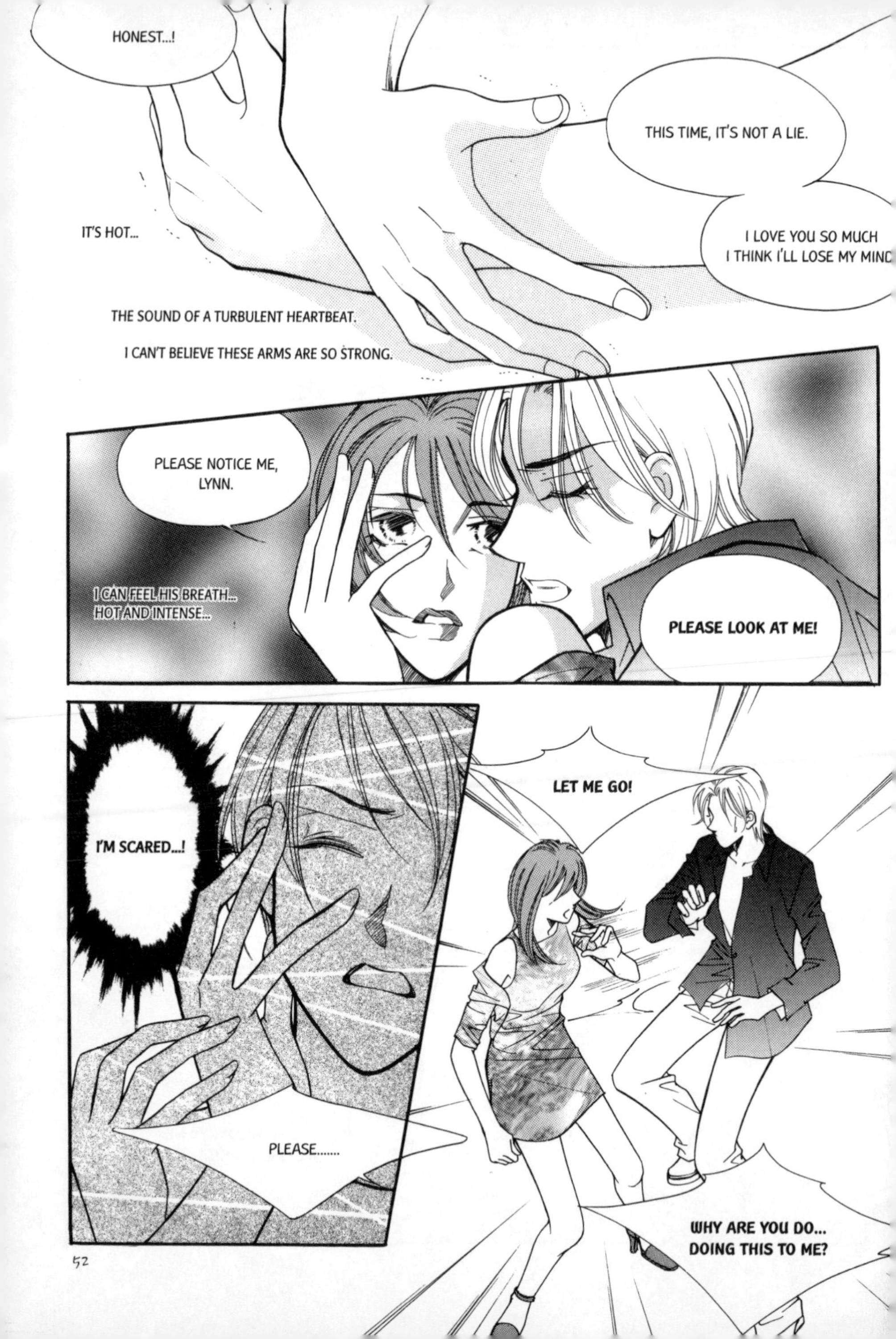
HONEST...!
THIS TIME, IT'S NOT A LIE.
IT'S HOT...
I LOVE YOU SO MUCH
I THINK I'LL LOSE MY MIND
THE SOUND OF A TURBULENT HEARTBEAT.
I CAN'T BELIEVE THESE ARMS ARE SO STRONG.
PLEASE NOTICE ME, LYNN.
I CAN FEEL HIS BREATH...
HOT AND INTENSE...
PLEASE LOOK AT ME!
I'M SCARED...!
PLEASE.......
LET ME GO!
WHY ARE YOU DO...
DOING THIS TO ME?

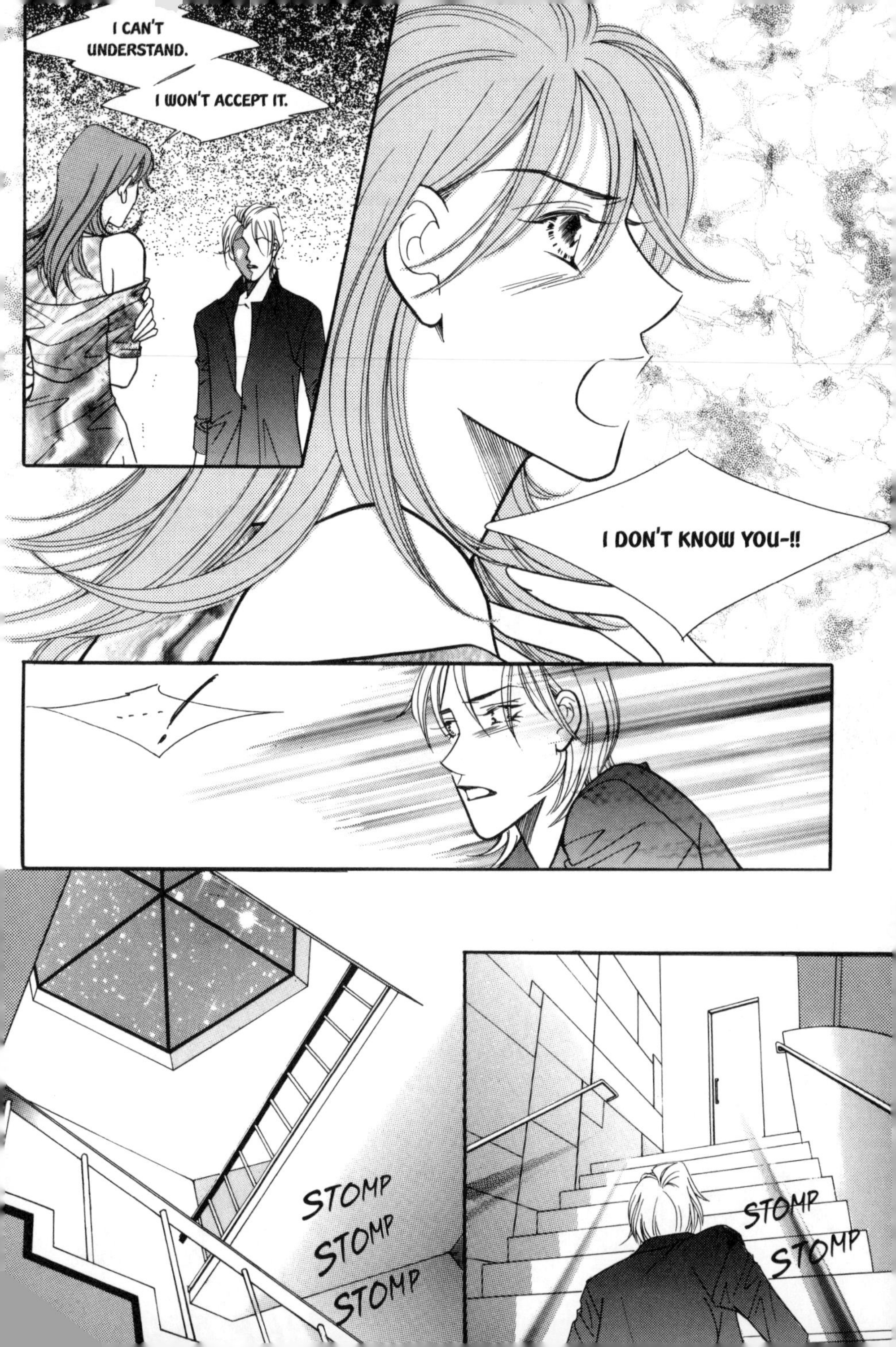
I CAN'T UNDERSTAND.
I WON'T ACCEPT IT.
I DON'T KNOW YOU-!!
--- !
STOMP
STOMP
STOMP
STOMP
STOMP

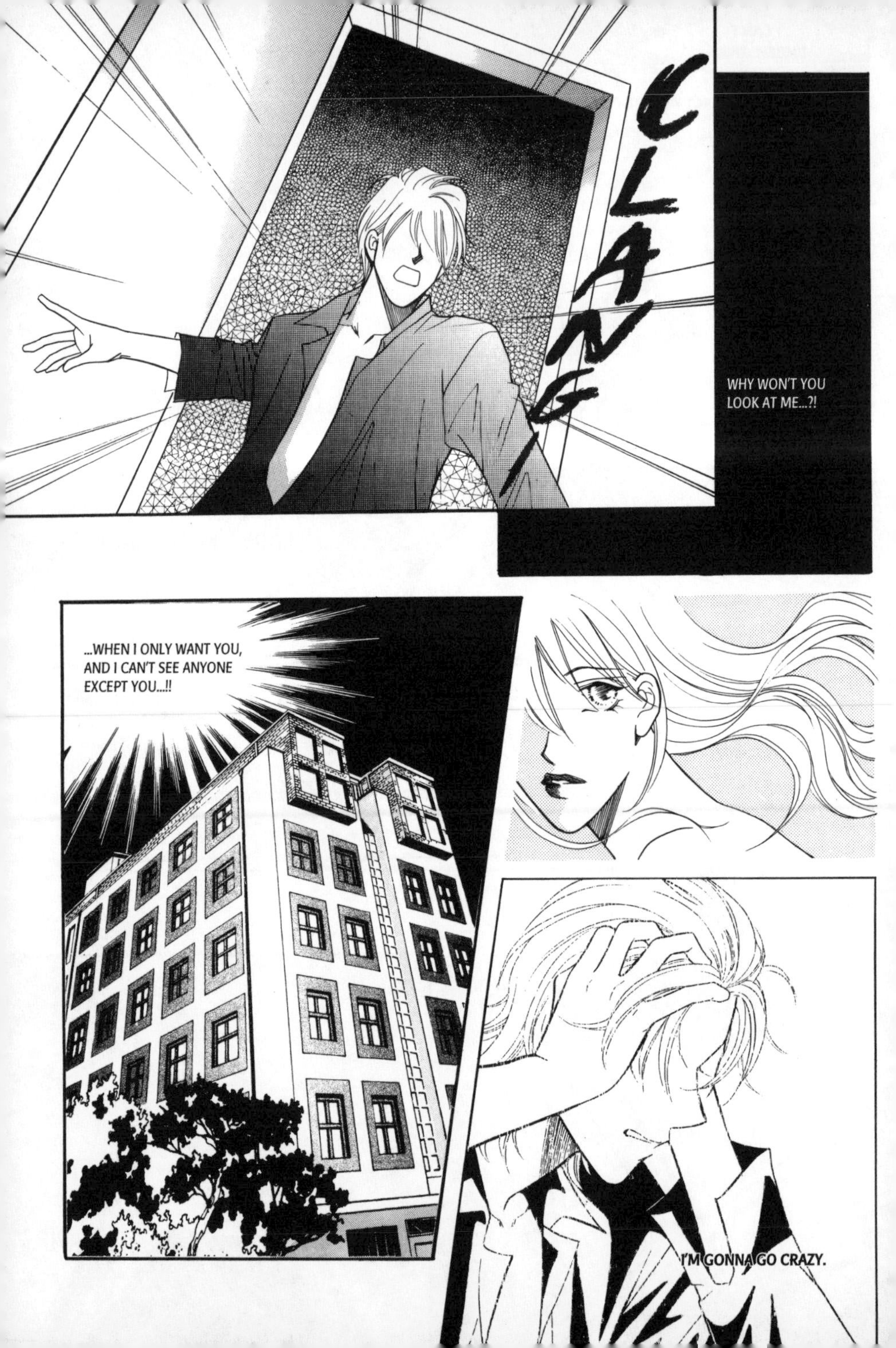
CLANG!
WHY WON'T YOU LOOK AT ME...?!
...WHEN I ONLY WANT YOU, AND I CAN'T SEE ANYONE EXCEPT YOU...!!
I'M GONNA GO CRAZY.

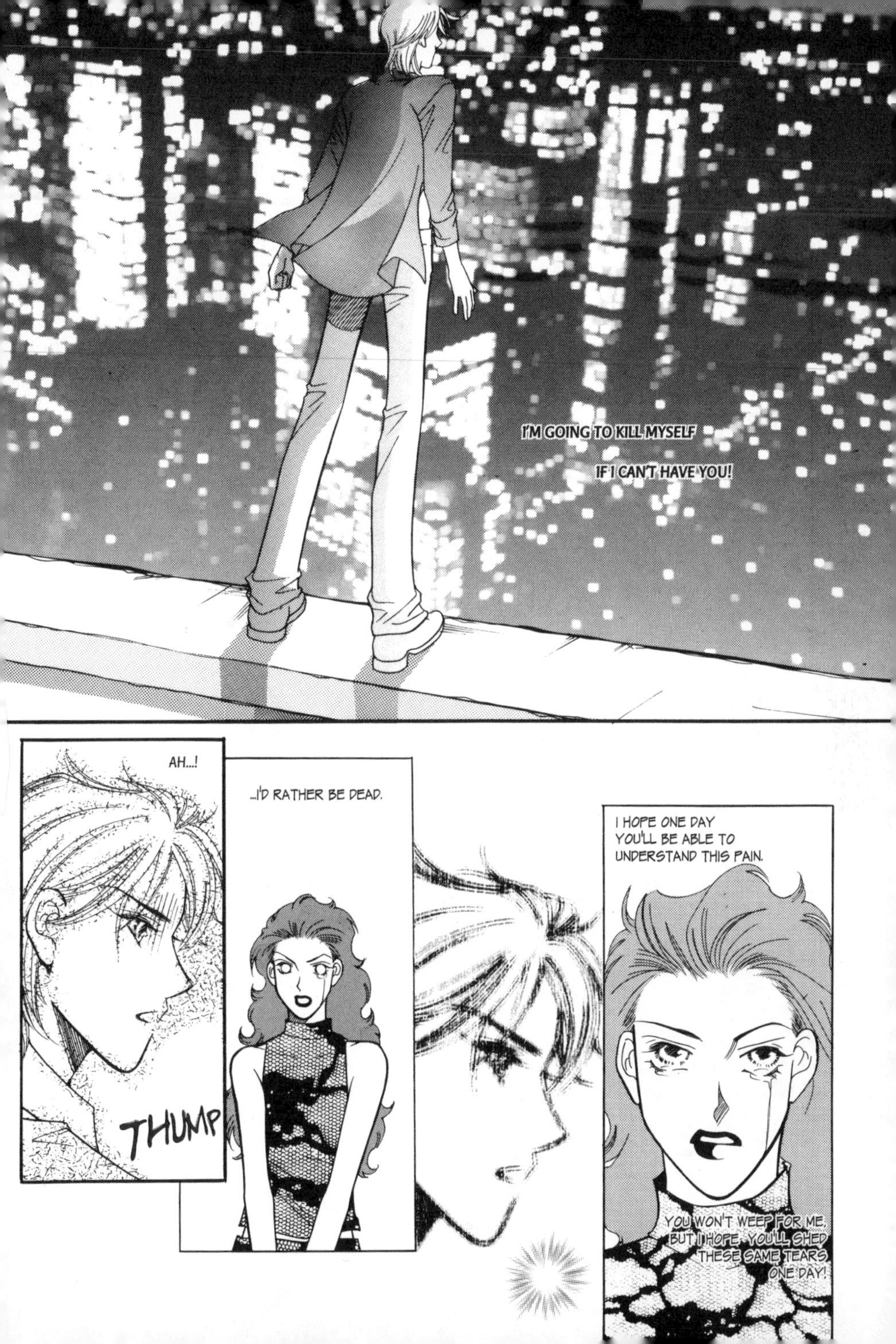
I'M GOING TO KILL MYSELF
IF I CAN'T HAVE YOU!
AH...!
THUMP
...I'D RATHER BE DEAD.
I HOPE ONE DAY YOU'LL BE ABLE TO UNDERSTAND THIS PAIN.
YOU WON'T WEEP FOR ME, BUT I HOPE YOU'LL SHED THESE SAME TEARS ONE DAY!

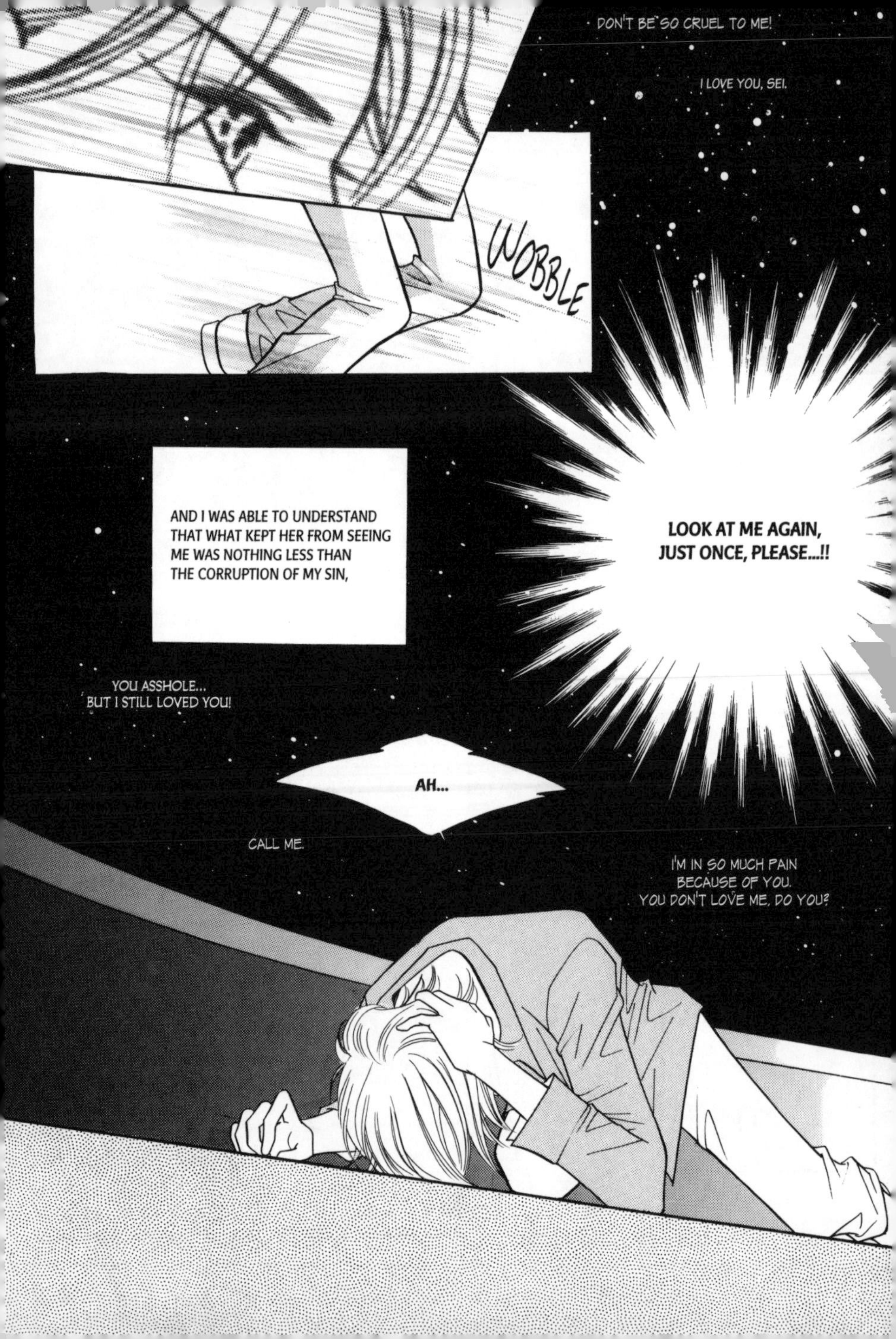
WOBBLE
DON'T BE SO CRUEL TO ME!
I LOVE YOU, SEI.
AND I WAS ABLE TO UNDERSTAND THAT WHAT KEPT HER FROM SEEING ME WAS NOTHING LESS THAN THE CORRUPTION OF MY SIN,
LOOK AT ME AGAIN, JUST ONCE, PLEASE...!!
YOU ASSHOLE... BUT I STILL LOVED YOU!
AH...
CALL ME.
I'M IN SO MUCH PAIN BECAUSE OF YOU. YOU DON'T LOVE ME, DO YOU?

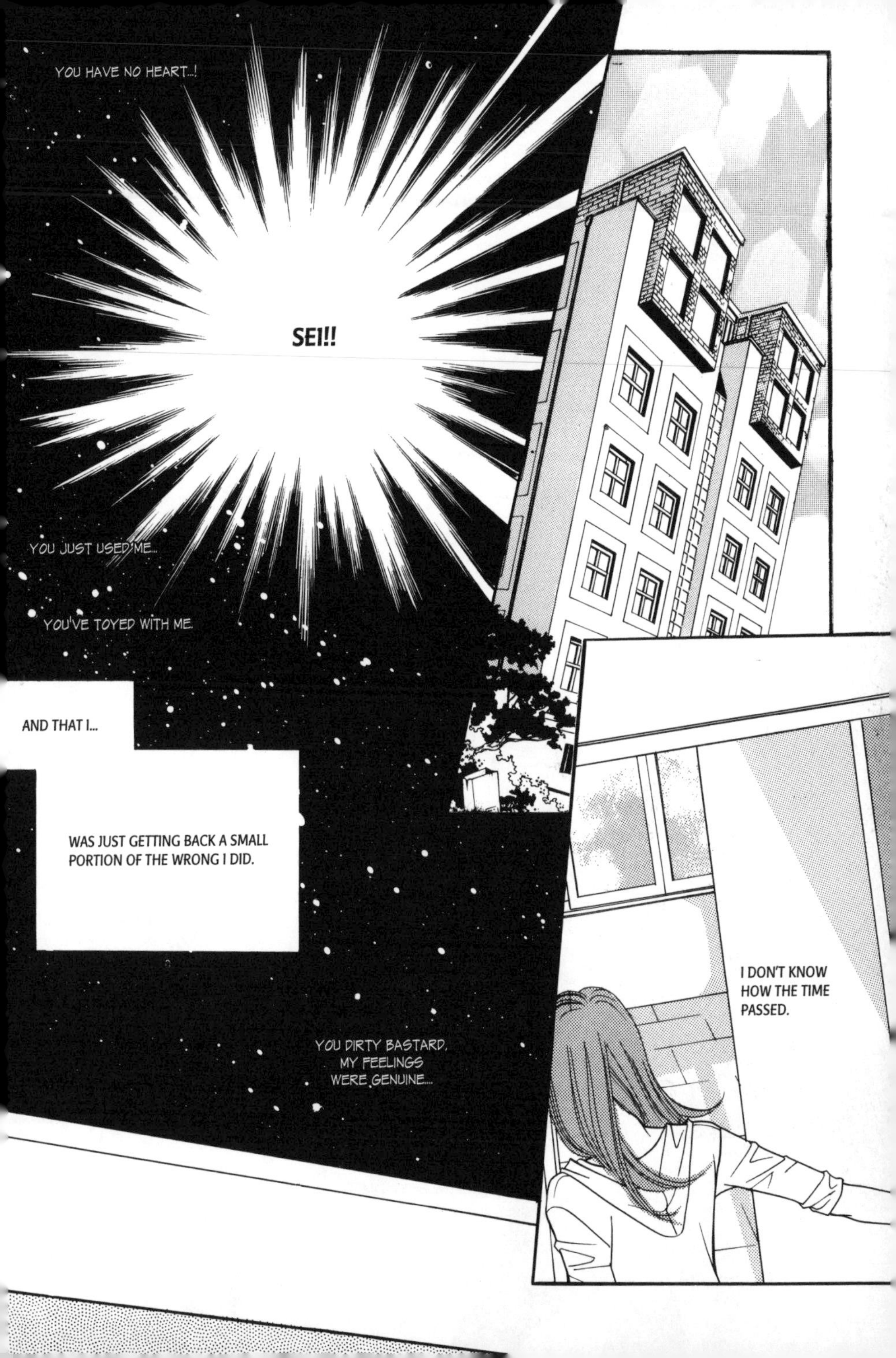
YOU HAVE NO HEART...!
SEI!!
YOU JUST USED ME...
YOU'VE TOYED WITH ME.
AND THAT I...
WAS JUST GETTING BACK A SMALL PORTION OF THE WRONG I DID.
YOU DIRTY BASTARD, MY FEELINGS WERE GENUINE....
I DON'T KNOW HOW THE TIME PASSED.

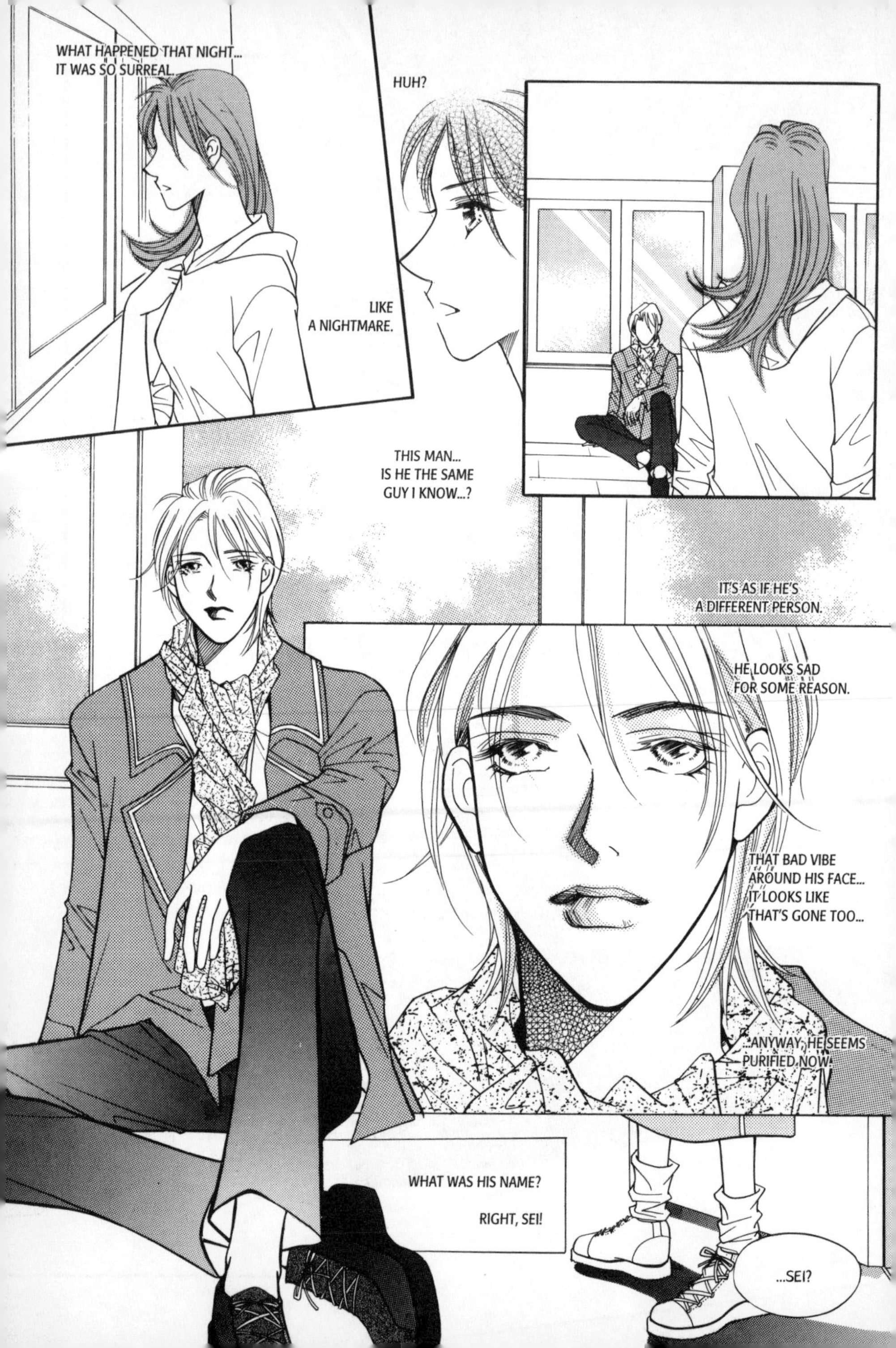
WHAT HAPPENED THAT NIGHT... IT WAS SO SURREAL.
LIKE A NIGHTMARE.
HUH?
THIS MAN... IS HE THE SAME GUY I KNOW...?
IT'S AS IF HE'S A DIFFERENT PERSON.
HE LOOKS SAD FOR SOME REASON.
THAT BAD VIBE AROUND HIS FACE... IT LOOKS LIKE THAT'S GONE TOO...
...ANYWAY, HE SEEMS PURIFIED NOW.
WHAT WAS HIS NAME?
RIGHT, SEI!
...SEI?

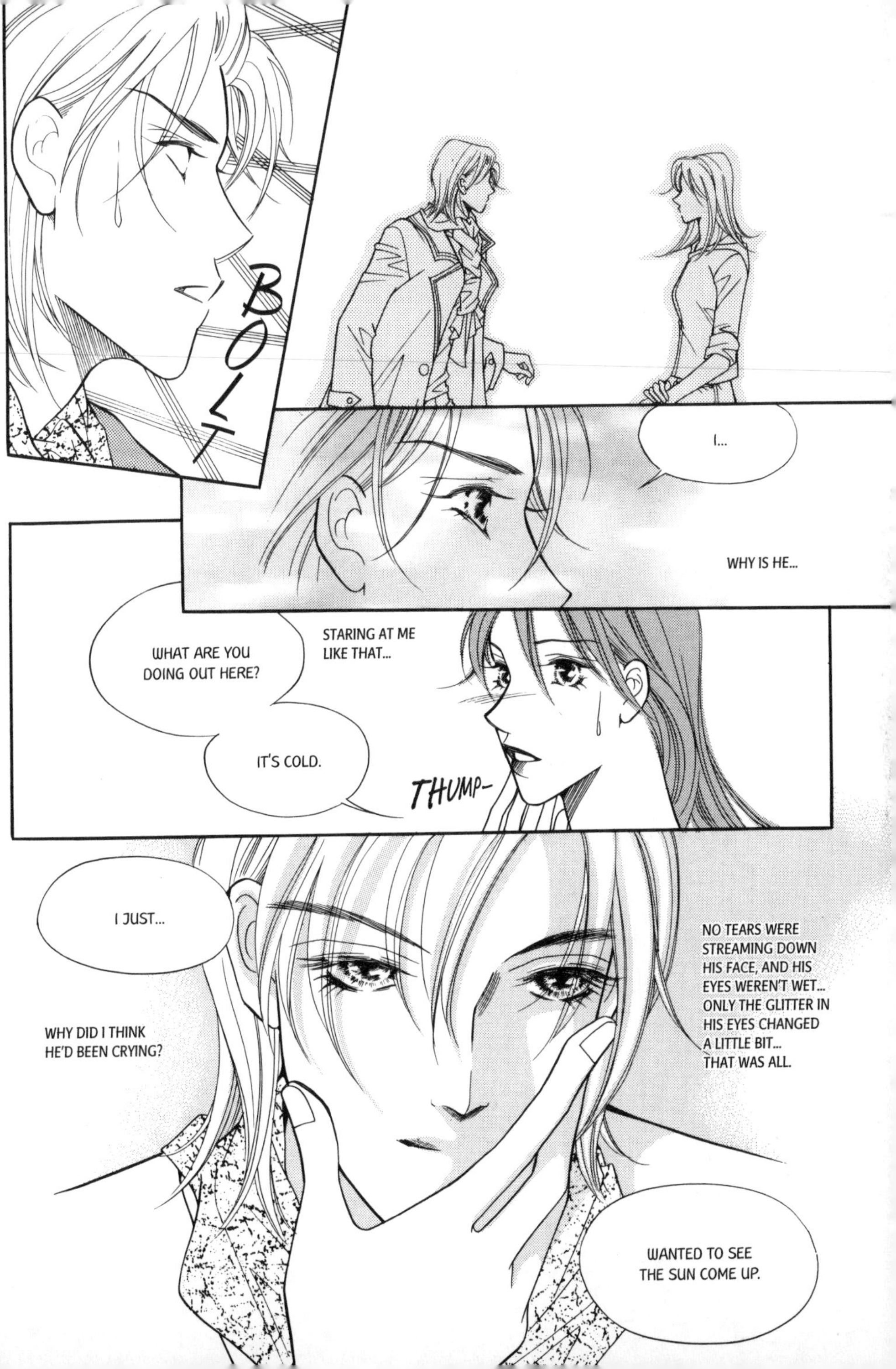
BOLT
I...
WHY IS HE...
WHAT ARE YOU DOING OUT HERE?
STARING AT ME LIKE THAT...
IT'S COLD.
THUMP-
I JUST...
WHY DID I THINK HE'D BEEN CRYING?
NO TEARS WERE STREAMING DOWN HIS FACE, AND HIS EYES WEREN'T WET... ONLY THE GLITTER IN HIS EYES CHANGED A LITTLE BIT... THAT WAS ALL.
WANTED TO SEE THE SUN COME UP.

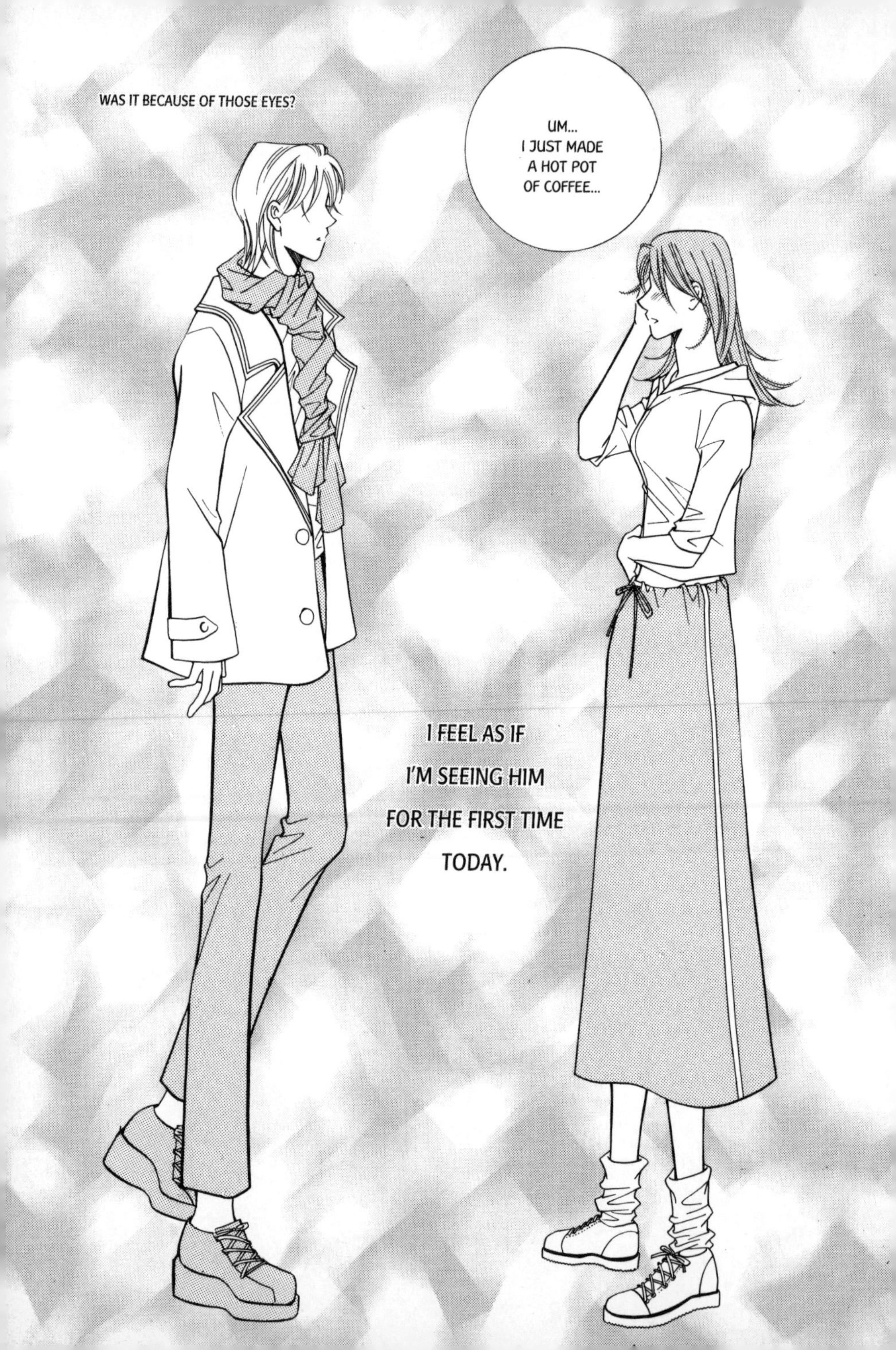
WAS IT BECAUSE OF THOSE EYES?
UM... I JUST MADE A HOT POT OF COFFEE...
I FEEL AS IF I'M SEEING HIM FOR THE FIRST TIME TODAY.

A SHORT GAME ABOUT A CHANCE ENCOUNTER

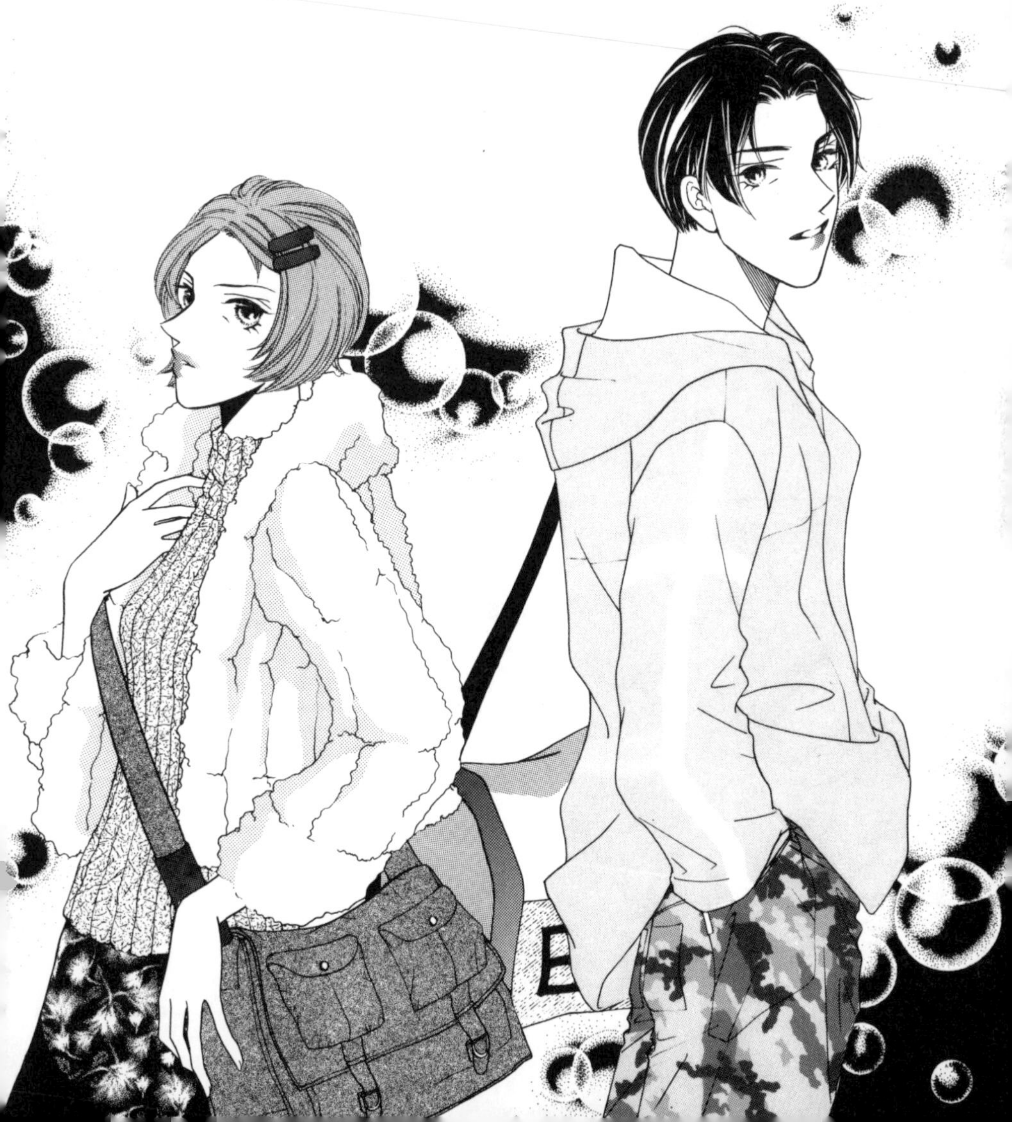

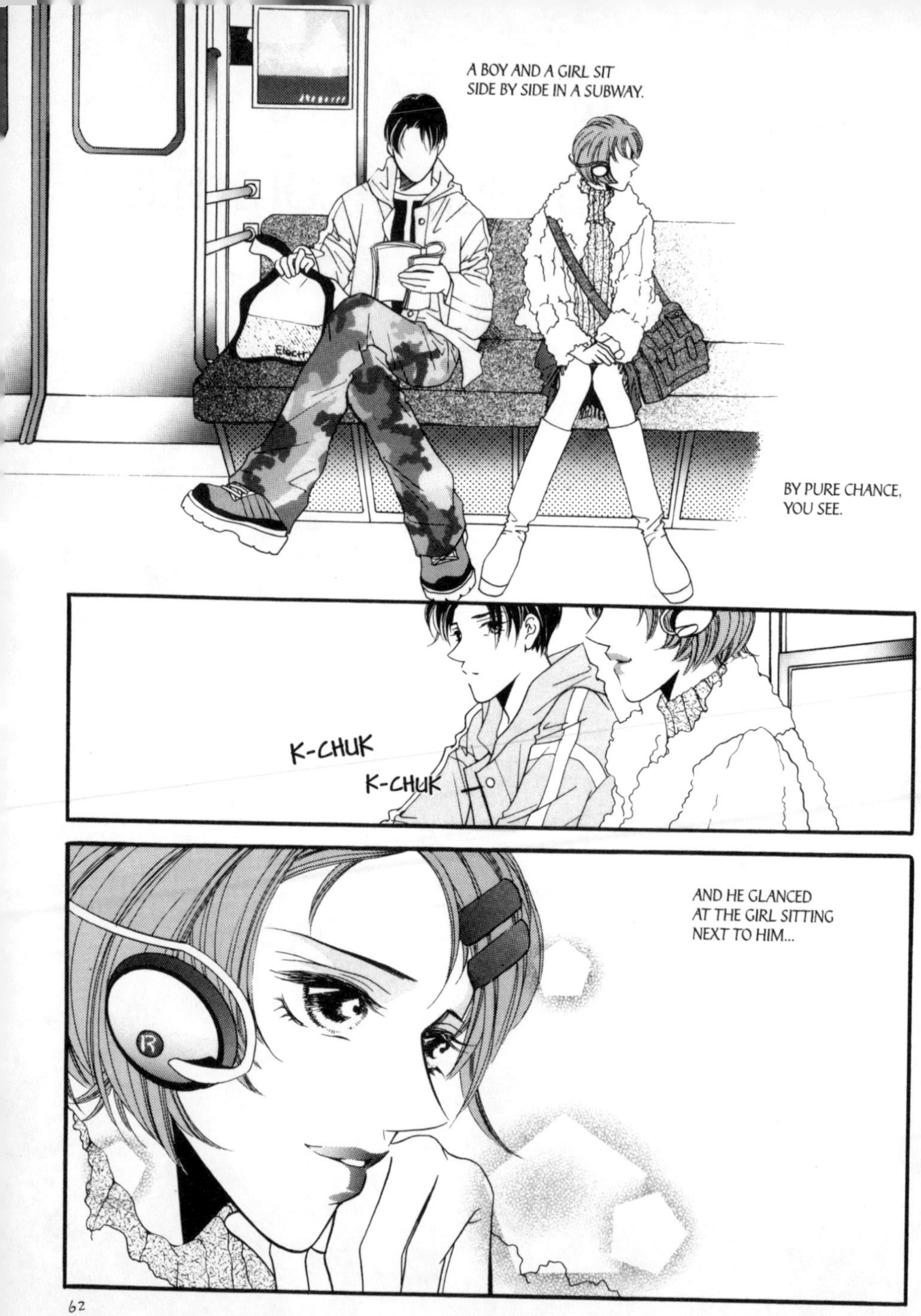
A BOY AND A GIRL SIT
SIDE BY SIDE IN A SUBWAY.
BY PURE CHANCE,
YOU SEE.
K-CHUK
K-CHUK
AND HE GLANCED
AT THE GIRL SITTING
NEXT TO HIM...

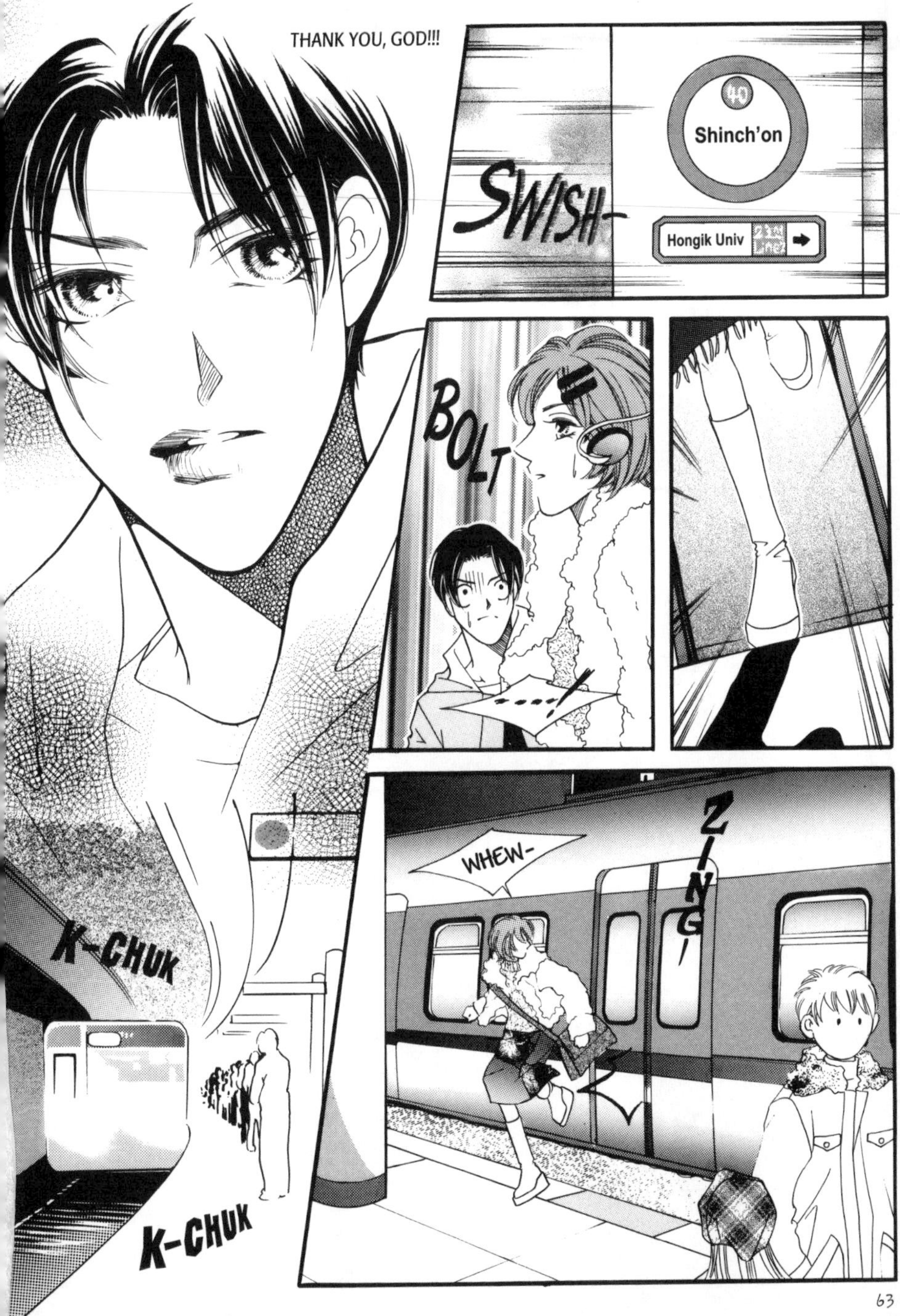
THANK YOU, GOD!!!
SWISH-
40
Shinch'on
Hongik Univ
BOLT
WHEW-
ZING!
K-CHUK
K-CHUK

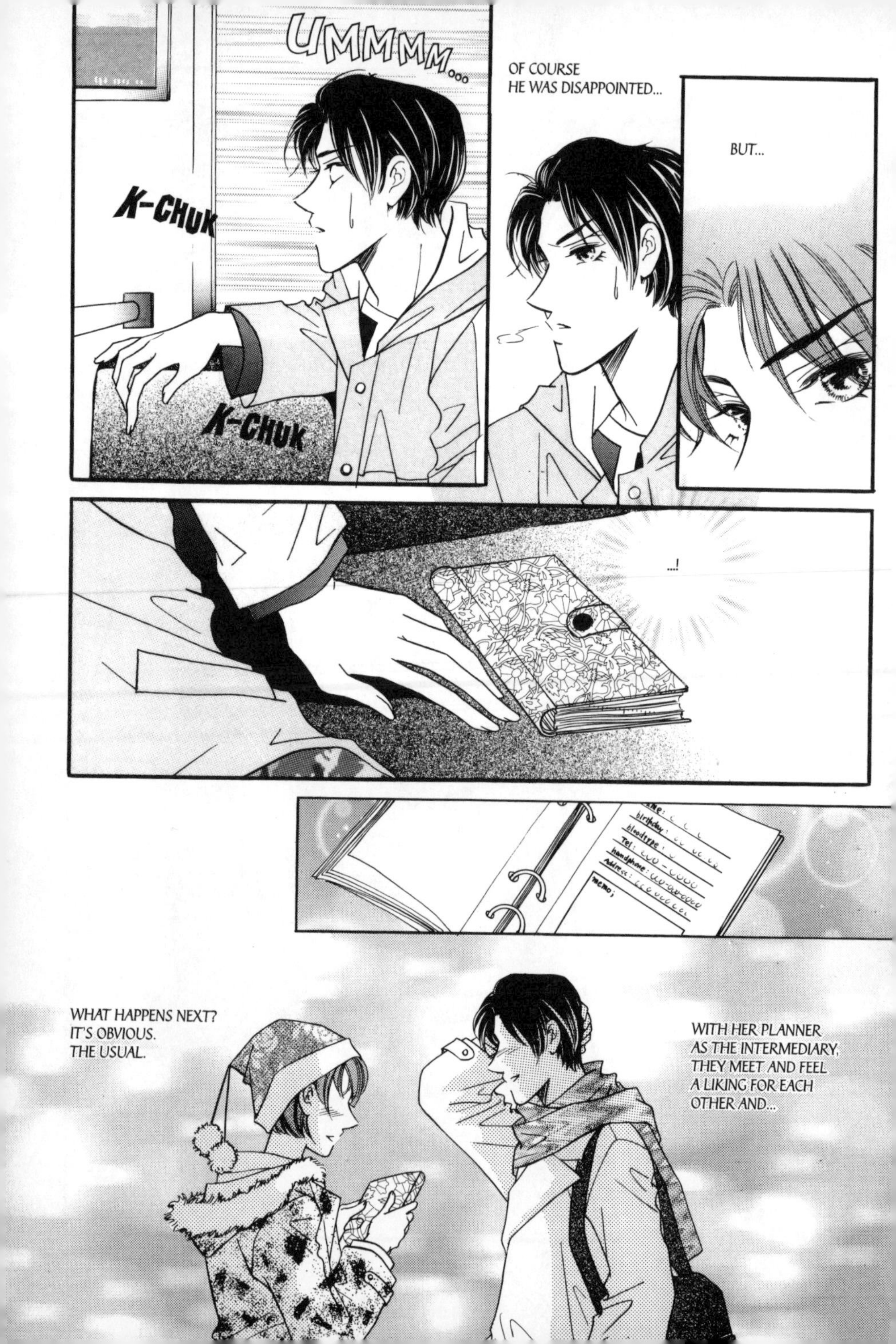
UMMMM...
K-CHUK
K-CHUK
OF COURSE HE WAS DISAPPOINTED...
BUT...
...!
birthday :
bloodtype :
Tel :
handphone :
address :
memo ;
WHAT HAPPENS NEXT? IT'S OBVIOUS. THE USUAL.
WITH HER PLANNER AS THE INTERMEDIARY, THEY MEET AND FEEL A LIKING FOR EACH OTHER AND...

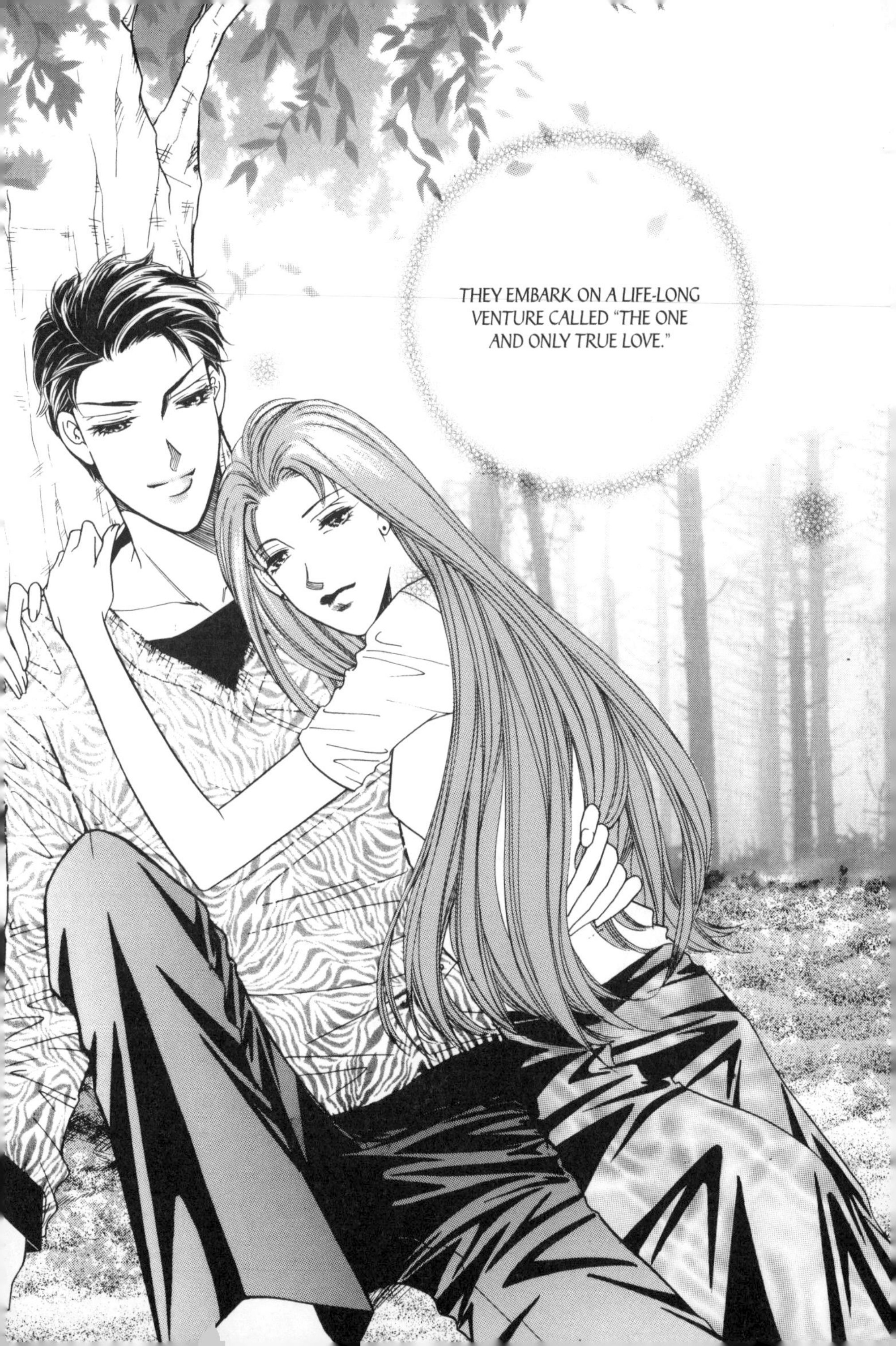
THEY EMBARK ON A LIFE-LONG VENTURE CALLED "THE ONE AND ONLY TRUE LOVE."

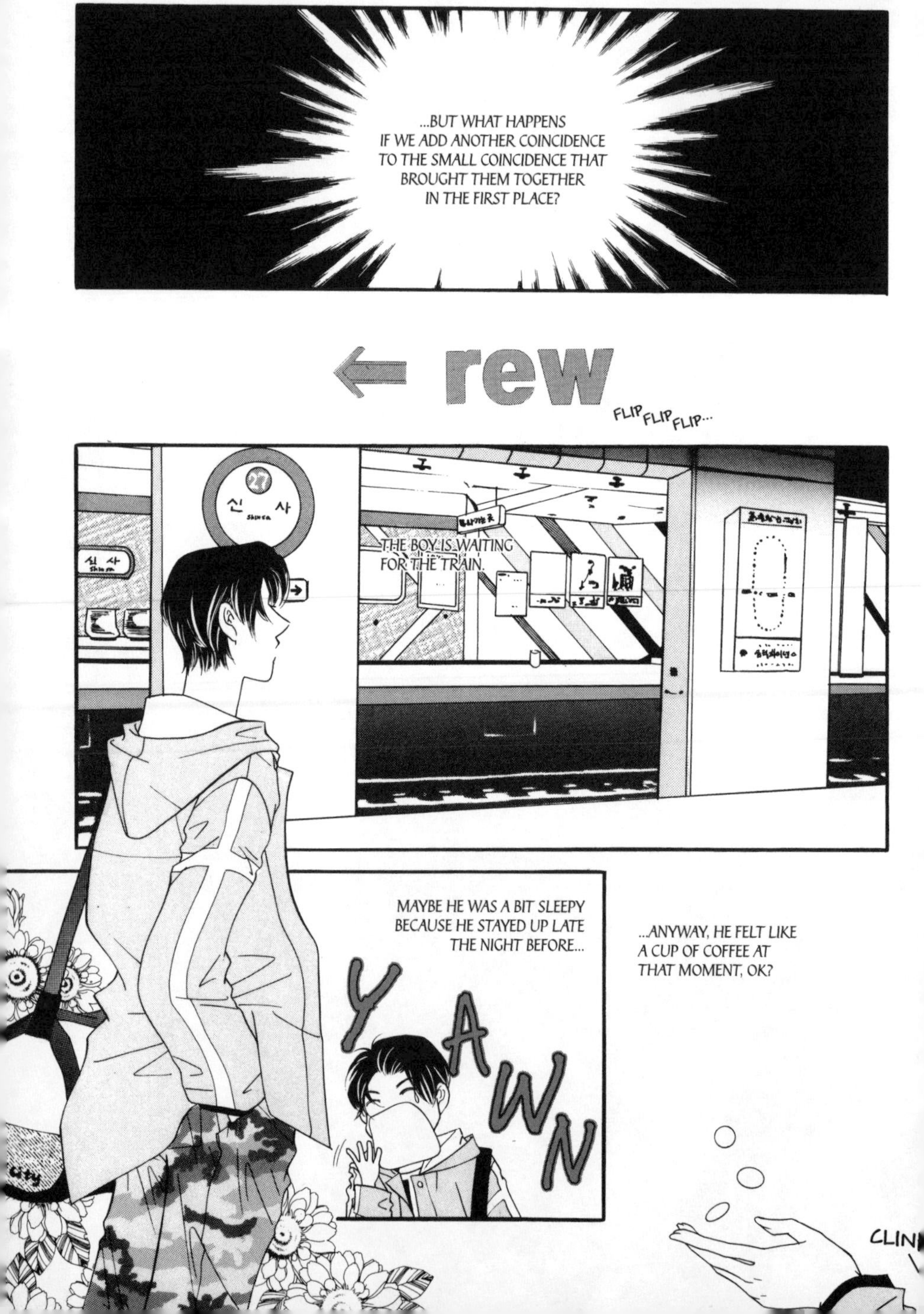
...BUT WHAT HAPPENS
IF WE ADD ANOTHER COINCIDENCE
TO THE SMALL COINCIDENCE THAT
BROUGHT THEM TOGETHER
IN THE FIRST PLACE?
rew
FLIP FLIP FLIP...
신 사
THE BOY IS WAITING
FOR THE TRAIN.
MAYBE HE WAS A BIT SLEEPY
BECAUSE HE STAYED UP LATE
THE NIGHT BEFORE...
YAWN
...ANYWAY, HE FELT LIKE
A CUP OF COFFEE AT
THAT MOMENT, OK?
CLIN

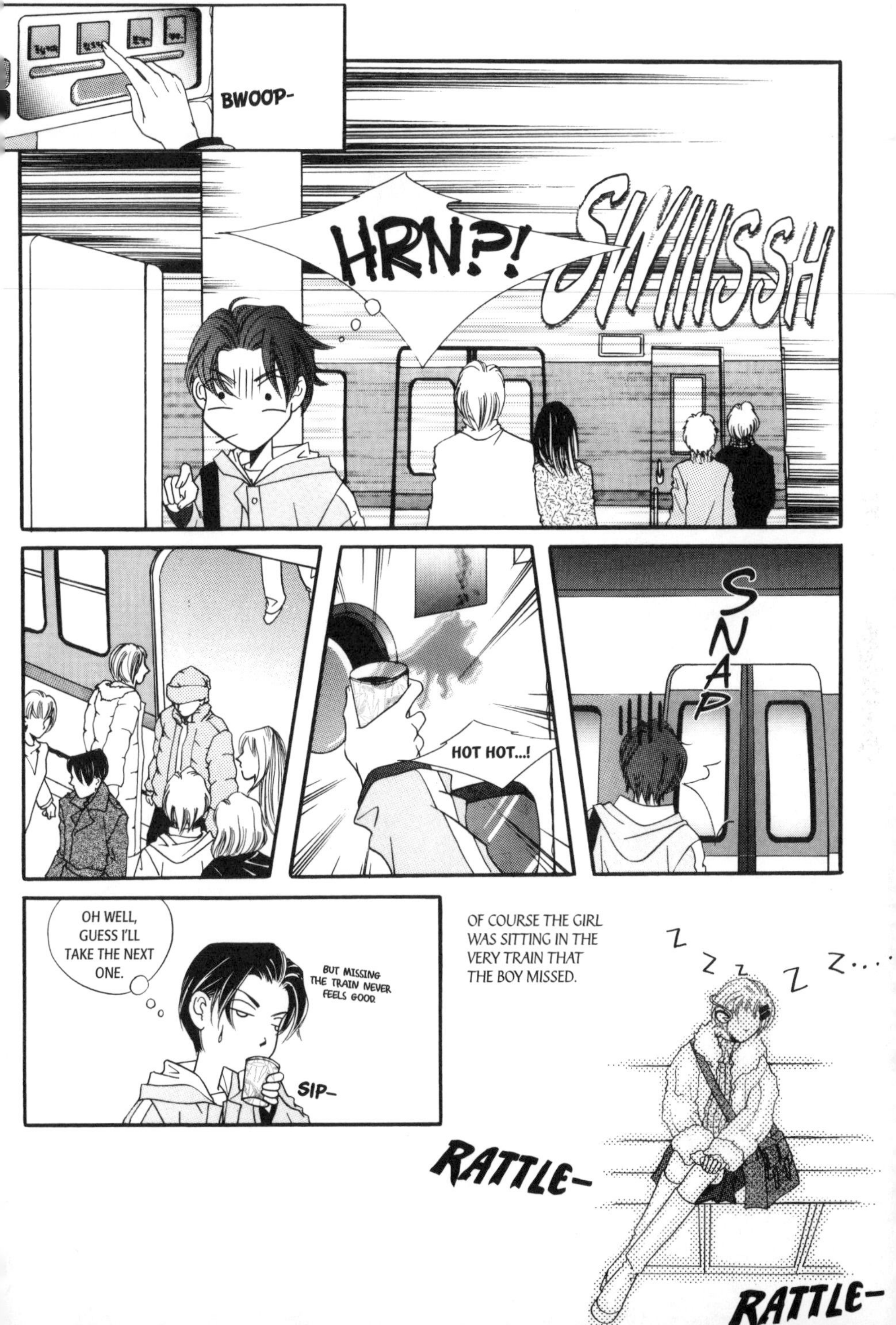
BWOOP-
HRN?!
SWIISSH
HOT HOT...!
SNAP
OH WELL, GUESS I'LL TAKE THE NEXT ONE.
BUT MISSING THE TRAIN NEVER FEELS GOOD.
SIP-
OF COURSE THE GIRL WAS SITTING IN THE VERY TRAIN THAT THE BOY MISSED.
Z Z Z Z Z...
RATTLE-
RATTLE-

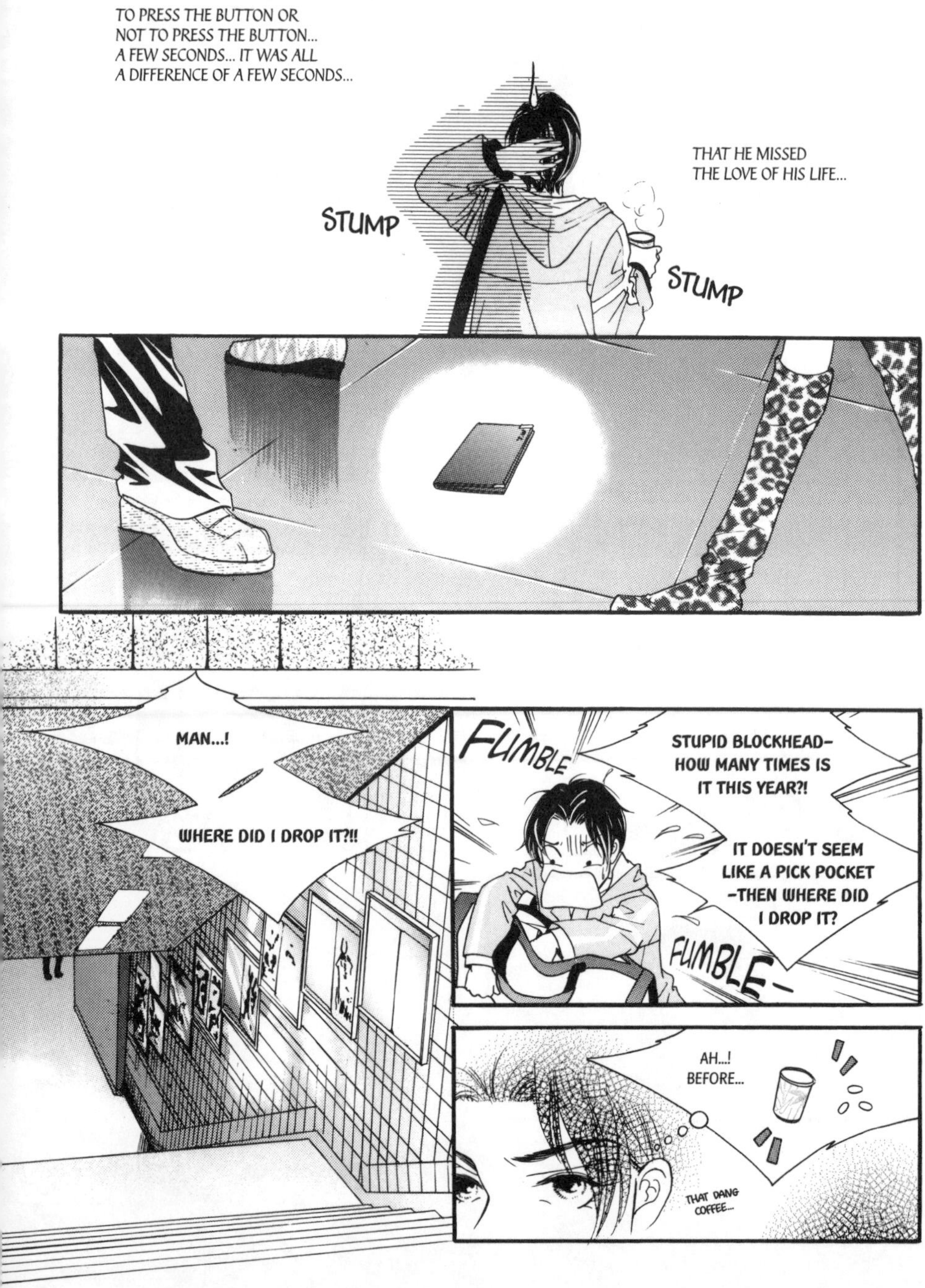
TO PRESS THE BUTTON OR NOT TO PRESS THE BUTTON... A FEW SECONDS... IT WAS ALL A DIFFERENCE OF A FEW SECONDS...
STUMP
THAT HE MISSED THE LOVE OF HIS LIFE...
STUMP
MAN...!
WHERE DID I DROP IT?!!
FUMBLE
STUPID BLOCKHEAD– HOW MANY TIMES IS IT THIS YEAR?!
IT DOESN'T SEEM LIKE A PICK POCKET –THEN WHERE DID I DROP IT?
FUMBLE–
AH...! BEFORE...
THAT DANG COFFEE...

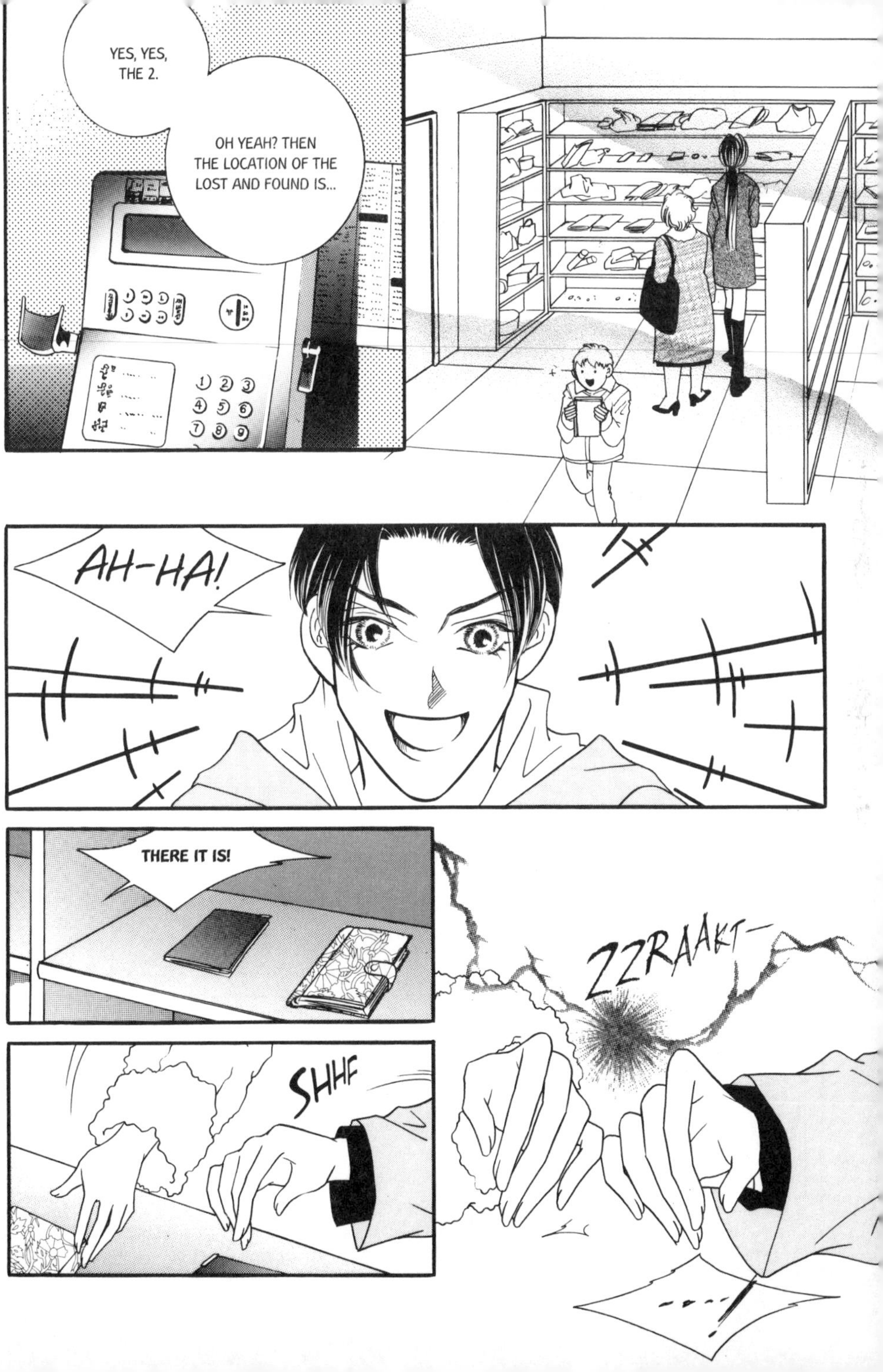
YES, YES, THE 2.
OH YEAH? THEN THE LOCATION OF THE LOST AND FOUND IS...
AH-HA!
THERE IT IS!
ZZRAAKT—
SHHF

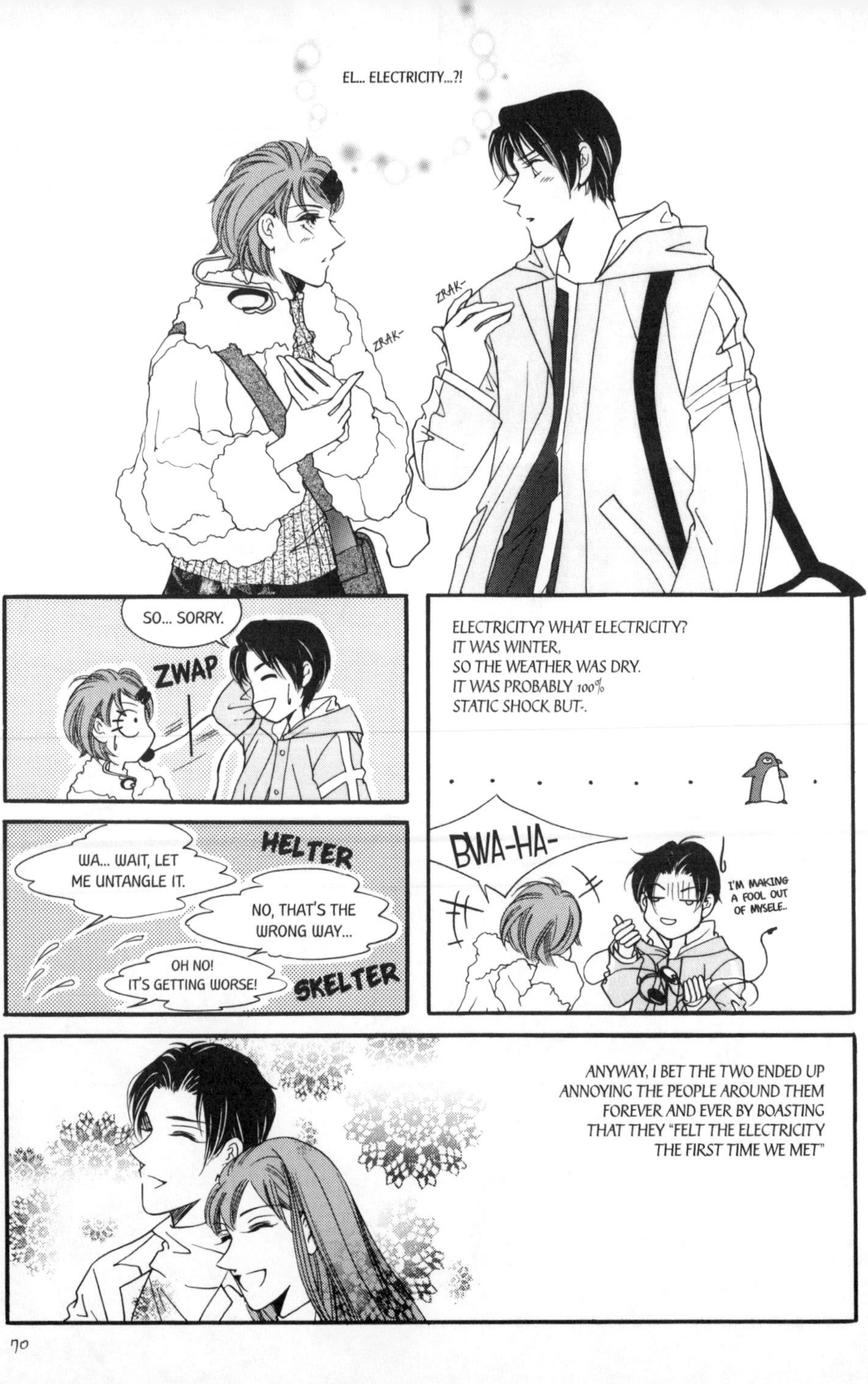
EL... ELECTRICITY...?!
ZRAK-
ZRAK-
SO... SORRY.
ZWAP
WA... WAIT, LET ME UNTANGLE IT.
HELTER
NO, THAT'S THE WRONG WAY...
OH NO! IT'S GETTING WORSE!
SKELTER
ELECTRICITY? WHAT ELECTRICITY?
IT WAS WINTER,
SO THE WEATHER WAS DRY.
IT WAS PROBABLY 100%
STATIC SHOCK BUT-.
. . . .
BWA-HA-
I'M MAKING A FOOL OUT OF MYSELF...
ANYWAY, I BET THE TWO ENDED UP ANNOYING THE PEOPLE AROUND THEM FOREVER AND EVER BY BOASTING THAT THEY "FELT THE ELECTRICITY THE FIRST TIME WE MET"

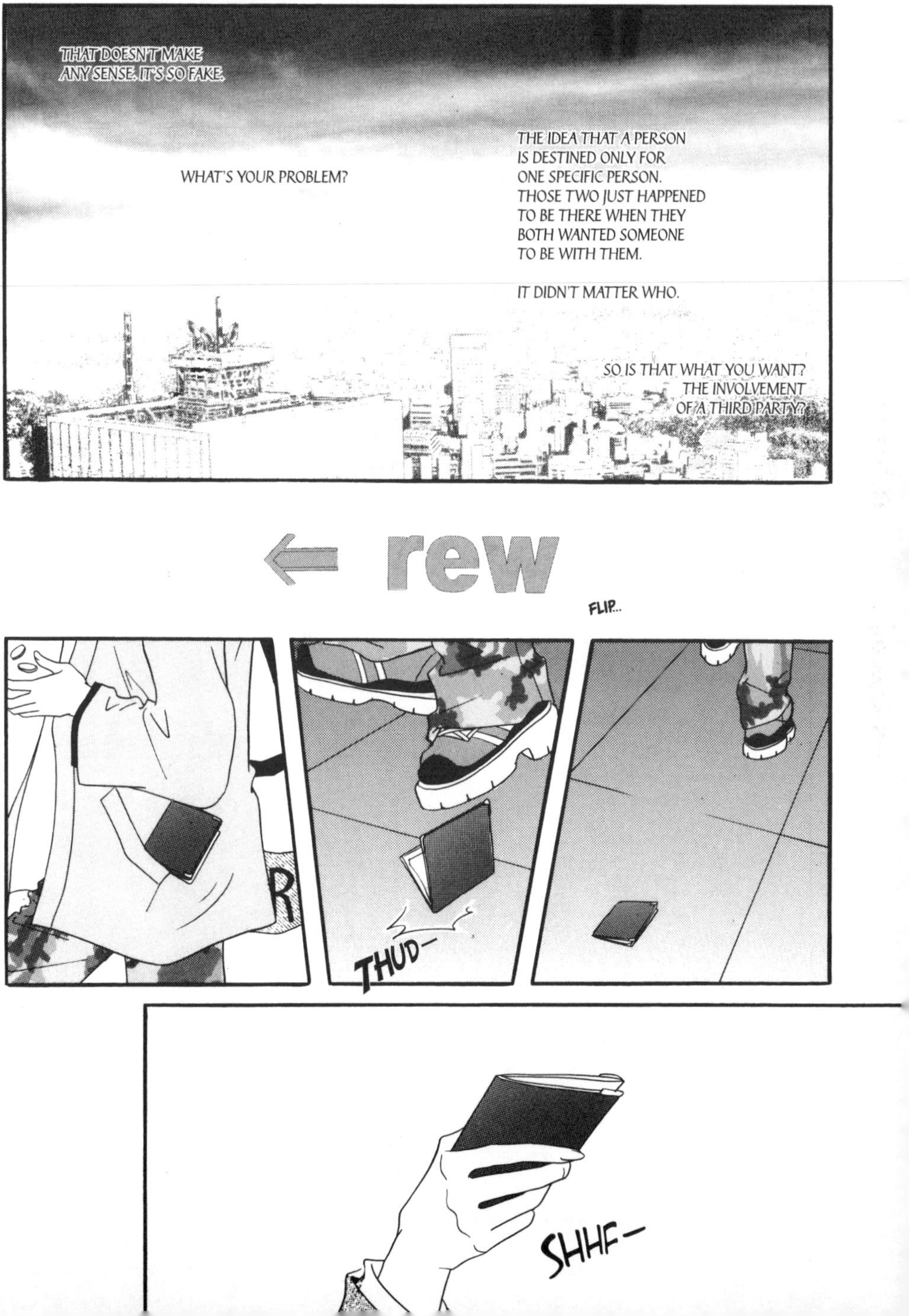
THAT DOESN'T MAKE ANY SENSE. IT'S SO FAKE.
WHAT'S YOUR PROBLEM?
THE IDEA THAT A PERSON IS DESTINED ONLY FOR ONE SPECIFIC PERSON. THOSE TWO JUST HAPPENED TO BE THERE WHEN THEY BOTH WANTED SOMEONE TO BE WITH THEM.
IT DIDN'T MATTER WHO.
SO IS THAT WHAT YOU WANT? THE INVOLVEMENT OF A THIRD PARTY?
rew
FLIP...
THUD-
SHHF-

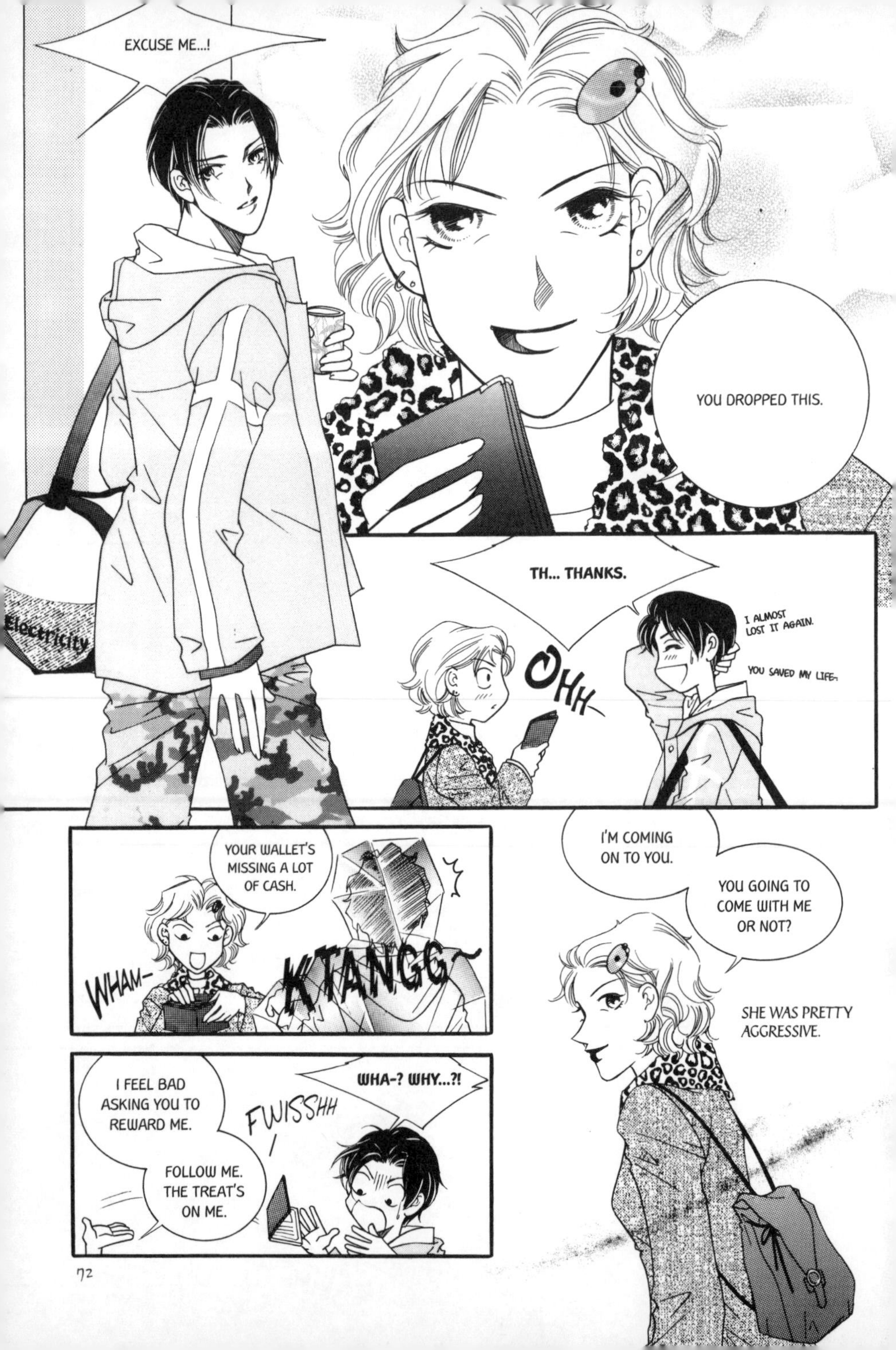
EXCUSE ME...!
YOU DROPPED THIS.
TH... THANKS.
OHH
I ALMOST LOST IT AGAIN.
YOU SAVED MY LIFE.
YOUR WALLET'S MISSING A LOT OF CASH.
WHAM-
KTANGG
I FEEL BAD ASKING YOU TO REWARD ME.
FOLLOW ME. THE TREAT'S ON ME.
WHA-? WHY...?!
FWISSHH
I'M COMING ON TO YOU.
YOU GOING TO COME WITH ME OR NOT?
SHE WAS PRETTY AGGRESSIVE.

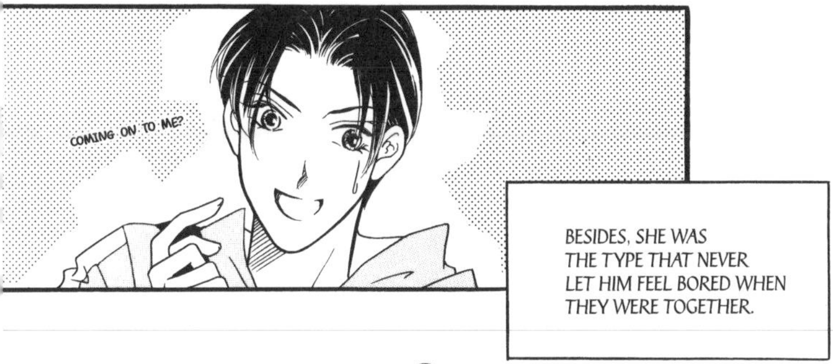
COMING ON TO ME?
BESIDES, SHE WAS THE TYPE THAT NEVER LET HIM FEEL BORED WHEN THEY WERE TOGETHER.

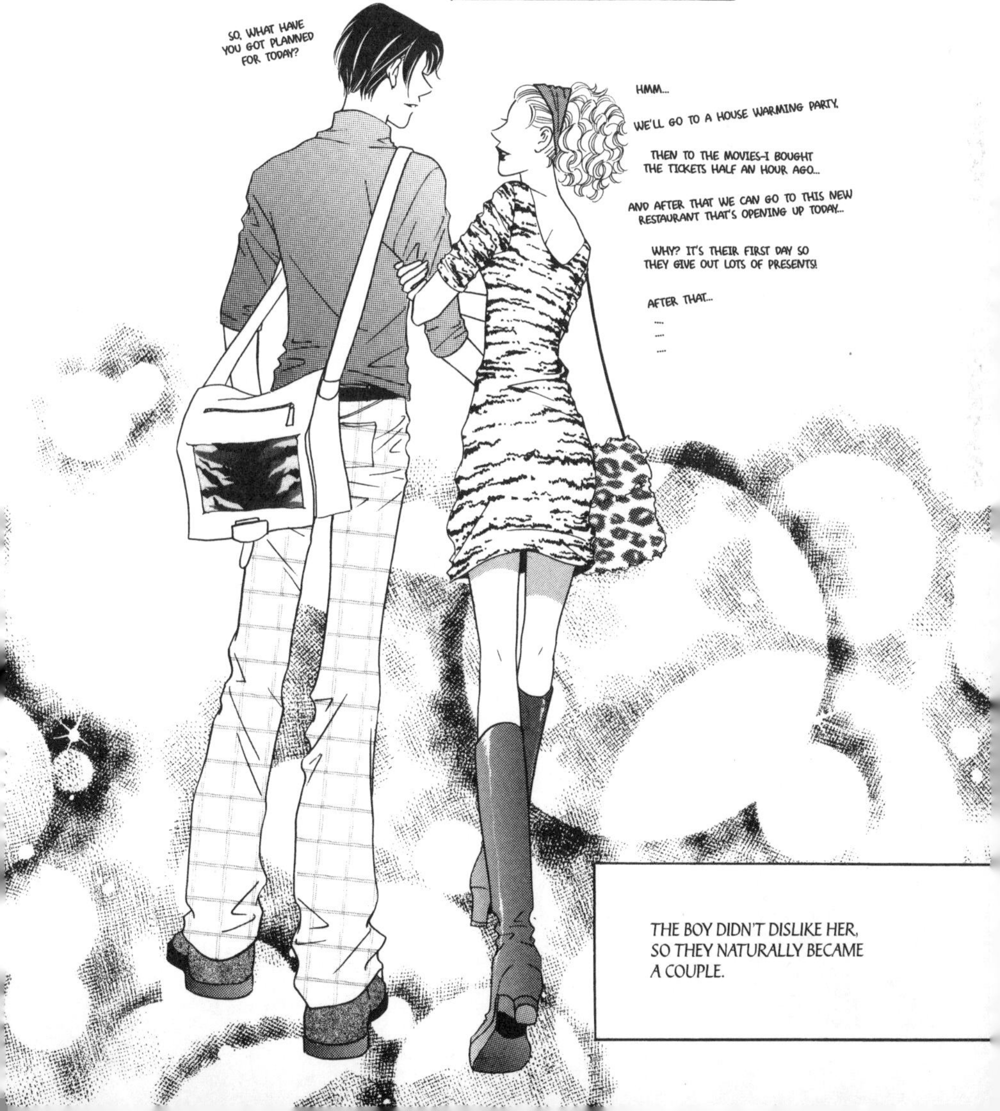
SO, WHAT HAVE YOU GOT PLANNED FOR TODAY?
HMM...
WE'LL GO TO A HOUSE WARMING PARTY.
THEN TO THE MOVIES–I BOUGHT THE TICKETS HALF AN HOUR AGO...
AND AFTER THAT WE CAN GO TO THIS NEW RESTAURANT THAT'S OPENING UP TODAY...
WHY? IT'S THEIR FIRST DAY SO THEY GIVE OUT LOTS OF PRESENTS!
AFTER THAT...
....
....
....
THE BOY DIDN'T DISLIKE HER, SO THEY NATURALLY BECAME A COUPLE.

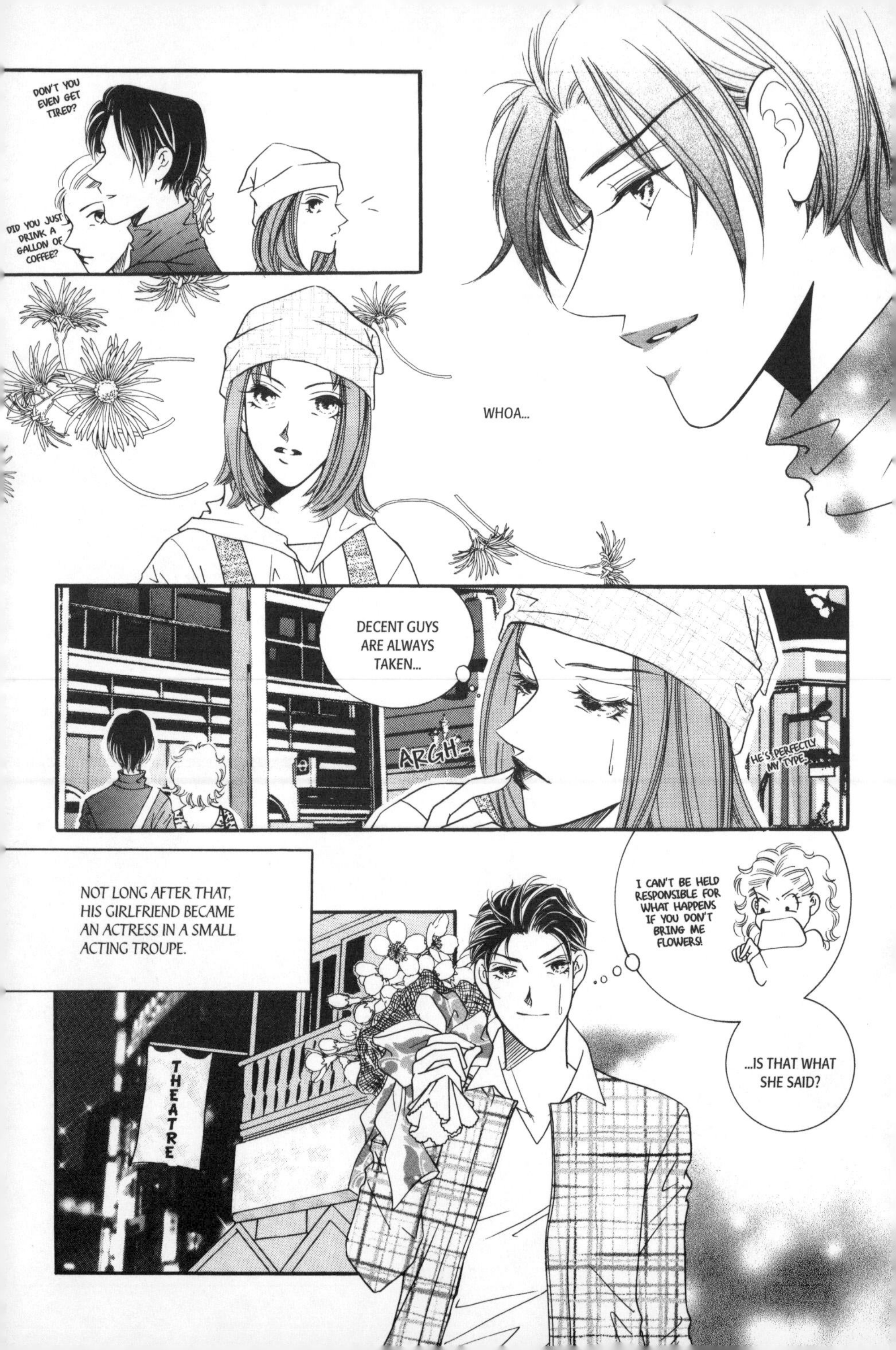

DON'T YOU EVEN GET TIRED?
DID YOU JUST DRINK A GALLON OF COFFEE?
WHOA...
DECENT GUYS ARE ALWAYS TAKEN...
ARGH-
HE'S PERFECTLY MY TYPE.
NOT LONG AFTER THAT, HIS GIRLFRIEND BECAME AN ACTRESS IN A SMALL ACTING TROUPE.
THEATRE
I CAN'T BE HELD RESPONSIBLE FOR WHAT HAPPENS IF YOU DON'T BRING ME FLOWERS!
...IS THAT WHAT SHE SAID?

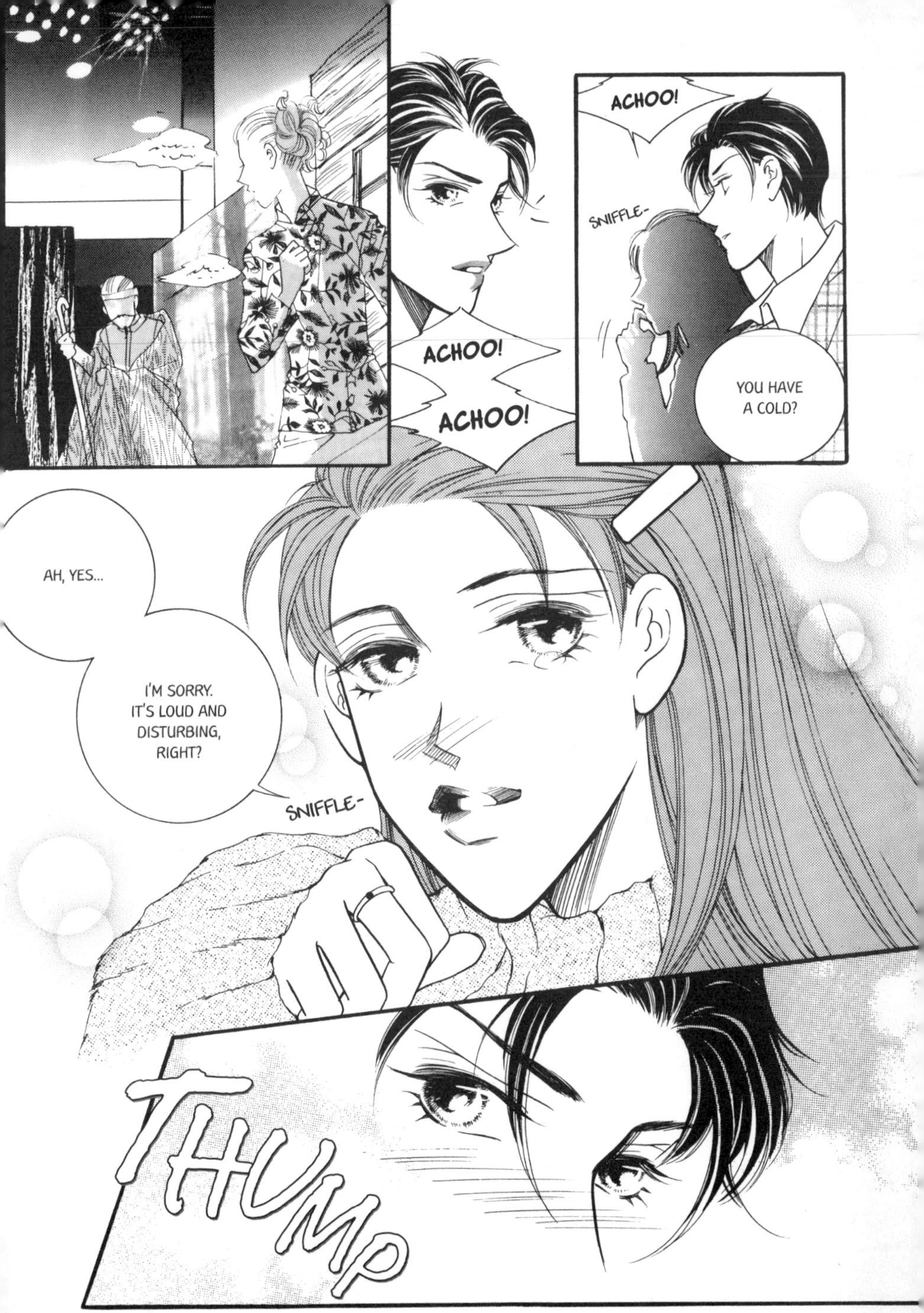
ACHOO!
ACHOO!
ACHOO!
SNIFFLE-
YOU HAVE A COLD?
AH, YES...
I'M SORRY. IT'S LOUD AND DISTURBING, RIGHT?
SNIFFLE-
THUMP

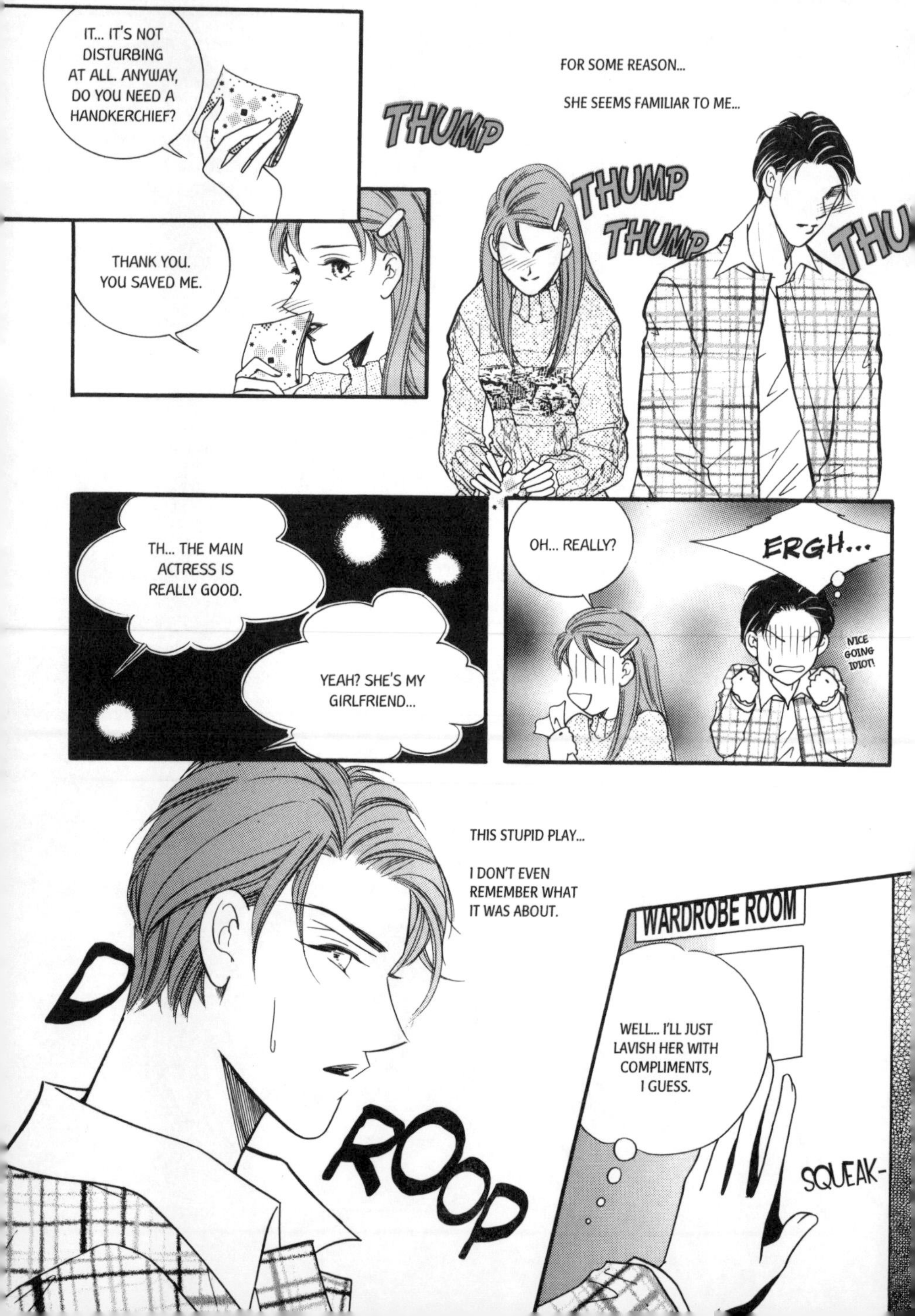
IT... IT'S NOT DISTURBING AT ALL. ANYWAY, DO YOU NEED A HANDKERCHIEF?
THANK YOU. YOU SAVED ME.
THUMP
FOR SOME REASON...
SHE SEEMS FAMILIAR TO ME...
THUMP
THUMP
THU
TH... THE MAIN ACTRESS IS REALLY GOOD.
YEAH? SHE'S MY GIRLFRIEND...
OH... REALLY?
ERGH...
NICE GOING IDIOT!
THIS STUPID PLAY...
I DON'T EVEN REMEMBER WHAT IT WAS ABOUT.
WARDROBE ROOM
WELL... I'LL JUST LAVISH HER WITH COMPLIMENTS, I GUESS.
D
ROOP
SQUEAK-

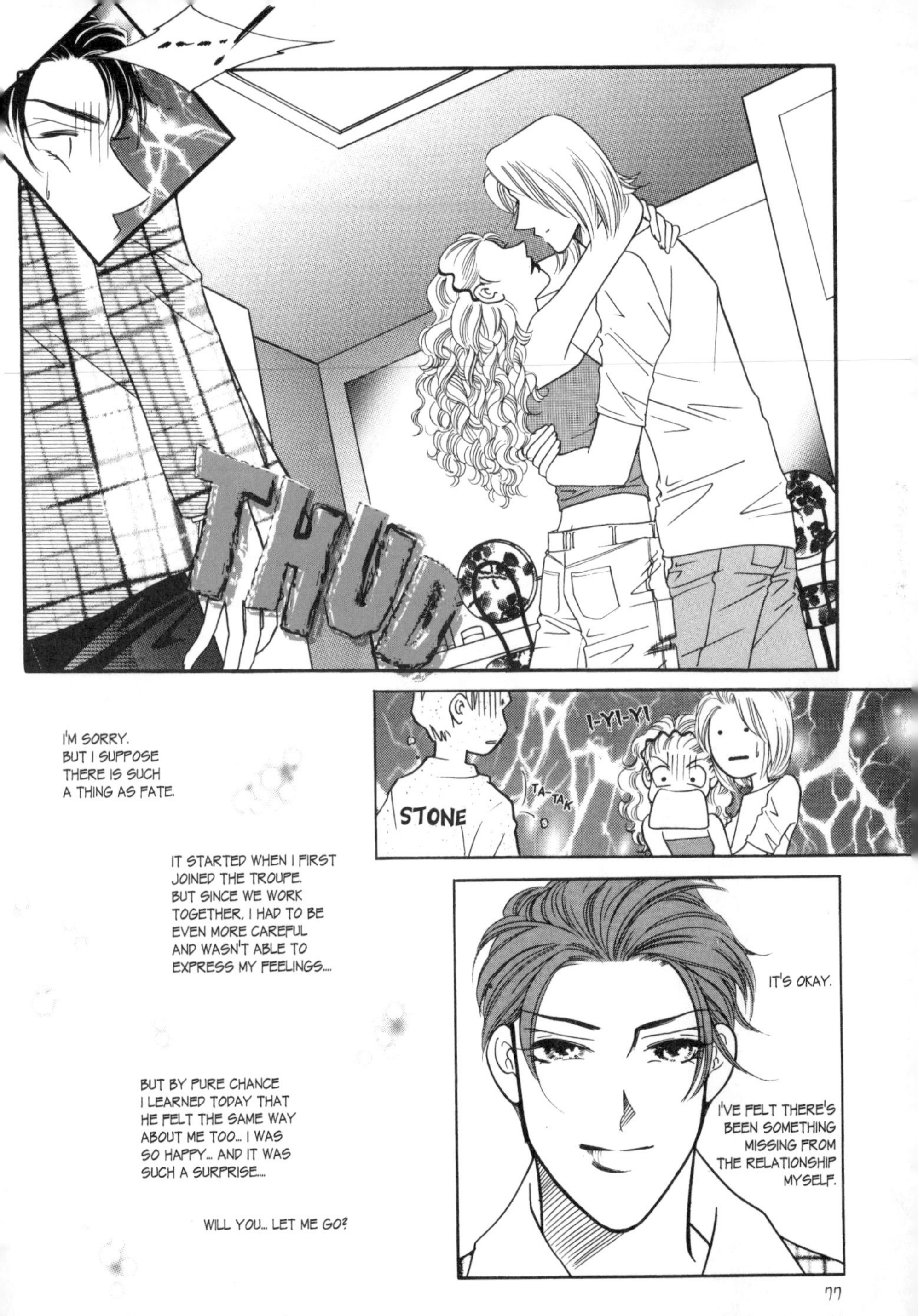
THUD
I'M SORRY.
BUT I SUPPOSE
THERE IS SUCH
A THING AS FATE.
I-YI-YI
STONE
TA-TAK
IT STARTED WHEN I FIRST
JOINED THE TROUPE.
BUT SINCE WE WORK
TOGETHER, I HAD TO BE
EVEN MORE CAREFUL
AND WASN'T ABLE TO
EXPRESS MY FEELINGS....
BUT BY PURE CHANCE
I LEARNED TODAY THAT
HE FELT THE SAME WAY
ABOUT ME TOO... I WAS
SO HAPPY... AND IT WAS
SUCH A SURPRISE....
WILL YOU... LET ME GO?
IT'S OKAY.
I'VE FELT THERE'S
BEEN SOMETHING
MISSING FROM
THE RELATIONSHIP
MYSELF.

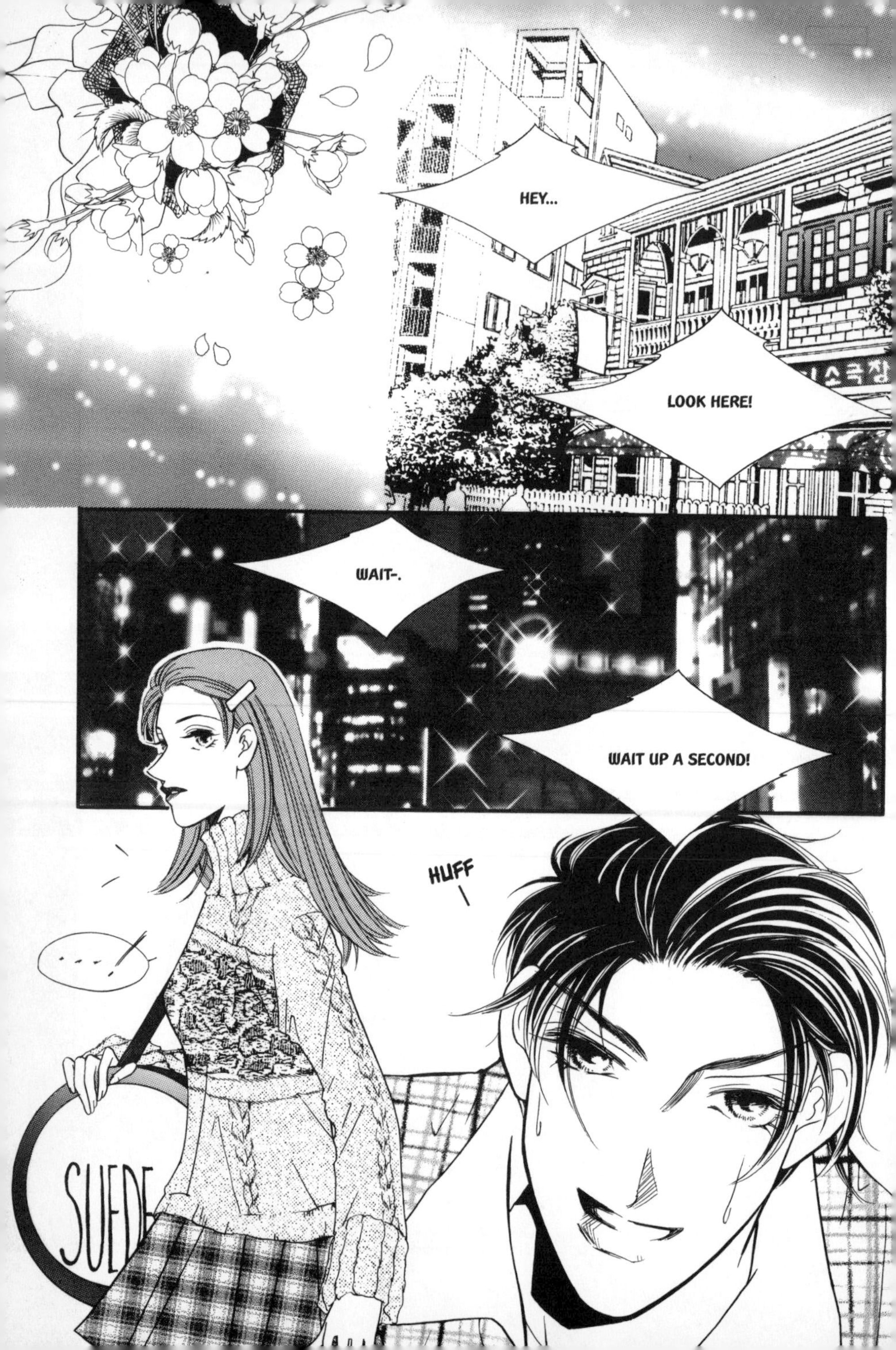
HEY...
LOOK HERE!
WAIT-.
WAIT UP A SECOND!
HUFF
...

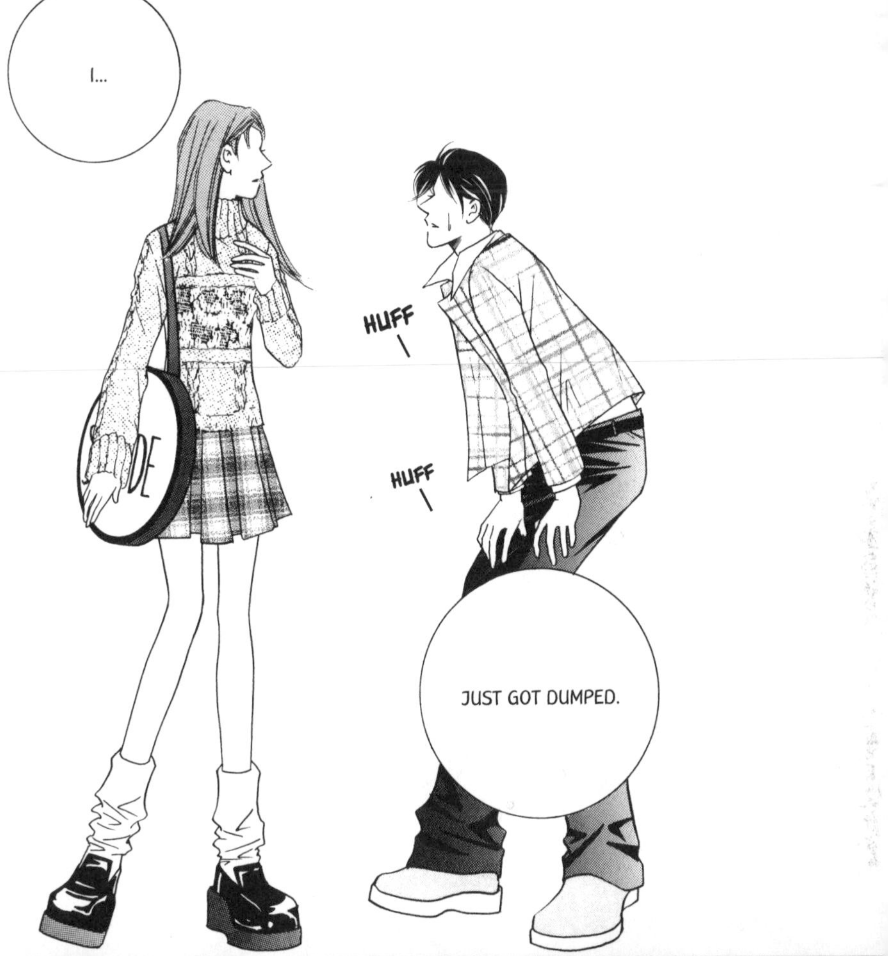
I...
HUFF
HUFF
JUST GOT DUMPED.

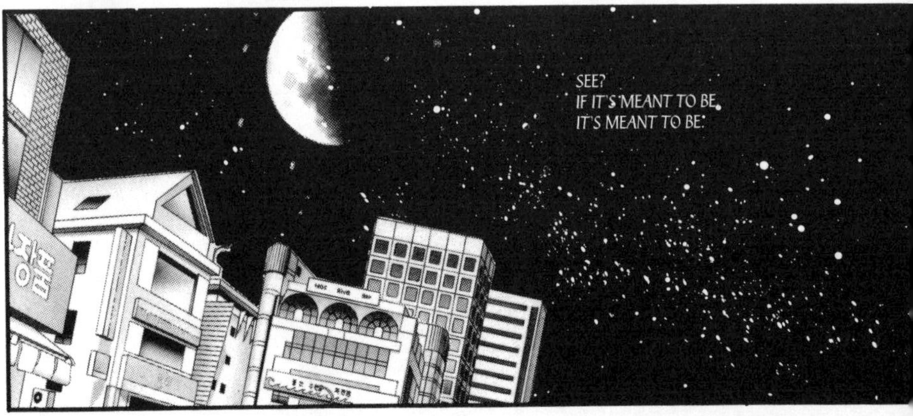
SEE?
IF IT'S MEANT TO BE,
IT'S MEANT TO BE.

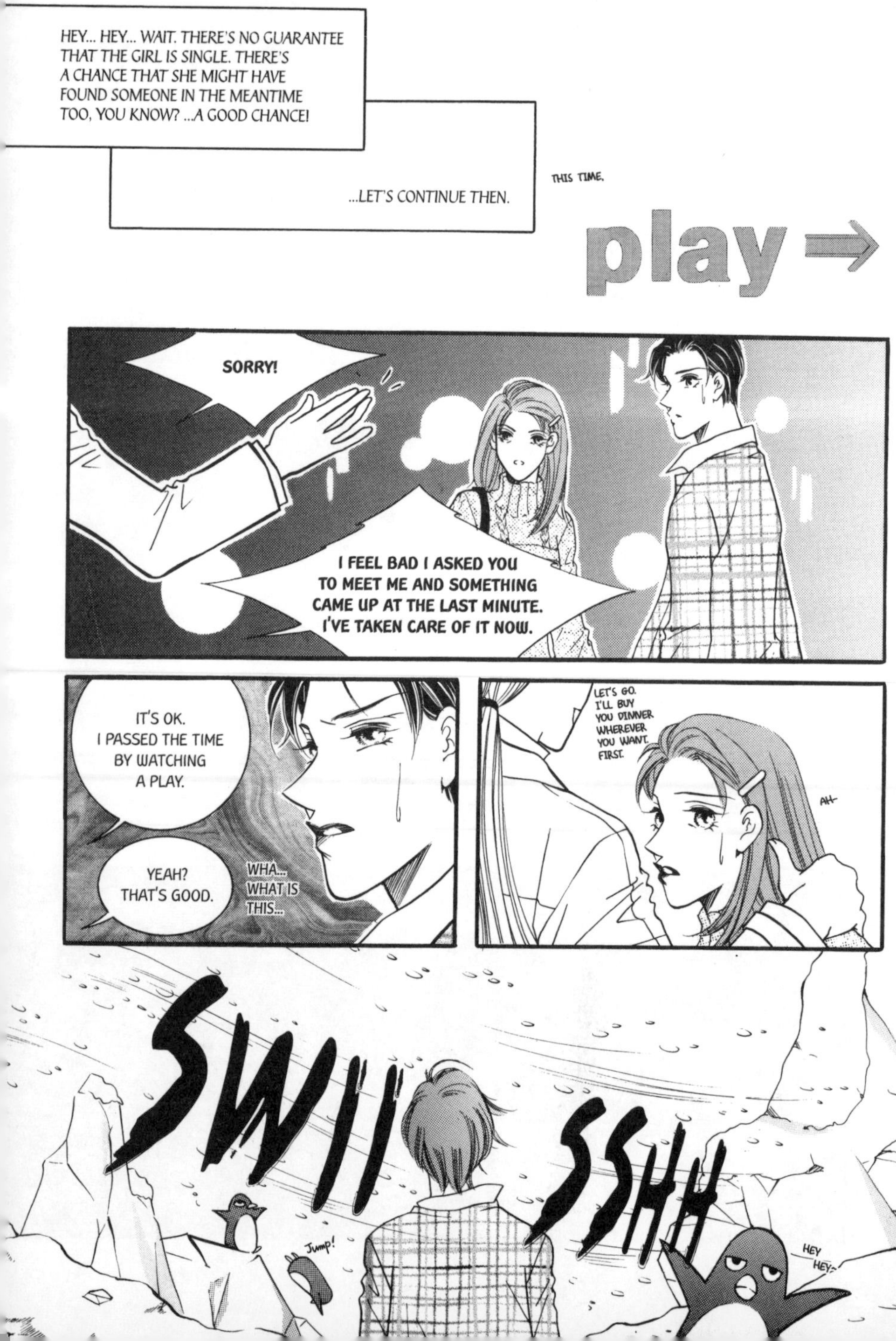
HEY... HEY... WAIT. THERE'S NO GUARANTEE THAT THE GIRL IS SINGLE. THERE'S A CHANCE THAT SHE MIGHT HAVE FOUND SOMEONE IN THE MEANTIME TOO, YOU KNOW? ...A GOOD CHANCE!
...LET'S CONTINUE THEN.
THIS TIME.
play→
SORRY!
I FEEL BAD I ASKED YOU TO MEET ME AND SOMETHING CAME UP AT THE LAST MINUTE. I'VE TAKEN CARE OF IT NOW.
IT'S OK. I PASSED THE TIME BY WATCHING A PLAY.
YEAH? THAT'S GOOD.
WHA... WHAT IS THIS...
LET'S GO. I'LL BUY YOU DINNER WHEREVER YOU WANT. FIRST.
AH-
SWII SSHH
Jump!
HEY HEY~

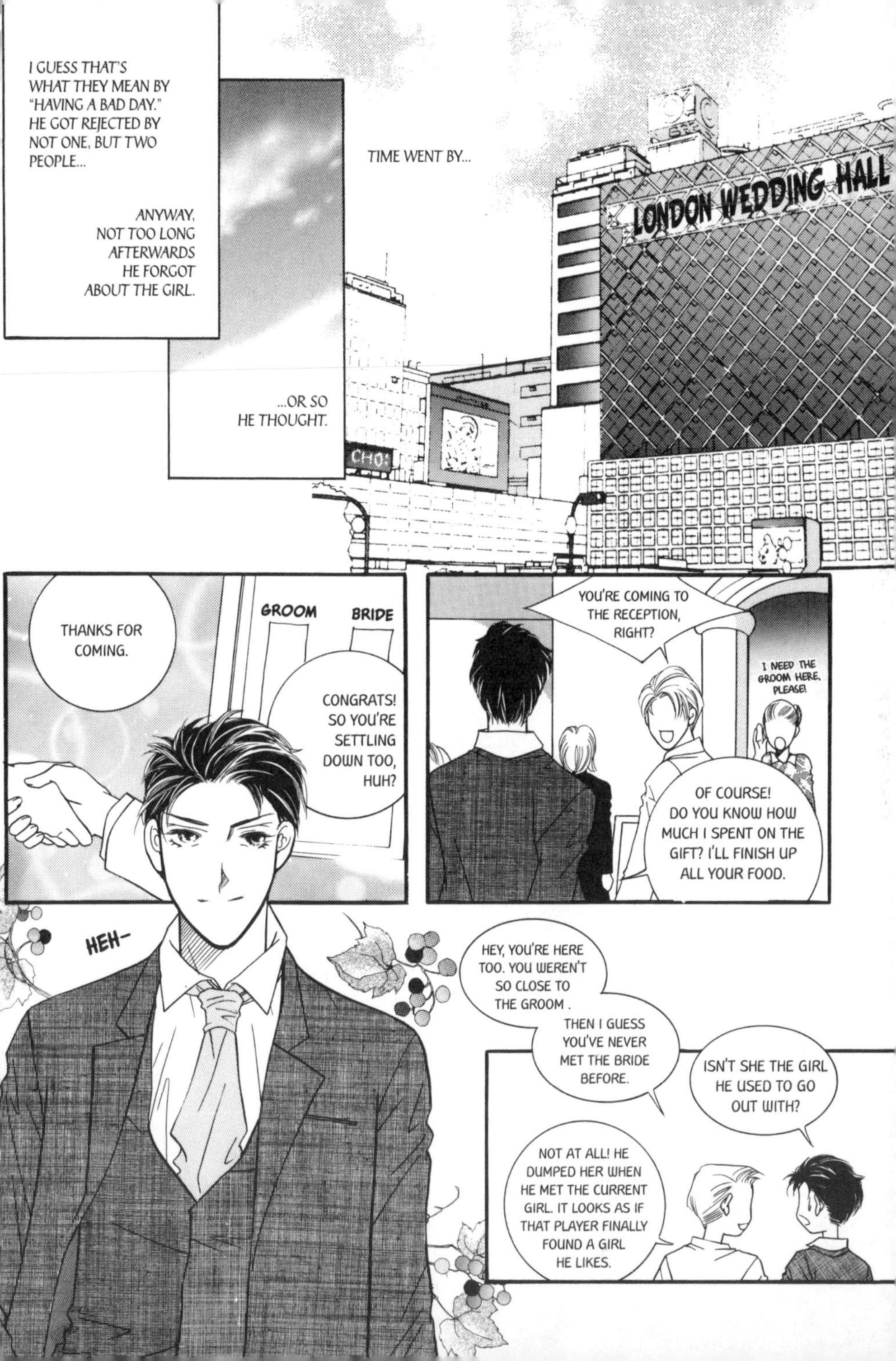
I GUESS THAT'S WHAT THEY MEAN BY "HAVING A BAD DAY." HE GOT REJECTED BY NOT ONE, BUT TWO PEOPLE...
ANYWAY, NOT TOO LONG AFTERWARDS HE FORGOT ABOUT THE GIRL.
...OR SO HE THOUGHT.
TIME WENT BY...
LONDON WEDDING HALL
CHO!
GROOM
BRIDE
THANKS FOR COMING.
CONGRATS! SO YOU'RE SETTLING DOWN TOO, HUH?
YOU'RE COMING TO THE RECEPTION, RIGHT?
I NEED THE GROOM HERE, PLEASE!
OF COURSE! DO YOU KNOW HOW MUCH I SPENT ON THE GIFT? I'LL FINISH UP ALL YOUR FOOD.
HEH-
HEY, YOU'RE HERE TOO. YOU WEREN'T SO CLOSE TO THE GROOM .
THEN I GUESS YOU'VE NEVER MET THE BRIDE BEFORE.
ISN'T SHE THE GIRL HE USED TO GO OUT WITH?
NOT AT ALL! HE DUMPED HER WHEN HE MET THE CURRENT GIRL. IT LOOKS AS IF THAT PLAYER FINALLY FOUND A GIRL HE LIKES.

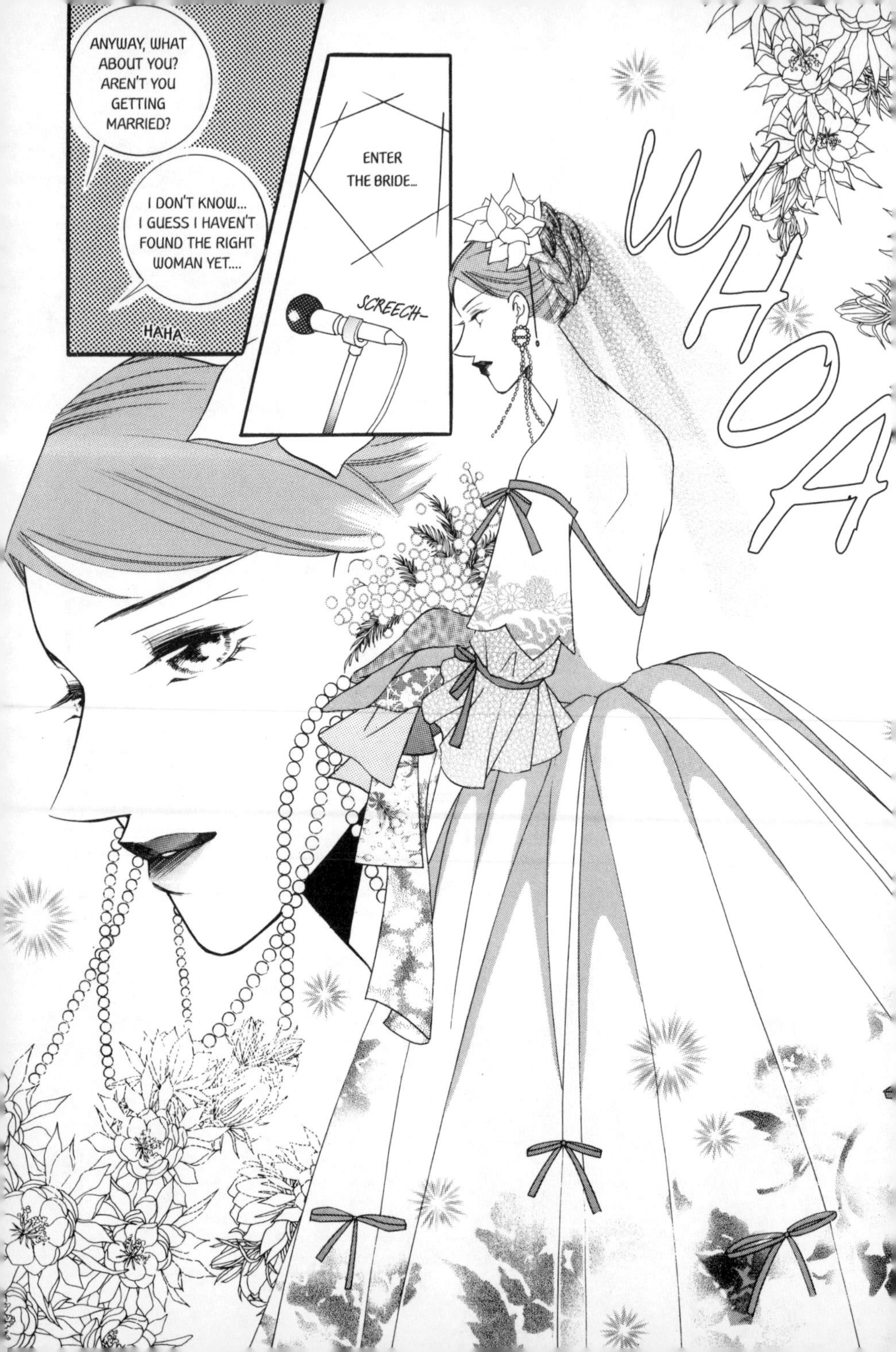
ANYWAY, WHAT ABOUT YOU? AREN'T YOU GETTING MARRIED?
I DON'T KNOW... I GUESS I HAVEN'T FOUND THE RIGHT WOMAN YET....
HAHA
ENTER THE BRIDE...
SCREECH-
WHOA

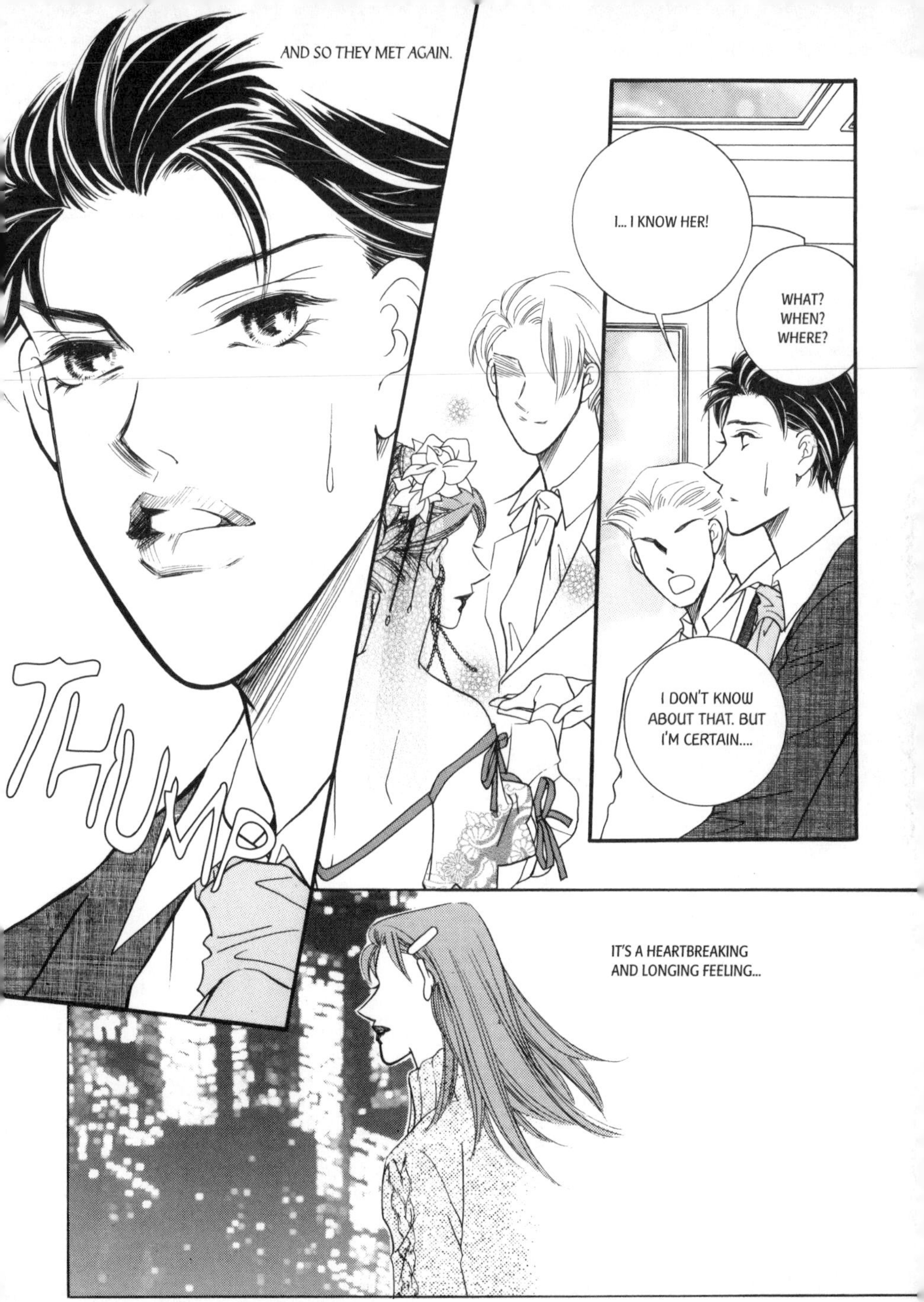
AND SO THEY MET AGAIN.
THUMP
I... I KNOW HER!
WHAT? WHEN? WHERE?
I DON'T KNOW ABOUT THAT. BUT I'M CERTAIN....
IT'S A HEARTBREAKING AND LONGING FEELING...

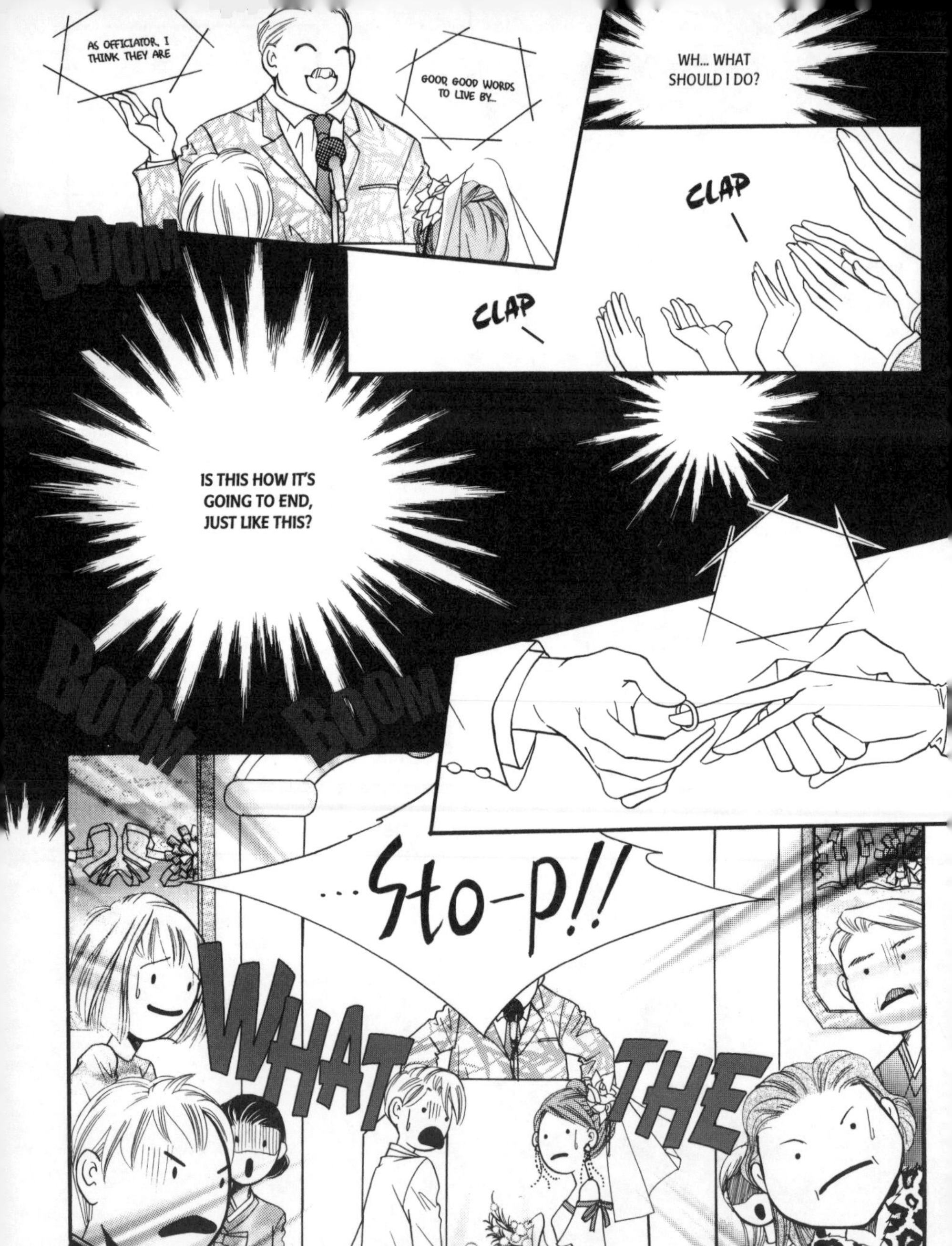
AS OFFICIATOR, I THINK THEY ARE
GOOD, GOOD WORDS TO LIVE BY...
WH... WHAT SHOULD I DO?
BOOM
CLAP
CLAP
IS THIS HOW IT'S GOING TO END, JUST LIKE THIS?
BOOM
BOOM
...Sto-p!!
WHAT THE

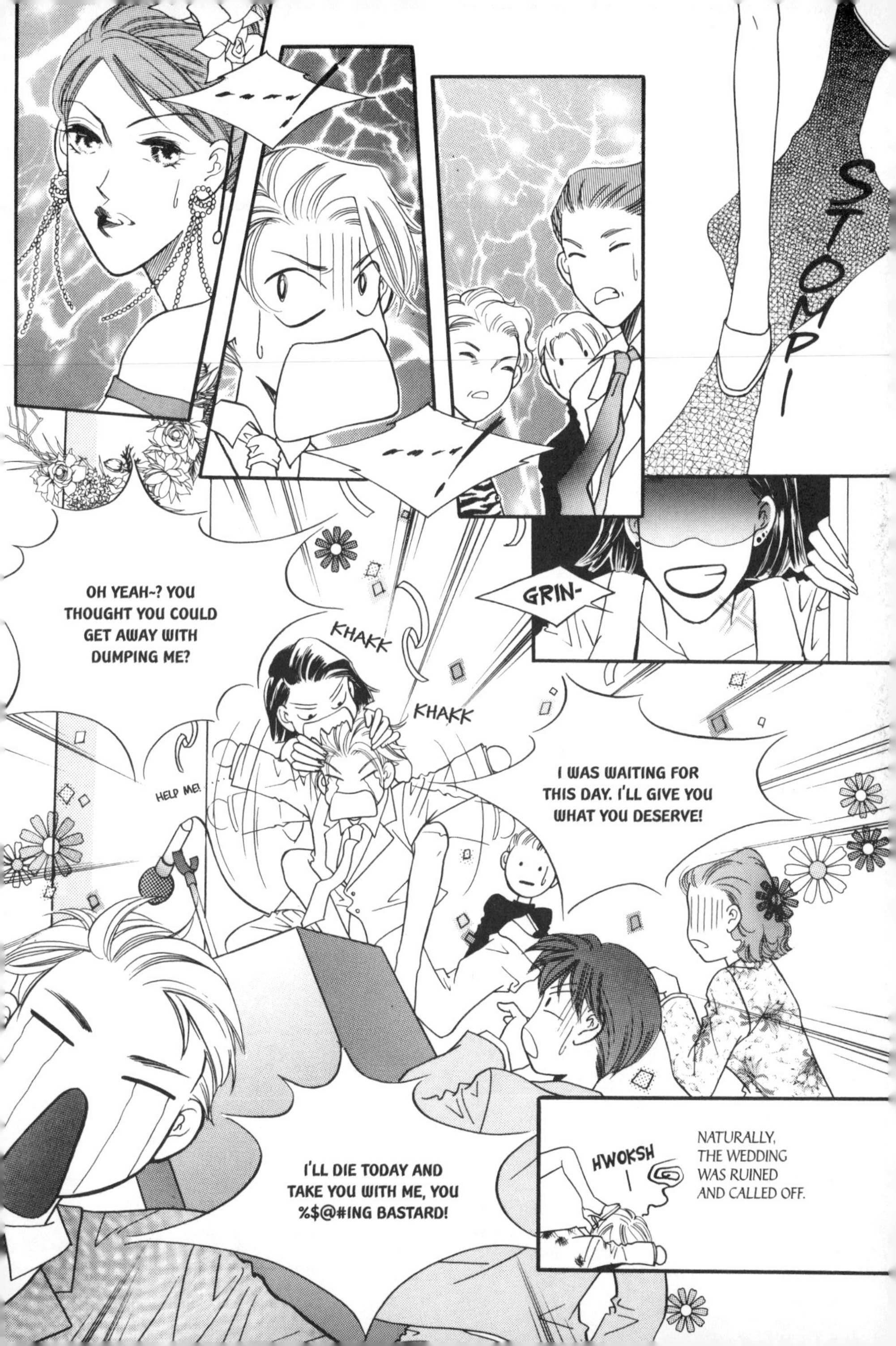

STOMP!
GRIN-
OH YEAH~? YOU THOUGHT YOU COULD GET AWAY WITH DUMPING ME?
KHAKK
KHAKK
HELP ME!
I WAS WAITING FOR THIS DAY. I'LL GIVE YOU WHAT YOU DESERVE!
I'LL DIE TODAY AND TAKE YOU WITH ME, YOU %$@#ING BASTARD!
HWOKSH
NATURALLY, THE WEDDING WAS RUINED AND CALLED OFF.

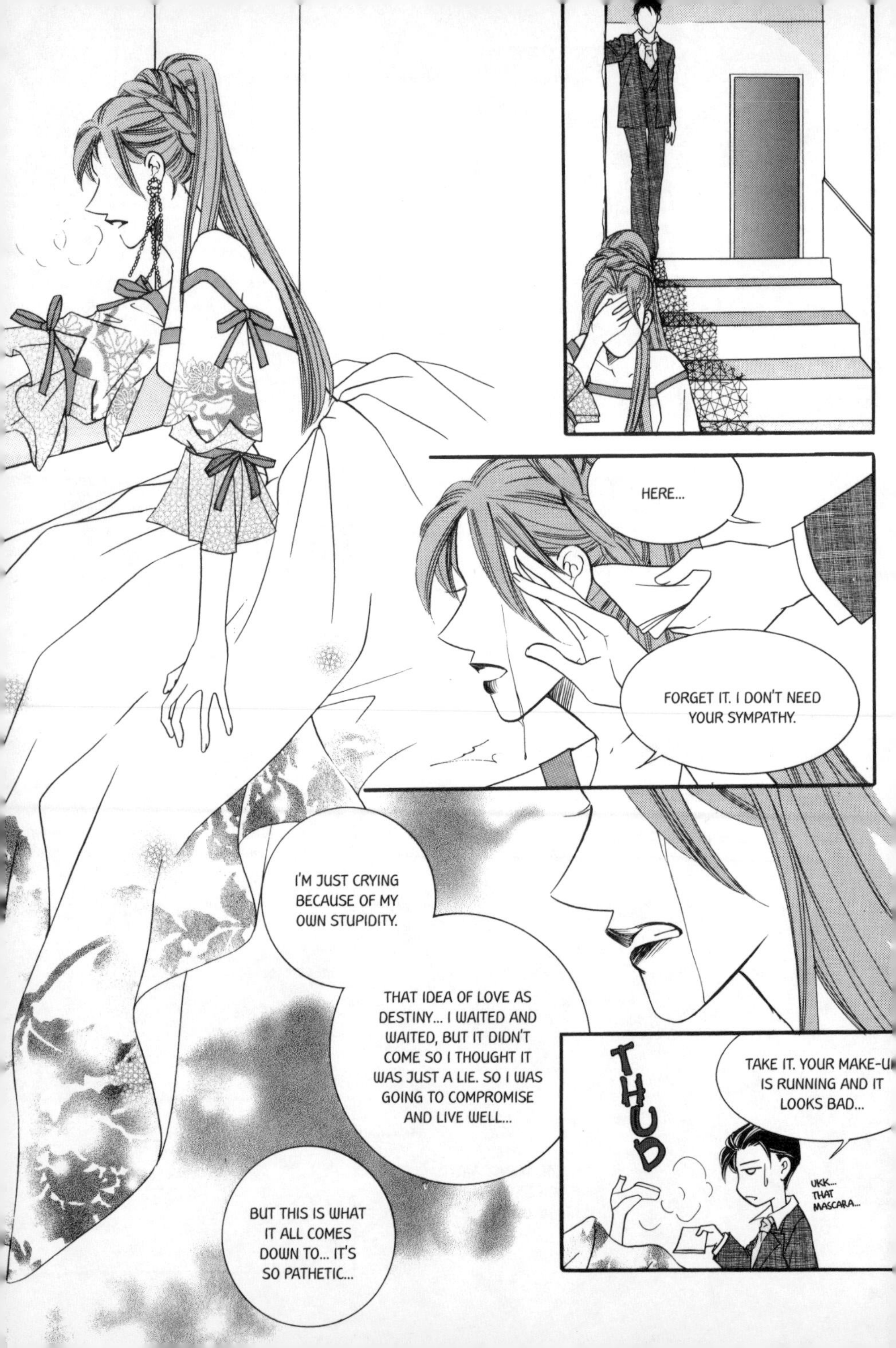
HERE...
FORGET IT. I DON'T NEED YOUR SYMPATHY.
I'M JUST CRYING BECAUSE OF MY OWN STUPIDITY.
THAT IDEA OF LOVE AS DESTINY... I WAITED AND WAITED, BUT IT DIDN'T COME SO I THOUGHT IT WAS JUST A LIE. SO I WAS GOING TO COMPROMISE AND LIVE WELL...
BUT THIS IS WHAT IT ALL COMES DOWN TO... IT'S SO PATHETIC...
THUD
TAKE IT. YOUR MAKE-U IS RUNNING AND IT LOOKS BAD...
UKK... THAT MASCARA...

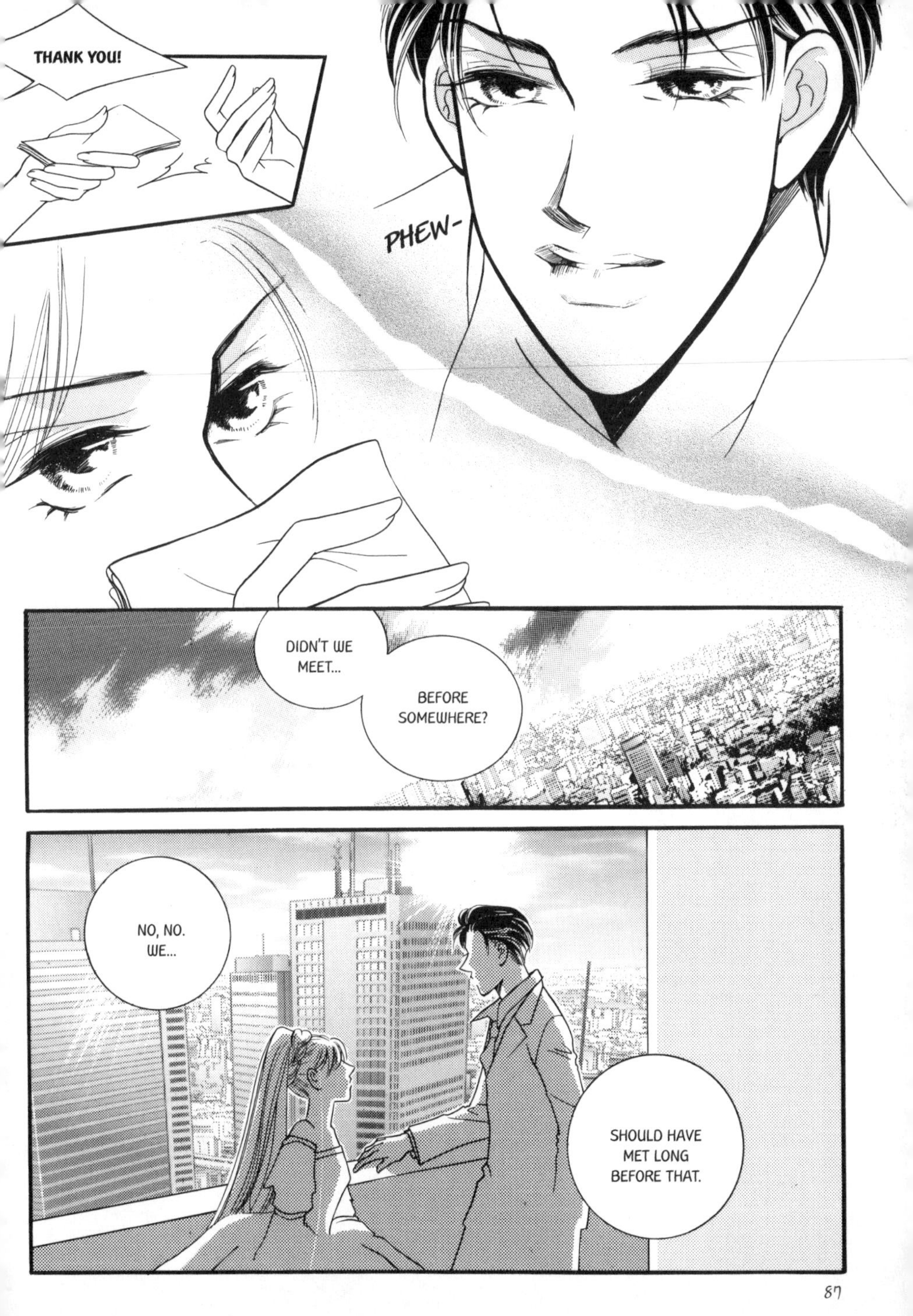
THANK YOU!
PHEW-
DIDN'T WE MEET...
BEFORE SOMEWHERE?
NO, NO. WE...
SHOULD HAVE MET LONG BEFORE THAT.

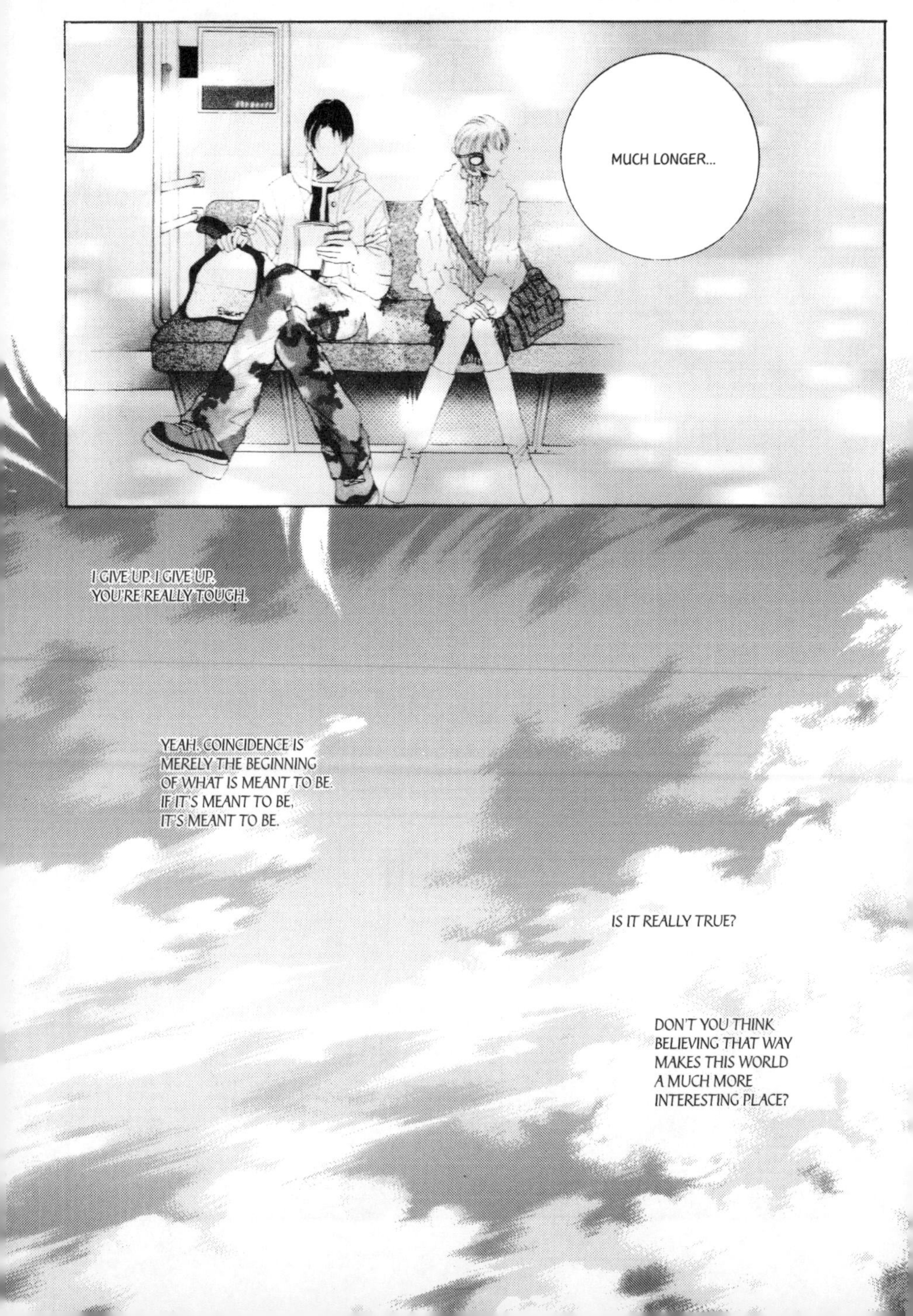
MUCH LONGER...
I GIVE UP. I GIVE UP.
YOU'RE REALLY TOUGH.
YEAH. COINCIDENCE IS MERELY THE BEGINNING OF WHAT IS MEANT TO BE. IF IT'S MEANT TO BE, IT'S MEANT TO BE.
IS IT REALLY TRUE?
DON'T YOU THINK BELIEVING THAT WAY MAKES THIS WORLD A MUCH MORE INTERESTING PLACE?

AUTOMATON

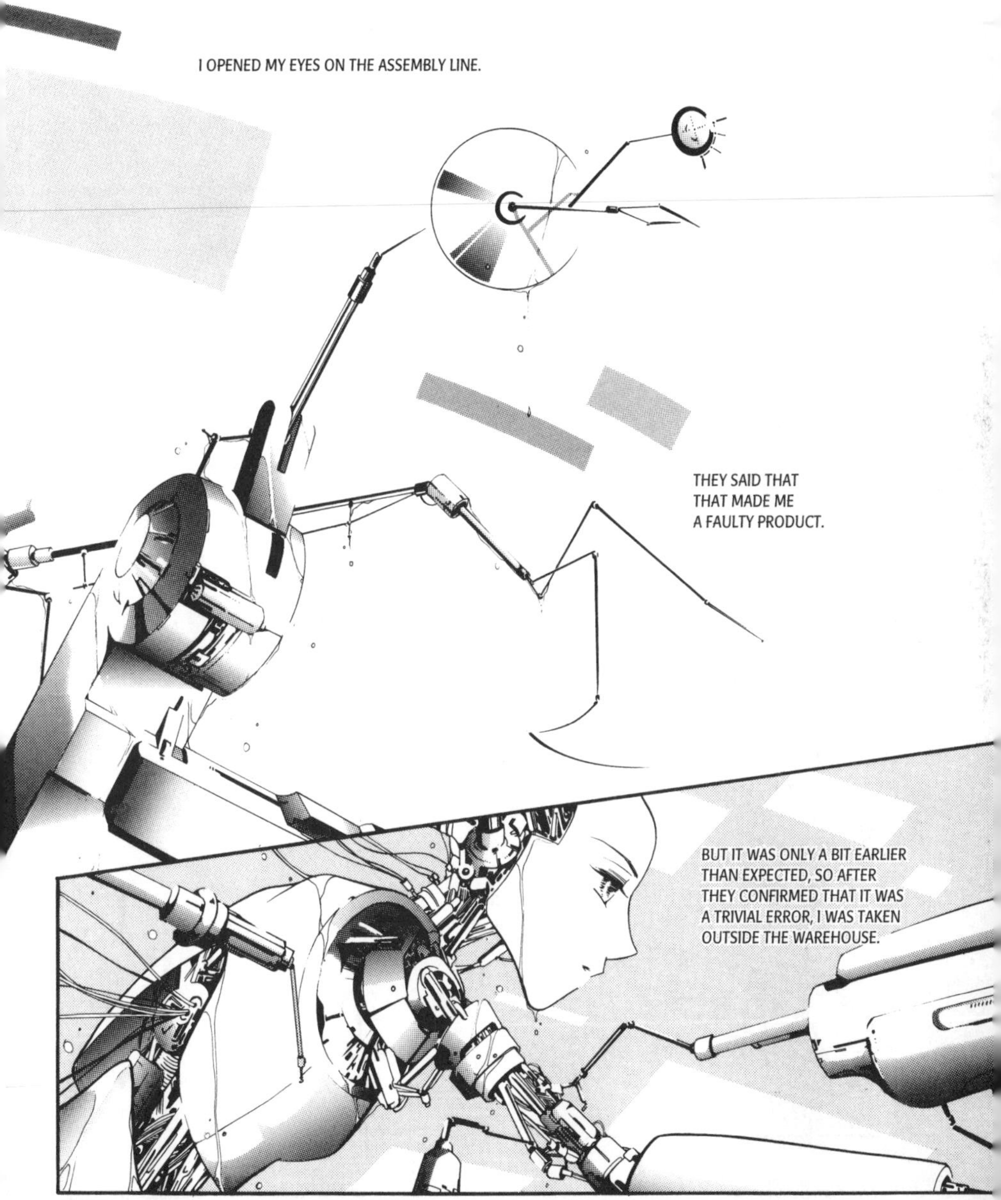
I OPENED MY EYES ON THE ASSEMBLY LINE.
THEY SAID THAT THAT MADE ME A FAULTY PRODUCT.
BUT IT WAS ONLY A BIT EARLIER THAN EXPECTED, SO AFTER THEY CONFIRMED THAT IT WAS A TRIVIAL ERROR, I WAS TAKEN OUTSIDE THE WAREHOUSE.

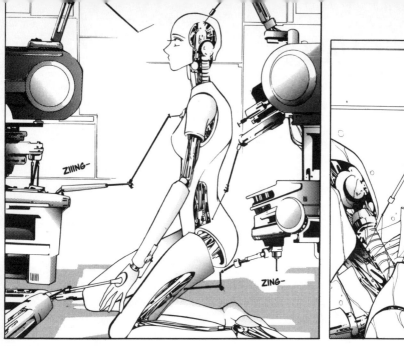

ZIIING—

ZING—

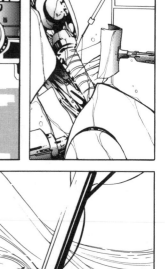

AND...

SHAA OPENED
HER EYES.

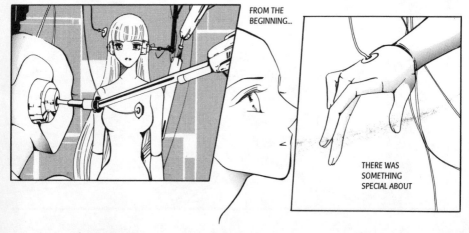

FROM THE
BEGINNING...

THERE WAS
SOMETHING
SPECIAL ABOUT

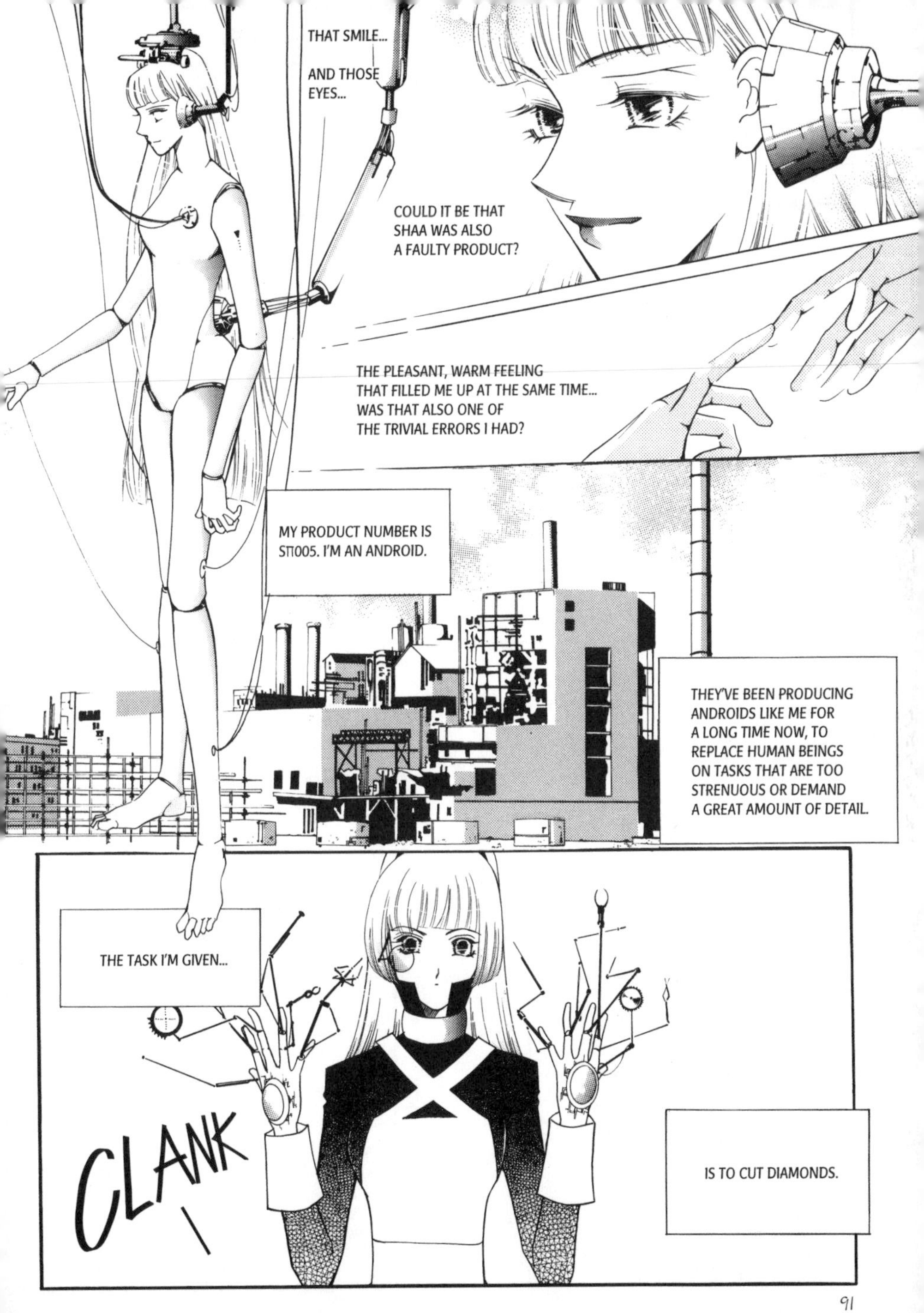
THAT SMILE...
AND THOSE EYES...
COULD IT BE THAT SHAA WAS ALSO A FAULTY PRODUCT?
THE PLEASANT, WARM FEELING THAT FILLED ME UP AT THE SAME TIME... WAS THAT ALSO ONE OF THE TRIVIAL ERRORS I HAD?
MY PRODUCT NUMBER IS ST1005. I'M AN ANDROID.
THEY'VE BEEN PRODUCING ANDROIDS LIKE ME FOR A LONG TIME NOW, TO REPLACE HUMAN BEINGS ON TASKS THAT ARE TOO STRENUOUS OR DEMAND A GREAT AMOUNT OF DETAIL.
THE TASK I'M GIVEN...
CLANK
IS TO CUT DIAMONDS.

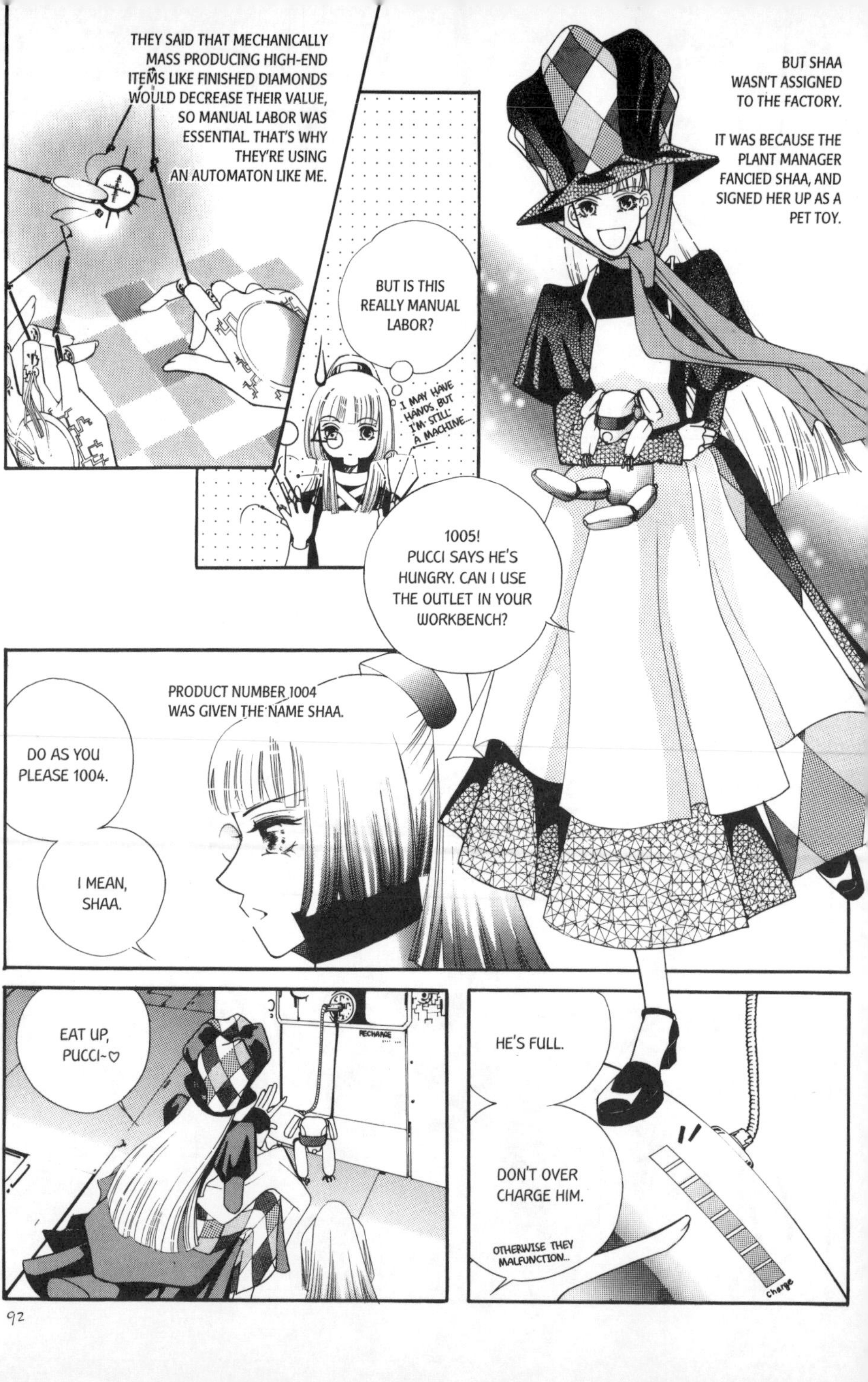
THEY SAID THAT MECHANICALLY MASS PRODUCING HIGH-END ITEMS LIKE FINISHED DIAMONDS WOULD DECREASE THEIR VALUE, SO MANUAL LABOR WAS ESSENTIAL. THAT'S WHY THEY'RE USING AN AUTOMATON LIKE ME.
BUT IS THIS REALLY MANUAL LABOR?
I MAY HAVE HANDS, BUT I'M STILL A MACHINE...
BUT SHAA WASN'T ASSIGNED TO THE FACTORY.
IT WAS BECAUSE THE PLANT MANAGER FANCIED SHAA, AND SIGNED HER UP AS A PET TOY.
1005! PUCCI SAYS HE'S HUNGRY. CAN I USE THE OUTLET IN YOUR WORKBENCH?
PRODUCT NUMBER 1004 WAS GIVEN THE NAME SHAA.
DO AS YOU PLEASE 1004.
I MEAN, SHAA.
EAT UP, PUCCI~♡
RECHARGE
HE'S FULL.
DON'T OVER CHARGE HIM.
OTHERWISE THEY MALFUNCTION...
Charge

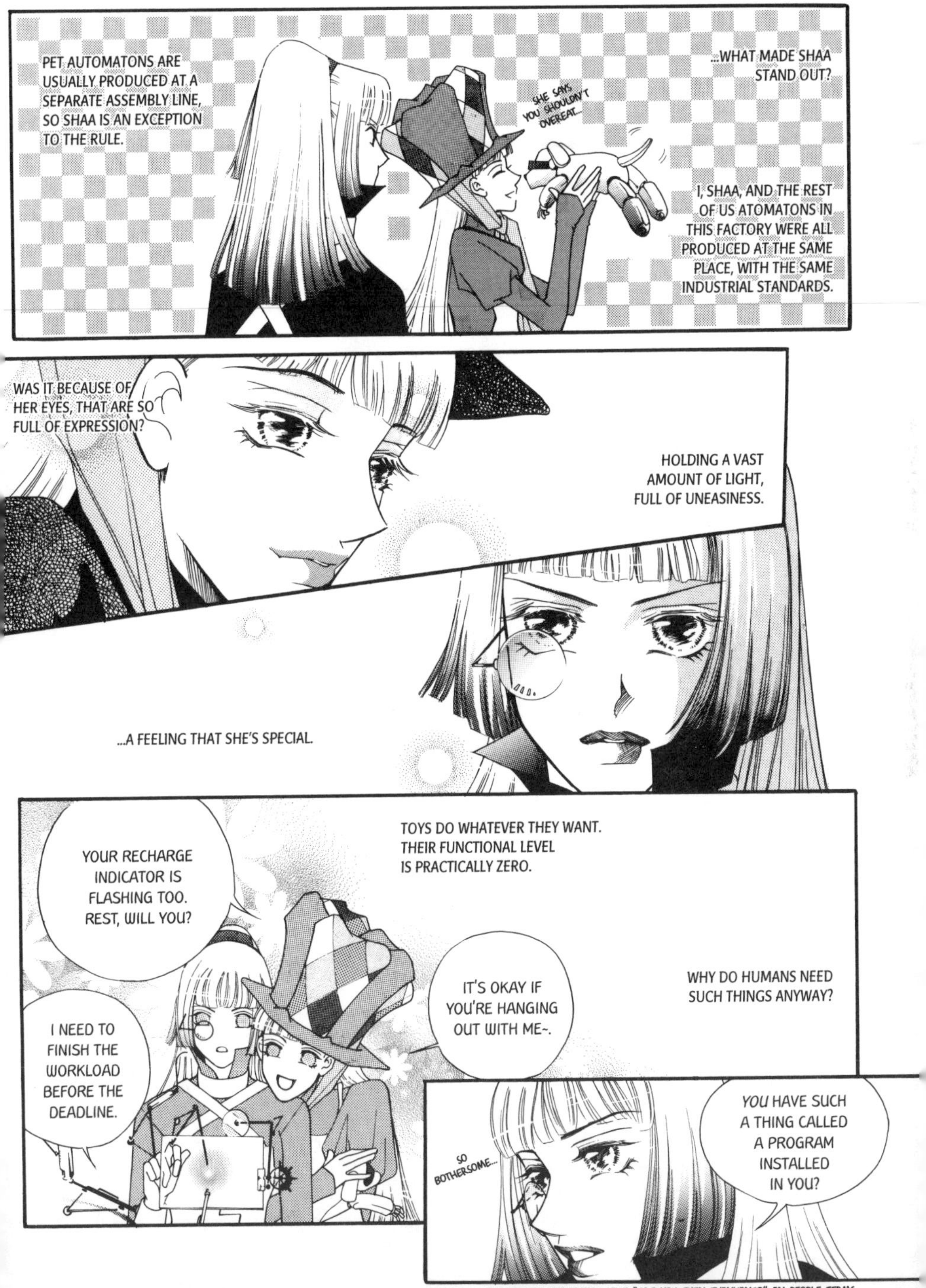
PET AUTOMATONS ARE USUALLY PRODUCED AT A SEPARATE ASSEMBLY LINE, SO SHAA IS AN EXCEPTION TO THE RULE.
SHE SAYS YOU SHOULDN'T OVEREAT...
...WHAT MADE SHAA STAND OUT?
I, SHAA, AND THE REST OF US ATOMATONS IN THIS FACTORY WERE ALL PRODUCED AT THE SAME PLACE, WITH THE SAME INDUSTRIAL STANDARDS.
WAS IT BECAUSE OF HER EYES, THAT ARE SO FULL OF EXPRESSION?
HOLDING A VAST AMOUNT OF LIGHT, FULL OF UNEASINESS.
...A FEELING THAT SHE'S SPECIAL.
YOUR RECHARGE INDICATOR IS FLASHING TOO. REST, WILL YOU?
TOYS DO WHATEVER THEY WANT. THEIR FUNCTIONAL LEVEL IS PRACTICALLY ZERO.
I NEED TO FINISH THE WORKLOAD BEFORE THE DEADLINE.
IT'S OKAY IF YOU'RE HANGING OUT WITH ME~.
WHY DO HUMANS NEED SUCH THINGS ANYWAY?
SO BOTHERSOME...
YOU HAVE SUCH A THING CALLED A PROGRAM INSTALLED IN YOU?

PROBABLY TRANSLATES TO SOMETHING LIKE "ARE YOU EVEN THINKING?" IN PEOPLE TERMS...

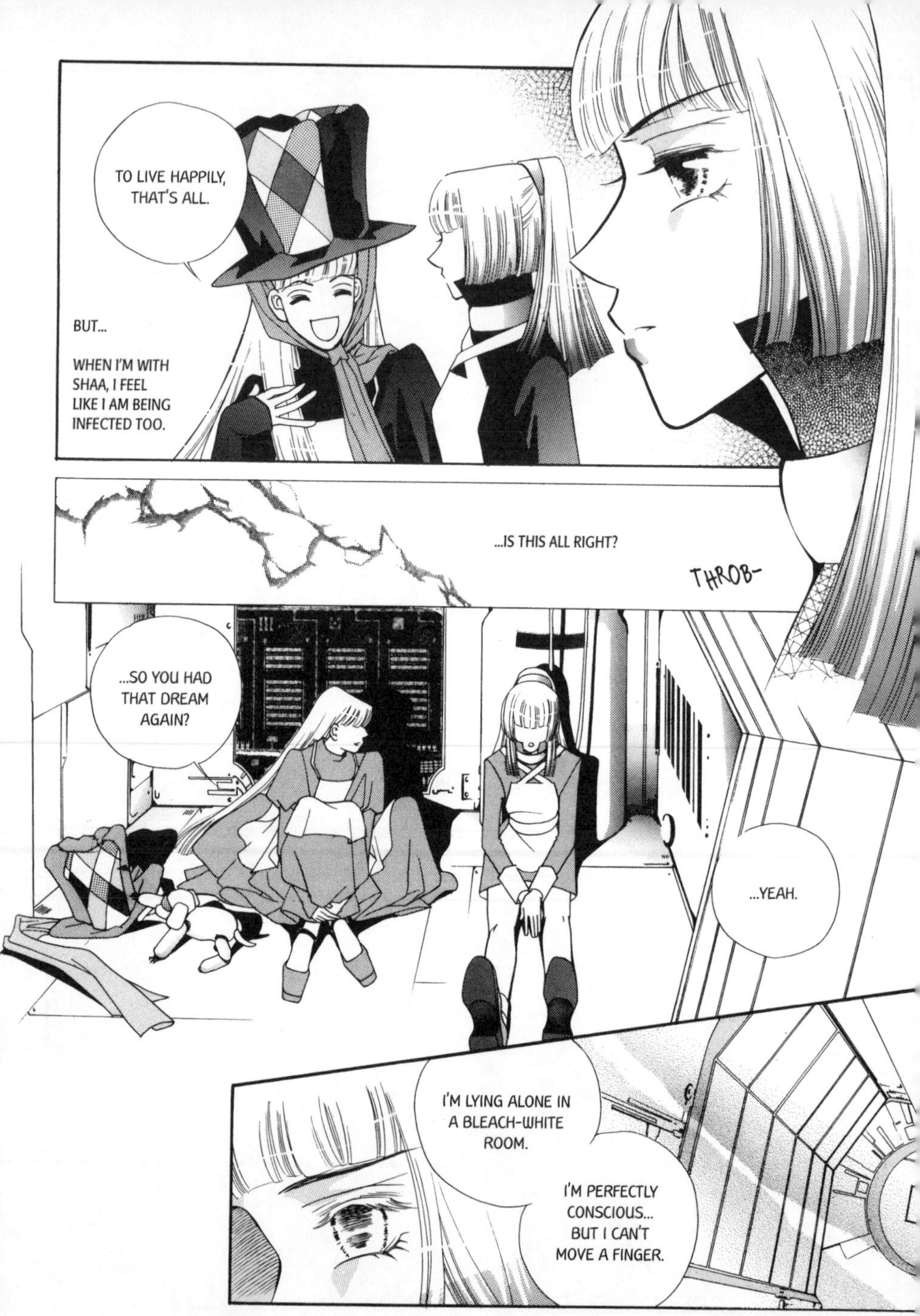
TO LIVE HAPPILY, THAT'S ALL.
BUT...
WHEN I'M WITH SHAA, I FEEL LIKE I AM BEING INFECTED TOO.
...IS THIS ALL RIGHT?
THROB-
...SO YOU HAD THAT DREAM AGAIN?
...YEAH.
I'M LYING ALONE IN A BLEACH-WHITE ROOM.
I'M PERFECTLY CONSCIOUS... BUT I CAN'T MOVE A FINGER.

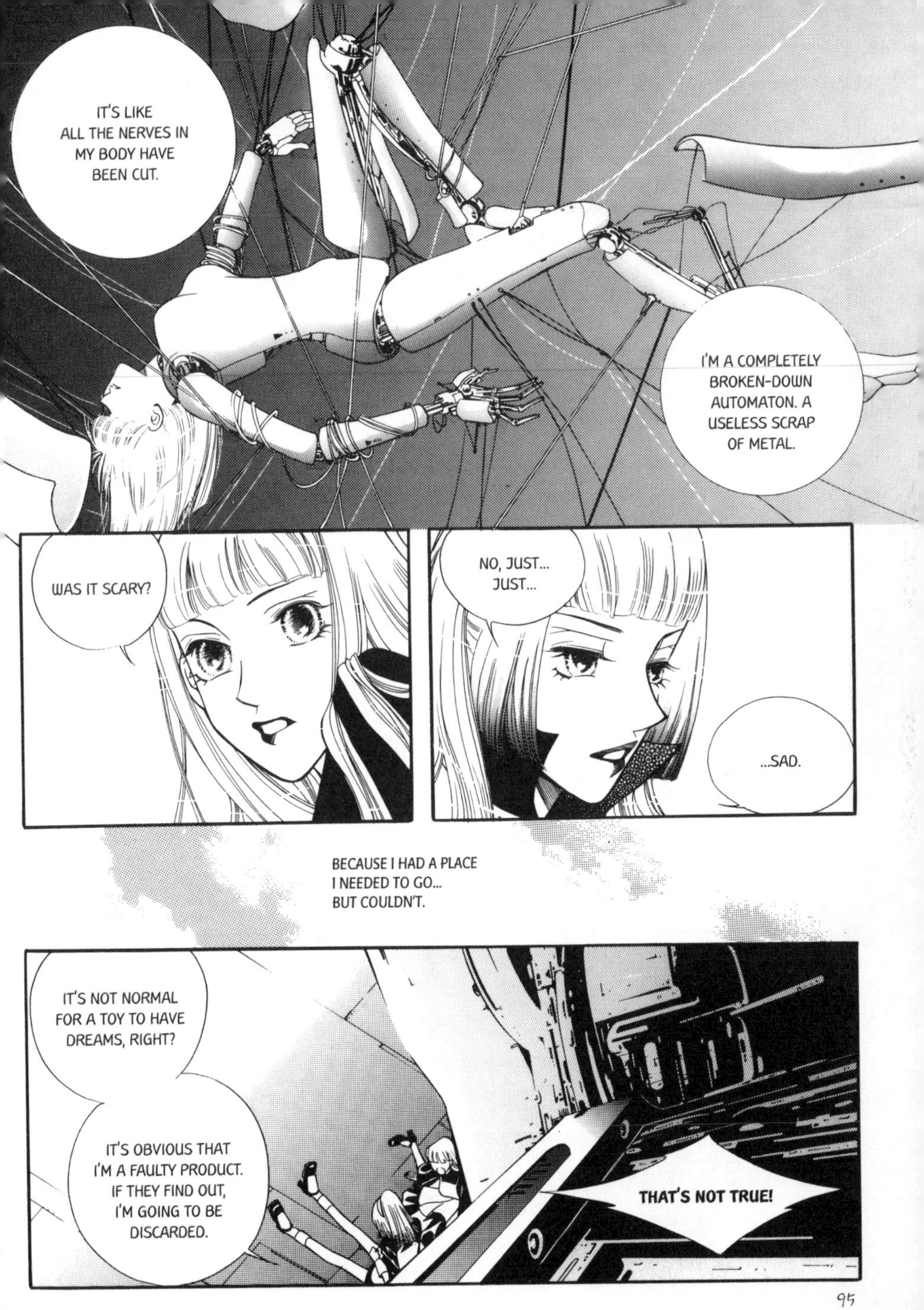
IT'S LIKE ALL THE NERVES IN MY BODY HAVE BEEN CUT.
I'M A COMPLETELY BROKEN-DOWN AUTOMATON. A USELESS SCRAP OF METAL.
WAS IT SCARY?
NO, JUST... JUST...
...SAD.
BECAUSE I HAD A PLACE I NEEDED TO GO... BUT COULDN'T.
IT'S NOT NORMAL FOR A TOY TO HAVE DREAMS, RIGHT?
IT'S OBVIOUS THAT I'M A FAULTY PRODUCT. IF THEY FIND OUT, I'M GOING TO BE DISCARDED.
THAT'S NOT TRUE!

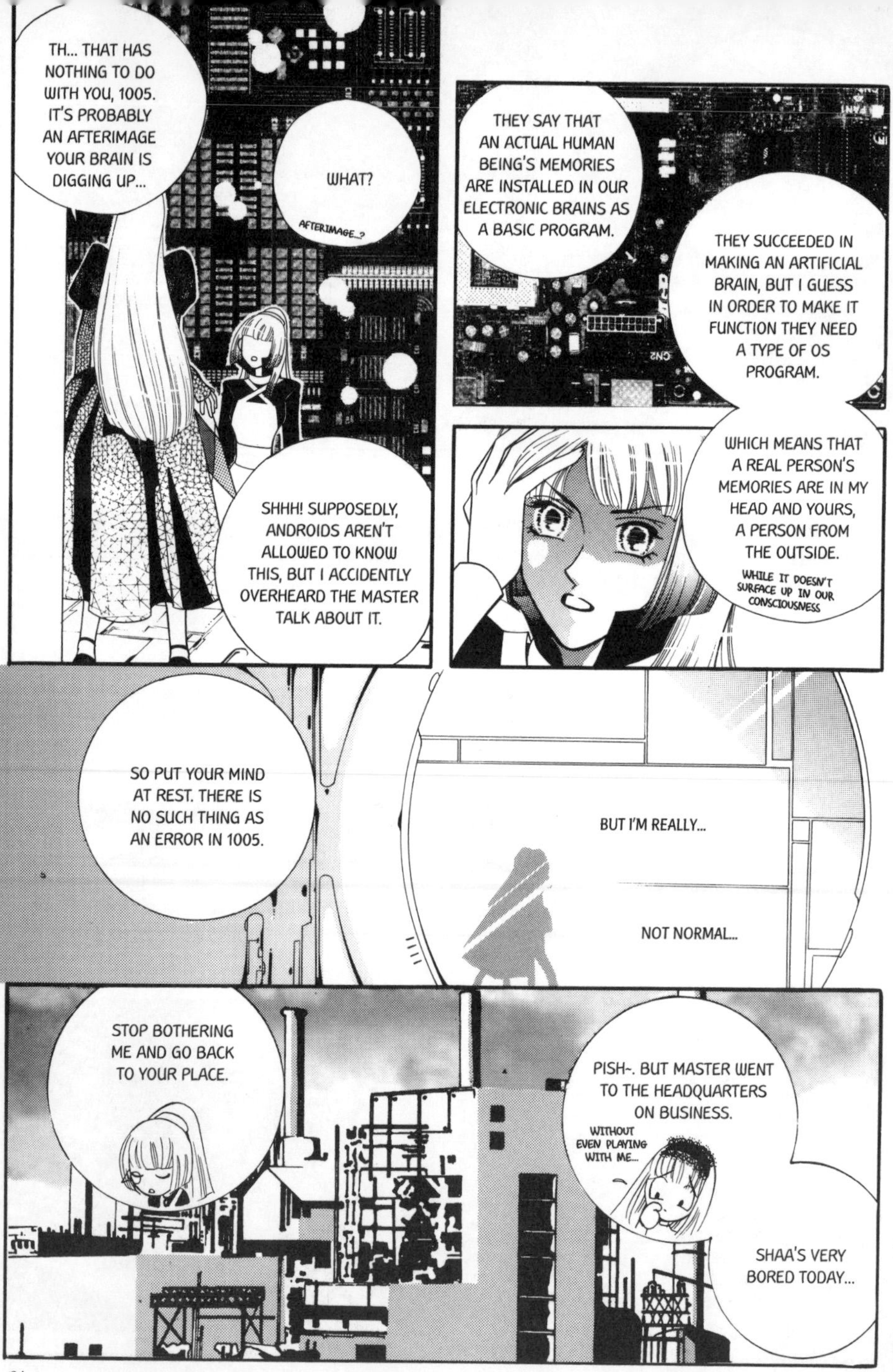
TH... THAT HAS NOTHING TO DO WITH YOU, 1005. IT'S PROBABLY AN AFTERIMAGE YOUR BRAIN IS DIGGING UP...
WHAT?
AFTERIMAGE...?
SHHH! SUPPOSEDLY, ANDROIDS AREN'T ALLOWED TO KNOW THIS, BUT I ACCIDENTLY OVERHEARD THE MASTER TALK ABOUT IT.
THEY SAY THAT AN ACTUAL HUMAN BEING'S MEMORIES ARE INSTALLED IN OUR ELECTRONIC BRAINS AS A BASIC PROGRAM.
THEY SUCCEEDED IN MAKING AN ARTIFICIAL BRAIN, BUT I GUESS IN ORDER TO MAKE IT FUNCTION THEY NEED A TYPE OF OS PROGRAM.
WHICH MEANS THAT A REAL PERSON'S MEMORIES ARE IN MY HEAD AND YOURS, A PERSON FROM THE OUTSIDE.
WHILE IT DOESN'T SURFACE UP IN OUR CONSCIOUSNESS
SO PUT YOUR MIND AT REST. THERE IS NO SUCH THING AS AN ERROR IN 1005.
BUT I'M REALLY...
NOT NORMAL...
STOP BOTHERING ME AND GO BACK TO YOUR PLACE.
PISH~. BUT MASTER WENT TO THE HEADQUARTERS ON BUSINESS.
WITHOUT EVEN PLAYING WITH ME...
SHAA'S VERY BORED TODAY...

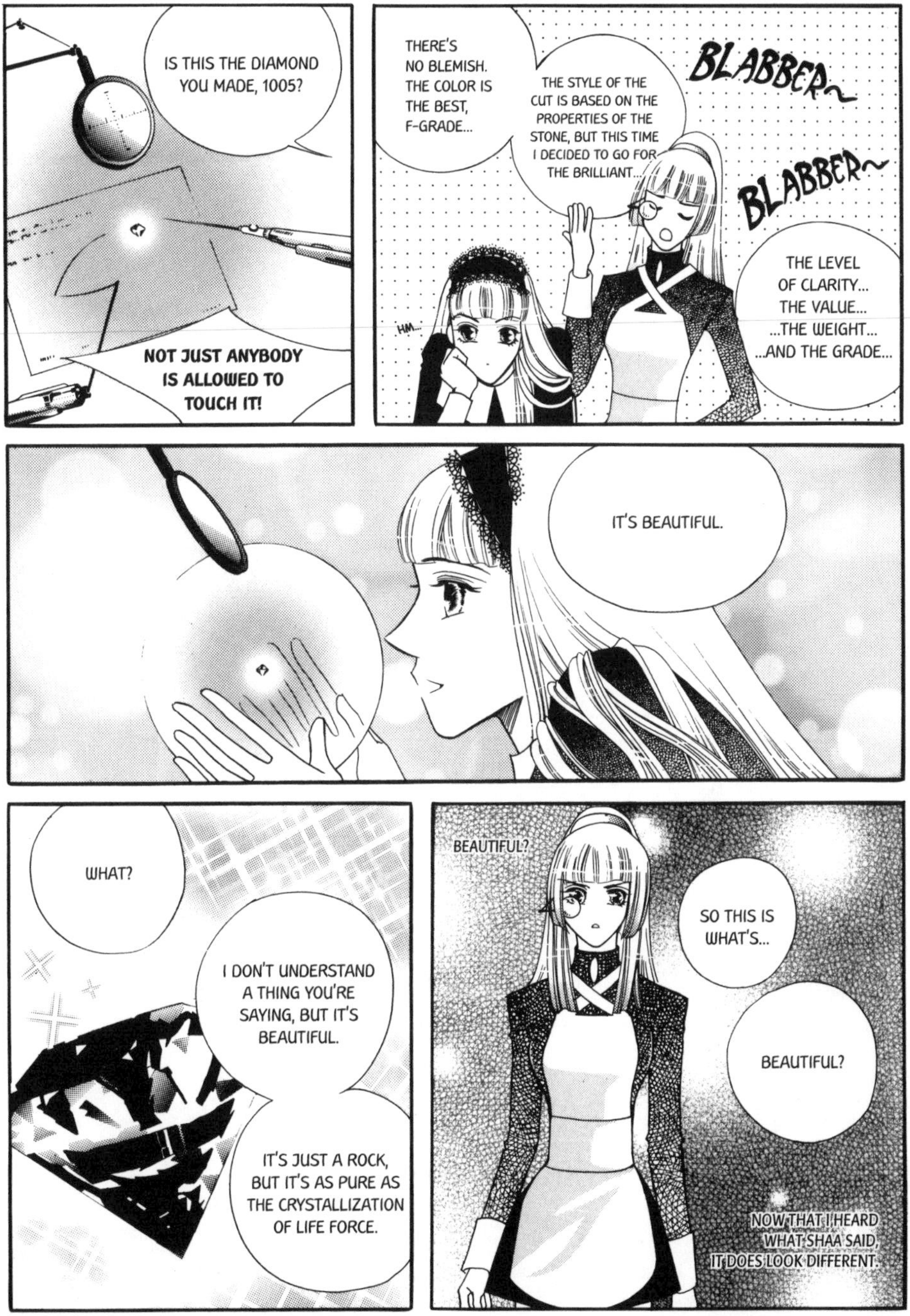
IS THIS THE DIAMOND YOU MADE, 1005?
NOT JUST ANYBODY IS ALLOWED TO TOUCH IT!
THERE'S NO BLEMISH. THE COLOR IS THE BEST, F-GRADE...
THE STYLE OF THE CUT IS BASED ON THE PROPERTIES OF THE STONE, BUT THIS TIME I DECIDED TO GO FOR THE BRILLIANT...
BLABBER~
BLABBER~
HM...
THE LEVEL OF CLARITY... THE VALUE... ...THE WEIGHT... ...AND THE GRADE...
IT'S BEAUTIFUL.
WHAT?
I DON'T UNDERSTAND A THING YOU'RE SAYING, BUT IT'S BEAUTIFUL.
IT'S JUST A ROCK, BUT IT'S AS PURE AS THE CRYSTALLIZATION OF LIFE FORCE.
BEAUTIFUL?
SO THIS IS WHAT'S...
BEAUTIFUL?
NOW THAT I HEARD WHAT SHAA SAID, IT DOES LOOK DIFFERENT.

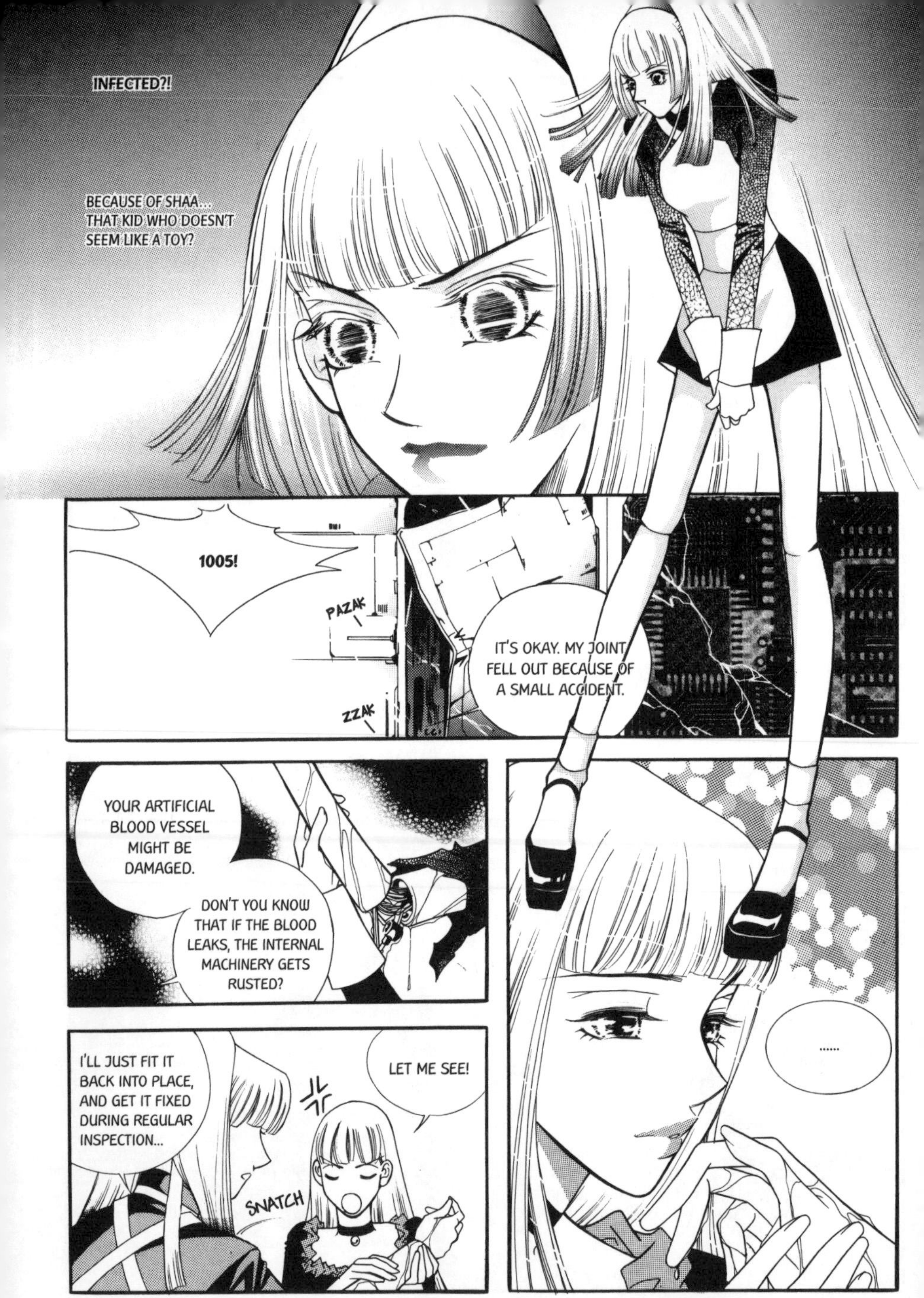

INFECTED?!
BECAUSE OF SHAA... THAT KID WHO DOESN'T SEEM LIKE A TOY?
1005!
PAZAK
ZZAK
IT'S OKAY. MY JOINT FELL OUT BECAUSE OF A SMALL ACCIDENT.
YOUR ARTIFICIAL BLOOD VESSEL MIGHT BE DAMAGED.
DON'T YOU KNOW THAT IF THE BLOOD LEAKS, THE INTERNAL MACHINERY GETS RUSTED?
I'LL JUST FIT IT BACK INTO PLACE, AND GET IT FIXED DURING REGULAR INSPECTION...
LET ME SEE!
SNATCH
......

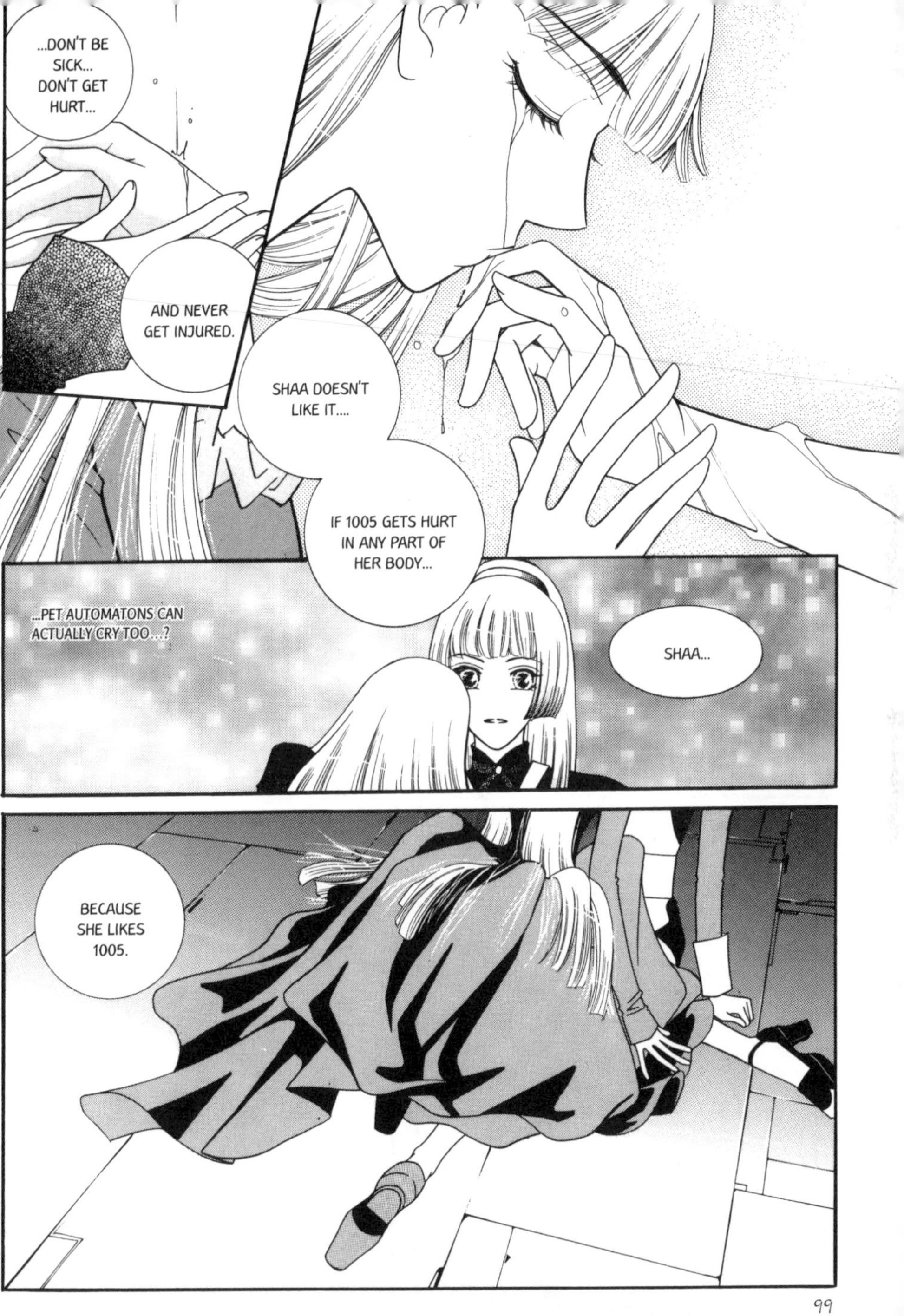
...DON'T BE SICK... DON'T GET HURT...
AND NEVER GET INJURED.
SHAA DOESN'T LIKE IT....
IF 1005 GETS HURT IN ANY PART OF HER BODY...
...PET AUTOMATONS CAN ACTUALLY CRY TOO...?
SHAA...
BECAUSE SHE LIKES 1005.

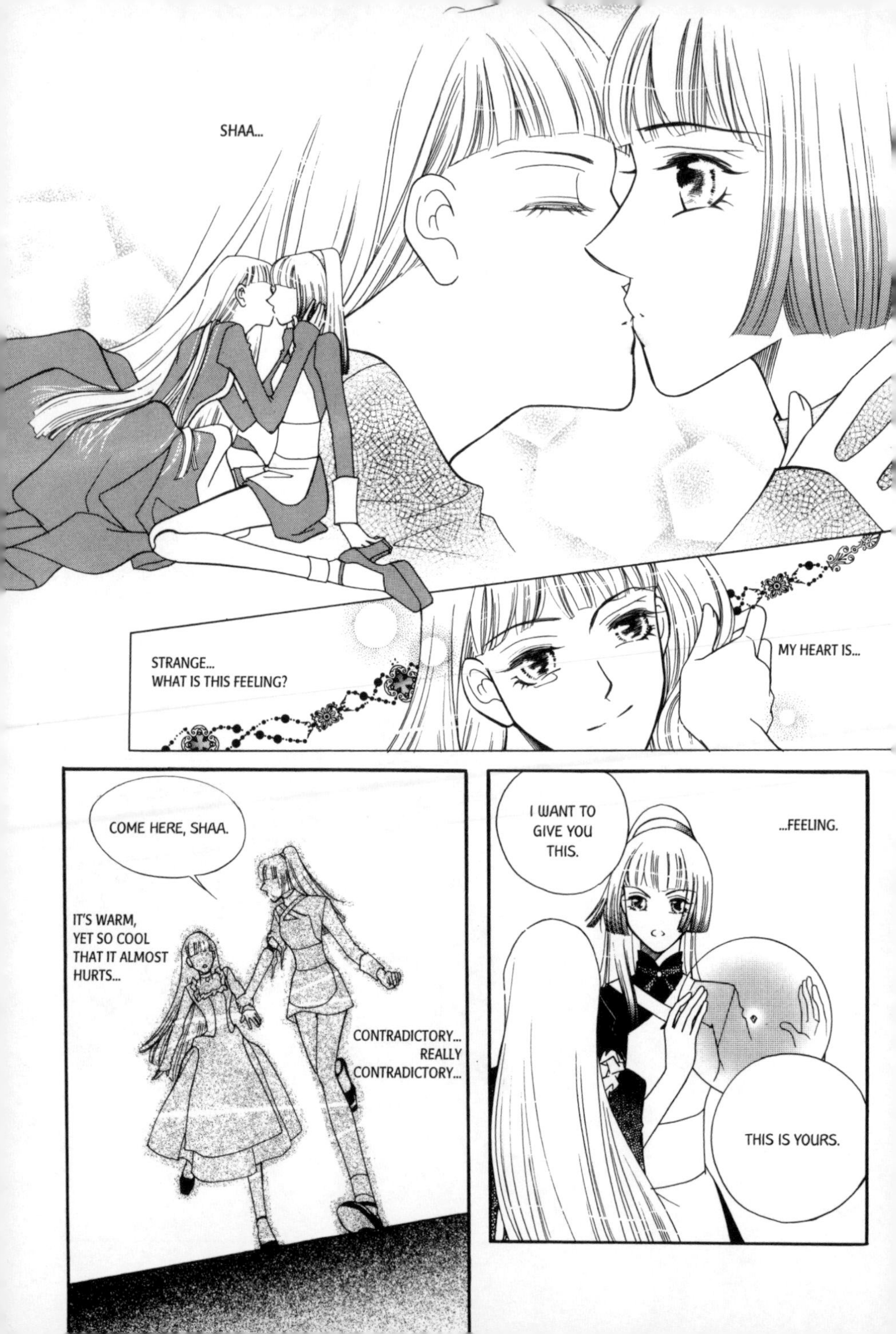
SHAA...
STRANGE...
WHAT IS THIS FEELING?
MY HEART IS...
COME HERE, SHAA.
IT'S WARM,
YET SO COOL
THAT IT ALMOST
HURTS...
CONTRADICTORY...
REALLY
CONTRADICTORY...
I WANT TO
GIVE YOU
THIS.
...FEELING.
THIS IS YOURS.

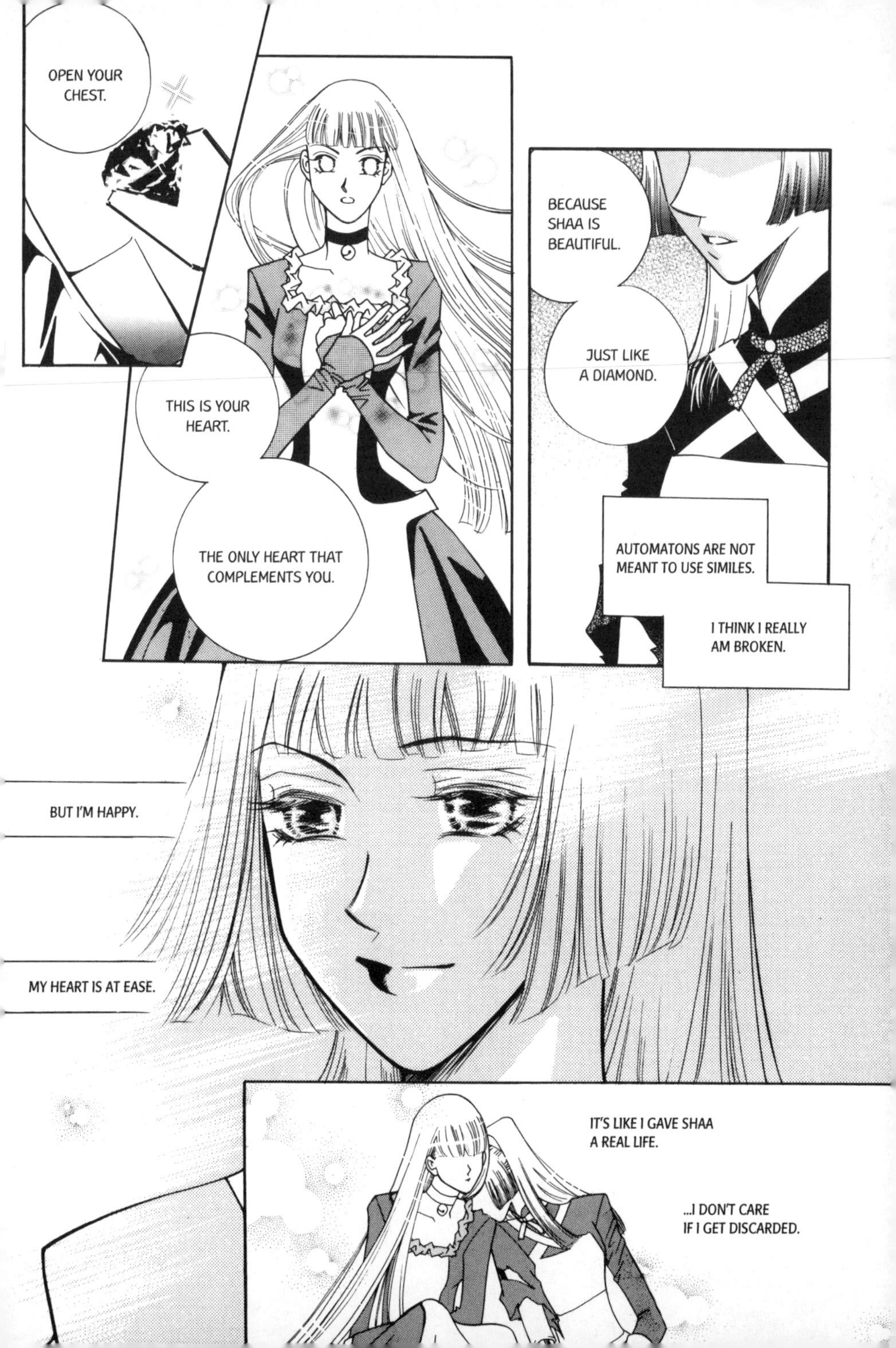
OPEN YOUR CHEST.
THIS IS YOUR HEART.
THE ONLY HEART THAT COMPLEMENTS YOU.
BECAUSE SHAA IS BEAUTIFUL.
JUST LIKE A DIAMOND.
AUTOMATONS ARE NOT MEANT TO USE SIMILES.
I THINK I REALLY AM BROKEN.
BUT I'M HAPPY.
MY HEART IS AT EASE.
IT'S LIKE I GAVE SHAA A REAL LIFE.
...I DON'T CARE IF I GET DISCARDED.

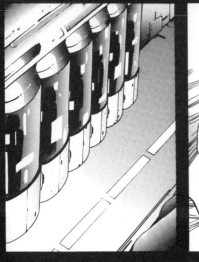

HAHH-!

THWAP

IT'S THAT DREAM AGAIN.

THE WHITE ROOM...

THE BROKEN LIMBS...

FREE ME!

KBANG

KBANG

SHAA...

KBANG

KBANG

SHAA...!

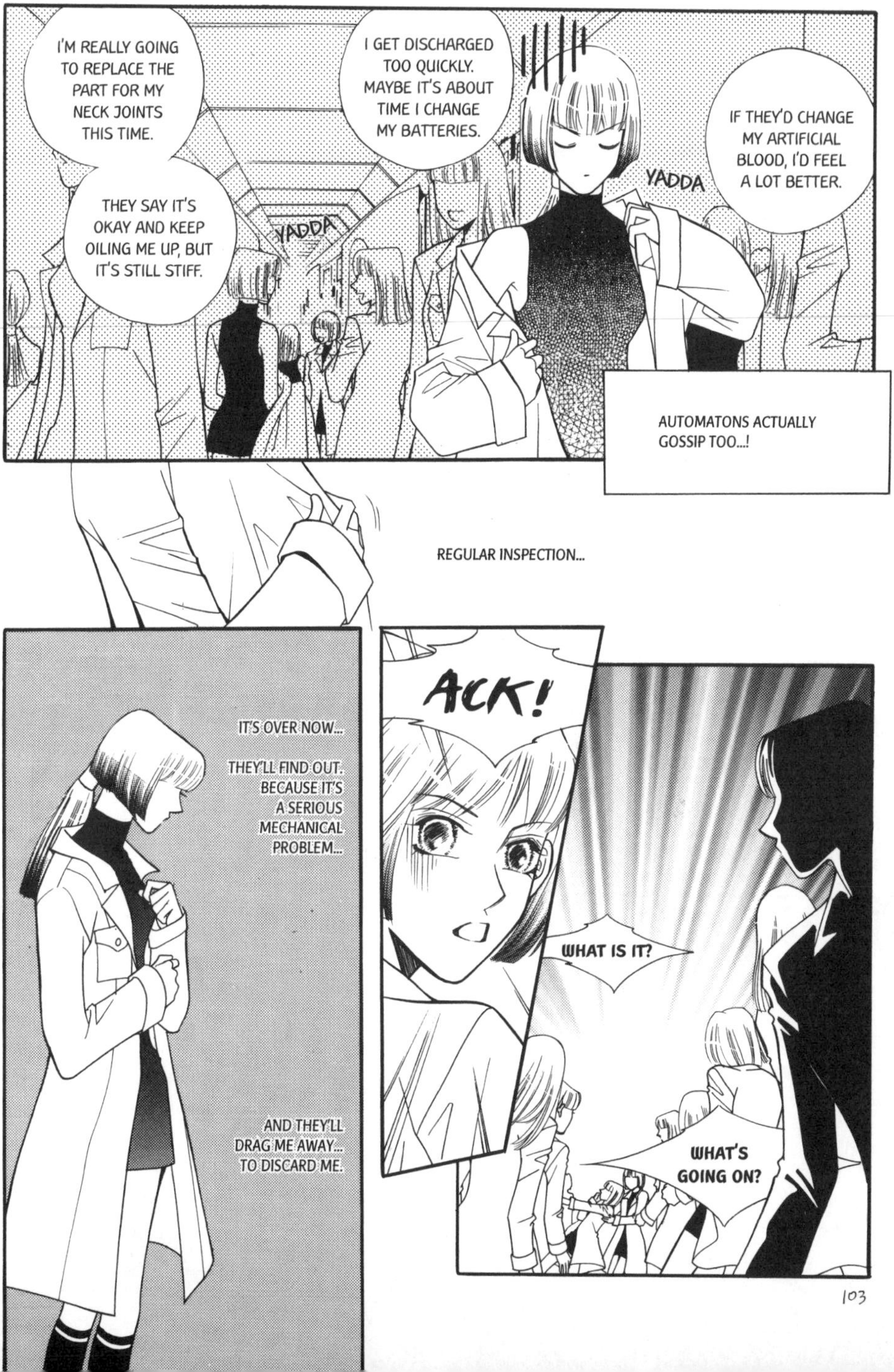
I'M REALLY GOING TO REPLACE THE PART FOR MY NECK JOINTS THIS TIME.
THEY SAY IT'S OKAY AND KEEP OILING ME UP, BUT IT'S STILL STIFF.
YADDA
I GET DISCHARGED TOO QUICKLY. MAYBE IT'S ABOUT TIME I CHANGE MY BATTERIES.
YADDA
IF THEY'D CHANGE MY ARTIFICIAL BLOOD, I'D FEEL A LOT BETTER.
AUTOMATONS ACTUALLY GOSSIP TOO...!
REGULAR INSPECTION...
IT'S OVER NOW...
THEY'LL FIND OUT. BECAUSE IT'S A SERIOUS MECHANICAL PROBLEM...
AND THEY'LL DRAG ME AWAY... TO DISCARD ME.
ACK!
WHAT IS IT?
WHAT'S GOING ON?

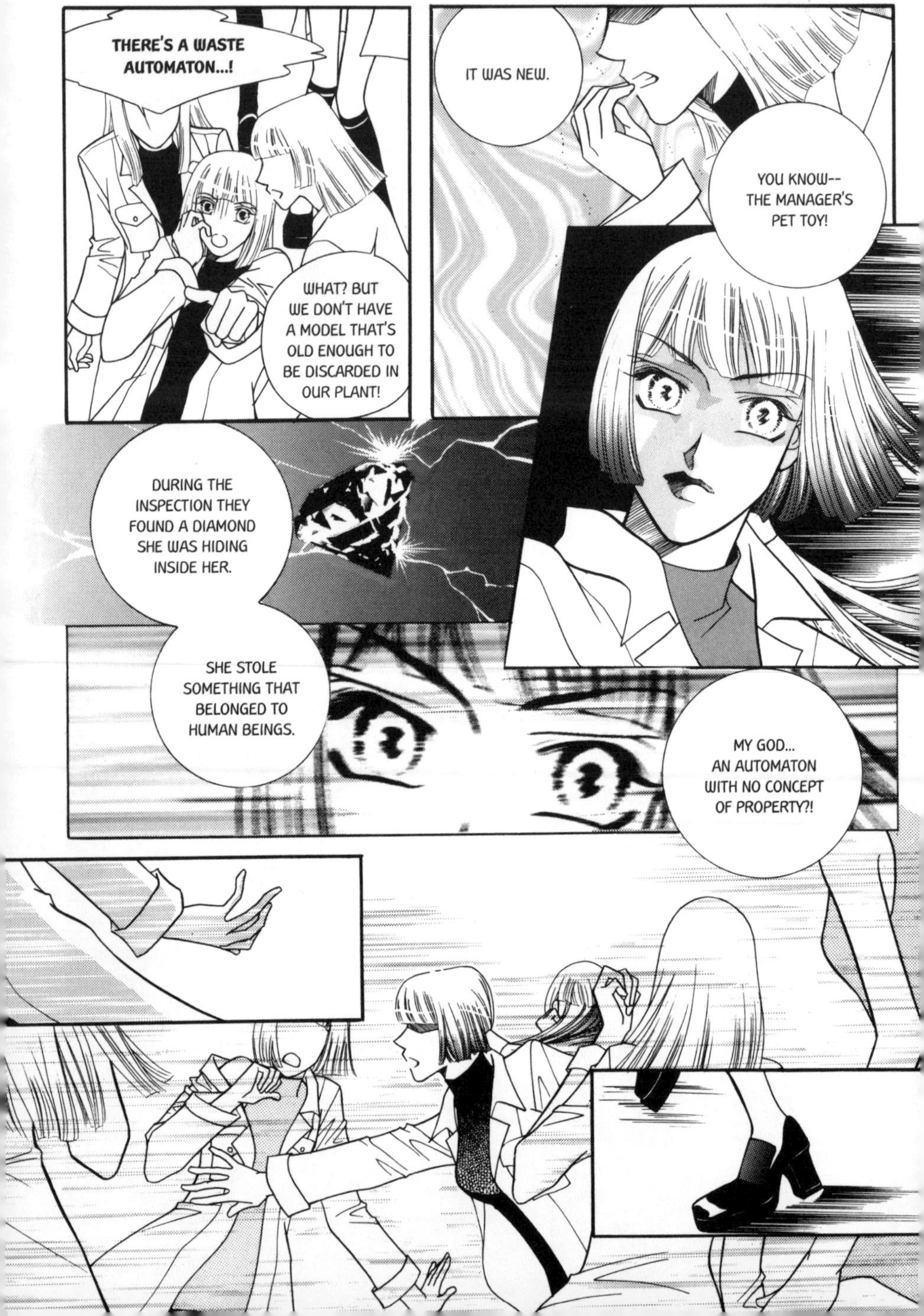

THERE'S A WASTE AUTOMATON...!
WHAT? BUT WE DON'T HAVE A MODEL THAT'S OLD ENOUGH TO BE DISCARDED IN OUR PLANT!
IT WAS NEW.
YOU KNOW-- THE MANAGER'S PET TOY!
DURING THE INSPECTION THEY FOUND A DIAMOND SHE WAS HIDING INSIDE HER.
SHE STOLE SOMETHING THAT BELONGED TO HUMAN BEINGS.
MY GOD... AN AUTOMATON WITH NO CONCEPT OF PROPERTY?!

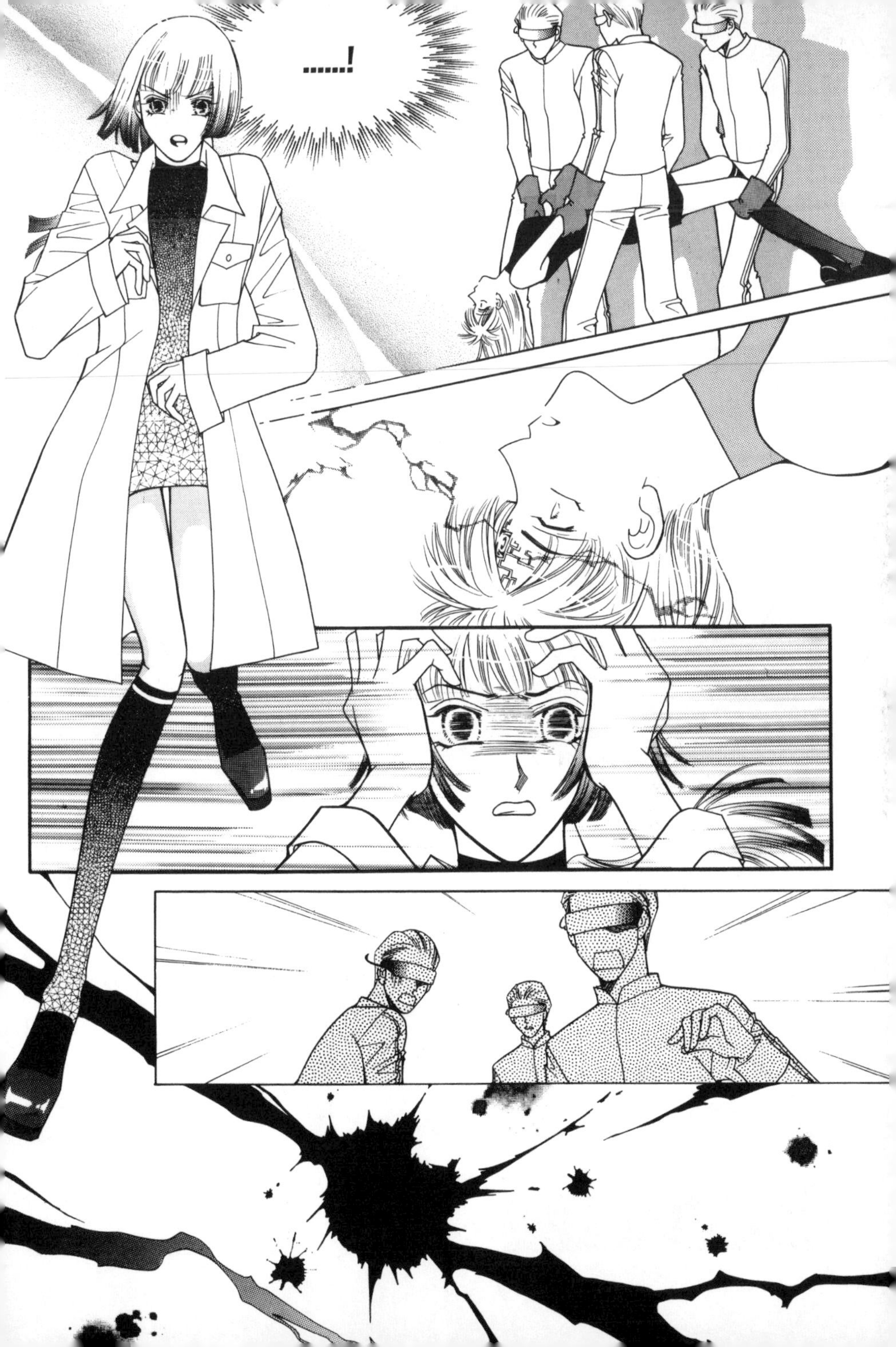
......!

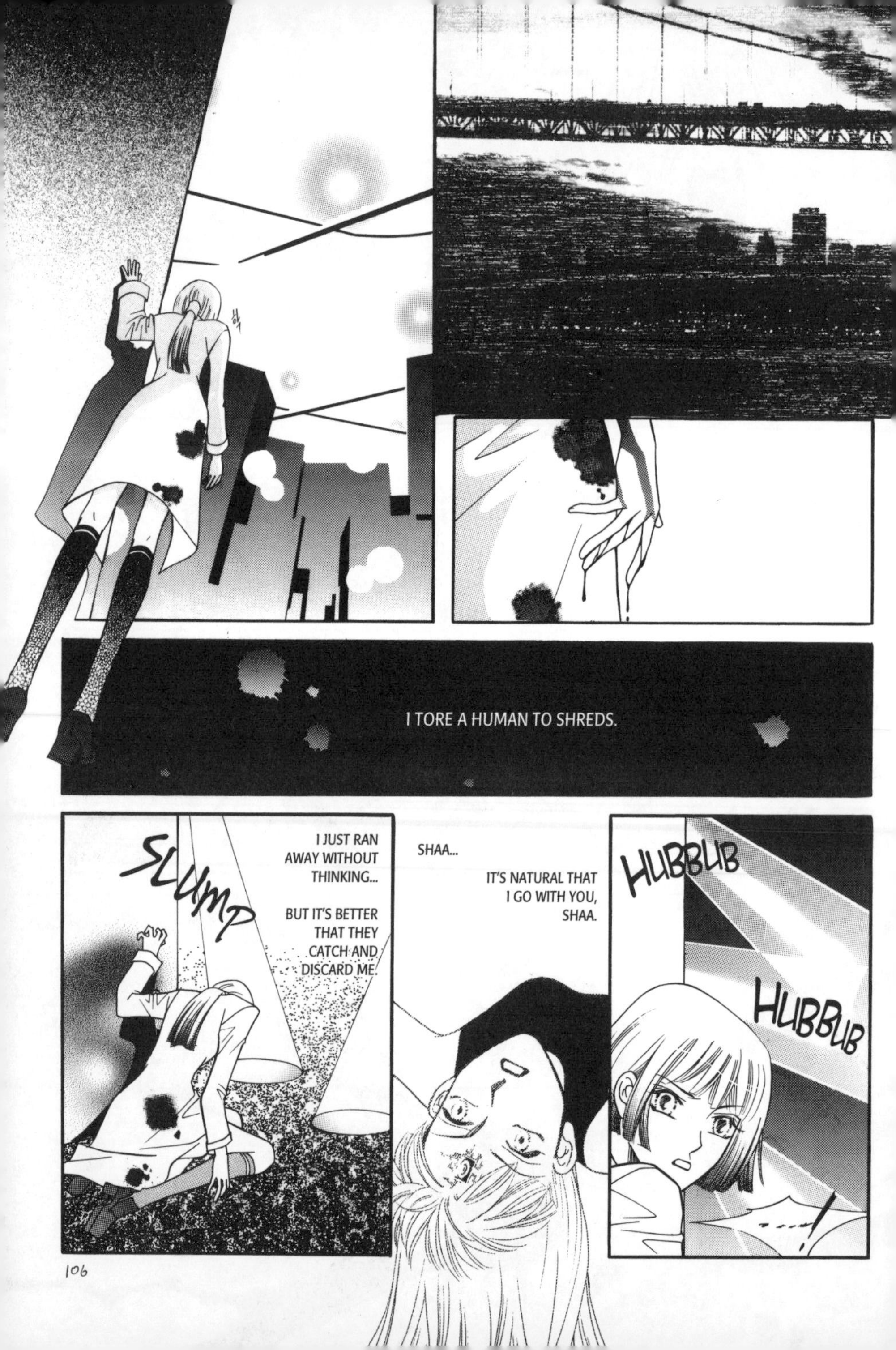
I TORE A HUMAN TO SHREDS.
SLUMP
I JUST RAN AWAY WITHOUT THINKING...
BUT IT'S BETTER THAT THEY CATCH AND DISCARD ME.
SHAA...
IT'S NATURAL THAT I GO WITH YOU, SHAA.
HUBBUB
HUBBUB

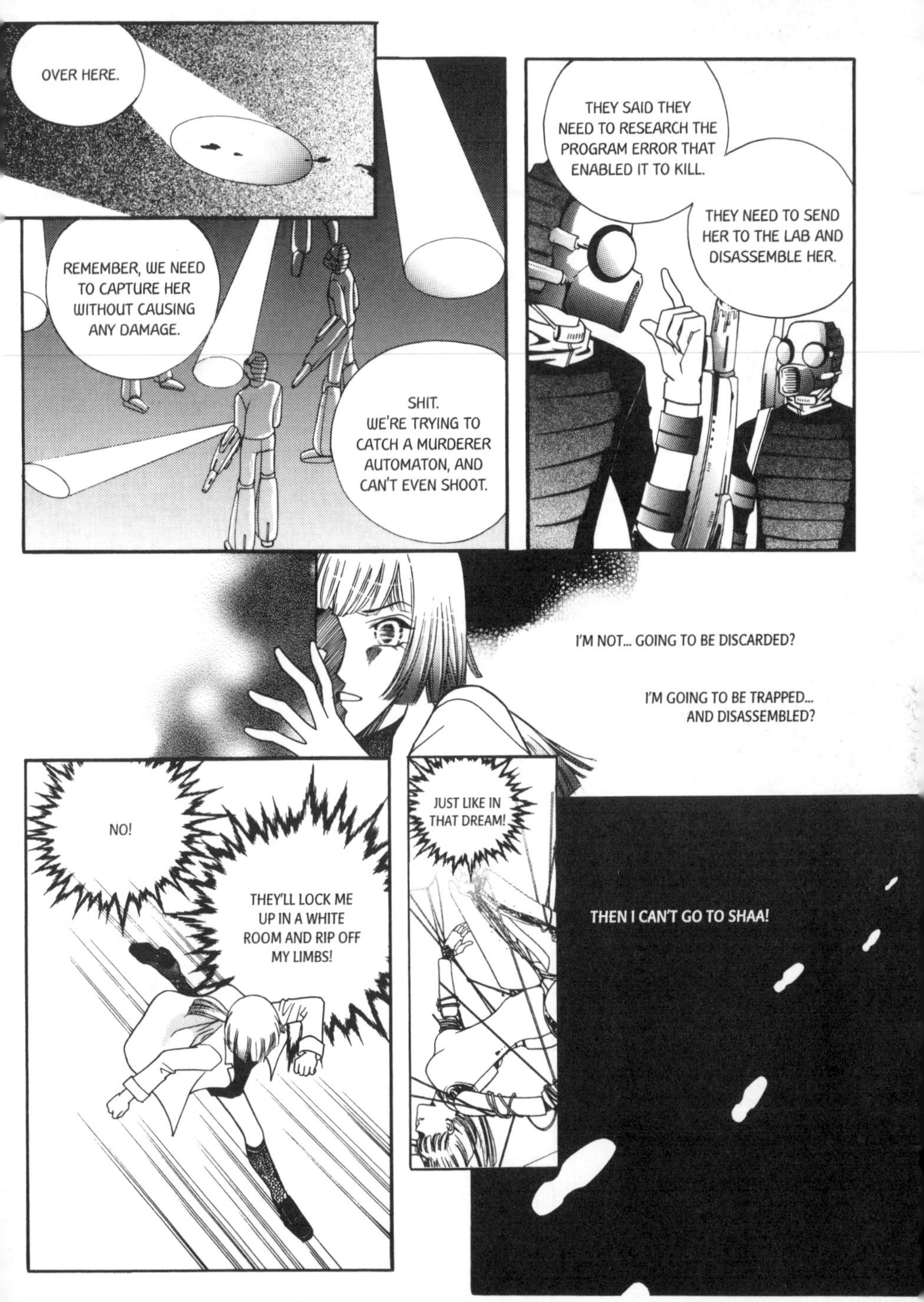
OVER HERE.
THEY SAID THEY NEED TO RESEARCH THE PROGRAM ERROR THAT ENABLED IT TO KILL.
REMEMBER, WE NEED TO CAPTURE HER WITHOUT CAUSING ANY DAMAGE.
SHIT. WE'RE TRYING TO CATCH A MURDERER AUTOMATON, AND CAN'T EVEN SHOOT.
THEY NEED TO SEND HER TO THE LAB AND DISASSEMBLE HER.
I'M NOT... GOING TO BE DISCARDED?
I'M GOING TO BE TRAPPED... AND DISASSEMBLED?
NO!
THEY'LL LOCK ME UP IN A WHITE ROOM AND RIP OFF MY LIMBS!
JUST LIKE IN THAT DREAM!
THEN I CAN'T GO TO SHAA!

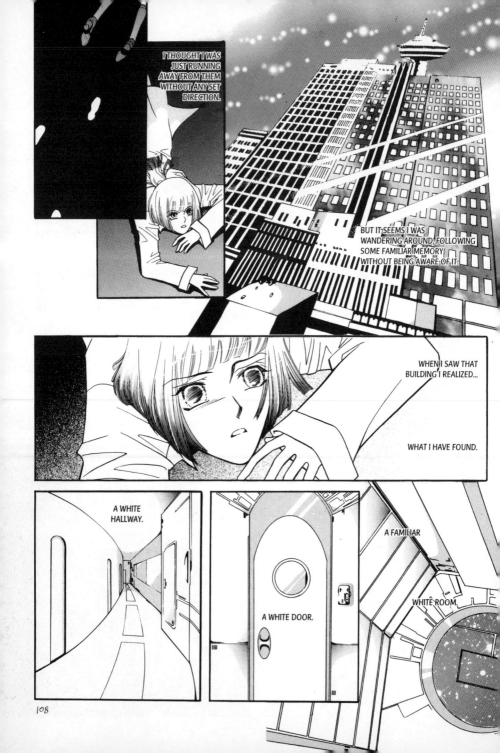

I THOUGHT I WAS JUST RUNNING AWAY FROM THEM WITHOUT ANY SET DIRECTION.

BUT IT SEEMS I WAS WANDERING AROUND, FOLLOWING SOME FAMILIAR MEMORY WITHOUT BEING AWARE OF IT.

WHEN I SAW THAT BUILDING I REALIZED...

WHAT I HAVE FOUND.

A WHITE HALLWAY.

A WHITE DOOR.

A FAMILIAR

WHITE ROOM.

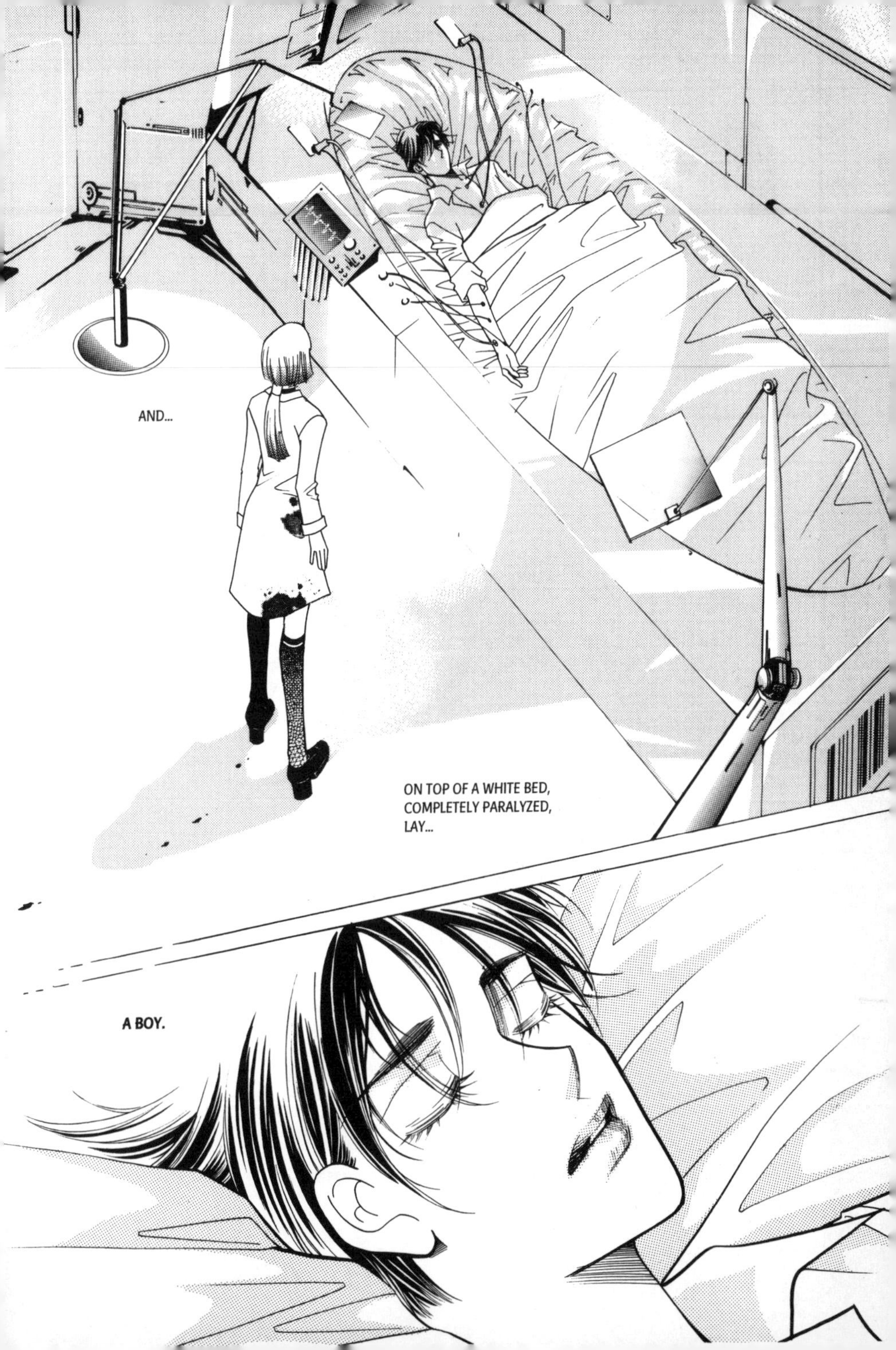
AND...
ON TOP OF A WHITE BED, COMPLETELY PARALYZED, LAY...
A BOY.

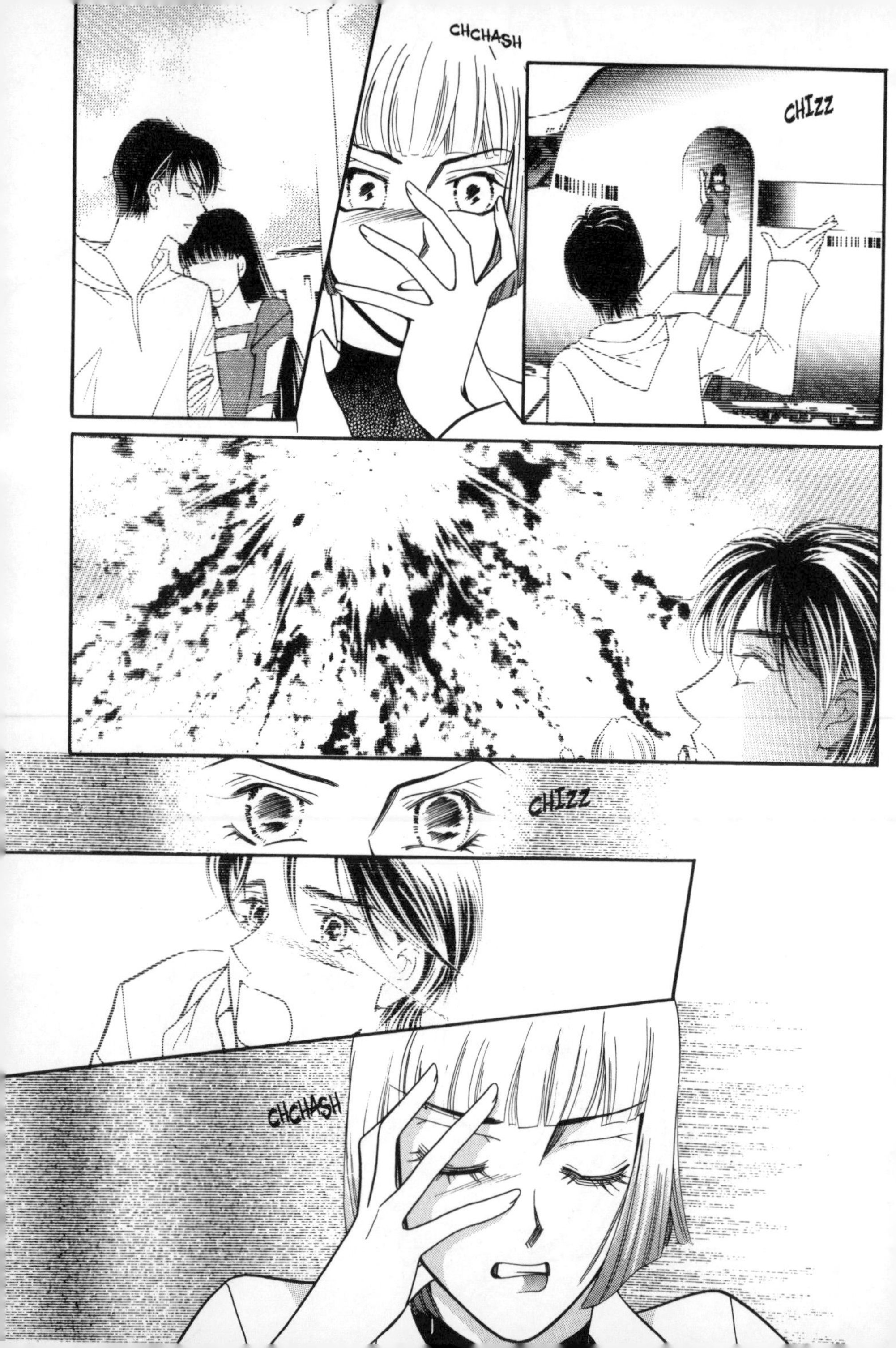
CHCHASH
CHIZZ
CHIZZ
CHCHASH

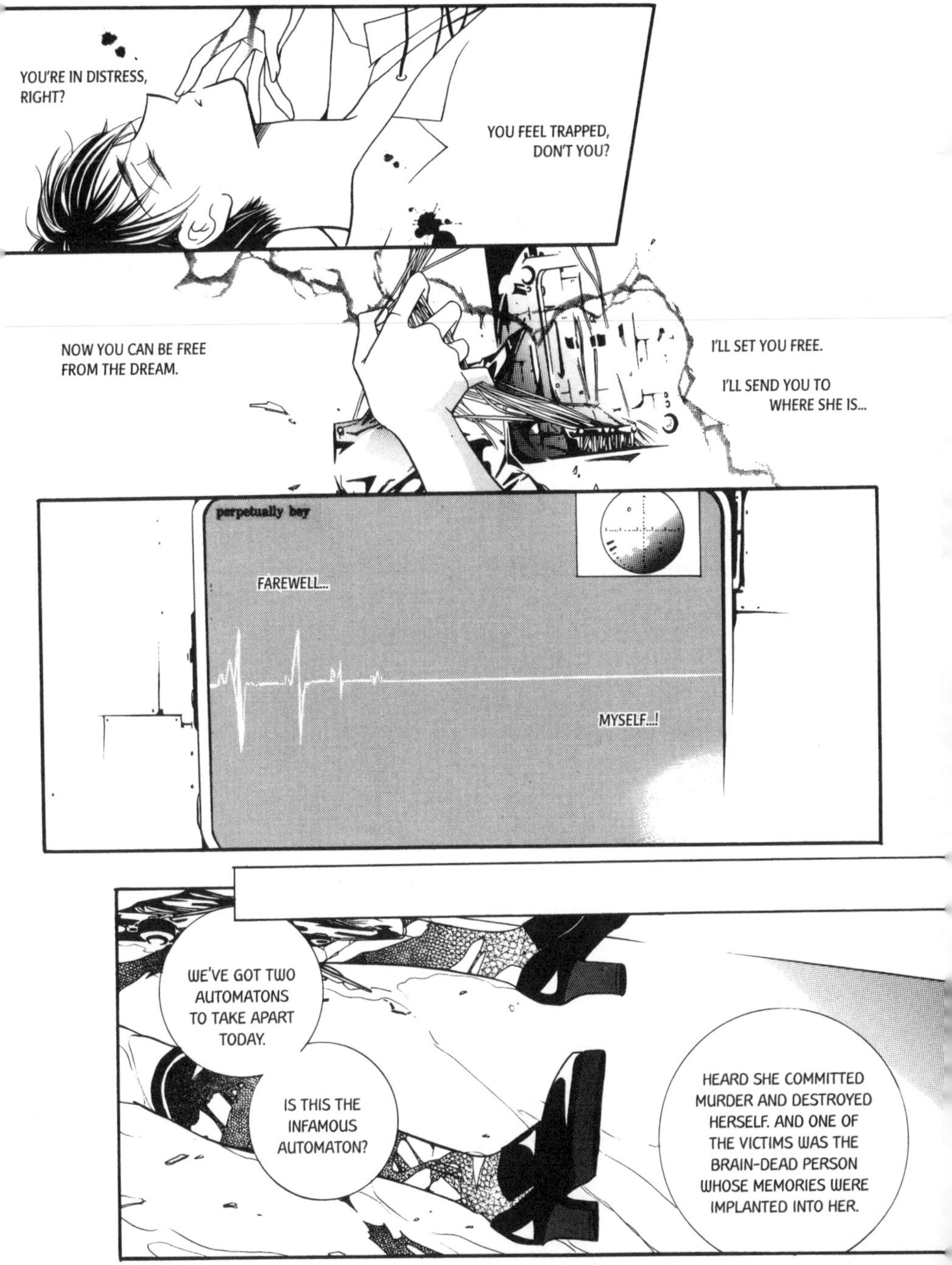
YOU'RE IN DISTRESS, RIGHT?
YOU FEEL TRAPPED, DON'T YOU?
NOW YOU CAN BE FREE FROM THE DREAM.
I'LL SET YOU FREE.
I'LL SEND YOU TO WHERE SHE IS...
perpetually bey
FAREWELL...
MYSELF...!
WE'VE GOT TWO AUTOMATONS TO TAKE APART TODAY.
IS THIS THE INFAMOUS AUTOMATON?
HEARD SHE COMMITTED MURDER AND DESTROYED HERSELF. AND ONE OF THE VICTIMS WAS THE BRAIN-DEAD PERSON WHOSE MEMORIES WERE IMPLANTED INTO HER.

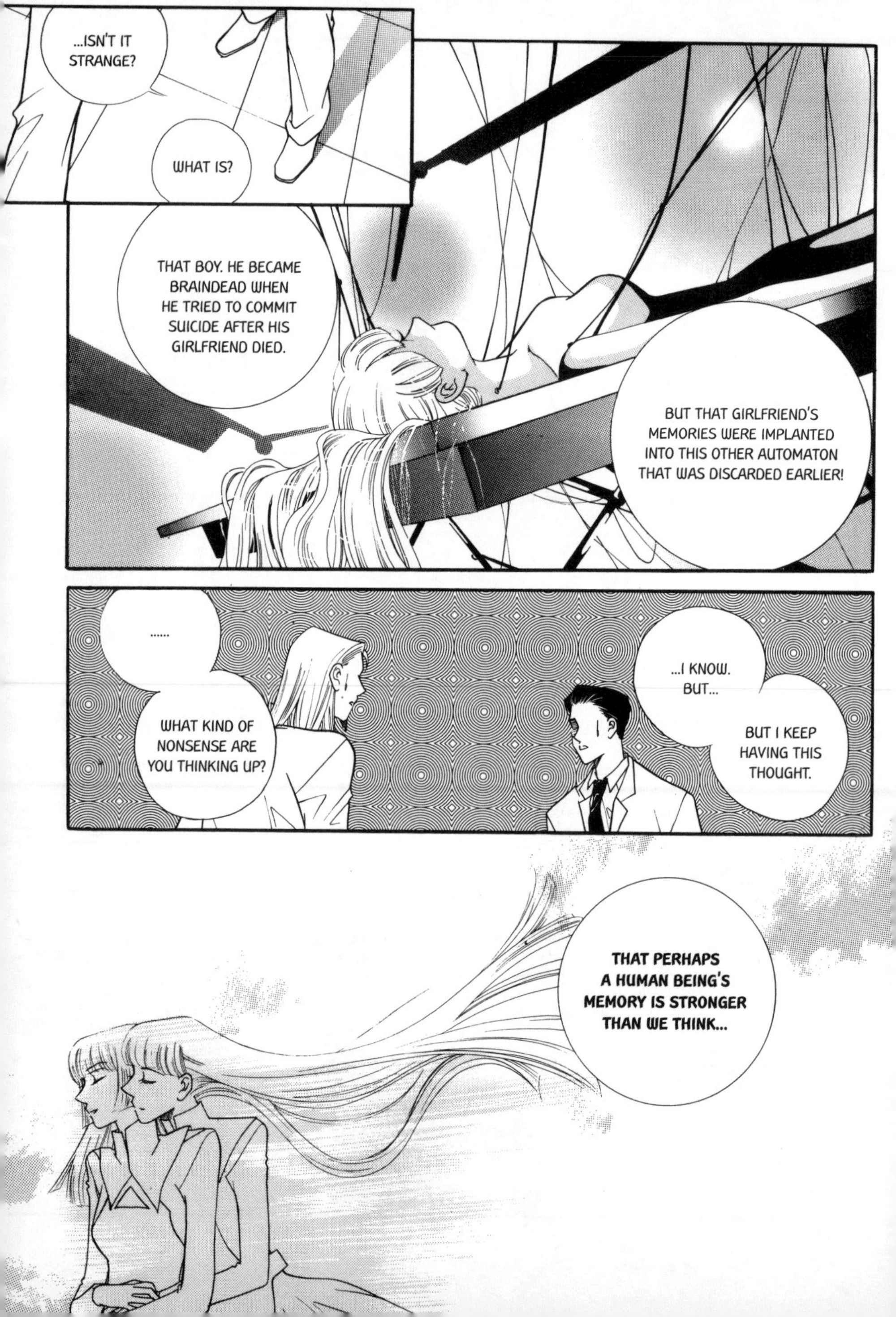
...ISN'T IT STRANGE?
WHAT IS?
THAT BOY. HE BECAME BRAINDEAD WHEN HE TRIED TO COMMIT SUICIDE AFTER HIS GIRLFRIEND DIED.
BUT THAT GIRLFRIEND'S MEMORIES WERE IMPLANTED INTO THIS OTHER AUTOMATON THAT WAS DISCARDED EARLIER!
......
WHAT KIND OF NONSENSE ARE YOU THINKING UP?
...I KNOW. BUT...
BUT I KEEP HAVING THIS THOUGHT.
THAT PERHAPS A HUMAN BEING'S MEMORY IS STRONGER THAN WE THINK...

A COLD

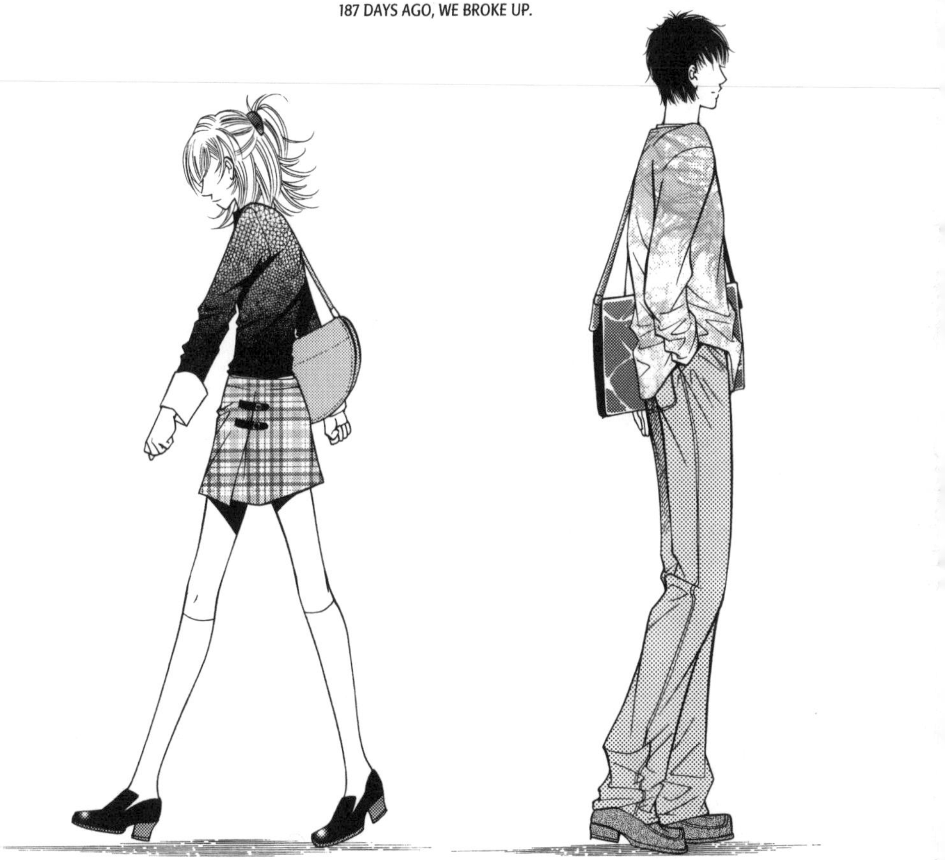
187 DAYS AGO, WE BROKE UP.

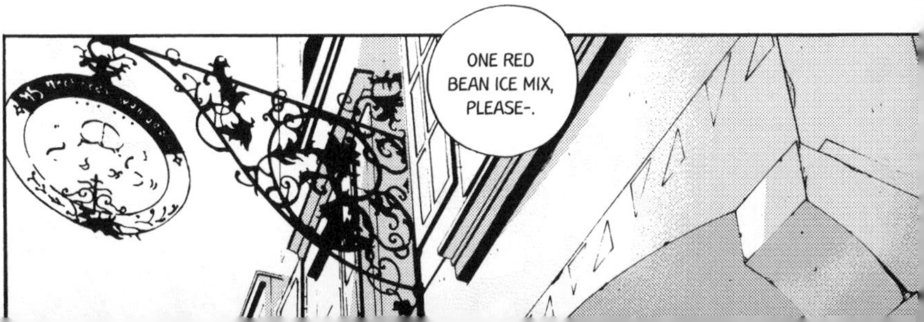
ONE RED BEAN ICE MIX, PLEASE-.

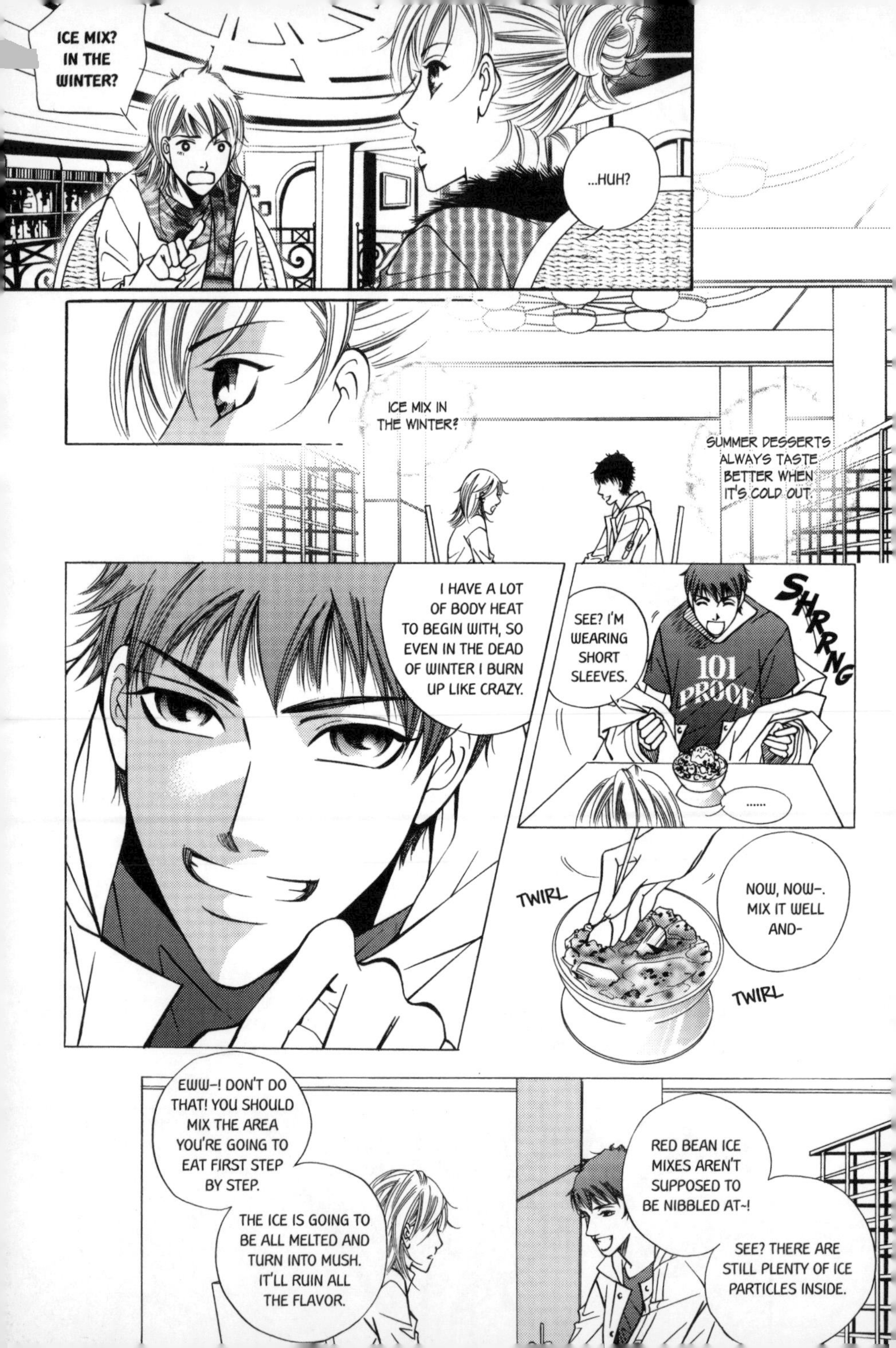
ICE MIX? IN THE WINTER?
...HUH?
ICE MIX IN THE WINTER?
SUMMER DESSERTS ALWAYS TASTE BETTER WHEN IT'S COLD OUT.
I HAVE A LOT OF BODY HEAT TO BEGIN WITH, SO EVEN IN THE DEAD OF WINTER I BURN UP LIKE CRAZY.
SEE? I'M WEARING SHORT SLEEVES.
SHRRNG
101 PROOF
......
TWIRL
NOW, NOW~. MIX IT WELL AND-
TWIRL
EWW~! DON'T DO THAT! YOU SHOULD MIX THE AREA YOU'RE GOING TO EAT FIRST STEP BY STEP.
THE ICE IS GOING TO BE ALL MELTED AND TURN INTO MUSH. IT'LL RUIN ALL THE FLAVOR.
RED BEAN ICE MIXES AREN'T SUPPOSED TO BE NIBBLED AT~!
SEE? THERE ARE STILL PLENTY OF ICE PARTICLES INSIDE.

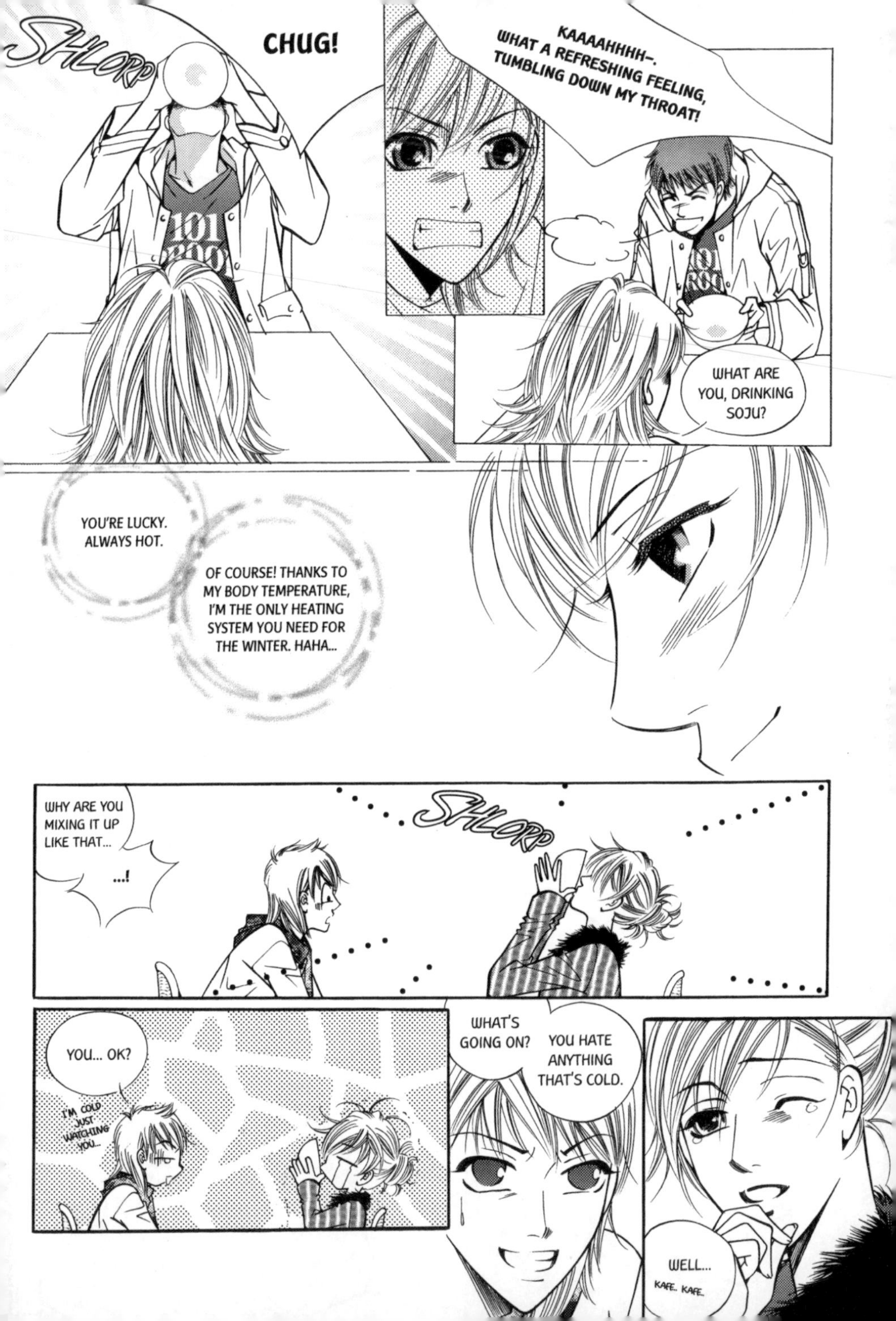
SHLORP
CHUG!
KAAAAHHHH-.
WHAT A REFRESHING FEELING,
TUMBLING DOWN MY THROAT!
WHAT ARE YOU, DRINKING SOJU?
YOU'RE LUCKY. ALWAYS HOT.
OF COURSE! THANKS TO MY BODY TEMPERATURE, I'M THE ONLY HEATING SYSTEM YOU NEED FOR THE WINTER. HAHA...
WHY ARE YOU MIXING IT UP LIKE THAT...
...!
SHLORP
YOU... OK?
I'M COLD JUST WATCHING YOU...
WHAT'S GOING ON?
YOU HATE ANYTHING THAT'S COLD.
WELL...
KAFE.. KAFE.

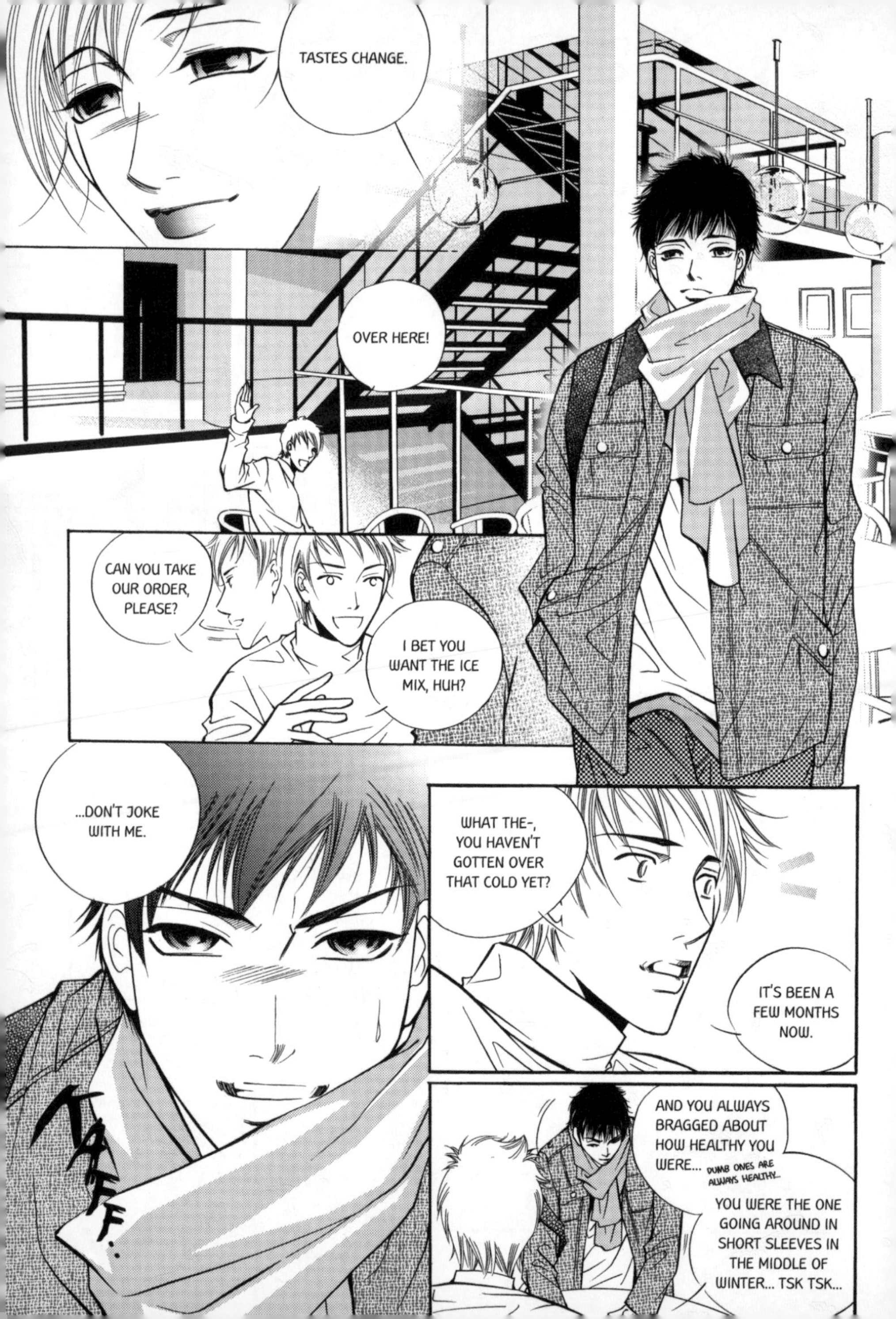
TASTES CHANGE.
OVER HERE!
CAN YOU TAKE OUR ORDER, PLEASE?
I BET YOU WANT THE ICE MIX, HUH?
...DON'T JOKE WITH ME.
KAFF.
WHAT THE-, YOU HAVEN'T GOTTEN OVER THAT COLD YET?
IT'S BEEN A FEW MONTHS NOW.
AND YOU ALWAYS BRAGGED ABOUT HOW HEALTHY YOU WERE...
DUMB ONES ARE ALWAYS HEALTHY...
YOU WERE THE ONE GOING AROUND IN SHORT SLEEVES IN THE MIDDLE OF WINTER... TSK TSK...

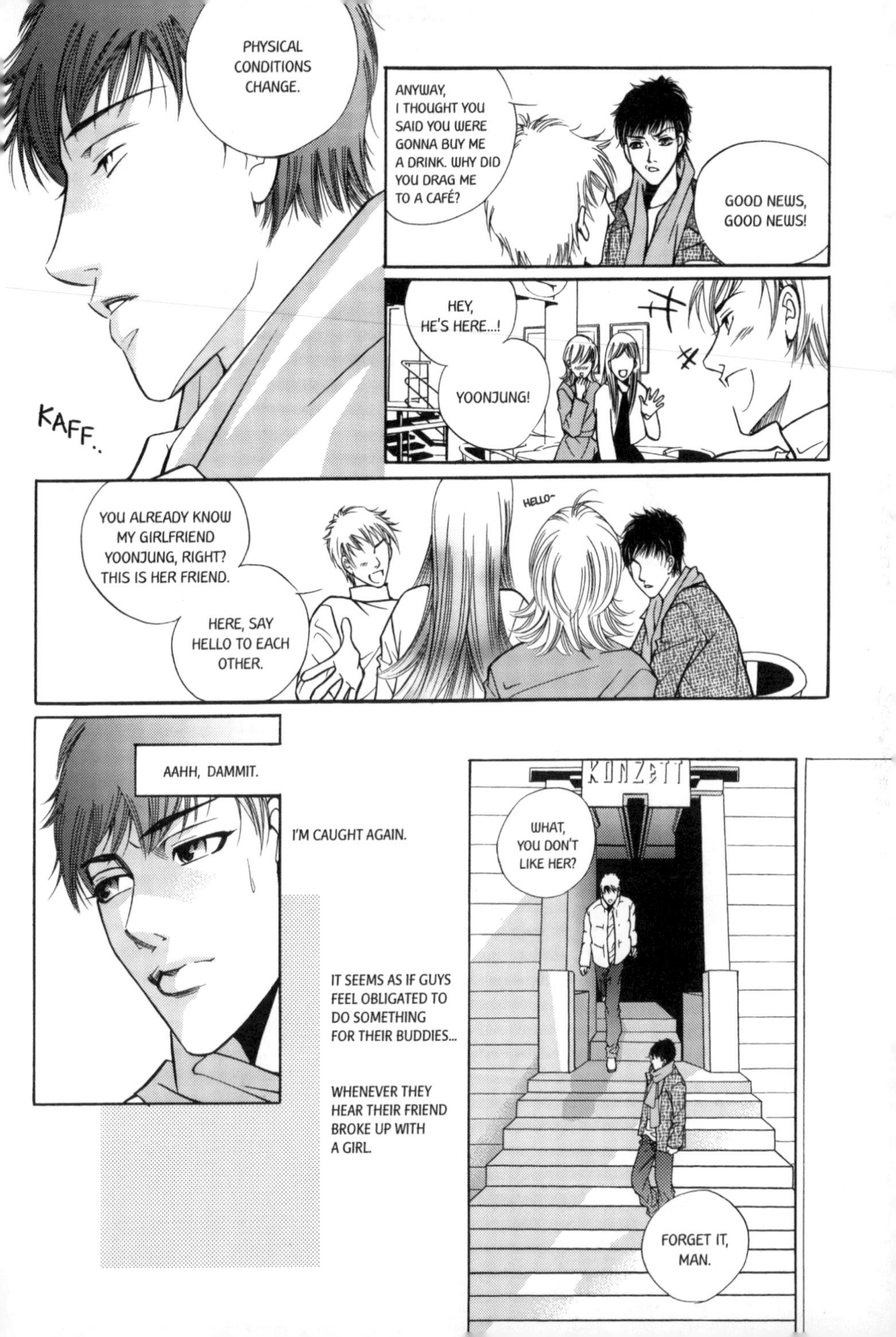
PHYSICAL CONDITIONS CHANGE.
KAFF..
ANYWAY, I THOUGHT YOU SAID YOU WERE GONNA BUY ME A DRINK. WHY DID YOU DRAG ME TO A CAFÉ?
GOOD NEWS, GOOD NEWS!
HEY, HE'S HERE...!
YOONJUNG!
YOU ALREADY KNOW MY GIRLFRIEND YOONJUNG, RIGHT? THIS IS HER FRIEND.
HERE, SAY HELLO TO EACH OTHER.
HELLO~
AAHH, DAMMIT.
I'M CAUGHT AGAIN.
IT SEEMS AS IF GUYS FEEL OBLIGATED TO DO SOMETHING FOR THEIR BUDDIES...
WHENEVER THEY HEAR THEIR FRIEND BROKE UP WITH A GIRL.
KONZETT
WHAT, YOU DON'T LIKE HER?
FORGET IT, MAN.

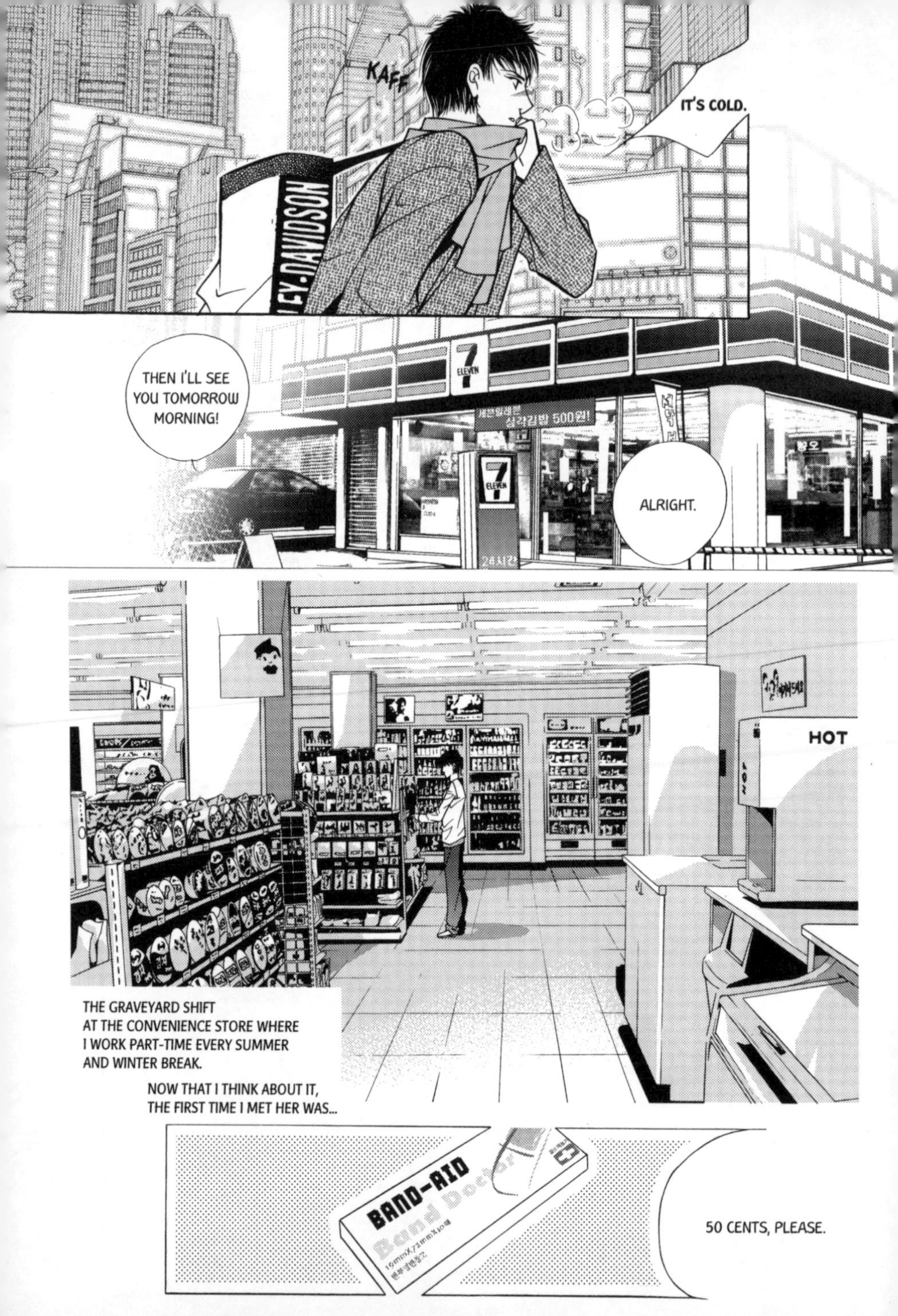
KAFF
IT'S COLD.
THEN I'LL SEE YOU TOMORROW MORNING!
ALRIGHT.
HOT
THE GRAVEYARD SHIFT AT THE CONVENIENCE STORE WHERE I WORK PART-TIME EVERY SUMMER AND WINTER BREAK.
NOW THAT I THINK ABOUT IT, THE FIRST TIME I MET HER WAS...
BAND-AID
Band Doctor
50 CENTS, PLEASE.

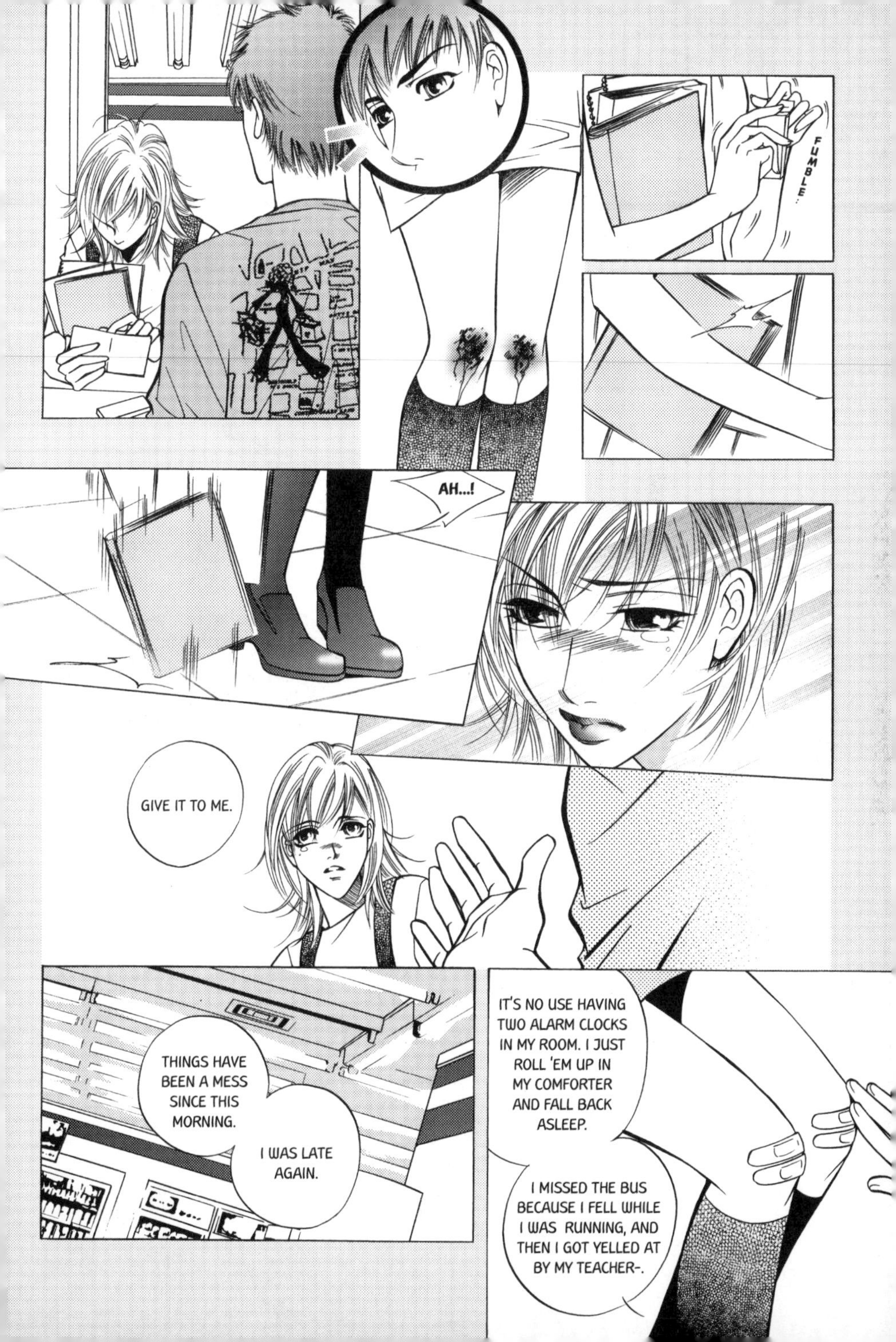
FUMBLE..
AH...!
GIVE IT TO ME.
THINGS HAVE BEEN A MESS SINCE THIS MORNING.
I WAS LATE AGAIN.
IT'S NO USE HAVING TWO ALARM CLOCKS IN MY ROOM. I JUST ROLL 'EM UP IN MY COMFORTER AND FALL BACK ASLEEP.
I MISSED THE BUS BECAUSE I FELL WHILE I WAS RUNNING, AND THEN I GOT YELLED AT BY MY TEACHER-.

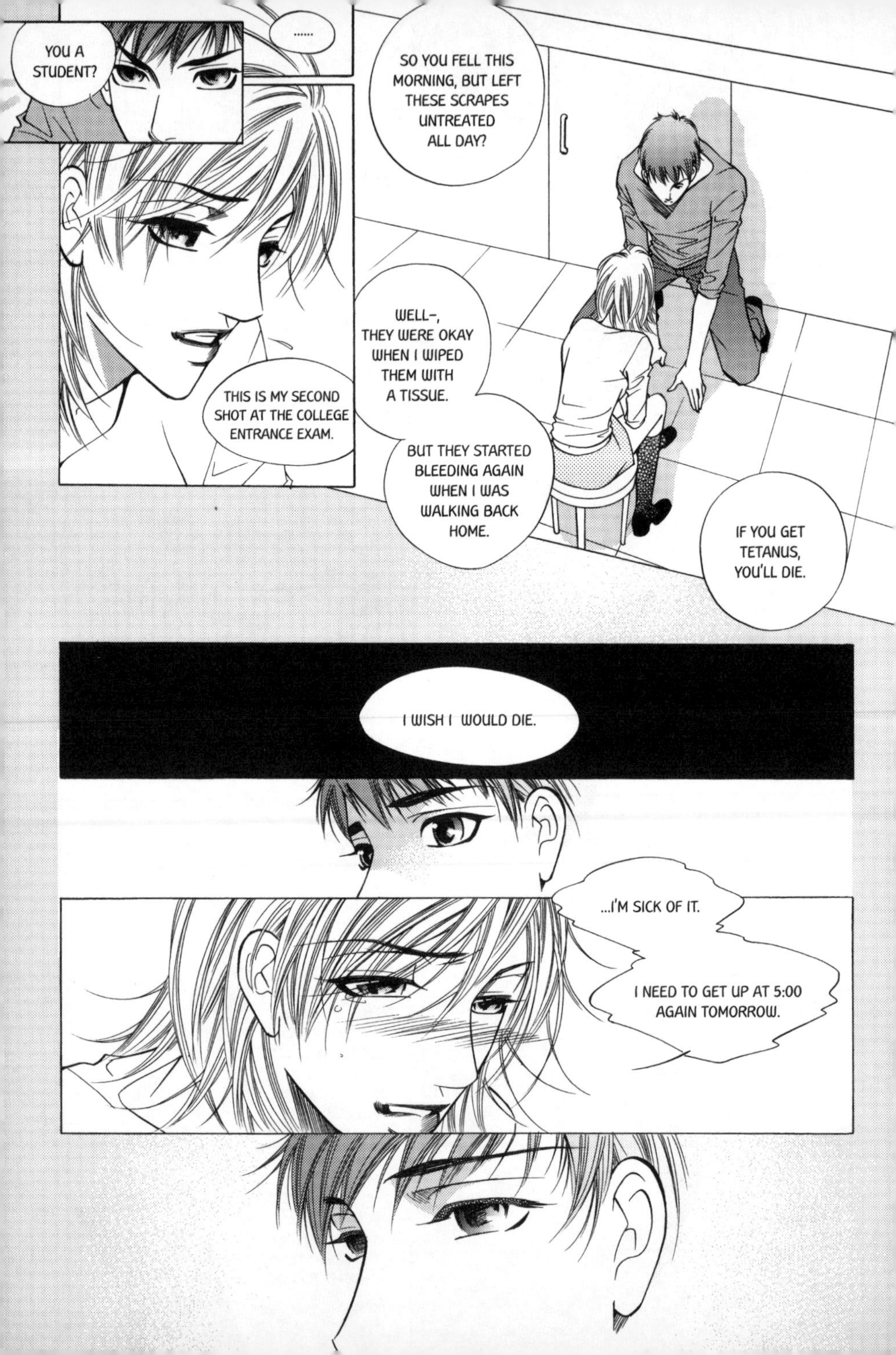
YOU A STUDENT?
......
THIS IS MY SECOND SHOT AT THE COLLEGE ENTRANCE EXAM.
SO YOU FELL THIS MORNING, BUT LEFT THESE SCRAPES UNTREATED ALL DAY?
WELL-, THEY WERE OKAY WHEN I WIPED THEM WITH A TISSUE.
BUT THEY STARTED BLEEDING AGAIN WHEN I WAS WALKING BACK HOME.
IF YOU GET TETANUS, YOU'LL DIE.
I WISH I WOULD DIE.
...I'M SICK OF IT.
I NEED TO GET UP AT 5:00 AGAIN TOMORROW.

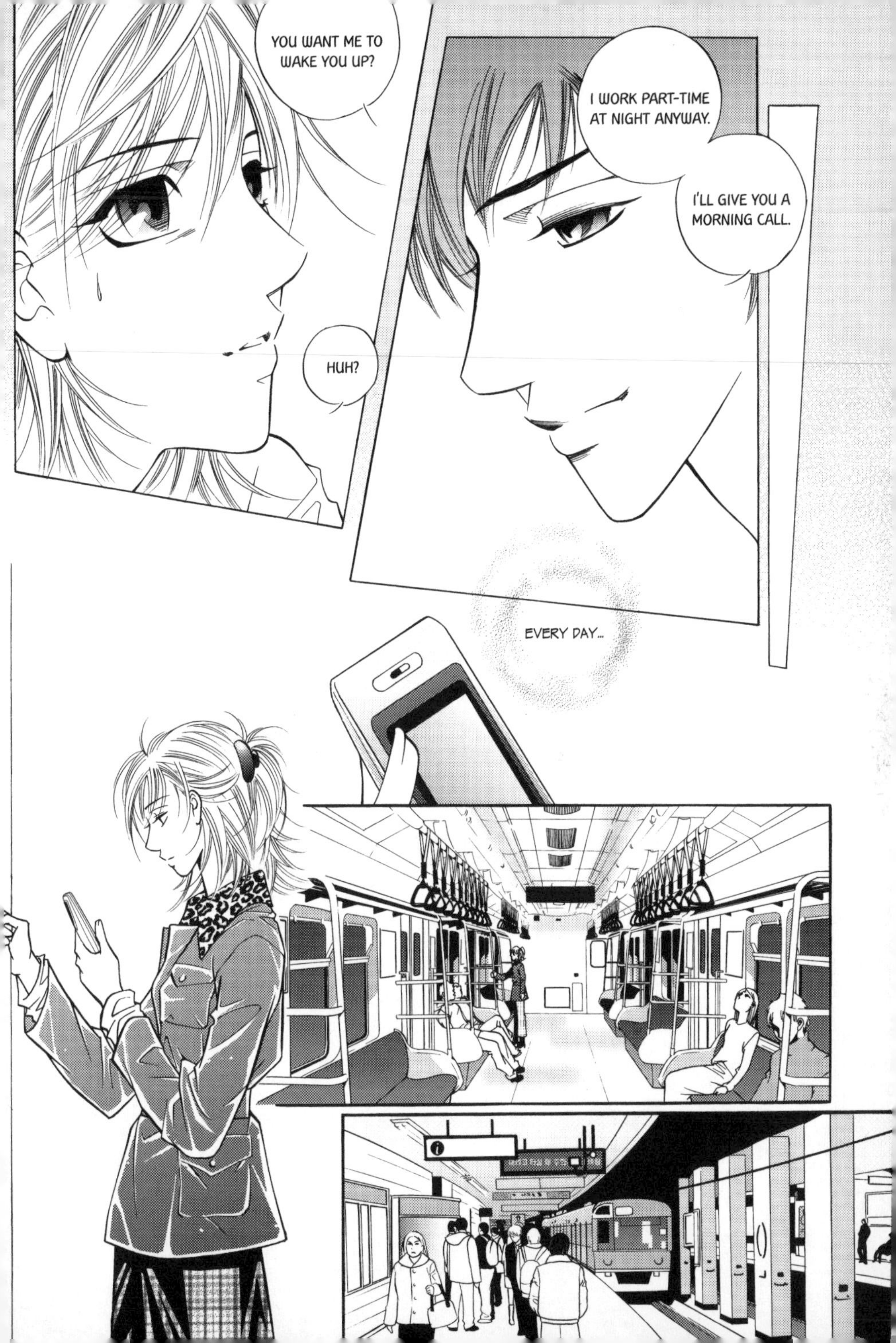
YOU WANT ME TO WAKE YOU UP?
HUH?
I WORK PART-TIME AT NIGHT ANYWAY.
I'LL GIVE YOU A MORNING CALL.
EVERY DAY...

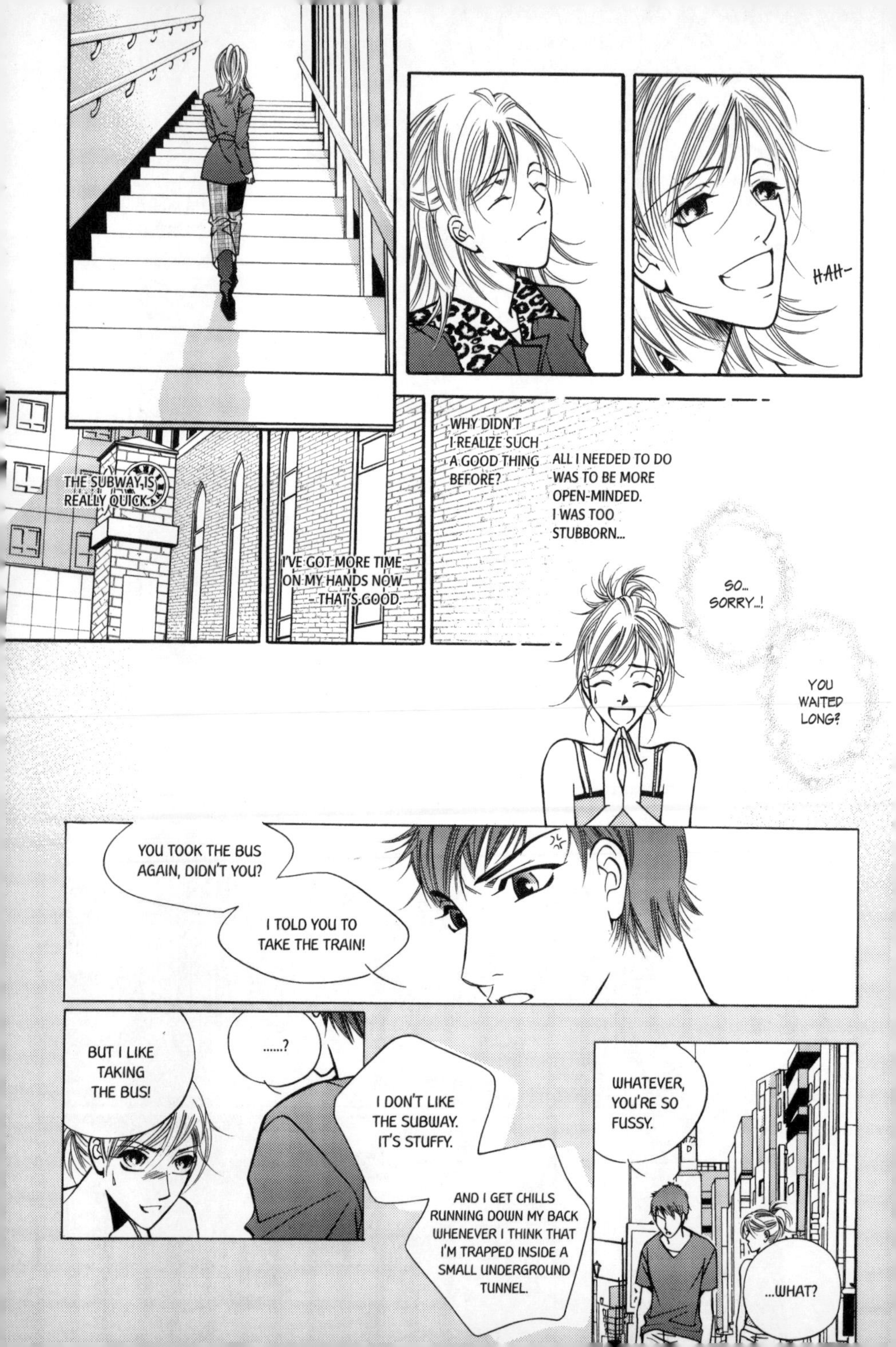
HAH-
THE SUBWAY IS REALLY QUICK.
I'VE GOT MORE TIME ON MY HANDS NOW -THAT'S GOOD.
WHY DIDN'T I REALIZE SUCH A GOOD THING BEFORE?
ALL I NEEDED TO DO WAS TO BE MORE OPEN-MINDED. I WAS TOO STUBBORN...
SO... SORRY...!
YOU WAITED LONG?
YOU TOOK THE BUS AGAIN, DIDN'T YOU?
I TOLD YOU TO TAKE THE TRAIN!
BUT I LIKE TAKING THE BUS!
......?
I DON'T LIKE THE SUBWAY. IT'S STUFFY.
AND I GET CHILLS RUNNING DOWN MY BACK WHENEVER I THINK THAT I'M TRAPPED INSIDE A SMALL UNDERGROUND TUNNEL.
WHATEVER, YOU'RE SO FUSSY.
...WHAT?

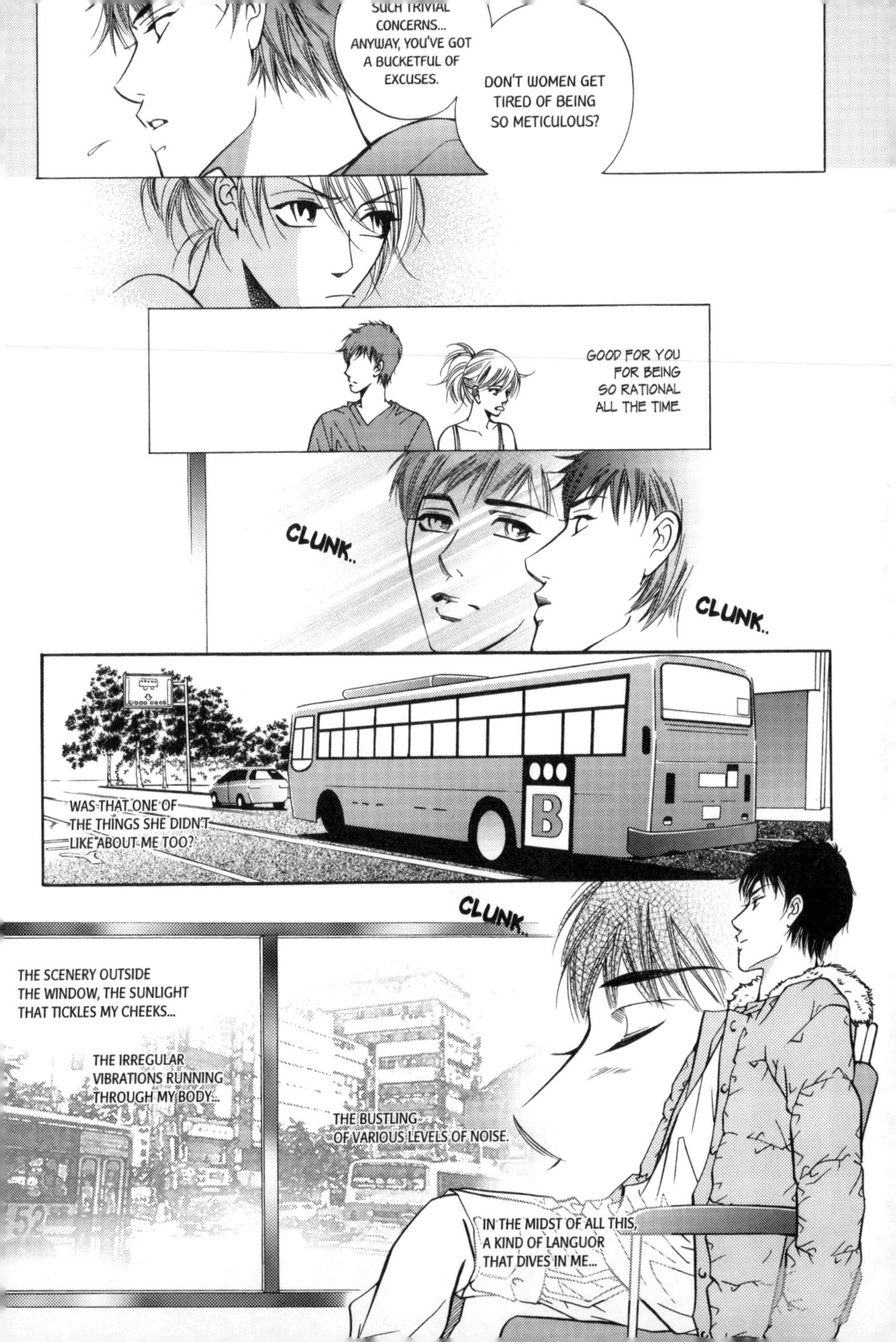
SUCH TRIVIAL CONCERNS... ANYWAY, YOU'VE GOT A BUCKETFUL OF EXCUSES.
DON'T WOMEN GET TIRED OF BEING SO METICULOUS?
GOOD FOR YOU FOR BEING SO RATIONAL ALL THE TIME.
CLUNK..
CLUNK..
WAS THAT ONE OF THE THINGS SHE DIDN'T LIKE ABOUT ME TOO?
B
CLUNK..
THE SCENERY OUTSIDE THE WINDOW, THE SUNLIGHT THAT TICKLES MY CHEEKS...
THE IRREGULAR VIBRATIONS RUNNING THROUGH MY BODY...
THE BUSTLING OF VARIOUS LEVELS OF NOISE.
IN THE MIDST OF ALL THIS, A KIND OF LANGUOR THAT DIVES IN ME...

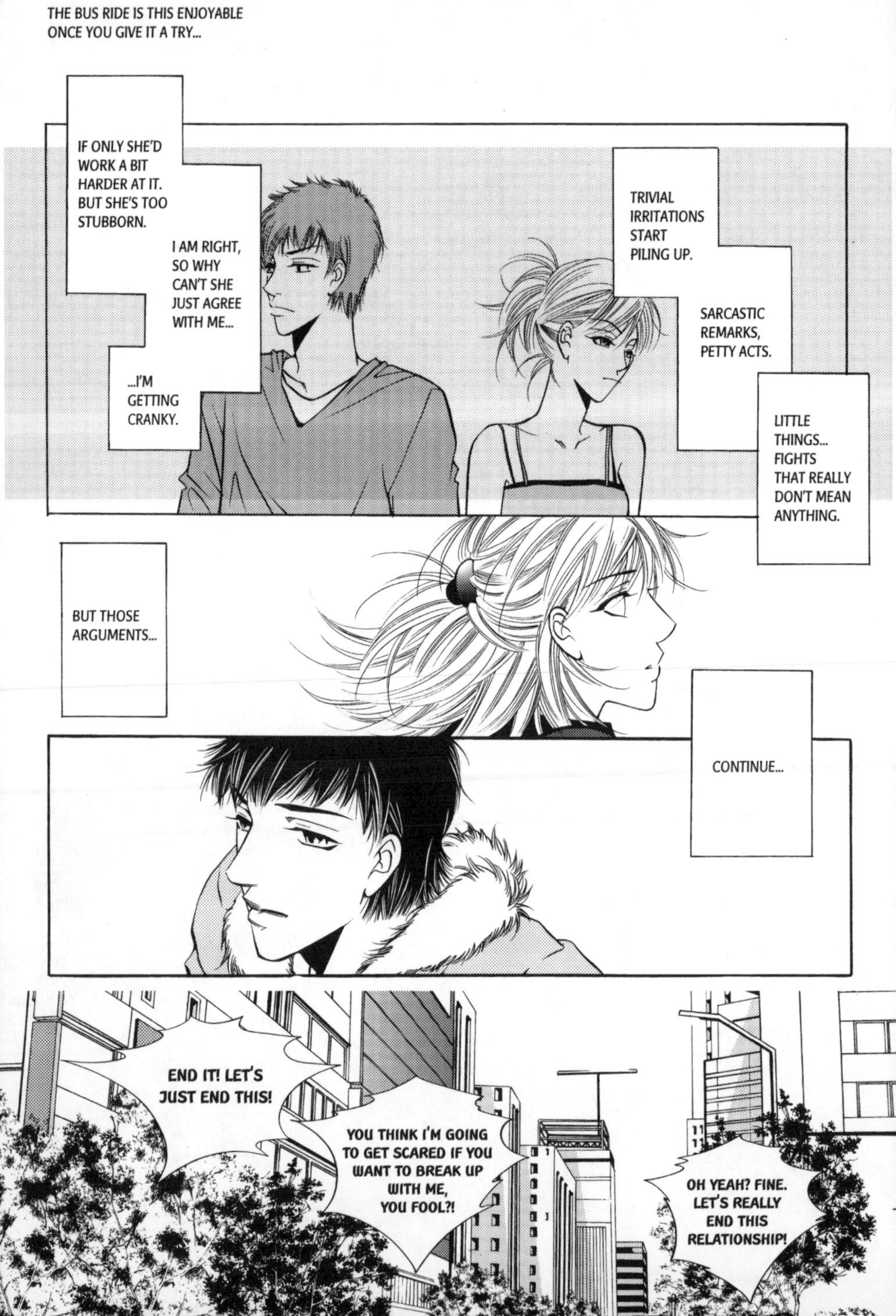

THE BUS RIDE IS THIS ENJOYABLE ONCE YOU GIVE IT A TRY...
IF ONLY SHE'D WORK A BIT HARDER AT IT. BUT SHE'S TOO STUBBORN.
I AM RIGHT, SO WHY CAN'T SHE JUST AGREE WITH ME...
...I'M GETTING CRANKY.
TRIVIAL IRRITATIONS START PILING UP.
SARCASTIC REMARKS, PETTY ACTS.
LITTLE THINGS... FIGHTS THAT REALLY DON'T MEAN ANYTHING.
BUT THOSE ARGUMENTS...
CONTINUE...
END IT! LET'S JUST END THIS!
YOU THINK I'M GOING TO GET SCARED IF YOU WANT TO BREAK UP WITH ME, YOU FOOL?!
OH YEAH? FINE. LET'S REALLY END THIS RELATIONSHIP!

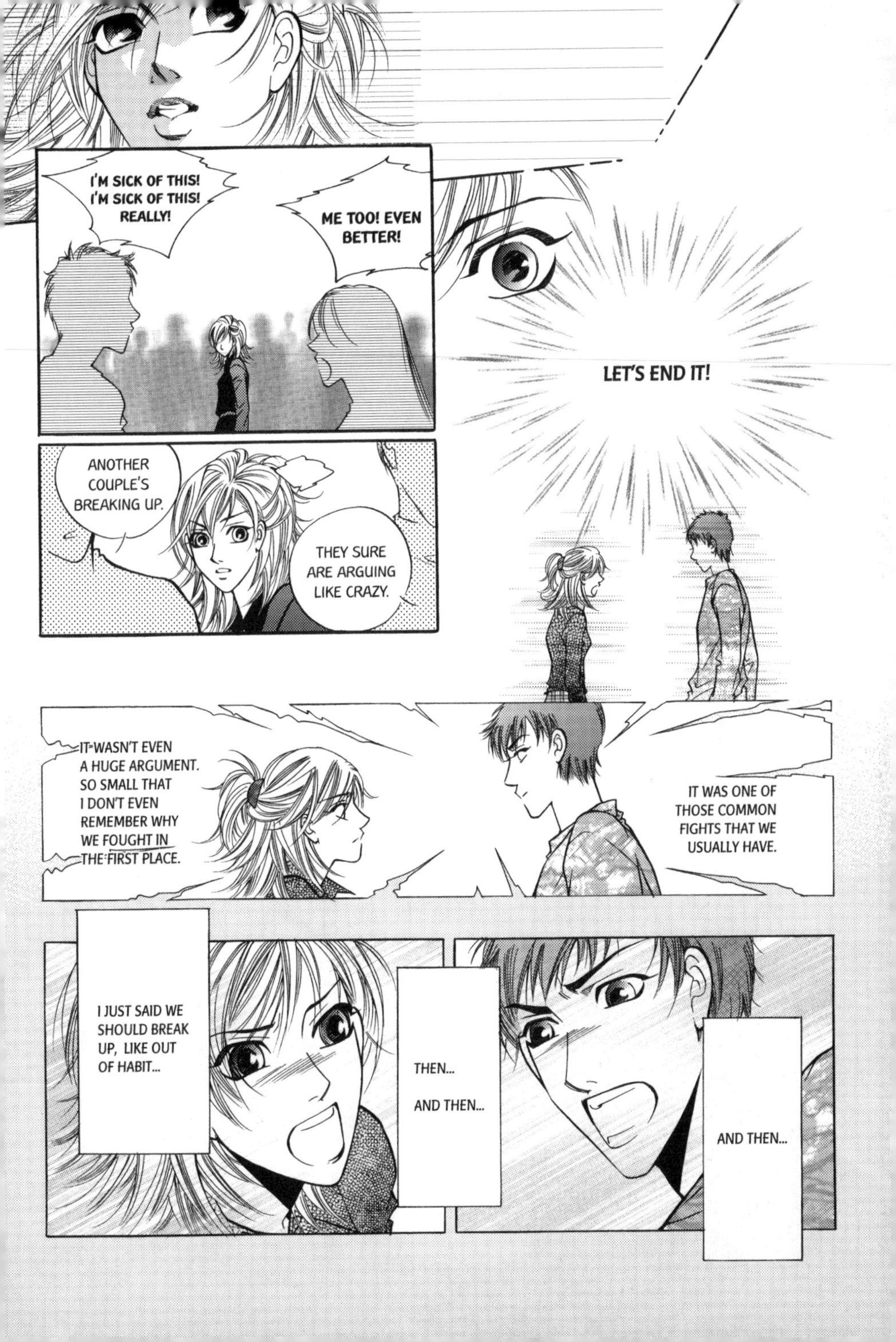
I'M SICK OF THIS! I'M SICK OF THIS! REALLY!
ME TOO! EVEN BETTER!
LET'S END IT!
ANOTHER COUPLE'S BREAKING UP.
THEY SURE ARE ARGUING LIKE CRAZY.
IT WASN'T EVEN A HUGE ARGUMENT. SO SMALL THAT I DON'T EVEN REMEMBER WHY WE FOUGHT IN THE FIRST PLACE.
IT WAS ONE OF THOSE COMMON FIGHTS THAT WE USUALLY HAVE.
I JUST SAID WE SHOULD BREAK UP, LIKE OUT OF HABIT...
THEN...
AND THEN...
AND THEN...

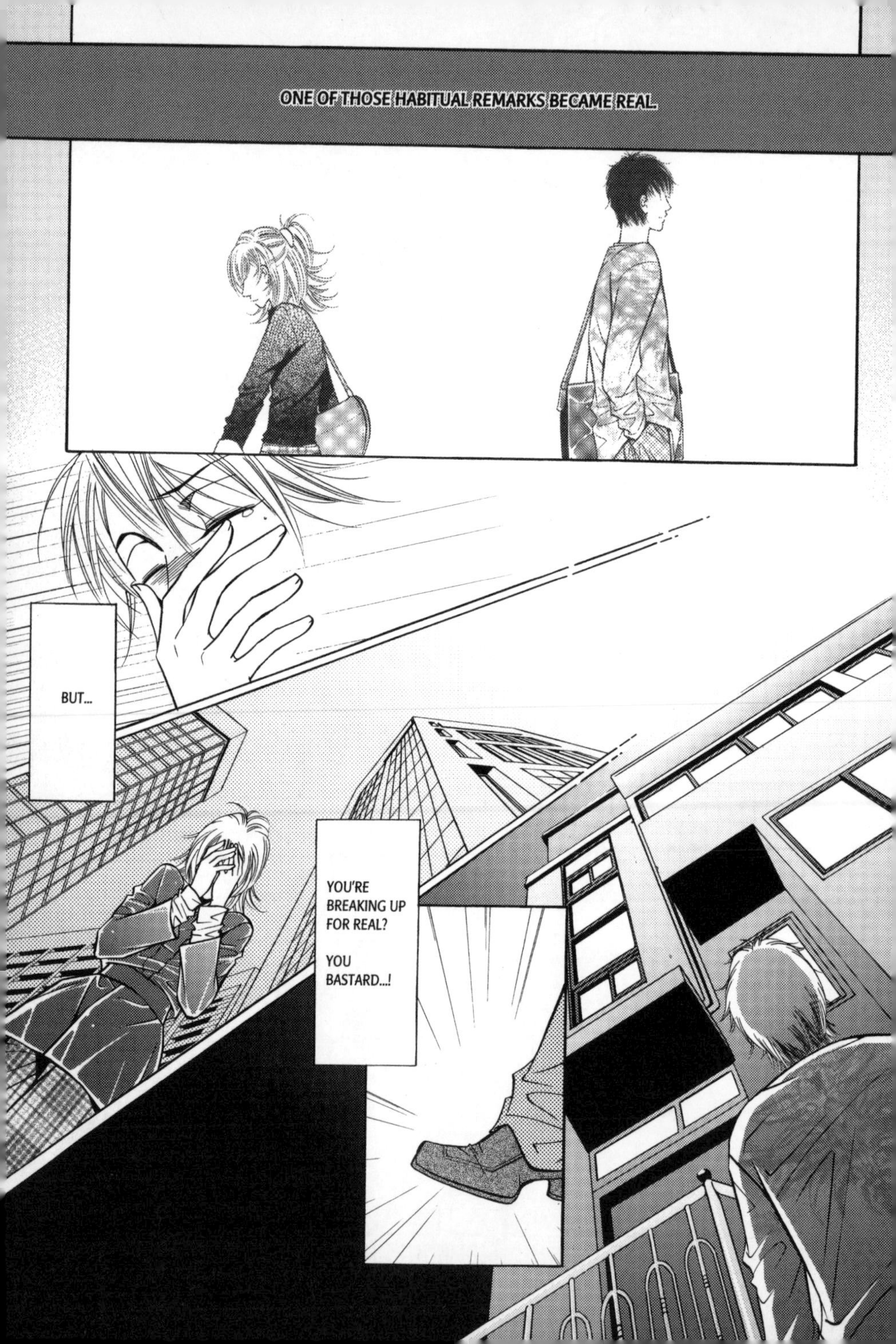
ONE OF THOSE HABITUAL REMARKS BECAME REAL.
BUT...
YOU'RE BREAKING UP FOR REAL?
YOU BASTARD...!

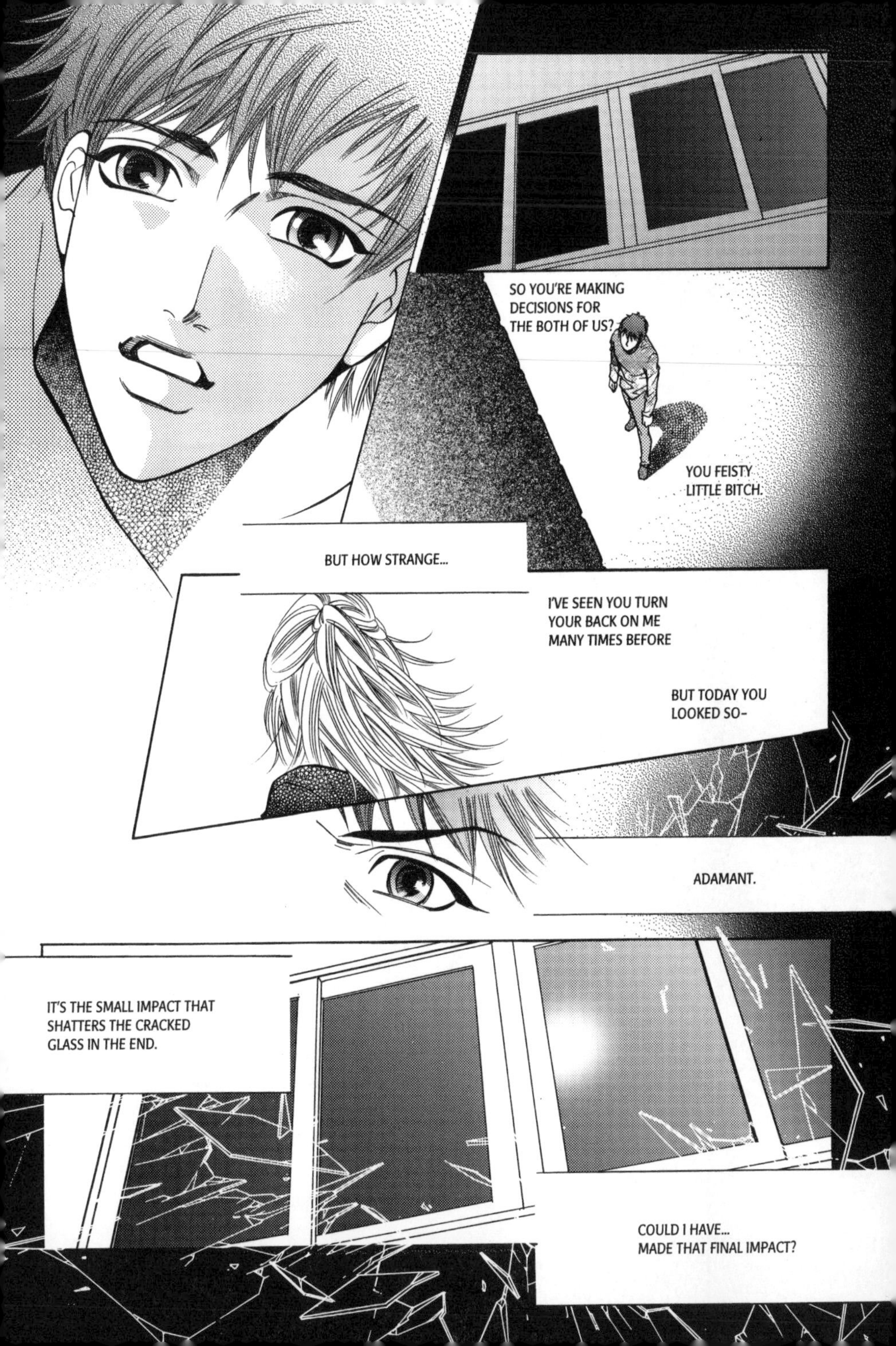
SO YOU'RE MAKING DECISIONS FOR THE BOTH OF US?
YOU FEISTY LITTLE BITCH.
BUT HOW STRANGE...
I'VE SEEN YOU TURN YOUR BACK ON ME MANY TIMES BEFORE
BUT TODAY YOU LOOKED SO-
ADAMANT.
IT'S THE SMALL IMPACT THAT SHATTERS THE CRACKED GLASS IN THE END.
COULD I HAVE... MADE THAT FINAL IMPACT?

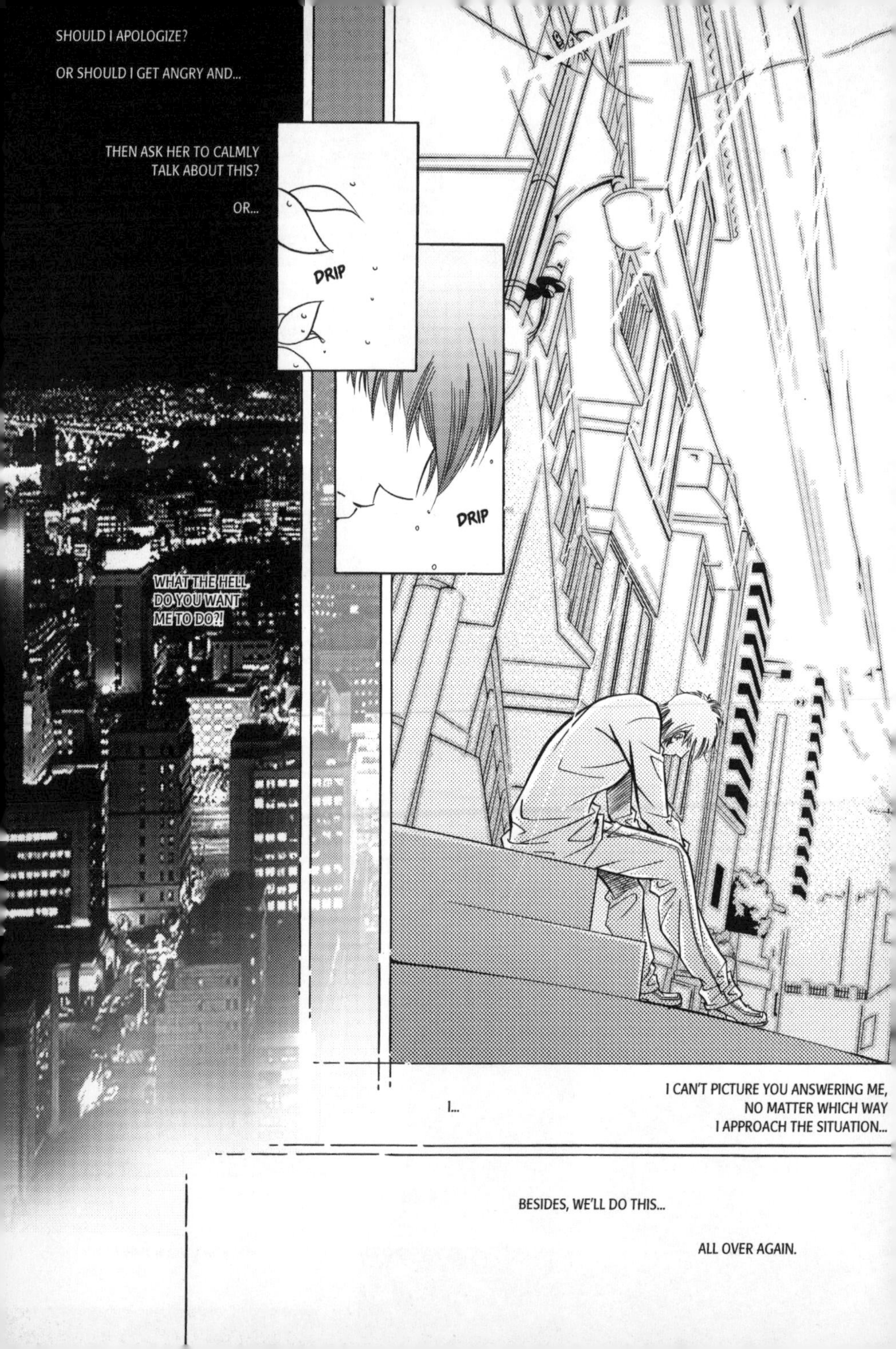
SHOULD I APOLOGIZE?
OR SHOULD I GET ANGRY AND...
THEN ASK HER TO CALMLY TALK ABOUT THIS?
OR...
DRIP
DRIP
WHAT THE HELL DO YOU WANT ME TO DO?!
I CAN'T PICTURE YOU ANSWERING ME, NO MATTER WHICH WAY I APPROACH THE SITUATION...
I...
BESIDES, WE'LL DO THIS...
ALL OVER AGAIN.

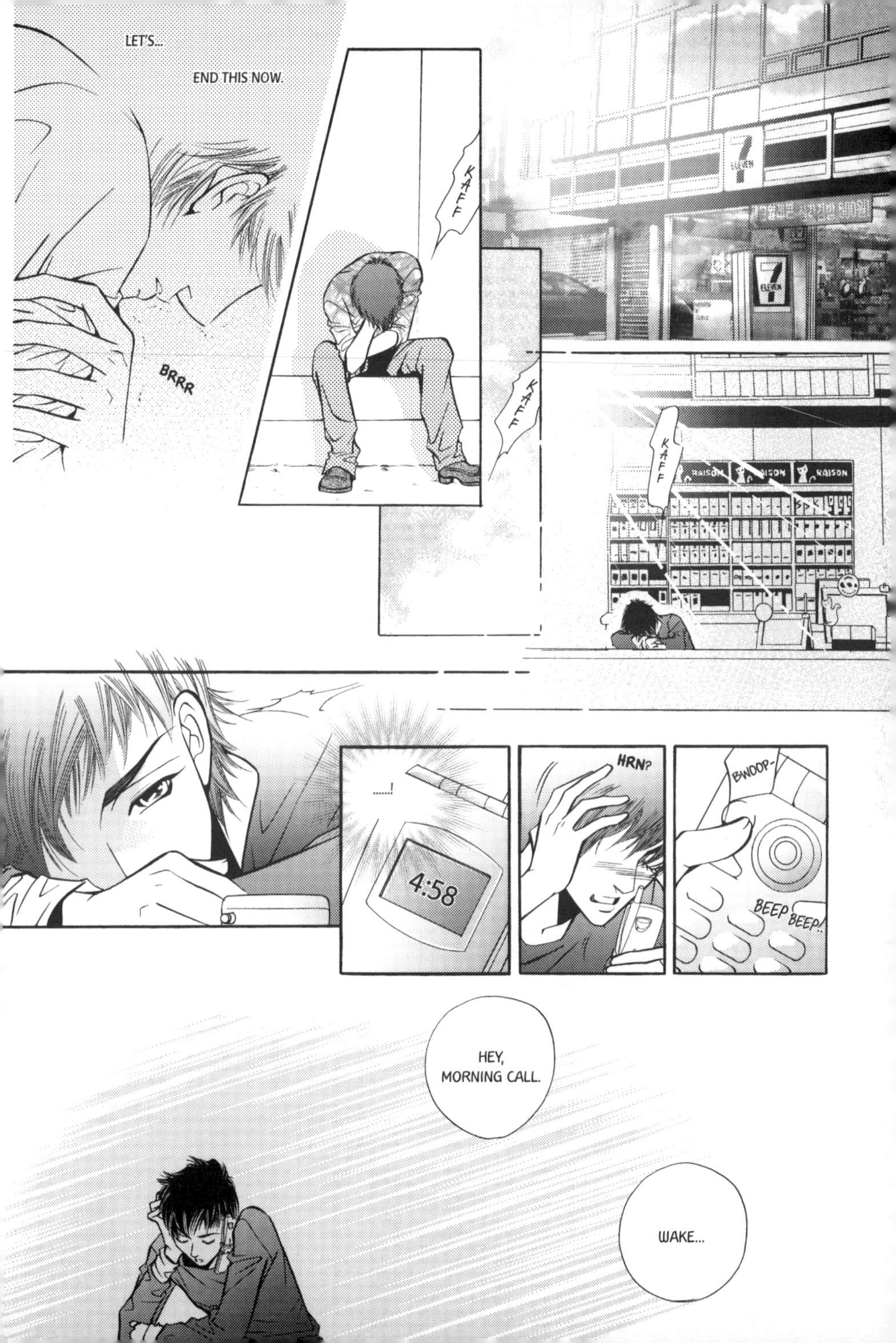
LET'S...
END THIS NOW.
BRRR
KAFF
KAFF
KAFF
......!
4:58
HRN?
BWOOP-
BEEP BEEP!
HEY, MORNING CALL.
WAKE...

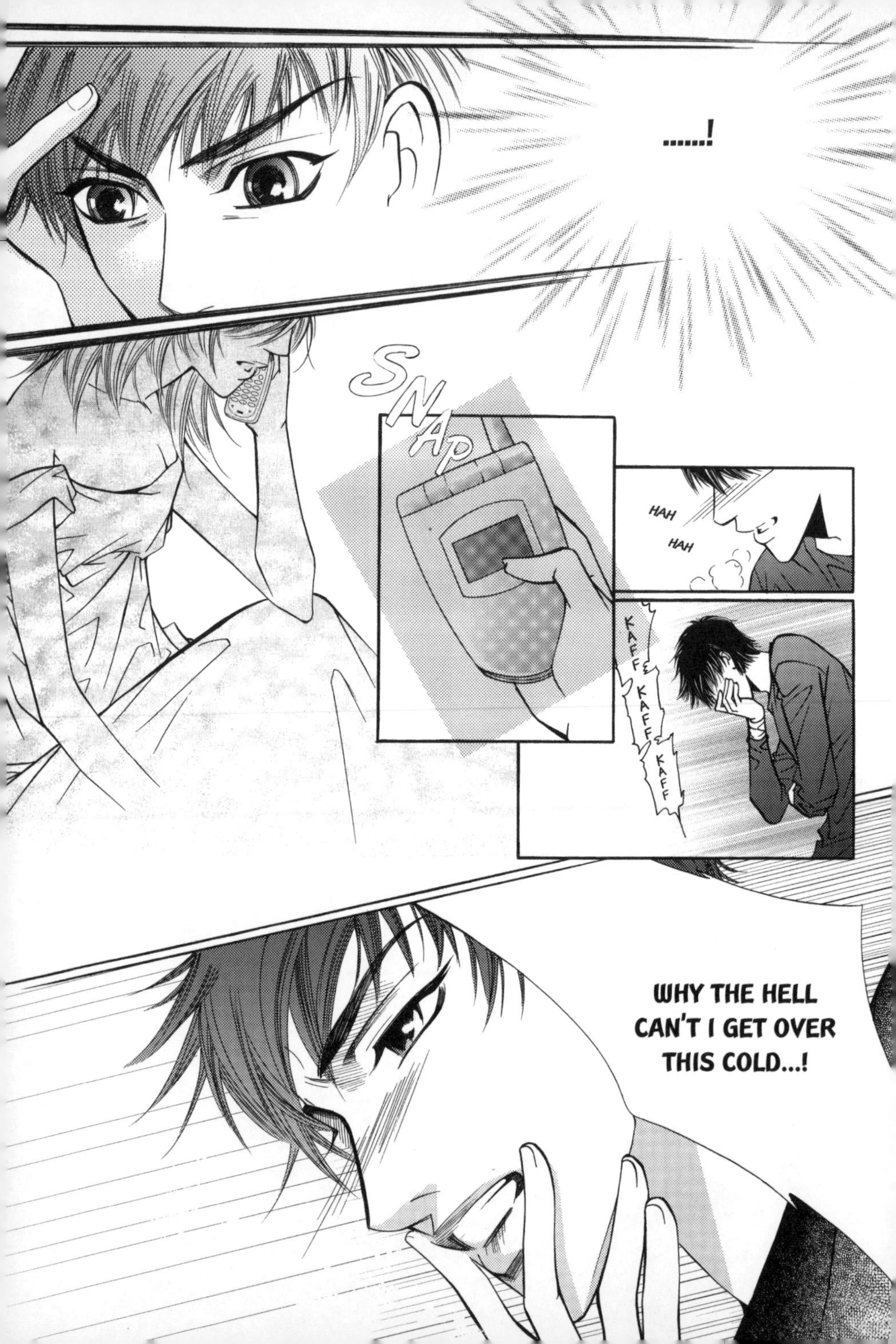

......!
SNAP
HAH
HAH
KAFF
KAFF
KAFF
KAFF
WHY THE HELL CAN'T I GET OVER THIS COLD...!

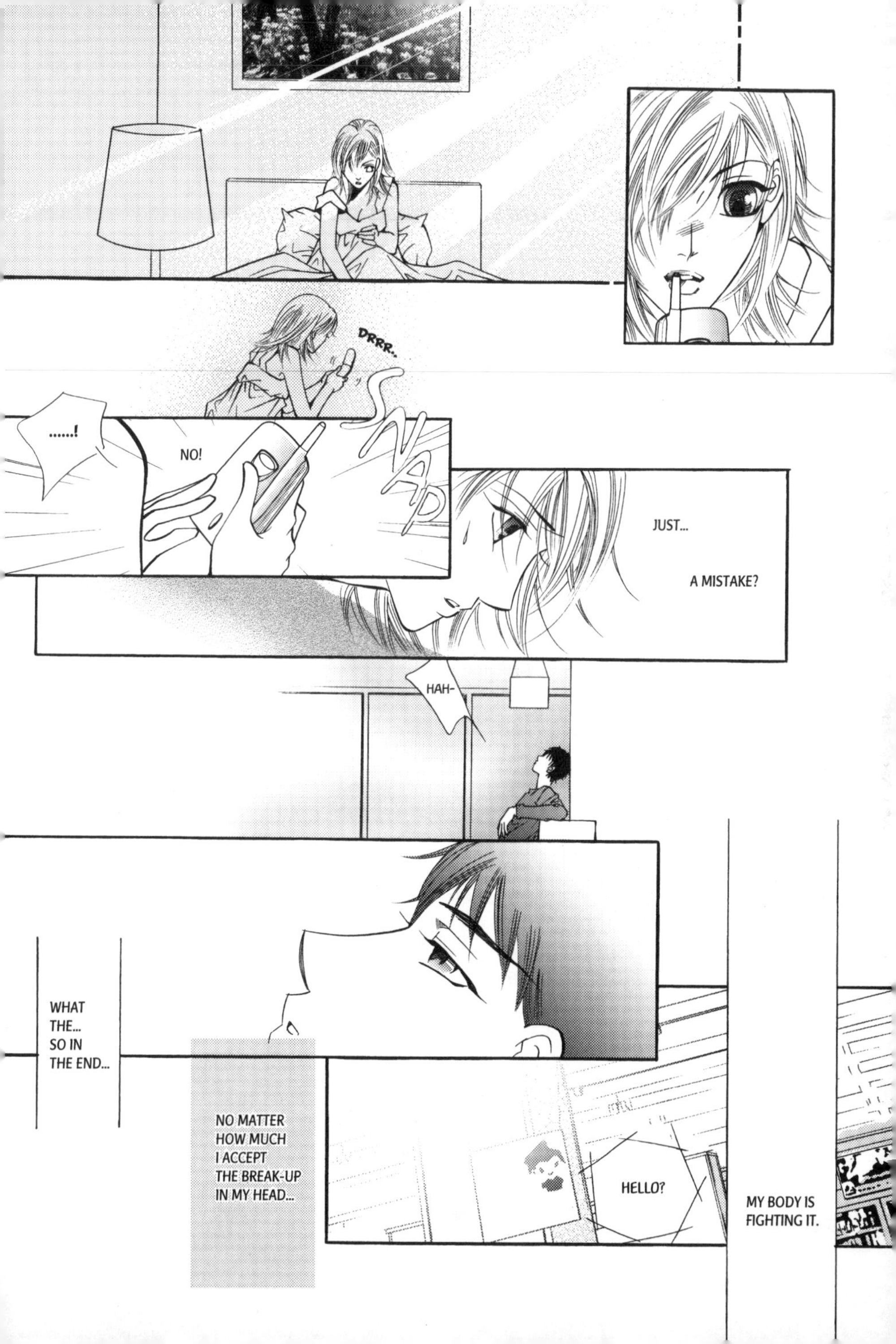

DRRR..
......!
NO!
SNAP
JUST...
A MISTAKE?
HAH-
WHAT THE... SO IN THE END...
NO MATTER HOW MUCH I ACCEPT THE BREAK-UP IN MY HEAD...
HELLO?
MY BODY IS FIGHTING IT.

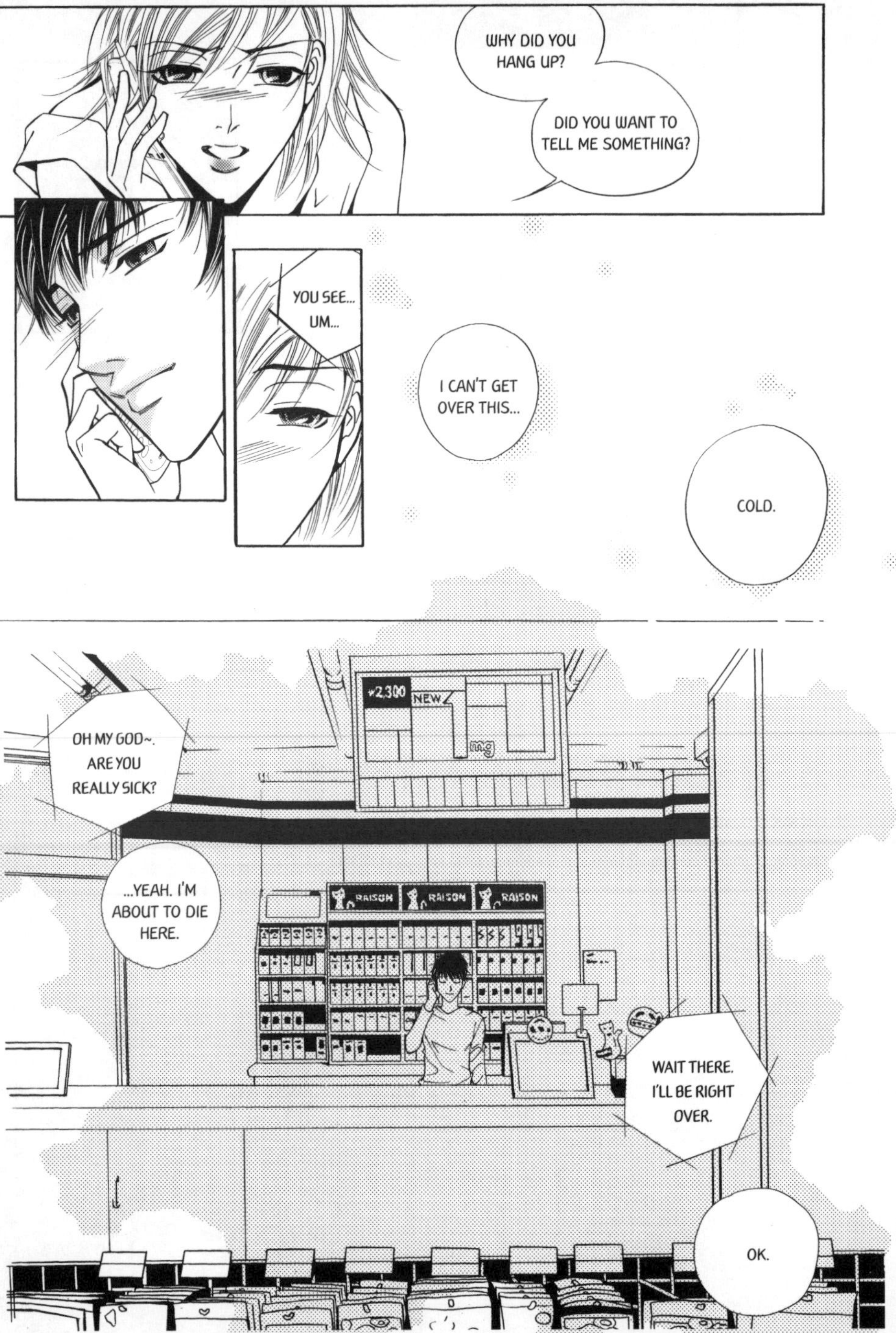
WHY DID YOU HANG UP?
DID YOU WANT TO TELL ME SOMETHING?
YOU SEE... UM...
I CAN'T GET OVER THIS...
COLD.
OH MY GOD~. ARE YOU REALLY SICK?
¥2,300
NEW
mg
RAISON
RAISON
RAISON
...YEAH. I'M ABOUT TO DIE HERE.
WAIT THERE. I'LL BE RIGHT OVER.
OK.

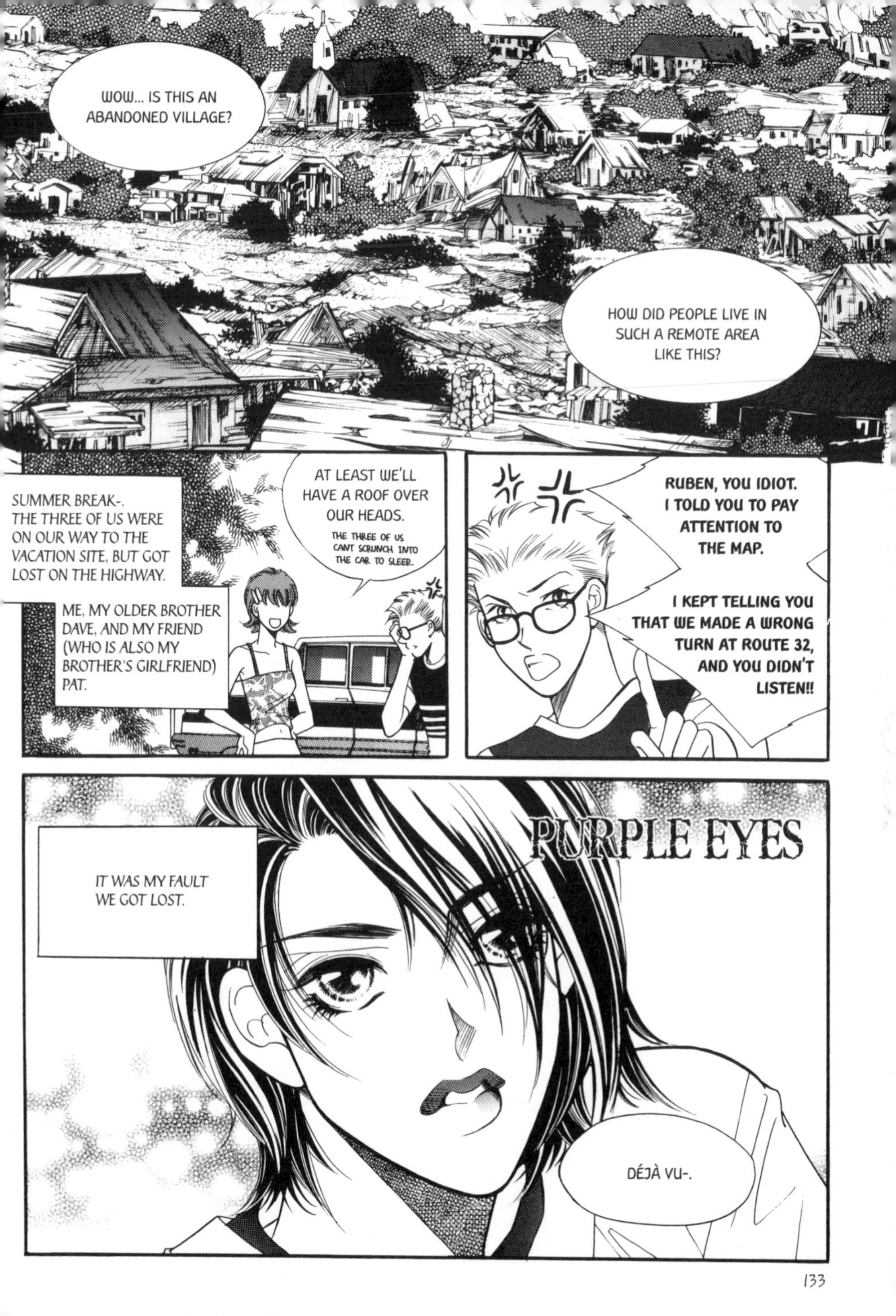
WOW... IS THIS AN ABANDONED VILLAGE?
HOW DID PEOPLE LIVE IN SUCH A REMOTE AREA LIKE THIS?
SUMMER BREAK-. THE THREE OF US WERE ON OUR WAY TO THE VACATION SITE, BUT GOT LOST ON THE HIGHWAY.
ME, MY OLDER BROTHER DAVE, AND MY FRIEND (WHO IS ALSO MY BROTHER'S GIRLFRIEND) PAT.
AT LEAST WE'LL HAVE A ROOF OVER OUR HEADS.
THE THREE OF US CANT SCRUNCH INTO THE CAR TO SLEEP...
RUBEN, YOU IDIOT. I TOLD YOU TO PAY ATTENTION TO THE MAP.
I KEPT TELLING YOU THAT WE MADE A WRONG TURN AT ROUTE 32, AND YOU DIDN'T LISTEN!!
PURPLE EYES
IT WAS MY FAULT WE GOT LOST.
DÉJÀ VU-.

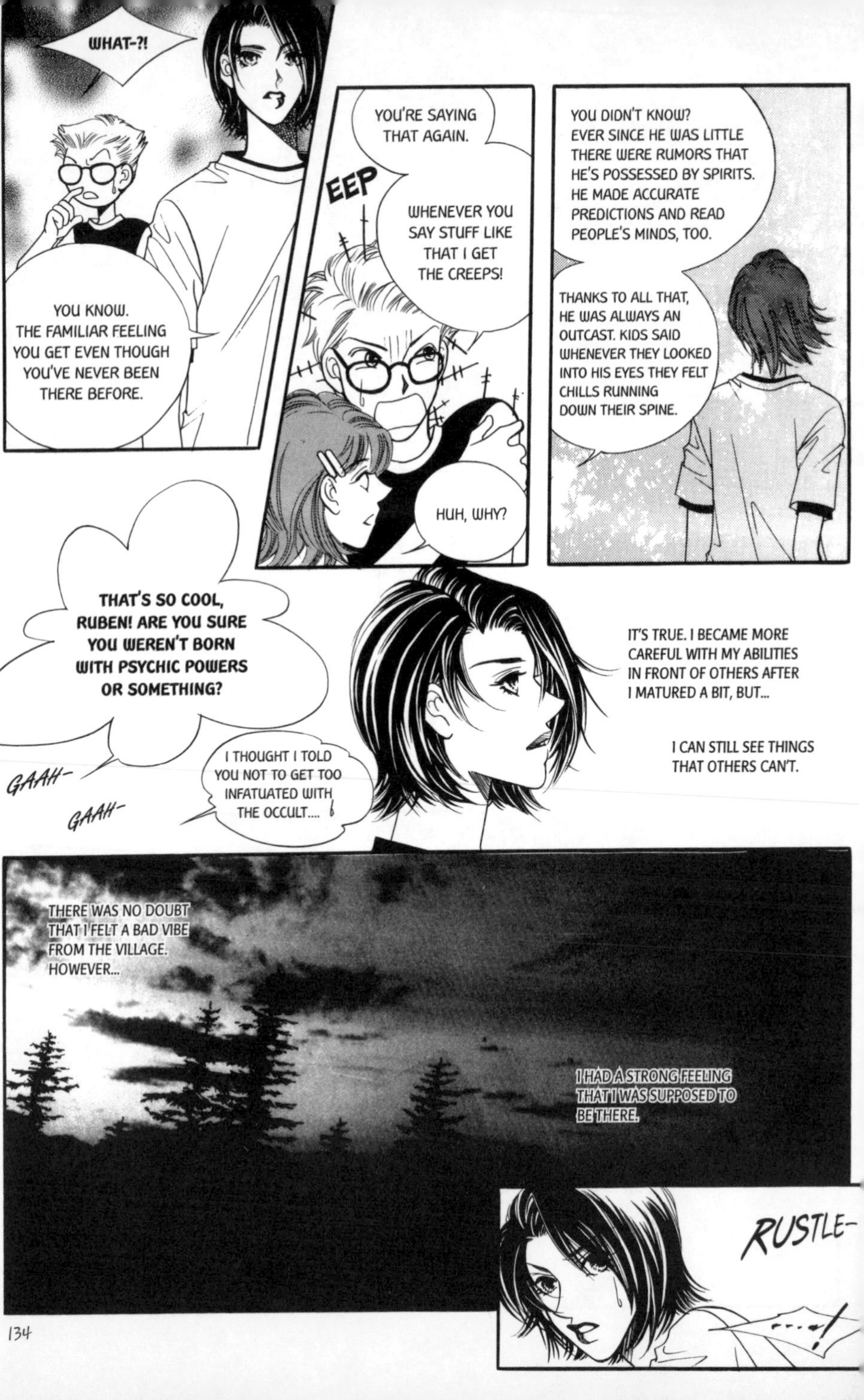
WHAT-?!
YOU KNOW. THE FAMILIAR FEELING YOU GET EVEN THOUGH YOU'VE NEVER BEEN THERE BEFORE.
YOU'RE SAYING THAT AGAIN.
EEP
WHENEVER YOU SAY STUFF LIKE THAT I GET THE CREEPS!
HUH, WHY?
YOU DIDN'T KNOW? EVER SINCE HE WAS LITTLE THERE WERE RUMORS THAT HE'S POSSESSED BY SPIRITS. HE MADE ACCURATE PREDICTIONS AND READ PEOPLE'S MINDS, TOO.
THANKS TO ALL THAT, HE WAS ALWAYS AN OUTCAST. KIDS SAID WHENEVER THEY LOOKED INTO HIS EYES THEY FELT CHILLS RUNNING DOWN THEIR SPINE.
THAT'S SO COOL, RUBEN! ARE YOU SURE YOU WEREN'T BORN WITH PSYCHIC POWERS OR SOMETHING?
GAAH-
GAAH-
I THOUGHT I TOLD YOU NOT TO GET TOO INFATUATED WITH THE OCCULT....
IT'S TRUE. I BECAME MORE CAREFUL WITH MY ABILITIES IN FRONT OF OTHERS AFTER I MATURED A BIT, BUT...
I CAN STILL SEE THINGS THAT OTHERS CAN'T.
THERE WAS NO DOUBT THAT I FELT A BAD VIBE FROM THE VILLAGE. HOWEVER...
I HAD A STRONG FEELING THAT I WAS SUPPOSED TO BE THERE.
RUSTLE-
...!

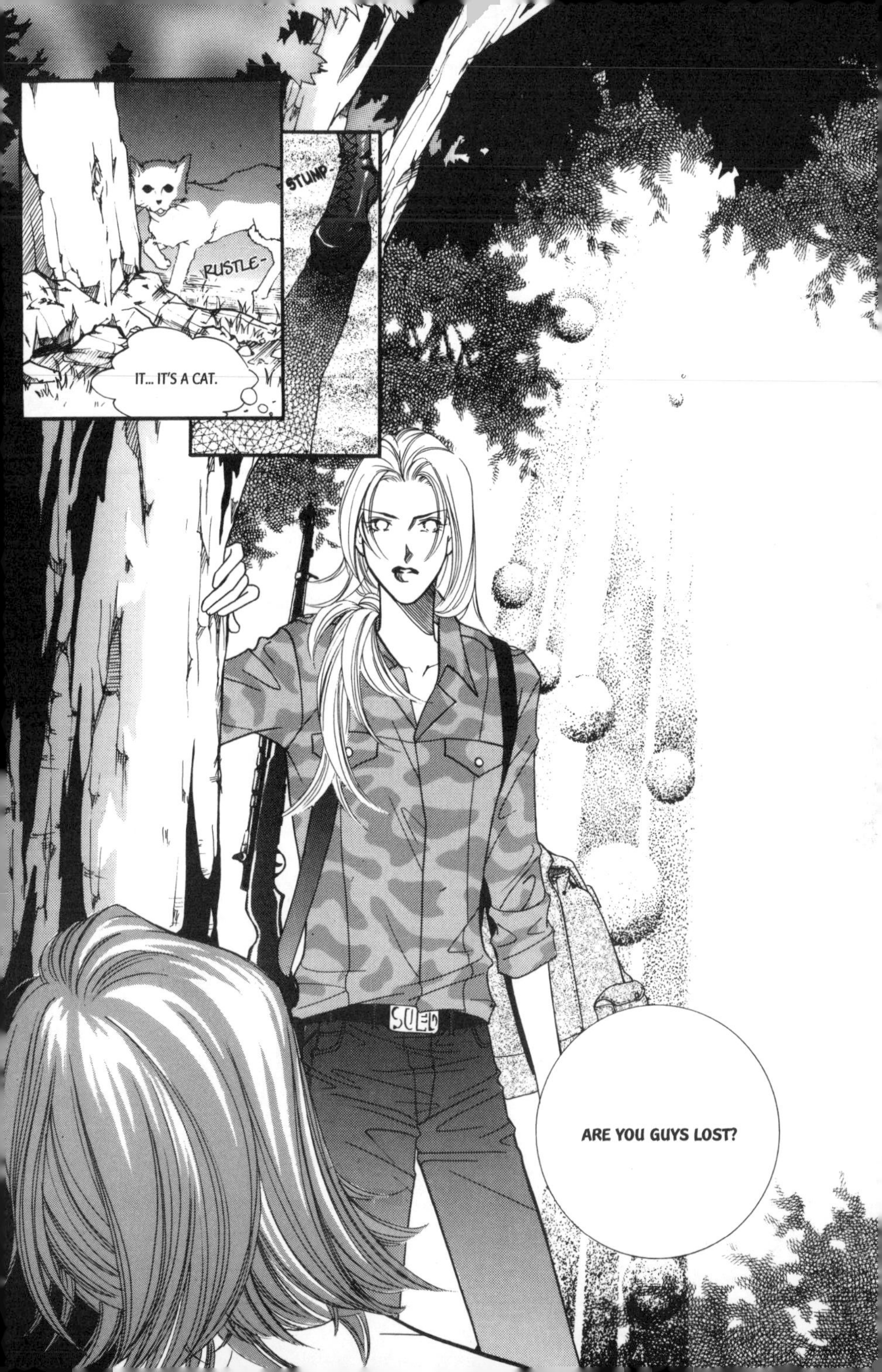
RUSTLE-
IT... IT'S A CAT.
STUMP-
ARE YOU GUYS LOST?

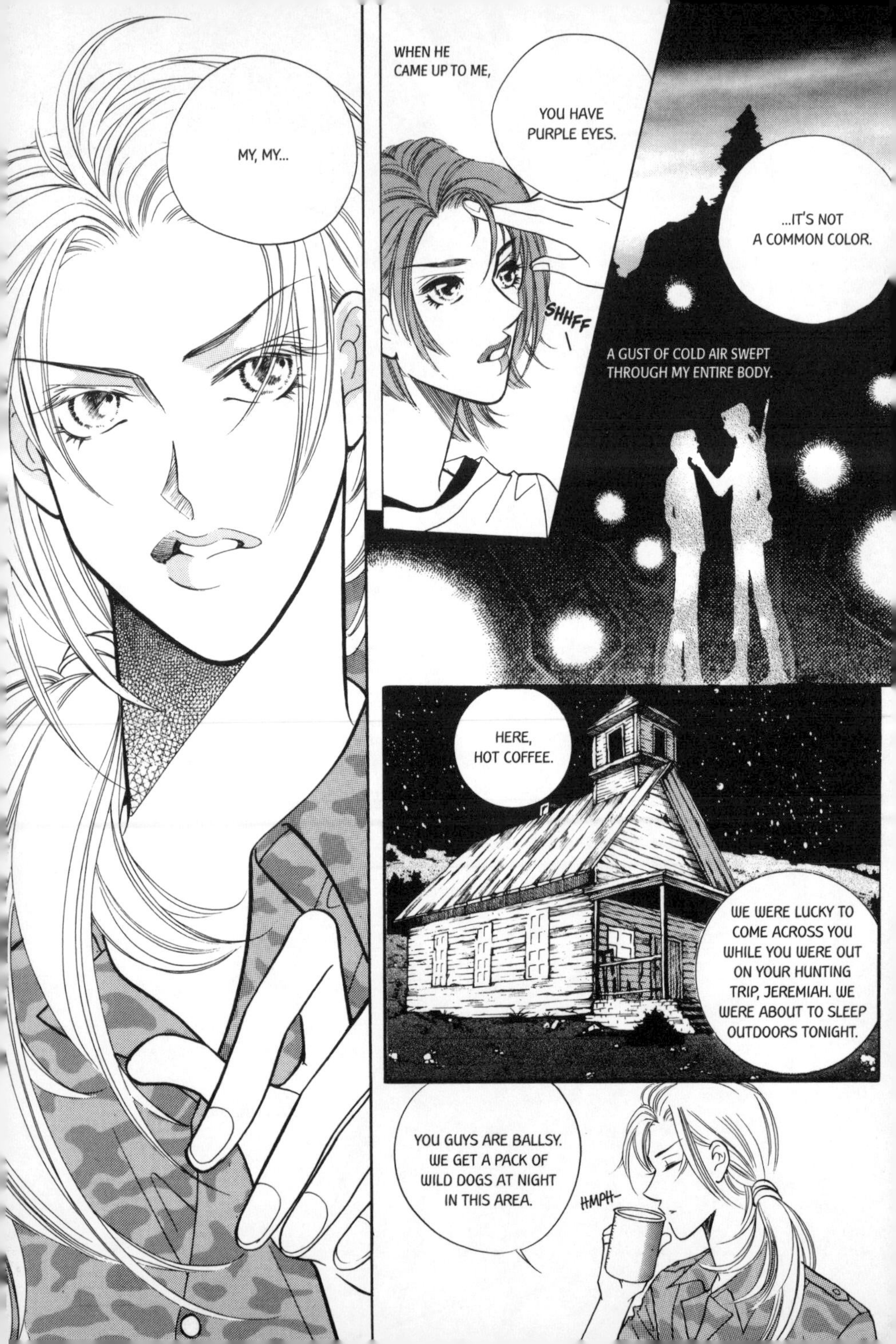
MY, MY...
WHEN HE CAME UP TO ME,
YOU HAVE PURPLE EYES.
...IT'S NOT A COMMON COLOR.
SHHFF
A GUST OF COLD AIR SWEPT THROUGH MY ENTIRE BODY.
HERE, HOT COFFEE.
WE WERE LUCKY TO COME ACROSS YOU WHILE YOU WERE OUT ON YOUR HUNTING TRIP, JEREMIAH. WE WERE ABOUT TO SLEEP OUTDOORS TONIGHT.
YOU GUYS ARE BALLSY. WE GET A PACK OF WILD DOGS AT NIGHT IN THIS AREA.
HMPH-

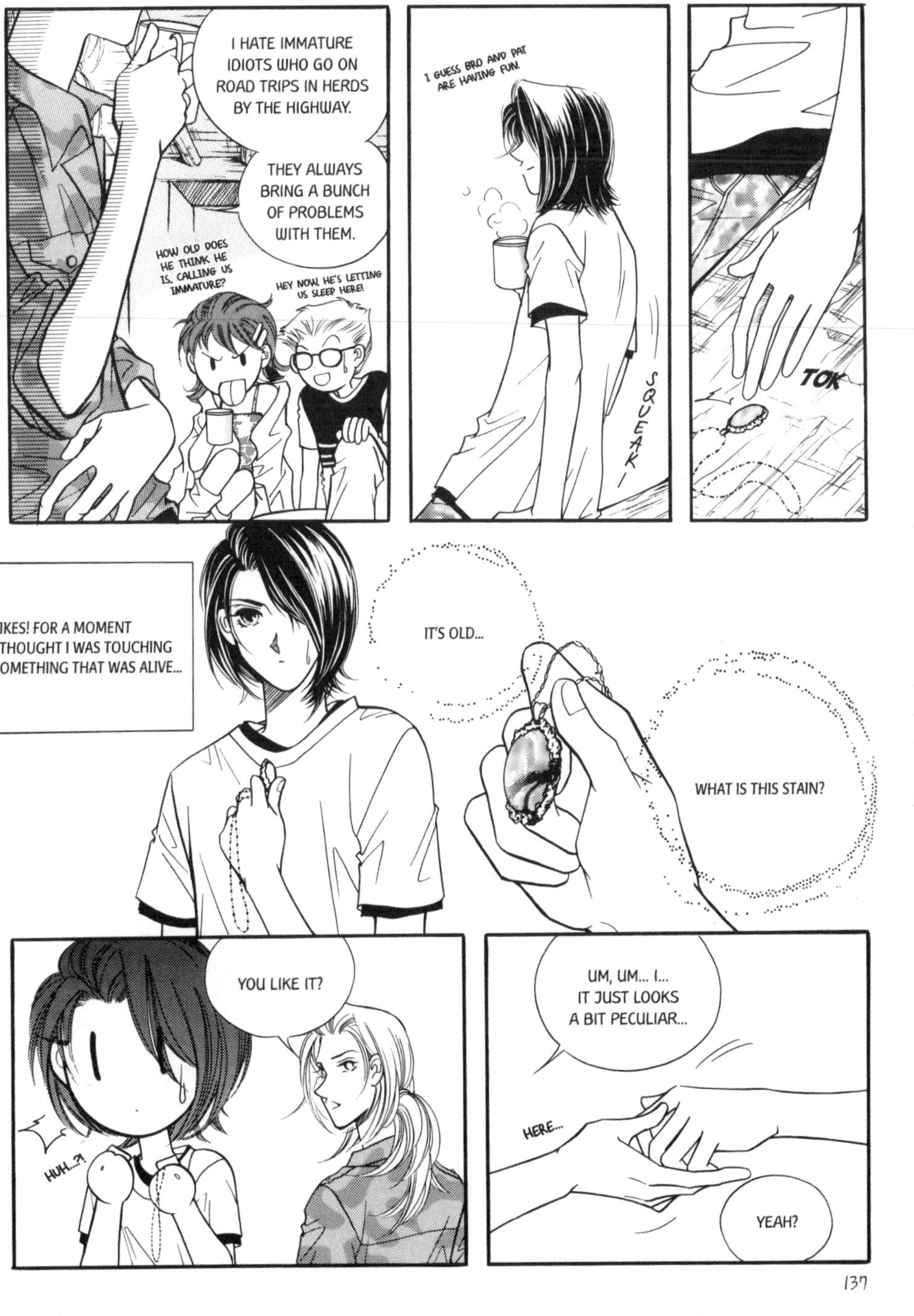
I HATE IMMATURE IDIOTS WHO GO ON ROAD TRIPS IN HERDS BY THE HIGHWAY.
THEY ALWAYS BRING A BUNCH OF PROBLEMS WITH THEM.
HOW OLD DOES HE THINK HE IS, CALLING US IMMATURE?
HEY NOW, HE'S LETTING US SLEEP HERE!
I GUESS BRO AND PAT ARE HAVING FUN.
SQUEAK!
TOK
YIKES! FOR A MOMENT I THOUGHT I WAS TOUCHING SOMETHING THAT WAS ALIVE...
IT'S OLD...
WHAT IS THIS STAIN?
YOU LIKE IT?
HUH...?!
UM, UM... I... IT JUST LOOKS A BIT PECULIAR...
HERE...
YEAH?

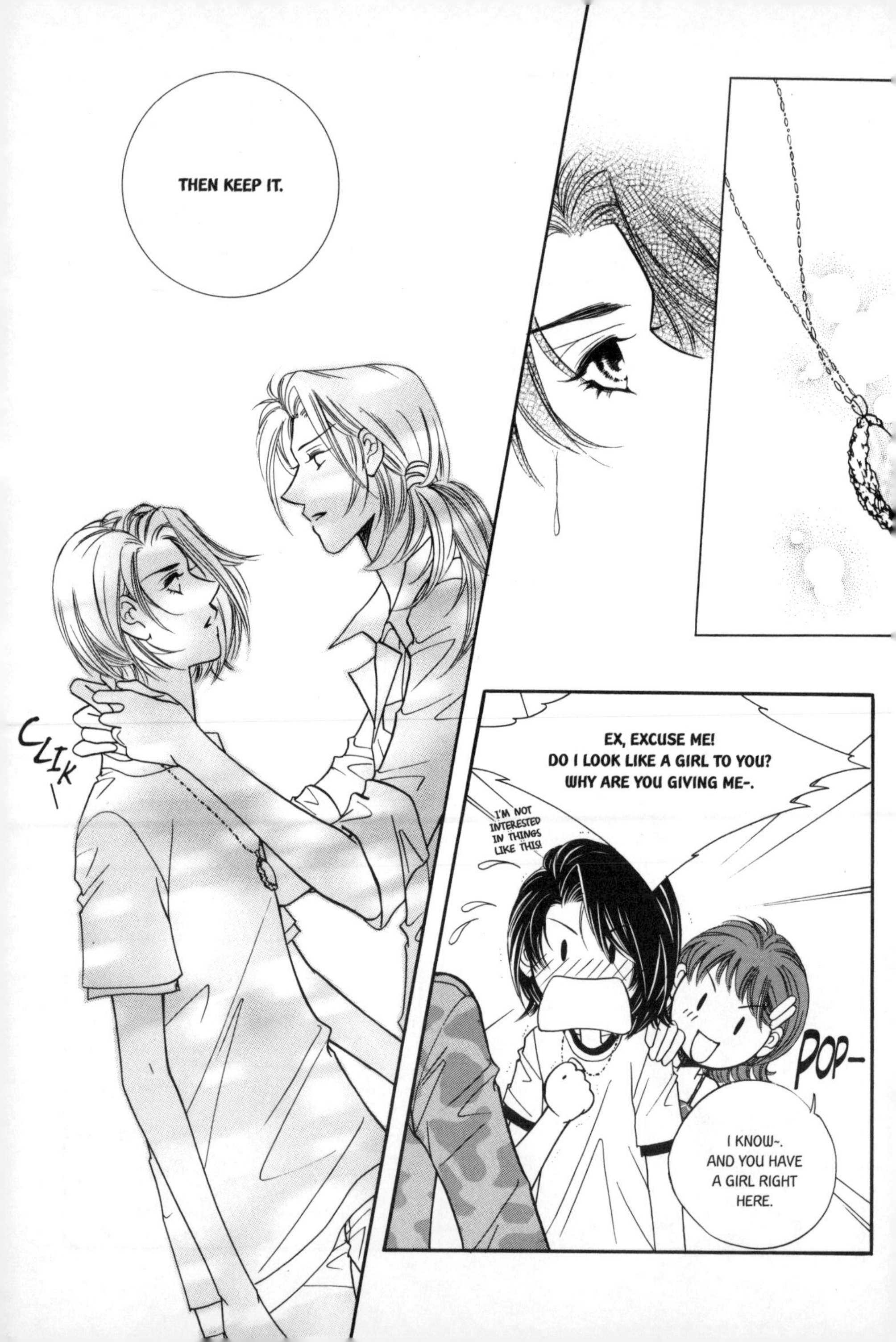
THEN KEEP IT.
CLIK
EX, EXCUSE ME! DO I LOOK LIKE A GIRL TO YOU? WHY ARE YOU GIVING ME-.
I'M NOT INTERESTED IN THINGS LIKE THIS!
POP-
I KNOW~. AND YOU HAVE A GIRL RIGHT HERE.

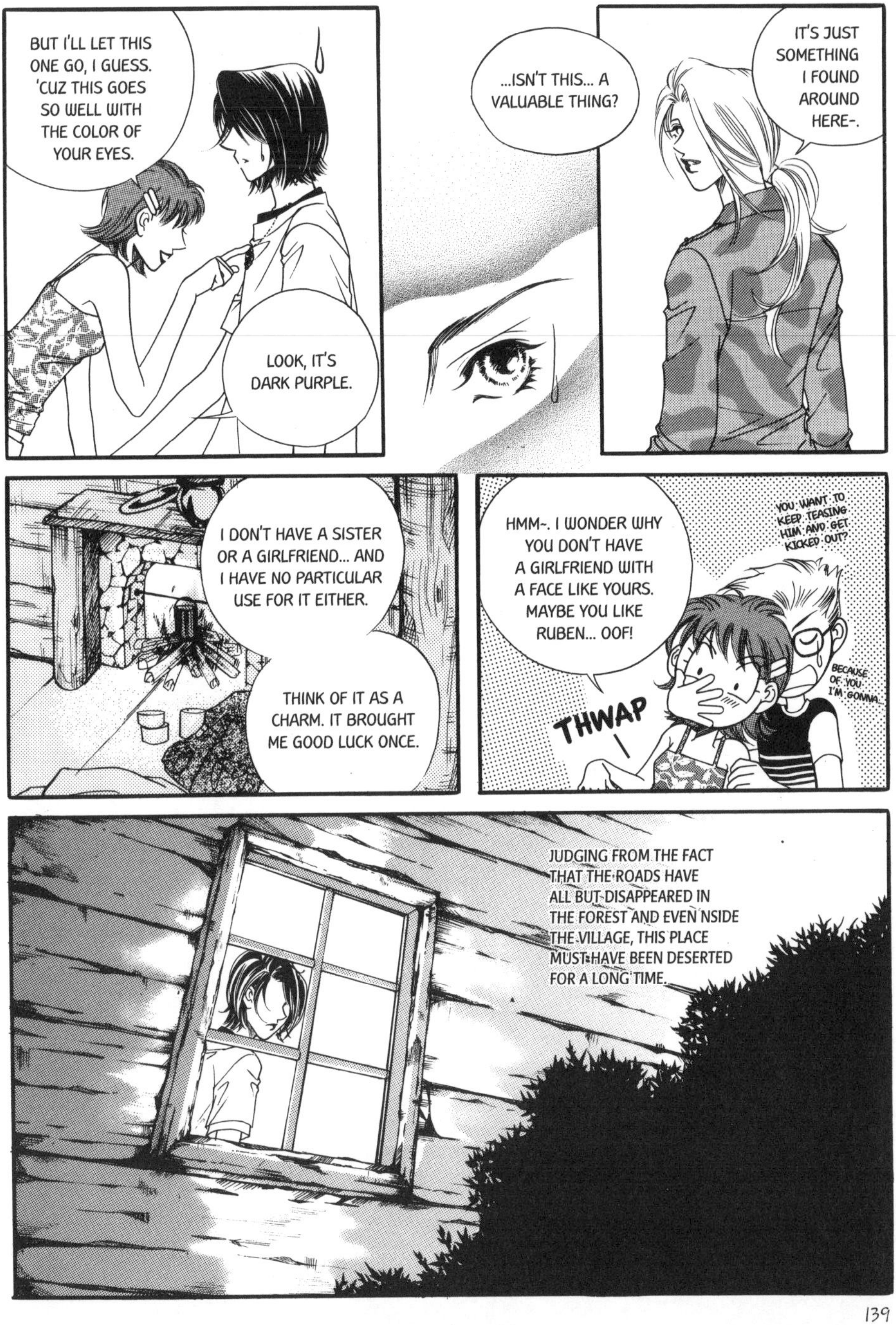
BUT I'LL LET THIS ONE GO, I GUESS. 'CUZ THIS GOES SO WELL WITH THE COLOR OF YOUR EYES.
LOOK, IT'S DARK PURPLE.
...ISN'T THIS... A VALUABLE THING?
IT'S JUST SOMETHING I FOUND AROUND HERE-.
I DON'T HAVE A SISTER OR A GIRLFRIEND... AND I HAVE NO PARTICULAR USE FOR IT EITHER.
THINK OF IT AS A CHARM. IT BROUGHT ME GOOD LUCK ONCE.
HMM~. I WONDER WHY YOU DON'T HAVE A GIRLFRIEND WITH A FACE LIKE YOURS. MAYBE YOU LIKE RUBEN... OOF!
YOU WANT TO KEEP TEASING HIM AND GET KICKED OUT?
THWAP
BECAUSE OF YOU I'M GONNA...
JUDGING FROM THE FACT THAT THE ROADS HAVE ALL BUT DISAPPEARED IN THE FOREST AND EVEN NSIDE THE VILLAGE, THIS PLACE MUST HAVE BEEN DESERTED FOR A LONG TIME.

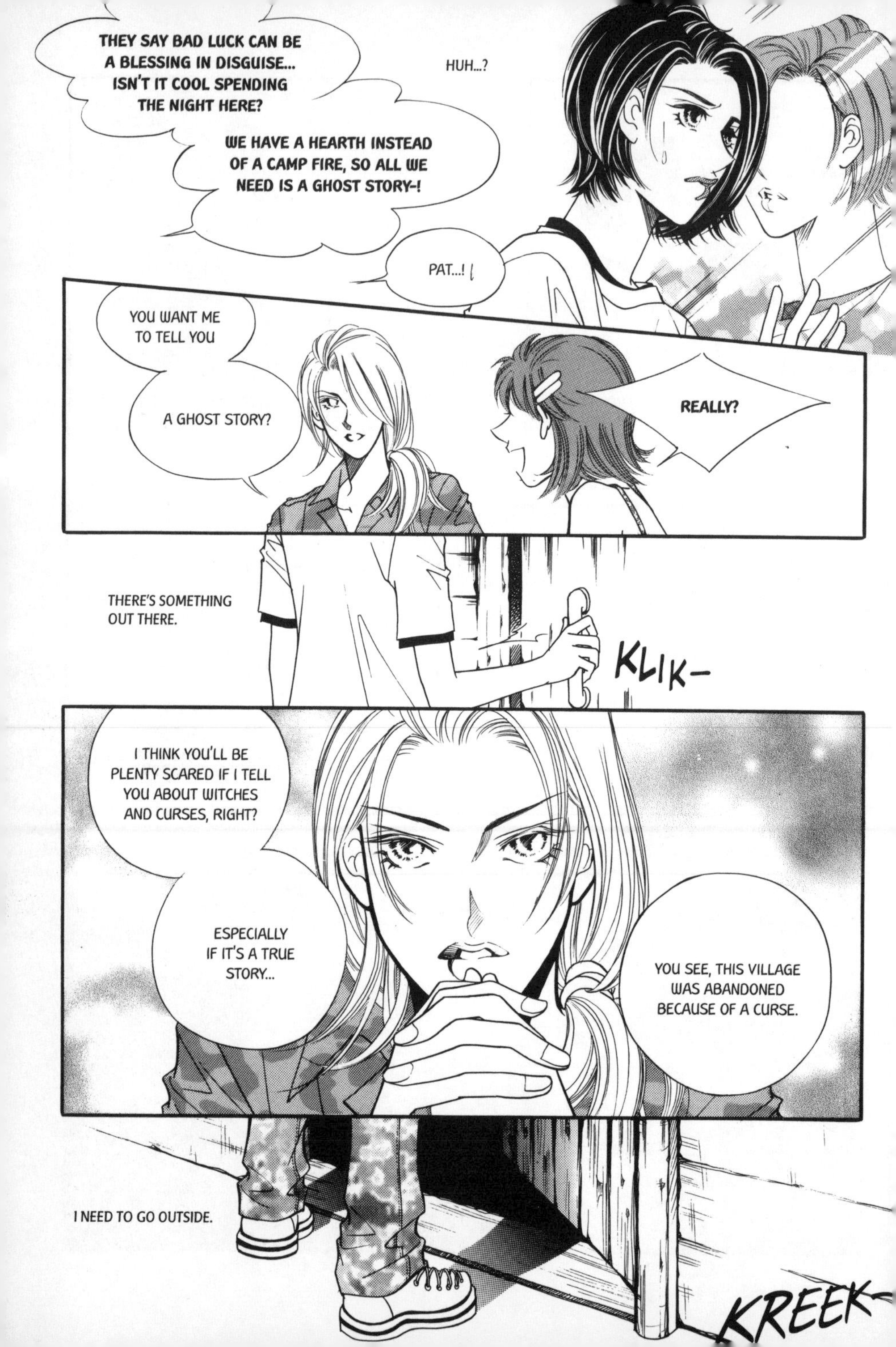
THEY SAY BAD LUCK CAN BE A BLESSING IN DISGUISE... ISN'T IT COOL SPENDING THE NIGHT HERE?
WE HAVE A HEARTH INSTEAD OF A CAMP FIRE, SO ALL WE NEED IS A GHOST STORY-!
HUH...?
PAT...!
YOU WANT ME TO TELL YOU
A GHOST STORY?
REALLY?
THERE'S SOMETHING OUT THERE.
KLIK-
I THINK YOU'LL BE PLENTY SCARED IF I TELL YOU ABOUT WITCHES AND CURSES, RIGHT?
ESPECIALLY IF IT'S A TRUE STORY...
YOU SEE, THIS VILLAGE WAS ABANDONED BECAUSE OF A CURSE.
I NEED TO GO OUTSIDE.
KREEK-

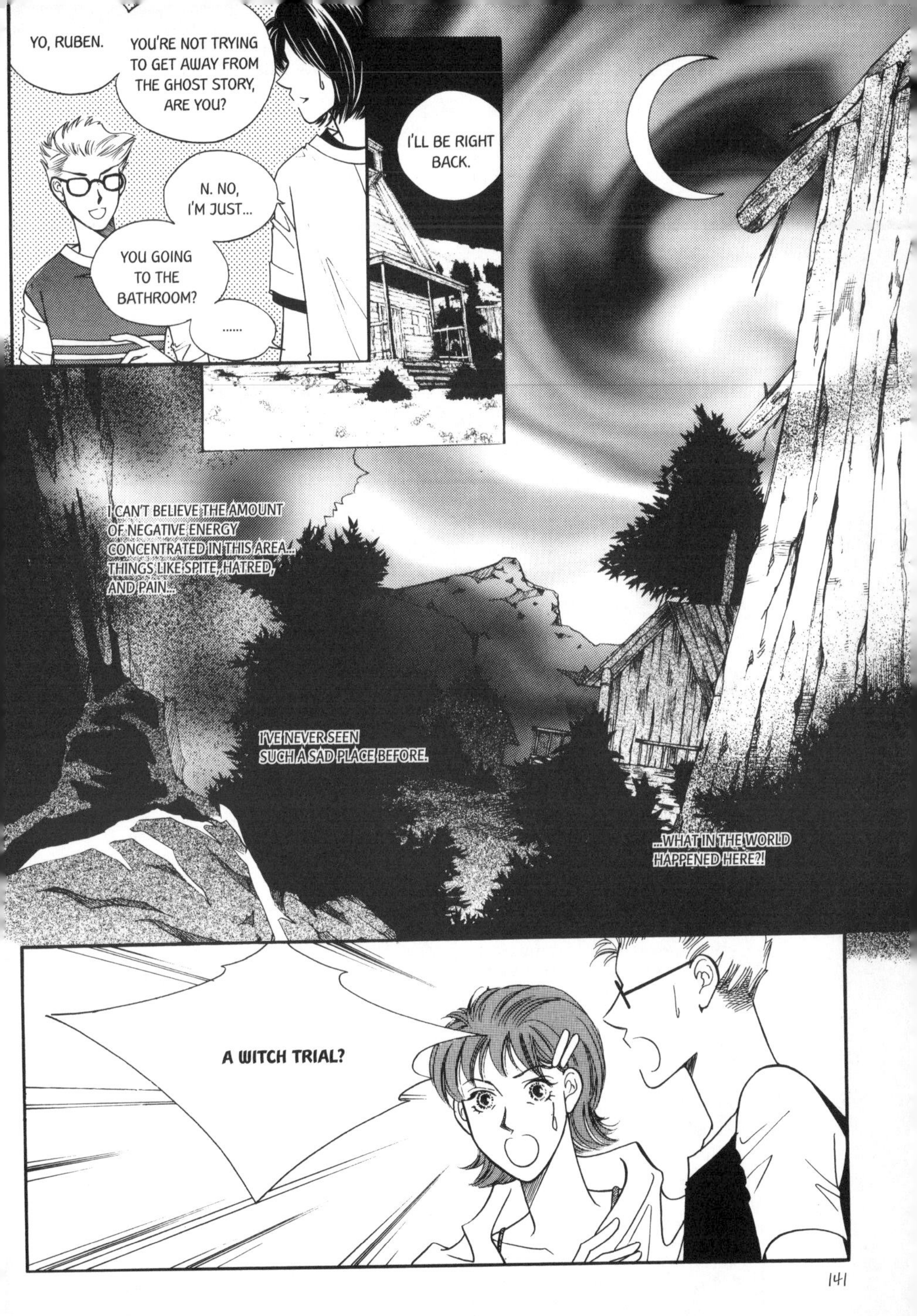
YO, RUBEN.
YOU'RE NOT TRYING TO GET AWAY FROM THE GHOST STORY, ARE YOU?
N. NO, I'M JUST...
YOU GOING TO THE BATHROOM?
......
I'LL BE RIGHT BACK.
I CAN'T BELIEVE THE AMOUNT OF NEGATIVE ENERGY CONCENTRATED IN THIS AREA... THINGS LIKE SPITE, HATRED, AND PAIN...
I'VE NEVER SEEN SUCH A SAD PLACE BEFORE.
...WHAT IN THE WORLD HAPPENED HERE?!
A WITCH TRIAL?

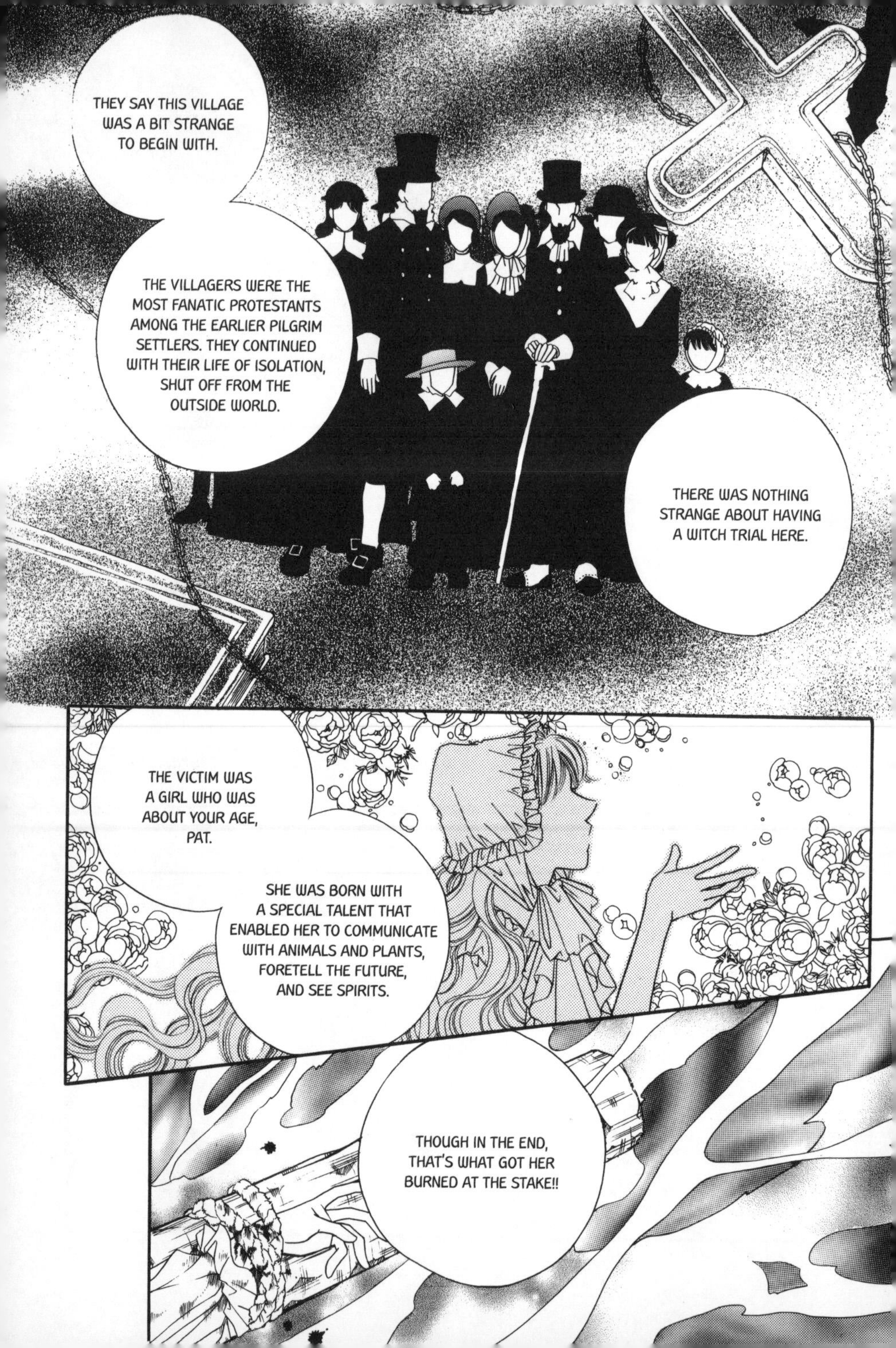

THEY SAY THIS VILLAGE WAS A BIT STRANGE TO BEGIN WITH.
THE VILLAGERS WERE THE MOST FANATIC PROTESTANTS AMONG THE EARLIER PILGRIM SETTLERS. THEY CONTINUED WITH THEIR LIFE OF ISOLATION, SHUT OFF FROM THE OUTSIDE WORLD.
THERE WAS NOTHING STRANGE ABOUT HAVING A WITCH TRIAL HERE.
THE VICTIM WAS A GIRL WHO WAS ABOUT YOUR AGE, PAT.
SHE WAS BORN WITH A SPECIAL TALENT THAT ENABLED HER TO COMMUNICATE WITH ANIMALS AND PLANTS, FORETELL THE FUTURE, AND SEE SPIRITS.
THOUGH IN THE END, THAT'S WHAT GOT HER BURNED AT THE STAKE!!

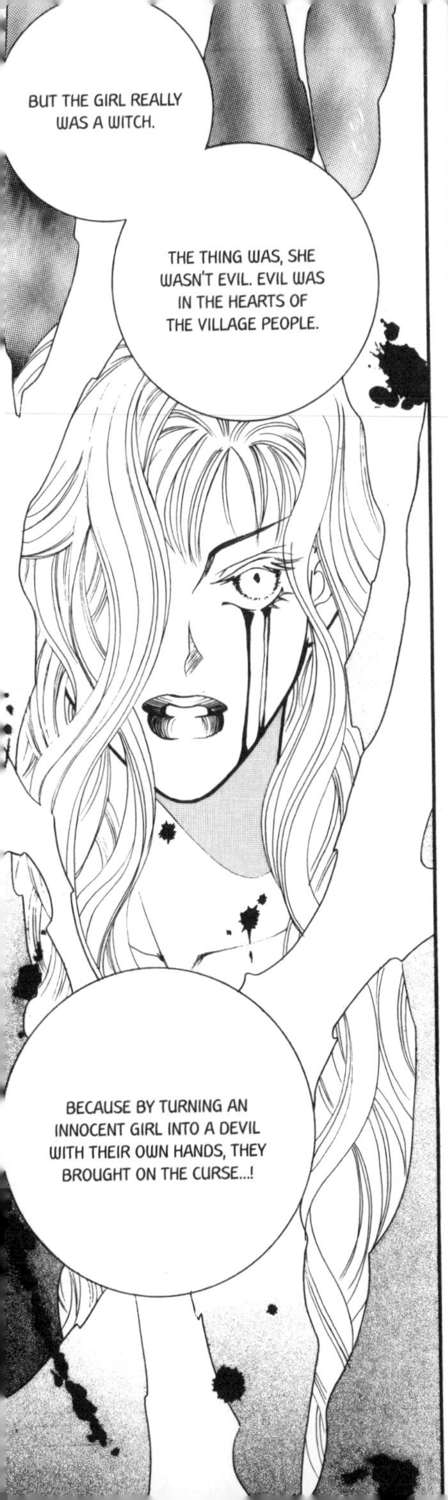
BUT THE GIRL REALLY WAS A WITCH.
THE THING WAS, SHE WASN'T EVIL. EVIL WAS IN THE HEARTS OF THE VILLAGE PEOPLE.
BECAUSE BY TURNING AN INNOCENT GIRL INTO A DEVIL WITH THEIR OWN HANDS, THEY BROUGHT ON THE CURSE...!

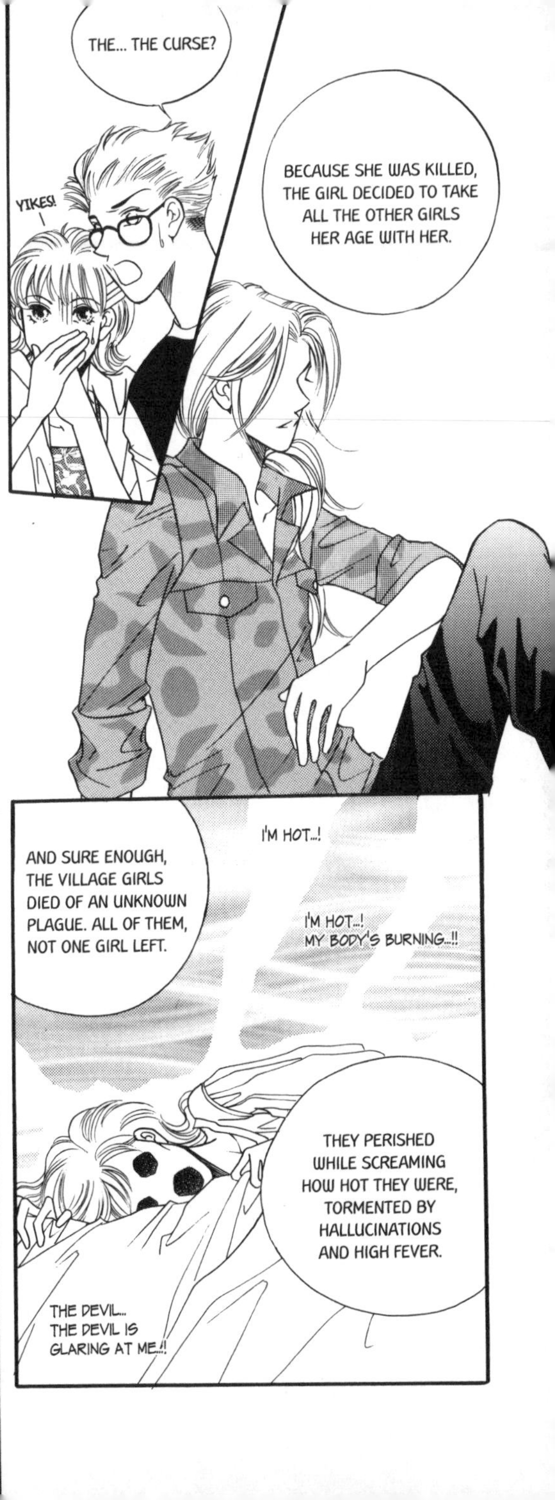
THE... THE CURSE?
YIKES!
BECAUSE SHE WAS KILLED, THE GIRL DECIDED TO TAKE ALL THE OTHER GIRLS HER AGE WITH HER.
AND SURE ENOUGH, THE VILLAGE GIRLS DIED OF AN UNKNOWN PLAGUE. ALL OF THEM, NOT ONE GIRL LEFT.
I'M HOT...!
I'M HOT...! MY BODY'S BURNING...!!
THEY PERISHED WHILE SCREAMING HOW HOT THEY WERE, TORMENTED BY HALLUCINATIONS AND HIGH FEVER.
THE DEVIL... THE DEVIL IS GLARING AT ME...!!

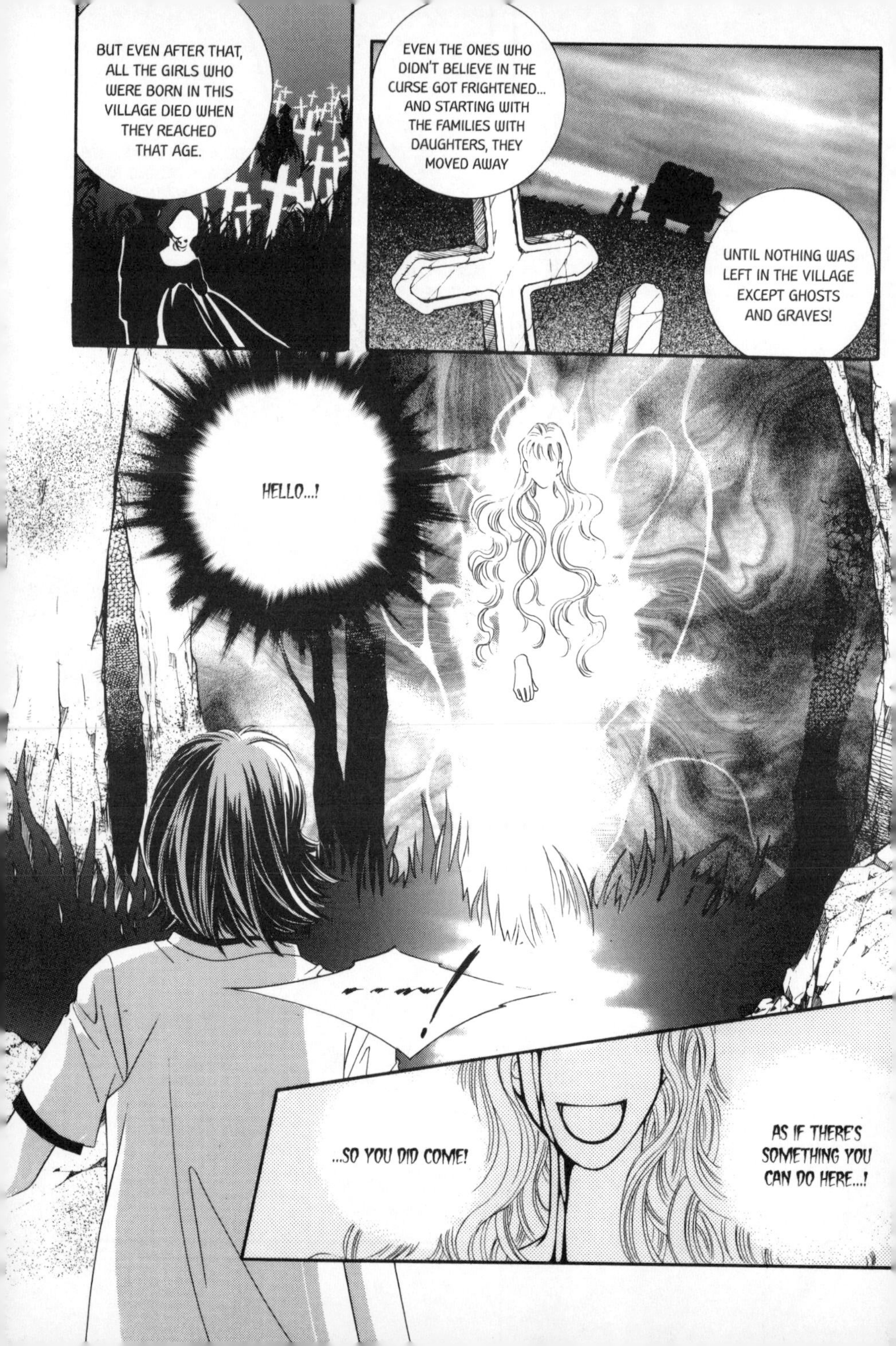
BUT EVEN AFTER THAT, ALL THE GIRLS WHO WERE BORN IN THIS VILLAGE DIED WHEN THEY REACHED THAT AGE.
EVEN THE ONES WHO DIDN'T BELIEVE IN THE CURSE GOT FRIGHTENED... AND STARTING WITH THE FAMILIES WITH DAUGHTERS, THEY MOVED AWAY
UNTIL NOTHING WAS LEFT IN THE VILLAGE EXCEPT GHOSTS AND GRAVES!
HELLO...!
...SO YOU DID COME!
AS IF THERE'S SOMETHING YOU CAN DO HERE...!

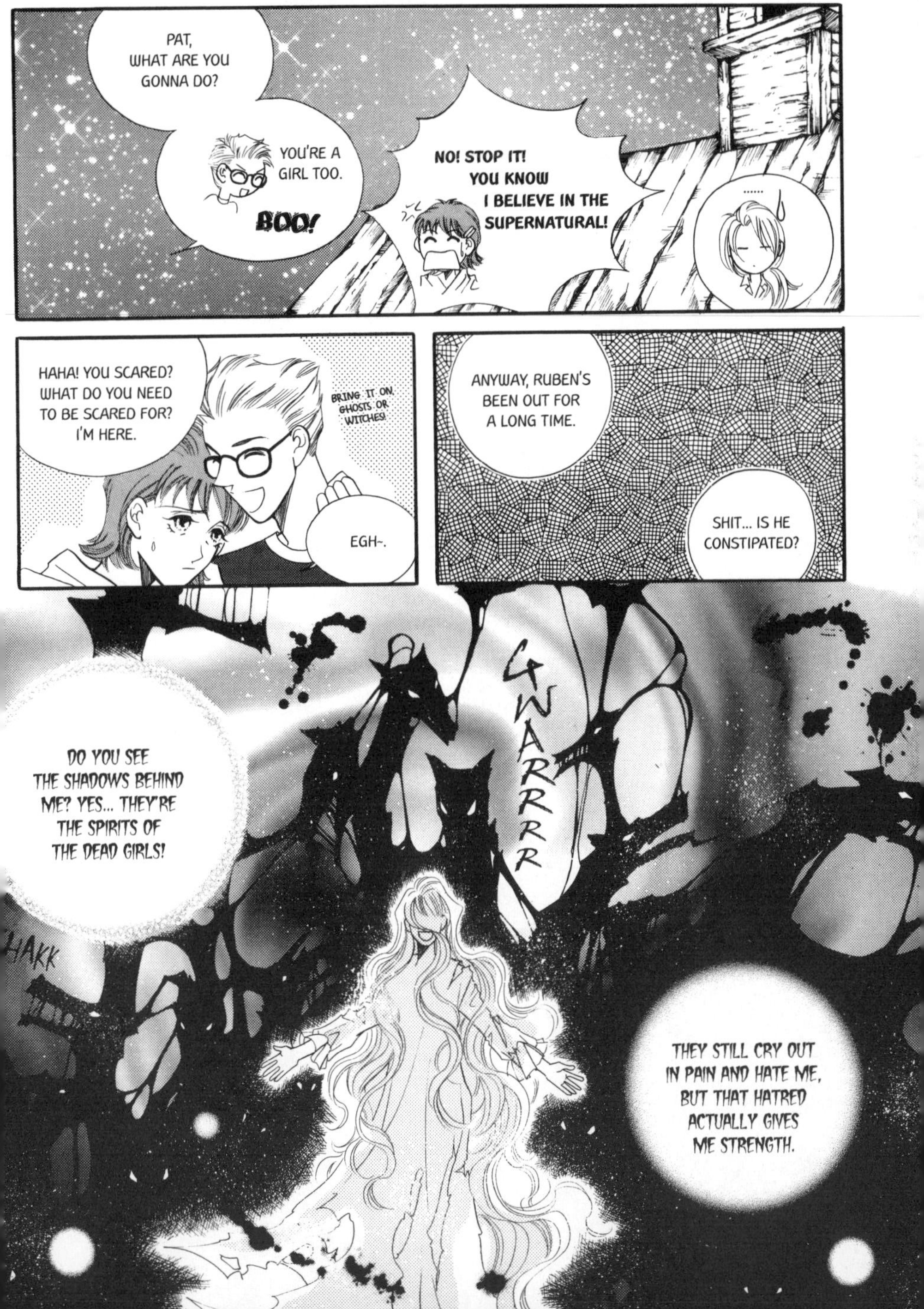
PAT, WHAT ARE YOU GONNA DO?
YOU'RE A GIRL TOO.
BOO!
NO! STOP IT! YOU KNOW I BELIEVE IN THE SUPERNATURAL!
......
HAHA! YOU SCARED? WHAT DO YOU NEED TO BE SCARED FOR? I'M HERE.
BRING IT ON, GHOSTS OR WITCHES!
EGH~.
ANYWAY, RUBEN'S BEEN OUT FOR A LONG TIME.
SHIT... IS HE CONSTIPATED?
DO YOU SEE THE SHADOWS BEHIND ME? YES... THEY'RE THE SPIRITS OF THE DEAD GIRLS!
GWARRRR
HAKK
THEY STILL CRY OUT IN PAIN AND HATE ME, BUT THAT HATRED ACTUALLY GIVES ME STRENGTH.

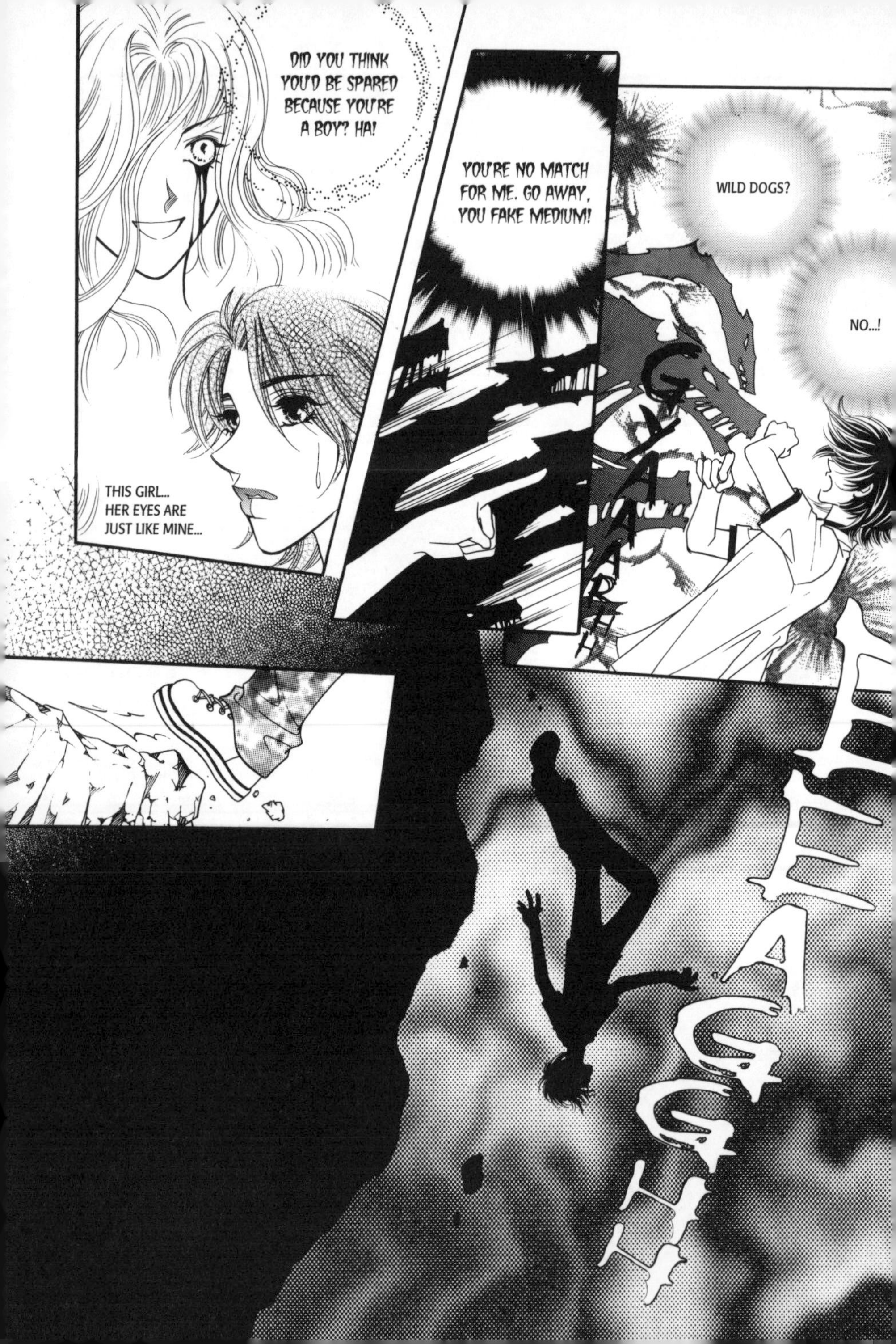
DID YOU THINK YOU'D BE SPARED BECAUSE YOU'RE A BOY? HA!
THIS GIRL... HER EYES ARE JUST LIKE MINE...
YOU'RE NO MATCH FOR ME. GO AWAY, YOU FAKE MEDIUM!
GYAAARH
WILD DOGS?
NO...!
EEAGGHH

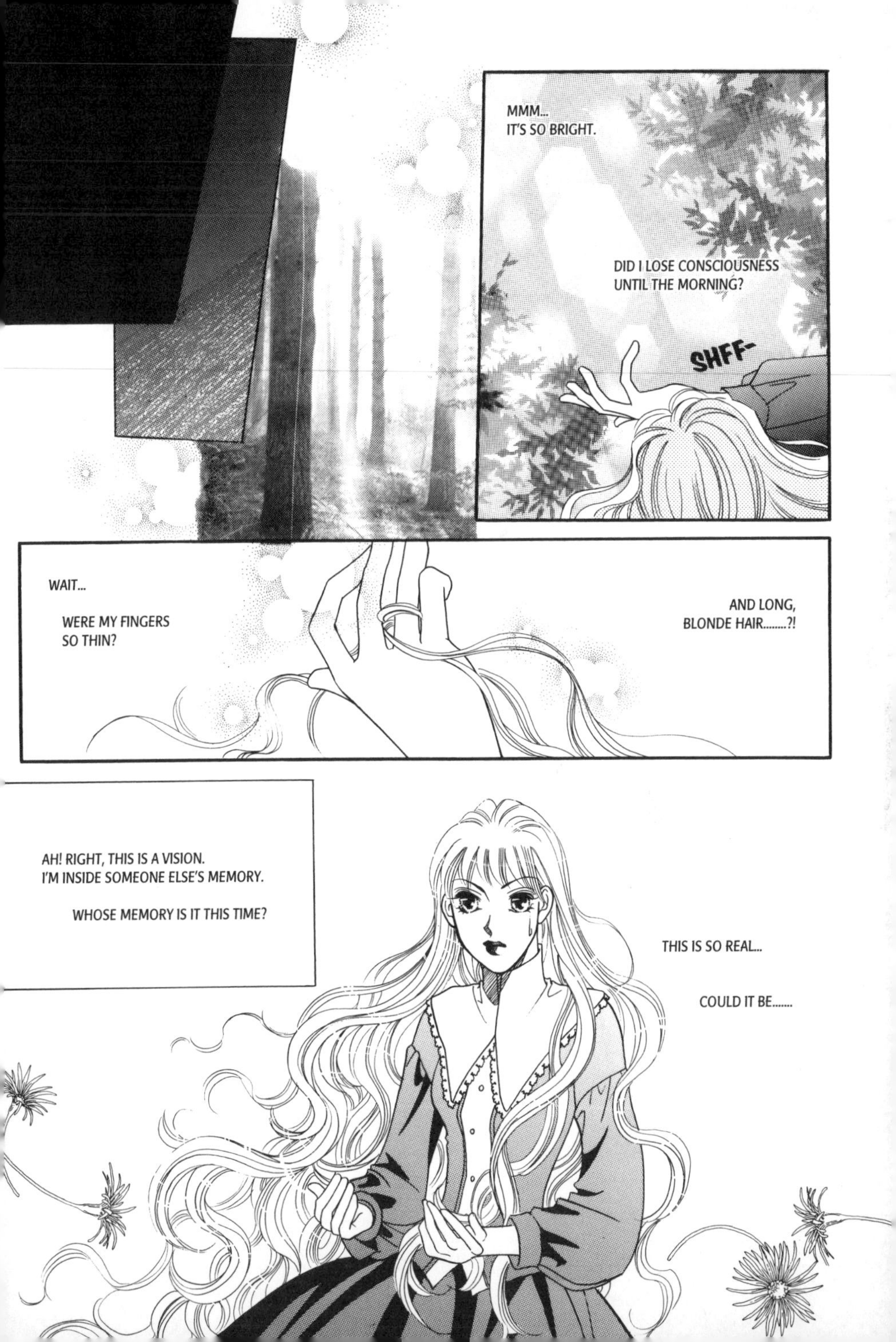
MMM...
IT'S SO BRIGHT.
DID I LOSE CONSCIOUSNESS
UNTIL THE MORNING?
SHFF-
WAIT...
WERE MY FINGERS
SO THIN?
AND LONG,
BLONDE HAIR........?!
AH! RIGHT, THIS IS A VISION.
I'M INSIDE SOMEONE ELSE'S MEMORY.
WHOSE MEMORY IS IT THIS TIME?
THIS IS SO REAL...
COULD IT BE.......

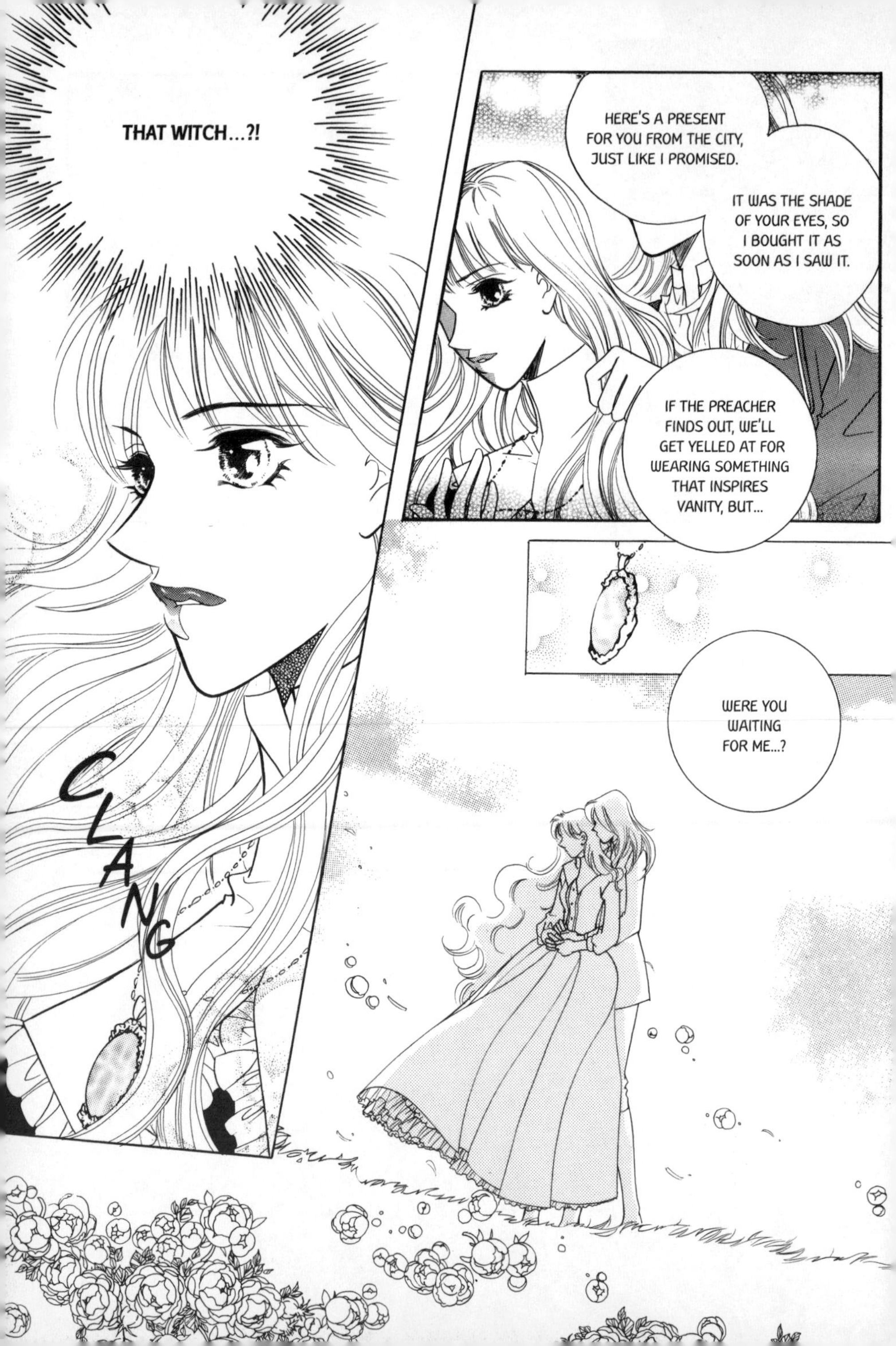
THAT WITCH...?!
CLANG
HERE'S A PRESENT FOR YOU FROM THE CITY, JUST LIKE I PROMISED.
IT WAS THE SHADE OF YOUR EYES, SO I BOUGHT IT AS SOON AS I SAW IT.
IF THE PREACHER FINDS OUT, WE'LL GET YELLED AT FOR WEARING SOMETHING THAT INSPIRES VANITY, BUT...
WERE YOU WAITING FOR ME...?

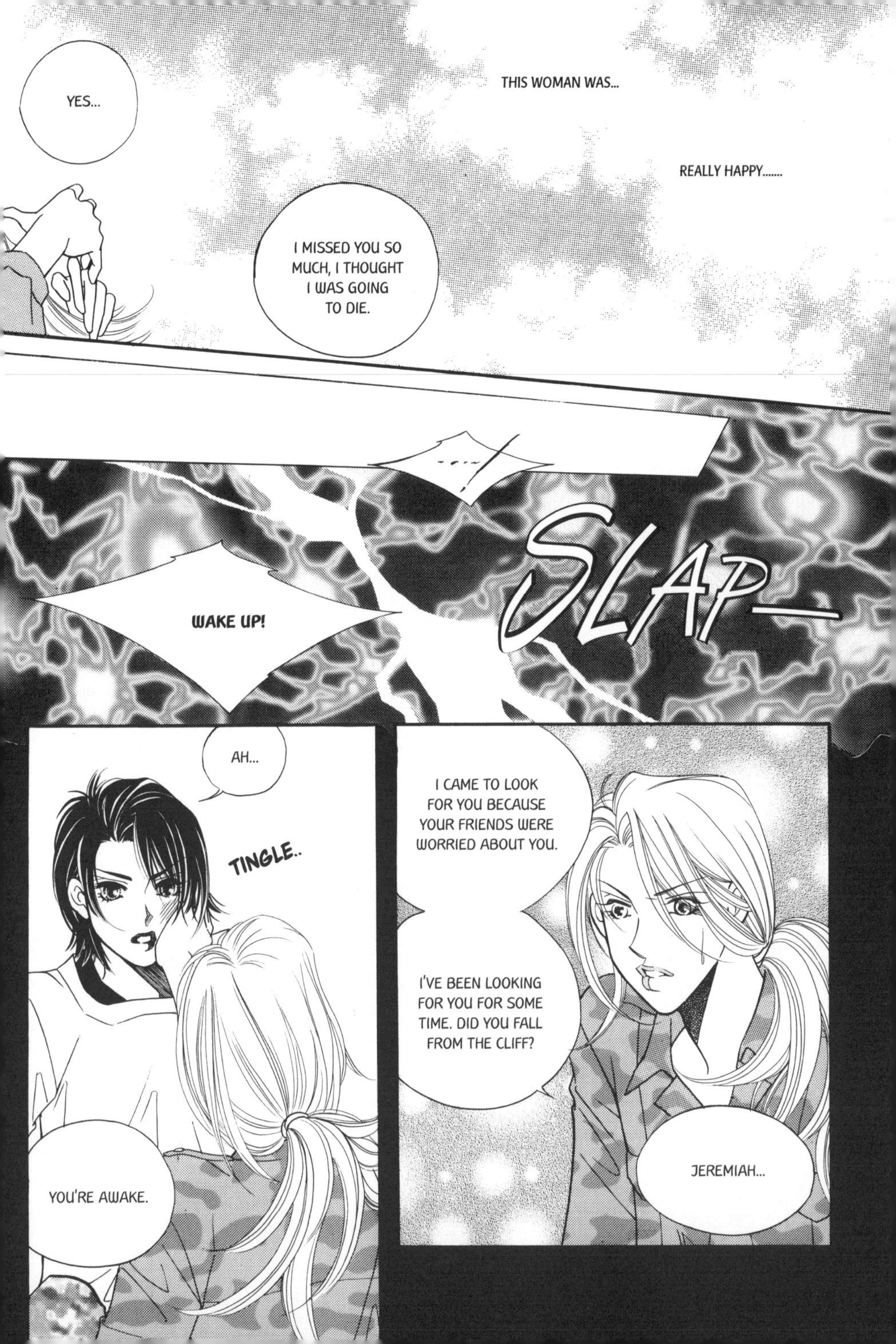

YES...
I MISSED YOU SO MUCH, I THOUGHT I WAS GOING TO DIE.
THIS WOMAN WAS...
REALLY HAPPY.......
WAKE UP!
SLAP—
AH...
TINGLE..
YOU'RE AWAKE.
I CAME TO LOOK FOR YOU BECAUSE YOUR FRIENDS WERE WORRIED ABOUT YOU.
I'VE BEEN LOOKING FOR YOU FOR SOME TIME. DID YOU FALL FROM THE CLIFF?
JEREMIAH...

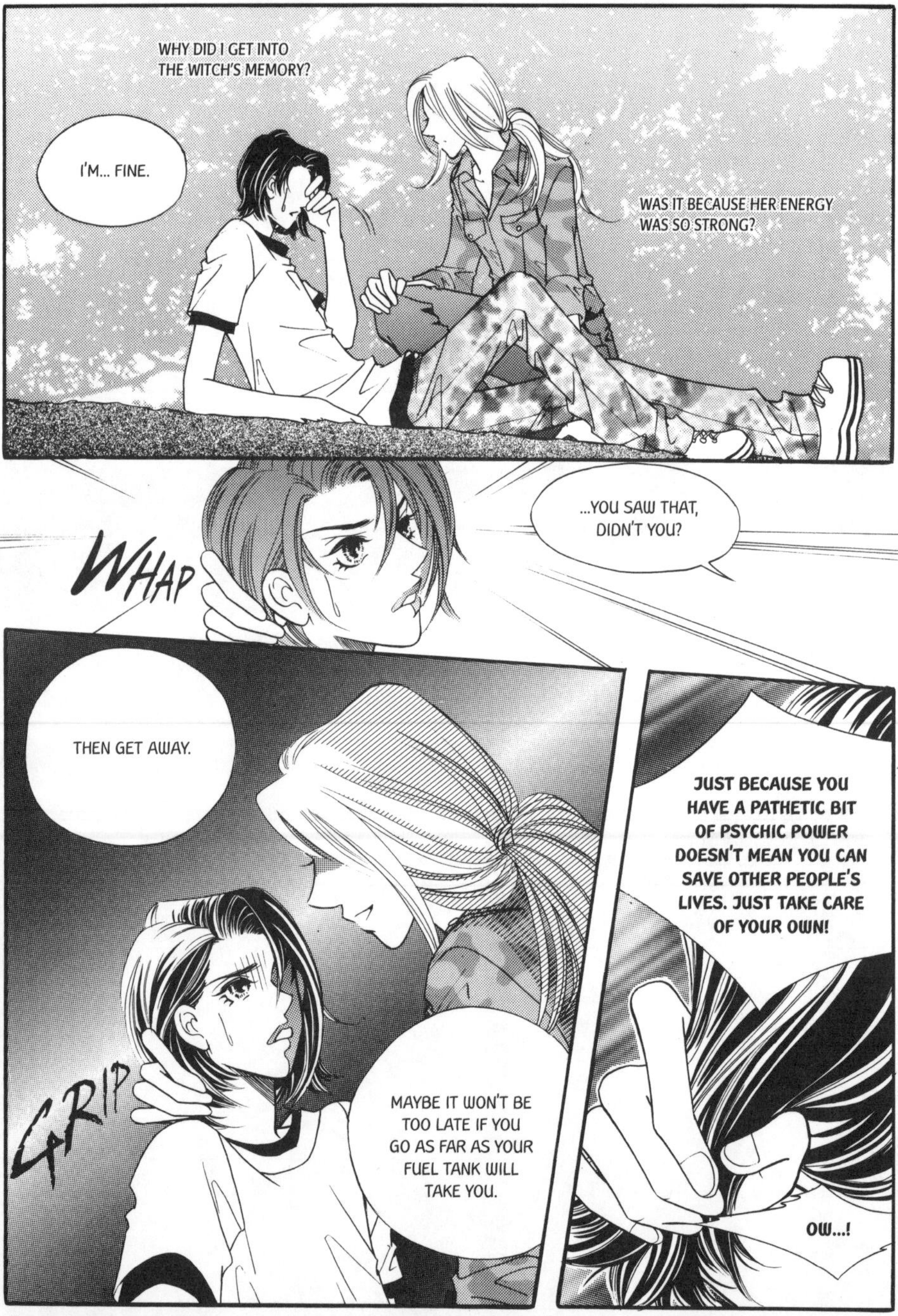
WHY DID I GET INTO THE WITCH'S MEMORY?
I'M... FINE.
WAS IT BECAUSE HER ENERGY WAS SO STRONG?
WHAP
...YOU SAW THAT, DIDN'T YOU?
THEN GET AWAY.
GRIP
MAYBE IT WON'T BE TOO LATE IF YOU GO AS FAR AS YOUR FUEL TANK WILL TAKE YOU.
JUST BECAUSE YOU HAVE A PATHETIC BIT OF PSYCHIC POWER DOESN'T MEAN YOU CAN SAVE OTHER PEOPLE'S LIVES. JUST TAKE CARE OF YOUR OWN!
OW...!

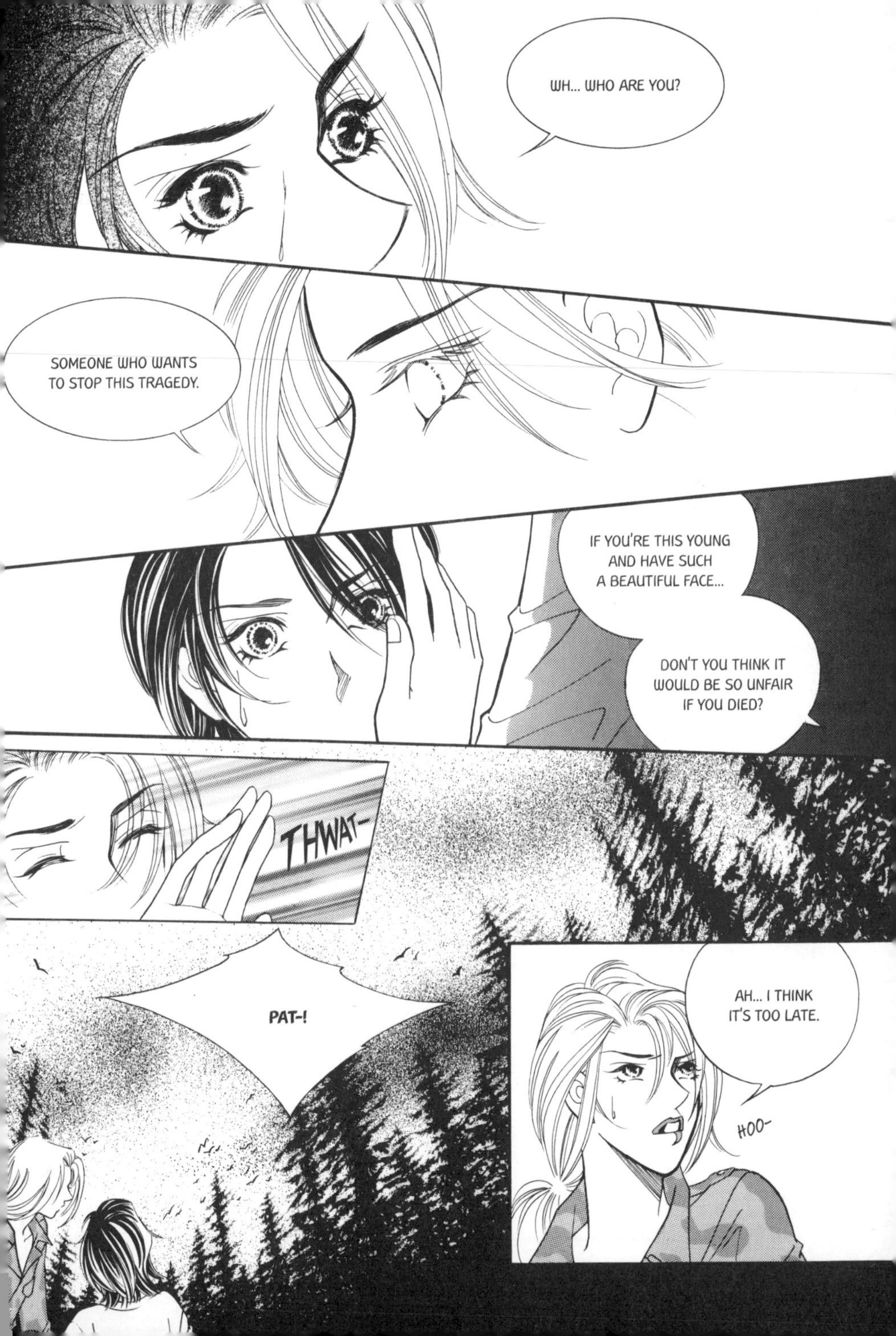
WH... WHO ARE YOU?
SOMEONE WHO WANTS TO STOP THIS TRAGEDY.
IF YOU'RE THIS YOUNG AND HAVE SUCH A BEAUTIFUL FACE...
DON'T YOU THINK IT WOULD BE SO UNFAIR IF YOU DIED?
THWAT-
PAT-!
AH... I THINK IT'S TOO LATE.
HOO-

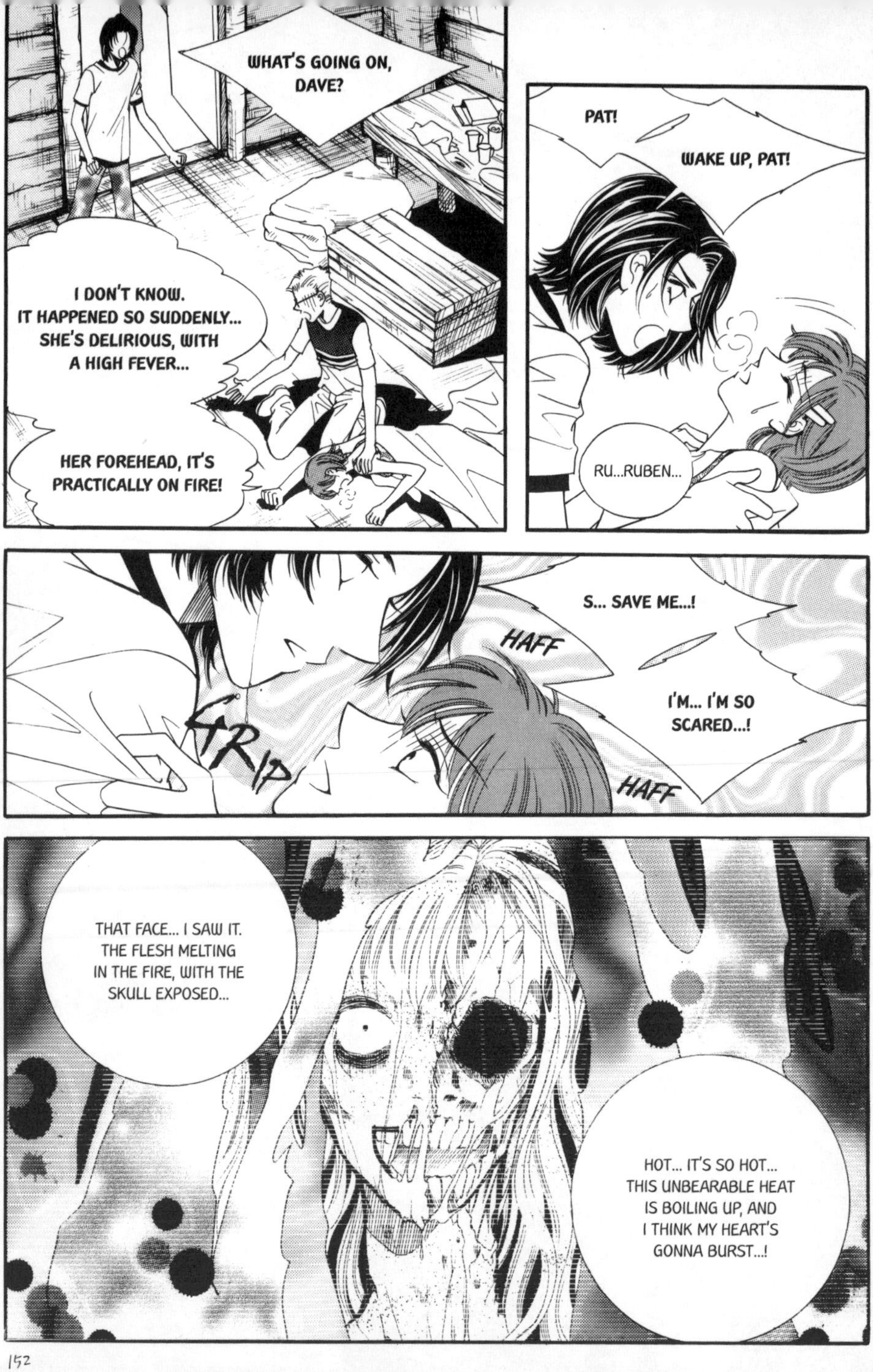
WHAT'S GOING ON, DAVE?
I DON'T KNOW. IT HAPPENED SO SUDDENLY... SHE'S DELIRIOUS, WITH A HIGH FEVER...
HER FOREHEAD, IT'S PRACTICALLY ON FIRE!
PAT!
WAKE UP, PAT!
RU...RUBEN...
GRIP
HAFF
S... SAVE ME...!
I'M... I'M SO SCARED...!
HAFF
THAT FACE... I SAW IT. THE FLESH MELTING IN THE FIRE, WITH THE SKULL EXPOSED...
HOT... IT'S SO HOT... THIS UNBEARABLE HEAT IS BOILING UP, AND I THINK MY HEART'S GONNA BURST...!

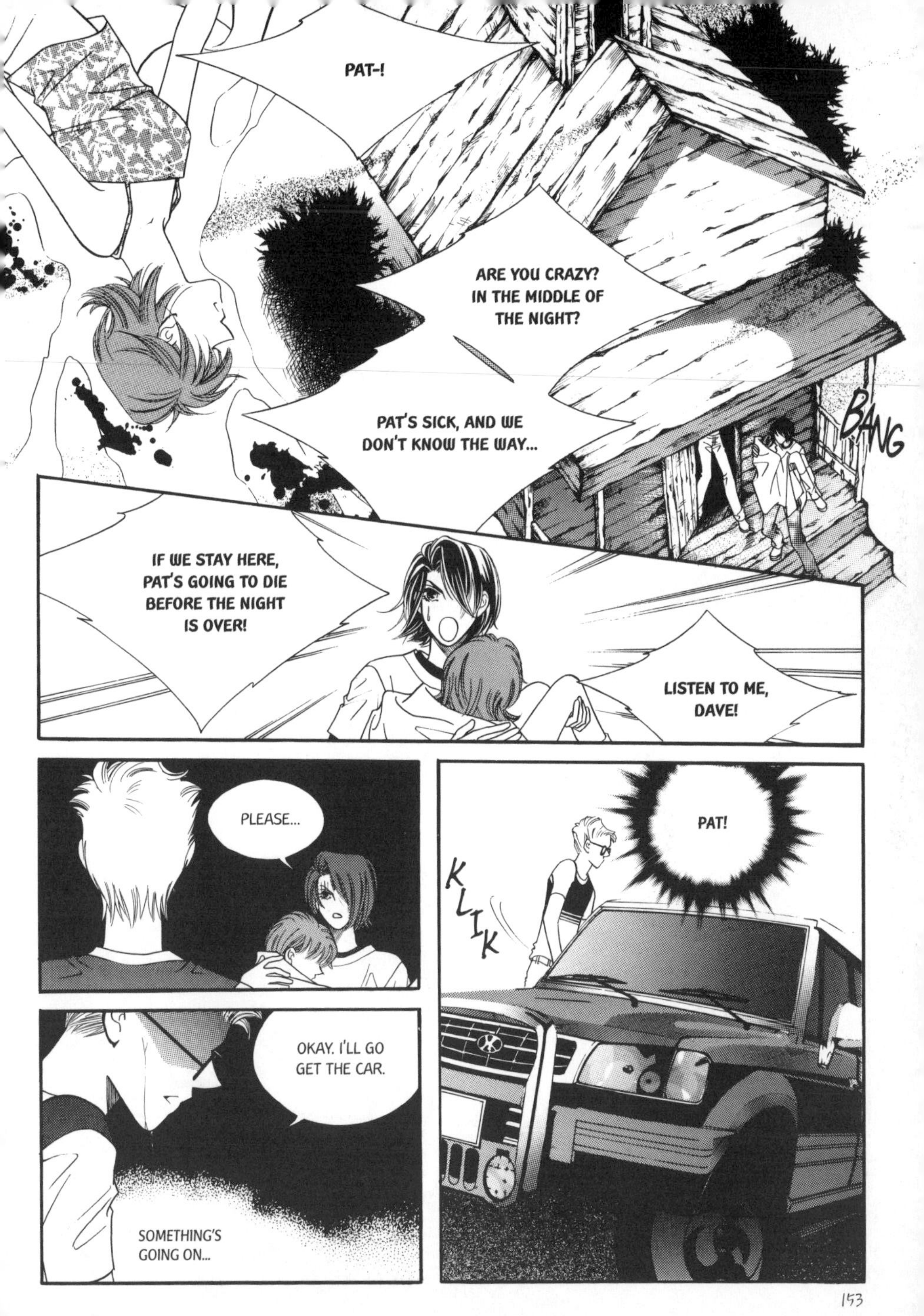
PAT-!
ARE YOU CRAZY? IN THE MIDDLE OF THE NIGHT?
PAT'S SICK, AND WE DON'T KNOW THE WAY...
BANG
IF WE STAY HERE, PAT'S GOING TO DIE BEFORE THE NIGHT IS OVER!
LISTEN TO ME, DAVE!
PLEASE...
OKAY. I'LL GO GET THE CAR.
SOMETHING'S GOING ON...
PAT!
KLIK

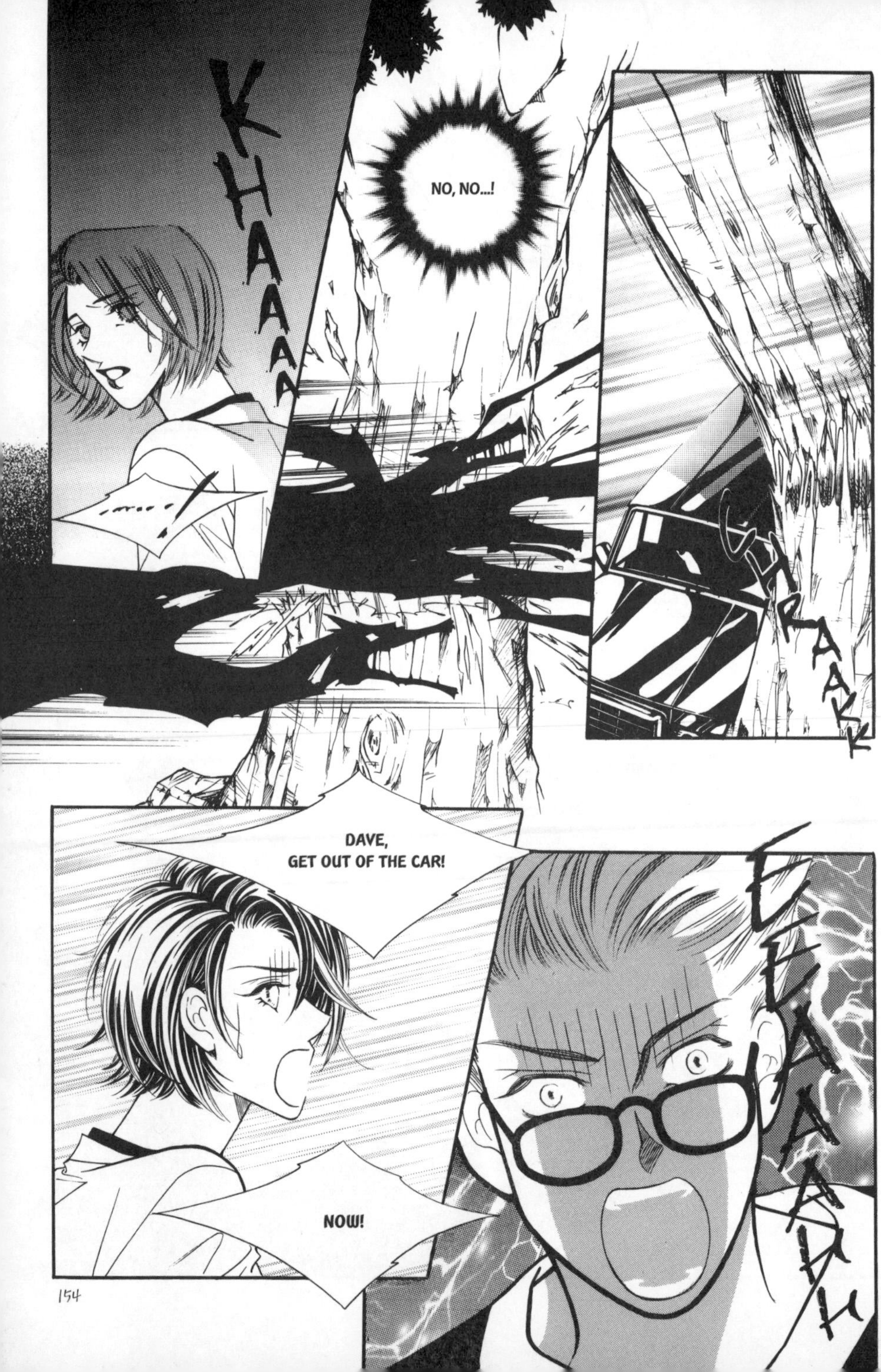
KHAAAA
NO, NO...!
DAVE,
GET OUT OF THE CAR!
NOW!

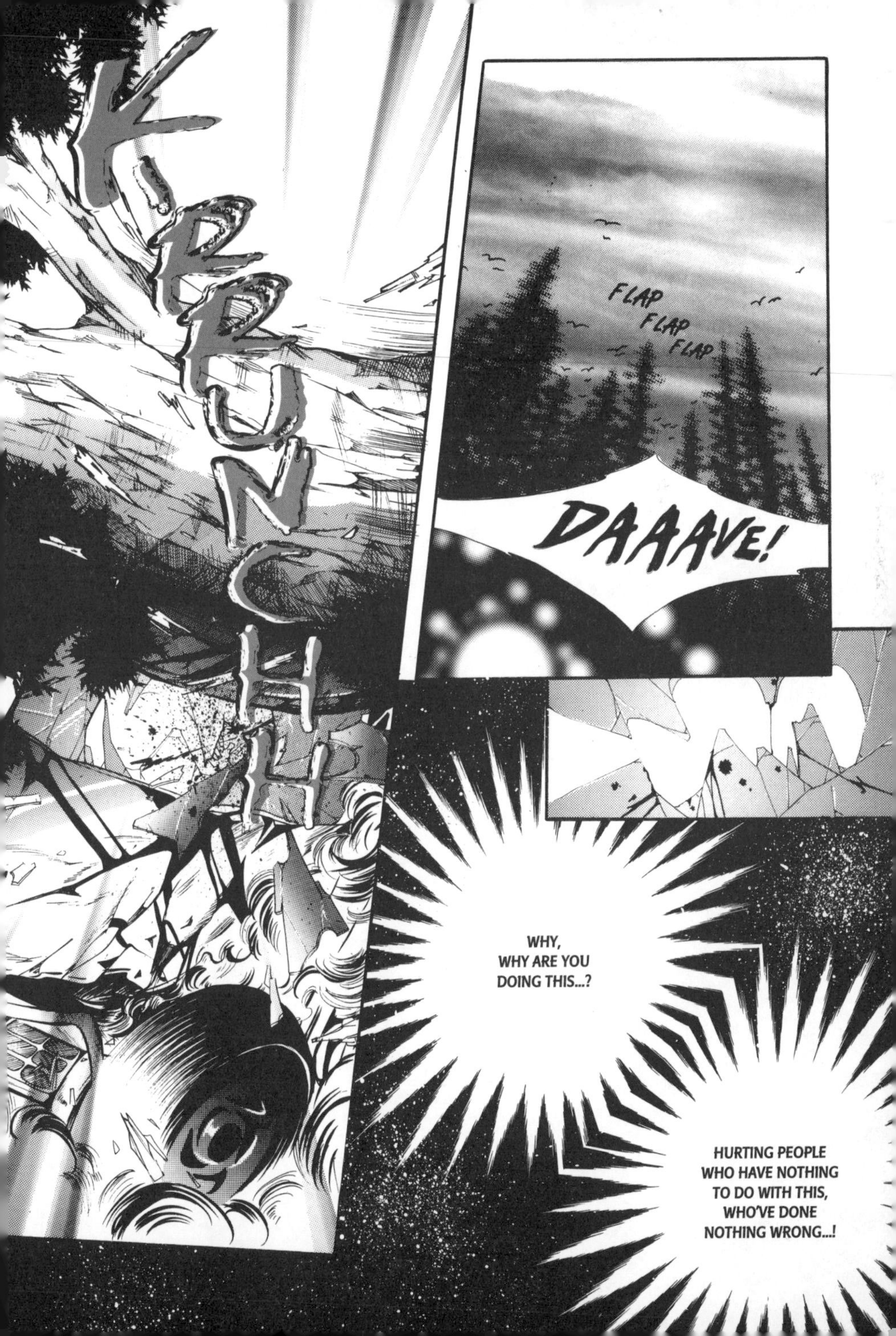
KRRUNCHHH
FLAP
FLAP
FLAP
DAAAVE!
WHY,
WHY ARE YOU
DOING THIS...?
HURTING PEOPLE
WHO HAVE NOTHING
TO DO WITH THIS,
WHO'VE DONE
NOTHING WRONG...!

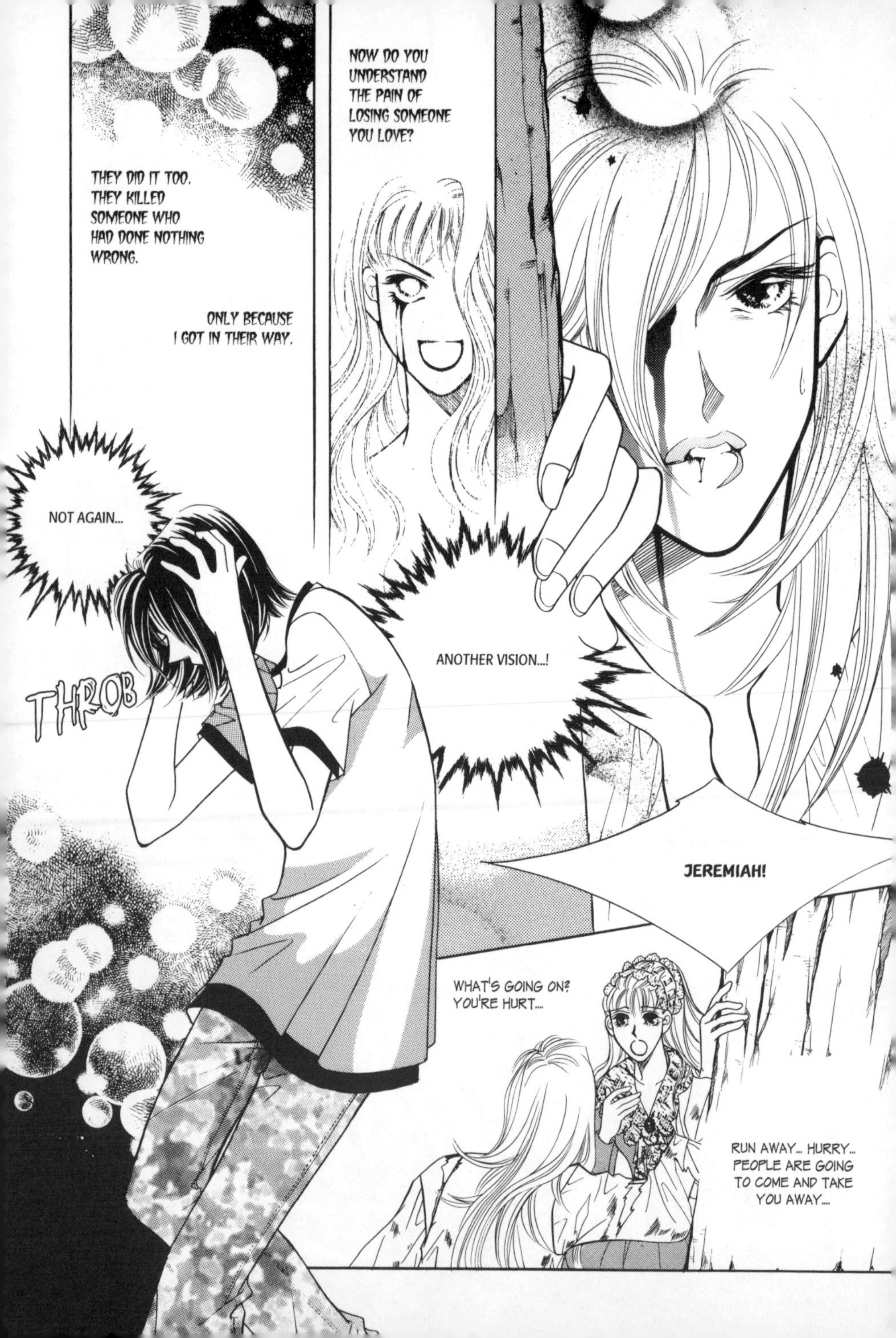
THEY DID IT TOO. THEY KILLED SOMEONE WHO HAD DONE NOTHING WRONG.
ONLY BECAUSE I GOT IN THEIR WAY.
NOW DO YOU UNDERSTAND THE PAIN OF LOSING SOMEONE YOU LOVE?
NOT AGAIN...
THROB
ANOTHER VISION...!
JEREMIAH!
WHAT'S GOING ON? YOU'RE HURT....
RUN AWAY... HURRY... PEOPLE ARE GOING TO COME AND TAKE YOU AWAY....

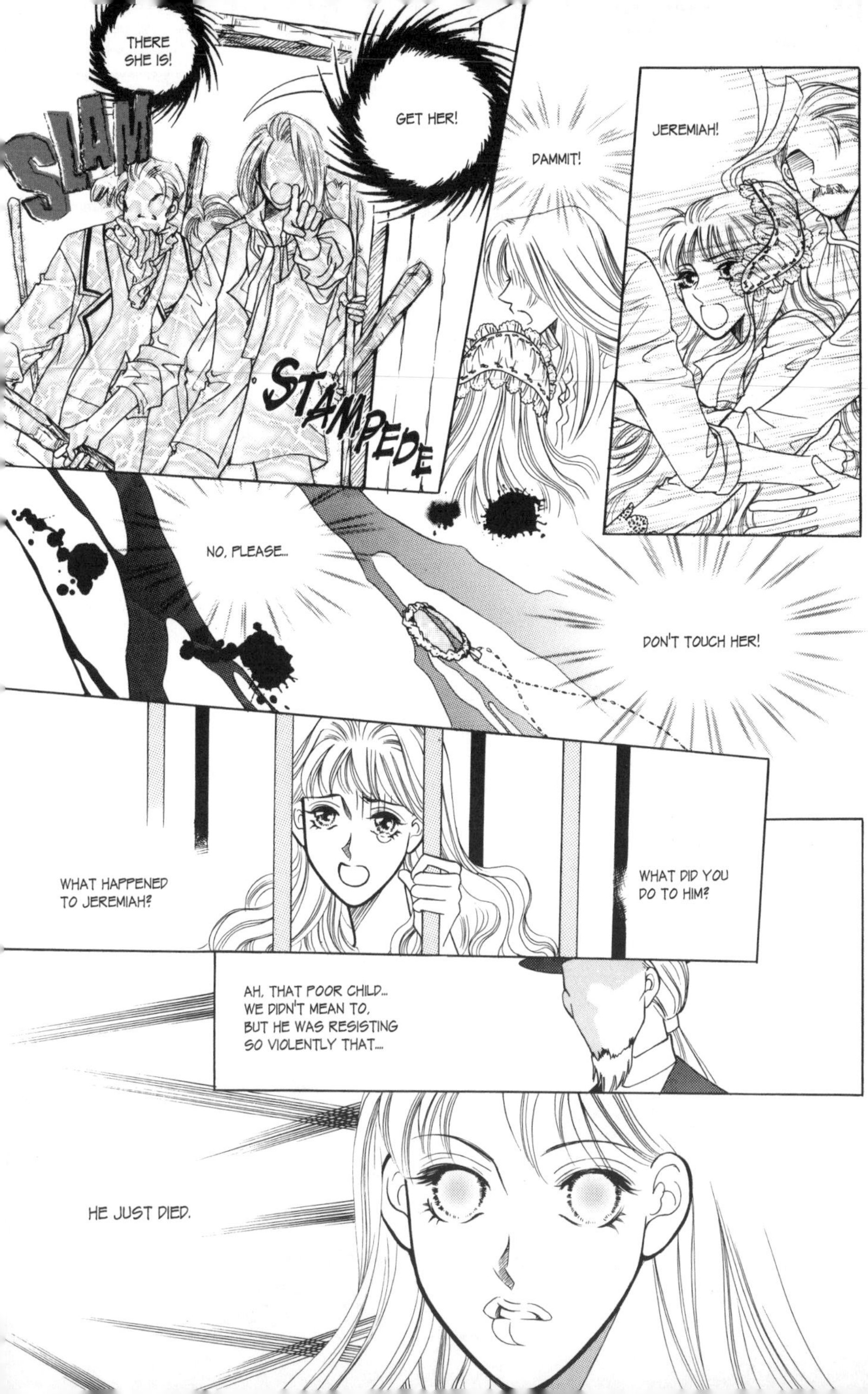
THERE SHE IS!
SLAM
GET HER!
STAMPEDE
DAMMIT!
JEREMIAH!
NO, PLEASE...
DON'T TOUCH HER!
WHAT HAPPENED TO JEREMIAH?
WHAT DID YOU DO TO HIM?
AH, THAT POOR CHILD... WE DIDN'T MEAN TO, BUT HE WAS RESISTING SO VIOLENTLY THAT....
HE JUST DIED.

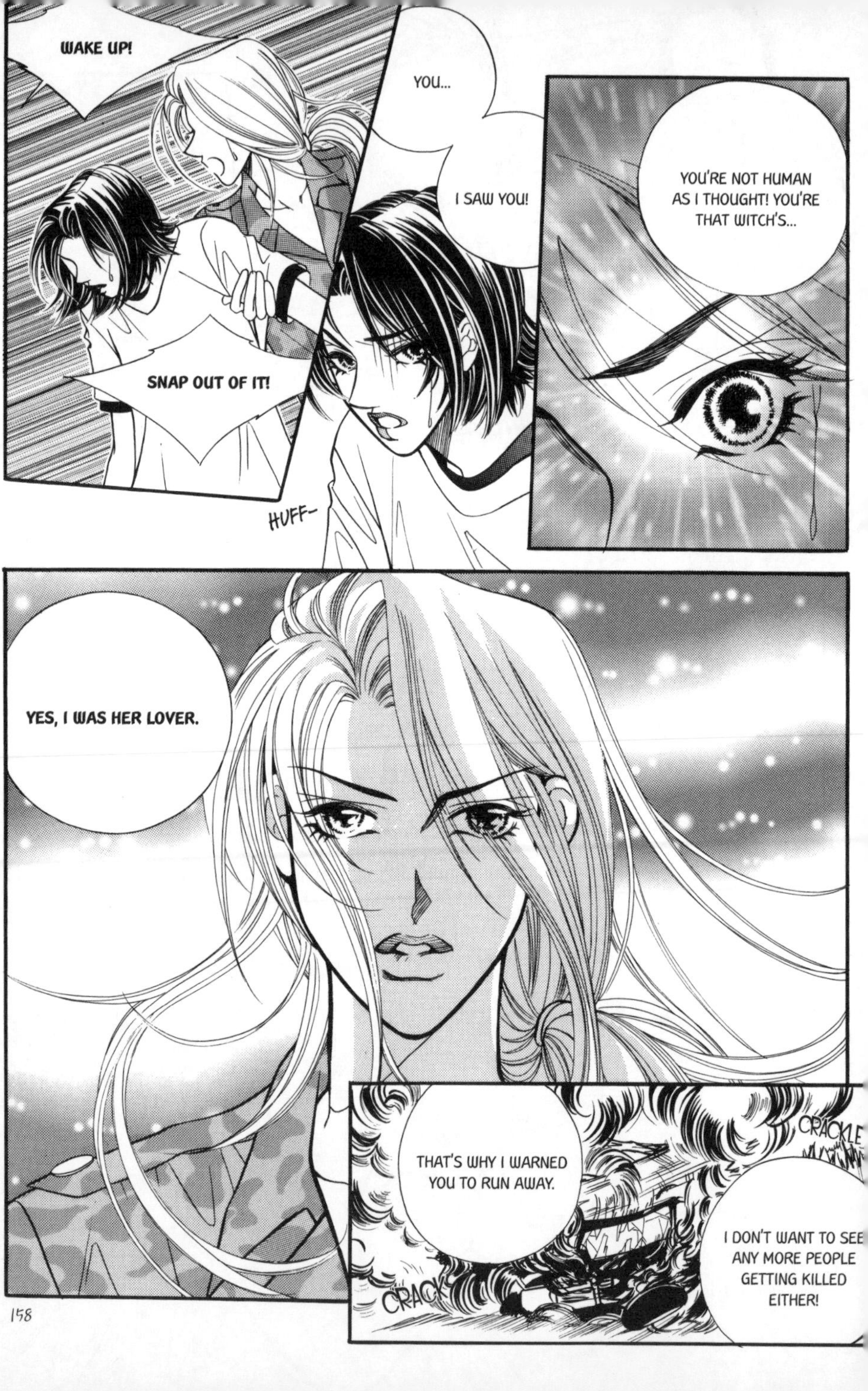
WAKE UP!
SNAP OUT OF IT!
YOU...
I SAW YOU!
HUFF-
YOU'RE NOT HUMAN AS I THOUGHT! YOU'RE THAT WITCH'S...
YES, I WAS HER LOVER.
THAT'S WHY I WARNED YOU TO RUN AWAY.
CRACKLE
I DON'T WANT TO SEE ANY MORE PEOPLE GETTING KILLED EITHER!
CRACK

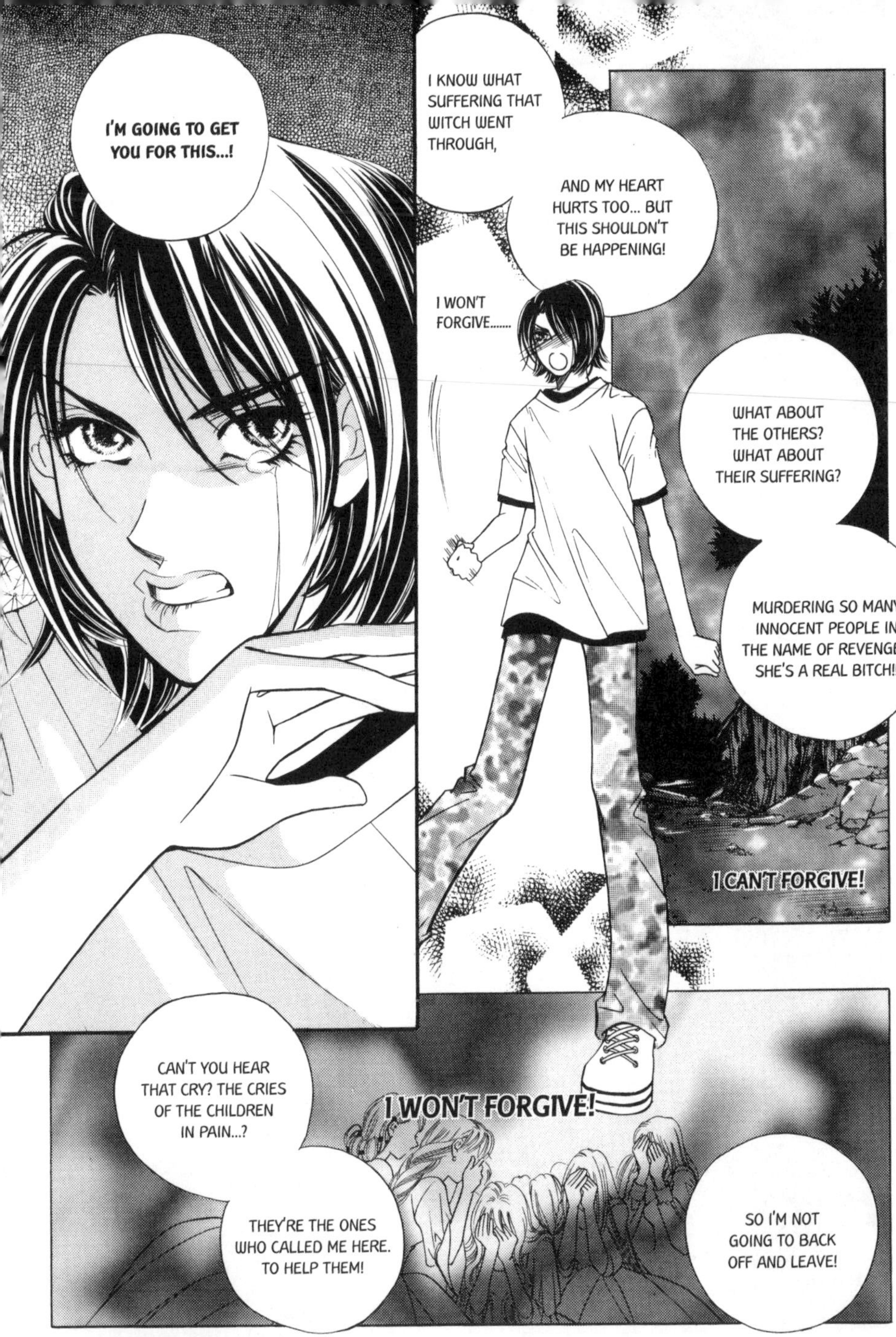
I'M GOING TO GET YOU FOR THIS...!
I KNOW WHAT SUFFERING THAT WITCH WENT THROUGH,
AND MY HEART HURTS TOO... BUT THIS SHOULDN'T BE HAPPENING!
I WON'T FORGIVE.......
WHAT ABOUT THE OTHERS? WHAT ABOUT THEIR SUFFERING?
MURDERING SO MANY INNOCENT PEOPLE IN THE NAME OF REVENGE... SHE'S A REAL BITCH!!
I CAN'T FORGIVE!
CAN'T YOU HEAR THAT CRY? THE CRIES OF THE CHILDREN IN PAIN...?
I WON'T FORGIVE!
THEY'RE THE ONES WHO CALLED ME HERE. TO HELP THEM!
SO I'M NOT GOING TO BACK OFF AND LEAVE!

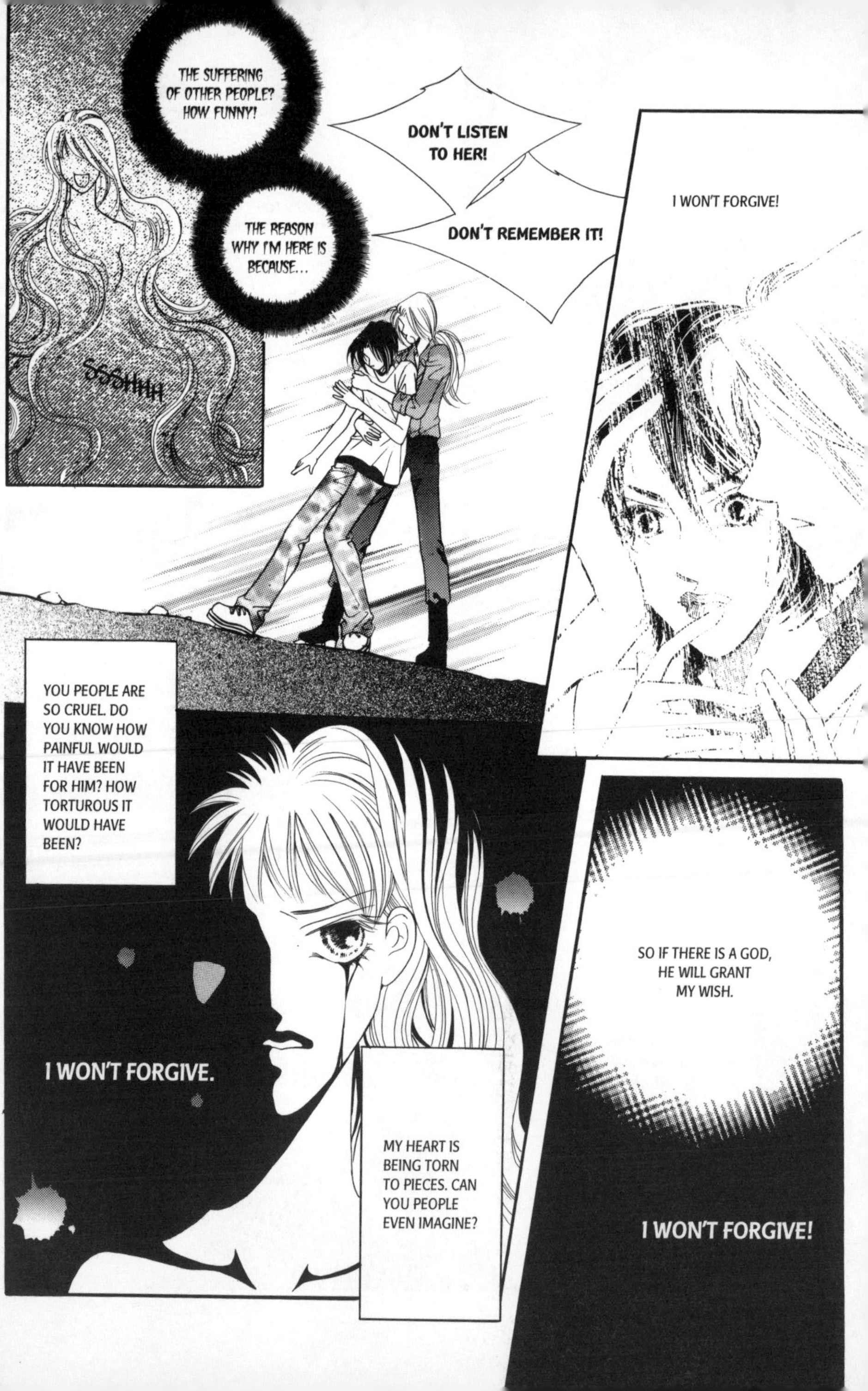

THE SUFFERING OF OTHER PEOPLE? HOW FUNNY!
THE REASON WHY I'M HERE IS BECAUSE...
SSSHHH
DON'T LISTEN TO HER!
DON'T REMEMBER IT!
I WON'T FORGIVE!
YOU PEOPLE ARE SO CRUEL. DO YOU KNOW HOW PAINFUL WOULD IT HAVE BEEN FOR HIM? HOW TORTUROUS IT WOULD HAVE BEEN?
I WON'T FORGIVE.
MY HEART IS BEING TORN TO PIECES. CAN YOU PEOPLE EVEN IMAGINE?
SO IF THERE IS A GOD, HE WILL GRANT MY WISH.
I WON'T FORGIVE!

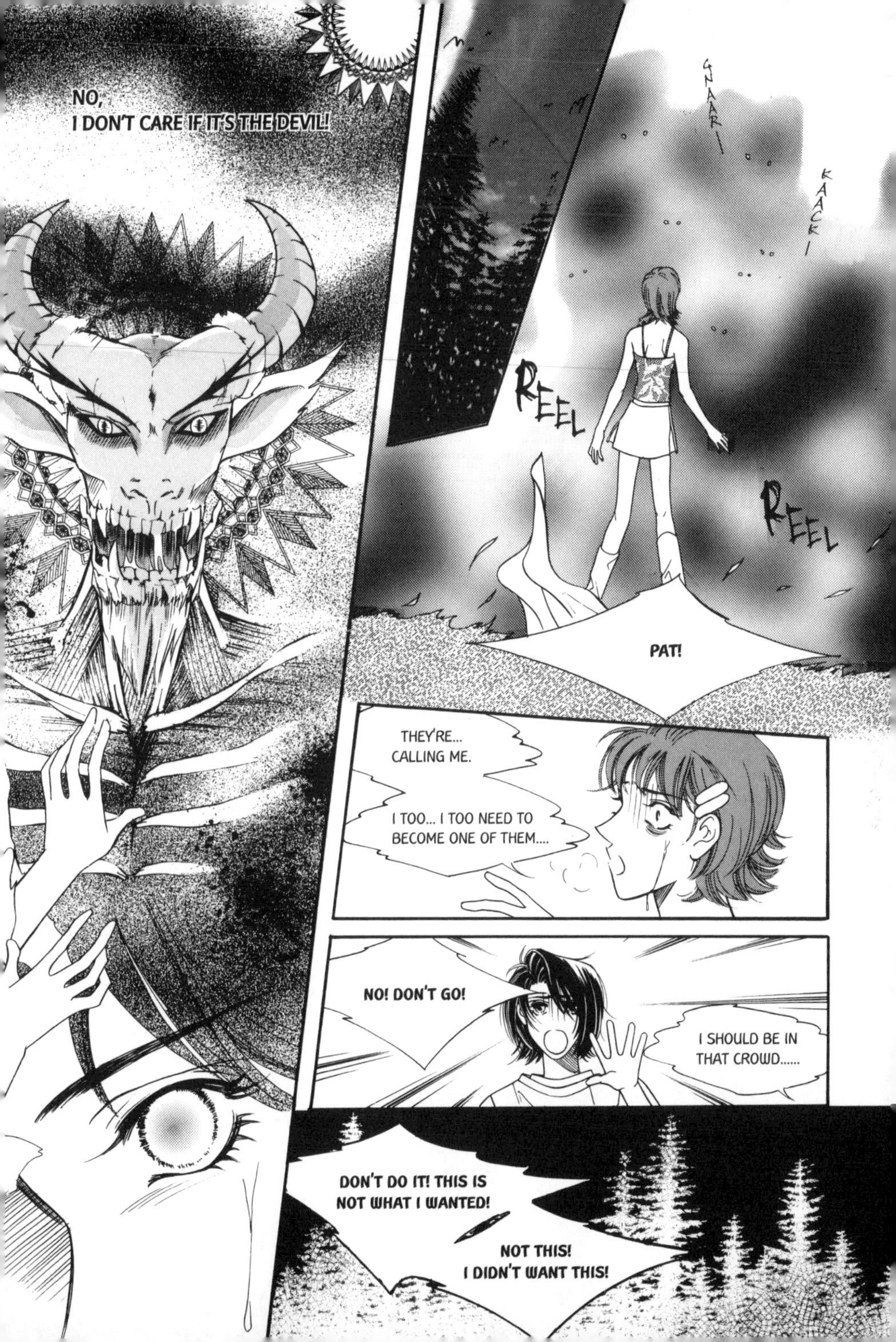
NO,
I DON'T CARE IF IT'S THE DEVIL!
GNAAR!
KAACK!
REEL
REEL
PAT!
THEY'RE... CALLING ME.
I TOO... I TOO NEED TO BECOME ONE OF THEM....
NO! DON'T GO!
I SHOULD BE IN THAT CROWD......
DON'T DO IT! THIS IS NOT WHAT I WANTED!
NOT THIS! I DIDN'T WANT THIS!

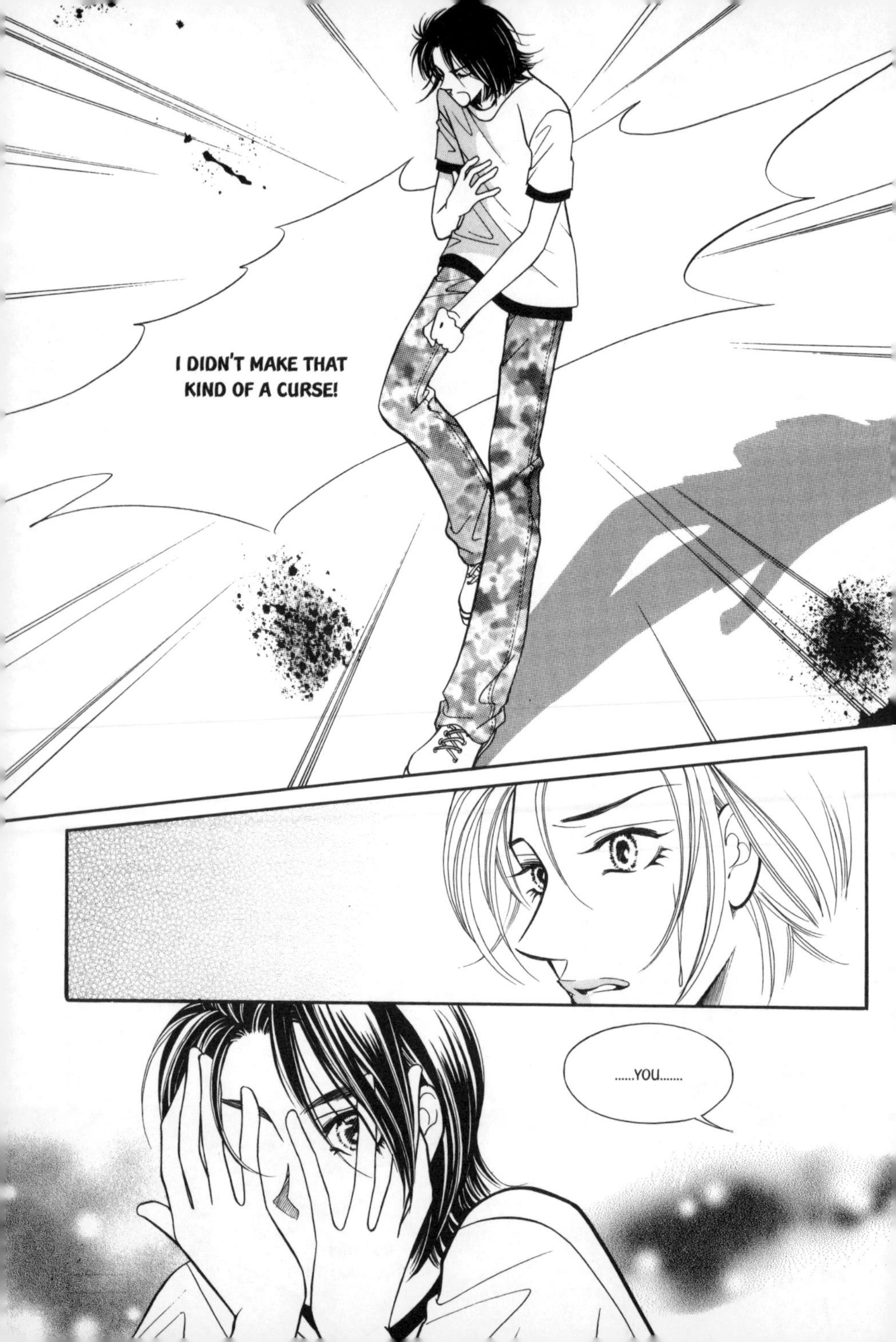
I DIDN'T MAKE THAT KIND OF A CURSE!
......YOU.......

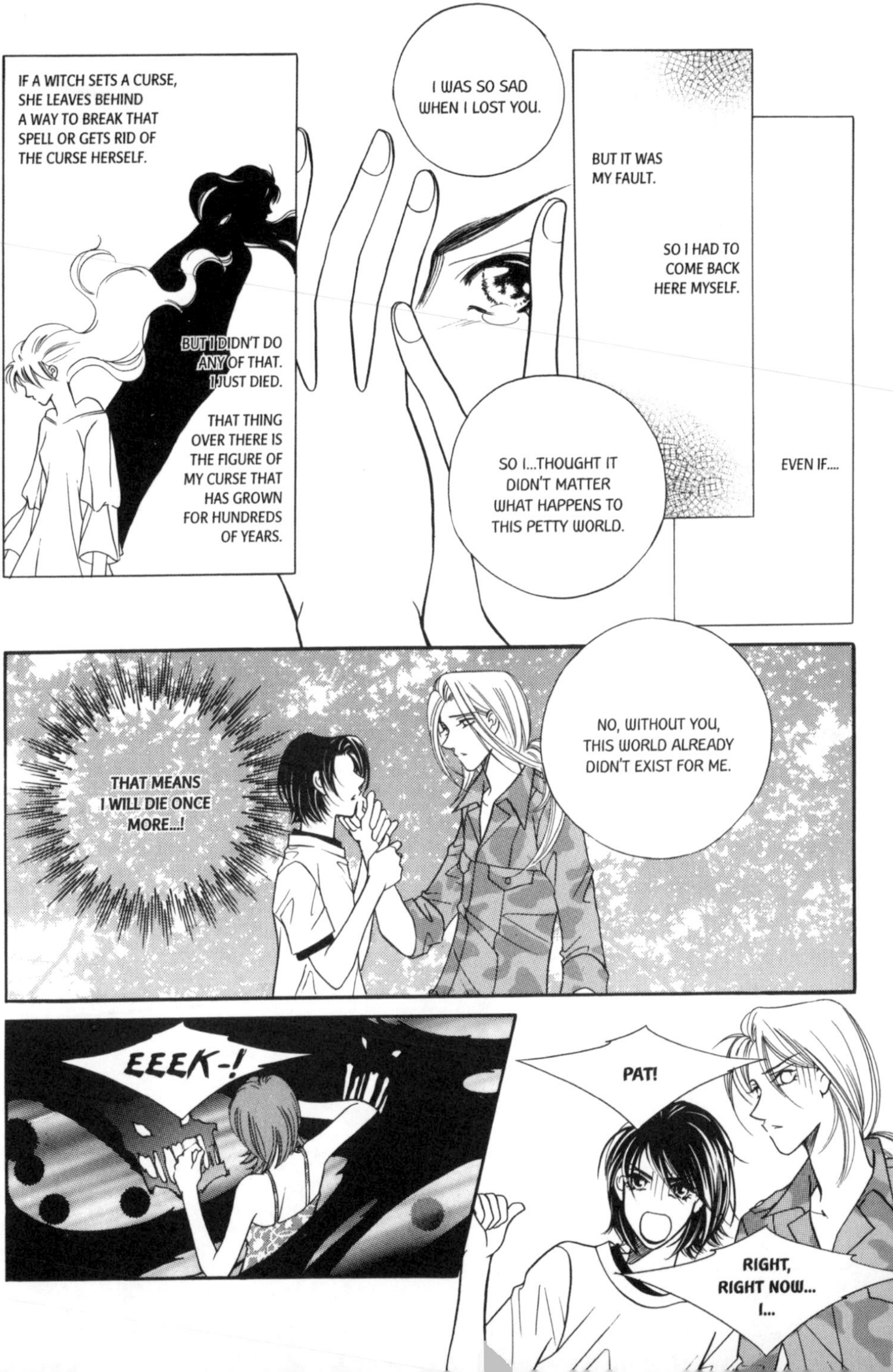
IF A WITCH SETS A CURSE, SHE LEAVES BEHIND A WAY TO BREAK THAT SPELL OR GETS RID OF THE CURSE HERSELF.
BUT I DIDN'T DO ANY OF THAT. I JUST DIED.
THAT THING OVER THERE IS THE FIGURE OF MY CURSE THAT HAS GROWN FOR HUNDREDS OF YEARS.
I WAS SO SAD WHEN I LOST YOU.
SO I...THOUGHT IT DIDN'T MATTER WHAT HAPPENS TO THIS PETTY WORLD.
BUT IT WAS MY FAULT.
SO I HAD TO COME BACK HERE MYSELF.
EVEN IF....
THAT MEANS I WILL DIE ONCE MORE...!
NO, WITHOUT YOU, THIS WORLD ALREADY DIDN'T EXIST FOR ME.
EEEK-!
PAT!
RIGHT, RIGHT NOW... I...

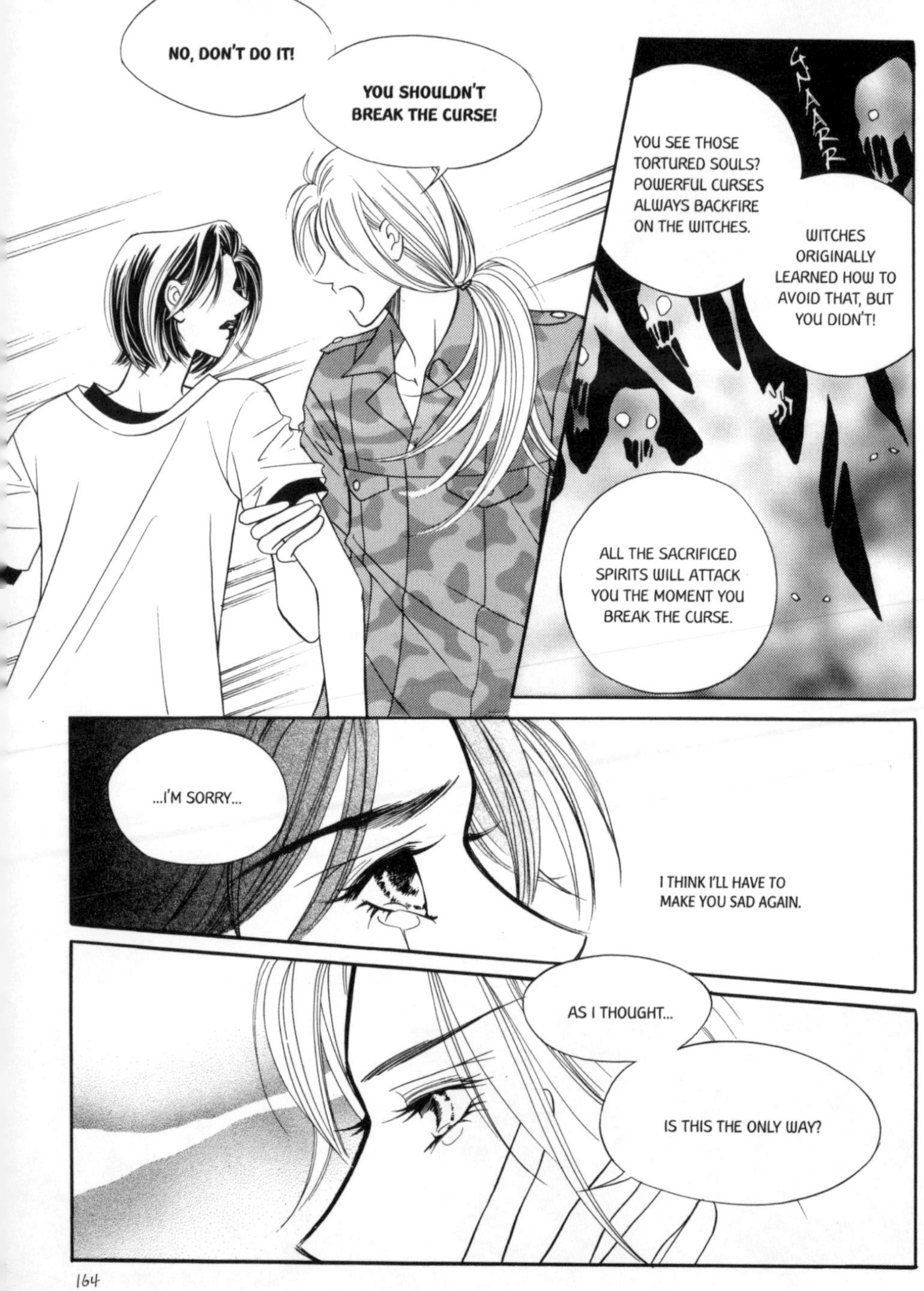
NO, DON'T DO IT!
YOU SHOULDN'T BREAK THE CURSE!
GNAARR
YOU SEE THOSE TORTURED SOULS? POWERFUL CURSES ALWAYS BACKFIRE ON THE WITCHES.
WITCHES ORIGINALLY LEARNED HOW TO AVOID THAT, BUT YOU DIDN'T!
ALL THE SACRIFICED SPIRITS WILL ATTACK YOU THE MOMENT YOU BREAK THE CURSE.
...I'M SORRY...
I THINK I'LL HAVE TO MAKE YOU SAD AGAIN.
AS I THOUGHT...
IS THIS THE ONLY WAY?

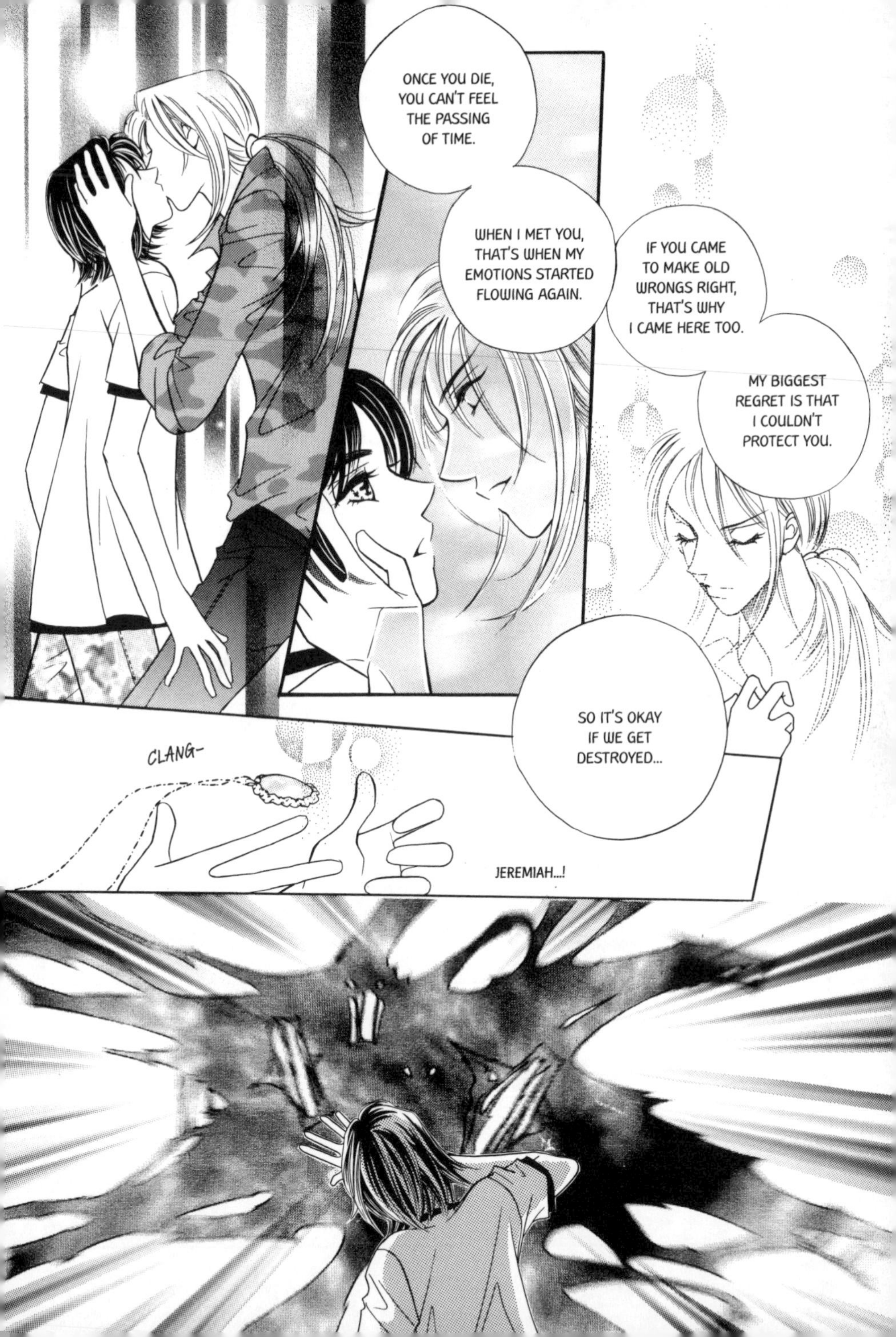
ONCE YOU DIE, YOU CAN'T FEEL THE PASSING OF TIME.
WHEN I MET YOU, THAT'S WHEN MY EMOTIONS STARTED FLOWING AGAIN.
IF YOU CAME TO MAKE OLD WRONGS RIGHT, THAT'S WHY I CAME HERE TOO.
MY BIGGEST REGRET IS THAT I COULDN'T PROTECT YOU.
CLANG-
SO IT'S OKAY IF WE GET DESTROYED...
JEREMIAH...!

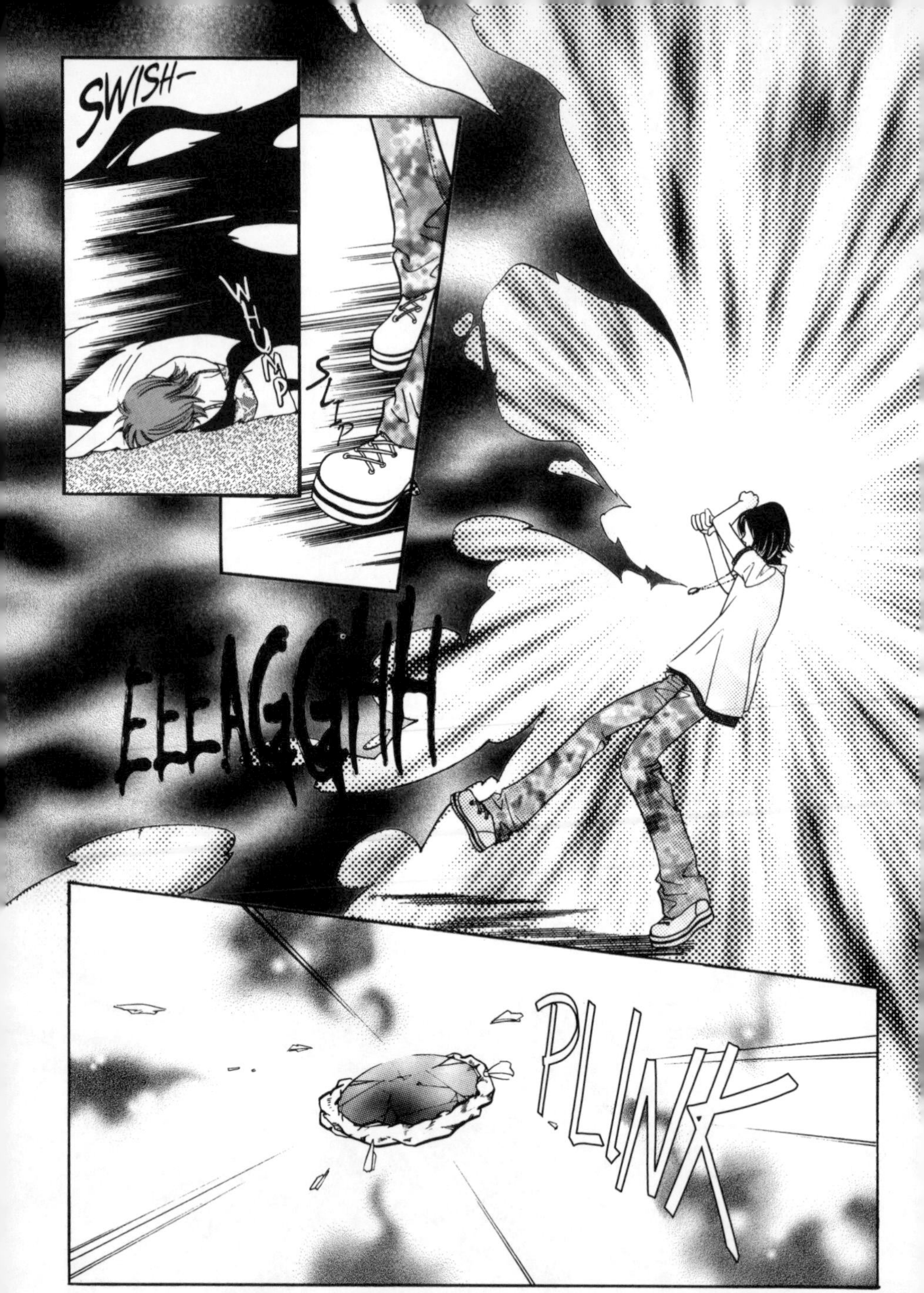
SWISH-
WHUMP
SLIP
EEEAGGHH
PLINK

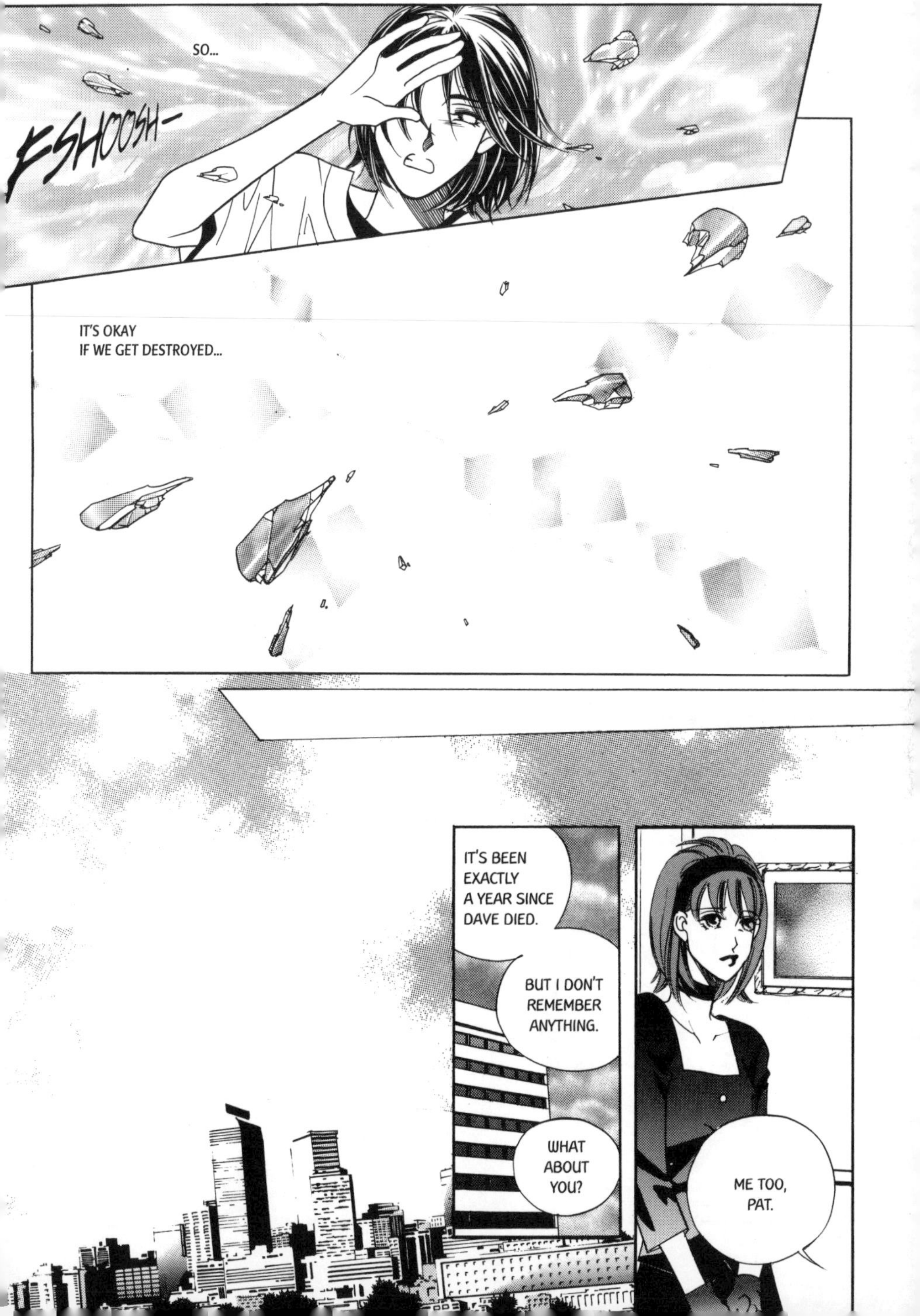
SO...
FSHOOSH-
IT'S OKAY IF WE GET DESTROYED...
IT'S BEEN EXACTLY A YEAR SINCE DAVE DIED.
BUT I DON'T REMEMBER ANYTHING.
WHAT ABOUT YOU?
ME TOO, PAT.

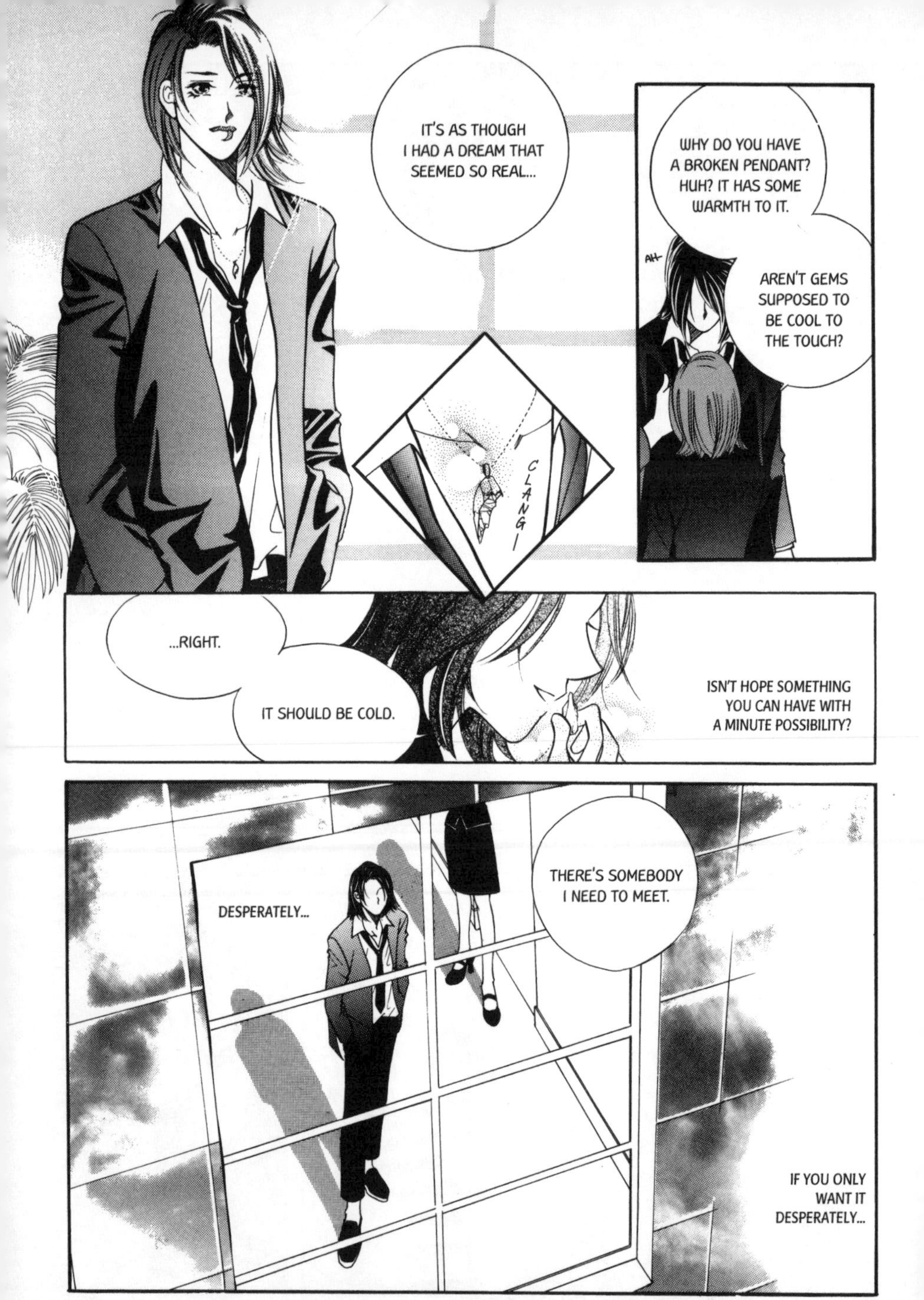
IT'S AS THOUGH I HAD A DREAM THAT SEEMED SO REAL...
CLANG!
WHY DO YOU HAVE A BROKEN PENDANT? HUH? IT HAS SOME WARMTH TO IT.
AH
AREN'T GEMS SUPPOSED TO BE COOL TO THE TOUCH?
...RIGHT.
IT SHOULD BE COLD.
ISN'T HOPE SOMETHING YOU CAN HAVE WITH A MINUTE POSSIBILITY?
DESPERATELY...
THERE'S SOMEBODY I NEED TO MEET.
IF YOU ONLY WANT IT DESPERATELY...

LEUCADIAN

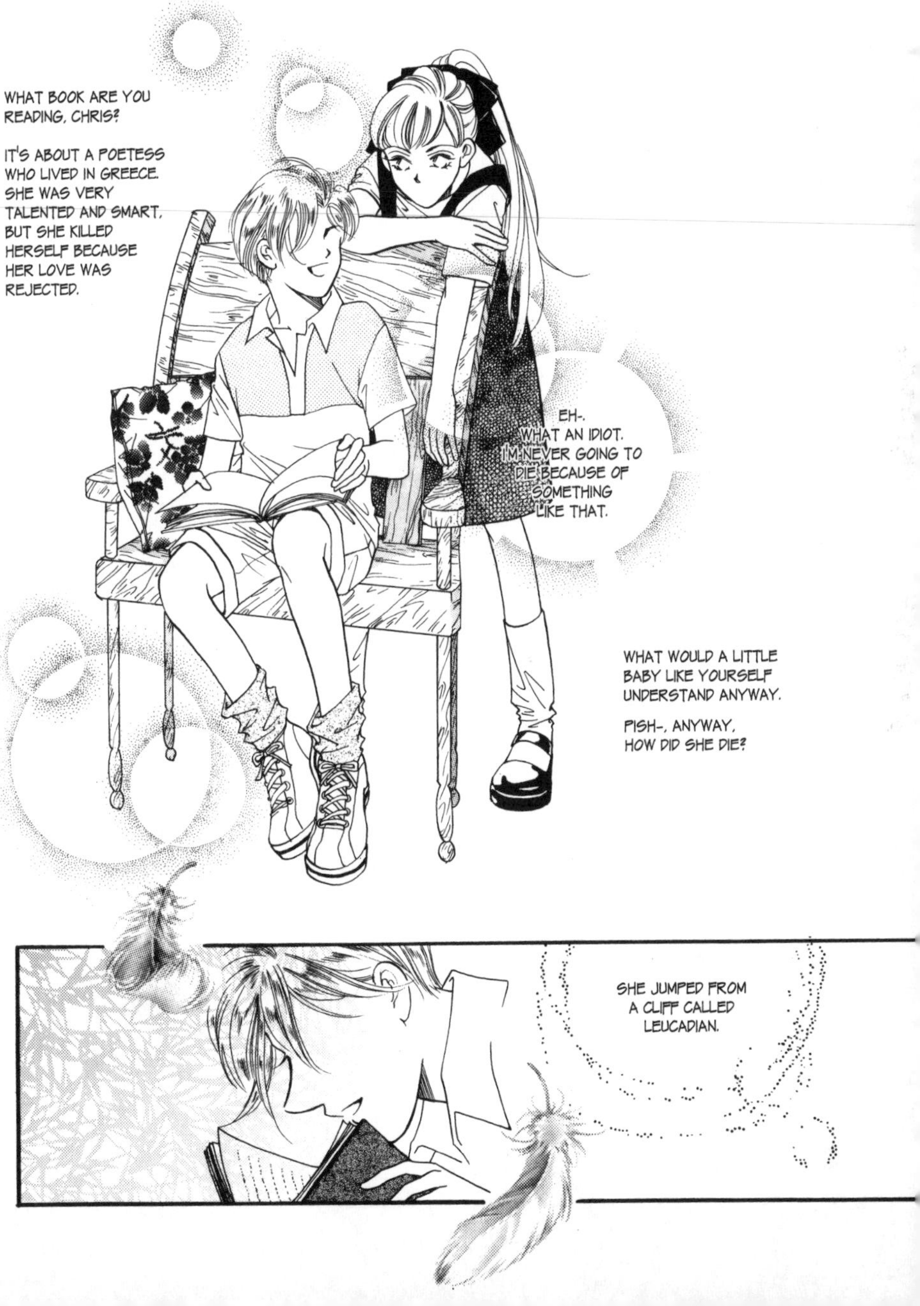
WHAT BOOK ARE YOU READING, CHRIS?
IT'S ABOUT A POETESS WHO LIVED IN GREECE. SHE WAS VERY TALENTED AND SMART, BUT SHE KILLED HERSELF BECAUSE HER LOVE WAS REJECTED.
EH-. WHAT AN IDIOT. I'M NEVER GOING TO DIE BECAUSE OF SOMETHING LIKE THAT.
WHAT WOULD A LITTLE BABY LIKE YOURSELF UNDERSTAND ANYWAY.
PISH-, ANYWAY, HOW DID SHE DIE?
SHE JUMPED FROM A CLIFF CALLED LEUCADIAN.

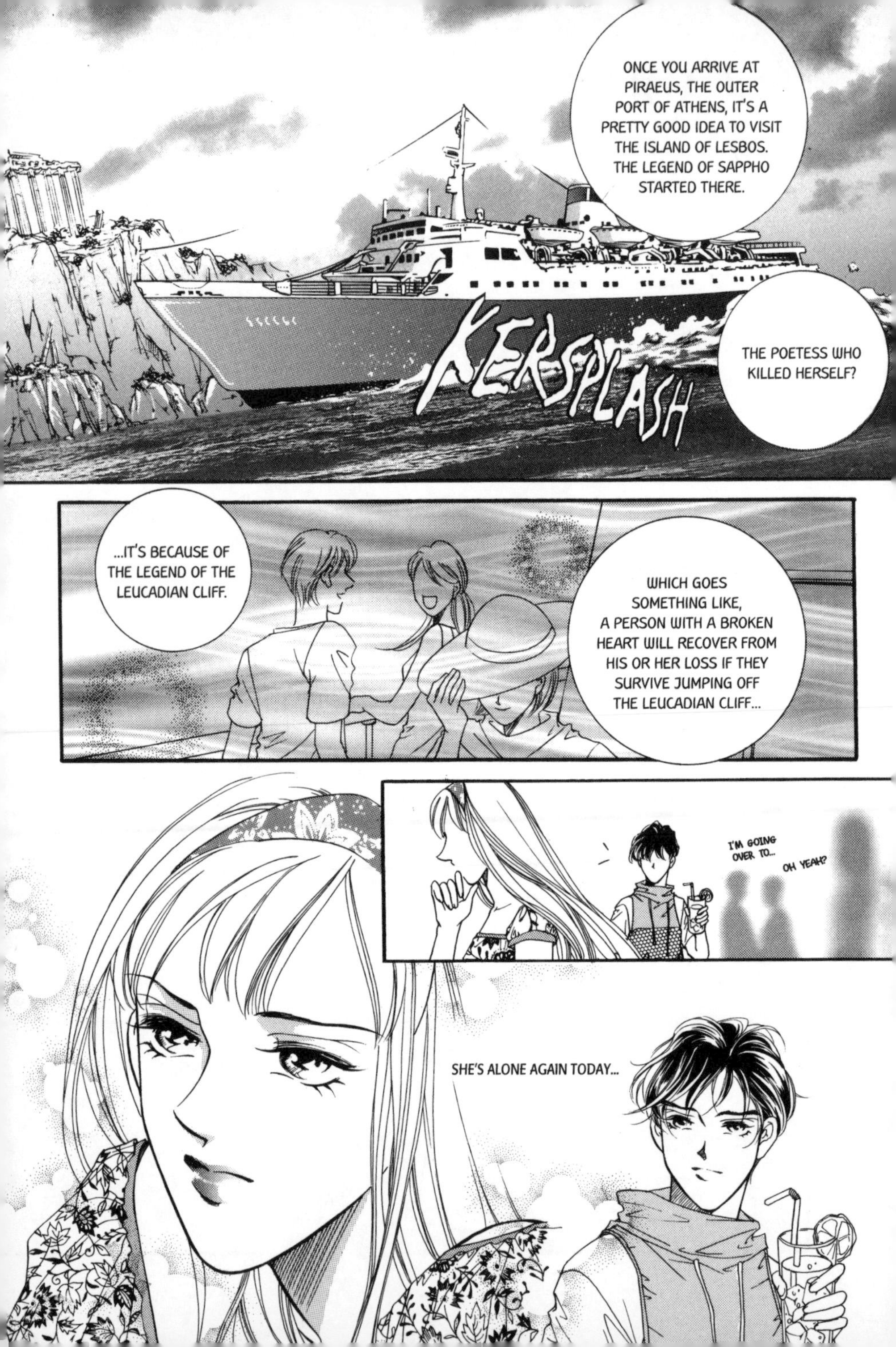
ONCE YOU ARRIVE AT PIRAEUS, THE OUTER PORT OF ATHENS, IT'S A PRETTY GOOD IDEA TO VISIT THE ISLAND OF LESBOS. THE LEGEND OF SAPPHO STARTED THERE.
KERSPLASH
THE POETESS WHO KILLED HERSELF?
...IT'S BECAUSE OF THE LEGEND OF THE LEUCADIAN CLIFF.
WHICH GOES SOMETHING LIKE, A PERSON WITH A BROKEN HEART WILL RECOVER FROM HIS OR HER LOSS IF THEY SURVIVE JUMPING OFF THE LEUCADIAN CLIFF...
I'M GOING OVER TO...
OH YEAH?
SHE'S ALONE AGAIN TODAY...

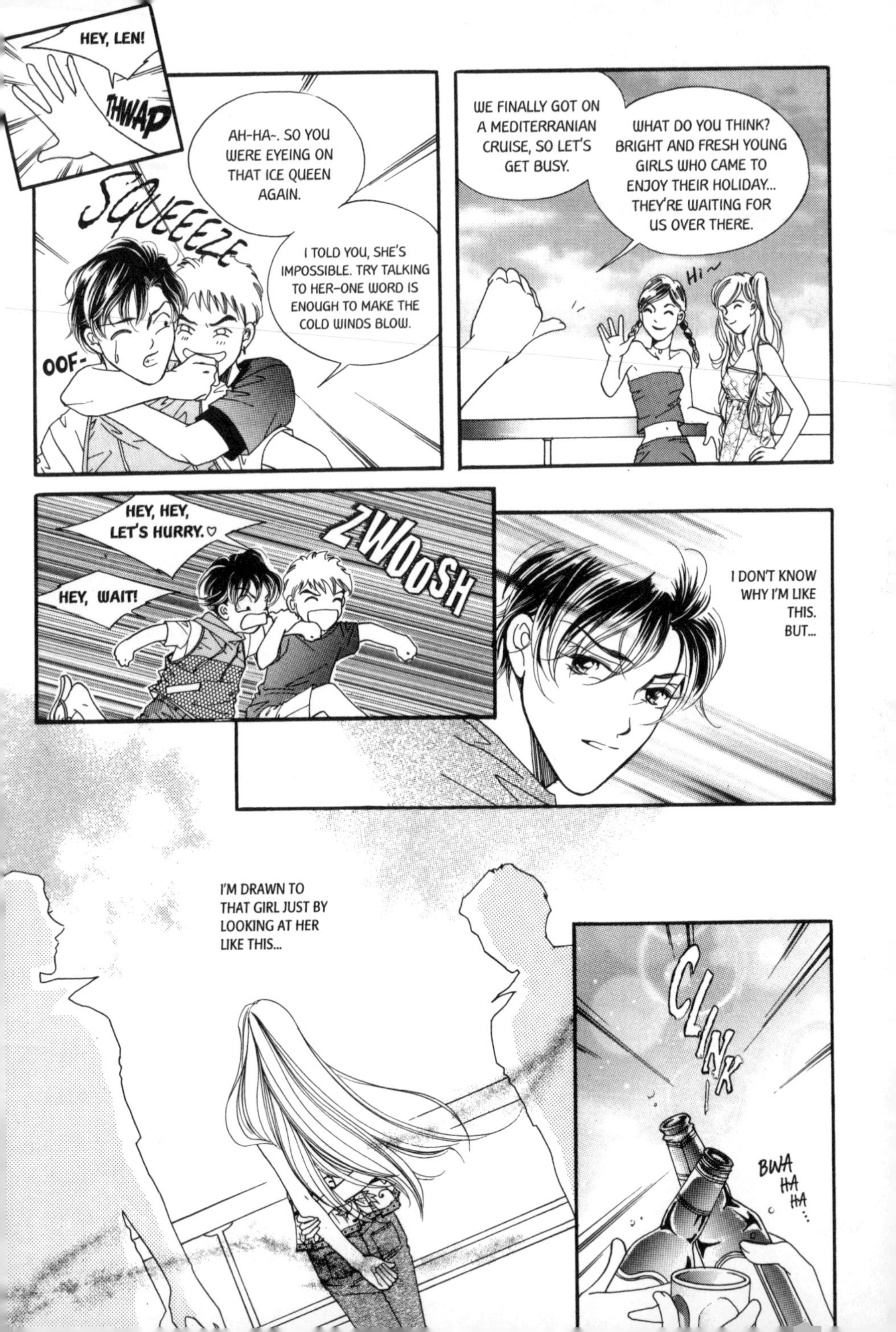

HEY, LEN!
THWAP
AH-HA-. SO YOU WERE EYEING ON THAT ICE QUEEN AGAIN.
SQUEEEEZE
I TOLD YOU, SHE'S IMPOSSIBLE. TRY TALKING TO HER-ONE WORD IS ENOUGH TO MAKE THE COLD WINDS BLOW.
OOF-
WE FINALLY GOT ON A MEDITERRANIAN CRUISE, SO LET'S GET BUSY.
WHAT DO YOU THINK? BRIGHT AND FRESH YOUNG GIRLS WHO CAME TO ENJOY THEIR HOLIDAY... THEY'RE WAITING FOR US OVER THERE.
Hi~
HEY, HEY, LET'S HURRY.♡
ZWOOSH
HEY, WAIT!
I DON'T KNOW WHY I'M LIKE THIS. BUT...
I'M DRAWN TO THAT GIRL JUST BY LOOKING AT HER LIKE THIS...
CLINK
BWA HA HA...

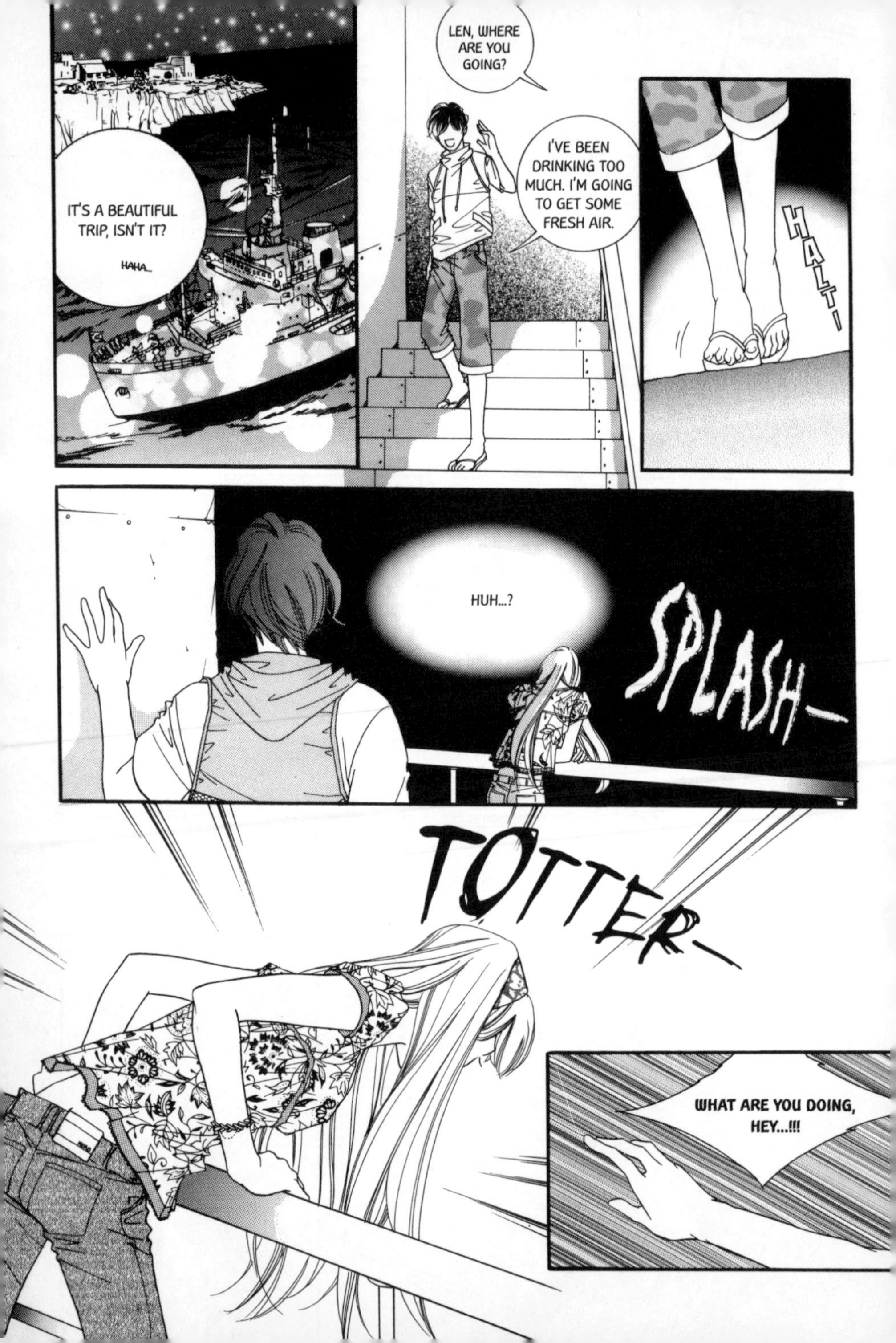
IT'S A BEAUTIFUL TRIP, ISN'T IT?
HAHA...
LEN, WHERE ARE YOU GOING?
I'VE BEEN DRINKING TOO MUCH. I'M GOING TO GET SOME FRESH AIR.
HALT!
HUH...?
SPLASH—
TOTTER—
WHAT ARE YOU DOING, HEY...!!!

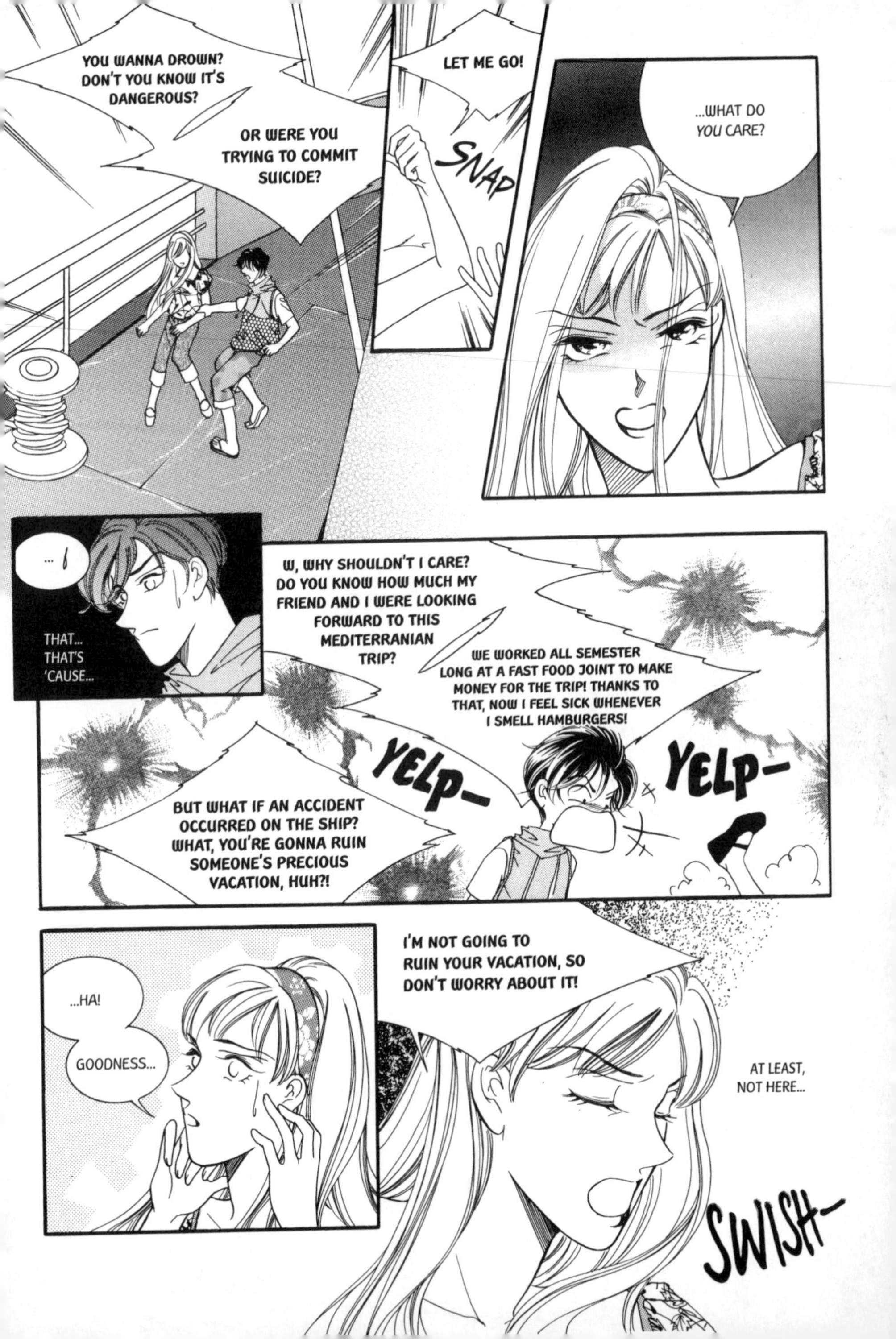
YOU WANNA DROWN? DON'T YOU KNOW IT'S DANGEROUS?
OR WERE YOU TRYING TO COMMIT SUICIDE?
LET ME GO!
SNAP
...WHAT DO YOU CARE?
...!
THAT... THAT'S 'CAUSE...
W, WHY SHOULDN'T I CARE? DO YOU KNOW HOW MUCH MY FRIEND AND I WERE LOOKING FORWARD TO THIS MEDITERRANIAN TRIP?
WE WORKED ALL SEMESTER LONG AT A FAST FOOD JOINT TO MAKE MONEY FOR THE TRIP! THANKS TO THAT, NOW I FEEL SICK WHENEVER I SMELL HAMBURGERS!
YELP-
BUT WHAT IF AN ACCIDENT OCCURRED ON THE SHIP? WHAT, YOU'RE GONNA RUIN SOMEONE'S PRECIOUS VACATION, HUH?!
YELP-
...HA!
GOODNESS...
I'M NOT GOING TO RUIN YOUR VACATION, SO DON'T WORRY ABOUT IT!
AT LEAST, NOT HERE...
SWISH-

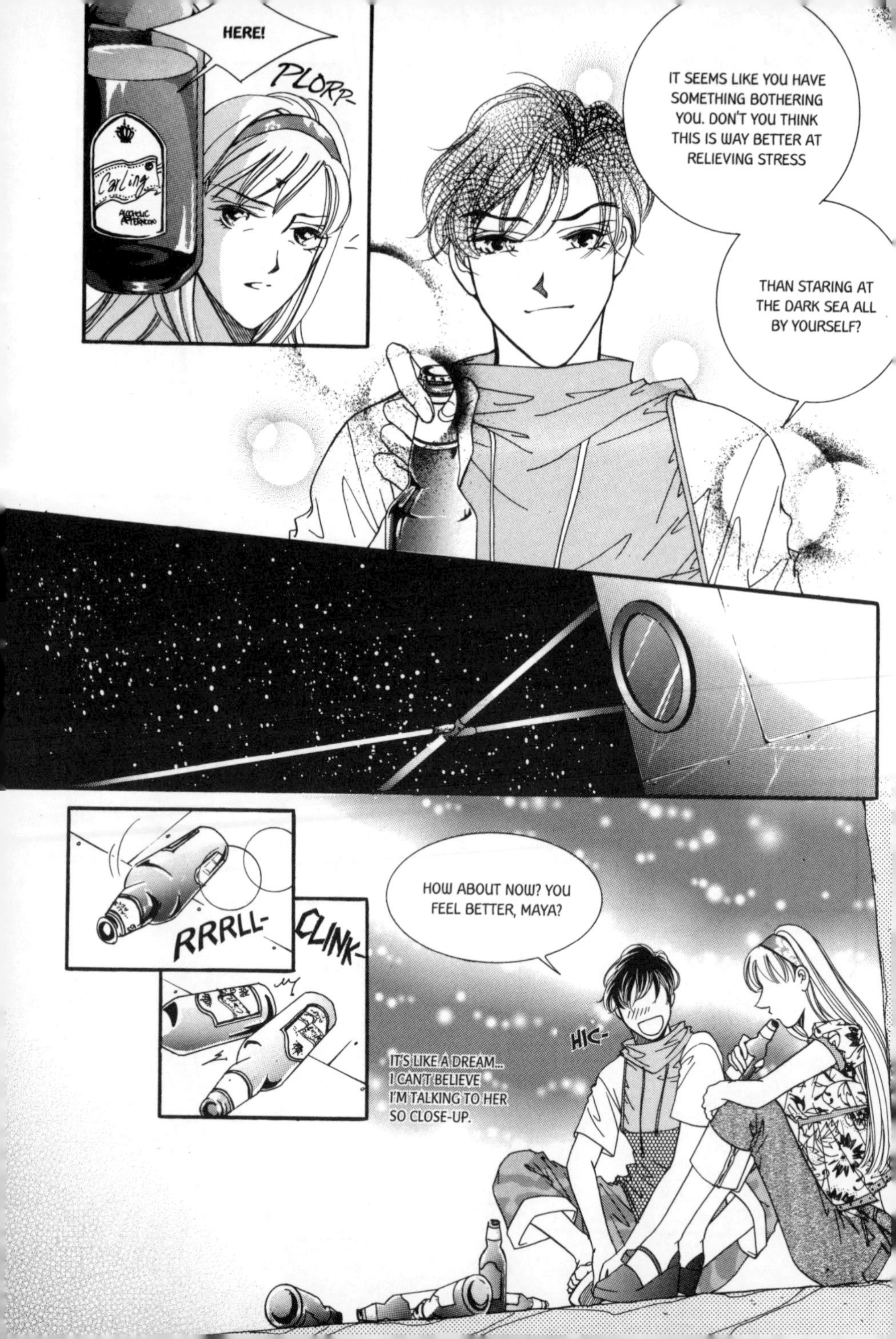
HERE!
PLORP-
IT SEEMS LIKE YOU HAVE SOMETHING BOTHERING YOU. DON'T YOU THINK THIS IS WAY BETTER AT RELIEVING STRESS
THAN STARING AT THE DARK SEA ALL BY YOURSELF?
RRRLL-
CLINK-
HOW ABOUT NOW? YOU FEEL BETTER, MAYA?
HIC-
IT'S LIKE A DREAM... I CAN'T BELIEVE I'M TALKING TO HER SO CLOSE-UP.

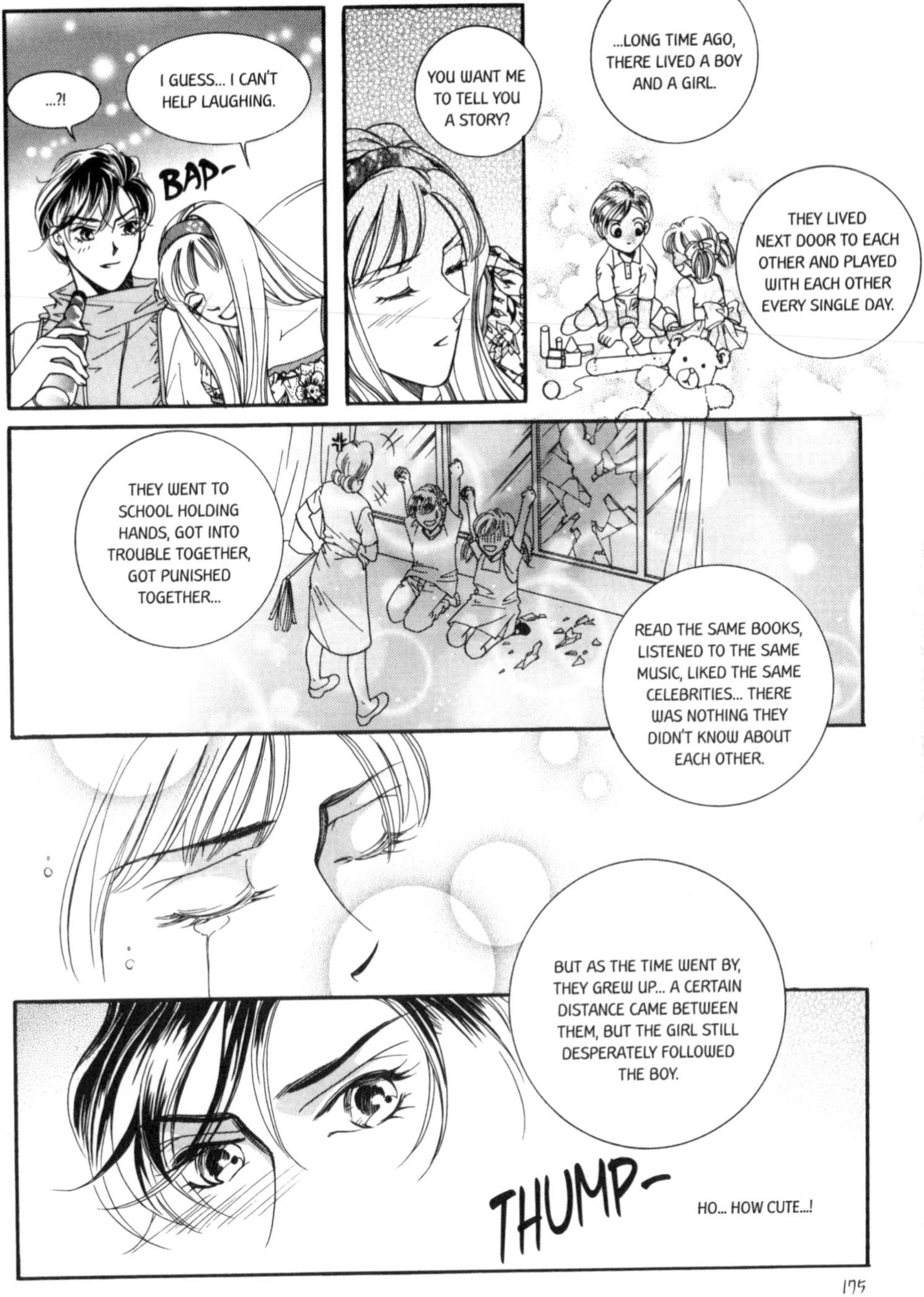

...?!
I GUESS... I CAN'T HELP LAUGHING.
BAP-
YOU WANT ME TO TELL YOU A STORY?
...LONG TIME AGO, THERE LIVED A BOY AND A GIRL.
THEY LIVED NEXT DOOR TO EACH OTHER AND PLAYED WITH EACH OTHER EVERY SINGLE DAY.
THEY WENT TO SCHOOL HOLDING HANDS, GOT INTO TROUBLE TOGETHER, GOT PUNISHED TOGETHER...
READ THE SAME BOOKS, LISTENED TO THE SAME MUSIC, LIKED THE SAME CELEBRITIES... THERE WAS NOTHING THEY DIDN'T KNOW ABOUT EACH OTHER.
BUT AS THE TIME WENT BY, THEY GREW UP... A CERTAIN DISTANCE CAME BETWEEN THEM, BUT THE GIRL STILL DESPERATELY FOLLOWED THE BOY.
THUMP-
HO... HOW CUTE...!

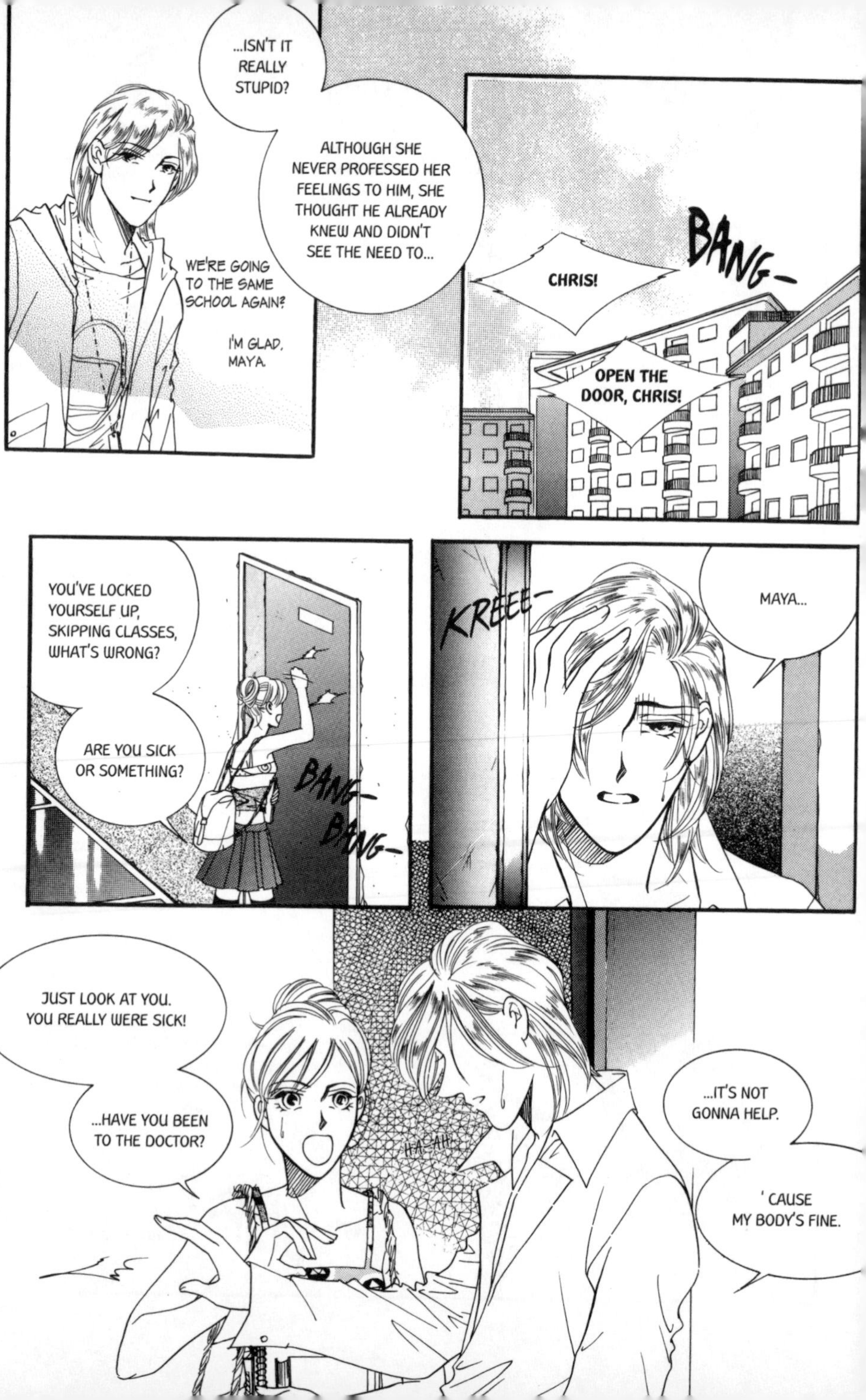
...ISN'T IT REALLY STUPID?
ALTHOUGH SHE NEVER PROFESSED HER FEELINGS TO HIM, SHE THOUGHT HE ALREADY KNEW AND DIDN'T SEE THE NEED TO...
WE'RE GOING TO THE SAME SCHOOL AGAIN?
I'M GLAD, MAYA.
BANG-
CHRIS!
OPEN THE DOOR, CHRIS!
YOU'VE LOCKED YOURSELF UP, SKIPPING CLASSES, WHAT'S WRONG?
ARE YOU SICK OR SOMETHING?
BANG-
BANG-
KREEE-
MAYA...
JUST LOOK AT YOU. YOU REALLY WERE SICK!
...HAVE YOU BEEN TO THE DOCTOR?
HA-AH
...IT'S NOT GONNA HELP.
'CAUSE MY BODY'S FINE.

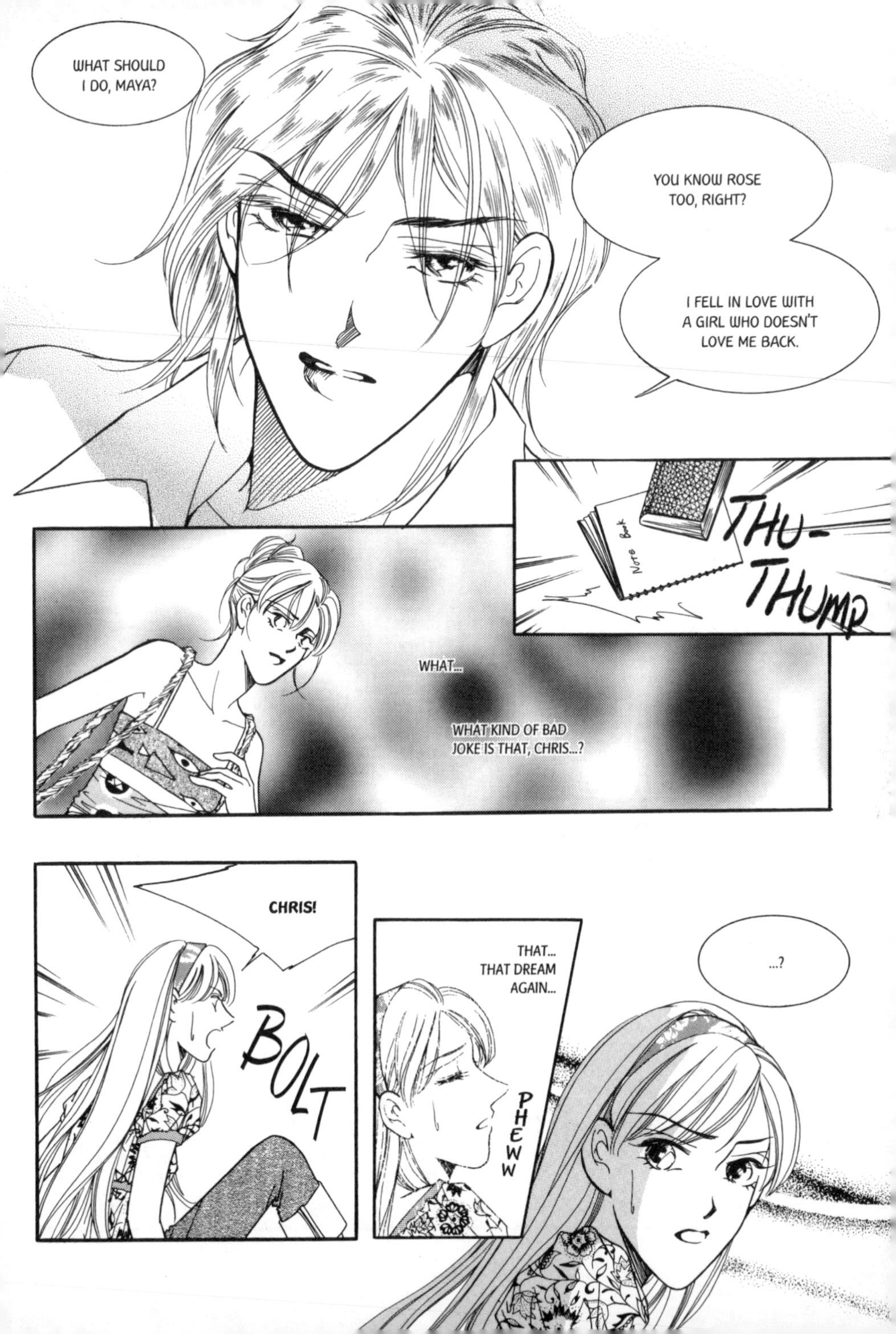
WHAT SHOULD I DO, MAYA?
YOU KNOW ROSE TOO, RIGHT?
I FELL IN LOVE WITH A GIRL WHO DOESN'T LOVE ME BACK.
Note Book
THU-THUMP
WHAT...
WHAT KIND OF BAD JOKE IS THAT, CHRIS...?
CHRIS!
BOLT
THAT... THAT DREAM AGAIN...
PHEWW
...?

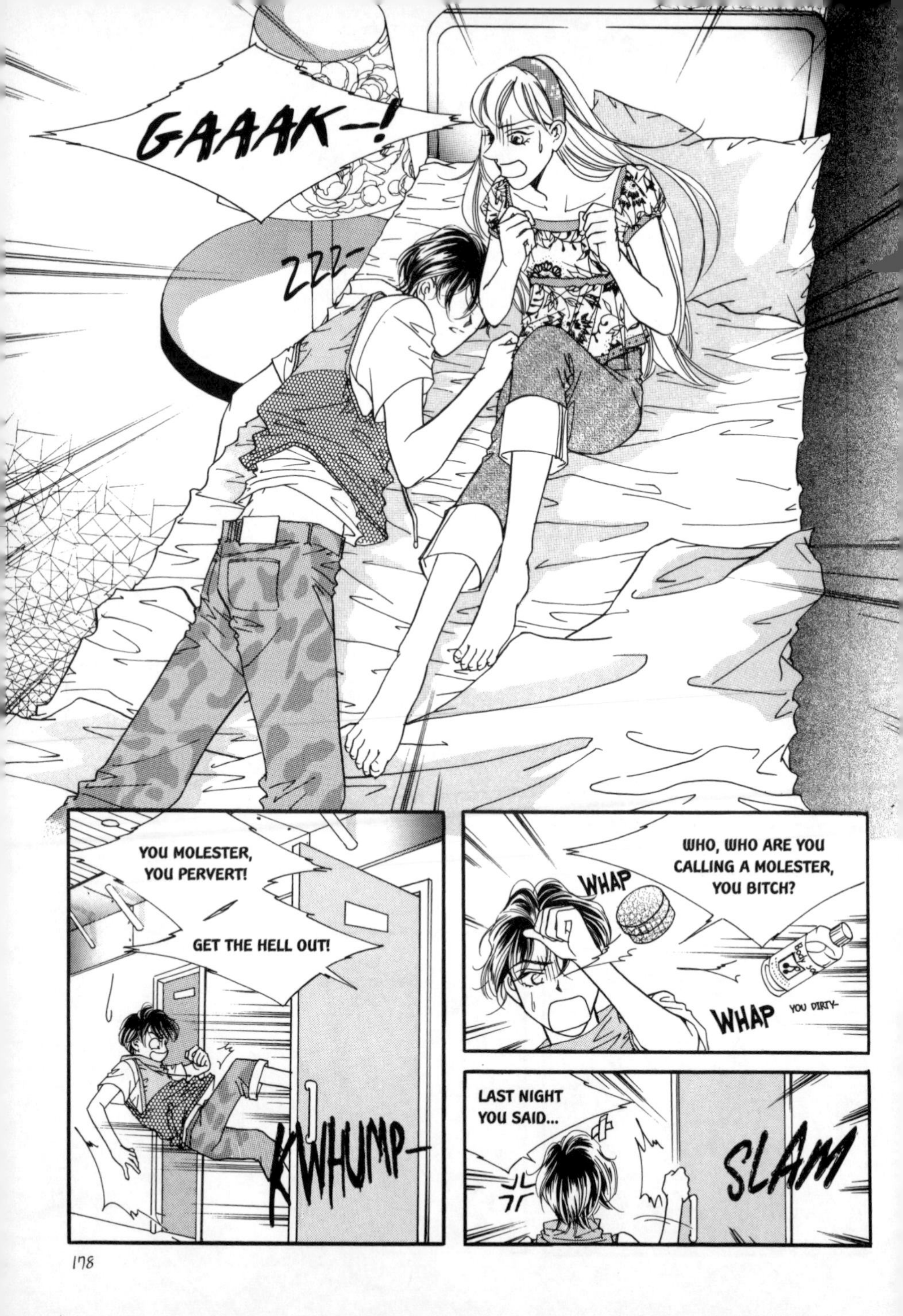
GAAAK—!
ZZZ—
YOU MOLESTER, YOU PERVERT!
GET THE HELL OUT!
KWHUMP—
WHAP
WHO, WHO ARE YOU CALLING A MOLESTER, YOU BITCH?
WHAP
YOU DIRTY-
LAST NIGHT YOU SAID...
SLAM

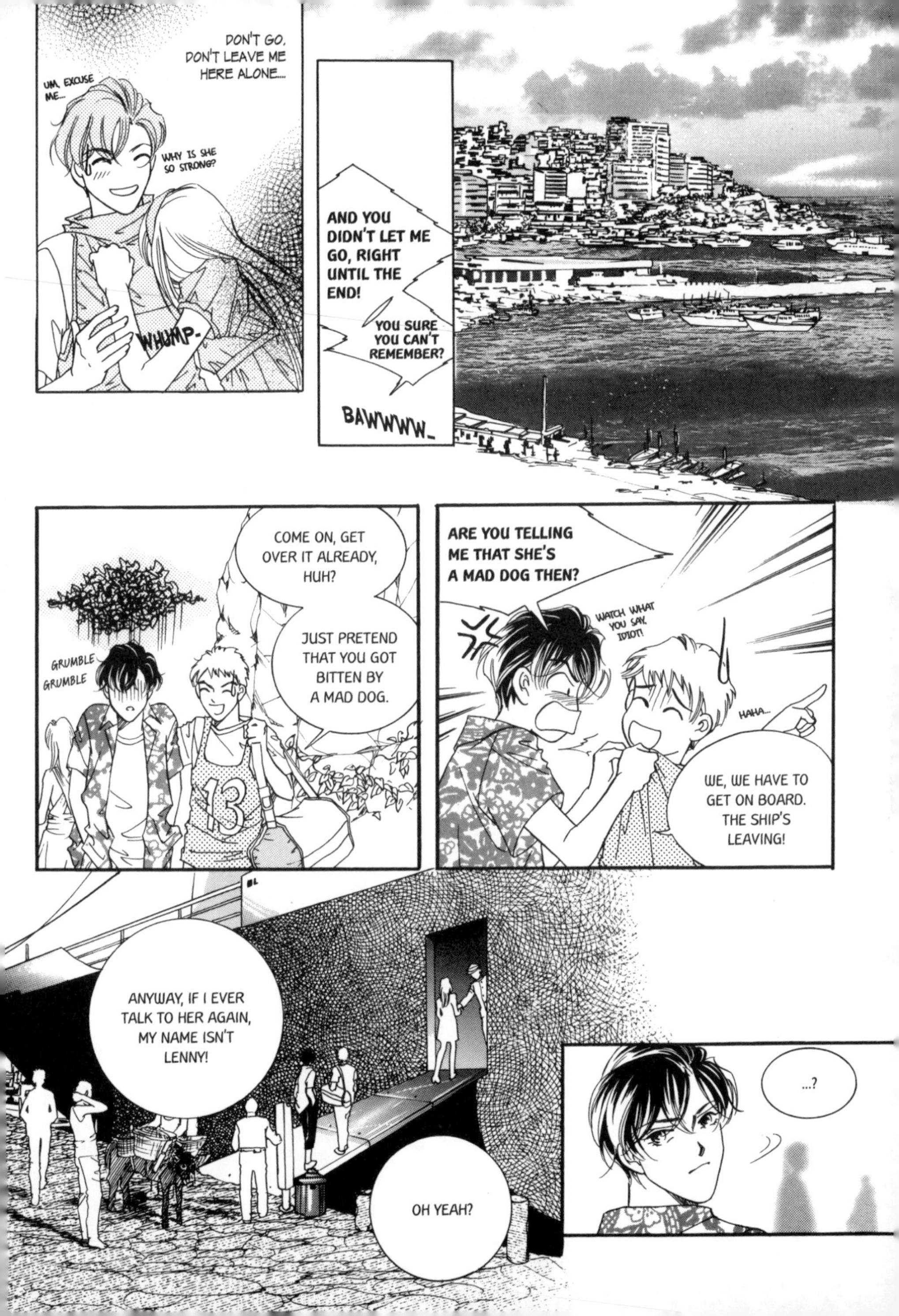
DON'T GO. DON'T LEAVE ME HERE ALONE....
UM, EXCUSE ME...
WHY IS SHE SO STRONG?
WHUMP-
AND YOU DIDN'T LET ME GO, RIGHT UNTIL THE END!
YOU SURE YOU CAN'T REMEMBER?
BAWWWW-
COME ON, GET OVER IT ALREADY, HUH?
JUST PRETEND THAT YOU GOT BITTEN BY A MAD DOG.
GRUMBLE GRUMBLE
13
ARE YOU TELLING ME THAT SHE'S A MAD DOG THEN?
WATCH WHAT YOU SAY, IDIOT!
HAHA...
WE, WE HAVE TO GET ON BOARD. THE SHIP'S LEAVING!
ANYWAY, IF I EVER TALK TO HER AGAIN, MY NAME ISN'T LENNY!
OH YEAH?
...?

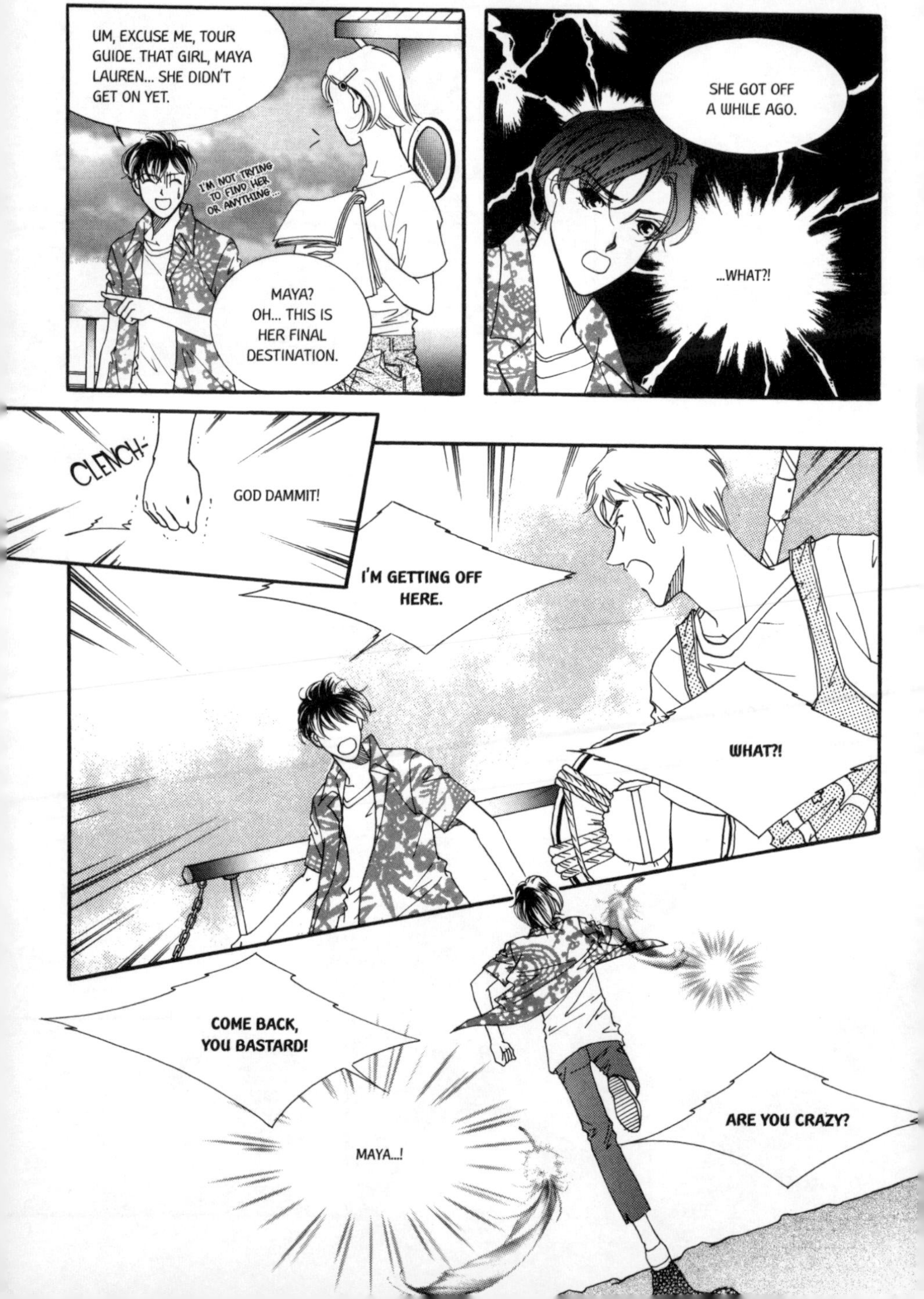
UM, EXCUSE ME, TOUR GUIDE. THAT GIRL, MAYA LAUREN... SHE DIDN'T GET ON YET.
I'M NOT TRYING TO FIND HER OR ANYTHING...
MAYA? OH... THIS IS HER FINAL DESTINATION.
SHE GOT OFF A WHILE AGO.
...WHAT?!
CLENCH-
GOD DAMMIT!
I'M GETTING OFF HERE.
WHAT?!
COME BACK, YOU BASTARD!
MAYA...!
ARE YOU CRAZY?

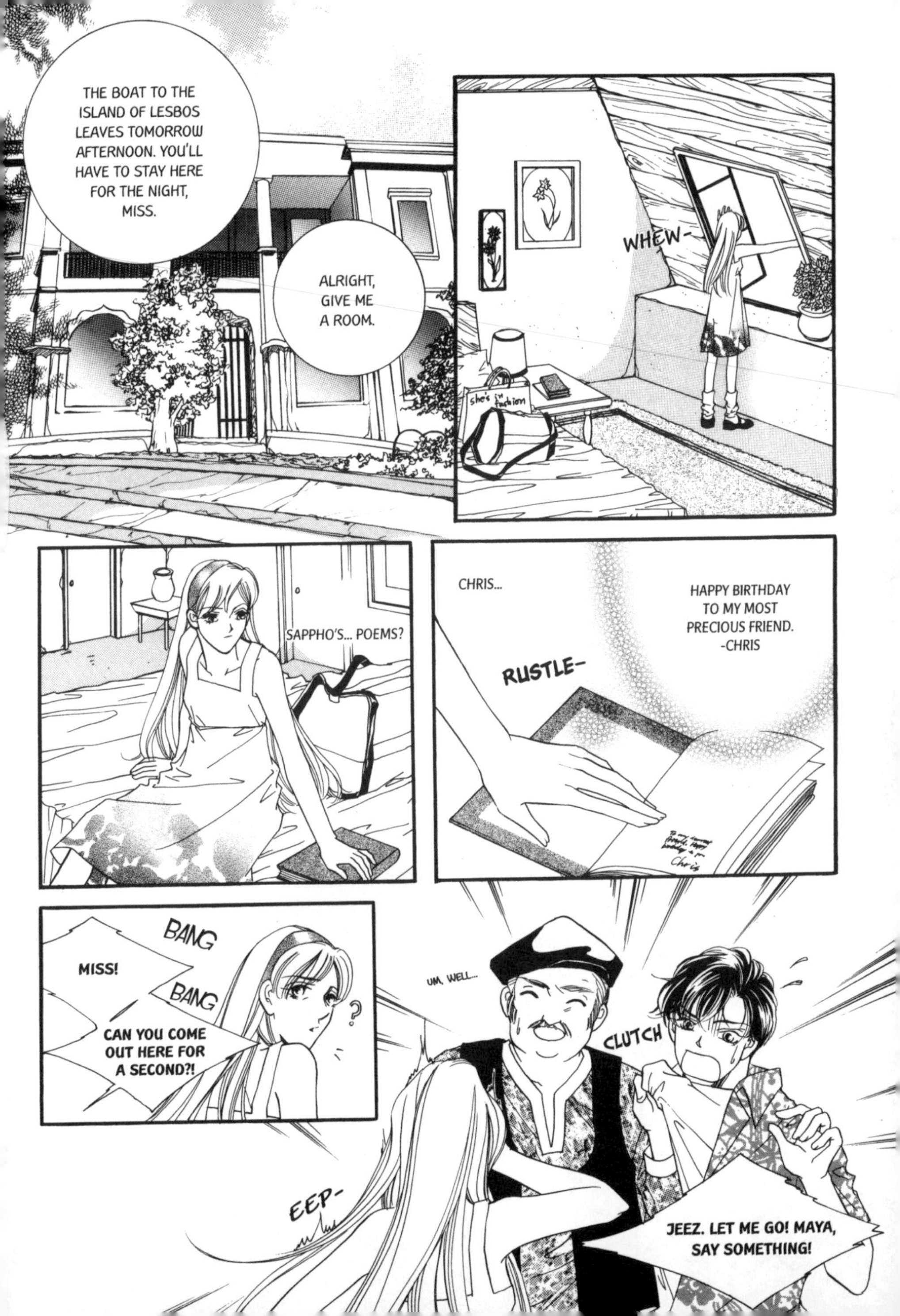
THE BOAT TO THE ISLAND OF LESBOS LEAVES TOMORROW AFTERNOON. YOU'LL HAVE TO STAY HERE FOR THE NIGHT, MISS.
ALRIGHT, GIVE ME A ROOM.
she's in fashion
WHEW-
SAPPHO'S... POEMS?
CHRIS...
HAPPY BIRTHDAY TO MY MOST PRECIOUS FRIEND. -CHRIS
RUSTLE-
BANG
MISS!
BANG
CAN YOU COME OUT HERE FOR A SECOND?!
UM, WELL...
CLUTCH
EEP-
JEEZ. LET ME GO! MAYA, SAY SOMETHING!

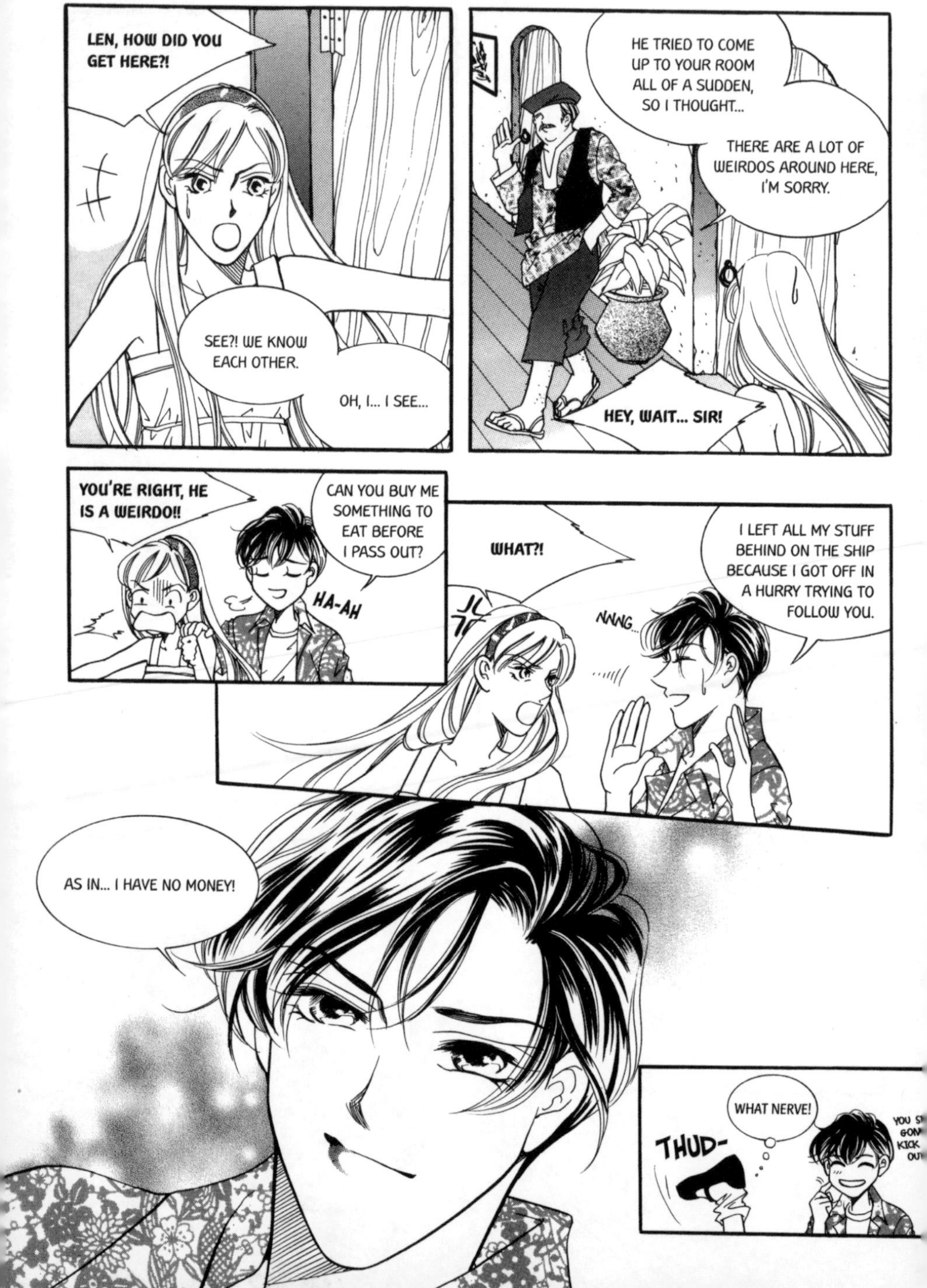
LEN, HOW DID YOU GET HERE?!
SEE?! WE KNOW EACH OTHER.
OH, I... I SEE...
HE TRIED TO COME UP TO YOUR ROOM ALL OF A SUDDEN, SO I THOUGHT...
THERE ARE A LOT OF WEIRDOS AROUND HERE, I'M SORRY.
HEY, WAIT... SIR!
YOU'RE RIGHT, HE IS A WEIRDO!!
CAN YOU BUY ME SOMETHING TO EAT BEFORE I PASS OUT?
HA-AH
WHAT?!
NNNG...
I LEFT ALL MY STUFF BEHIND ON THE SHIP BECAUSE I GOT OFF IN A HURRY TRYING TO FOLLOW YOU.
AS IN... I HAVE NO MONEY!
THUD-
WHAT NERVE!

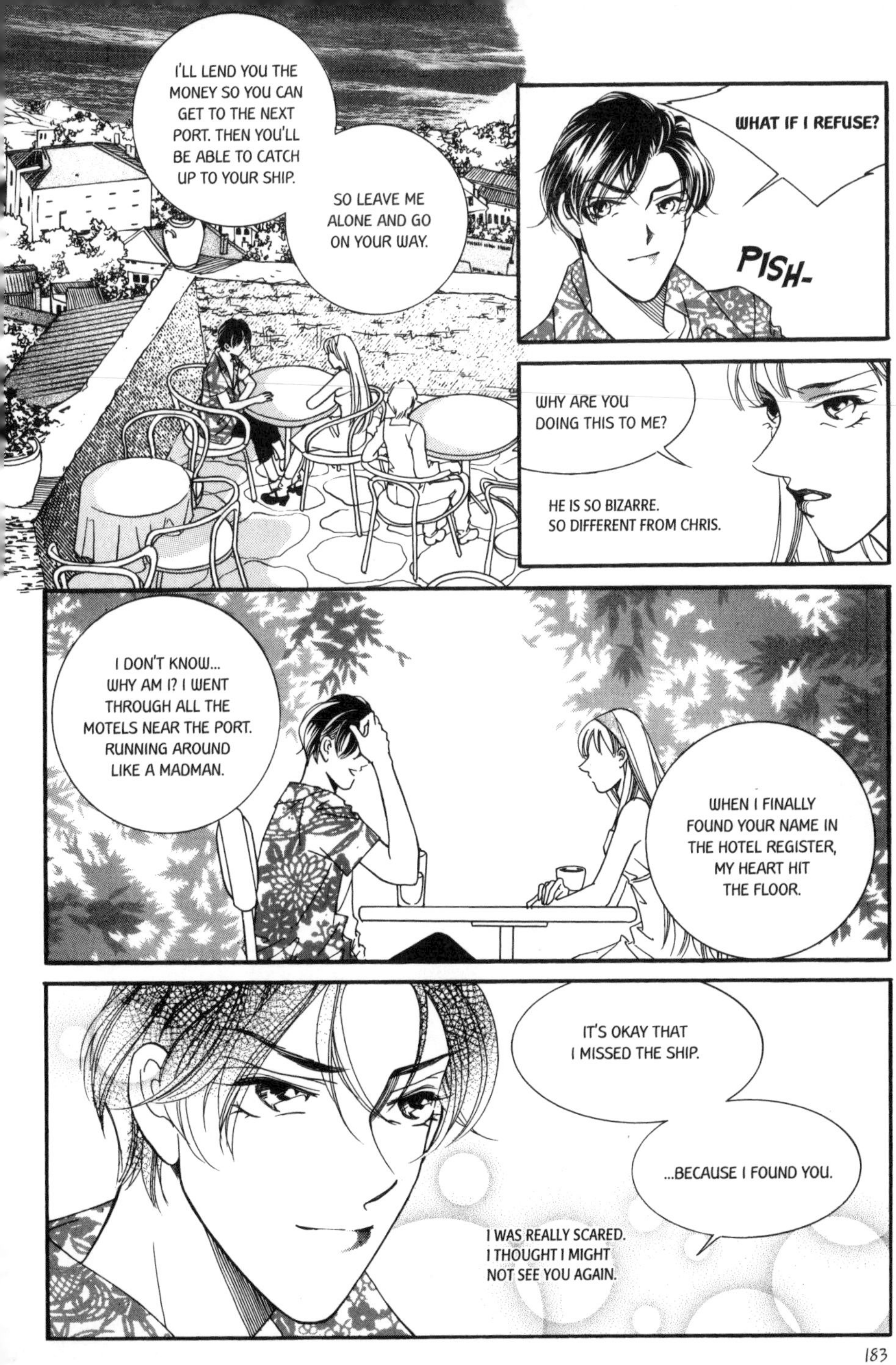
I'LL LEND YOU THE MONEY SO YOU CAN GET TO THE NEXT PORT. THEN YOU'LL BE ABLE TO CATCH UP TO YOUR SHIP.
SO LEAVE ME ALONE AND GO ON YOUR WAY.
WHAT IF I REFUSE?
PISH-
WHY ARE YOU DOING THIS TO ME?
HE IS SO BIZARRE. SO DIFFERENT FROM CHRIS.
I DON'T KNOW... WHY AM I? I WENT THROUGH ALL THE MOTELS NEAR THE PORT. RUNNING AROUND LIKE A MADMAN.
WHEN I FINALLY FOUND YOUR NAME IN THE HOTEL REGISTER, MY HEART HIT THE FLOOR.
IT'S OKAY THAT I MISSED THE SHIP.
...BECAUSE I FOUND YOU.
I WAS REALLY SCARED. I THOUGHT I MIGHT NOT SEE YOU AGAIN.

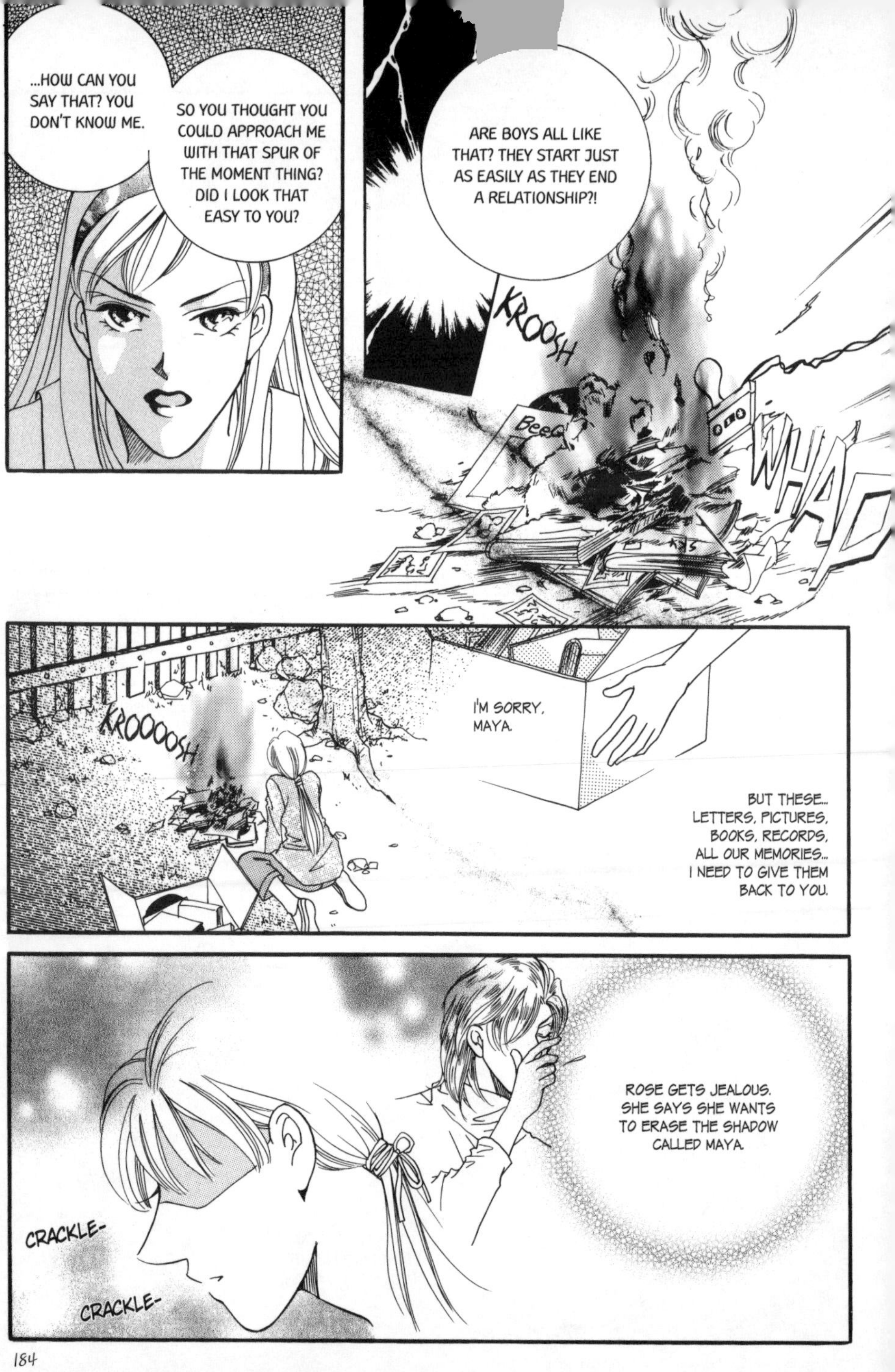
...HOW CAN YOU SAY THAT? YOU DON'T KNOW ME.
SO YOU THOUGHT YOU COULD APPROACH ME WITH THAT SPUR OF THE MOMENT THING? DID I LOOK THAT EASY TO YOU?
ARE BOYS ALL LIKE THAT? THEY START JUST AS EASILY AS THEY END A RELATIONSHIP?!
KROOSH
WHAD
KROOOOSH
I'M SORRY, MAYA.
BUT THESE... LETTERS, PICTURES, BOOKS, RECORDS, ALL OUR MEMORIES... I NEED TO GIVE THEM BACK TO YOU.
ROSE GETS JEALOUS. SHE SAYS SHE WANTS TO ERASE THE SHADOW CALLED MAYA.
CRACKLE-
CRACKLE-

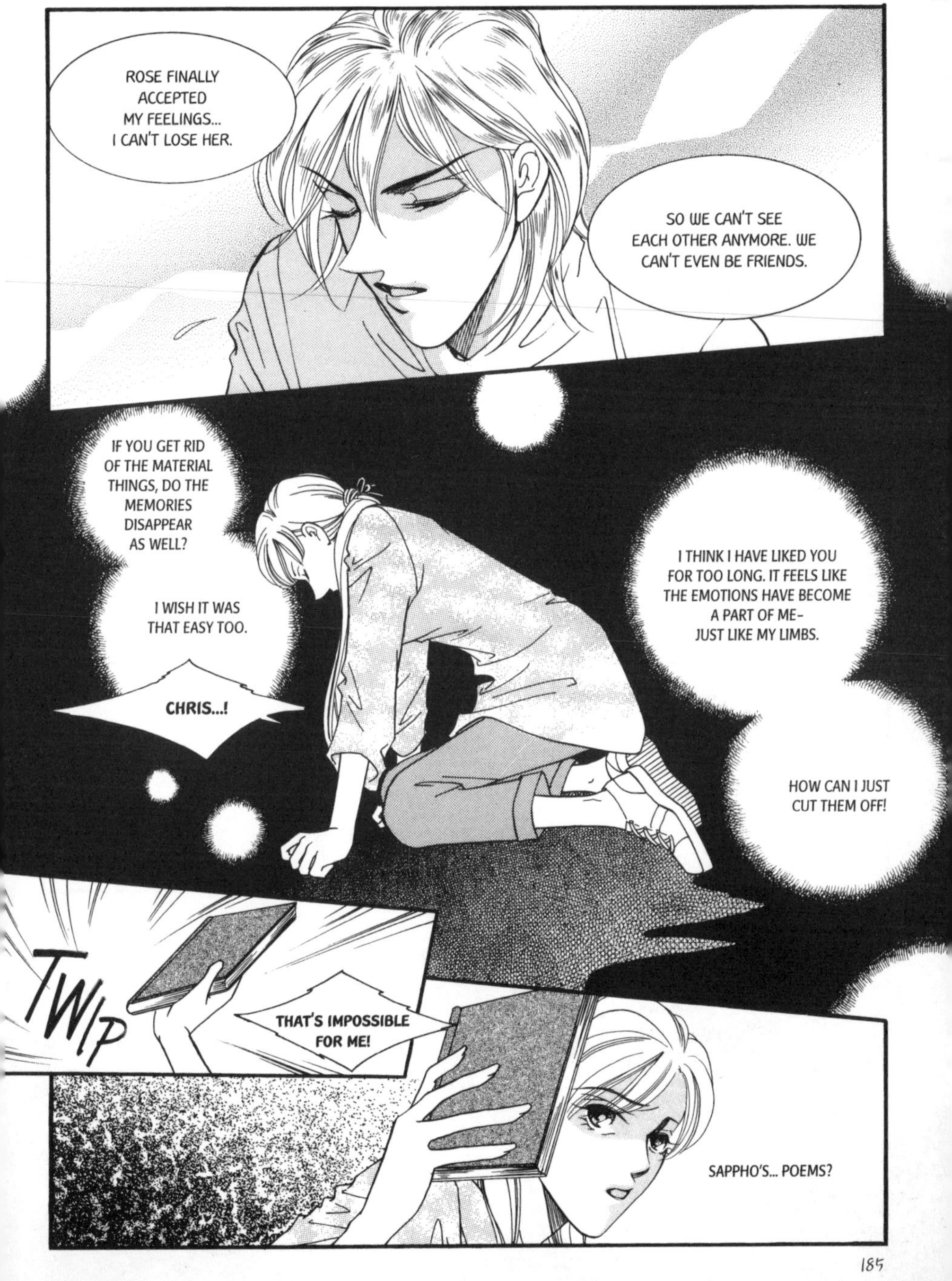

ROSE FINALLY ACCEPTED MY FEELINGS... I CAN'T LOSE HER.
SO WE CAN'T SEE EACH OTHER ANYMORE. WE CAN'T EVEN BE FRIENDS.
IF YOU GET RID OF THE MATERIAL THINGS, DO THE MEMORIES DISAPPEAR AS WELL?
I WISH IT WAS THAT EASY TOO.
I THINK I HAVE LIKED YOU FOR TOO LONG. IT FEELS LIKE THE EMOTIONS HAVE BECOME A PART OF ME- JUST LIKE MY LIMBS.
CHRIS...!
HOW CAN I JUST CUT THEM OFF!
TWIP
THAT'S IMPOSSIBLE FOR ME!
SAPPHO'S... POEMS?

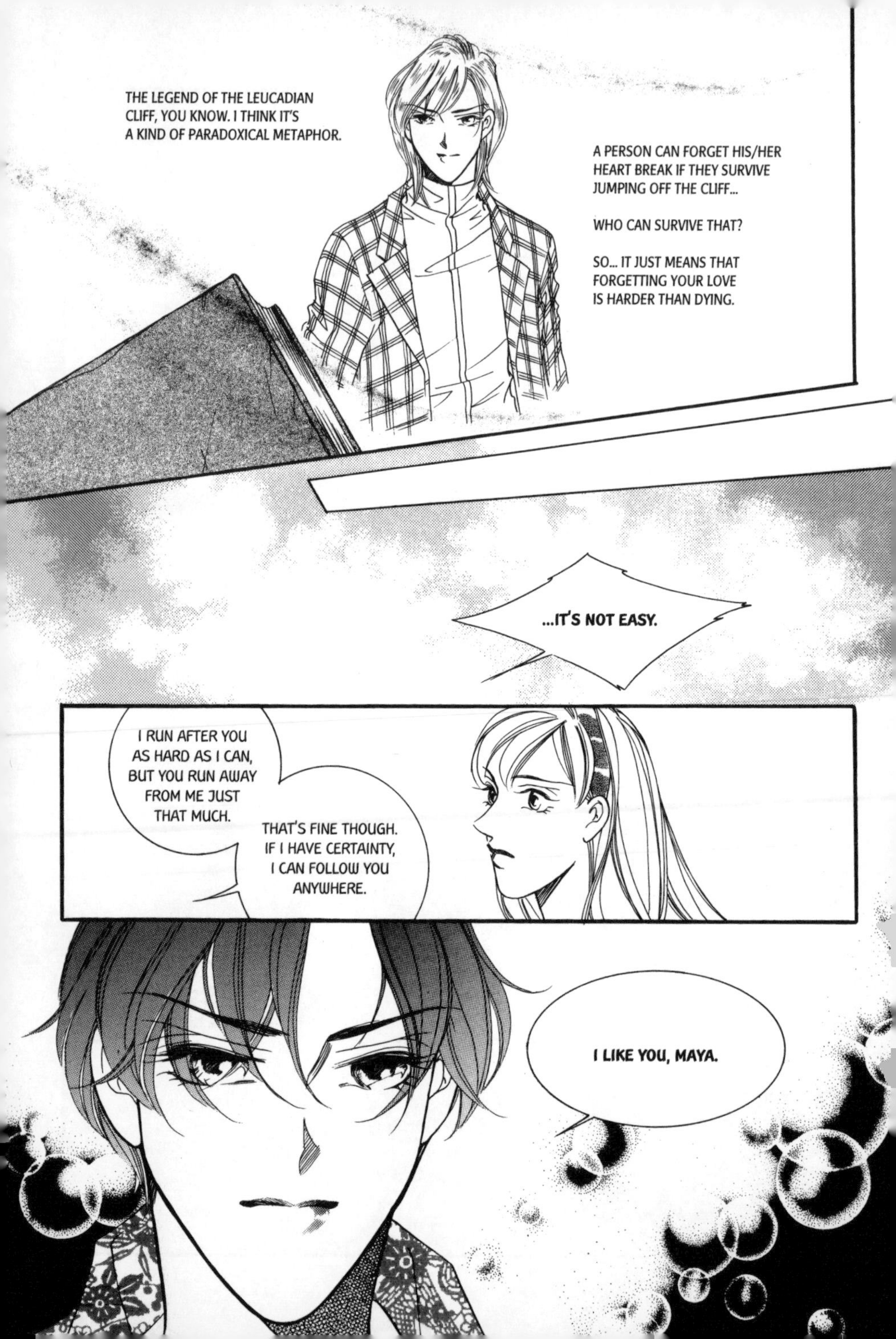
THE LEGEND OF THE LEUCADIAN CLIFF, YOU KNOW. I THINK IT'S A KIND OF PARADOXICAL METAPHOR.
A PERSON CAN FORGET HIS/HER HEART BREAK IF THEY SURVIVE JUMPING OFF THE CLIFF...
WHO CAN SURVIVE THAT?
SO... IT JUST MEANS THAT FORGETTING YOUR LOVE IS HARDER THAN DYING.
...IT'S NOT EASY.
I RUN AFTER YOU AS HARD AS I CAN, BUT YOU RUN AWAY FROM ME JUST THAT MUCH.
THAT'S FINE THOUGH. IF I HAVE CERTAINTY, I CAN FOLLOW YOU ANYWHERE.
I LIKE YOU, MAYA.

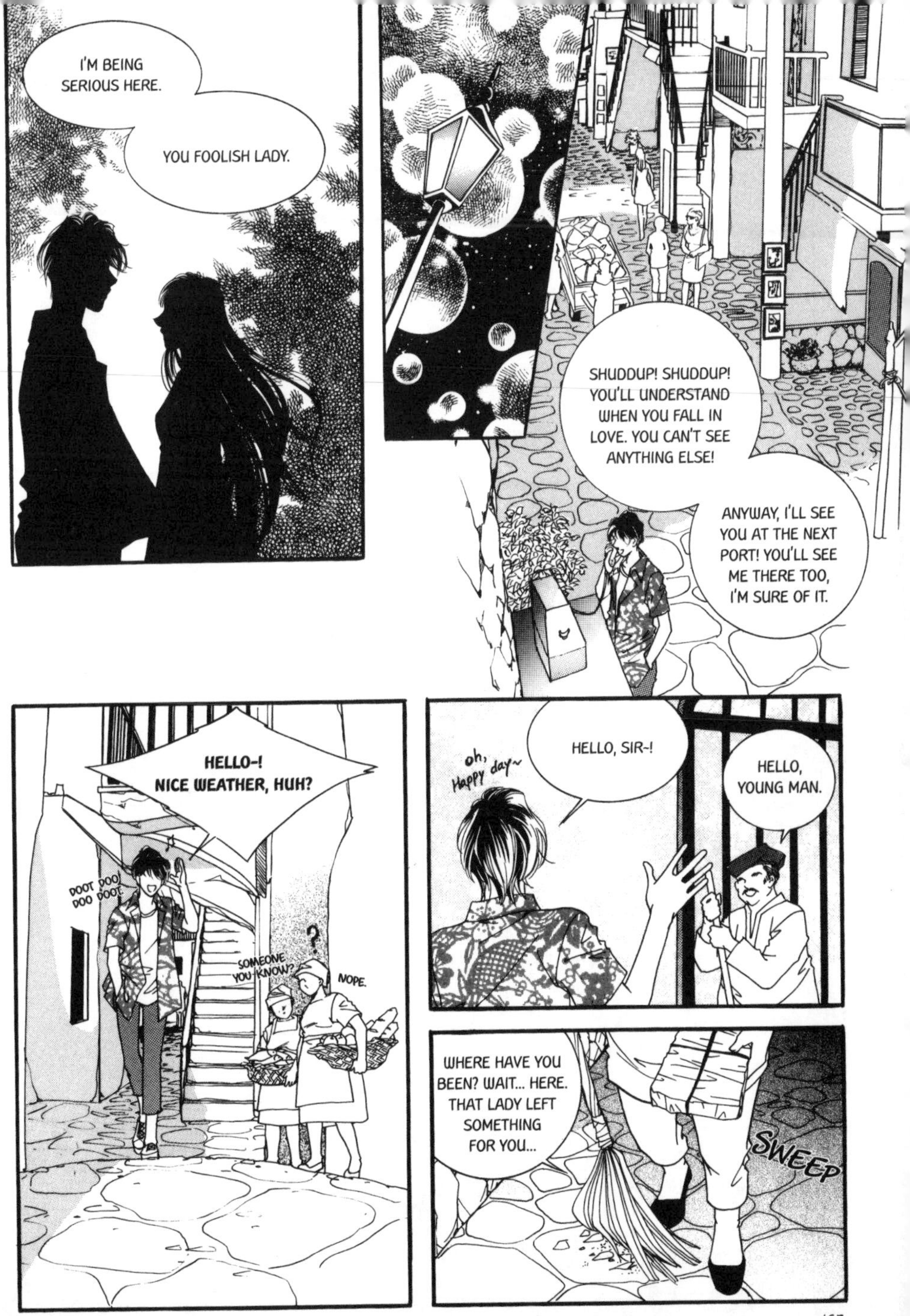
I'M BEING SERIOUS HERE.
YOU FOOLISH LADY.
SHUDDUP! SHUDDUP! YOU'LL UNDERSTAND WHEN YOU FALL IN LOVE. YOU CAN'T SEE ANYTHING ELSE!
ANYWAY, I'LL SEE YOU AT THE NEXT PORT! YOU'LL SEE ME THERE TOO, I'M SURE OF IT.
HELLO~! NICE WEATHER, HUH?
DOOT DOO DOO DOOT
SOMEONE YOU KNOW?
NOPE.
oh, Happy day~
HELLO, SIR~!
HELLO, YOUNG MAN.
WHERE HAVE YOU BEEN? WAIT... HERE. THAT LADY LEFT SOMETHING FOR YOU...
SWEEP

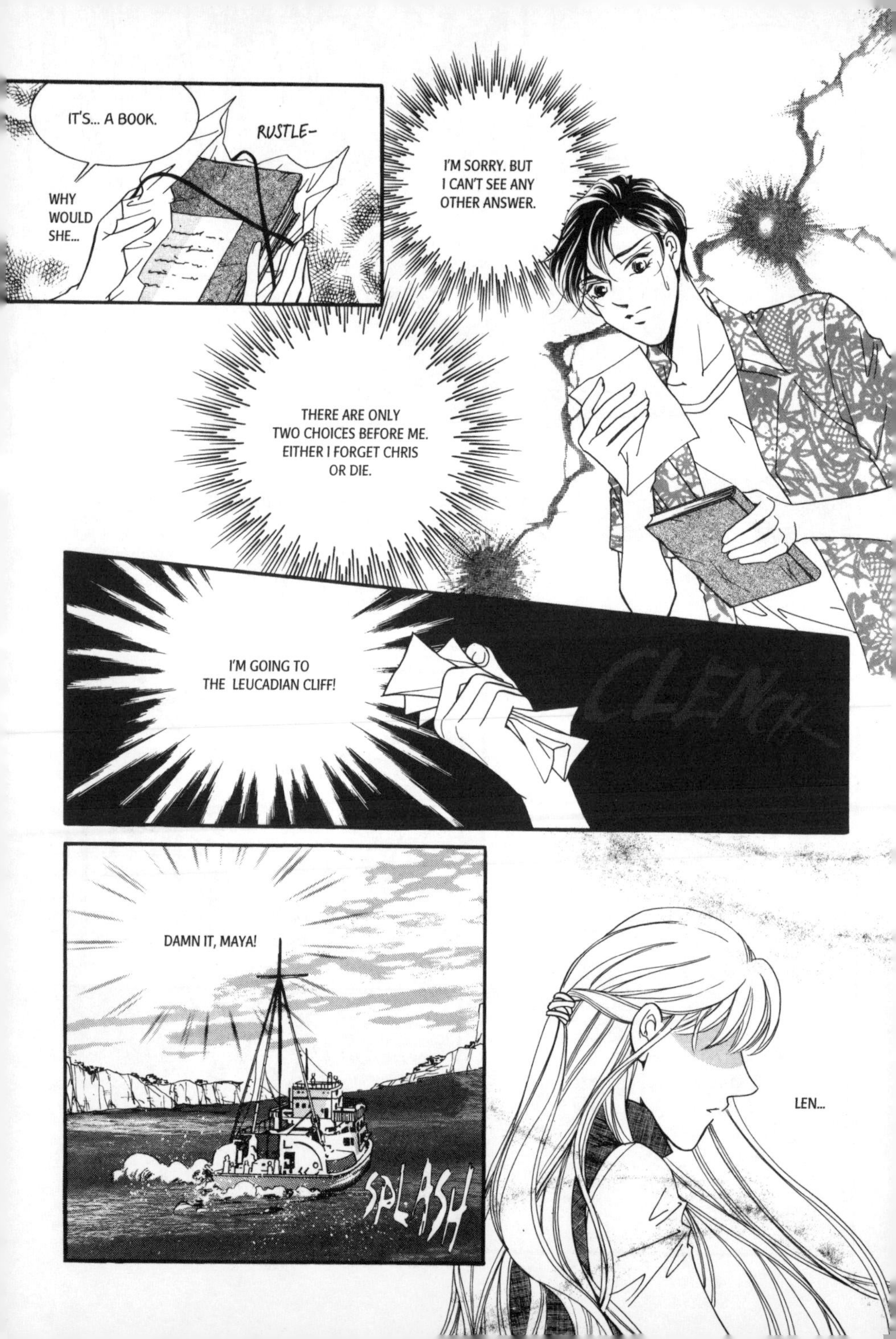

IT'S... A BOOK.
RUSTLE-
WHY WOULD SHE...
I'M SORRY. BUT I CAN'T SEE ANY OTHER ANSWER.
THERE ARE ONLY TWO CHOICES BEFORE ME. EITHER I FORGET CHRIS OR DIE.
I'M GOING TO THE LEUCADIAN CLIFF!
CLENCH
DAMN IT, MAYA!
SPLASH
LEN...

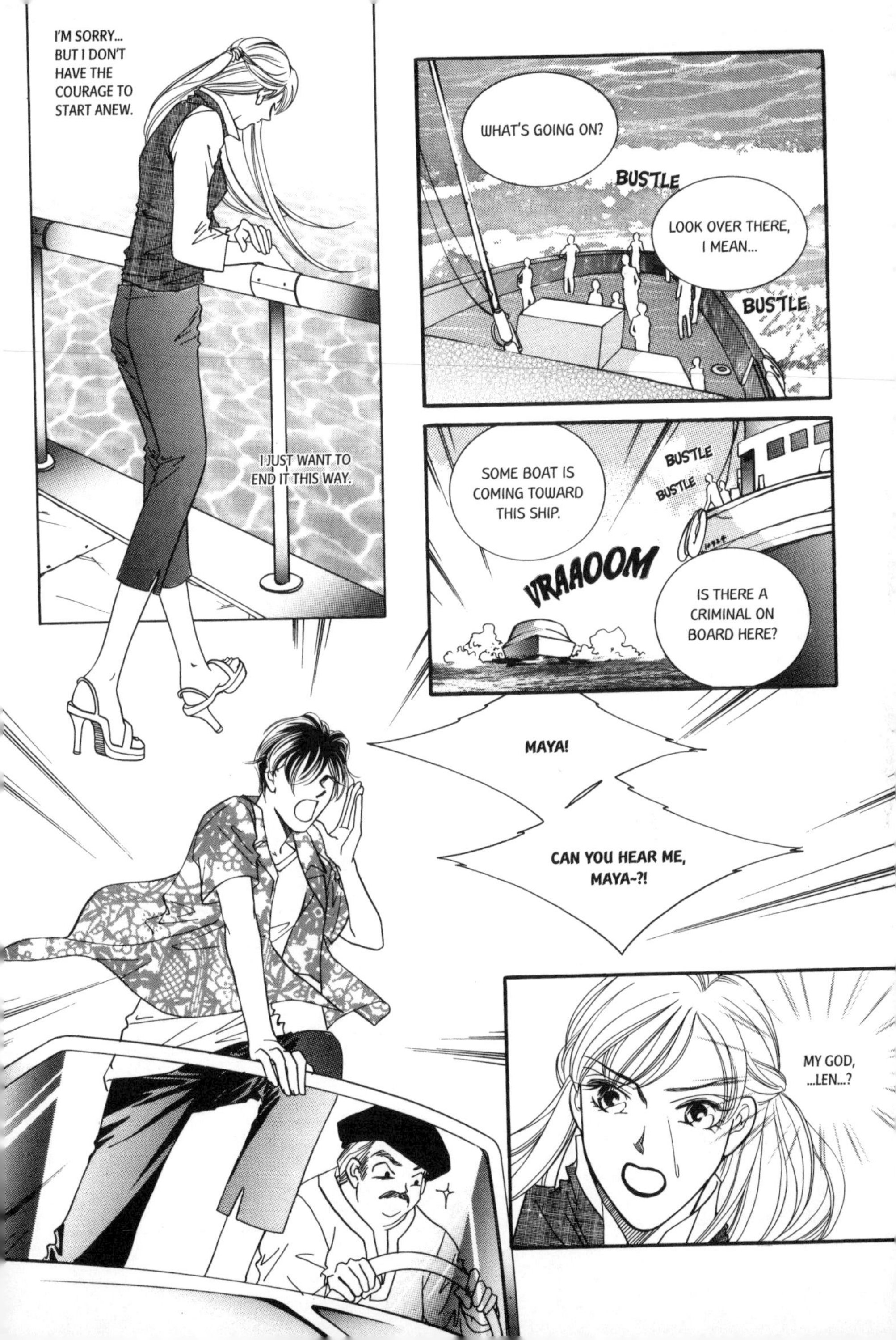
I'M SORRY... BUT I DON'T HAVE THE COURAGE TO START ANEW.
I JUST WANT TO END IT THIS WAY.
WHAT'S GOING ON?
BUSTLE
LOOK OVER THERE, I MEAN...
BUSTLE
SOME BOAT IS COMING TOWARD THIS SHIP.
BUSTLE
BUSTLE
VRAAOOM
IS THERE A CRIMINAL ON BOARD HERE?
MAYA!
CAN YOU HEAR ME, MAYA~?!
MY GOD, ...LEN...?

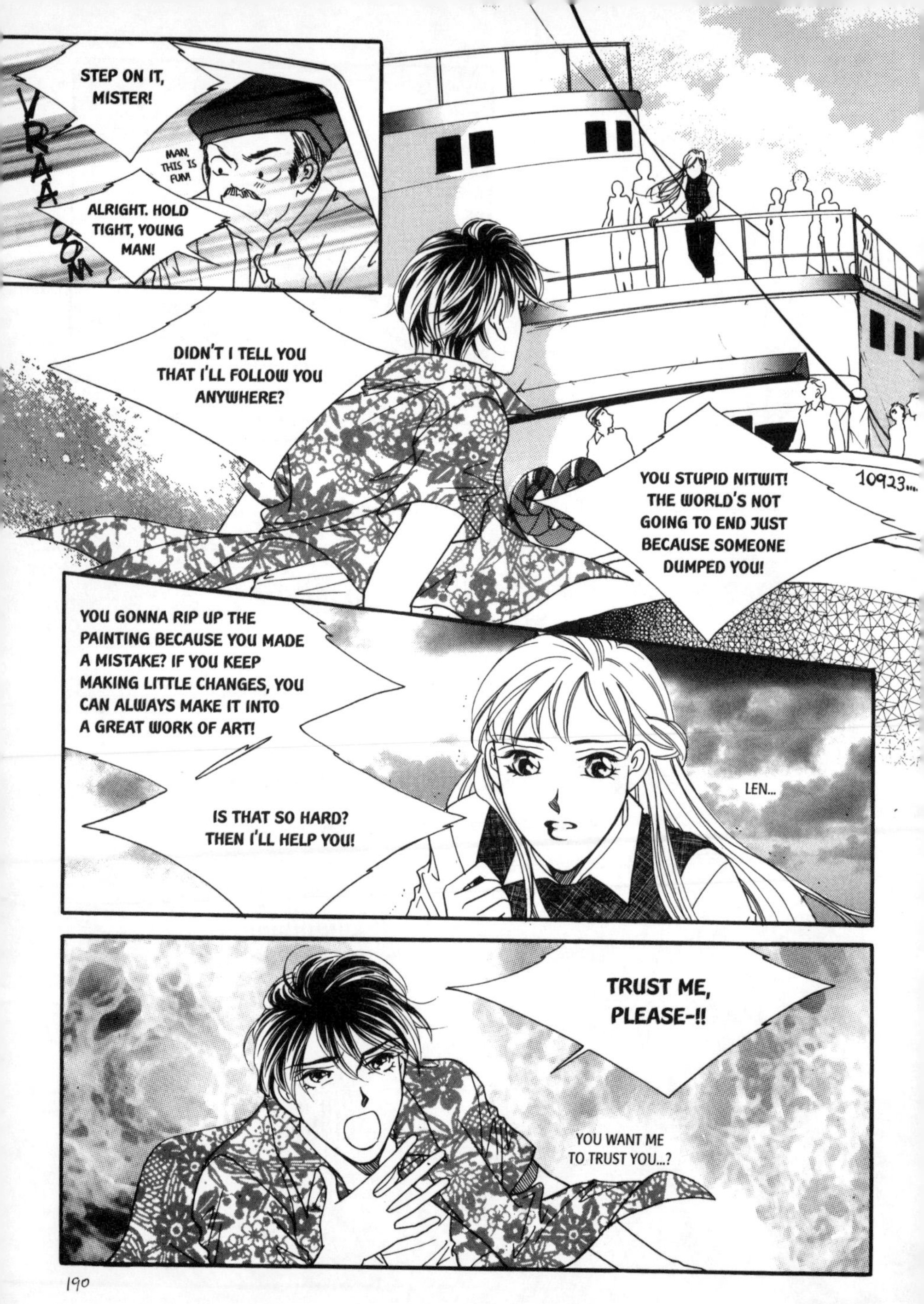
STEP ON IT, MISTER!
VRAAOOM
MAN, THIS IS FUN!
ALRIGHT. HOLD TIGHT, YOUNG MAN!
DIDN'T I TELL YOU THAT I'LL FOLLOW YOU ANYWHERE?
YOU STUPID NITWIT! THE WORLD'S NOT GOING TO END JUST BECAUSE SOMEONE DUMPED YOU!
10923...
YOU GONNA RIP UP THE PAINTING BECAUSE YOU MADE A MISTAKE? IF YOU KEEP MAKING LITTLE CHANGES, YOU CAN ALWAYS MAKE IT INTO A GREAT WORK OF ART!
IS THAT SO HARD? THEN I'LL HELP YOU!
LEN...
TRUST ME, PLEASE-!!
YOU WANT ME TO TRUST YOU...?

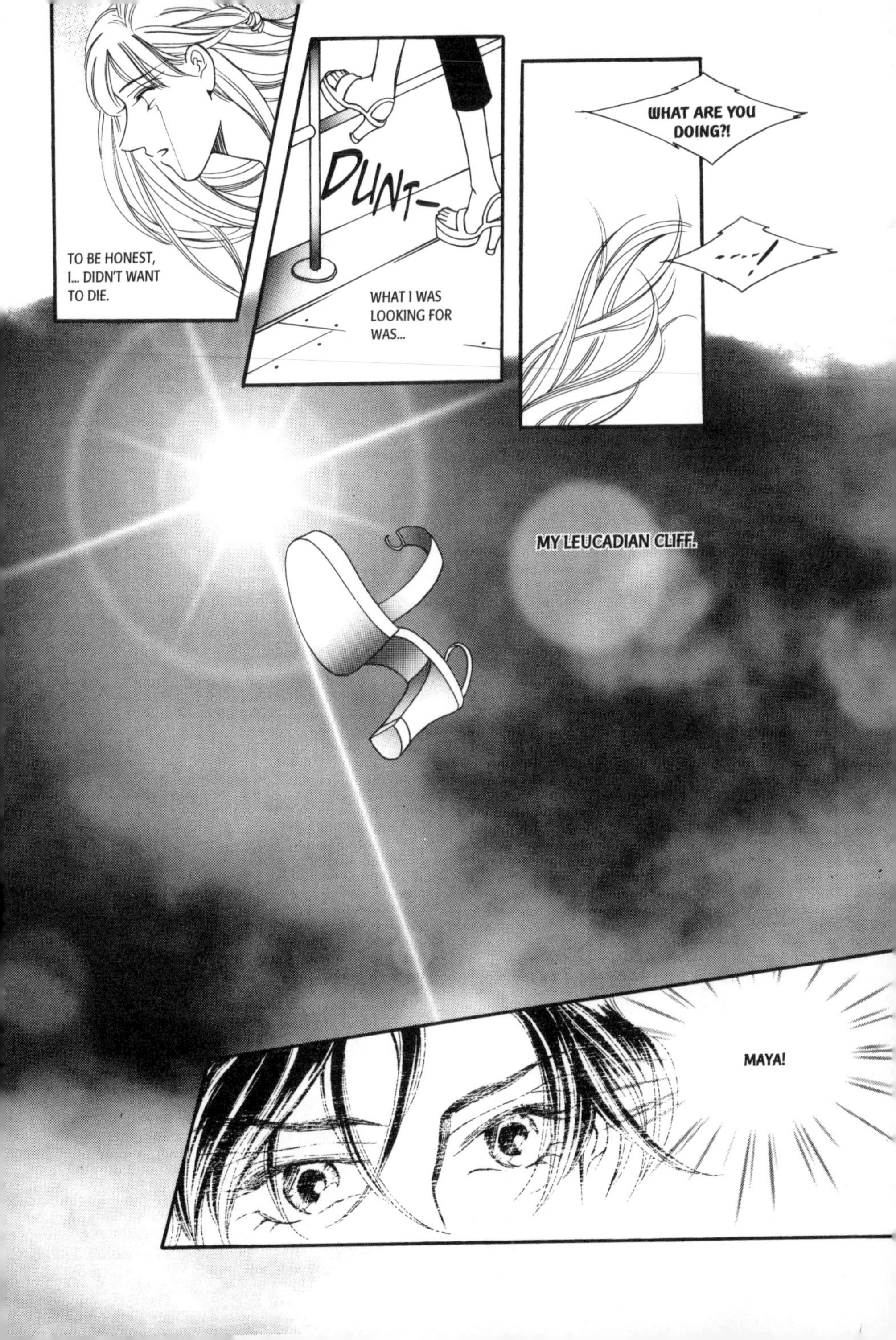
TO BE HONEST, I... DIDN'T WANT TO DIE.
DUNT-
WHAT I WAS LOOKING FOR WAS...
WHAT ARE YOU DOING?!
...!
MY LEUCADIAN CLIFF.
MAYA!

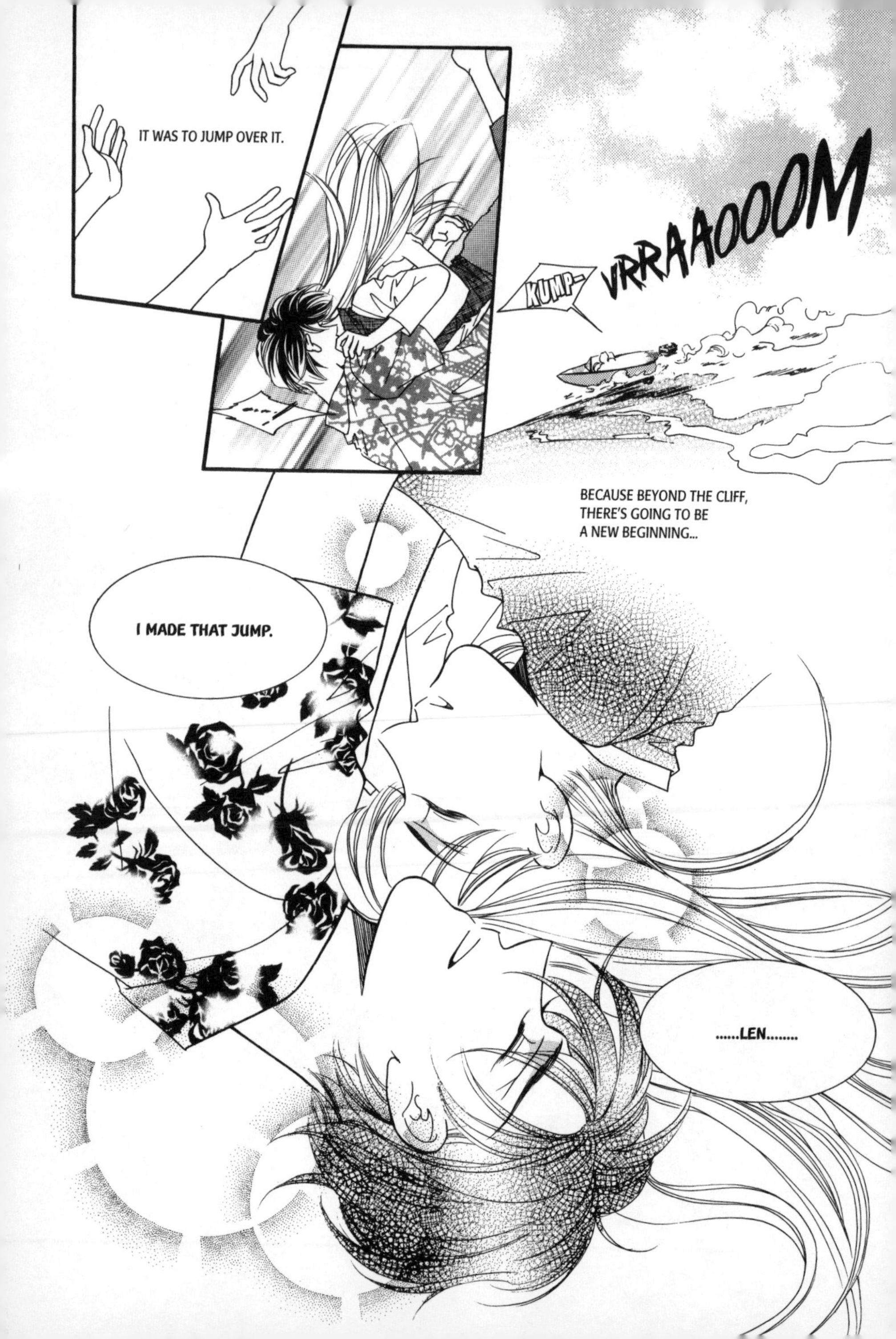

IT WAS TO JUMP OVER IT.
KUMP-
VRRAAOOOM
BECAUSE BEYOND THE CLIFF, THERE'S GOING TO BE A NEW BEGINNING...
I MADE THAT JUMP.
......LEN........

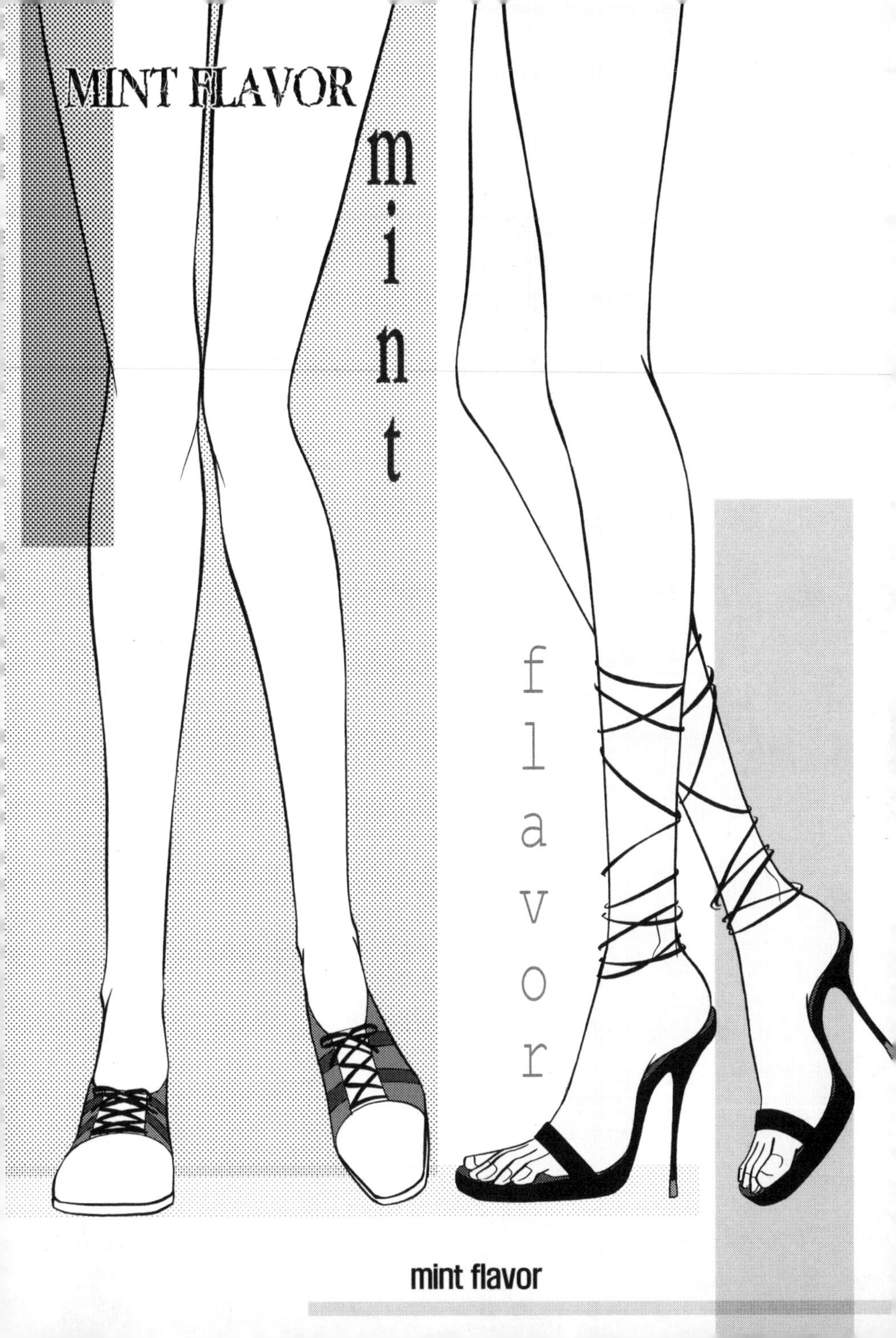
MINT FLAVOR
mint
flavor

mint flavor

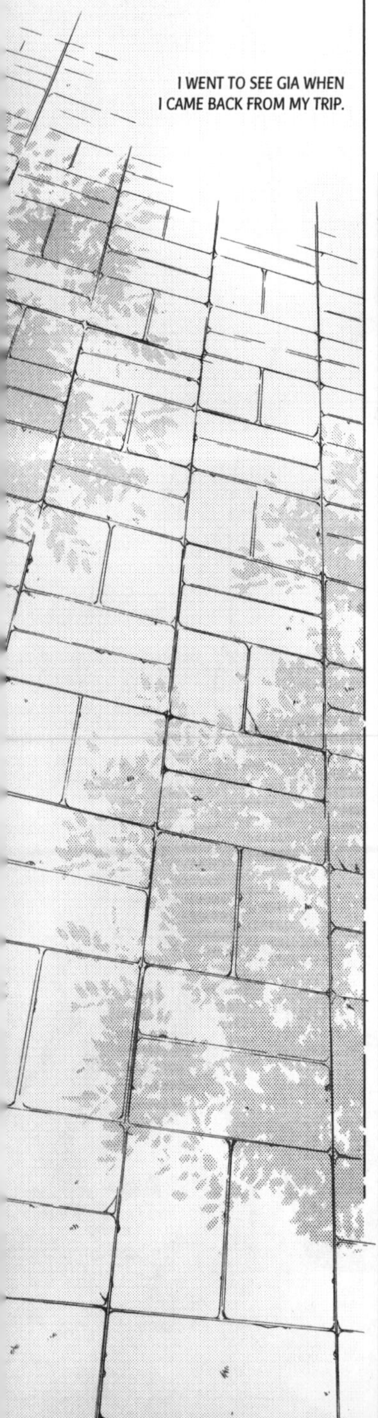
I WENT TO SEE GIA WHEN
I CAME BACK FROM MY TRIP.

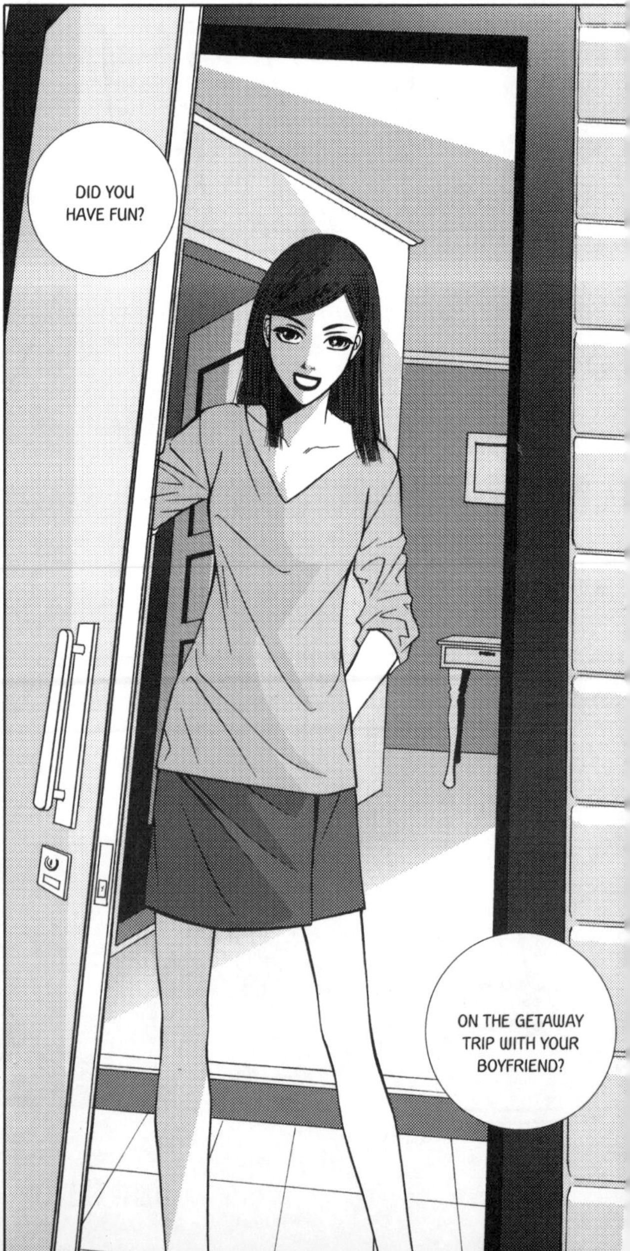
DID YOU
HAVE FUN?
ON THE GETAWAY
TRIP WITH YOUR
BOYFRIEND?

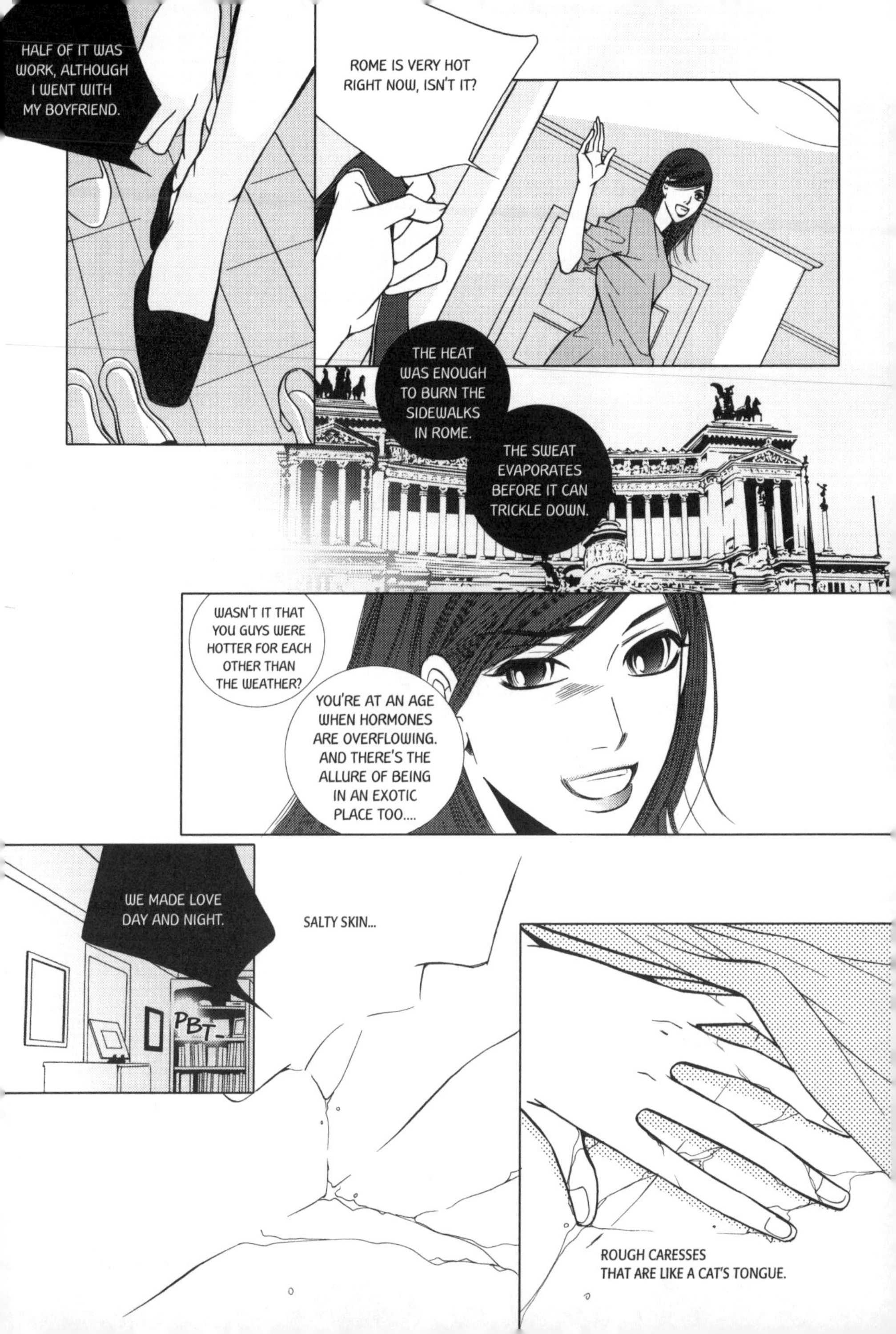
HALF OF IT WAS WORK, ALTHOUGH I WENT WITH MY BOYFRIEND.
ROME IS VERY HOT RIGHT NOW, ISN'T IT?
THE HEAT WAS ENOUGH TO BURN THE SIDEWALKS IN ROME.
THE SWEAT EVAPORATES BEFORE IT CAN TRICKLE DOWN.
WASN'T IT THAT YOU GUYS WERE HOTTER FOR EACH OTHER THAN THE WEATHER?
YOU'RE AT AN AGE WHEN HORMONES ARE OVERFLOWING. AND THERE'S THE ALLURE OF BEING IN AN EXOTIC PLACE TOO....
WE MADE LOVE DAY AND NIGHT.
PBT_
SALTY SKIN...
ROUGH CARESSES THAT ARE LIKE A CAT'S TONGUE.

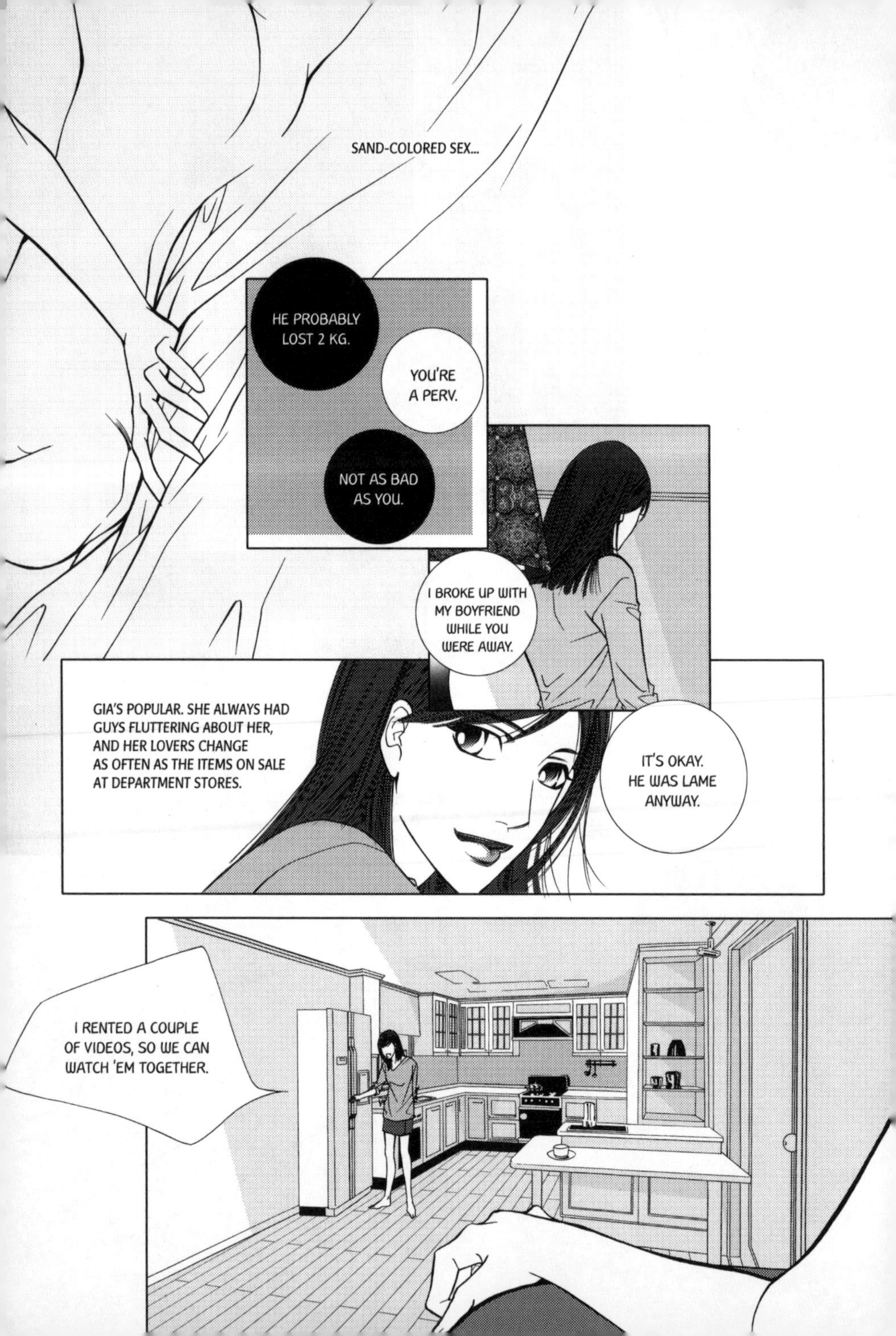
SAND-COLORED SEX...
HE PROBABLY LOST 2 KG.
YOU'RE A PERV.
NOT AS BAD AS YOU.
I BROKE UP WITH MY BOYFRIEND WHILE YOU WERE AWAY.
GIA'S POPULAR. SHE ALWAYS HAD GUYS FLUTTERING ABOUT HER, AND HER LOVERS CHANGE AS OFTEN AS THE ITEMS ON SALE AT DEPARTMENT STORES.
IT'S OKAY. HE WAS LAME ANYWAY.
I RENTED A COUPLE OF VIDEOS, SO WE CAN WATCH 'EM TOGETHER.

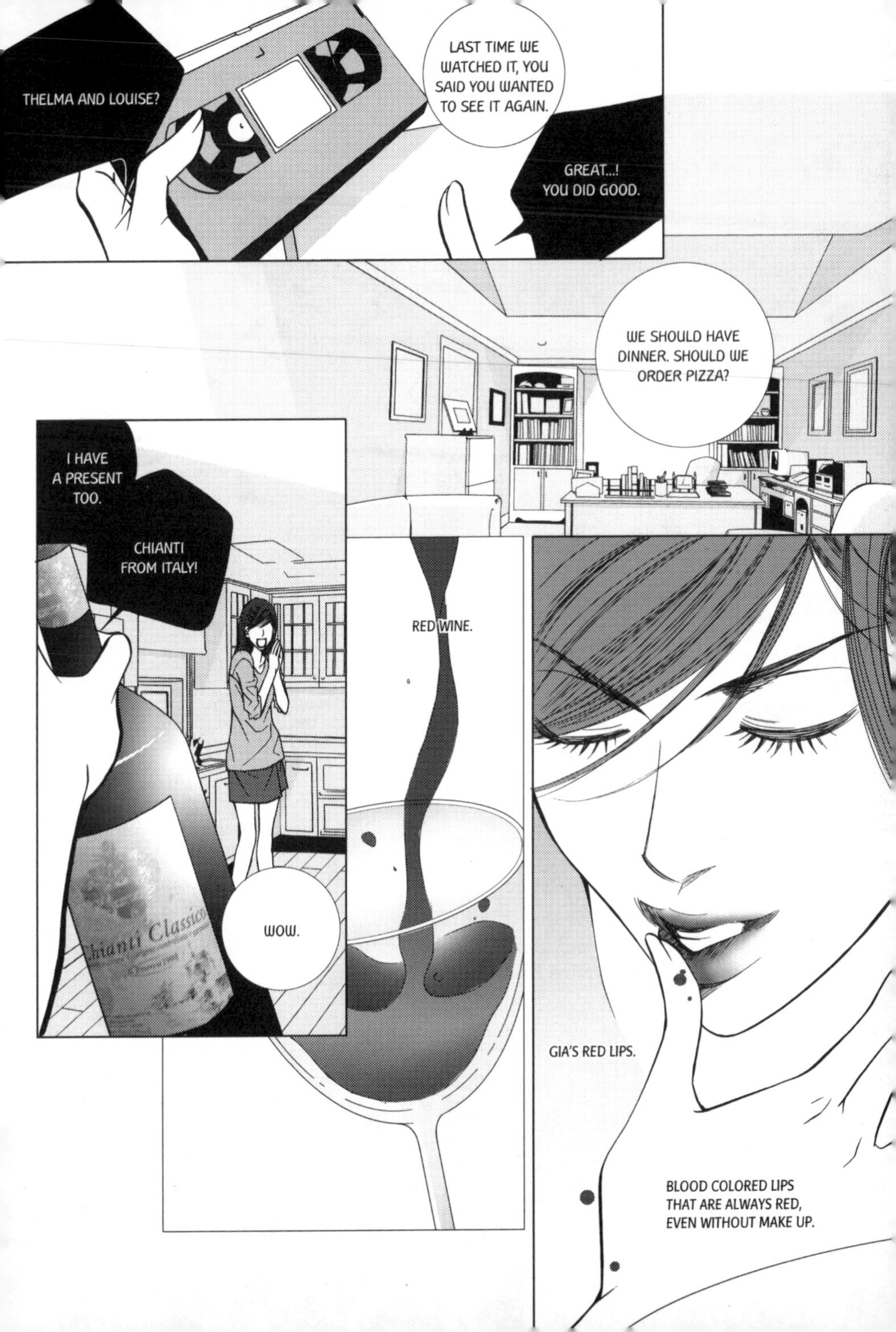
THELMA AND LOUISE?
LAST TIME WE WATCHED IT, YOU SAID YOU WANTED TO SEE IT AGAIN.
GREAT...! YOU DID GOOD.
WE SHOULD HAVE DINNER. SHOULD WE ORDER PIZZA?
I HAVE A PRESENT TOO.
CHIANTI FROM ITALY!
Chianti Classico
WOW.
RED WINE.
GIA'S RED LIPS.
BLOOD COLORED LIPS THAT ARE ALWAYS RED, EVEN WITHOUT MAKE UP.

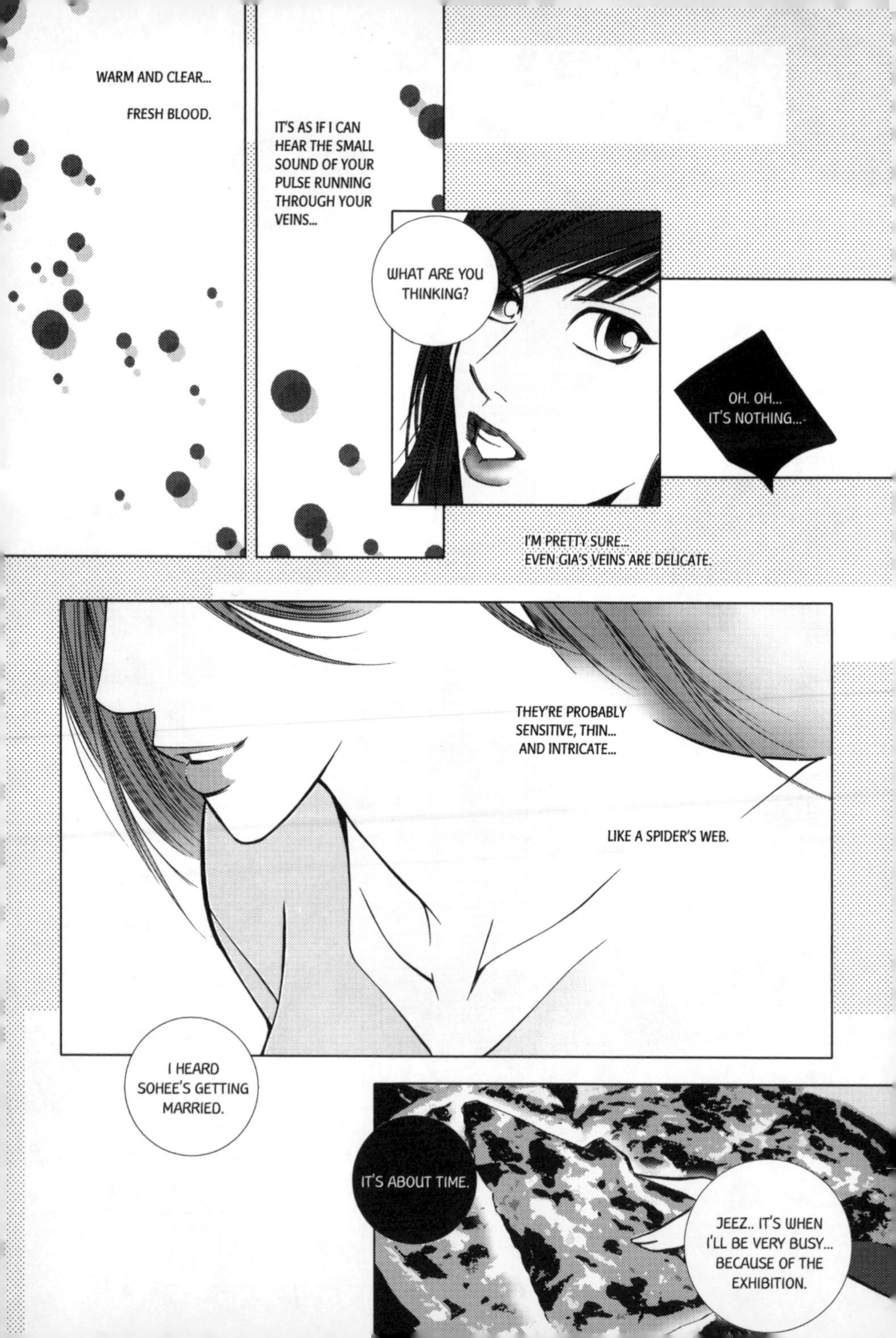
WARM AND CLEAR...
FRESH BLOOD.
IT'S AS IF I CAN HEAR THE SMALL SOUND OF YOUR PULSE RUNNING THROUGH YOUR VEINS...
WHAT ARE YOU THINKING?
OH. OH... IT'S NOTHING...
I'M PRETTY SURE... EVEN GIA'S VEINS ARE DELICATE.
THEY'RE PROBABLY SENSITIVE, THIN... AND INTRICATE...
LIKE A SPIDER'S WEB.
I HEARD SOHEE'S GETTING MARRIED.
IT'S ABOUT TIME.
JEEZ.. IT'S WHEN I'LL BE VERY BUSY... BECAUSE OF THE EXHIBITION.

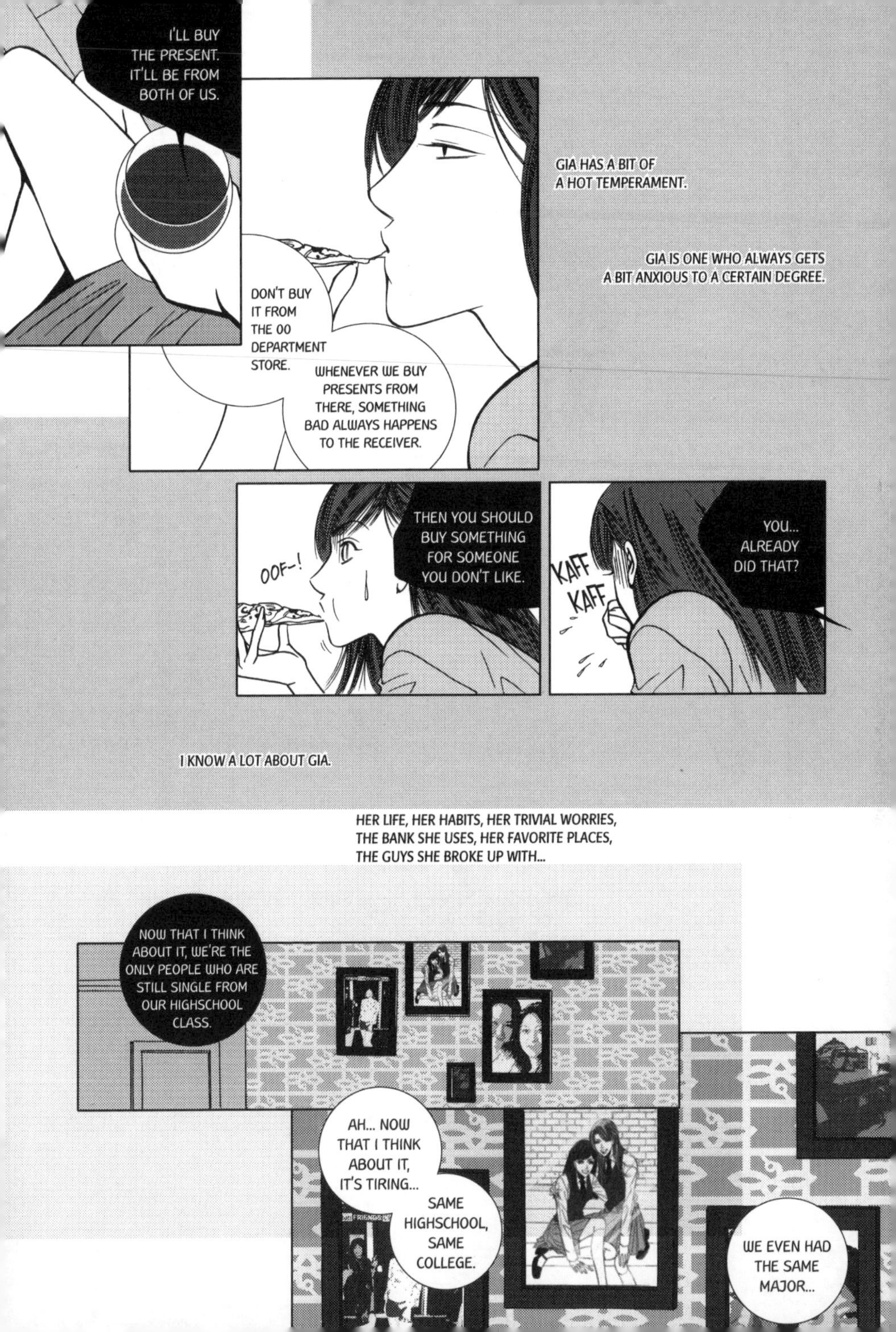

I'LL BUY THE PRESENT. IT'LL BE FROM BOTH OF US.
DON'T BUY IT FROM THE OO DEPARTMENT STORE.
WHENEVER WE BUY PRESENTS FROM THERE, SOMETHING BAD ALWAYS HAPPENS TO THE RECEIVER.
GIA HAS A BIT OF A HOT TEMPERAMENT.
GIA IS ONE WHO ALWAYS GETS A BIT ANXIOUS TO A CERTAIN DEGREE.
OOF-!
THEN YOU SHOULD BUY SOMETHING FOR SOMEONE YOU DON'T LIKE.
KAFF KAFF
YOU... ALREADY DID THAT?
I KNOW A LOT ABOUT GIA.
HER LIFE, HER HABITS, HER TRIVIAL WORRIES, THE BANK SHE USES, HER FAVORITE PLACES, THE GUYS SHE BROKE UP WITH...
NOW THAT I THINK ABOUT IT, WE'RE THE ONLY PEOPLE WHO ARE STILL SINGLE FROM OUR HIGHSCHOOL CLASS.
AH... NOW THAT I THINK ABOUT IT, IT'S TIRING...
SAME HIGHSCHOOL, SAME COLLEGE.
WE EVEN HAD THE SAME MAJOR...

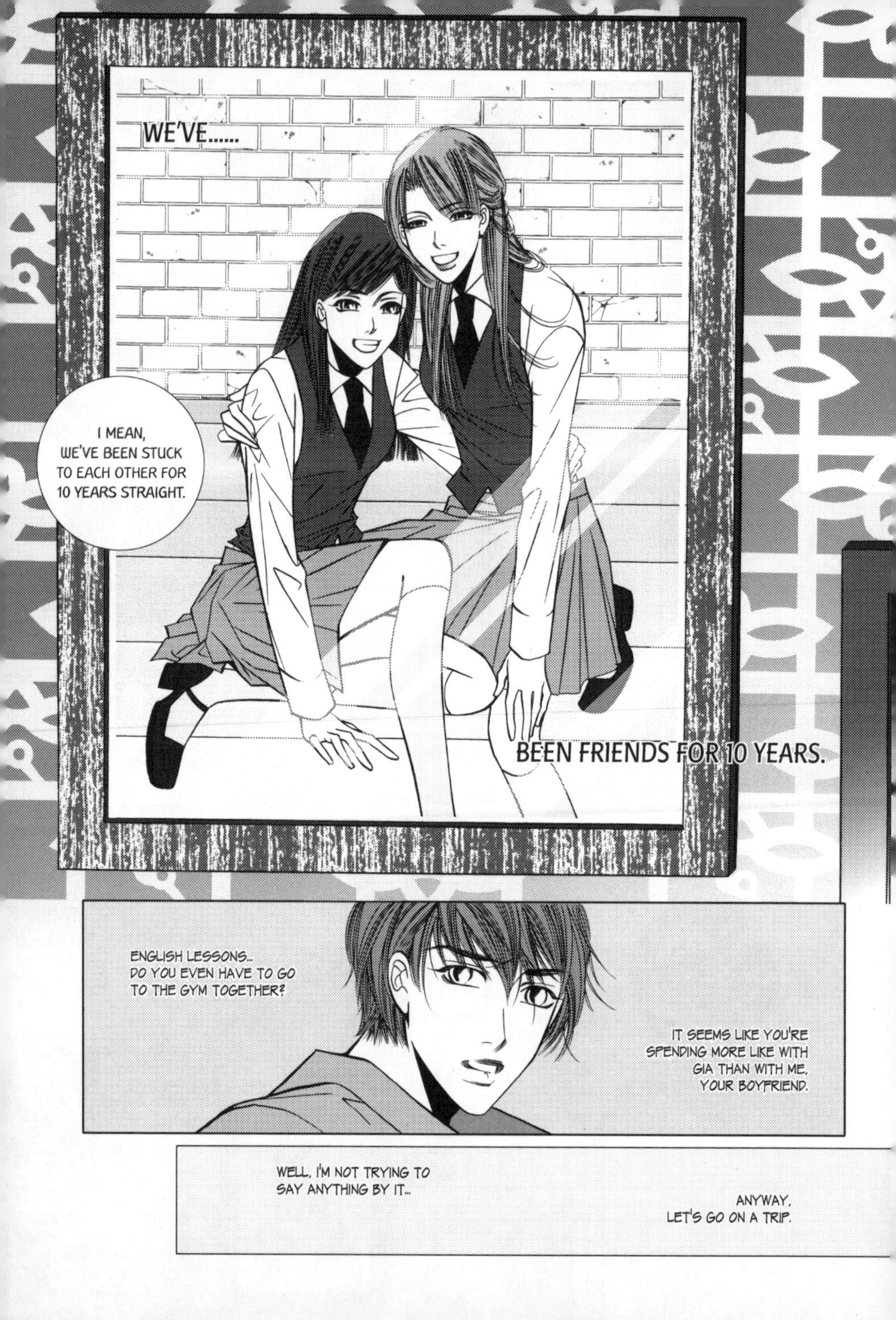
WE'VE......
I MEAN, WE'VE BEEN STUCK TO EACH OTHER FOR 10 YEARS STRAIGHT.
BEEN FRIENDS FOR 10 YEARS.
ENGLISH LESSONS... DO YOU EVEN HAVE TO GO TO THE GYM TOGETHER?
IT SEEMS LIKE YOU'RE SPENDING MORE LIKE WITH GIA THAN WITH ME, YOUR BOYFRIEND.
WELL, I'M NOT TRYING TO SAY ANYTHING BY IT...
ANYWAY, LET'S GO ON A TRIP.

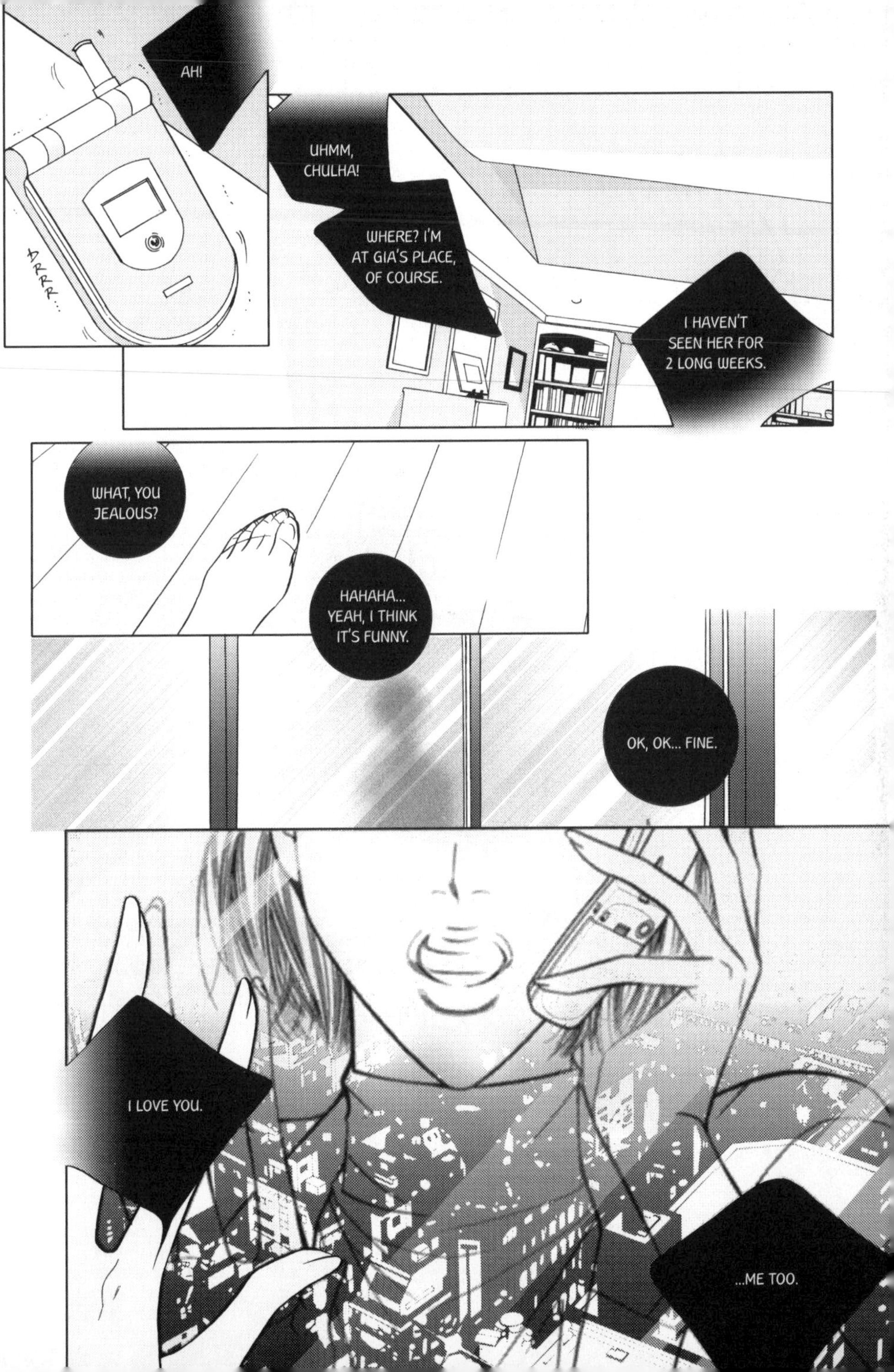
AH!
DRRR...
UHMM, CHULHA!
WHERE? I'M AT GIA'S PLACE, OF COURSE.
I HAVEN'T SEEN HER FOR 2 LONG WEEKS.
WHAT, YOU JEALOUS?
HAHAHA... YEAH, I THINK IT'S FUNNY.
OK, OK... FINE.
I LOVE YOU.
...ME TOO.

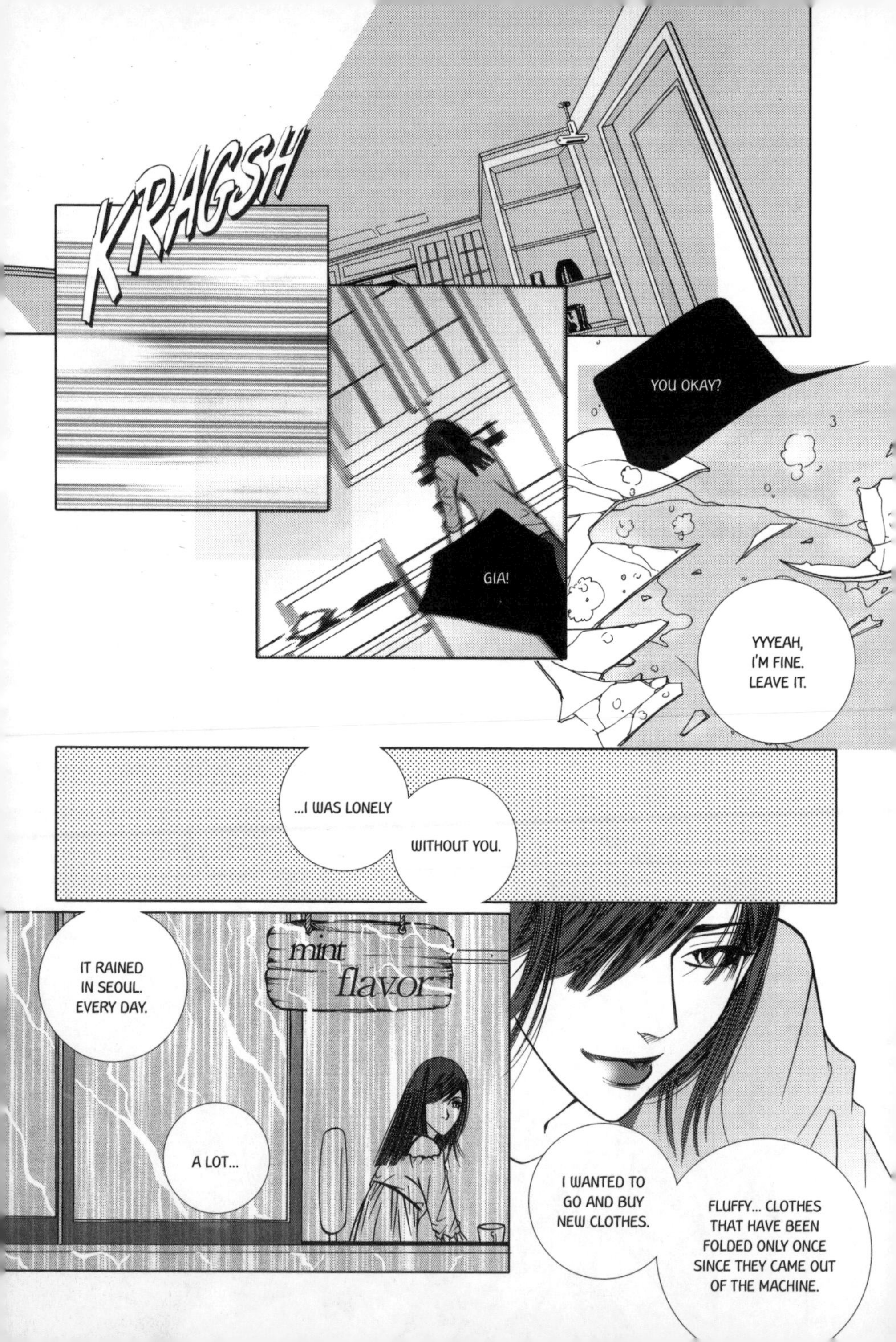
KRAGSH
GIA!
YOU OKAY?
YYYEAH, I'M FINE. LEAVE IT.
...I WAS LONELY
WITHOUT YOU.
IT RAINED IN SEOUL. EVERY DAY.
mint flavor
A LOT...
I WANTED TO GO AND BUY NEW CLOTHES.
FLUFFY... CLOTHES THAT HAVE BEEN FOLDED ONLY ONCE SINCE THEY CAME OUT OF THE MACHINE.

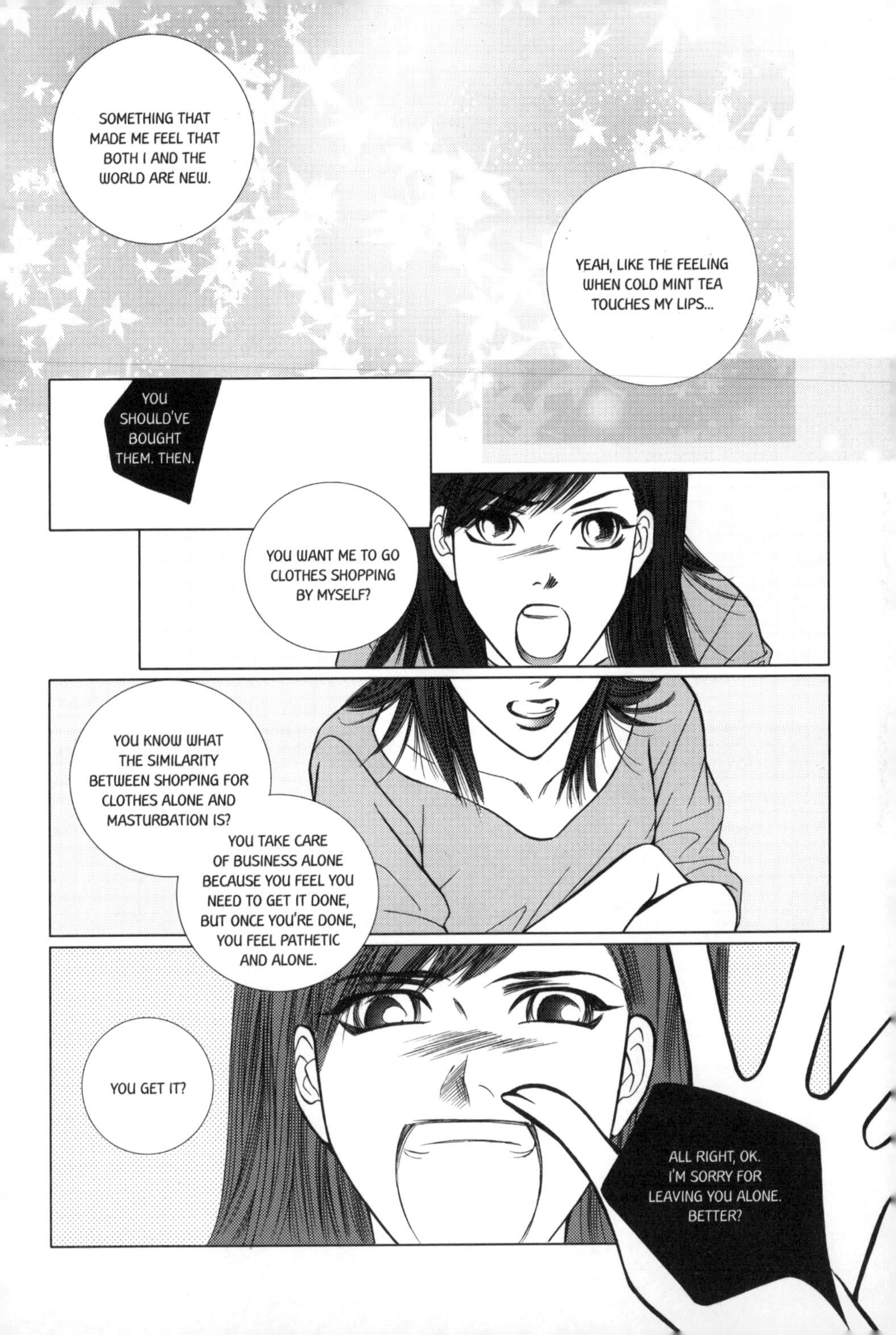
SOMETHING THAT MADE ME FEEL THAT BOTH I AND THE WORLD ARE NEW.
YEAH, LIKE THE FEELING WHEN COLD MINT TEA TOUCHES MY LIPS...
YOU SHOULD'VE BOUGHT THEM. THEN.
YOU WANT ME TO GO CLOTHES SHOPPING BY MYSELF?
YOU KNOW WHAT THE SIMILARITY BETWEEN SHOPPING FOR CLOTHES ALONE AND MASTURBATION IS?
YOU TAKE CARE OF BUSINESS ALONE BECAUSE YOU FEEL YOU NEED TO GET IT DONE, BUT ONCE YOU'RE DONE, YOU FEEL PATHETIC AND ALONE.
YOU GET IT?
ALL RIGHT, OK. I'M SORRY FOR LEAVING YOU ALONE. BETTER?

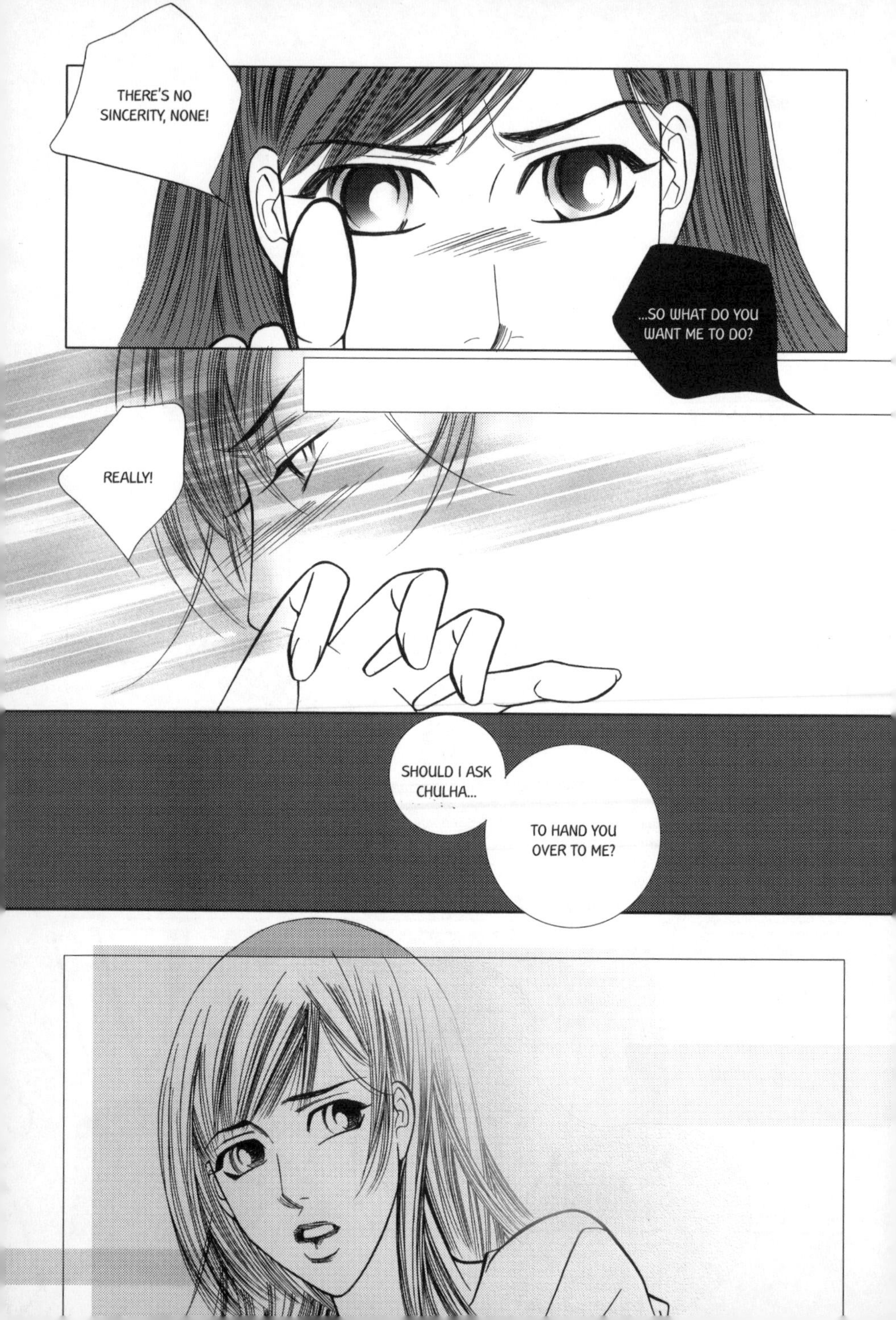
THERE'S NO SINCERITY, NONE!
...SO WHAT DO YOU WANT ME TO DO?
REALLY!
SHOULD I ASK CHULHA...
TO HAND YOU OVER TO ME?

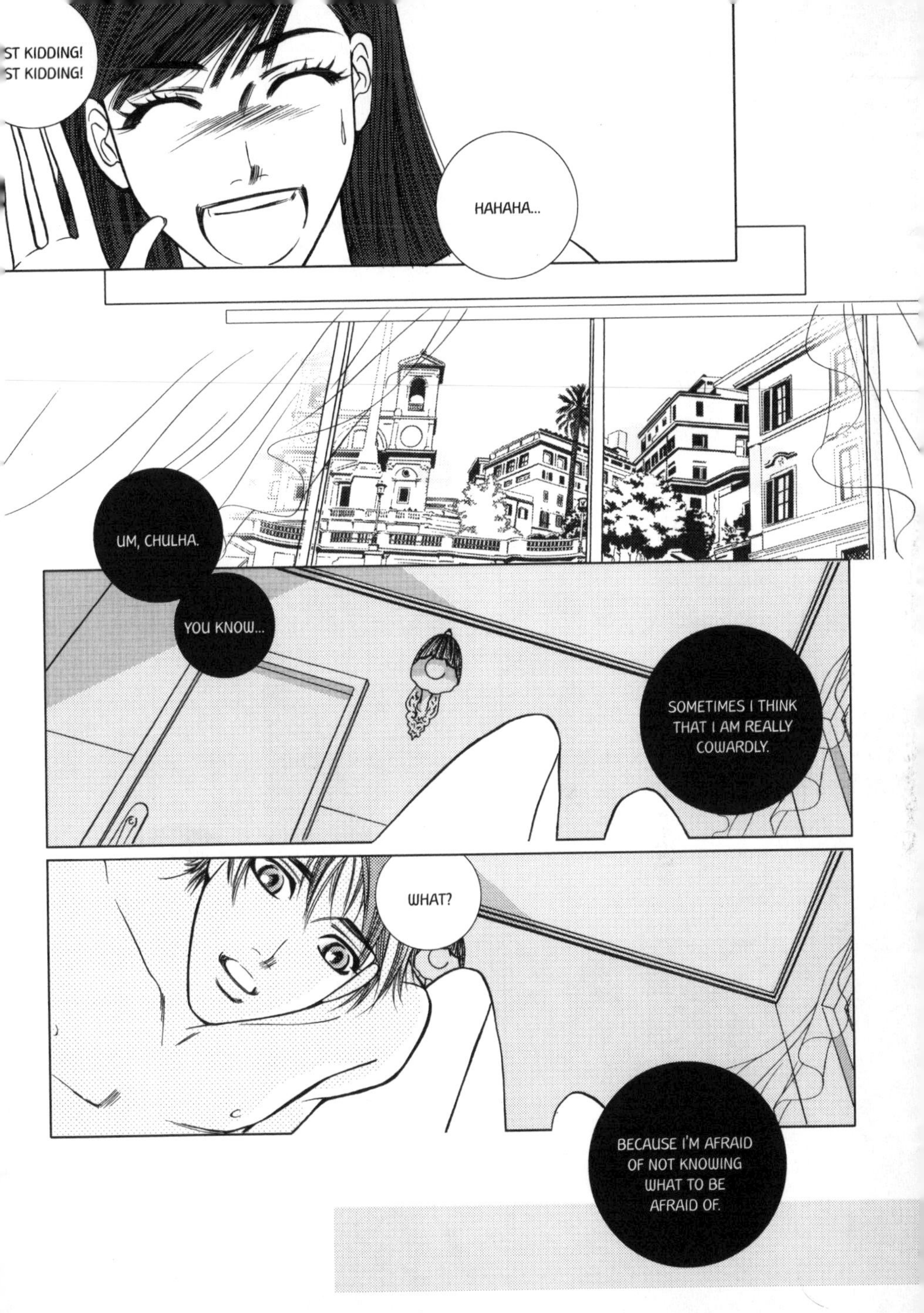
ST KIDDING!
ST KIDDING!
HAHAHA...
UM, CHULHA.
YOU KNOW...
SOMETIMES I THINK THAT I AM REALLY COWARDLY.
WHAT?
BECAUSE I'M AFRAID OF NOT KNOWING WHAT TO BE AFRAID OF.

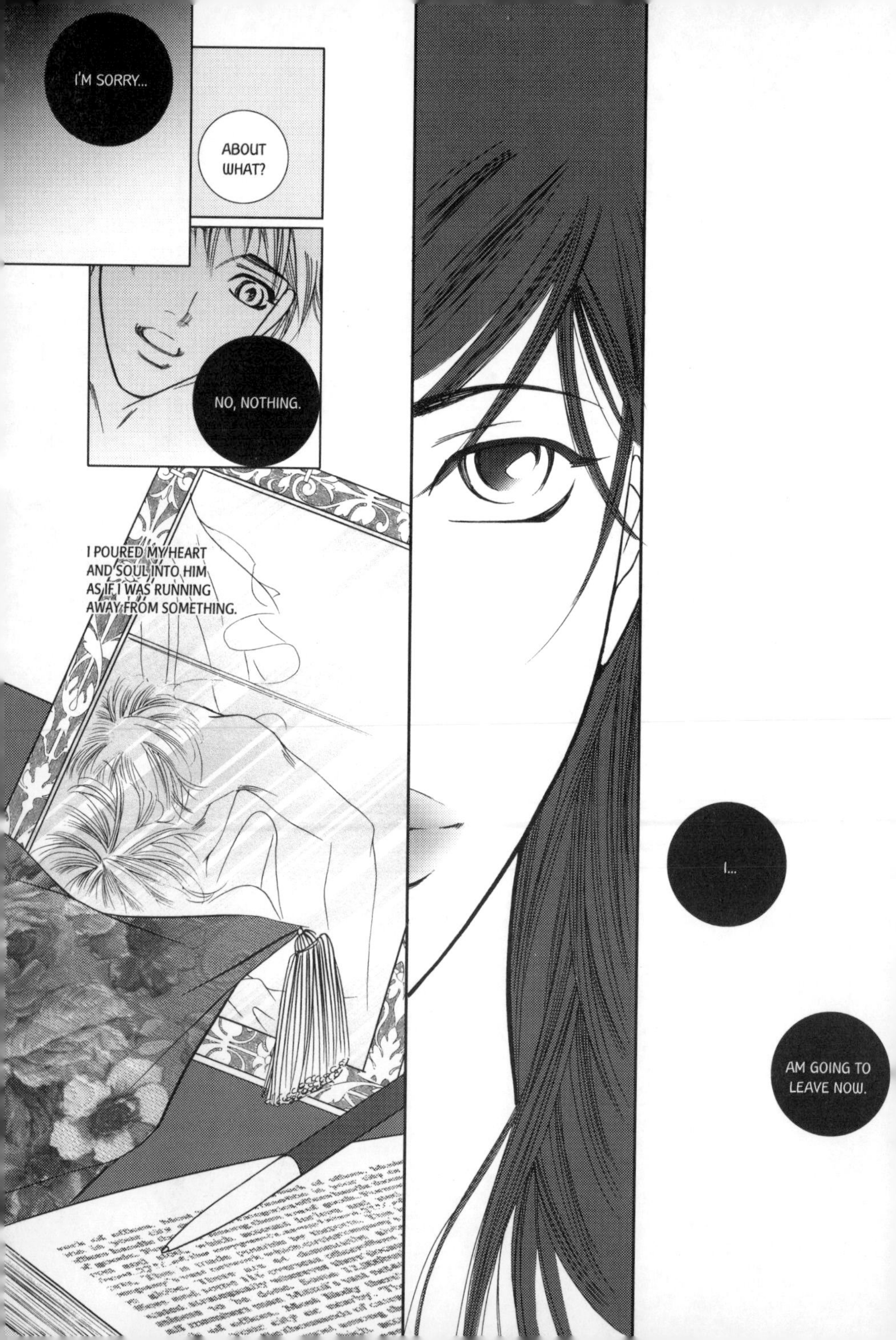
I'M SORRY...
ABOUT WHAT?
NO, NOTHING.
I POURED MY HEART AND SOUL INTO HIM AS IF I WAS RUNNING AWAY FROM SOMETHING.
I...
AM GOING TO LEAVE NOW.

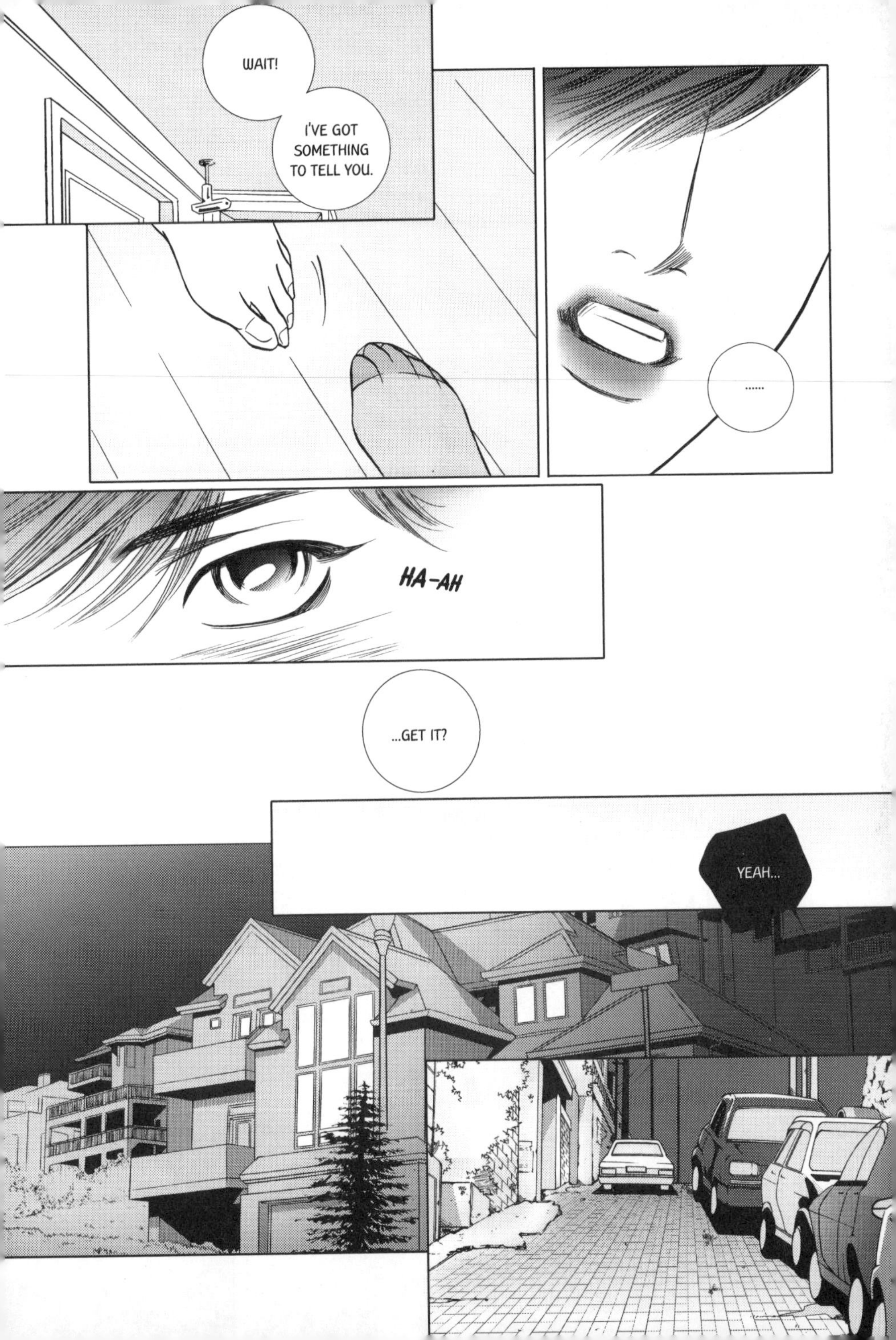
WAIT!
I'VE GOT SOMETHING TO TELL YOU.
......
HA-AH
...GET IT?
YEAH...

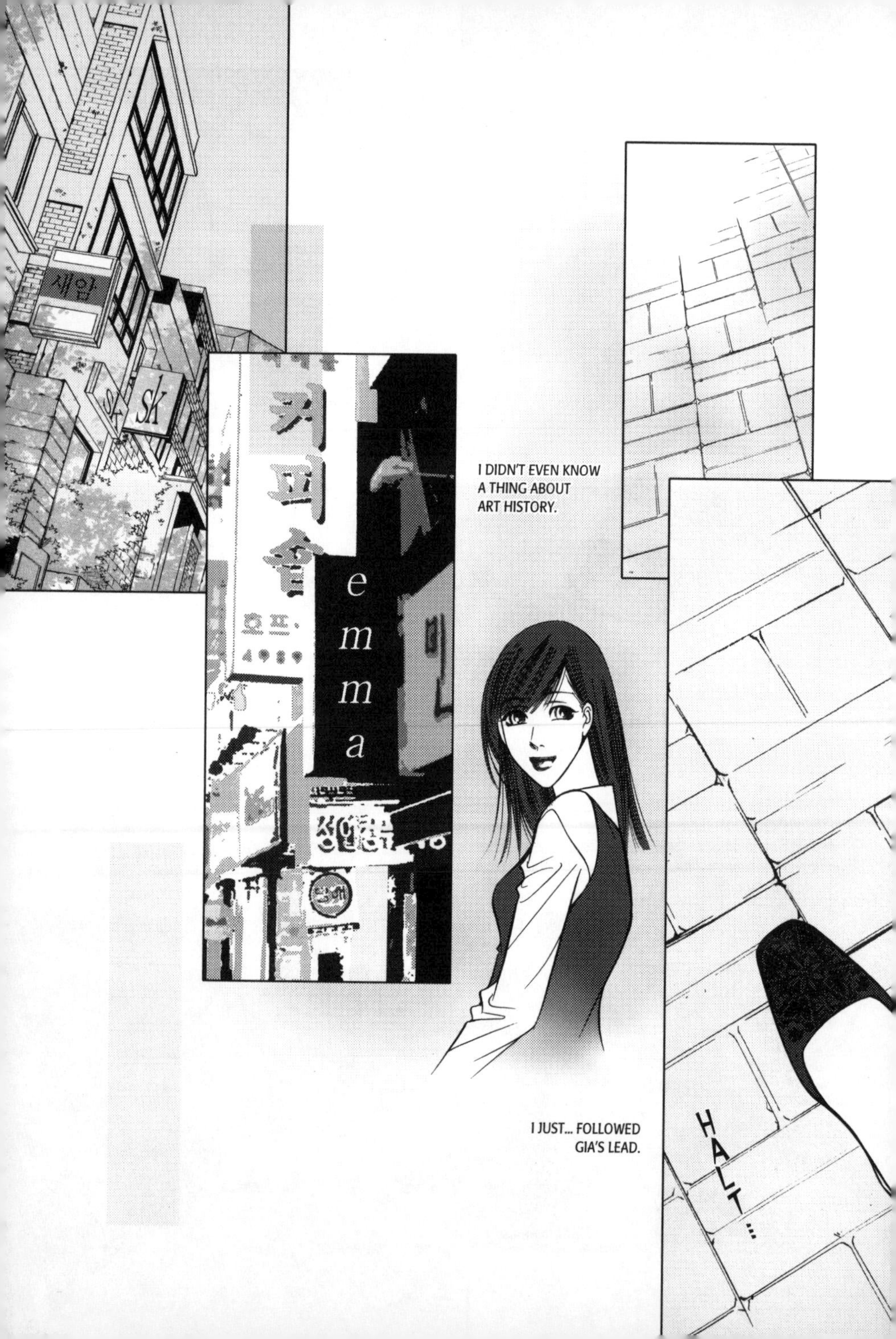
SK
emma
I DIDN'T EVEN KNOW A THING ABOUT ART HISTORY.
I JUST... FOLLOWED GIA'S LEAD.
HALT...

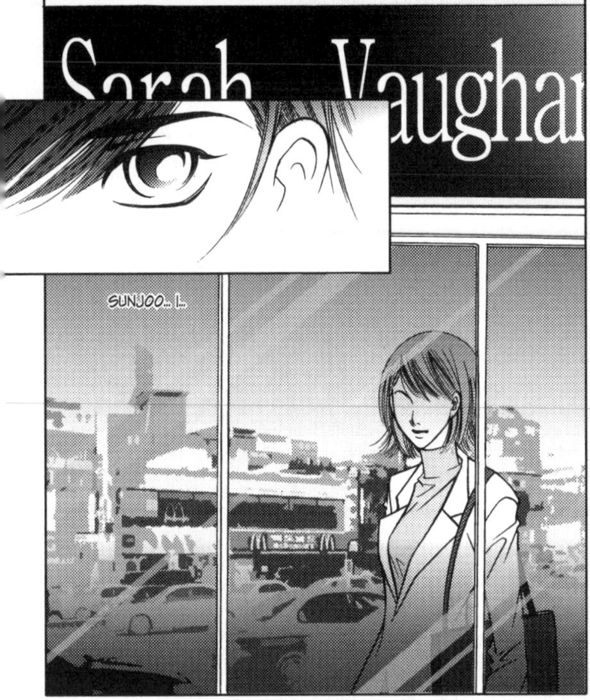
SUNJOO... I...

AM NOT GOING TO HAVE ANY MORE
BOYFRIENDS FROM NOW ON...

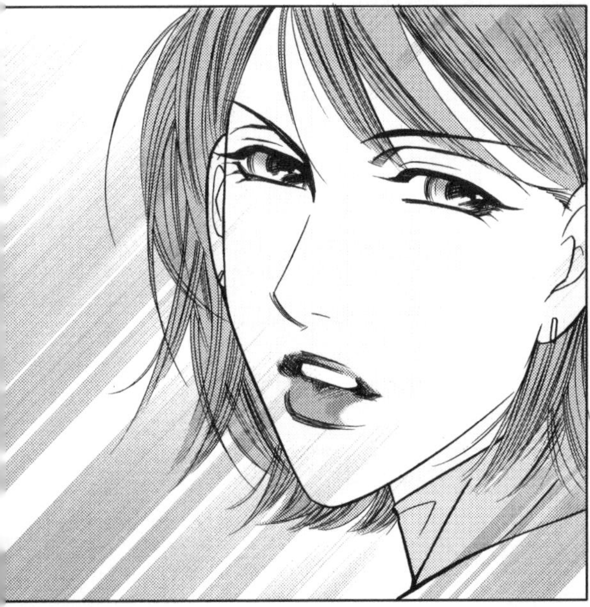

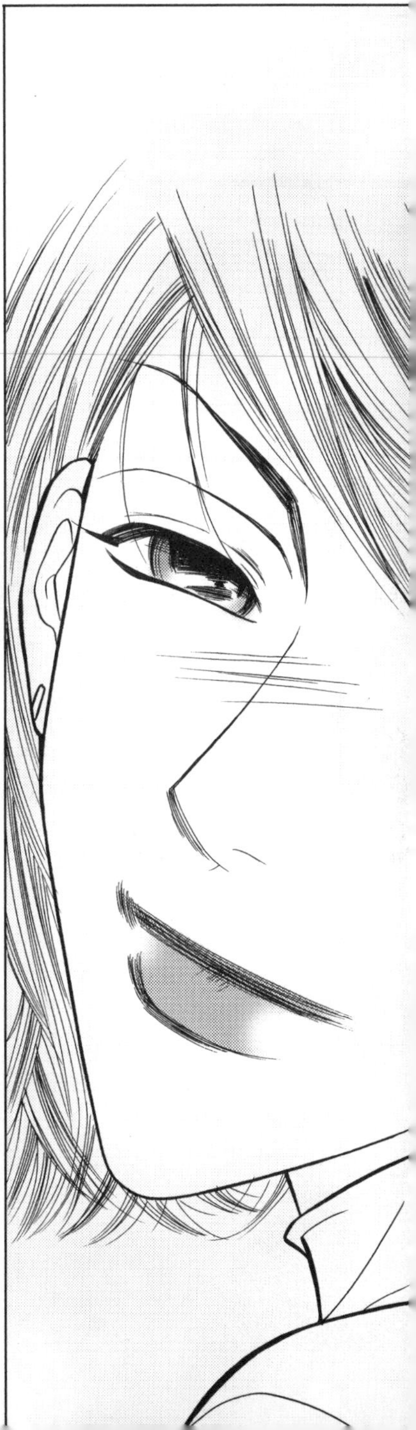

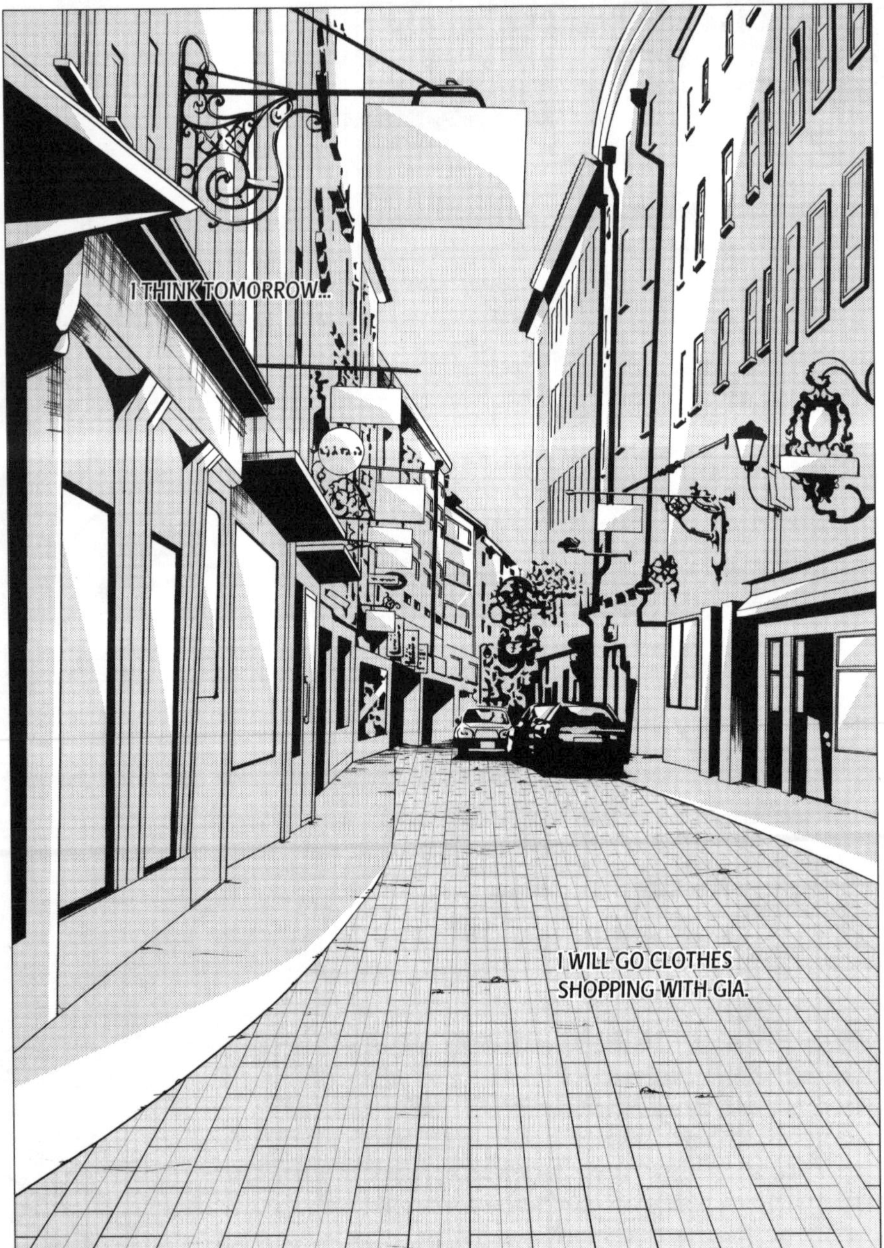
I THINK TOMORROW...
I WILL GO CLOTHES SHOPPING WITH GIA.

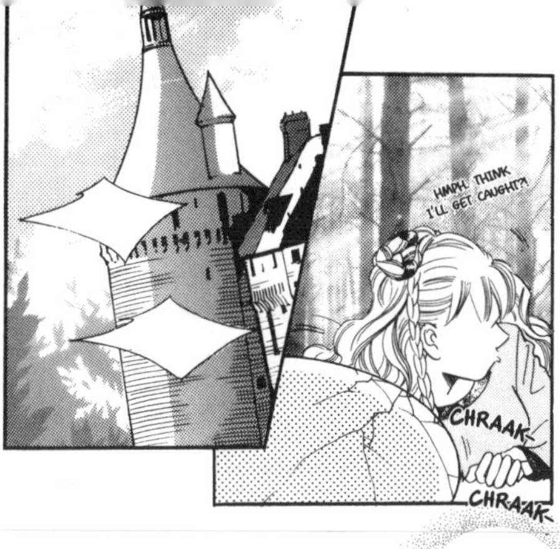
HMPH. THINK I'LL GET CAUGHT?!
CHRAAK-
CHRA'AK-

IN THE FOREST OF MY FATHER'S DOMINION, WHERE I RAN AWAY TO ESCAPE MY TUTOR...

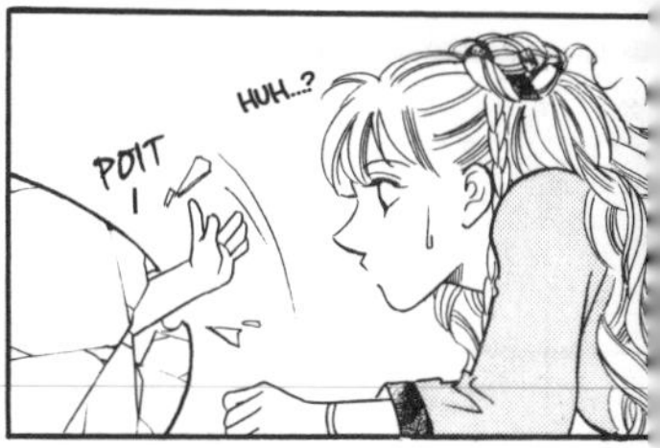
POIT
HUH..?

A FLYING LESSON

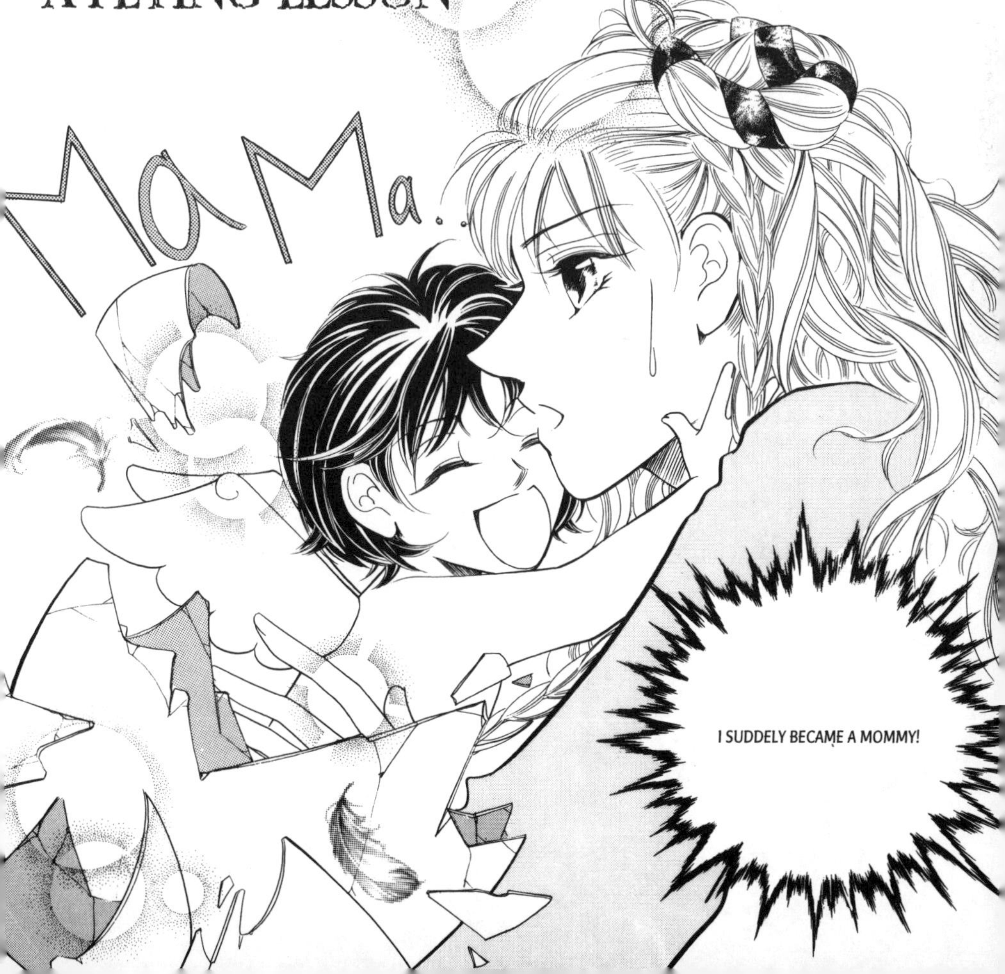
MaMa...
I SUDDELY BECAME A MOMMY!

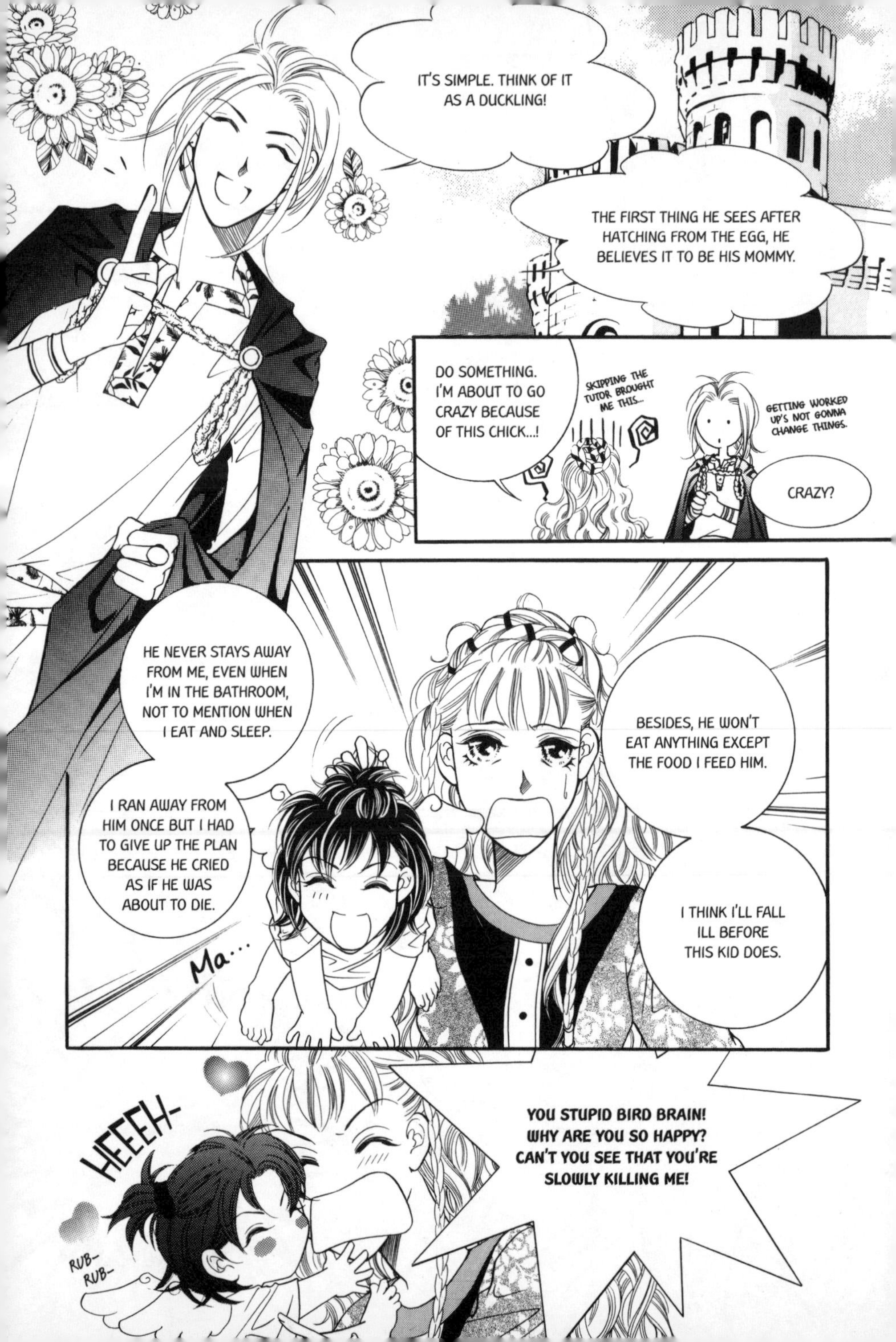
IT'S SIMPLE. THINK OF IT AS A DUCKLING!
THE FIRST THING HE SEES AFTER HATCHING FROM THE EGG, HE BELIEVES IT TO BE HIS MOMMY.
DO SOMETHING. I'M ABOUT TO GO CRAZY BECAUSE OF THIS CHICK...!
SKIPPING THE TUTOR BROUGHT ME THIS...
GETTING WORKED UP'S NOT GONNA CHANGE THINGS.
CRAZY?
HE NEVER STAYS AWAY FROM ME, EVEN WHEN I'M IN THE BATHROOM, NOT TO MENTION WHEN I EAT AND SLEEP.
I RAN AWAY FROM HIM ONCE BUT I HAD TO GIVE UP THE PLAN BECAUSE HE CRIED AS IF HE WAS ABOUT TO DIE.
Ma...
BESIDES, HE WON'T EAT ANYTHING EXCEPT THE FOOD I FEED HIM.
I THINK I'LL FALL ILL BEFORE THIS KID DOES.
HEEEH-
RUB- RUB-
YOU STUPID BIRD BRAIN! WHY ARE YOU SO HAPPY? CAN'T YOU SEE THAT YOU'RE SLOWLY KILLING ME!

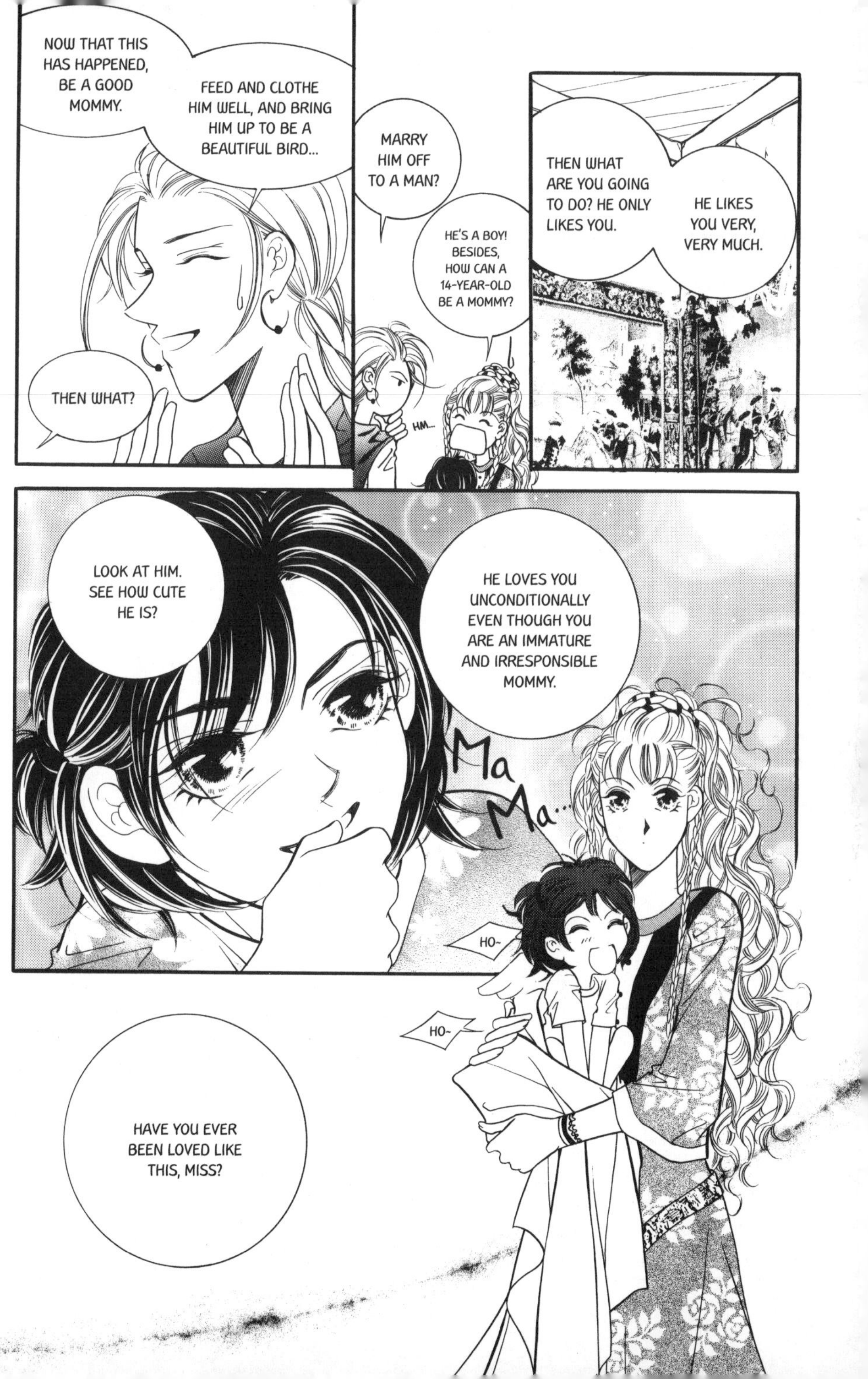
NOW THAT THIS HAS HAPPENED, BE A GOOD MOMMY.
FEED AND CLOTHE HIM WELL, AND BRING HIM UP TO BE A BEAUTIFUL BIRD...
THEN WHAT?
MARRY HIM OFF TO A MAN?
HE'S A BOY! BESIDES, HOW CAN A 14-YEAR-OLD BE A MOMMY?
HM...
THEN WHAT ARE YOU GOING TO DO? HE ONLY LIKES YOU.
HE LIKES YOU VERY, VERY MUCH.
LOOK AT HIM. SEE HOW CUTE HE IS?
HE LOVES YOU UNCONDITIONALLY EVEN THOUGH YOU ARE AN IMMATURE AND IRRESPONSIBLE MOMMY.
Ma Ma...
HO~
HO~
HAVE YOU EVER BEEN LOVED LIKE THIS, MISS?

YEAH. TO BE HONEST,

I'M A BIT THANKFUL AND AMAZED THAT HE'S SO ATTACHED TO ME, ONLY ME.

BESIDES, HE'S REALLY CUTE.

ER...HERMAN...

LOOK, HE SAID MY NAME!

A CHILD WITH A CHILD...

ALRIGHT, PLEASE ANSWER.

WHAT'S THE GERMANIC TRIBE THAT DESTROYED THE WEST ROMAN EMPIRE?

THA... THAT'S...

DESPAIR~

YOU LEARNED IT JUST YESTERDAY...

UM... UM... UM...

ODOACER!

HE'S PRETTY SMART FOR A BIRD BRAIN.

I THINK HE MIGHT BE SMARTER THAN YOU, MISS.

LESS INTELLIGENT THAN A BIRD.

I DID WELL, RIGHT?

FINE, FINE, STEP ALL OVER ME.

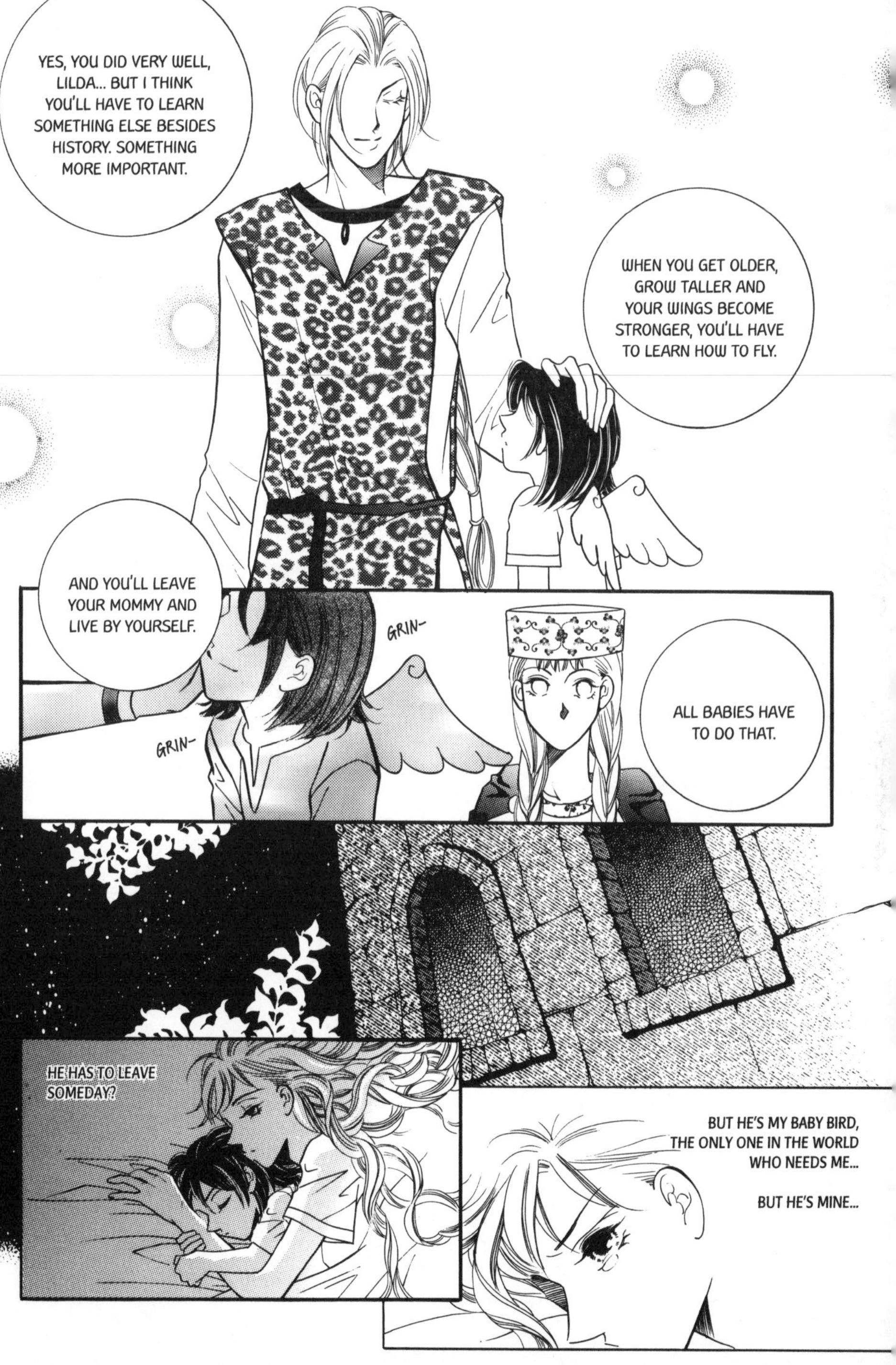
YES, YOU DID VERY WELL, LILDA... BUT I THINK YOU'LL HAVE TO LEARN SOMETHING ELSE BESIDES HISTORY. SOMETHING MORE IMPORTANT.
WHEN YOU GET OLDER, GROW TALLER AND YOUR WINGS BECOME STRONGER, YOU'LL HAVE TO LEARN HOW TO FLY.
AND YOU'LL LEAVE YOUR MOMMY AND LIVE BY YOURSELF.
GRIN-
GRIN-
ALL BABIES HAVE TO DO THAT.
HE HAS TO LEAVE SOMEDAY?
BUT HE'S MY BABY BIRD, THE ONLY ONE IN THE WORLD WHO NEEDS ME...
BUT HE'S MINE...

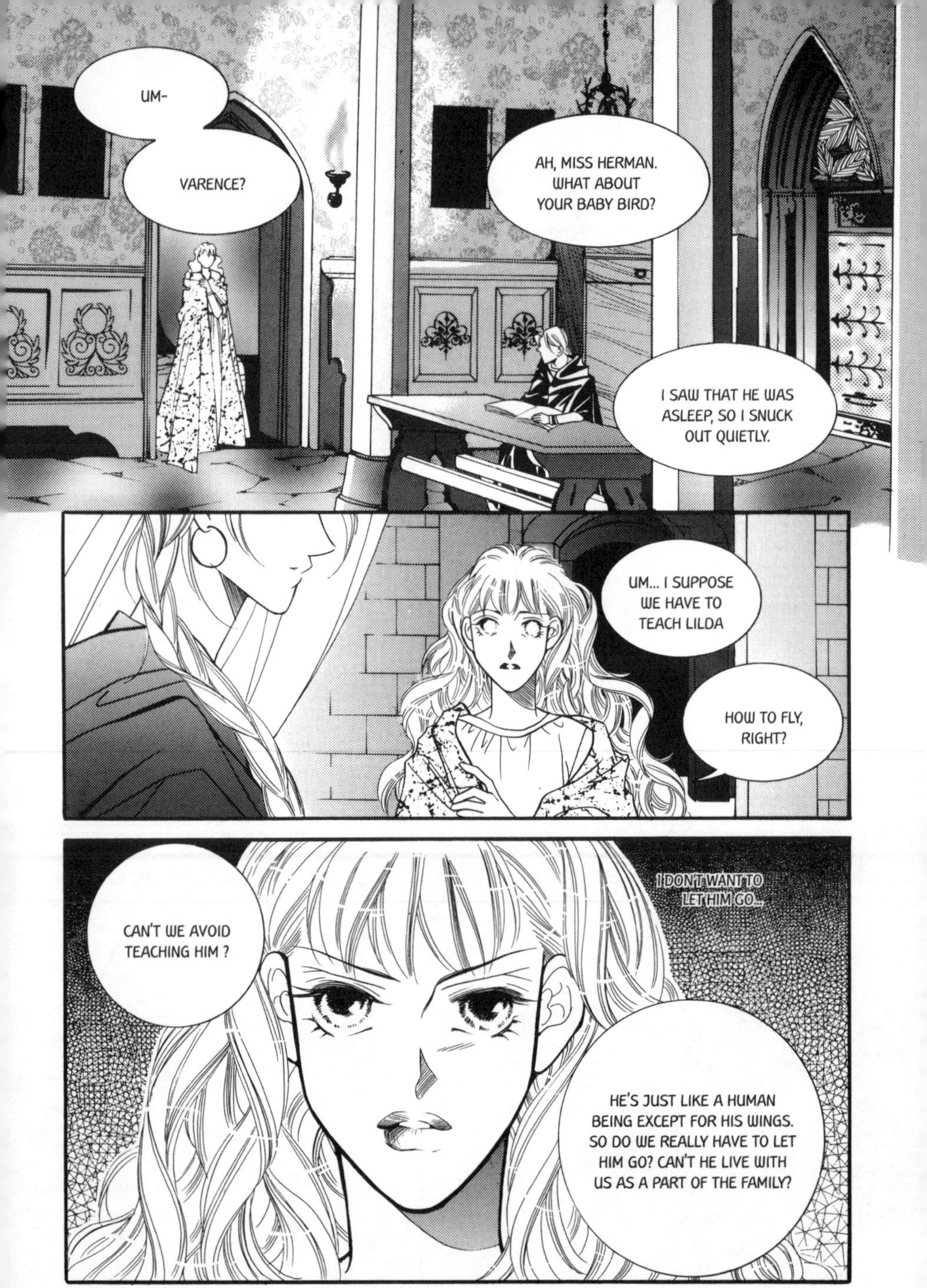
UM-
VARENCE?
AH, MISS HERMAN. WHAT ABOUT YOUR BABY BIRD?
I SAW THAT HE WAS ASLEEP, SO I SNUCK OUT QUIETLY.
UM... I SUPPOSE WE HAVE TO TEACH LILDA
HOW TO FLY, RIGHT?
CAN'T WE AVOID TEACHING HIM ?
I DON'T WANT TO LET HIM GO...
HE'S JUST LIKE A HUMAN BEING EXCEPT FOR HIS WINGS. SO DO WE REALLY HAVE TO LET HIM GO? CAN'T HE LIVE WITH US AS A PART OF THE FAMILY?

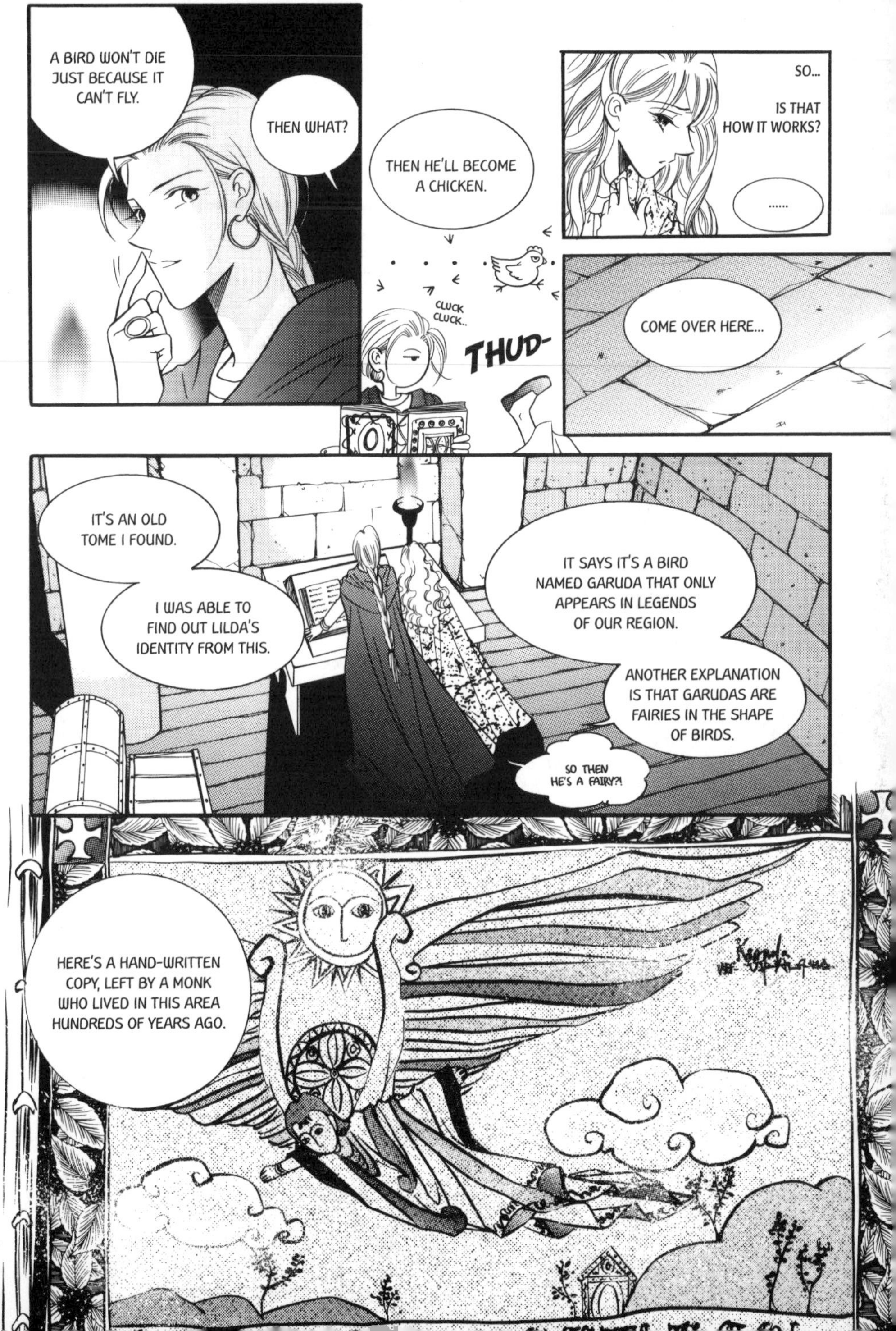

A BIRD WON'T DIE JUST BECAUSE IT CAN'T FLY.
THEN WHAT?
THEN HE'LL BECOME A CHICKEN.
SO...
IS THAT HOW IT WORKS?
......
CLUCK CLUCK..
THUD-
COME OVER HERE...
IT'S AN OLD TOME I FOUND.
I WAS ABLE TO FIND OUT LILDA'S IDENTITY FROM THIS.
IT SAYS IT'S A BIRD NAMED GARUDA THAT ONLY APPEARS IN LEGENDS OF OUR REGION.
ANOTHER EXPLANATION IS THAT GARUDAS ARE FAIRIES IN THE SHAPE OF BIRDS.
SO THEN HE'S A FAIRY?!
HERE'S A HAND-WRITTEN COPY, LEFT BY A MONK WHO LIVED IN THIS AREA HUNDREDS OF YEARS AGO.

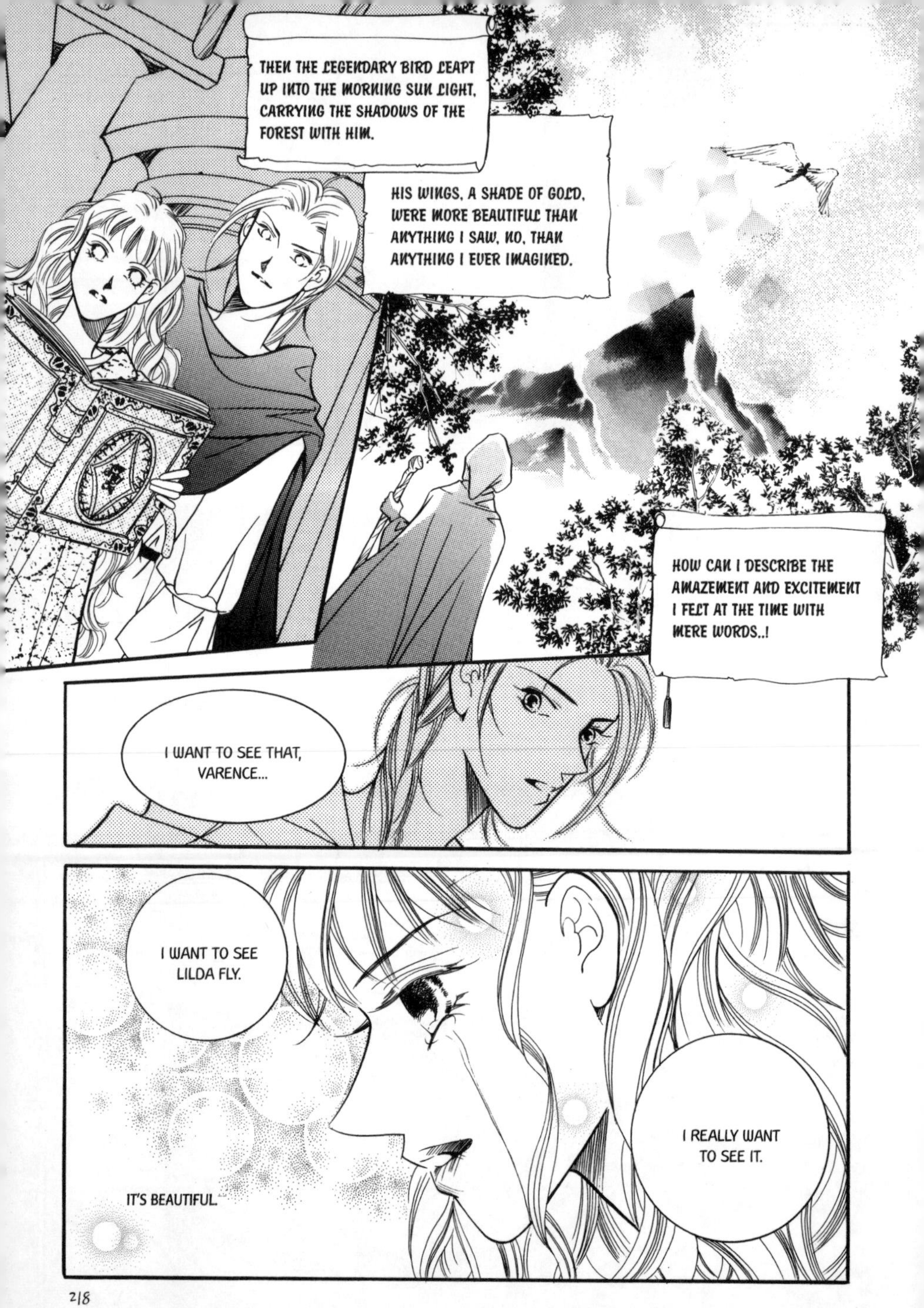
THEN THE LEGENDARY BIRD LEAPT UP INTO THE MORNING SUN LIGHT, CARRYING THE SHADOWS OF THE FOREST WITH HIM.
HIS WINGS, A SHADE OF GOLD, WERE MORE BEAUTIFUL THAN ANYTHING I SAW, NO, THAN ANYTHING I EVER IMAGINED.
HOW CAN I DESCRIBE THE AMAZEMENT AND EXCITEMENT I FELT AT THE TIME WITH MERE WORDS..!
I WANT TO SEE THAT, VARENCE...
I WANT TO SEE LILDA FLY.
IT'S BEAUTIFUL.
I REALLY WANT TO SEE IT.

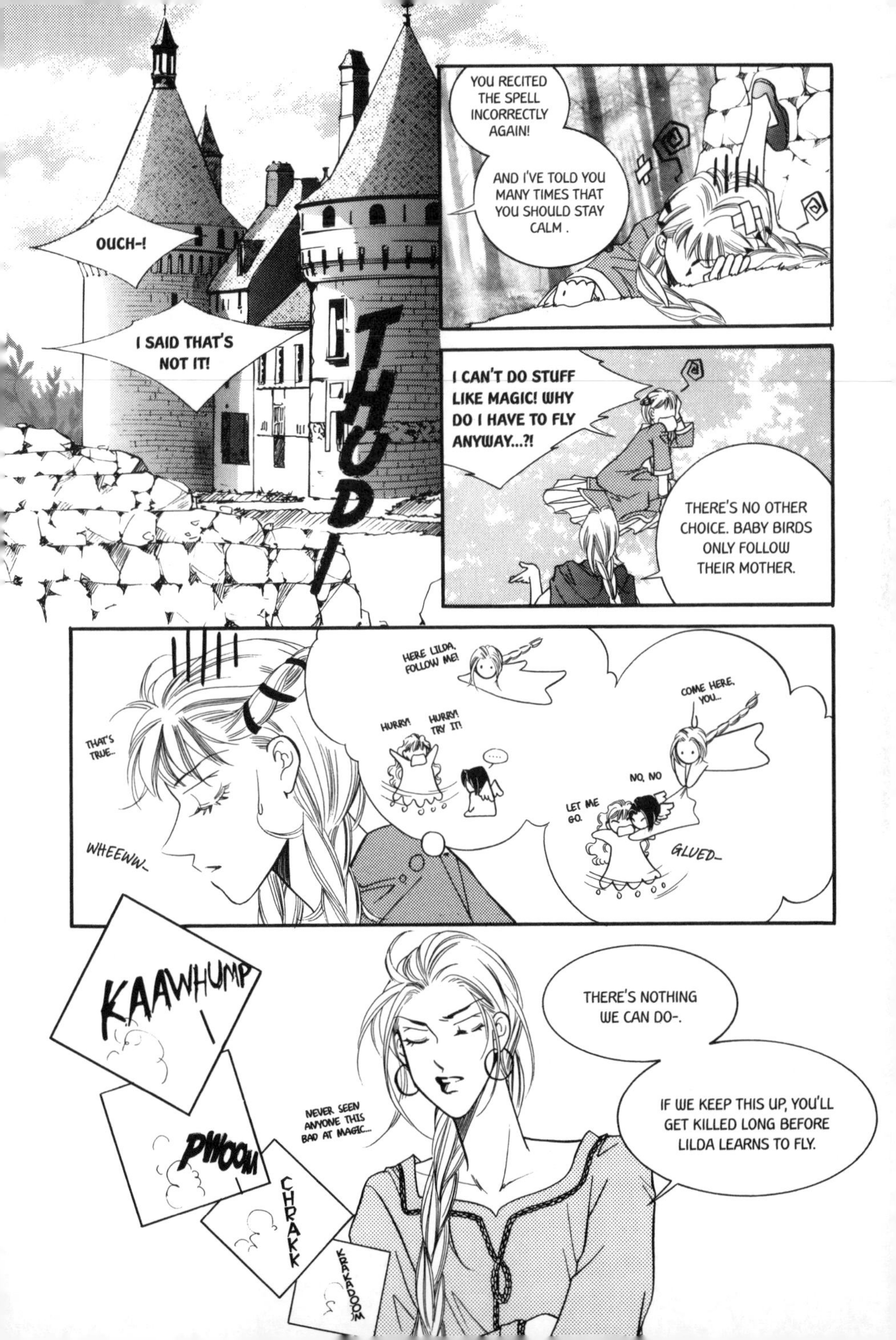
OUCH-!
I SAID THAT'S NOT IT!
THUD!
YOU RECITED THE SPELL INCORRECTLY AGAIN!
AND I'VE TOLD YOU MANY TIMES THAT YOU SHOULD STAY CALM .
I CAN'T DO STUFF LIKE MAGIC! WHY DO I HAVE TO FLY ANYWAY...?!
THERE'S NO OTHER CHOICE. BABY BIRDS ONLY FOLLOW THEIR MOTHER.
THAT'S TRUE..
HERE LILDA, FOLLOW ME!
HURRY!
HURRY! TRY IT!
....
COME HERE, YOU..
NO, NO
LET ME GO.
GLUED-
WHEEWW-
KAAWHUMP
PWOOM
CHRAKK
KRAKADOOM
NEVER SEEN ANYONE THIS BAD AT MAGIC...
THERE'S NOTHING WE CAN DO-.
IF WE KEEP THIS UP, YOU'LL GET KILLED LONG BEFORE LILDA LEARNS TO FLY.

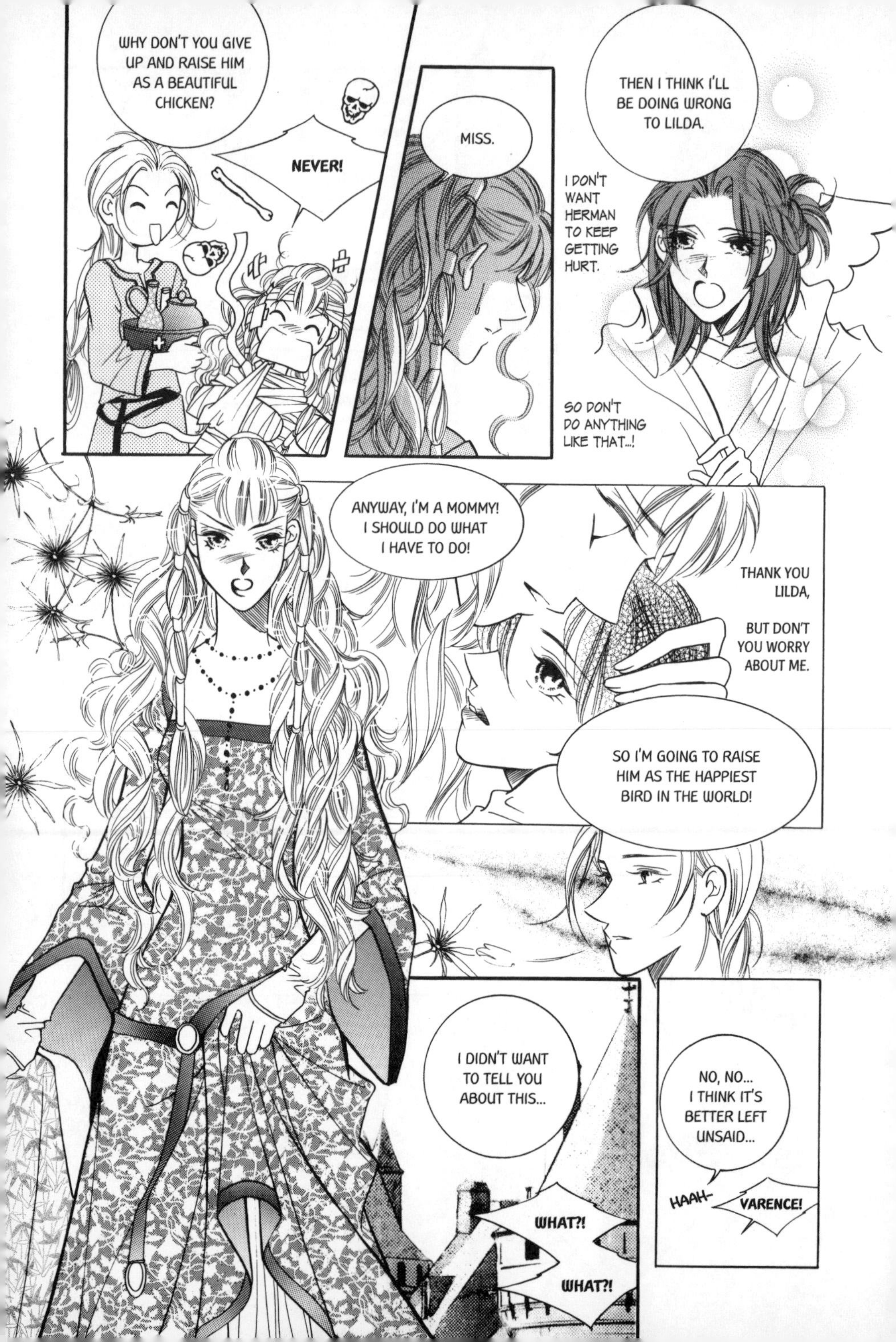
WHY DON'T YOU GIVE UP AND RAISE HIM AS A BEAUTIFUL CHICKEN?
NEVER!
MISS.
THEN I THINK I'LL BE DOING WRONG TO LILDA.
I DON'T WANT HERMAN TO KEEP GETTING HURT.
SO DON'T DO ANYTHING LIKE THAT...!
ANYWAY, I'M A MOMMY! I SHOULD DO WHAT I HAVE TO DO!
THANK YOU LILDA,
BUT DON'T YOU WORRY ABOUT ME.
SO I'M GOING TO RAISE HIM AS THE HAPPIEST BIRD IN THE WORLD!
I DIDN'T WANT TO TELL YOU ABOUT THIS...
WHAT?!
WHAT?!
NO, NO... I THINK IT'S BETTER LEFT UNSAID...
HAAH-
VARENCE!

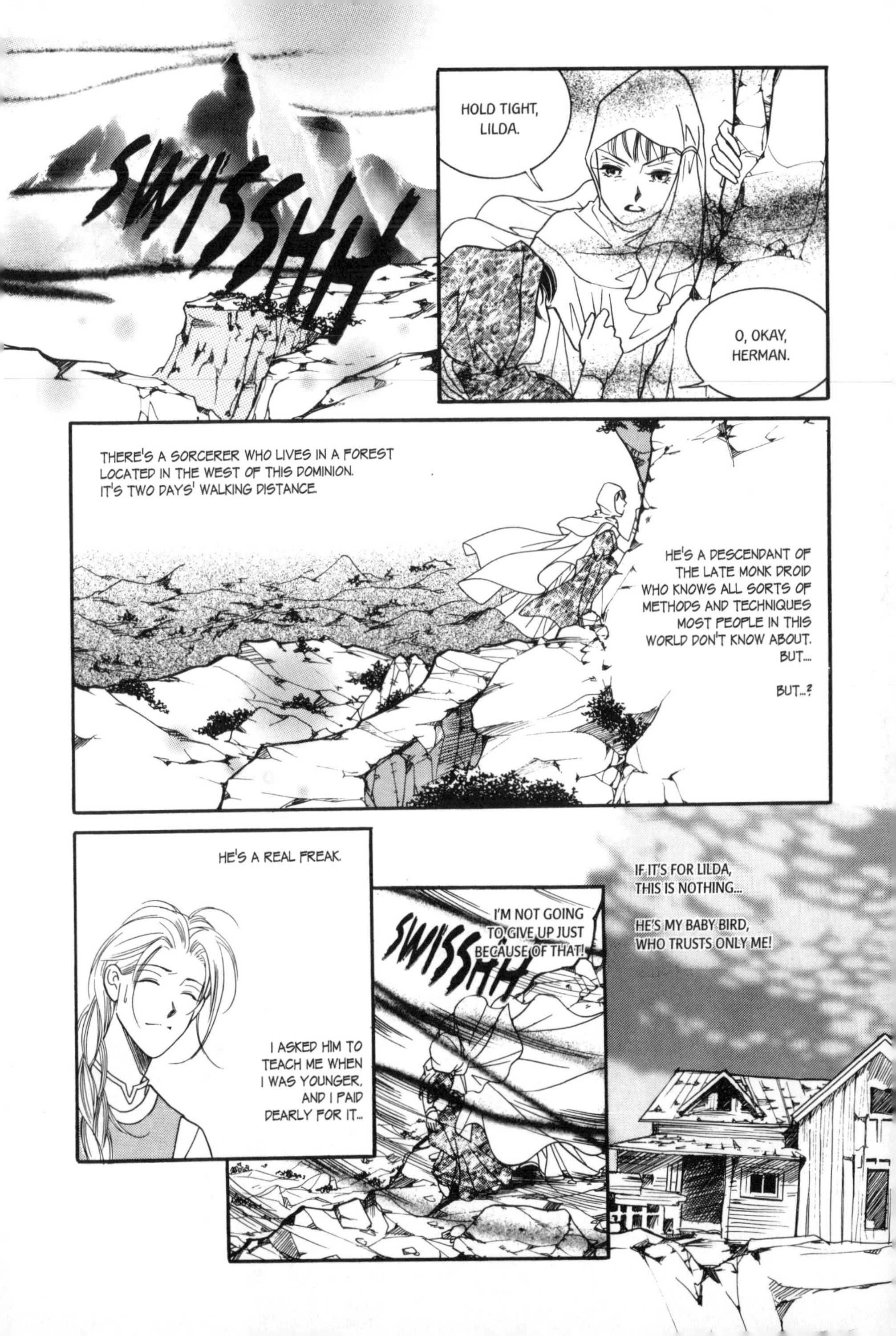
SWISSHH
HOLD TIGHT, LILDA.
O, OKAY, HERMAN.
THERE'S A SORCERER WHO LIVES IN A FOREST LOCATED IN THE WEST OF THIS DOMINION. IT'S TWO DAYS' WALKING DISTANCE.
HE'S A DESCENDANT OF THE LATE MONK DROID WHO KNOWS ALL SORTS OF METHODS AND TECHNIQUES MOST PEOPLE IN THIS WORLD DON'T KNOW ABOUT. BUT...
BUT...?
HE'S A REAL FREAK.
I ASKED HIM TO TEACH ME WHEN I WAS YOUNGER, AND I PAID DEARLY FOR IT...
SWISSHH
I'M NOT GOING TO GIVE UP JUST BECAUSE OF THAT!
IF IT'S FOR LILDA, THIS IS NOTHING...
HE'S MY BABY BIRD, WHO TRUSTS ONLY ME!

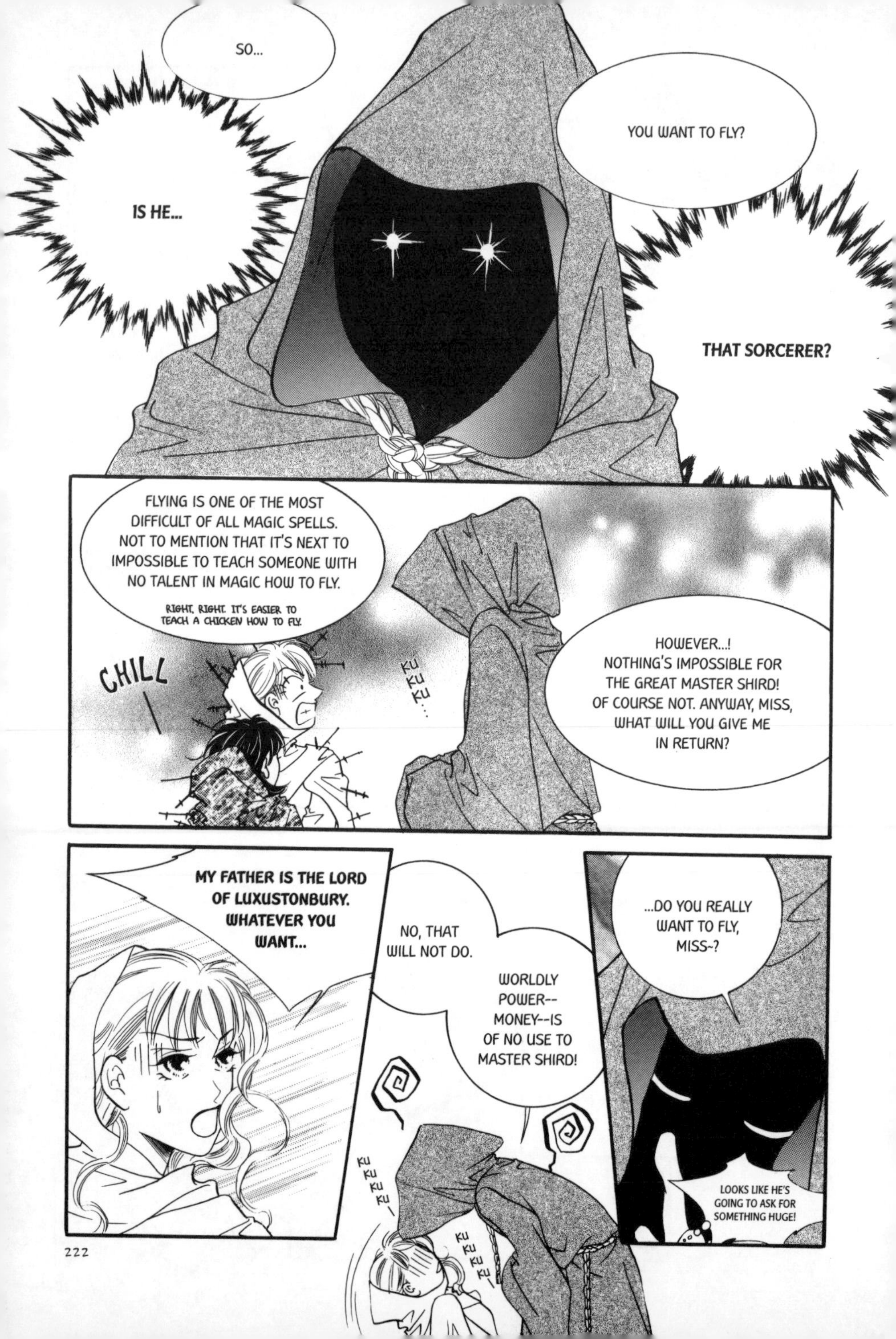

SO...
IS HE...
YOU WANT TO FLY?
THAT SORCERER?
FLYING IS ONE OF THE MOST DIFFICULT OF ALL MAGIC SPELLS. NOT TO MENTION THAT IT'S NEXT TO IMPOSSIBLE TO TEACH SOMEONE WITH NO TALENT IN MAGIC HOW TO FLY.
RIGHT, RIGHT. IT'S EASIER TO TEACH A CHICKEN HOW TO FLY.
CHILL
KU KU KU...
HOWEVER...! NOTHING'S IMPOSSIBLE FOR THE GREAT MASTER SHIRD! OF COURSE NOT. ANYWAY, MISS, WHAT WILL YOU GIVE ME IN RETURN?
MY FATHER IS THE LORD OF LUXUSTONBURY. WHATEVER YOU WANT...
NO, THAT WILL NOT DO.
WORLDLY POWER--MONEY--IS OF NO USE TO MASTER SHIRD!
KU KU KU KU
KU KU KU KU
...DO YOU REALLY WANT TO FLY, MISS~?
LOOKS LIKE HE'S GOING TO ASK FOR SOMETHING HUGE!

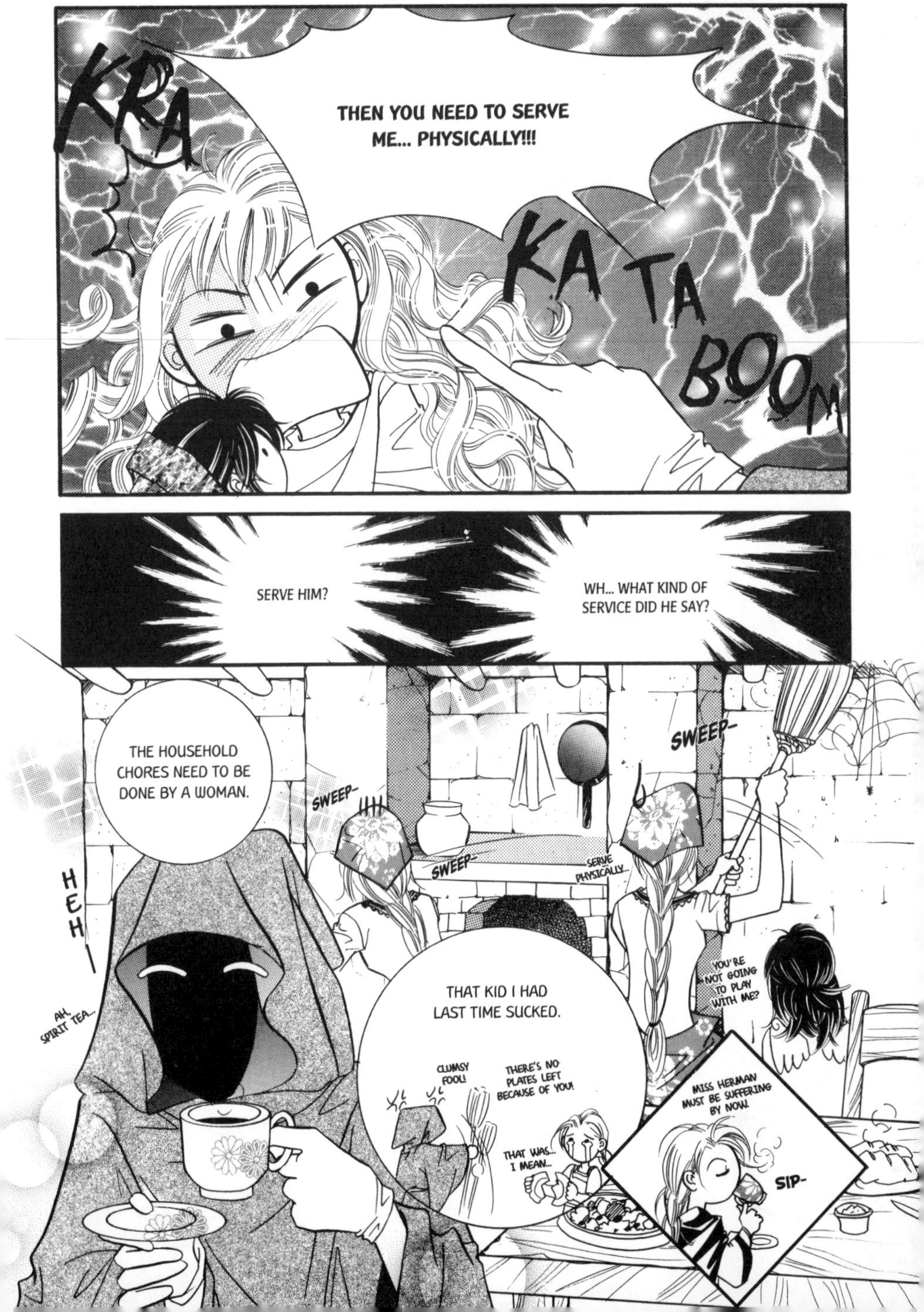
KRA
THEN YOU NEED TO SERVE ME... PHYSICALLY!!!
KA TA BOOM
SERVE HIM?
WH... WHAT KIND OF SERVICE DID HE SAY?
THE HOUSEHOLD CHORES NEED TO BE DONE BY A WOMAN.
HEH
SWEEP-
SWEEP-
SWEEP-
SERVE PHYSICALLY...
AH, SPIRIT TEA...
THAT KID I HAD LAST TIME SUCKED.
YOU'RE NOT GOING TO PLAY WITH ME?
CLUMSY FOOL!
THERE'S NO PLATES LEFT BECAUSE OF YOU!
THAT WAS... I MEAN...
MISS HERMAN MUST BE SUFFERING BY NOW.
SIP-

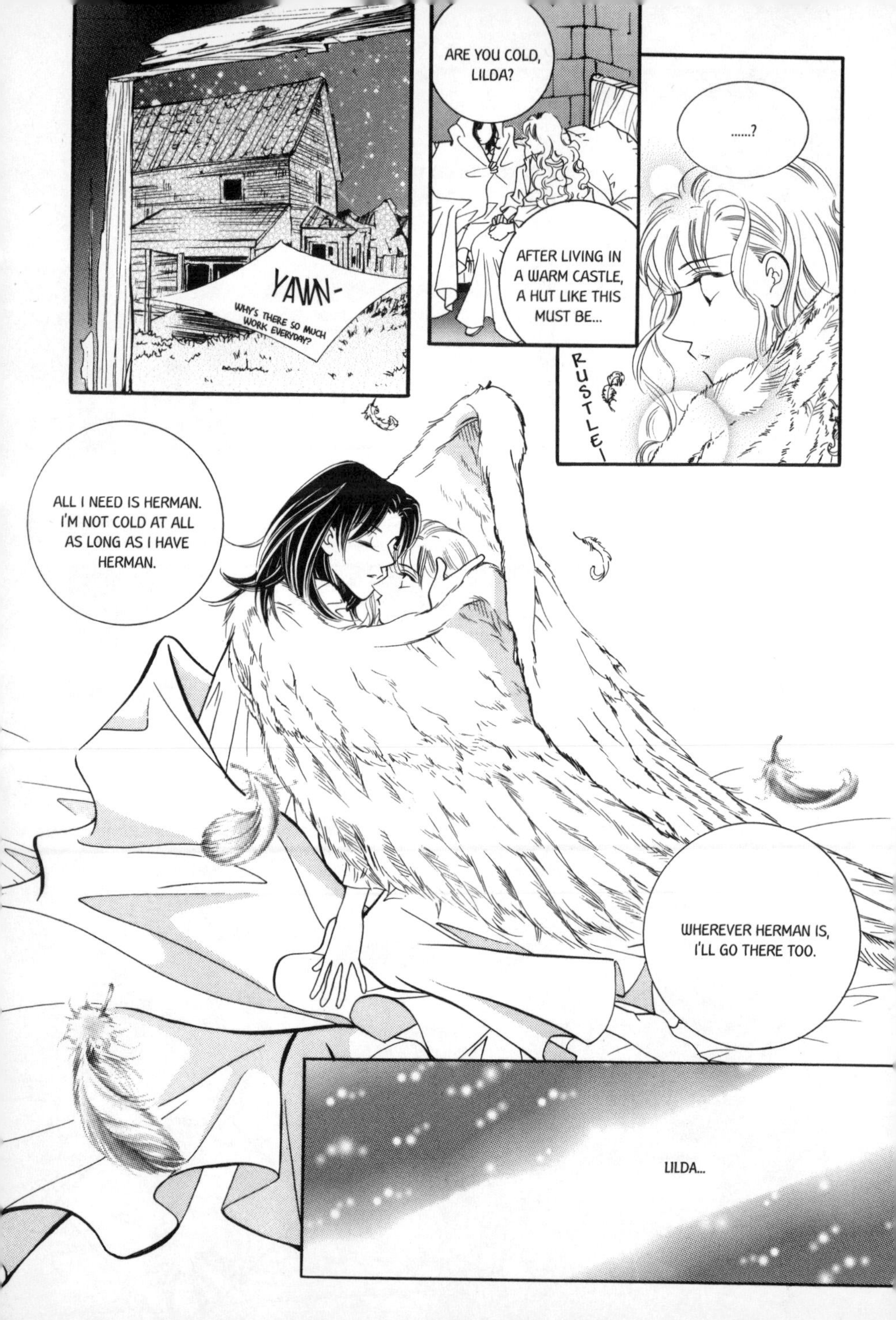
YAWN-
WHY'S THERE SO MUCH WORK EVERYDAY?
ARE YOU COLD, LILDA?
AFTER LIVING IN A WARM CASTLE, A HUT LIKE THIS MUST BE...
......?
RUSTLE!
ALL I NEED IS HERMAN. I'M NOT COLD AT ALL AS LONG AS I HAVE HERMAN.
WHEREVER HERMAN IS, I'LL GO THERE TOO.
LILDA...

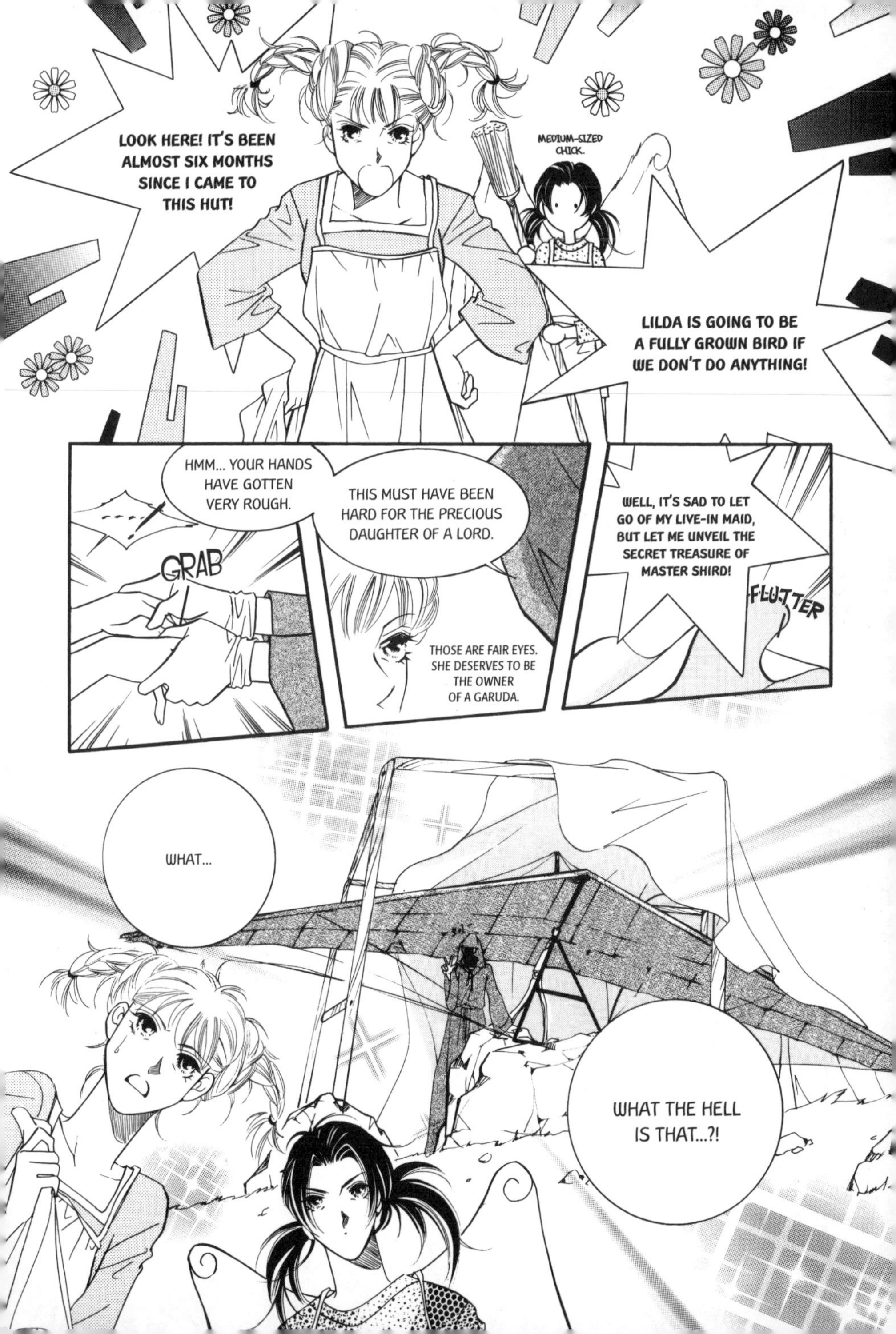
LOOK HERE! IT'S BEEN ALMOST SIX MONTHS SINCE I CAME TO THIS HUT!
MEDIUM-SIZED CHICK.
LILDA IS GOING TO BE A FULLY GROWN BIRD IF WE DON'T DO ANYTHING!
HMM... YOUR HANDS HAVE GOTTEN VERY ROUGH.
GRAB
THIS MUST HAVE BEEN HARD FOR THE PRECIOUS DAUGHTER OF A LORD.
THOSE ARE FAIR EYES. SHE DESERVES TO BE THE OWNER OF A GARUDA.
WELL, IT'S SAD TO LET GO OF MY LIVE-IN MAID, BUT LET ME UNVEIL THE SECRET TREASURE OF MASTER SHIRD!
FLUTTER
WHAT...
WHAT THE HELL IS THAT...?!

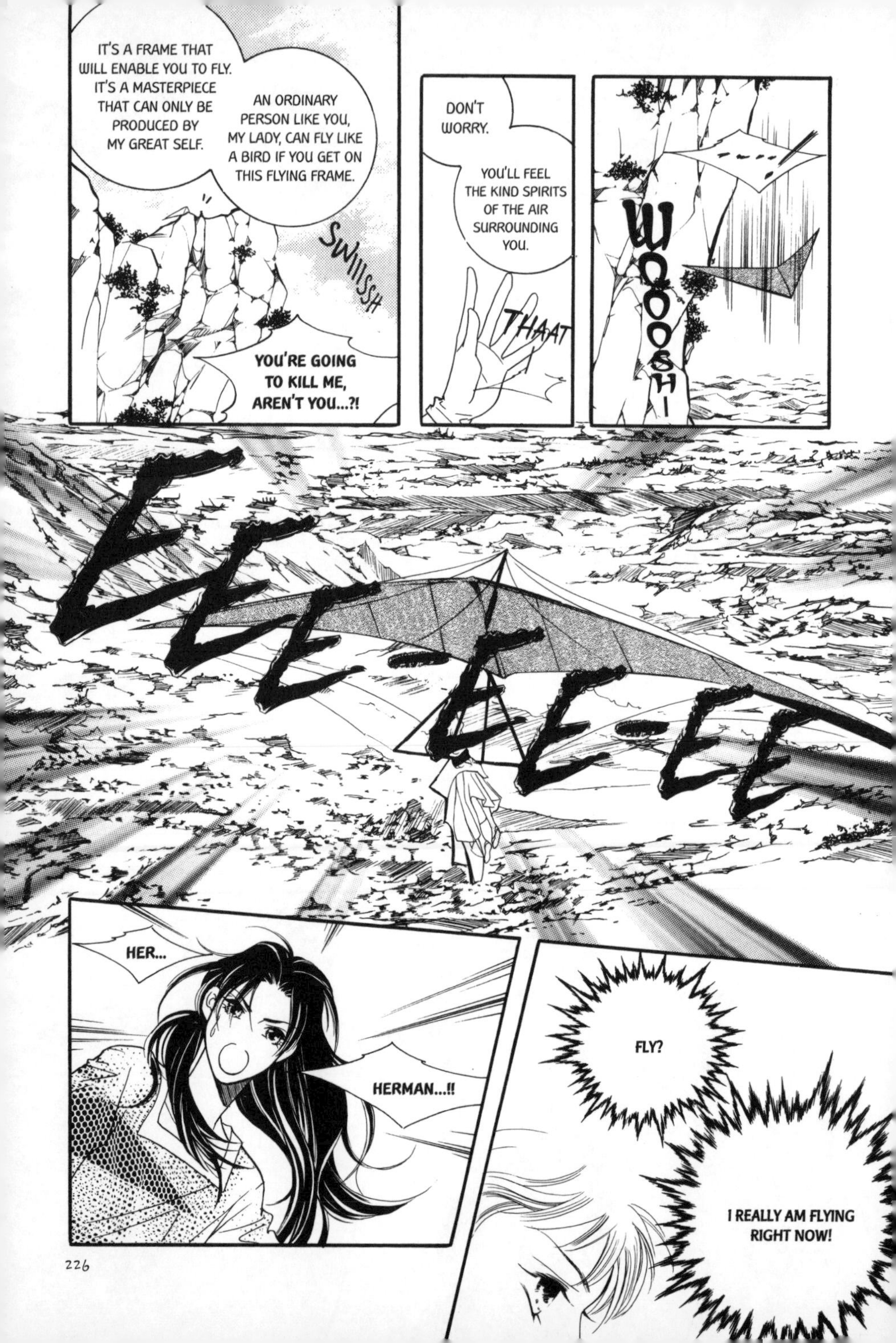
IT'S A FRAME THAT WILL ENABLE YOU TO FLY. IT'S A MASTERPIECE THAT CAN ONLY BE PRODUCED BY MY GREAT SELF.
AN ORDINARY PERSON LIKE YOU, MY LADY, CAN FLY LIKE A BIRD IF YOU GET ON THIS FLYING FRAME.
SWIIISSH
YOU'RE GOING TO KILL ME, AREN'T YOU...?!
DON'T WORRY.
YOU'LL FEEL THE KIND SPIRITS OF THE AIR SURROUNDING YOU.
THAAT
WOOOSH
EEE-EE-EEE
HER...
HERMAN...!!
FLY?
I REALLY AM FLYING RIGHT NOW!

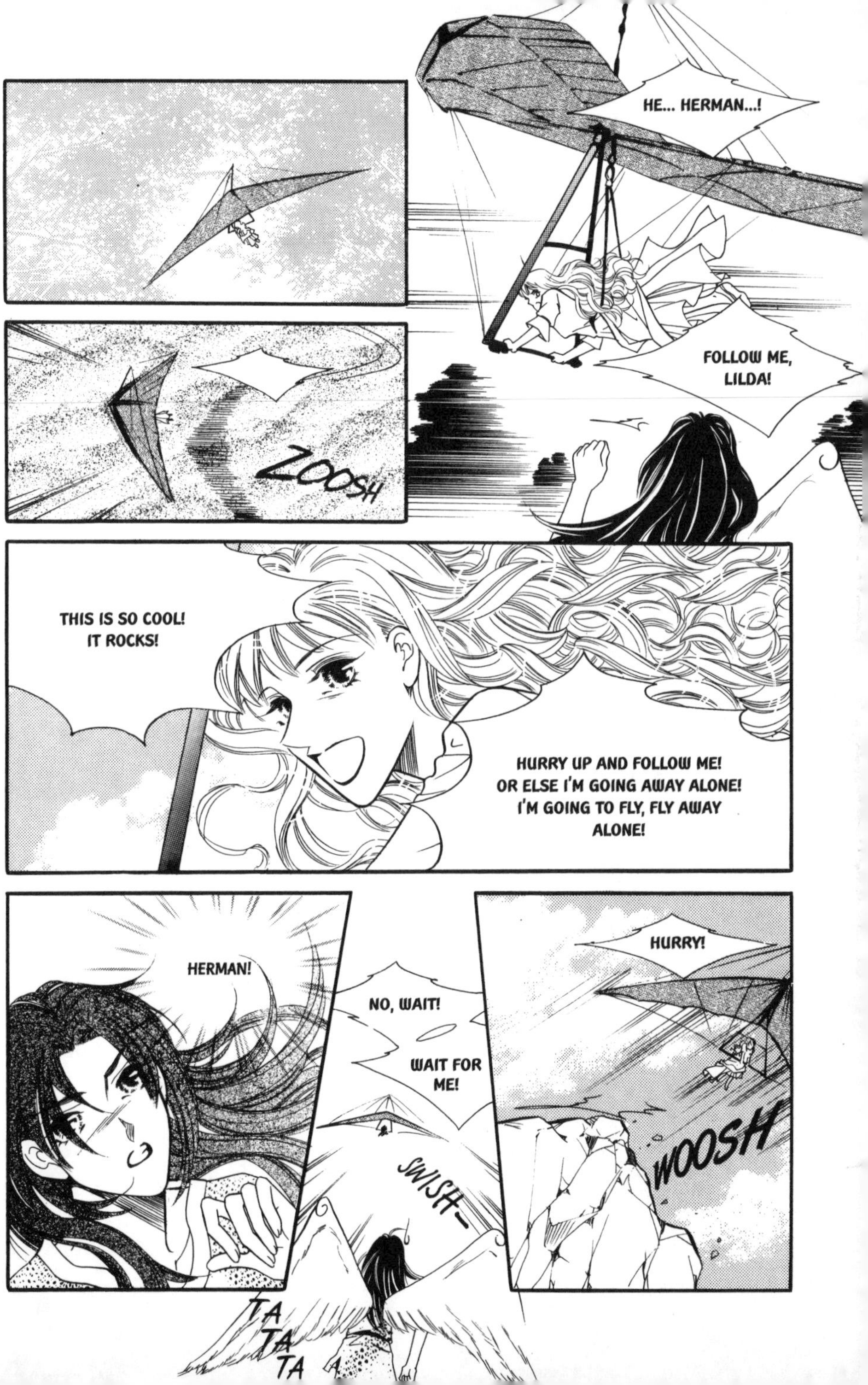
HE... HERMAN...!
FOLLOW ME, LILDA!
ZOOSH
THIS IS SO COOL! IT ROCKS!
HURRY UP AND FOLLOW ME! OR ELSE I'M GOING AWAY ALONE! I'M GOING TO FLY, FLY AWAY ALONE!
HERMAN!
NO, WAIT!
WAIT FOR ME!
SWISH-
TA TA TA TA
HURRY!
WOOSH

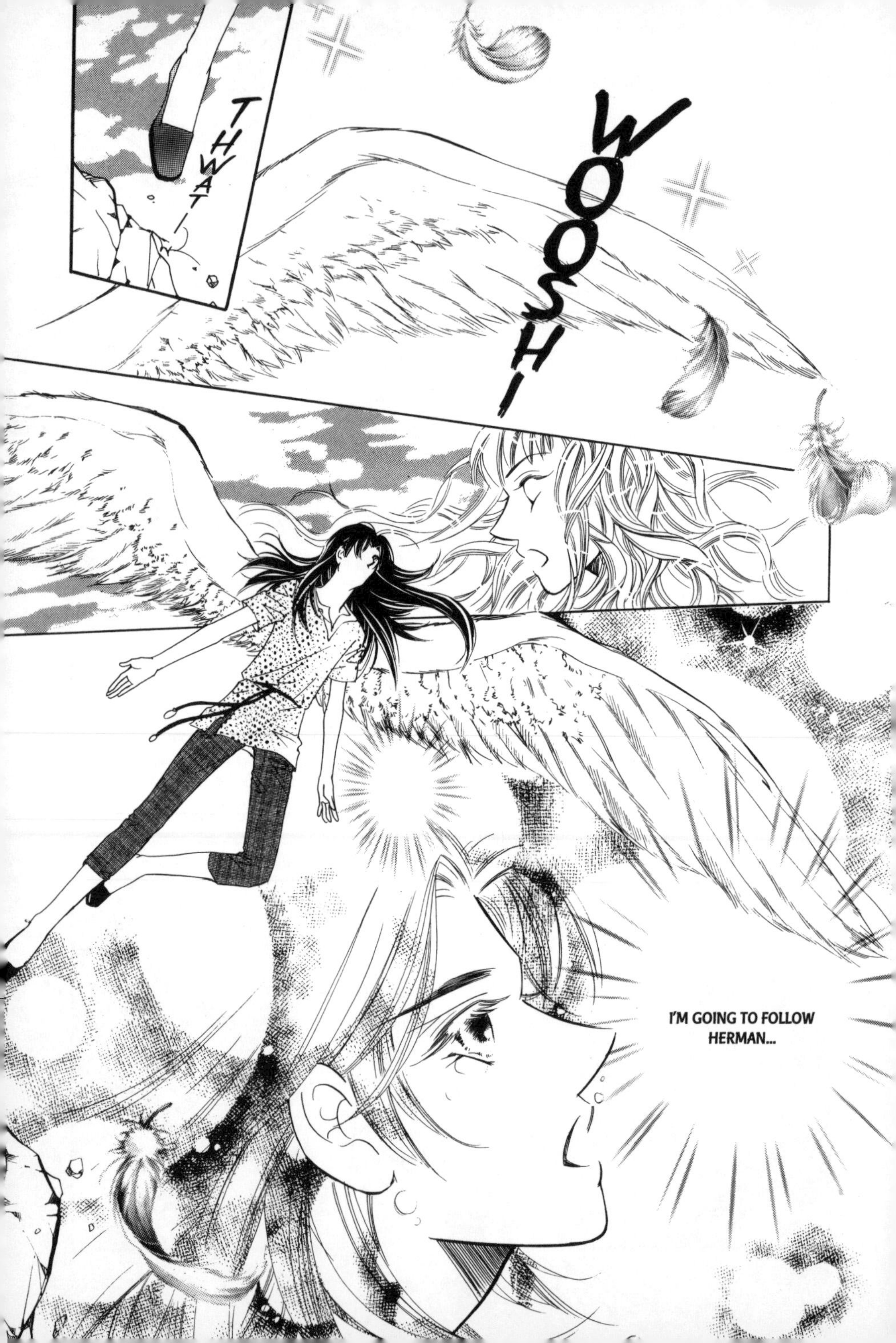
THWAT!
WOOSH!
I'M GOING TO FOLLOW HERMAN...

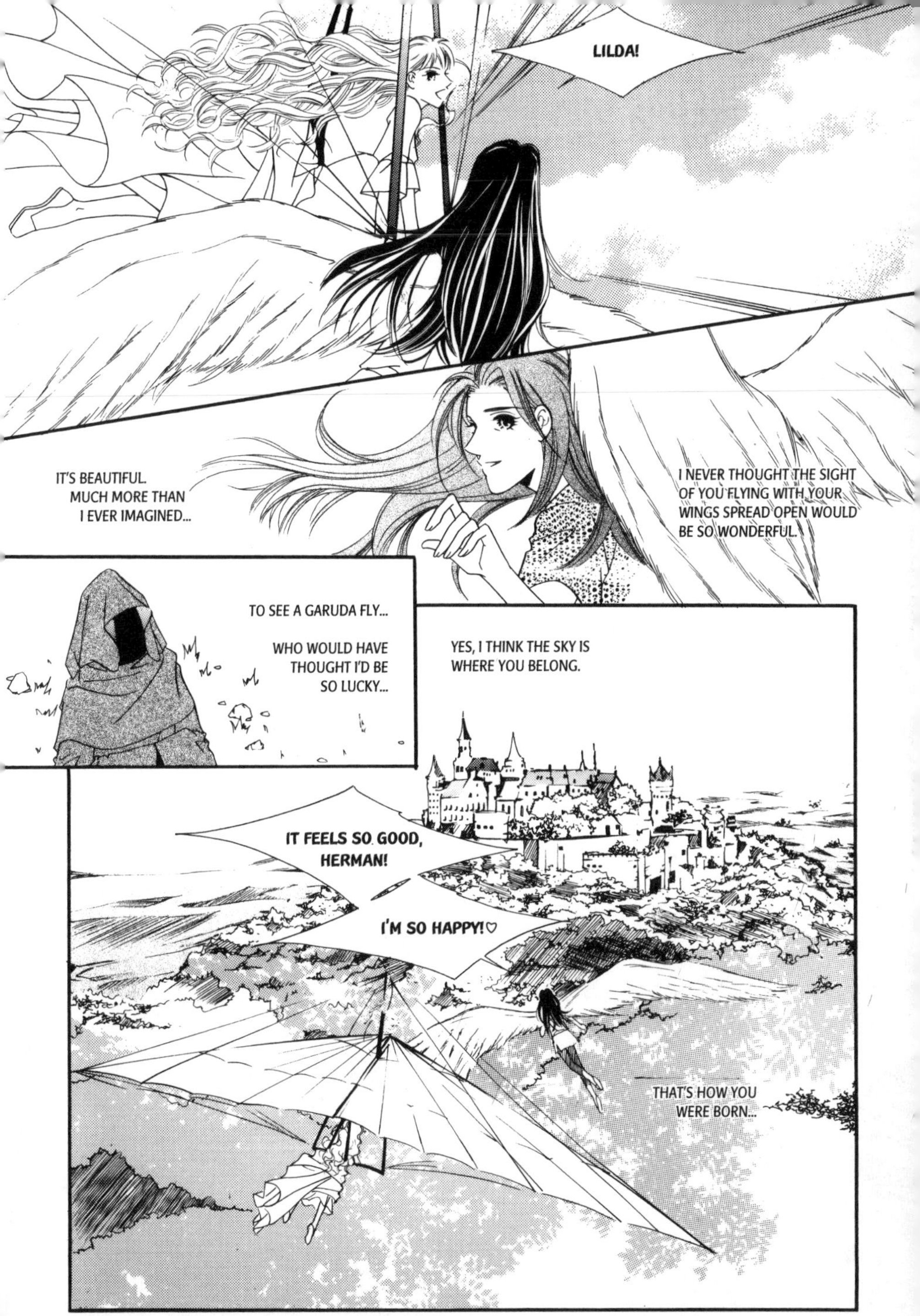
LILDA!
IT'S BEAUTIFUL. MUCH MORE THAN I EVER IMAGINED...
I NEVER THOUGHT THE SIGHT OF YOU FLYING WITH YOUR WINGS SPREAD OPEN WOULD BE SO WONDERFUL.
TO SEE A GARUDA FLY...
WHO WOULD HAVE THOUGHT I'D BE SO LUCKY...
YES, I THINK THE SKY IS WHERE YOU BELONG.
IT FEELS SO GOOD, HERMAN!
I'M SO HAPPY!♡
THAT'S HOW YOU WERE BORN...

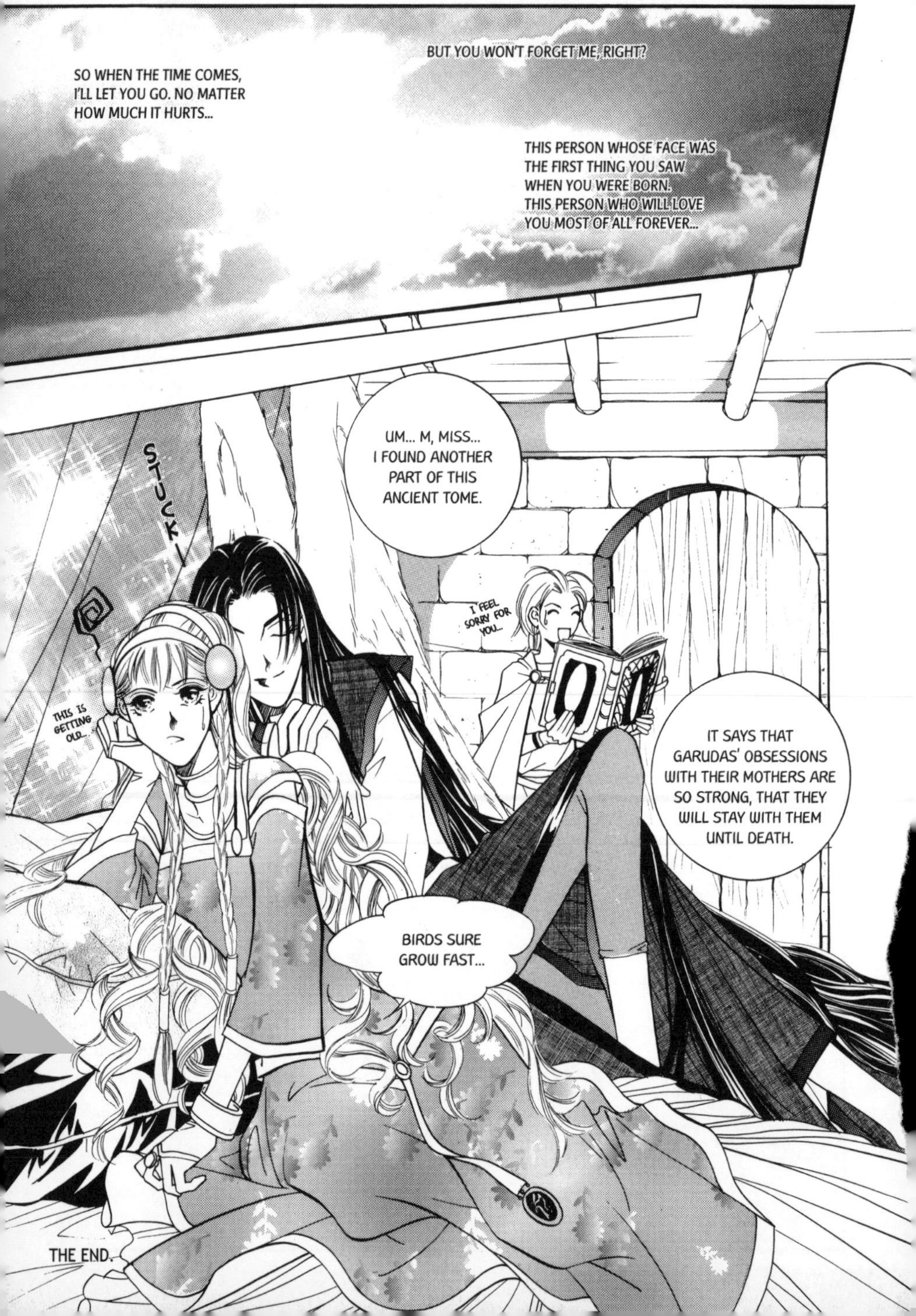
SO WHEN THE TIME COMES, I'LL LET YOU GO. NO MATTER HOW MUCH IT HURTS...
BUT YOU WON'T FORGET ME, RIGHT?
THIS PERSON WHOSE FACE WAS THE FIRST THING YOU SAW WHEN YOU WERE BORN. THIS PERSON WHO WILL LOVE YOU MOST OF ALL FOREVER...
STUCK
UM... M, MISS... I FOUND ANOTHER PART OF THIS ANCIENT TOME.
I FEEL SORRY FOR YOU...
THIS IS GETTING OLD...
IT SAYS THAT GARUDAS' OBSESSIONS WITH THEIR MOTHERS ARE SO STRONG, THAT THEY WILL STAY WITH THEM UNTIL DEATH.
BIRDS SURE GROW FAST...
THE END.

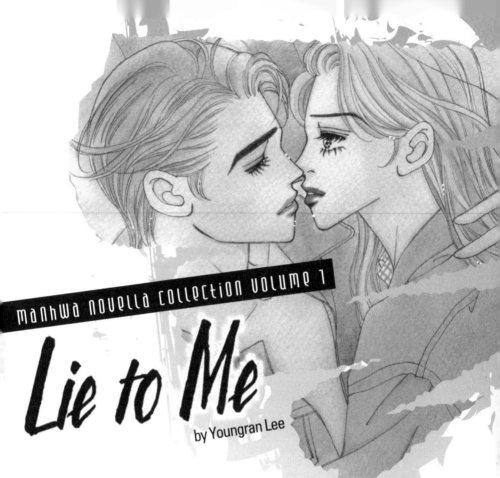

MANHWA NOVELLA COLLECTION VOLUME 1

Lie to Me

by Youngran Lee

NETCOMICS presents Manhwa Novella Collection-an anthology of shorter works from the most prominent Korean comic authors! Volume 1: Lie to Me contains three popular shorter works by Youngran Lee, one of the most famous shojo writers in Korea.

Lie to Me : Hyunjin plays a cruel trick on Gangjae, who's lost his memory in a car accident. But how will Gangjae react when he regains his memory and discovers Hyungjin's treachery?

French Kiss : When catty Jooyoung dares shy Yoonha to kiss anyone in the café, their victim, Joonsuh, turns out to be both exceptionally handsome and hopelessly naïve. Yoonha's bold act draws Joonsuh to her and what began as a mean-spirited dare takes an unexpected turn...

Conspiring with the Enemy : Out on a group date, Myunghae fights with a stranger... only to learn the next day that the man she quarreled with is also her new math teacher!

NETCOMICS August 2006 Release

the great
CATSBY

Created by
Doha

VOLUME 3 FINDS OUR HERO SLOWLY HEADING DOWN
THE ROAD TO MATURITY. BUT IT WOULDN'T BE CATSBY
WITHOUT PLENTY OF HILARIOUS AND TOUCHING DETOURS
ALONG THE WAY—LIKE AN ILL-FATED JOB INTERVIEW,
LEARNING TO SHOP FOR WINTER CLOTHES,
AND DISCOVERING THAT YOUR "SHADOW" HAPPENS TO
LOOK A LOT LIKE YOUR EX-GIRLFRIEND. MEANWHILE, THE NEARBY HOUSING DEVELOPMENT IS
GOING TO BE CALLED "PROVENCE"—BUT AS CATSBY LEARNS, HE CAN TRAVEL TO A PROVENCE
OF THE MIND WHENEVER HE'S ALONE WITH A CERTAIN SOMEONE. WILL TRUE LOVE FIND
A WAY? FIND OUT IN THE RICHEST CATSBY YET!

NATIONAL WINNER OF THE 3 MOST PRESTIGIOUS AWARDS FOR MANHWA IN 2005!

Doha's often hilarious color drawings (almost everybody's a cat)
are infused with a rich humanity and vivid,
expressive faces. This is an honest delineation of
the anxiety of youth wrapped in the innocent
style of anthropomorphic animals.

- Publishers Weekly

"The Great Catsby is twisted,
funny and beautiful.
Can't wait to read more."

- Scott McCloud, Author,
Understanding Comics

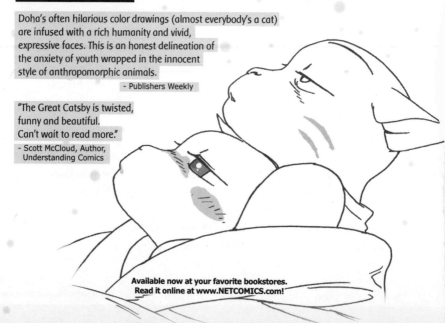

Available now at your favorite bookstores.
Read it online at www.NETCOMICS.com!